postmodernism & china

a b o u n d a r y 2 b o o k

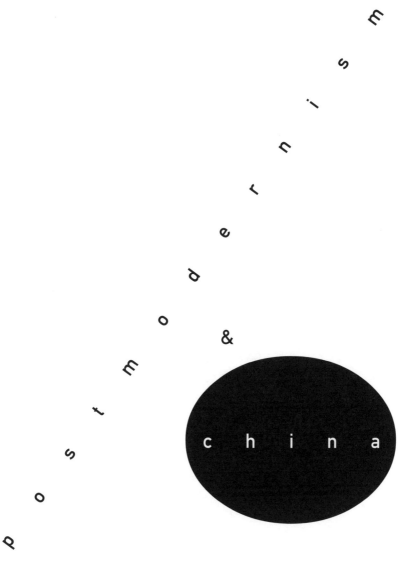

postmodernism & china

Edited by Arif Dirlik and Xudong Zhang

Duke University Press   Durham and London 2000

© 2000 Duke University Press

All rights reserved

Printed in the United States of America on acid-free paper ∞

Typeset in Quadraat by Tseng Information Systems, Inc.

Library of Congress Cataloging-in-Publication Data

appear on the last printed page of this book.

contents

postmodernism & china

arif dirlik & xudong zhang

Introduction: Postmodernism and China

This collection of discussions on postmodernism and China undertakes two tasks. The first task is to map out the terrain of what might be construed as postmodern in intellectual and creative activity, focusing for the most part on the People's Republic of China (PRC). The second task is to engage the question of whether postmodernity and postmodernism are relevant concepts for grasping the condition of contemporary Chinese societies, including but not restricted to the PRC.

Postmodernism as a concept was introduced to Chinese intellectual circles in the mid-eighties, with the works of Fredric Jameson playing an important part in the Chinese appreciation of postmodernism (other important figures contributing to the Chinese appreciation of postmodernism were Jürgen Habermas, Ihab Hassan, Linda Hutcheon, Jean-François Lyotard, and William V. Spanos).[1] Since then, there has been a proliferation of work that either views itself as self-consciously postmodernist or is labeled as such by others. We do not, however, have a clear appreciation of the scope and significance of such work. The first task, therefore, is to define the terrain of the postmodern in China, which also requires an examination of the Chinese situation with reference to the modernity-postmodernity shift globally. While the argument for a passage from the modern to the postmodern remains contested even within the postindustrial West, it nevertheless offers a context against which to evaluate the historical notion of Chinese postmodernity. The juxtaposition of a Chinese postmodernity and a Euro-American postmodernity is of theoretical interest because it may provide a supplement to the conditions of postmodernism in general.

The obvious continuity (or discontinuity) of the modern and the postmodern, and the somewhat parasitic relationship of discussions of postmodernism to notions of modernism, calls for the guarded use of critical perspectives from studies of modernism, if only to achieve a momentary sense-certainty through which the encounter with Chinese postmodernism becomes sensible. In his *All That Is Solid Melts into Air*, Marshall Berman differentiates modernity as (1) a socioeconomic transformation, (2) a historical experience coping with social change, and (3) the "cultural vision" based on that historical experience.[2] If Berman's useful differentiation of questions concerning the modern can be transplanted with some qualification into the inquiry into the postmodern, the issue of postmodernism and China may be pursued on three conceptually distinct, but socially and critically interrelated, planes. But first, a few words on the necessary qualifications, which also offer clues as to why we think it may be productive to postulate a Chinese postmodern.

A fundamental problem with Berman's approach to modernity is his restriction of the problems it presents for Euro-America. Berman has little to say about the ways in which colonization of the world may have contributed to the Euro-American experience of modernity. Conversely, as he evades the question, except for brief references to Russia, he has even less to say about the experience of modernity among those who were compelled into modernity by Euro-American coercion, who experienced it as domination from the outside, and whose own projects of modernity included a fundamental preoccupation with the recovery of local/national subjectivities.[3]

This distinction points to ways in which the postmodern may serve productively to illuminate the contemporary situation in the relationship of Third World societies to Euro-America. As we will elaborate below, there are plausible objections to the use of the postmodern as a category to explain this situation. Temporally speaking, if the postmodern is indeed a condition of late capitalism, it does not make much sense to apply it to situations where even the modern, as an economic and political category, remains to be achieved. Spatially, in a society such as China, where precapitalist economic relations (and corresponding social and political forms) coexist with capitalist and socialist relations, a category such as the postmodern may be applicable only to a limited sector of society, leaving out large segments of territory and population. Under these circumstances, using the term *postmodern* may seem at best to evade fundamental economic, social, political, and cultural problems, at worst as a Eurocentric recolonization of a Third World terrain marked by uneven development.

We would like to suggest, to the contrary, that it is precisely such a situation of spatial fracturing and temporal desynchronization that justifies the use of the postmodern against the spatial (as in the nation-form) and temporal (as in the development of a national market and culture) teleologies of modernity. The coexistence of the precapitalist, the capitalist, and the postsocialist economic, political, and social forms represents a significant departure from the assumptions of a Chinese modernity, embodied above all in the socialist revolutionary project.

Most objections to the use of postmodernism within a Chinese context presuppose the nation-form as the unit of analysis, which is misleading because of the increasingly problematic status of the nation as a unit of analysis, as it is undermined by forces from both within and without. The unevenness of regional development in China is no longer a manifestation only of past legacies; those legacies are being reconfigured by the incorporation of China into a global economy that both nourishes and generates differences on the same national terrain. At the same time, Chinese populations around the world have acquired enormous economic power and assert their own sense of Chineseness against the claims of the territorial Chinese state embodied in the PRC. This contestation involves not only the three Chinese or Chinese-dominated states of the PRC, Taiwan, and Singapore but also the stateless Chinese ethnicities encompassed by the term *diaspora*. Such contestation itself is a significant departure from Chinese modernity as it has been enunciated through a century of revolution. The contradiction between identities that may be marked as Chinese and their dispersal into many localities around the world forces a rethinking of modernist notions of a unified and unquestioned Chinese identity, which is represented by the socialist state.

Postmodernism, at the very least, has heuristic uses for dealing with this situation of simultaneous unity and dispersal. We may also usefully think of this condition of Chineseness as a generator of postmodernity. Under conditions of a global capitalism, Chinese states and populations are no longer merely the "objects" of forces emanating from Euro-America but are themselves significant contributors to the operations of capitalism; hence the seemingly contradictory representations of China and Chinese at once in conventional orientalist (or self-orientalist) terms as a location of the exotic other but also as the carriers of values expanding the frontiers of capitalism. The tradition of the modern/traditional dichotomy may still be there, but the tradition now appears as a means to transcend the modern.[4]

Akbar Ahmed's observation that postmodernism is both a beneficiary and a generator of ethnicity may be paraphrased here (without altering his sense in any way): Chinese ethnicity is at once a beneficiary and a generator of postmodernism.[5] What we need to keep in mind, especially with reference to the PRC, is that postmodernity is not just what comes after the modern but rather what comes after particular manifestations of the modern in China's historical circumstances, that the postmodern is also the postrevolutionary and the postsocialist. One of the ironies of postmodernity in China, visible in some of the contributions in this volume, is that while the ultimate justification for the use of the term may lie in spatial fracturing and temporal dissonance, which call into question any claims to cultural authenticity, Chinese postmodernists insist nevertheless on marking Chinese postmodernity as something authentically Chinese.

With these qualifications in mind, let us return to the various levels at which a Chinese postmodernity may be conceived. The first is post-modernization as a socioeconomic transformation, which is embodied in new information and computer technology, the global mobility of capital and labor, post-Fordist or flexible production, and all the technologies associated with contemporary global capitalism. The particularity of the Chinese socioeconomic transformation in the post-Mao era lies in the socialist reforms aimed at technological innovation and integration with the global economy. From the beginning, the impact of the postindustrial revolution on the socialist infrastructure was a political as well as an economic event. In other words, the technological and organizational efficacy associated with the market has always been defined vis-à-vis socialist, more precisely, Soviet-style, industrialization or modernization; its application has always been introduced by intense political and ideological operations and maneuvered and orchestrated by the state bureaucracy and the intelligentsia. Throughout the 1980s, decentralization, the "invisible hand" of the market, global operation and competition, and the whole cornucopia of neoliberal economic doctrines were engaged ideologically and theoretically in order to create a "socialist market economy."

The socioeconomic change that sets the platform for discussions of Chinese postmodernity and postmodernism is, therefore, historically a state project. And it is the history of the particular state ideology or ideologies that provides the temporal as well as the social framework by which the process of Chinese "postmodernization" acquires concrete meaning as a postrevolu-

tionary secularization. While Chinese leaders like to speak of "using capitalism to develop socialism," the current reality may well be the reverse: the use
of "socialism" to achieve capitalist development. Under the guise of socialism, China has become a source of cheap labor, with far-reaching implications for economies globally. At the same time, it is the socialistic policies of
the regime (such as keeping down the costs of everyday life) that make possible the sustenance of a low-wage labor force. China's massive size makes
it a force in the global economy and in politics, but in terms of income per
capita, China is still a very poor country. It remains to be seen whether, in
the Chinese context, socialism is a necessary, even preferable, condition for
a thriving market economy, and whether it is the task of a postmodern authoritarianism, so to speak, to provide social stability, job training, and a welfare system, and to protect the domestic market while engaging in an export-
oriented economy.[6] The recent birth of a new brand of Chinese nationalism
in the marketplace seems to have everything to do with this residual socialism lending itself to the most unrelenting forces of late capitalism. Yet, from
a different subject-position (and a different set of ideological fantasies), the
market is also becoming an indispensable, not to mention more effective,
means to an end of socialism understood as a utopian notion of the state
per se.

One of the most stunning and least theorized accomplishments in post-
Mao Chinese economic growth, a modernization in the form of postmodernization, is the creation of a diverse, decentralized network of rural- or
communal-based township enterprises (*xiangzhen qiye*), which now collectively represent more than a third of the Chinese GNP and export volume. Indeed, the township enterprise seems to epitomize the historical as well as the
theoretical contradictions and paradoxes of at least one aspect of the Chinese
economy. Here, one sees that the industrial penetration of the rural also gives
rise to a posturban, decentralized, and place-based mode of development that
promises to narrow rural-urban disparity and to rebuild rural communities in
the market environment. At the same time, decollectivization allows earlier
(including socialist) structures of production and social and cultural forms
to reclaim parts of the reorganization of rural China in terms of a neocollec-
tivism.[7] The integration with the global (as many township enterprises are
export oriented) reinvents the local, and *culture* in the broadest sense of the
term becomes an essential "natural resource" for capitalization. In a contrary direction, ironically, in the vast terrain of the rural economy, the specters
of Mao are increasingly visible in a people's war of (post-)modernization.
These contradictions divide a locally bound population (which is not necessarily anti-Western, since the West provides a model of economic wealth

even at that level) from an elite that already seeks to become part of a global elite (without necessarily being antistate or pro-Western). They also keep alive memories of socialism, while problematizing the meanings of modernity and postmodernity.

The relationship between a new market environment and an old nation-form is also, or perhaps mainly, being redefined in terms of the post-modern. The integration of the Chinese economy with global markets has had multiple effects on Chinese social life. On the one hand, it exposes the Chinese market and the realm of daily life to global capital and to international fashions and ideologies. This has created the impression that cities such as Shanghai, Beijing, and Shenzhen, now with cityscapes punctuated by the golden arches of McDonald's and giant Panasonic advertisements, are nothing more than Chinese enclaves of a global consumer society. On the other hand, the world market's spread into China, and China's willing entry into it, enables Chinese consumers to encounter a world of difference, unevenness, inequality, and hierarchy, often delineated in terms of nation-state borders. Against the universal claims of the world market, these differences are constant reminders of location, boundary, and community. Thus, amid the euphoria of globalization and integration, Chinese must also be experiencing what Ernest Gellner calls the "fatalistic" sense of belonging (and loyalty and love as a valorization of or "supplement" to what you cannot choose), namely, an enhanced communal identity in terms of birthplace, natural environment, color, economic condition, political culture, common history, and language.[8] Both the sense of integration and the sense of difference (if not isolation) manifest themselves in the emerging discourse of Chinese postmodernism, which in turn makes its own symbolic space available to one or the other tendency, yielding different formal/ideological products under different social circumstances. While the emergence of global capitalism has called the nation-form into question globally, the Chinese case presents challenges of its own, not just because of the proliferation of Chinese states as part of the historical legacy of modern China but also because of an increasingly visible Chinese diaspora that has its roots in this same historical legacy but is also dynamized by contemporary economic and political forces. These social/political phenomena have created problems in the search for a Chinese identity and also pose serious challenges to narrativizing China as a historical entity. A full accounting of Chinese postmodernity ultimately cannot be restricted to any one Chinese location but must also account for motions of populations that are global and that present the very contemporary problem of contradictions in the global and the local. It is important to emphasize here that these observations pertain to problems of identity within the so-called Han ethnicity and appear to be even more complex when non-Han groups are introduced into the portrayal of Chineseness.

The very real economic success of the Chinese, centered in Pacific Asia but achieving a global reach through diasporic populations, has added to the already existing questions of Euro-American hegemony, which for a long time defined modernity. With their newly found economic success, Chinese elites have also explicitly challenged the ideology of Eurocentric modernity by reasserting native ideologies (such as Confucianism) or ideologies of an Asian mode of development (such as that of Lee Kuan Yew, the former prime minister of Singapore, who is particularly active in promoting an antidemocratic capitalist developmentalism). In this sense, too, the economic success of Chinese populations may be viewed as a generator of postmodernity.

If postsocialism is central to the historical experience of Chinese postmodernity, its centrality lies in the social, political, and cultural vocabulary it provides, through which the more general or standard grammar of the postmodern experience—decentralization, transnational mobility, economic and cultural diversity, consumerism, and some emerging or renewed sense of locality, individuality, and diversity—can be imagined, confronted, and assimilated.

This constitutes the second topology of our discussion of Chinese postmodernism. If Chinese society experienced modernity as revolution and socialism, Chinese postmodernity is to be grasped not only in its relationship to modernity in general but also in its relationship to a socialist and revolutionary modernity. Much more clearly than in societies where postmodernity and modernity are both encompassed within the history of capitalism, Chinese postmodernism may reveal the antirevolutionary thrust of postmodernism as well as its contradictions. For while China disengages from its revolutionary past, as a postrevolutionary and postsocialist society, it still bears strong traces of that past, which serve as reminders of an earlier challenge to the capitalist world-system. The contradictions are most evident in the anomalous situation of a state that still claims socialism to legitimize itself, but must nevertheless demonstrate that legitimacy by being more successful at capitalism than capitalist societies (which to some extent it has demonstrated by registering enormous rates of growth). While Chinese postmodernism may be most striking as an antirevolutionary repudiation of a socialist modernity, what may make Chinese postmodernity unique is that, within a postsocialist situation, postmodernity itself may serve as a site of struggle between the legacy of the past and the forces of the present.

Here Chinese postmodernity may serve as a periodizing concept. Since the end of the nineteenth century, thinking about history and culture in China has been dominated by the categories of modernity and the enlightenment. Chinese communism was arguably the most forceful, and ultimately most successful, expression of an ideological commitment to modernity. Since 1978, a radical break with the revolutionary past has called into question the earlier framework of experiences, values, and ideologies. This questioning has itself been overwhelmed by new patterns of production and consumption that have accompanied China's integration into the global capitalist system, exacerbating the problem of representation in a radically unstable situation of everyday life and culture. Market, consumption, and media, all conceived in global rather than merely national terms, have replaced revolutionary mobilization as the dynamizing force of social change, announcing the triumph of the ideology of consumerism, but also opening the way for the liberation of peoples and localities by a plurality of worldviews, for the assertion of difference, and for the revision of the past and the creation of the future. Dizzying change and bewildering fragmentation not only undermine inherited narratives but call into question the very possibility of encapsulation within a coherent narrative of the past, the present, and the future. If postmodernity as a concept helps grasp this condition, the condition also suggests reasons why the Chinese facing this experience should find in postmodernism a discourse that speaks to their experience.

The third and last terrain of interrogation is the cultural vision that is developed out of the experience of postmodernity, or cultural postmodernism, as illustrated in fashion, music, architecture, video, art, literature, and theoretical discourses. It may be a truism to say that, in China in the 1980s, the issue of postmodernism first emerged not as a theoretical challenge (as the cliché goes) but as an aesthetic expectation. This observation, far from dismissing the problematics of Chinese postmodernism as those of mere borrowed forms and homegrown fantasies, should open up discussions of the historical and theoretical implications of the expectation for a *houxiandai zhuyi* (postmodernism) as a self-fulfilling prophesy and should unravel the aesthetic complex that becomes the surest sign, indeed a conspicuous stage, of the changing economic, social, political, and cultural relations in post-Mao China.[9]

Any honest student of the brief, yet convoluted, history of Chinese postmodernism would have to admit that, during most of the 1980s, postmodernism as a discourse preceded postmodernism as a reality, and that the intense collective experience of change, similar to that of the West on a macrohistorical scale, did not give rise to the Euro-American feeling that "the modern was now over."[10] If the history of post-Mao China can be seen as a speeding up of the socioeconomic evolution of the postwar West, recorded by a historical camera, then modernity with a vengeance is clearly the force that shaped the same libidinal and ideological landscape that gave rise to both a high modernism and a parasitic postmodernism at the same time.

These preliminary differentiations may help us focus more historically on the central issues of Chinese postmodernism by disengaging from some heated, yet ultimately unproductive, debates regarding Chinese postmodernism. The first of these debates is about China's qualifications to be a postmodern society and, by implication, about the "authenticity" of a Chinese-style post-modernism. Cultural conservatives, realists, and modernists in China tend to see Chinese postmodernism as comically out of touch with Chinese reality— as defined by common sense, that is, in terms of income per capita; the illiter-acy rate; the vast rural population; the socialist economic, social, and political infrastructure; and so forth—and therefore unwarranted. Meanwhile, apolo-gists of Chinese postmodernism are busy pointing out the presence in the Chinese cities of postmodern enclaves and logos that are in every respect as authentic as their Western originals. The result is an escalating antagonism along the battle lines that might be called "postmodernism for postmod-ernism's own sake." Under these circumstances, any critical account of the issue would be forced into the corners of empiricism and nominalism, both of which in turn feed the prevalent suspicion that Chinese postmodernism is produced by the social (and particularly intellectual) fantasy of, and a pro-longed obsession with, catching up with the West.

This is to some extent valid, as is evidenced by the insistence of Chinese postmodernists on the authenticity of Chinese postmodernism, which conve-niently overlooks the fact that *authenticity* is a term that is called into question by postmodernism. Authenticity also implies holding on to the idea of an au-thentic Chinese national terrain, which is hardly tenable, since even those Chinese critics who participate in the conversation about a Chinese moder-nity or postmodernity are widely dispersed globally, bringing to bear on the discussion the cultural orientations and prejudices of their many locations. It is more productive, under the circumstances, to approach the question of Chinese postmodernity as one aspect of a global postmodernity mediated by the terrains and histories identifiable as Chinese. Finally, it is also important to bear in mind in these discussions a distinction between postmodernism as a description of some social and cultural reality, and postmodernism as a concept with which to grasp and make sense of a complex reality that does not lend itself to comprehension through categories marked by the spatial and temporal teleologies of modernity.

A more constructive response to the accusations brought against Chi-nese postmodernism is perhaps to avoid dutifully characterizing the causal relationship between a certain material condition and a certain cultural-theoretical expression, all of which are, in effect, based on the particular body of experience of the West—above all, the United States. Rather, what can be derived from the Bermanian differentiation is that all three (conceptual) levels of the process of postmodernity could, and in fact did, function relatively autonomously and claim their own empirical, ideological, and historical authenticities. The cultural vision of postmodernism, for example, once available to individuals and communities, could produce a historical experience of its own, which would in turn define its own socioeconomic truthfulness. The postmodern rhetoric of the disappearance of center, origin, teleology, and depth is as much an appropriation by the postmodern secularization as it is an articulation of it; the Derridean game of the sign and the text is not so much a space in which a postsocialist subjectivity grows as the very grammar by which it is constituted. Desire and pleasure, considered in the market or consumer context, are integral parts of material and social production as is the production of more desire and pleasure. The political economy of Chinese postmodernism offers, therefore, more than a hint that the reform bureaucracy of post-Mao China not only has grasped the market mechanism but also has managed to legitimize it in terms of human nature, as the liberation of the forces of production. This has become more apparent since the Tiananmen tragedy of 1989, but especially since the nearly total release of market forces following Deng Xiaoping's "imperial" visit to the south, when he gave his blessings to the total release of market forces without worrying about their consequences for socialism. The message clearly was that the market economy and the promotion of consumption would serve as distractions from politics, which were always fraught with the danger of a repeat of the events of 1989. To the extent that Chinese postmodernism celebrates a mass-consumer culture, it then appears in its complicity with the strategy of the regime, much as postmodernism in the United States is complicit with the unfolding of a global capitalism.

Here, the causal relationship is found not between the economic and the cultural, or the base and the superstructure, but rather within the respective histories of economy and ideology, of content and forms. And it is the historical chain of signification, with all its gaps, omissions, repressions, and contradictions, that becomes the location for a critical diagnosis and a dialectical narrative. In an environment that nourishes "the identification of the commodity with its image" and the "symbiosis between the market and the media,"[11] the structural rather than the mechanical relationship between economy, experience, and culture becomes all the more important. In the postmodern condition, production and culture mingle with one another through a dialectical third: commodification and consumption. Thus, the encounter with postmodernity is first and foremost a cultural encounter; in other words, the contact with global capitalism is to a great extent the contact with its culture, discourse, ideology, and vice versa. If postmodernism is, paraphrasing Jameson to eliminate teleology, the cultural logic of global capitalism, then in the Chinese context it must also be at one and the same time the cultural logic of a postrevolutionary, yet residually socialist, Chinese form of life.

Historicization necessarily leads to a political understanding of the issue. In fact, the discourse of Chinese postmodernism has become one of the focal points of recent cultural-political debates among Chinese intellectuals. While the question of the authenticity of Chinese postmodernism receded from the front line of theoretical debate (but certainly not from the public discourse), it was replaced by questions concerning its political implications. This shift has less to do with the internal theoretical evolution in the Chinese field and more with the tidal wave of marketization unleashed in the early 1990s. Ironically, when consumerism and mass-consumer culture swept the country and reshaped the Chinese landscape, postmodernism as a descriptive paradigm, or, better still, as a sign of a collective anticipation, became a useful political label. As the theoretical interest in Western writings on postmodernism yields to a critical urgency of mapping out the dizzying changes in Chinese culture, or, more precisely, popular culture, categories that used to be the building blocks of the discourse of postmodernism—global capital, the international market, consumption, mobility, decenteredness—all melt into the background of an avalanche of case studies on topics ranging from TV soap operas to advertisements, from social fashions (such as nostalgia) to "the new state of affairs" (xinzhuangtai) of everyday life. In a sense, one may say that the discussion of Chinese postmodernism flourished only in its afterlife, namely, as Chinese culture studies. Most of the essays included in this collection fall into this category.

Like its Western—in particular, American—counterparts, Chinese culture studies has as its explicit goal the study of mass culture and various forms of everyday life. And like its Western counterparts again, underlying Chinese culture studies is a paradigmatic shift from intellectual discourse to mass culture, from high theory to "low" text, from literature to other media, especially visual media. Unlike culture studies in the West, however, the Chinese encounter with the booming everyday world and its cultural manifestations overlapped with the most brutal moment of an all-out effort to establish a market economy and to integrate with global capitalism. The deconstruction of the aesthetic-philosophical discourse of humanism and the high modernism of the 1980s, which for Chinese postmodernists is nothing more than the last mythology of the New Era, allows a more concrete context in which a decisively postmodern critical sensibility takes shape.[12] The rejection of total submission to the intellectual genealogy of universal modernity here also gives rise to a postcolonial perspective from which to look at Western discourse. The Chinese discourse of postcolonial criticism, often framed in nativist terms, both indicates the heightened awareness of power relationships in cultural production and manifests the kind of confidence derived from the Chinese economic success in the global market. While the Chinese critique of hegemonic hierarchy and teleological progress are theoretically valid, the main thrust of such a critique lies clearly in its assertion, sometimes celebration, of the legitimacy and richness of the present—of secularization, locality, the everyday world, and, ultimately, "the people," whose invention is conditioned as much by the emergent market as by the residual (socialist) state.

Thus, the sociological specificity of a Chinese postmodern culture may lie in the fact that, in critic Zhang Yiwu's words, "the poetic aspirations for a 'civilization' and 'life of abundance' designed by the discourse of modernity now become a realistic choice in the everyday sphere itself." [13] The demise of intellectual high culture in the face of consumerism then gives rise to a whole variety of *jouissance* that is derived from the public's widespread belief that they are decidedly putting something behind them and shifting all kinds of socialist or modernist paradigms of social value, psychological pattern, cultural mode, and stylistic fashion. The critical affirmation of mass culture obviously draws its theoretical inspiration from postmodernism, postcolonialism, critical theory, and cultural studies in the West, particularly in the United States. But to determine the historical meaning of Chinese postmodernism is to determine the correlation and differentiation between various forms of post-isms that form a linguistic maze in contemporary Chinese cultural criticism: post-Maoism, postrevolutionism, postcolonialism, postsocialism, postmetaphysicalism, postutopianism, post–New Eraism, postexperimentalism, post-Fordism, postallegoricalism, post–Fifth Generationism, and so forth. Nearly eight decades ago, during the May Fourth New Culture movement, the first Chinese "cultural revolution" was driven by a "pathos of novelty," when every publication carried in its title the adjective *new*. The third "cultural revolution" of the present day is marked by *post-* as its signifier. Against the background of the first and the second (socialist) cultural revolutions, this third cultural revolution may signify exhaustion with the promise of modernity, even as China would seem to be achieving the long elusive goal of modernization and moving beyond.

Yet, the disengagement from intellectual high culture and the embrace of the everyday pose two challenges to the pioneers of Chinese culture studies. First, there is the need to formulate a theoretical qualification of globalization, or global capitalism, as a Chinese experience, and to perform a close analysis of its relationship to the state as well as to the everyday sphere. Second, there is the need to use theory itself, which contains its own historicization, self-reflexively. However, in meeting these challenges, Chinese postmodernists are often put on the defensive by their liberal and conservative opponents, partly because of the postmodernists' almost total absorption in mapping out an explosive new cultural space, and partly because of a structural separation between critics on the front line of cultural studies (and cultural journalism) and theoreticians in the traditional disciplines of philosophy, aesthetics, and literary theory, a pattern that formed during the 1980s, when theory enjoyed unchallenged authority in developing a semiautonomous intellectual discourse vis-à-vis the state ideological apparatus. Last but not least, the theoretical discourse of mass culture has yet to clarify its own stand in a differentiated social and intellectual sphere in specific fundamental ideological and political terms.

Not surprisingly, from these weak spots, liberals have waged their attack on the new critical discourse, which they playfully, and somewhat contemptuously, have labeled "postology" (houxue, the Chinese term for theories with the prefix of post-, but it can also mean postscholarship or "late-born learning"). In a frequently quoted article by Lei Yi published in Dushu, the author accuses the "post-" critics of confusing First World problematics with Third World situations, and of universalizing theoretical discourses of postmodernism without a much needed process of nativization. The general validity of Lei Yi's point is obvious on a superficial level. However, his call for a "study of the Chinese context" has a political implication that reveals what is truly at stake in this debate. By rhetorically praising the courage of confronting the epistemological hegemony of the West through the works of Michel Foucault and Edward Said, Lei Yi is in fact deploring the lack of such courage in Chinese post- critics to confront the hegemony and power in their own Chinese environment.[14]

This position and strategy are shared by other liberals. In an article published in Hong Kong, Henry Y-H. Zhao discerns an unholy alliance between Chinese postmodernism and mass culture that aims to "destroy elite culture." By a self-positioning of elite intellectuals as a critical priesthood on the margins of modern society, Zhao defines the rise of mass culture and its theoretical discourse as "neoconservatism." For him, there seems to be a short circuit between a "conscious challenge to the global victory of late capitalism" and "an apology for the degradation of contemporary culture."[15] Xu Ben, another critic, further argues that a premodern-modern distinction is more crucial than an East-West opposition, and that the "chief form of oppression" in China is not the imperial or "postcolonial" West but the totalitarian regime at home. Based on his suspicion that the Chinese discourse of postcolonialism is centered on a celebration of indigenousness, and not on critical resistance (its resistance is directed to the "discursive oppression from the First World"), Xu immediately subjects Chinese postmodernism to a political trial of ideological identity with or loyalty to the Chinese regime, or to the universal West. The verdict is by no means unpredictable. Criticizing the Chinese discourse of postcolonialism, Xu Ben writes:

> [Chinese postcolonialism] is out of touch with Chinese reality. By elevating the discursive oppression from the First World into the chief form of oppression experienced in China today, it shuns—unwittingly or not—the violence and oppression that exist in native social reality. Although "Third World" criticism from China takes pains to keep a distance from the official discourse of nationalism, it nonetheless avoids any critical analysis of it. Its antagonism has only an international edge and no domestic pointedness. Therefore, not only can this discourse coexist peacefully with the official discourse of nationalism; it accommodates the interests of the latter. By ignoring immediate oppression at home and criticizing a "global" one at a distance, it developed a phony mode of resistance-criticism in the humanities that is extremely conducive to the state's ideological control and appropriation.[16]

By placing the Chinese debate over theory, mass culture, and nationalism against the global background of capitalist euphoria and ideological homogeneity, liberal criticism (which no doubt has its own version of postmodern reality) nevertheless shows the implicit link between the cultural vision of Chinese postmodernism and the historical experience of postrevolutionary China. It is necessary to underline here that the debate over postmodernism is not to be grasped in terms of contrasts between East and West, First World and Third World, politics and antipolitics, et cetera. Not the least important aspect of these debates may be that postmodernism is an issue in intra-elite struggles, in which it serves as an intellectual weapon for those among the Chinese elite who are willing to recognize globalization and mass culture as irreducible moments of a contemporary Chinese reality, who find in postmodernism a means to grasp critically both the legacies of past hierarchies and their reconfigurations under a regime of global capitalism, and whose antipolitical politics may not lead to radical resistance to oppression and exploitation but at the very least may open up cultural spaces in which such resistance assumes new forms. Postmodernity in China confronts a historical legacy that differs from its Euro-American counterparts. Having experienced modernity as colonialism from the outside and as a coercive state project from the inside, postmodernity may allow for the emergence of alternative social and cultural formations that do not so much signal the end of modernity as mark the beginning of imagining alternatives to it.

This collection of essays is aimed at making the problems of a Chinese postmodernity explicit and available to critical interrogation. In doing so, it acknowledges the fundamental ambiguity of the issue of Chinese postmodernism, namely, its possible complicity in the culture of global capitalism, its origins in mass participation in economic life, and its evasion of issues of political participation. Thus, the critical effort at redefining the national culture in terms of enhanced freedom and a new logic of imagination in the everyday world both prefigures new paradigms of Chinese culture studies and is hampered by its internal difficulties and external resistances. Culture studies in China may share with its Euro-American counterparts an evasion of politics or even the depoliticization of everyday life. If this problem appears with greater urgency in the Chinese case, it may be because of the centrality to Chinese postmodernism of the intricate relationship between the everyday sphere, the state, the (elite) intellectuals, and the omnipresent ideology and culture of global capitalism. Yet, ambiguity, understood dialectically, is not only the mode in which Chinese postmodernism is articulated; it also points to the directions in which we may engage this problematic and the search for cultural and social alternatives. In Walter Benjamin's words, it is "the figurative appearance of the dialectic, the law of the dialectic at a standstill." [17]

The essays in this volume grapple with the intriguing problems that may render Chinese postmodernism unique historically and that therefore make it all the more relevant to grasp "the condition of postmodernity" in both Chinese and global contexts. In all of these senses, it is possible to suggest that postmodernism as a way of grasping contemporary China must account not only for commonalities between China and others in a global condition of postmodernity but also for the ways in which China itself may be a generator of postmodernity as a result of its own unique historical experience and the contradictions that are the legacy of that experience. Obviously, this is a question that is far too broad and weighty to be encompassed within one volume, but we have made an effort through preliminary inquiries into selected aspects of the question to open up a terrain for future inquiry.

The theoretical and political concerns discussed above are reflected in the essays that follow. While postmodernism in the PRC or the cultural form of Chinese postsocialism remains the focus of the volume, there are also substantive analyses of postmodernism in Taiwan and Hong Kong. Rather than merely examples from the Chinese "peripheries," the five essays that address this topic contribute directly to our understandings of the central problematic of Chinese postmodernism as a historical phenomenon rooted in uneven development of the modern world system and conditioned by radically different collective experiences, memories, and imaginations at a sub- or transnational level. To this extent, the intricate relationship between postmodernism and a new brand of nationalism in Taiwan, or the role that colonialism, neocolonialism, and postcolonialism play in the making of the postmodernism in Hong Kong, is internal to the question of postsocialism in the mainland rather than external.

Thematically, the essays fall into four broad areas. Wang Ning, Ping-hui Liao, Anthony King and Abidin Kusno, and Xiaoying Wang map the terrain of the postmodern in the PRC, Taiwan, and Hong Kong respectively. Liu Kang, Sheldon Hsiao-peng Lu, and Sebastian Liao provide a contour of the politicality of the issue of postmodernism in different locales, as it is entangled with the rise of the mass culture, the decline of the enlightenment intellectuals, the forces of globalization, and the new wave of nation making after the end of the Cold War. More detailed analyses follow, as Dai Jinhua, Chen Xiaoming, Jeroen de Kloet, Chao-yang Liao, and Evans Chan look into the cultural manifestations of Chinese postmodernism as particular forms of innovation, production, consumption, and fashion. The cultural scenes and their political implications are further explored by the studies of the paradigmatic change in contemporary Chinese literature by Zhang Yiwu, Wendy Larson, Xiaobing Tang, and Xiaobin Yang. Finally, Xudong Zhang seeks to bring the issue of Chinese postmodernism a theoretical narrative by rethinking its politics and historicity through its challenge to the establishment of Chinese modernism and its ambiguous relationship to the Chinese postsocialism as both an everyday reality and a discursive intervention.

Notes

1 Fredric Jameson visited China in 1985 and taught at Beijing University during the fall semester. The Chinese translation of the transcribed lectures was subsequently published under the title *Houxiandai zhuyi yu wenhua lilun* (Postmodernism and cultural theory) in 1986 (and in Taiwan in 1989). The lectures remain to this day the most widely read and quoted work in Chinese discussions of postmodernism.

2 See Marshall Berman, *All That Is Solid Melts into Air* (New York: Penguin Books, 1988), 15–37.

3 For further discussion of this problem, see Arif Dirlik, "Modernism and Antimodernism in Mao Zedong's Marxism," in *Critical Perspectives on Mao Zedong's Thought*, ed. Arif Dirlik, Paul Healy, and Nick Knight (Atlantic Highlands, N.J.: Humanities Press, 1997), 59–83.

4 We are referring here to the recent "Confucian revival" that has had such an impact on mainland scholars and that finds in Confucianism the key to the recent rapid development of Chinese societies. See Arif Dirlik, "Confucius in the Borderlands: Global Capitalism and the Reinvention of Confucianism," *boundary 2* 22, no. 3 (fall 1995): 229–73.

5 Ahmed states: "Ethno-religious revivalism is both cause and effect of postmodernism." See Akbar S. Ahmed, *Postmodernism and Islam: Predicament and Promise* (New York: Routledge, 1992), 13. What Ahmed has in mind is that even as the reassertion of ethnicity challenges a Eurocentric modernity, postmodernism allows for and legitimizes the reemergence of ethnicities and cultural forms suppressed under regimes of modernity.

6 For a sharply critical discussion of the Chinese economic miracle, see Richard Smith, "Creative Destruction: Capitalist Development and China's Environment," *New Left Review* 222 (1997): 3–41.

7 For a compelling study of postsocialist industrialization and social organization in rural China, see Wang Ying, *Xin jitizhuyi* (New collectivism) (Beijing: Jingji Guanli Chuban-she, 1996).

8 Gellner suggests that the flourishing of modern nationalisms depends both on a prevailing "universal high culture" (industrialization, rationalization, etc.) and on some social, cultural, and natural barriers that are insurmountable by individuals. This dual basis, according to Gellner, gives rise to "resentments and discontents" that are always at work in nationalist discourses and bestows on nationalism a "fated" atmosphere. See Ernest Gellner, *Nations and Nationalism* (Ithaca, N.Y.: Cornell University Press, 1983), 61–62.

9 It might be useful to point out here a particular feature of the Chinese term *houxiandai zhuyi* (postmodernism), which has somewhat different implications in a Chinese historical context than it has in a Euro-American context. In periodizing the "modern" in Chinese history, dating back to the initial encounter with Euro-America during the Opium War (1839–1842), Chinese historians have used two terms, *jindai* (recent) and *xiandai* (contemporary), the former referring to the period 1839–1919, and the latter referring to the period since 1919 (the May Fourth movement), but even more specifically to the period since 1921, when the Communist Party was founded. In historical periodization, therefore, *xiandai* refers specifically to the period of the Communist Revolution. The Chinese term for *postmodernism*, therefore, may be viewed generally as meaning *postmodern*, but it also carries strong connotations of *postrevolutionary*.

10 Paul Bové, preface to *Early Postmodernism: Foundational Essays*, ed. Paul A. Bové (Durham, N.C.: Duke University Press, 1995), 4.

11 Fredric Jameson, *Postmodernism, or, The Cultural Logic of Late Capitalism* (Durham, N.C.: Duke University Press, 1991), 275.

12 See Zhang Yiwu, "Zuihoude shenhua" (The last mythology), in *Renwen jingshen xunsi lu* (In search of the human spirit), ed. Wang Xiaoming (Shanghai: Wenhui Chubanshe, 1995), 137–41.

13 Zhang Yiwu, "Xin zhuangtaide jueqi" (The emergence of the new state of affairs), *Zhongshan* 2 (1994): 115; translation by Xudong Zhang.

14 Lei Yi, "Beijing yu cuowei" (Background and dislocation), *Dushu* (Reading) 4 (1995): 16–19.

15 Zhao Yiheng, " 'Post-ism' and the New Conservatism in China," *Ershiyi shiji* (Twenty-first century) 27 (Feb. 1995): 11; translation by Xudong Zhang.

16 Xu Ben, " 'Disan shijie piping' zai dangjin Zhongguode chujing" (The situation of "Third World criticism" in contemporary China), *Ershiyi shiji* (Twenty-first century) 27 (Feb. 1995): 17; translation by Xudong Zhang.

17 Walter Benjamin, *Charles Baudelaire: A Lyric Poet in the Era of High Capitalism* (London: Verso, 1983), 171.

i mapping the postmodern

wang ning

1   The Mapping of Chinese Postmodernity

Whether there is such a thing as postmodernism has been, and continues to be, controversial. In this essay, I argue that postmodernity as a cultural phenomenon in the contemporary era exists not only in the West but in the East as well—as evidenced by recent debates on the question of postmodernity and the "postmodern fad" in China and in other Asian and Third World societies. For the past thirty years, the debate about postmodernity has been of acute interest to major European and American scholars and critics in the humanities and social sciences.[1] Some, moreover, have extended the consideration of postmodernity to Asian and other Third World cultures and literatures. Until recently, many Western scholars who think that postmodernism does, in fact, exist have held nevertheless that it is a Western phenomenon that is irrelevant to Third World and Asian societies, which lack the conditions for postmodernity.[2] Frequent cultural and academic exchanges in recent years have inclined increasing numbers of Western scholars to think of postmodernity as a universal phenomenon, even if it germinated in the cultural soil of Western postindustrial society.[3] These days, when debates about postmodernism overlap with questions of postcolonialism or postcoloniality in the non-Western world, the relevance of postmodernism to scholars, writers, and literary critics in the East is enhanced even further.[4]

The global extension of postmodernism has other consequences. As a Chinese scholar studying postmodernism from within its current creative and critical practices in the Chinese context, I would argue that postmodernism is no longer a monolithic phenomenon but rather has generated different forms both in the West and in the East.[5] So to observe postmodernism—as either a cultural phenomenon, a contemporary episteme or weltanschauung, a literary current, or something else—it is necessary to construct this concept at different levels in a pluralistic way. In this essay, I try to avoid using the term *postmodernism*, as it is undoubtedly a Western cultural product that is characterized by postindustrial symptoms.[6] Instead, I use the more inclusive terms *postmodern* and *postmodernity* to map its travel, spread, and development in China. In mapping out the Chinese postmodern, one of my primary goals is to elucidate the similarities and differences between Chinese "postmodernism" and its Western counterpart. Before I get into these complex issues, however, I would like to say a few words by way of introduction about the various forms this postmodern has assumed.[7]

Postmodernism, or Postmodernity Redescribed

Since the beginning of the international postmodernism debate, postmodernism has undergone continual redefinition and redescription. Jean-François Lyotard, Fredric Jameson, Matei Calinescu, Ihab Hassan, Leslie Fiedler, Douwe Fokkema, Hans Bertens, Linda Hutcheon, Jonathan Arac, and Brian McHale, among others, have offered their own definitions and descriptions of postmodernism. Their constructs are based largely on Western practices, seldom touching on Asian or Third World cultures and literatures. Jameson and Fokkema, whose descriptions and criticisms of postmodernism are the most influential in China with regard to Third World cultures and Chinese literature and literary criticism, are nevertheless unable to redefine it on the basis of a knowledge of Chinese culture and literature. Jameson's construction of postmodernism, in particular, based as it is on a periodization of capitalism, would automatically exclude China, for China is still a developing country in the Third World and is far from attaining the standards of a postindustrial society. But in reality, uneven development in its politics, economy, and culture undoubtedly manifests postindustrial symptoms in the economy and postmodern elements in political life and culture. Beginning with Jameson's and Fokkema's descriptions of the actual situation in China, postmodernism could be redescribed in terms of the following eight forms it has assumed within the scope of literature and culture alone: (1) a fundamental cultural phenomenon in highly developed capitalist countries or post-industrial societies that occasionally appears in unevenly developed regions within underdeveloped countries; (2) a kind of worldview, or a way of looking at the world and life, in which the world is no longer a world of totality but rather one of plurality, fragmentation, and decentralization; (3) a main current of literature and art after the fall of modernism, both continuous and discontinuous with modernism, and relevant both to avant-garde experimentation and to popular literature; (4) a narrative style or kind of discourse that is characterized by suspicion of "master narratives," or "metanarratives," and that resorts to nonselective or quasi-nonselective devices and to a certain "schizophrenic" structure of the text, in which meaning is actually decentralized in the course of a fragmentary narration; (5) an interpretive code or a reading strategy with which earlier and even non-Western texts can be analyzed from the perspective of postmodernity; (6) a philosophical trend that is contrary, in the current postindustrial and consumer society, to the elite preoccupation with the Enlightenment, or as a sort of post-Enlightenment phenomenon characterized by the crisis of legitimation and representation; (7) a cultural strategy adopted by Asian and Third World critics during their economic modernization and struggle against cultural colonialism and linguistic hegemonism; and (8) a critical mode that emerged after the failure of structuralism and that is characterized by Foucauldian and Derridean poststructuralist approaches to literary texts, which dominate current cultural criticism and cultural studies.[8] This is how I have recently come to understand postmodernism in the current global context—as a sort of extended modernism, but one that needs to be distinguished from modernism.

Juxtaposing postmodernism with modernism may not be novel for Western scholars. Many Chinese readers and critics still think that there is little difference between the two,[9] but others maintain that postmodernism actually marks a distinctive break from all modernist conventions and even a powerful challenge against modernism. For those who take the latter position, modernism is canonical and thus conservative, while postmodernism is avant-garde and thus very progressive. I would rather view the relationship between the two from a diachronic and a synchronic perspective. That is, as a movement that follows modernism, postmodernism evidently has something in common with the latter; but it differs from postmodernism in its philosophical foundation, aesthetic ideals, artistic representation, as well as in the cultural context in which it originated and developed. It is true that in their debts to the irrationalist trends of culture and philosophy, modernism and postmodernism are quite similar. But modernism is based largely on the assumptions and ideas of Schopenhauer, Bergson, Kierkegaard (partly), Nietzsche, and Freud, while postmodernism is more indebted to existentialists such as Nietzsche (as rediscovered by Foucault), Kierkegaard (partly), Heidegger, Sartre, and Freud (as reinterpreted by Lacan). Thus, it is not surprising that they are more different than alike in many respects.

In an earlier essay, I identified eleven major differences between modernism and postmodernism.[10] Further examination would probably reveal more differences between the two, but these are sufficient to indicate that postmodernism not only appears after modernism but also runs counter to the dominant code of modernism in content. As an undercurrent, postmodernity can be traced back in history, for it is anticipated by the baroque period, by realism, and by the historical avant-garde in Western literature and art. But it emerged completely only after World War II, when modernism became more canonical and exhausted itself. In its belatedness, postmodernism might well be interpreted as a "culture of secondarity." [11] While in recent years, postmodernism has lost some of its popularity in the West, it has been gradually penetrating Third World and Asian societies as a globalized cultural phenomenon and as a literary and artistic current responding to the frustration with modernism. Nevertheless, modernism is the logical starting point of postmodernism; as Lyotard has observed, the postmodern is essentially "part of the modern" and is an inevitable product of the development of modernism. We cannot neglect the intrinsic connection between the two, but instead must understand the postmodern according to the paradox of the "post" and the "modo."

In discussing the Chinese postmodern, the more inclusive term *postmodernity* is preferable to *postmodernism*, for, unlike the latter, it does not presuppose a certain cultural tradition (which is lacking in China) nor is it subject to the assumption of a solid modernity as a precondition for postmodernity. I do not wish to negate the fact that although it has something to do with an intrinsic logic in the development of Chinese culture and literature, Chinese postmodernity is chiefly a "borrowed thing" from the West. Mapping its presence in China may help us understand what Chinese postmodernity means in a world of global capital and a globalized cultural context, how it is different from its original form(s) in the cultural context of Western society, the extent to which this borrowed thing has assumed indigenous characteristics, and how it has functioned in the current Post–New Period (*hou xinshiqi*) Chinese culture and literature as well as in contemporary Chinese society, which is colored by the market economy and a sort of postsocialism.[12]

The Reception of Postmodernism in Chinese Literature

We can easily trace the origin and development of postmodernism in China by considering the literary field. Postmodernism was introduced and discussed in the Chinese cultural and literary context in the early 1980s, concurrently with the revival of modernism in literature of the New Period (*xin shiqi*, 1978–1989). The introduction and translation of modernist writings in China is by no means a contemporary event. Modernism first arrived in China in the 1920s, and almost all of the major writers and critics at the time either were involved in the "modernist" movement, were more or less influenced by it, were interested in the debate on it, or reacted to it with their own individual stand,[13] which paved the way for its second high tide in the New Period. But in the late 1930s, with the increasing influence of Marxist doctrine among Chinese intellectuals, modernism, along with other expressions of Western thought, such as Nietzsche's philosophy and Freud's psychoanalysis, subsided and was of little interest among literary circles. It was not "recovered" until after 1978, when it flourished for a second time. During this period, there was a proliferation of polemical discussions of questions such as: What is modernism? Does modernism contain progressive ideas, or is it a totally decadent Western bourgeois ideology? Should modernism be introduced in China, or should it be rejected despite its strong influence and academic value in the West? Should socialist China have modernist culture and literature? The socialist realist doctrine of "Chinese characteristics" (as the organic combination of revolutionary realism and revolutionary romanticism) provided the standard for judging whether modernism was progressive or reactionary. It is not surprising that there was no definite conclusion to this debate, but scholars and writers seemed to agree that modernist literature should be critically and moderately introduced and studied, though not necessarily advocated.[14] It was in the course of this debate that issues concerning postmodernism were touched on, and the terms *postmodern* and *postmodernism* appeared occasionally in journals devoted to foreign literature (although they were translated inaccurately, despite the fact that the terms had already been discussed in the field of architecture).[15]

Generally speaking, postmodernism appeared in three forms: as a poststructuralist theoretical discourse, as an avant-garde intellectual rebellion against the modernist episteme, and as a contemporary consumer culture. There were signs of all three in Chinese culture, literature, and art, but the greatest impact seems to have occurred in literary circles, in part because writers and critics were most active in pursuing the most recent fads, and because they commanded the largest space for writing and publishing. As a literary movement, postmodernism was launched in China in 1980, with the publication of the Chinese translation of John Barth's essay "The Literature of Replenishment: Postmodernist Fiction" in *Report on Foreign Literature (Wai-guo wenxue baodao)*, a journal published in Shanghai that stopped publication in the late 1980s. Since then, other journals devoted to foreign literature — for instance, *World Literature* (*Shijie wenxue*), *Foreign Literature and Art* (*Waiguo wenyi*), the *Bulletin of Foreign Literature* (*Waiguo wenxue tongxun*), *Literature Abroad* (*Guowai wenxue*), *Foreign Literatures* (*Waiguo wenxue*), and *Contemporary Foreign Literature* (*Dangdai waiguo wenxue*) — have published literary works by postmodernists such as García Márquez, Borges, Nabokov, Barth, Barthelme, Salinger, Mailer, Heller, Beckett, Pynchon, Vonnegut, Robbe-Grillet, Calvino, and others. They were joined in short order by academic journals of literature and culture, such as the authoritative *Social Sciences in China* (*Zhongguo shehui kexue*), which was published in both Chinese and English; *Reading* (*Dushu*); *Peking University Journal* (*Beijing Daxue xuebao*); *Contemporary Cinema* (*Dangdai dianying*); *Studies of Literature and Art* (*Wenyi yanjiu*); *Literary Review* (*Wenxue pinglun*); *Foreign Literature Review* (*Waiguo wenxue pinglun*); *Literature and Art Gazette* (*Wenyi bao*); *Foreign Literature Studies* (*Waiguo wenxue yanjiu*); *People's Literature* (*Renmin wenxue*); *Shanghai Literature* (*Shanghai wenxue*), *Purple Mountain* (*Zhongshan*); and *Flower City* (*Huacheng*), all of which published translated articles on postmodernism by Western scholars such as Ihab Hassan, Jean-François Lyotard, Fredric Jameson, William Spanos, Douwe Fokkema, Jonathan Arac, Linda Hutcheon, and Hans Bertens, and included, as well, introductory and critical essays by Chinese scholars.

With regard to translated theoretical books, two books in postmodern studies deserve special mention: Jameson's *Postmodernism and Cultural Theories* (*Houxiandaizhuyi yu wenhua lilun*) (1987, in Chinese) [16] and Fokkema's and Bertens's edited volume, *Approaching Postmodernism* (*Zuoxiang houxiandaizhuyi*) (1991, in Chinese).[17] Jameson's book is quoted and discussed most often, simply because of its early publication and the author's international prestige. In fact, since Jameson has always adopted a Marxist critical attitude toward postmodernism, his work is quoted by both supporters and critics of postmodernism. Although the book is not a scholarly work written in a systematic manner, it has influenced Chinese critical circles and literary scholars about Western postmodernism and informed them about how it differs from modernism. Its role in enlightening Chinese scholars cannot be underestimated. Fokkema's and Bertens's book, because of its academic value and empirical approach to literature proper, is quoted mainly by literary critics and scholars, and has enabled Chinese scholars to further their exploration into literary postmodernism from both the linguistics and genre studies points of view. Currently, it is the most widely available book on postmodernism both on the mainland and in Taiwan.

In addition, such internationally prestigious scholars as Hassan, Jameson, Fokkema, Arac, Bertens, Ralph Cohen, and Terry Eagleton have been invited to participate in conferences or to lecture on postmodernism in China's universities and research institutes,[18] bringing with them the results of their most recent research and helping to push forward the study of postmodernism in China. Also, since 1990, a number of international conferences on postmodernism and its relation to contemporary Chinese literature have been held in Beijing, Dalian, and Nanjing, at which Chinese and foreign writers, critics, and scholars have engaged in discussions about the possibility of postmodernism in China, the characteristics of Chinese postmodernism, if it exists, and its differences from what appears in the West. The socialist market economy that has been practiced in China since the beginning of the 1990s has also promoted the growth of postmodern elements on the Chinese cultural soil, with TV production, the film industry, advertising enterprises, and other forms of mass media increasingly challenging elite literature. In some big cities and coastal areas, a sort of "postmodern aura" has even appeared. Quite a few young artists and scholars do welcome the arrival of the postmodern, which they feel helps them create a pluralistic cultural atmosphere and emancipates artists' imaginations. To the intellectuals of liberal humanism, the rise of postmodernism in China has certainly helped decentralize or deterritorialize the long-standing totalitarian cultural conventions and literary discourse. For a period, especially in Beijing, speaking of postmodernism or other "postist" concepts (hou de gainian) emerged as a fad in cultured society and intellectual life. We can say for certain that postmodernism has entered China through the joint efforts of Chinese and Western scholars and translators and has been gradually influencing present-day Chinese culture and literature in varying degrees, as evidenced by the reactions, responses, and reception of many writers and critics.[19] The critical and creative reception of postmodernism has generated various postmodern versions that are often mixed with the premodern, high-modern, realistic, postromantic, and even indigenous and primitive, since China's politics and economy have been developing in an uneven and pluralistic way. If we focus our attention on literature and culture, we may identify at least six versions of postmodernity in present-day China.

The Six Versions of Postmodernity in China

In my earlier essay, I identified four versions of postmodernity in current Chinese culture and literature. The so-called Post–New Period began with the development of postmodern studies and with the changing cultural situation that began in the early 1990s, when China entered a new stage of market economy both culturally and literarily. Today, literature is increasingly colored by contemporary commercialization, which distinguishes it from the cultural dominant in the New Period, which was characterized by humanism and enlightenment. It is no longer "pure," as it used to be, but rather is affected by, or even marked with, contemporary consumer culture. And the dominant tendency is no longer toward elite culture and literature in its traditional sense but toward popular culture. So in this present mapping, I will describe or redescribe six versions of postmodernity in China.[20] It should be noted that some of these versions of postmodernity have already been relegated to the past and will be of significance only to researchers of literary and cultural history. I should also emphasize here that unlike the eight forms of postmodernism I have described in accordance with international criteria, the six versions that I identify here are derived from developments within the Chinese cultural terrain.

The first version of postmodernity can be found in the so-called avant-garde fiction (xianfeng xiaoshuo) and experimental poetry (shiyanpai shige) of young novelists such as Liu Suola, Xu Xing, Wang Shuo, Sun Ganlu, Yu Hua, Ge Fei, Ye Zhaoyan, Hong Feng, Ma Yuan, Mo Yan, Can Xue, and Lü Xin, and avant-garde poets such as Daozi, Zhou Lunyou, and others of the so-called Feifeizhuyi shipai (Feifei school of poetry), who appeared after 1985 with experimental writings that challenged canonical realist and modernist writings. Some of them acknowledged frankly that they were more influenced by the Western postmodernists than by the modernists. For example, Yu Hua and Ge Fei acknowledged that they read many works by Borges and García Márquez, although they did not regard these Western authors as postmodernists at the time.[21] Western postmodernists stimulated the Chinese creative imagination and inspired Chinese authors and poets to write innovative literary works. The avant-gardists recognized that there were no forbidden areas to their artistic exploration and experimentation.

On the other hand, some, such as Ma Yuan, have been unwilling to admit their indebtedness to Western postmodernism.[22] At the present time, some of these avant-gardists, for instance Ge Fei, Su Tong, and Mo Yan, are seeking to compromise with the current trend of commercialization and to find a comfortable intermediate zone between writing for literature and writing for the market. Their bold experimentation in the eighties did anticipate a new tone and aesthetic attitude different from the cultural dominant of New Period Chinese literature.[23] Following their experiments, young women writers such as Zhao Mei, Xu Lan, Chen Ran, Lin Bai, Xu Xiaobin, Hai Nan, Hong Ying, and Xu Kun have applied various devices to their experimental writings, which are categorized as either the "new fiction of experience" (xin tiyan xiaoshuo) or "new fiction of stance" (xin zhuangtai xiaoshuo), but their impact has not been as significant as that of the male avant-gardists.[24] Because of a limited audience and a depressed literary market for radical literary ideas, the avant-garde poets of postmodernism rarely publish their works in leading journals.[25] But it is noteworthy that Daozi and Zhou Lunyou do identify themselves with the American postmodernist poets, and others shout out the radical slogan "Down with Beidao!" (*Dadao Beidao*).[26] On the whole, however, the avant-garde poets have much less influence than the avant-garde novelists.

The second version of postmodernity is marked by the rise of the "new realist school" (*xin xieshi pai*) and its practitioners' reaction to, and challenge against, the radical experimentation of the avant-gardists. The school appears to anticipate a return to tradition and representation but in reality indicates a parody of traditional realism and a transcendence of modernism. It is not in actuality a literary school, but some might consider it as such and include in its ranks novelists such as Chi Li, Fang Fang, Liu Zhenyun, Liu Heng, and even Su Tong and Ye Zhaoyan,[27] whose works are characterized as appealing to the "immediacy of experience" and as suspecting the master narrative by virtue of pursuing a sort of intermediary point at which popular literature and high literature can merge, thereby giving full play to a sense of the "commonality" (*pingmin yishi*). In the late 1980s, these new realists, with their almost "silent" writing practices and their dissatisfaction with the radical experimentation with language and narrative discourse practiced by the avant-gardists, provided Chinese literature with a certain new dynamic—a sense of commonality, namely, a sense of "describing one's real state of mind and ideas . . . and making everything look truthful, very truthful indeed." [28] This sense cannot help but remind us of the sense of commonality created by the Western postmodernists, who also tried to "cross the border" and "close the gap" so as to eliminate the demarcation between high literature and popular literature. It is true that in the writings of the new realists, the traditional master narrative obviously disappears, and the whole work is filled with trifling things and redundant descriptions. The author's tone is indifferent rather than subjective. These writers intend to explore the possibilities of fiction writing, always renewing their faith in imagination rather than in the notion of reality. They do not believe that the purpose of literature is to enlighten people but are instead engaged in writing a kind of "petites histoires"—namely, insignificant happenings that could take place anywhere, any time. They resort to what they have actually experienced in life rather than to the master narrative or metanarrative. Obviously, this practice has roused some controversy in critical circles, partly because of the indeterminacy of the term *new realism* and partly because of these authors' indifferent and overwritten descriptions and redundant narrative style.[29] In any event, whatever critics might read from these new realist texts, postmodernity is at least one of the many codes used in analyzing and interpreting them.

Since China entered the socialist market economy in the early 1990s, any form of revolution has become history, and many changes have taken place in literary circles and in intellectual life during this postrevolutionary period.[30]

Like anything in a consumer society, cultural production "is thereby driven back inside a mental space which is no longer that of some degraded collective 'objective spirit,' " and history, "by way of our own pop images and simulacra of that history, . . . itself remains forever out of reach." [31] Confronted by a commercial economy and a consumption-oriented creative and cultural life, intellectuals and men of letters increasingly feel in crisis. Thus, the question of the "crisis of the humanistic spirit" (renwen jingshen de weiji) is raised before them.[32] In the face of an emerging popular culture, some are shocked at first and then try desperately to maintain their elite stand; others, because of the temptation of money and commercialization, involve themselves in business, thus giving up their original aesthetic position; still others try to find the middle of the road by readjusting their position and analyzing popular culture in a theoretical way. Thus, the third version of postmodernity is unique: largely attacked by humanistic intellectuals but more popular among ordinary people, especially young university students. This is the controversial "Wang Shuo phenomenon," which represents a kind of commercializing orientation in literary creation and cultural life. This version is characterized by pastiche literature (pingcou wenxue), which combines many irrelevant events to make up a story; by the literature of entrustment (shou weituo de wenxue), in which an author writes about a certain company or enterprise in an exaggerated manner, usually for a considerable amount of money; by the literature of the mass media (chuanmei wenxue), which includes especially TV series and TV journalism; by the literature of consumption (xiaofei wenxue), where various popular newspapers flood the cultural market; and even by the literature of royalty bargaining (yijia wenxue) (as it is called by Wang Shuo), in which an author can name his price for a hot property. These are undoubtedly symptoms of the "crisis of representation" and of a "postindustrial culture." The reader can easily observe many postmodern elements in nonfiction, reportage, TV series, journalism, and popular histories, all of which strongly challenge serious or high literature. On the other hand, Wang Shuo, among others, by describing contemporary life in an ironic manner, tries to deconstruct all meaning by parodying or mocking anything serious and sublime. He and his cohorts openly announce that they are "playing" with literature, that they are merely "men of piled-up Chinese characters" (ma zi de ren) rather than men of letters. In this respect, it is easy to recognize the symptoms Jameson criticizes in his study of postmodernism. Although the literary value of their works is much less than that of avant-garde literature and the new realist fiction, their works are valuable for presenting a vast panorama of present-day Chinese society colored by postindustrial society and consumer culture.[33]

The fourth version of postmodernity is characterized by the "new historicist" attempt to recast historical figures in a parodic way or to create popular histories both in literary writing and in mass media production. For example, the characterization of Empress Wu (Wu Zetian) in novels, as well as in films and TV productions, made this controversial empress known to almost every household.[34] Thus, literary creation is subject even to film directors and TV producers.[35] Such an attempt is obviously inspired by the new historicist view that distinguishes historical events from historical narratives. Since history cannot repeat itself in an accurate way, it can only be represented in an allegorical way, or more specifically, in literary narration. Therefore, the demarcations between history and fiction, between a historical figure and a fictional character, and between historical truth and narrative truth are all obscured. Also, some writers, partly because they lack the raw material in their lives and partly because of the postmodern concept of parody or even collage, go to great lengths to rewrite canonical literary works or to recreate the story of controversial historical figures whose lives are full of legendary interest. Together with the mass media, including the television and film producers, and sometimes even advertising executives, the new historicist writers present a real challenge to elite literature. Culture becomes something to consume rather than a lofty artistic product, evidently a symptom of postmodern society. Although China is by no means a postmodern country at present, the uneven development of its economy, foreign trade, and even culture cannot help but endow it with elements of the postmodern. In this regard, China is, perhaps, unique among Third World societies.

The fifth version of postmodernity is completely different from the first four versions, in that it is closely related to the development of the international postmodernism debate. Along with the introduction and translation of contemporary Western critical theory in China, Chinese critics are increasingly indebted to the Foucauldian theory of power, knowledge, and discourse, with power at the axis, and to the Derridean theory of deconstruction; these theories help Chinese critics deconstruct the long-standing totalitarian or dominant master narrative discourse, thus setting free their theoretical imagination and creativity. There is interest in these postmodern theories among the young avant-garde and scholarly critics, but also among some older scholars. This increased awareness has developed a fifth version of postmodernity, which takes the form in current Chinese cultural life of poststructuralism. On the one hand, some scholars and critics of foreign literature studies, such as Wang Fengzhen, Zheng Min, Zhang Guofeng, Qian Jiaoru, and I, in taking pains to introduce poststructuralist theories to Chinese readers, engage in careful comparative studies; on the other hand, those scholars and critics with backgrounds in Chinese literature, such as Zheng Min, Chen Xiaoming, Zhang Yiwu, Dai Jinhua, and Wang Gan, although not necessarily familiar with the original theoretical texts in English or French, have shown interest in applying poststructuralist theories to their analysis of contemporary Chinese literary or film texts: Zheng, as an old poet and scholarly critic who has maintained an elite aesthetic view, always standing between the two stages of the modern and the postmodern, tries to give full play to a sort of postmodern or poststructuralist way of thinking, thus breaking through the traditional academic way of thinking; Chen, in his close reading of the avant-garde texts, conscientiously applies Derrida's theory of deconstruction to decode the postmodern narratives of the avant-gardists; Zhang, possessed by Jameson's postmodern theory with regard to Third World culture, seems more interested in the contemporary study of popular culture and is now deeply involved in the postcolonial debate and cultural studies; Dai and Wang deal with film and literature, respectively, from the perspectives of feminism and cultural deconstruction and critique. Their critical practice, whether successful or inadequate at the moment, has actually helped popularize postmodernism in Chinese literary criticism, taking the first step toward a critical academic dialogue between Chinese and Western theory and toward the establishment of a science of literary criticism. So it is not strange that the fifth version of postmodernity is apparently influenced by poststructuralism, which is characterized by a deconstructive way of thinking and the undermining, and even deconstruction, of the "totality" of discourse and power. Because of their efforts, and the recent debate on postcolonialism and Third World culture both domestically and overseas, a pluralistic realm of cultural and literary criticism and theoretical debate has evolved in the Chinese context.

Postcolonialism, especially as it relates to so-called Third World culture and Third World criticism, is another Western cultural trend that has been introduced in China. It is viewed as one of the joint forces of neoconservatism,[36] and it may also be considered the sixth version of postmodernity. Of course, this is a rather controversial and complicated case, and it has aroused heated debate in overseas Chinese journals.[37] Those engaged in postmodern studies and postmodern criticism in China are ironically accused of being neoconservatives (xin baoshouzhuyi zhe). Obviously, this sort of critique has been inspired by Habermas's critique of Lyotardian postmodernism. Since China has never been a completely colonized country, discussions of postcolonialism seem merely to be a cultural strategy in the struggle against Western cultural hegemonism and linguistic imperialism and against the overall process of modernizing China. Some overseas Chinese intellectuals, because of their dissatisfaction with the Eurocentric mode of thinking, Western discourse, and their current "outside" position, try to revive the traditional Chinese cultural spirit by reconsidering classical Chinese philosophical thinking. On the one hand, they are not satisfied with simply considering the question of postcoloniality in the Western context but would rather associate the anticolonialist struggle with the domestic reality on the level of the debate on modernity/postmodernity and current Chinese cultural reflection and critique. To Chinese intellectuals, postmodernism/postcolonialism is a powerful discourse that enables them to undermine not only the Western empire but the domestic totalitarian ideology. On the other hand, they are not satisfied with the accidental coincidence of a domestic postmodern studies that includes the prevailing official nationalist ideology, so they are confronted with the phenomenon of China's modernity/alternative modernity in a world of global capitalism. Studies by young overseas Chinese scholars such as Liu Kang, Xiaobing Tang, Henry Zhao, Xu Ben, Sheldon Lu, and Zhang Xudong, all of whom are very active in Anglo-American critical circles and are very interested in the domestic debate on postmodernism and postcolonialism, certainly have contributed to the international postmodernism debate, have helped push forward postmodern studies in the overseas Chinese context, and have enabled the academic dialogue on postmodern studies to continue between Chinese and Western scholars.[38]

(Re)Constructing Postmodernism in the Chinese Context

Through the above mapping and brief theoretical analysis, we can see that postmodernism undoubtedly has a marked presence in China, although it should be viewed first as a product of Western capitalist society and as an inevitable and logical reaction to the development of human culture, ideology, and literary representation. It came onto the scene of Chinese culture and intellectual life and influenced contemporary Chinese literature largely because of the logic of the Chinese economy and culture in a transitional period, the so-called Post–New Period, when everything was increasingly influenced by contemporary commercialization. It could thus be regarded as both a "borrowed thing" (bolaipin) as well as an indigenous product to some extent, for it is very relevant to the development of Chinese politics, economy, and culture. As Jean Baudrillard puts it in his recent book, "simulation is precisely this irresistible unfolding, this sequencing of things as though they had a meaning, when they are governed only by artificial montage and nonmeaning. Putting a price on the event up for auction by radical disinformation. Setting a price on the event, as against setting it in play, setting it in history."[39] This quotation expresses the current Chinese situation with regard to cultural life and society. But ironically, just as postmodernism, as a cultural phenomenon and a literary current, became almost exhausted or "canonized" in the West, and as academics seemed to become more interested in the question of postcoloniality with regard to gender studies, area studies, Third World criticism, and other "minority" or marginal discourse, it attracted the attention of scholars and critics in Asian societies such as China, India, Japan, and Korea, to whose cultural traditions and literary conventions it apparently runs counter. So the question of postmodernity is often associated with the "decolonization" of Asian indigenous cultures and literary discourses.[40] And the modernity/postmodernity/alternative modernity debate cannot ignore the issue of cultural identity and its reconstruction.

As we approach the fin de siècle, the world we face is one of detotalization, deterritorialization, and contingency, in which all "repressed things" have been released and human imagination has been totally emancipated. Will there appear such a phenomenon as cultural decadence, as was the case with the last turn of the century? I am not sure, although I am optimistic about the progress of history. It is indeed the case that "post-1968 politics has been revealed as a self-delusory project; all forms of liberation—sexual, political, aesthetic—engender only an escalation of networks of simulation which subsume, neutralize, or dissolve all meaning."[41] The same could be said of the current situation in China after the end of the 1980s, when elitist culture and mainstream ideology became less powerful as it was confronted with the rise of popular culture. It is no wonder that postmodernism, starting as a cultural phenomenon and a literary current in North America in the 1950s, has now become a very effective alternative discourse in Chinese cultural and literary circles, at the periphery rather than at the center.[42] There are probably still some Western scholars and critics who do not believe it is possible for postmodernism to emerge in non-Western cultures and literatures. In view of the striking differences between the East and the West, in both cultural traditions and literary conventions, and in view of the limitations of postmodernism in both chronology and geography, they are not entirely wrong. But the mapping of Chinese postmodernity that I have offered above makes a case to the contrary.

One may well say that postmodernism was produced in the West largely because of the right cultural soil and the long-standing project of modernity. In contrast, in Asian and Third World societies such as China, there is no such background for a gradually evolving cultural tradition and an increasingly innovative literary convention. The project of modernity in China is obviously incomplete, owing to various political, economic, cultural, and intellectual reasons. Furthermore, because of the inadequacy of the cultural soil and the unreceptive atmosphere, it would be almost impossible for postmodernism to be produced in a non-Western culture and literature. The fact is that China is still a Third World country in which various elements are blended: premodern, modern, postmodern, and even primitive. In a society such as this, which is subject to contingencies and uneven development, anything can happen at any time; so why not postmodernism? Moreover, postmodernism appears as a mutation, largely different from its original form(s) in the West. So Chinese postmodernity is a consequence of the encounter between Chinese and Western cultures; it encompasses a combination of both foreign and domestic elements.

Since postmodernity in China is most popular in the fields of literature and art, we could focus our attention on those areas. Western society allows artists an embarras de choix, a multiplicity of choices, in producing a work of art. But in an economically developing Third World society such as China, literary creation is strongly colored with a sort of utilitarianism and cognitive function, and it is obviously anachronistic to speak of "nonselective devices," characterized by the postmodern, under such premodern conditions, which seemingly confirm the view of Western scholars who do not think it is possible for postmodernism to be favorably received in China. Even Third World avant-gardists, or postmodernists, who have a clear sense of postmodernity and who are very eager to draw on something new, are still restricted in their living conditions and cultural life. But Chinese postmodernists such as Su Tong and Wang Shuo have managed to find a middle ground, a place between the avant-garde intellectual rebel and the consumer cultural market. They still have a choice in subject matter and can experiment, or even play with narrative discourse. However, they can never move from the periphery to the center in a country that remains ideologically totalitarian. Any attempt to overemphasize the deconstructive or conservative function of Chinese postmodernity will undoubtedly prove inadequate.

Furthermore, in view of its relations and partial continuity with modernism (since literary postmodernism as a movement emerged after the fall of modernism), it is quite natural to assume that postmodernism could appear only in the West; but in Asian and Third World societies, there was no such cultural foundation on which postmodernism could be supported. In these countries, modernism is either belated or regarded as a presumed existence whose significance has not yet been discovered by ordinary people, so postmodernism can hardly be imagined under such inadequate conditions. As far as the Chinese case is concerned, one can clearly find from my mapping that, along with the recent rapid development of the economy and cultural and academic exchanges, postmodernism has had no difficulty in coming onto the scene of such an incomplete modernity.

Hence, a tentative conclusion: postmodernism is not restricted to the Western model, even though it did originate in the West. It has not only taken different forms in the West but has also generated mutations and produced different versions in several non-Western countries, including China. What postmodernism means in the Chinese context, however, is very different from what it originally meant in the Western context. So in this sense, just as post-modernism is always incompatible with mainstream modernism in the West, it can never become a cultural dominant in Asian or Third World societies, especially China. The current postmodernist fad in some Third World countries is just a temporary phenomenon. Postmodernism will remain secondary, no matter how influential it is at the moment. On the other hand, confronted with mainstream culture and the dominant ideology, it may be assimilated into a new pluralistic context, and may instigate previously unanticipated cultural developments. It is in this sense that a mapping of postmodernity is both historically necessary and culturally significant.

Notes

I am very grateful to Arif Dirlik and Fredric Jameson, who not only invited me to present this essay at Duke University but made very insightful remarks and suggestions that certainly enabled me to revise it into the present form. I also thank the Center for Ibsen Studies at the University of Oslo, whose distinguished fellowship and excellent facilities undoubtedly made it possible for me to complete this essay.

1   It is true that since the beginning of the debate on postmodernism, leading American critics such as Irving Howe, John Barth, William Spanos, Susan Sontag, Leslie Fiedler, and Ihab Hassan were involved in the debate in the 1960s; and leading European scholars such as Jürgen Habermas and Jean-François Lyotard heatedly debated the concepts of modernity and postmodernity in the late 1970s and early 1980s, thus endowing postmodernism with a philosophical status; and in the 1980s and the early 1990s, important scholars and critics such as Alan Wilde, Fredric Jameson, Jonathan Arac, Norman Holland, Ralph Cohen, Linda Hutcheon, Matei Calinescu, Douwe Fokkema, and Hans Bertens were involved in the debate on and description of postmodernism as either a cultural phenomenon, a literary current in the twentieth century, or a political strategy. Chinese scholars and critics involved in the modernism debate in the early 1980s seemed to overlook or be ignorant of the concept of postmodernism. So it is not surprising that the debate on modernism in the Chinese context is contemporaneous with the discussion about postmodernism in the Western context.

2   For example, Alan Wilde, in *Horizons of Assent: Modernism, Postmodernism, and the Ironic Imagination* (Baltimore: Johns Hopkins University Press, 1981), regards postmodernism as essentially "an American event" (12); Douwe Fokkema, in *Literary History, Modernism, and Postmodernism* (Philadelphia: John Benjamins, 1974), affirms that it is inconceivable to "favorably receive postmodernism" in China (56); and Linda Hutcheon says in a personal letter to me that postmodernism is always thought of as a "typical Western model." But later, Fokkema changed his mind and invited me to write one chapter on the reception of postmodernism in China for the book *International Postmodernism* (Philadelphia: John Benjamins, 1997), which he and Hans Bertens edited.

3   Important Western scholars such as Jameson, Eagleton, Cohen, Arac, and Fokkema have expressed their ideas in conference presentations and lectures while in China.

4   This may be seen in the papers delivered at the workshop "Postmodernity?—An Examination of the Third World Countries' Avant-Garde Literature" during the 13th Congress

of the International Comparative Literature Association (Tokyo, August 1991). See the cluster of articles on the topic (which I edited) published in *Proceedings of XIII Congress of ICLA*, vol. 6 (Tokyo, 1995).

5 For instance, in India, talk about postmodernism is often connected to the country's modernization and decolonization, but in Japan, postmodern elements find particular embodiment in avant-garde literature and art. In the West, there are even more forms of postmodernism that have been defined and described by different scholars.

6 See Wang Ning, "Constructing Postmodernism: The Chinese Case and Its Different Versions," *Canadian Review of Comparative Literature* 20, no. 1/2 (1993): 49–61. In a public lecture delivered in Perth, Australia, in December 1996, Fredric Jameson also acknowledged that, thinking of the problem in global terms, he would rather use the word *postmodernity* than *postmodernism*.

7 I am particularly indebted to the theoretical constructions made by Jameson, Hassan, Arac, Fokkema, and Calinescu.

8 Here I have obviously revised my previous descriptions of postmodernism, which were published in English and Chinese, because of the development of the international postmodernism debate and its influence on Chinese cultural and intellectual life.

9 Yuan Kejia is responsible for the mistranslation of the term *literary modernism* into Chinese as *xiandaipai* (the modern school), which includes the historical avant-garde, such as Dadaism and surrealism, and postmodernist currents such as the French *nouveau roman* and Latin American magic realism.

10 See Wang Ning, "Constructing Postmodernism," 50–51.

11 See Virgil Nemoianu, *A Theory of the Secondarity: Literature, Progress, and Reaction* (Baltimore: Johns Hopkins University Press, 1989). Despite the fact that to many scholars, postmodernism is outside the mainstream Western culture, to Jameson, it is a "cultural dominant" during the postwar years.

12 With regard to the difference between the New Period and the Post–New Period, there are still controversies in the Chinese and overseas critical circles. For a description of the concept itself, see Wang Ning, "Confronting Western Influence: Rethinking Chinese Literature of the New Period," *New Literary History* 24, no. 4 (autumn 1993): 925–26; and "Hou xinshiqi: Yizhong lilun miaoshu" (Post–New Period: A theoretical description), *Huacheng* (Flower city) 3 (1995): 201–8.

13 See Wang Ning, "Confronting Western Influence"; and Yue Daiyun and Wang Ning, eds., *Xifang wenyi sichao yu ershi shiji Zhongguo wenxue* (Western trends of literary thought and twentieth-century Chinese literature) (Beijing: Zhongguo Shehui Kexue Chubanshee, 1990).

14 Some of the articles dealing with the debate are included in He Wangxian, ed., *Xifang xiandaipai wenxue wenti lunzheng ji* (Issues on the debate of Western modernist literature), 2 vols. (Beijing: People's Literature Press, 1984). Some of the essays in this book touch on the question of postmodernism.

15 The term *postmodernism* was at the time translated into Chinese as *hou xiandaipai* (the late modern school). It was used in Chinese architecture earlier than in literature because it was misinterpreted in literary circles, whereas in the field of architecture, scholars could easily distinguish the postmodern from the modern style.

16 Jameson's book, which was translated by Xiaobing Tang, was first published by Shaanxi Normal University Press in 1987 and then by Peking University Press in 1996. Apart from his groundbreaking translation, Tang has also been active in publishing relevant essays in English, such as "The Function of New Theory: What Does It Mean to Talk about

Postmodernism in China?" *Public Lecture* 4, no. 1 (fall 1991): 89–108; "Residual Modernism: Narratives of the Self in Contemporary Chinese Fiction," *Modern Chinese Literature* 7 (spring 1993): 2–34; and "Configuring the Modern Space: Cinematic Representation of Beijing and Its Politics," *East-West Film Journal* 8, no. 2 (July 1994): 47–69.

17   Fokkema's and Bertens's book was translated by Wang Ning, Gu Donghua, Huang Guiyou, and Zhao Baisheng, published first by Peking University Press in 1991 and Taiwan Shuxin Press in 1993. Since that time, two other edited books on postmodernism have appeared: Wang Yuechuan and Shang Shui, eds., *Houxiandaizhuyi wenhua yu meixue* (Postmodernist culture and aesthetics) (Beijing: Peking University Press, 1992); and Wang Ning and Zhang Yiwu, eds., *Houxiandai wenlun jingcui* (The postmodern theories reader) (Nanjing: Yilin Press, 1997).

18   Ihab Hassan was invited to lecture at Shandong University and Nanjing University in 1982, but he did not speak on postmodernism; Fredric Jameson gave a series of lectures on postmodernism and contemporary Western cultural theory at Peking University and Shenzhen University in 1985, and lectured again on issues relevant to the question of postmodernism in Shanghai and Beijing in May 1993; Douwe Fokkema lectured on postmodernism at Nanjing University and Nanjing Normal University in 1987, and at Peking University in September and October 1993; Hans Bertens gave a keynote speech at the International Conference on Postmodernism and Contemporary Chinese Literature in 1993 in Beijing; and Terry Eagleton and Jonathan Arac gave keynote speeches on postmodernism at the International Conference on Cultural Studies: China and the West, in Dalian in 1995.

19   During my talk on postmodernism at Duke University on 18 October 1996, Jameson pointed out in his remarks that apart from the joint efforts of Chinese and Western scholars in postmodern studies, the emergence of postmodernism in China is also due to three other factors: finances, or the operation of global capitalization; cyber time, or the popularization of computer and other high-tech advances; and consumer culture, which I regard as the third version of Chinese postmodernity. See also Fredric Jameson, *Postmodernism, or, The Cultural Logic of Late Capitalism* (Durham, N.C.: Duke University Press, 1991), 53–54.

20   In this essay, I have largely revised my original description of the four versions of postmodernity published in my essay "Constructing Postmodernism" and have added two new versions.

21   For a detailed description and analysis of postmodernity in contemporary Chinese avant-garde fiction, see Wang Ning, "Reception and Metamorphosis: Postmodernity in Contemporary Chinese Avant-Garde Fiction," *Social Sciences in China* 14, no. 1 (1993): 5–13.

22   This was acknowledged rather frankly at the workshop "Postmodernism and Contemporary Chinese Literature" sponsored by the Institute of Comparative Literature at Peking University on 11 July 1990.

23   For a radical view praising avant-garde fiction, see Zhang Yiwu, "Lixiangzhuyi de zhongjie: Shiyan xiaoshuo de wenhua tiaozhan" (An end to idealism: The cultural challenge of avant-garde fiction), in *Shengcun youxi de shuiquan* (Selected essays in Chinese postmodern criticism) ed. Zhang Guoyi (Beijing: Peking University Press, 1994), 106–21.

24   The "new fiction of experience" was advocated by the journal *Beijing wenxue* (Beijing literature) and the "new fiction of stance" was advocated jointly by the literary magazine *Zhongshan* and the critical journal *Wenyi zhengming* (Debate on literature and art), but neither has received much of a response from critical circles.

25   These experimental poems are largely published in the overseas literary magazine *Jin-*

tian (Today), which is not available on China's mainland but which is popular among the overseas literary circles. And many of these poems appear in the writers' own printed journal, *Feifei*.

26 The work of Beidao (Zhao Zhenkai), a well-known Chinese poet and editor of the journal *Jintian*, is regarded as representative of Chinese modernist poetry in the early 1980s.

27 The vague term *new realism* was first put forward by Wang Gan and some other critics who were closely related to the magazine *Zhongshan* (Purple mountain), in which quite a few new realist short stories and novelettes were published during 1990 and 1991. See Wang Gan, "Jinqi xiaoshuo de houxianshizhuyi qingxiang" (The postrealist tendency in recent fiction), in *Shengcun youxi de shuiquan*, 74–86.

28 See Fang Fang, "Yiqie doushi zhenshi" (All of them are real things), *Zhongpianxiaoshuo xuankan* (Selected novelettes) 2 (1992): 93.

29 For a radical critique of "new realist fiction," see Chen Xuguang, "Xin xieshi xiaoshuo de zhongjie: Jianlun 'houxiandaizhuyi' zai Zhongguo de mingyun" (The end of new realist fiction: On the fate of 'postmodernism' in Chinese literature), *Shengcun youxi de shuiquan*, 183–97.

30 See Arif Dirlik's description and theorization in his essay, "Reversals, Ironies, Hegemonies: Notes on the Contemporary Historiography of Modern China," *Modern China* 22, no. 3 (July 1996): 255–62.

31 See Jameson, *Postmodernism, or, The Cultural Logic of Late Capitalism*, 25.

32 This question was first raised in 1993 in the journals *Dushu* and *Shanghai wenxue* by young scholars such as Wang Xiaoming and Chen Sihe in Shanghai. At one time, this issue could generate a heated debate, but it is now out of fashion in contemporary cultural studies.

33 For a detailed description and theoretical analysis of the rise of popular culture in China, see Sheldon Hsiao-peng Lu, "Postmodernity, Popular Culture, and the Intellectual: A Report on Post-Tiananmen China," *boundary 2* 23, no. 2 (summer 1996): 139–69.

34 Owing to the influence and popularity of film and particularly TV, Empress Wu (Wu Zetian) has become much better known than any male emperor, in part because she has always been criticized and because there are several versions of her "story," each from the author's own perspective.

35 Director Zhang Yimou paid six novelists to write about Empress Wu. They did, although perhaps not always according to Zhang's instruction.

36 See Henry Zhao, "Post-Ism and Chinese New Conservatism," *New Literary History* 28, no. 1 (1997): 31–44. This essay, which was delivered at the Dalian conference in August 1995, provoked quite a debate among Chinese and Western participants.

37 See, for example, the articles appearing in *Ershiyi shiji* (Twenty-first century), published in Hong Kong, especially those articles published in 1995 and 1996. Because of its limited circulation, this journal has not had much influence in mainland critical circles.

38 See Liu Kang, "Postmodernism, the Avant-garde, and Chinese Cultural Reflection," *Proceedings of the XIII Congress of ICLA*, vol. 6 (Tokyo, 1995): 560–64; and "Is There an Alternative to (Capitalist) Globalization? The Debate about Modernity in China," *boundary 2* 23, no. 3 (fall 1996): 245–69; Sheldon Hsiao-peng Lu, "Postmodernity, Popular Culture, and the Intellectual"; Xu Ben, *Zouxiang houxiandai yu houzhimin* (Approaching postmodernity and postcoloniality) (Beijing: China Social Sciences Publishing House, 1996); and Zhang Xudong, *Chinese Modernism in the Era of Reforms: Cultural Fever, Avant-Garde Fiction, and the New Chinese Cinema* (Durham, N.C.: Duke University Press, 1997).

39 Jean Baudrillard, *The Illusion of the End*, trans. Chris Turner (Cambridge: Cambridge University Press, 1994), 14.

40 See Wang Ning, "Postcolonial Theory and the 'Decolonization' of Chinese Culture," *Ariel* 28, no. 4 (1997).

41 Rita Felsk, "Fin de siècle, Fin de sexe: Transsexuality, Postmodernism, and the Death of History," *New Literary History* 27, no. 2 (spring 1996): 339.

42 I should point out here that it is absolutely wrong of some overseas Chinese scholars to suggest that Chinese postmodern critics have interests in common with or even conspire with the government. Those postmodern critics, such as Zhang Yiwu, could be active only within very limited critical and academic circles that are far from the official discourse and mainstream ideology.

anthony d. king & abidin kusno

2   On Be(ij)ing in the World: "Postmodernism,"
"Globalization," and the Making of Transnational
Space in China

Huge swaths of Beijing are being cleared by real-estate developers to make way for high-rise
apartments, office buildings and shopping centers. The familiar syndrome of urban renewal
is drastically changing the face of an ancient city within a few years. Within a few years around
90 percent of the old neighborhoods will be cleared. — New York Times, 1 March 1998

What architectural or urban design practices give the cities of contemporary
China their distinctive visual identity? What are the social objectives, political
imaginings and economic agendas that provide contemporary urban transformations with their particular shape(s)? From where, at the end of the twentieth century, do the models and metaphors of (post)modernity in China's
cities actually derive? How, in a situation of multinational capitalism where
the nation-state is — despite all the supposed "withering away" — still a major
force for constructing cultural identity, do the market and the state influence
images of (post)modernity in the contemporary Chinese city?

In posing these questions we aim, first, to focus attention on the multiplicity of influences and constraints that are transforming the contemporary
city in China, especially in Beijing and Shanghai. We inquire into their new ar-

chitectural forms and building typologies, which, in different contexts, construct new ways in which to imagine their sociopolitical identities. Second, we aim to show how the construction of transnational space in China results from a response to both the regime of global capitalism and the Chinese state project of modernity in the Reform era. In the process, this construction necessarily helps to constitute individual and collective Chinese transnational subjectivities. Third, we argue that while the architectural references of the contemporary Chinese city are derived from a "Western" repertoire, the framework of comparison is more accurately constituted in relation to the urban centers in Asia undergoing similar transformations. And while suggesting that transnational architecture and urbanism in China are a cultural product of "Western" capitalism, we do not imply that they result from an attempt of China to "catch up with" the West. Instead, the specter of capitalism and its (post)modern representations appearing in the major cityscapes of China, are being staged in order to establish the central position of China vis-à-vis its Asian counterparts as well as the world at large.

Framing Chinese Postmodernism

The editors of this volume have aimed to capture the historical specificity of China without losing sight of its relations to the larger world. China's (re)entry into the world through capitalism is characterized by the editors as the moment of its "postmodernism." While we can agree with the framework, we nonetheless wish to avoid the dominant apolitical and ahistorical understandings associated with this concept, which, these days, can mean anything and everything, and hence, analytically nothing. Our own disaffection from the term stems from various concerns,[1] some of them shared by our editors: a Euro-Americocentric understanding of the world that "has little to say about the ways colonization may have contributed to the Euro-American experience of modernity"; the experience of (colonial) modernity "among those who were compelled into (it) by Euro-American coercion" and finally, by our use of the term "a Eurocentric recolonization" of what they call a "Third World terrain." [2] In short, what the use of "postmodernism" frequently reveals is a spatially and historically restricted understanding of what is conventionally referred to as "the modern," especially as it is represented in frequently cited texts on the topic.[3]

Writing about modernity, Arjun Appadurai suggests that "one of the problematical legacies of grand Western social science—Comte, Marx, Toennies, Weber—is that it has steadily reinforced the sense of some single moment—call it the modern moment—that by its appearance creates a dramatic and unprecedented break between tradition and modernity. . . . [T]his view has been shown repeatedly to distort the meanings of change and the politics of past-ness."[4] We need to recognize the relativity of the idea of "the modern," and its status, not as some temporal or historical category but rather as a cultural one. As our editors suggest, the cultural context of modernity and postmodernity has to be set within the specificity of China. In this sense, contemporary cultural production and consumption in China has less to do with American postmodernism than with its own historical shifts in political cultures. In the editors' formulation, "Chinese postmodernism is to be grasped not only in its relationship to modernity in general but also in its relationship to a socialist and revolutionary modernity."[5] The editors' objective, therefore, is to reveal the new landscape of power in contemporary China as "one aspect of a global postmodernity mediated by the terrains and histories identifiable as Chinese."[6] The purpose is not just to put China within the structural context of global capitalism but also to reveal the struggle of Chinese cultural politics over "the legacy of the past and the forces of the present."[7] The making of transnational space in contemporary China is, therefore, an instance of the ways in which China creates its own version of (post)modernity within the structure of global capitalism.

The spread of free-market mechanisms and practices worldwide, as the Chinese (or indeed, any other) case illustrates, poses a question of how the institutions and practices of capitalism work in any particular locality, and at any time, under what constraints and with what results. As Massey reminds us, economies are equally cultural practices,[8] shaped by distinct historical, political, geographical, and cultural conditions. The attraction of inward investment, as well as the foreign institutions, expertise, and personnel that goes with it—a central plank in contemporary Chinese economic strategy—also rests on assumptions of what a future kind of modernity would actually be, look like, and especially, as far as cities are concerned, what physical, spatial, and architectural form it would take.

Our concern is with the relationship between global forces and local-regional histories in the making of transnational space in China. We begin by discussing the crossing-over of certain Euro-American urban artifacts, such as the skyscraper office tower, the luxury apartment building, and the suburban villa, to the urban space of China. These three building types are not completely new in China. What has made them especially distinctive are the transnational meanings that have been invested in them by the China Daily (from which much of our evidence comes) as part of the official state-commercial project of modernity. Moreover, using these three building types also permits us to address aspects of a global (post)modernity in China whose contemporary histories demand a transformation of its architectural and urban traditions. We argue that these phenomena of global (post)modernity, mediated by the political cultures of the state, have also to be understood in the context of China's relations to its regional neighbors. In this sense, therefore, the global flow of building cultures is necessarily framed by the local histories of the region. Finally, we ask about the effects that the construction of transnational space might have on the formation of individual and collective identities.

Constructing Similitudes

Writing on the development and spread of the (Eurocentric) idea of the nation-state as the dominant form of governance, Mohammed Bamyeh draws our attention to the fact that "sovereign governance . . . is governed by the idea of constructing a similitude . . . whereby (on each occasion of the creation of a new state) one constructs a globally legitimate player. With the rise of the state as the standard form of governance, standard structures of domination and models of political behavior were created. The rise of total politics in modernity cannot thus be separated from their obsessive attention to each other, an attention which is itself a feature of globalization." [9]

Just as Bamyeh suggests that "one of the consequences of global modernity is that every state has to see itself in the context of other states," so, inherent in the same process, every "real" or aspiring world city strives to define itself in the context of other world cities. Within the realm of global capitalism, this is as true of financial districts or international hotels as the architectural or urban design shells in which they exist. In such a comparative context, the principal reference group for the development of these phenomena are the dominant urban centers of the capitalist economic and cultural ecumene— New York, Tokyo, and London. However, as we argue in the final section, these images of the "West" are subjected to a "horizontal" comparison with the regional centers of Asia, which, with China, are similar, though different. These regional mimicries have an effect of constituting difference. Local attributes are incorporated into the language of transnational architectural firms, producing as a result global architecture in the region with local characteristics. Though the imagery of these other centers does not feature in our discussion, they nonetheless figure as the ground against which China both imagines its entry into the capitalist network and registers its own performance.

Just as socially "marginal" subjects get themselves photographed in the company of prominent personalities in the expectation of raising their own status, developers adopt the same strategy with buildings. Thus, images of the new Sun Dong An Plaza in Beijing, described as "one of the most famous commercial centers in Beijing," strive to establish its comparable worth by

Ginza, **Tokyo.**   Manhattan, **New York.**   Canary Wharf, **London.**

Wangfujing Street, **Beijing.**

Offices and retail spaces are now available for leasing

Move into Sun Dong An Plaza, one of the most famous commercial centres in Beijing.

Figure 1   Advertisement for Sun Dong An Plaza, from
China Daily, 14 October 1997.

representing it alongside images of Ginza, Tokyo; Manhattan, New York; and
Canary Wharf, London (Figure 1).[10] In relocating these developments onto
one imaginary global plane, the expectation is that the accumulation of signified meaning, attached to familiar signs, will in some way drain off into
the one that is unknown. Elsewhere, similitude in design is accompanied
by similitude in name, glossy office developments, for example, being marketed as "Manhattan Building" (Figure 2), "Parkview Towers", or "Investment
Plaza." The advertisement for one such development, located in the district
"where most foreign embassies can be found," claims that it has "the same
importance as the 'Central District'" in Hong Kong, and lists, in proof of
that claim, the offices of the various multinational enterprises that can be
found there: BASF, Boeing, British Aerospace, Coopers and Lybrand, Daiwa,
Fujitsu, Honda, IBM, Toshiba, and others. One advertisement less modestly
even claims "We Have in Beijing What They Have in New York"—a statement

新中港万泰大厦
NCHK Manhattan Building
Completion by the end of 1997

High-tech intelligent office tower
Unique atrium design
Next to Swissotel on the 2nd Ring Rd. E.
Easy access to any point of contact

- Dongsishitiao subway outlet
- 15-storey grand office and commercial complex
- 1–3/Floors 9,000 sq.m. for shopping & entertainment
- 4/F 5000 sq.m. specially for luxurious Chinese restaurant
- 5/F for uptown western restaurant, club & business center
- 6–15/Floors main office tower with an atrium
- Colorful indoor garden on 5th floor
- 2 levels of basement car park providing 150 spaces

- 4 escalators and 2 bullet lifts from first to fifth floor serving shoppers
- 8 imported deluxe high-speed Mitsubishi lifts for office zone
- Able to meet corporate need up to 4,400 sq.m. per floor
- 2000 DDD & IDD lines
- CABD,. Satellite TV system and fiber optics network
- Full glass curtain wall and Building Management Control (BMC)

Pre-sale & Pre-leasing hotline:
(8610) 6552 8888

Developer: Beijing Xin Zhong Gang Building Co., Ltd
Property Management: Richard Ellis Co., Ltd

Address: 6 Chaoyangmen Beidajie, Dongcheng District, Beijing   Zip Code: 100027
Beijing Overseas Sales Permit No. 110

Figure 2   Advertisement for the Manhattan Building, from
China Daily, 1 September 1994.

that is apparently directed to other urban centers in Asia as well as to potential
investors elsewhere.

In this process of transplantation, however, it is a selective, not a total
or comprehensive "representative" world of global modernity that is cited,
one in which the influence of North America figures large.[11] As the profile of
the economy changes, new forms and shapes emerge in the architectural and

building typology of the city in relation to the very specific conditions and influences in which it develops. In this way, through the adoption of other forms, other symbols, and above all, the spatial language of other worlds, the Chinese capital moves itself into another universe of meaning.

We want, therefore, to discuss these transformations in relation to three architectural innovations in the built environment of the Chinese city, especially Beijing and Shanghai, introduced mainly from the United States and Europe and largely in the 1990s. In focusing on these three—the skyscraper, the luxury apartment block, and the suburban villa—we want to show how particular "modern" building types, produced in particular places (in the West) under the very specific historical, social, and cultural conditions of industrial capitalism each type invested in the country of its origin with specific social meanings are introduced into China to help construct a new "universe of an ordered whole."[12] And, to use a metaphor from computing, we show a process of "cut and paste" being performed on a global scale, in which urban and architectural forms are "cut" from the particular historic urban experience of some societies and cultures, "pasted" into another society and culture, and then "edited" in order to help construct new, though not necessarily seamless, transnational spaces in China's two most important cities, the capital and the metropolis.[13]

Metaphors of Modernity 1: The Skyscraper

The completion of what is currently the world's tallest building, Petronas Towers in Kuala Lumpur, in 1996 focused the world's attention during that year not only on the object itself but also on it was meant to symbolize. Media watchers were alerted to the fact that the tallest building on earth was no longer in the West but, for the first time since 1891, no longer in the United States.[14] Moreover, not only were six of the world's ten tallest buildings in Asia, six of the first fifteen were in China.[15] According to many reports, these new towers—virtually all designed by American architectural firms—were supposedly symbolic of Asia's entry onto the global stage of economic and political power over the next decade, not only marking the emergence of a powerful new space in the world economy, but also, at the close of the old millenium, a powerful new time, the "Asian Century." For the American architectural journal, *Progressive Architecture*, "a shift of historic proportions [was] taking place and architecture is the premier symbol of that transformation. . . . [T]he Chinese, as well as many other Asians, tend to want buildings as tall as possible and in as ostentatiously modern a style as can be found."

In the years since 1996, China has soared ahead in this supposedly global competition. Even before the completion of Shanghai's Jinmao Tower in August 1998, at 420 meters (36.5 meters taller than the previous Chinese record holder, the Diwang Commercial Mansion in Shenzhen), the Shanghai World Financial Center, which began construction in 1998, will, according to *China Daily*, "rise up from the city's Pudong district and" (imperial lackeys take note) "tower over the famed Bund." When the office tower and hotel is completed in 2001, it will rise 94 stories, or 460 meters, making it 10 meters taller than the current world leader, Petronas Towers (450 meters).[16] If this is not enough in itself, according to one *China Daily* report (3 Sept. 1997), since 1992 Shanghai has built 220 skyscrapers, at least twenty of which are 220 meters tall.

In dealing with these many stories, what we want to address is the development of the skyscraper as a particular metaphor of modernity and, more important, the development of the particular worlds in which such metaphors have meaning. What we aim to show is that particular signs of modernity have been generated at politically and geographically significant moments in the history of particular "worlds," and the relations among them at particular conjunctures in the emergence of advanced industrial capitalism. We want to ask about these different worlds in which, in this case, the competition for "the world's tallest building" is constituted and to place the present round of competition in a more historical perspective, across space.

In these displays of architectural spectacle, "the world" is primarily understood in economic, political, and cultural terms, and generally as a world of nation-states. For example, in an American atlas of 1889, a diagram purports to represent "the principal high buildings of the old world" (78 in all, mainly in Europe, though also in Asia, including China), the main aim of which is to demonstrate the superiority of the United States, its capital, and first president, by highlighting the height of the Washington Monument (completed 1885), which exceeds them all, at 555 feet.

Here, the distinction being made is between the "old world" and "the new." The main significance of the Washington Monument here, or rather, its height, as well as the discourses that circulate around it, is that they establish, without the consent or involvement of other states, cities, or jurisdictions, the notion of a "world" competition where none had existed before. In the process, they put into place the idea of a discursive global space in which other nations, cities, or organizations are positioned as competitors. In that context, the current phase of "world" competition seems to have begun with the invention of the American skyscraper, particularly those of New York City and Chicago in the 1890s. However, this is not an "international" competition between nations;[17] it may be confined either to the American corporate world, the world of individual business egos, or even representatives of particular religions. It is certainly not a "global" competition in that many individuals, corporations, cities, or nations eschew participation. For F. W. Woolworth, whose 1912 headquarters building was, when built, the "tallest office building in the world," it was principally a world of commerce confined to the United States.

There seems to be a general consensus in the literature that the emergence of the skyscraper in late-nineteenth and early-twentieth-century America has a great deal to do with nationalism as well as a search for a national architectural style embodying a distinctive American identity. The 306 skyscrapers that were built in New York between about 1890 and 1908 [18] become a paradigmatic statement, not only of American architecture and urbanism, but also of the economic ideology, mode of production, and the assumptions from which it was largely, if not entirely, derived: capitalist land values, speculative office development, and big business materialism in the United States. It also, of course, became a national symbol of modernity, represented especially by the three 1930s icons of New York City, the Chrysler, RCA, and Empire State Buildings.

That China, theoretically a communist state—though one pursuing capitalist economic policies—should, therefore, in the 1990s not only choose to symbolize its modernity within the world of nations through the language and architectural codes of American capitalism but also employ American architectural firms and design practices in order to achieve this may seem to be entirely logical. China's immediate capitalist predecessors, the neighboring countries of East and Southeast Asia, have already marked their urban centers with capitalist landmarks. Hong Kong, Malaysia, Indonesia, and Singapore established the architectural and spatial game, and when it entered this game, China not only merely "followed" these Asian confreres but overtook them, by re-centering the "middle kingdom" through the concentration of luxury skyscrapers designed by well-known "Western" architects. However, it can also be understood quite differently: the competition could demonstrate a complete transformation of China's architectural and spatial traditions.

Throughout its five thousand years of urban civilization, the Chinese architectural tradition has been especially represented by architectural principles that have emphasized harmony with the landscape, "building with nature," and the spiritual ecology of *feng shui*. In domestic as well as more formal architecture, single-story building has predominated, often with courtyard forms; and whether in imperial palaces, gardens, or temples, as in the Forbidden City of Beijing, the spatial representation of power and authority has been effected *horizontally* rather than *vertically*. The principles of Chinese design were rectilinearity and axiality, and with these, according to Kostof, went "the horizontal aesthetic, the conscious preference for a uniform range of heights that shifted the environmental burden of social distinctions to the placement of buildings in the general scheme of the city, the level of the terraces on which they invariably stood, the area they covered and the degree of their ornamentation."[19]

Even with the Communist Revolution, Mao's spatially symbolic commemorative space was horizontal, not vertical: the demolition of vast tracts of central Beijing aimed to enlarge Tiananmen Square in order to hold an assembly "of one billion" as "only the biggest public, thus the biggest square, could match the supreme power of the Chairman and the [Tiananmen] Gate."[20] Mao's square, in its massive horizontality, was both the symbolic center of a new Beijing and also of a new China, "the triumph of the proletarian revolution."[21] The only buildings that aspired to reach upward were the Soviet-inspired exhibition halls in Beijing and Shanghai, though the model here was their Soviet design rather than the question of "mere height" as such. The logic was imitative solidarity rather than competitive similitude.

In this long-term historical and cultural context, therefore, the shift away from a horizontal symbolic representation of power to a vertical one would seem to suggest an acceptance, by the Chinese political establishment, of an increasingly (and selectively) global system of architectural signification, produced by the logic of a private, for-profit system of capitalist land values, typically represented by Manhattan or Hong Kong. Just what the relevance of this change is as a symbolic signifier of modernity, we shall discuss below.

Metaphors of Modernity 2: The Apartment Building

The country that is more developed industrially only shows, to the less developed, the image of its own future. — Karl Marx, preface to *Capital*

According to a report from the London-based international property consultants Richard Ellis, Beijing had a stock of 21,000 units of residential property "designed for overseas buyers" early in 1998; it comprised 102 developments, of which 72 were high-rise, 24 low-rise, and the others mixed. Sixty percent of the apartments were in the Chaoyang district, "the most popular expatriate residential area in Beijing"; 14,000 of these units had come on stream in the previous three years (1994–1997). According to the report, the units were either largely "quality apartments" or "single-family houses" (cited in CD, 16 Feb. 1998).

Writing in 1980, city-planning historian John Hancock states,[22] "the history of the American apartment house can be seen as a case study of segmentation, affirmed and promulgated in an avowedly classless society." Although apartments house a wide cross-section of society, and also take various (collective) forms, "users past and present have at least two things in common: they are renters and are considered by society to be in at best a transient social state," with the majority having lived, or intending to live, within the dominant American housing culture of owned, separate houses. Though neither the term nor the type is of American origin, "the social function of the American apartment house . . . shows how various groups are 'housed apart.' " "What has held Americans together," according to historian Robert Wiebe, "was their ability to live apart." [23]

In the United States, the apartment house represents a phase in a series of fragmentations in the development of the city: by the mid-nineteenth century, separation had occurred between factory, commercial, and residential districts, the latter further divided along neighborhood lines by class, income, ethnic, religious, and racial groups. Early apartment houses, from the 1870s, housed the city's elite in new neighborhoods, in choice in-town as well as suburban sites, with the city splitting into two cities: one for managers, the other for workers. Along with downtown corporate buildings came tall luxury hotels and apartments, all part of the process of segregation and social filtering of the American city. In tracing three boom periods in the development of the apartment house, Hancock focuses his attention on five types: palatial apartments for the rich, luxury apartments for the affluent, owner-occupied apartments for both these groups, efficiency apartments for the middle class, and subsidized apartments for the poor. "The 'form of tenure,' " according to social critic Constance Perin, "is read as a primary social sign, used in categorizing people, in much the same as race, income, occupation and education." [24] The earliest apartment buildings in Manhattan date from the 1870s and were exclusively for the rich, built alongside mansions and elegant town houses. By the 1900s, all were identified by prestigious street addresses. Early prestigious apartments, such as the famous Dakota built in 1884, had wine cellars, a baronial dining hall for private parties, a large lawn for private parties (later converted into tennis courts), twenty units the size of family houses, and servants' rooms under the dormer roof. For the wealthy, the advantage of such apartment buildings was that they enabled them to live in fashionable areas. Hancock discusses examples of apartment buildings developed in the 1920s, with magnificently landscaped gardens, where the lowest rents were 75 percent of average annual earnings of American urban employees. By the 1970s, luxury apartments such as the high-rise Marina City in Chicago were "often on the scale of micro cities, with shopping arcades, restaurants, bars, offices, TV studios, a skating rink, plaza, and a parking garage for 900 cars for 896 apartments." By the 1990s apartments represented 90 percent of total housing in New York.

We cite this abbreviated history merely to show that, in whatever economic, social, historical, and cultural context, the design and social production of building form is not just intimately connected with social relations, social structures, and social meaning but is critical in *constituting* them. In this context, we can take note of apartment building in Beijing in the 1990s.

The construction of the first group of apartments "designed for overseas investors" was approved by Beijing in 1993. According to the *China Daily* (1 Sept. 1997), the major clients for these were "foreign-funded firms, employees of these, or overseas investors"; major domestic buyers were "highly profitable Chinese enterprises or rich people" for whom the attraction was "the excellent quality and management."[25] The production of residential property for "overseas buyers" has to be seen as part of larger property development projects, including business centers, office developments, shopping centers and arcades, trade exhibition halls, and the drive to attract multinationals and foreign direct investment.

As with the Beijing World Trade Center, Finance Street,[26] or the new Sun Dong An Plaza with its pagoda towers and "traditional" roof style, the marketing objective is to eliminate the distance between the unfamiliar and familiar, to create an equivalence, by the use of easily recognizable signs, between the comfortably known and the uncomfortably strange. Thus, for the (English-speaking) international business class, the names of apartment developments are as internationally recognizable, and exchangeable, as if they were in Boston, Berlin, or Birmingham: Manhattan Garden, Sunshine Plaza, Regent Court, Profit Tower, Roman Garden, City Plaza, Parkview Tower, Global Village, Rich and Famous, Golden Land, Green Lake Garden. The images of architectural design are equally interchangeable (Figure 3).[27] Like most of the other high-rise developments, the China World Apartments, within the grounds of the China World Center, with its five star-hotel, shopping arcade, and state-of-the-art recreational facilities, are a world apart from accommodation for the local inhabitants. The one-to-three-bedroom apartments offer extensive satellite TV networks, housekeeping, laundry, dry-cleaning services and a resident Montessori kindergarten (CD, 1 Sept. 1997).

In these advertisements, as also in the spaces they represent, two reciprocal processes are at work: the first, a distancing from the everyday conditions of the local Beijing social environment; the second, an attempt to reproduce, as far as possible, an "international" cultural space with which new investors or inhabitants are familiar. This takes place on three levels: first, in the neighborhood, by, for example, locating the Fuhua Mansion apartments close to the "Embassy area where more than a hundred organizations from different countries gather" (CD, 23 Sept. 1997) or by naming strategies, as with the Beijing International Friendship Garden in "the honorable diplomacy district."

The next level is the more immediate social and spatial environment, providing, as with the Sanquan apartments, again in the Chaoyang district ("where foreign embassies and five star hotels abound"), facilities for tennis,

Figure 3   Advertisement for Profit Tower apartment building, from
China Daily, 7 October 1997.

squash, and table tennis, along with an outdoor pool, a computer-simulated golf range, sauna, supermarket, restaurant, karaoke, central air conditioning, and twenty-four-hour security (*CD*, 10 Feb. 1998). Or, as at the Beijing Euro-village ("Your Ideal Home in Beijing"), the development is marketed as an "expatriate neighborhood" of "154 houses only" (*sic*) with "generous spacing between the houses" (*CD*, 4 Sept. 1997).

At the third level is the attention given to the needs of the body, the environment closest to the culturally conscious self and presumably most in need of familiar support. This might be in the form of "imported European furniture," as at the Sanquan apartments; "sanitary utensils, all with famous trade marks, imported from abroad," as at the Fuhua Mansion apartments; or the "Western fittings" in various villa advertisements. Or, to make sure that

European-style standards are maintained, the management is by the Swiss hotel chain, Swissotel.

Two developments help to explain the construction of this newly privileged space in the Chinese capital. On one hand, in the political sphere, as the nation-state has become in an era of global modernity the sole form of civil governance worldwide, the political, economic, spatial, and architectural representation of each sovereign state (which numbered fewer than seventy in 1945 and some two hundred half a century later), whether in embassies or diplomatic or trade missions, creates an economically privileged space where property values are set by the ability of *states* to pay them. These, located within a high-value, prestigious, and (often) administratively designated area, reproduce the conditions of what was earlier the world of the colonial city of Shanghai: foreign concessions, embassy compounds, and a certain "international culture" created by the accustomed habitus of an international social elite. On the other hand, in the economic sphere, with the rapid growth of multinational corporations (many of them larger, in terms of capital value, than many small states)—which have, in the twentieth century, become the most widespread, most powerful form of business organization worldwide— an even more powerful set of economic forces is at work in inflating both commercial and residential property values in the capital city.[28]

Such economic forces, however, are only one dimension of the phenomenon. Diplomatic and representative personnel, as well as multinational executives, have accommodation requirements not just in terms of space and facilities and standards commensurate with lifestyles characteristic of the richest countries in the world (frequently, though misleadingly, characterized in such advertisements as "world class") but also in terms of particular social and cultural expectations, not least those related to leisure and recreational habits. These relate to questions of internal design and fittings and also to visual, aural, olfactory, and gustatory preferences and, not least, to a design imagery in both the interior as well as the exterior environment, an imagery that is culturally familiar, such that the semi-itinerant occupants will, for the duration of their stay, feel both psychologically secure as well as culturally comfortable when they are at home. In this respect, though differing in some important ways, the world of the contemporary international business class has much in common with that of an earlier expatriate colonial community.[29] The making of the transnational space in China has thus concomitantly embodied the training of sentiments, emotions, and affections that contribute to the production of collective transnational historical subjects. These are some of the prerequisites behind the construction of transnational space, not only in Beijing but also in other capital cities worldwide. We can observe that all this represents a deeper colonization through cultural forms. It also suggests that, no matter how high the buildings are, countries such as China are always a step behind, as the (American and European) urban models that they emulate are now based on different values.

Metaphors of Modernity 3: The Villa

Leaving the crowded and noisy city, in just twenty minutes' drive you can get to the Beijing Dragon Villas, the beautiful American-Canadian residences . . . in fresh air, broad lawns and the beauty of nature. —Advertisement in China Daily, February 18, 1994

Just as the apartment building has a genealogy in the society and space of the American city, so also has the villa in a somewhat longer time and space of Europe.[30]

Villa came into the English language as a response to a renewed interest in the classics during the seventeenth century.[31] Early examples from the Oxford English Dictionary draw parallels between English life and architecture and the country estates of ancient Rome. But the term and architectural idea spread, from Italy, into the fashion-conscious vocabulary of the "beau monde" in England only from the second half of the eighteenth century. "Villa," to quote Pierre du Prey, "became synonymous with all that was chic, petite, a la mode or dernier cri."[32] Though villa had no precise definition, both the term and the architectural idea to which it was applied—"a smallish, free standing, block-like dwelling, set in ample grounds"—was to enter the vocabulary of English vernacular housing in the expansion of the bourgeois classes in the early phases of industrial capitalism. Architectural writers at the time were also aware—with prescience—of the Italian subcategory of the villa suburbana. According to one architectural writer of the time, the architectural category of villa was seen as being suitable for the social and economic category of a "gentleman of moderate fortune." By the early nineteenth century, the notion of the villa, with that social connotation, had become fully absorbed into the social, experiential, and architectural vocabulary of the nascent suburban bourgeois class, a social meaning and location it has retained, not least, with the growth of accumulation in property and urban development, from the Mediterranean to the Caribbean, in the form of the "residence secondaire."

What is most important about the villa, however, whether in Britain, Europe, or the United States, or other free-market landscapes in which it appeared, is its innate historical connection with the suburb, a form of (sub)urbanism that, in its characteristic American or Australian version, is intimately tied to individualized patterns of property ownership and consumption—in relation either to transport (automobiles), accommodation

Figure 4   Advertisement for Beijing Dragon Villas,
from *China Daily*, 18 February 1994.

(dwellings), consumer goods (electric appliances), or to recreational space (barbecue equipment, swimming pools, lawn tractors). The classic American suburb is a vast engine of consumption, a huge multiplier of consumer demand.[33]

In China, the villa is both transplanted and translated. Constructing a bridge of similitude over a trans-Pacific imaginary, images in the advertisements for the Beijing Dragon Villas, ("beautiful American-Canadian resi-

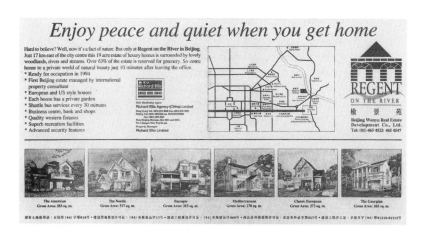

Figure 5   Advertisement for Regent on the River villas, from *China Daily.*

dences") are relocated in the upmarket spaces of prominent world cities in the West: "Just like Beverly Hills of California, Richmond of Vancouver, Bayview Hills of Toronto, Long Island of New York" (Figure 4). For prices from upward of $360,000, overseas investors can own 400 square meters of "deluxe villa" with 300 square meters of private garden (CD, 18 Feb. 1994). As an alternative choice, Regent on the River (Figure 5), seventeen kilometers east of the Beijing city center, is a nineteen-acre estate of luxury homes "surrounded by lovely woodlands, rivers and streams." The designs and nomenclature of these "European and U.S.-style houses," with gross area between 265 and 315 square meters, and managed by the international property consultants, London-based Richard Ellis,[34] are selected from a broader cultural register to reach a more differentiated, residentially discriminating, international Euro-American clientele: "the American," "the Nordic," "the Baroque," "the Mediterranean," "the Classic European," and "the Georgian" (Figure 5). Each house has its own private garden, "advanced security features," and "quality Western fixtures." Reference is also made to a business center, bank, shops, and a shuttle bus service to the city center every thirty minutes (CD, 24 Mar. 1994). Another major development, a kilometer from the Asian Games Village, is the Purple Jade Villas (offering "the most luxury European-style villa[s] in Beijing"): 328 villas, from 150 to 500 square meters in size, located in 1,000-square-meter gardens set in 6,000-square-meter woods, with 60,000 square meters of grass and 30,000 square meters of lake, in addition to a tennis court, angling club, and outdoor swimming pool. Either with an eye to security or simply to territorial identity, the attention of prospective investors is also drawn to "an enormous fence of 100 metres wide" (CD, 24 Mar. 1994).

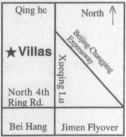

Figure 6   Feature photograph of River Garden villas,
from the business page of *China Daily*, 13 October 1997.

Other advertisements, for River Garden villas, for example ("tastefully designed in Euro-American style by a famous architectural firm from the USA"),
promise recreational facilities and restaurants in a clubhouse (CD, 1 Sept.
1994). Similarly, Phoenix Hill Villas ("eight different types in European style")
are located near the Beijing International Golf Club, "the only world-class 18
hole golf course built and managed by Japan Golf Promotions" (CD, 10 Mar.
1994). All of these developments, including also the more recent King's Garden Villas, with its business and shopping centers, indoor and outdoor sports,
and twenty-four-hour security, professional management (CD, 5 Sept. 1997),
draw particular reference to their location, generally near the expressway linking Beijing city proper and the Capital Airport (compare Figure 6).

In the ancient Chinese city, according to Liu[35], all was enclosed by walls,
with cities exhibiting an axial symmetry, roads running north-south and east-

west, forming a checker board grid, with the palace—as in ancient Peking—located precisely at the center. Writing about the Western metropolitan city, architectural critic Deyan Sudjic has suggested that, in recent decades, the symbolic center has shifted from the city hall and market square to the airport plaza.[36] If we substitute the royal palace for the hall and market, for the (possibly exogenous) community living in the newly developing suburban villas, the universe represented by the old Chinese city has become a spatial world turned inside out.[37]

The Worlds of Chinese Cities

One thing that is known, more generally, about the "traditional" Chinese city is that it is a cosmological representation, in space, of the Chinese universe. In the words of architectural and urban historian L. G. Liu, citing the ancient rules of *kao gong ji*, Chinese city planning was "closely linked with ideas of real and ideal social order and represented a structured vision of the universe. Builders aimed at making the city a true image of the universe as an ordered whole, a symbol of power, order and attuned to nature." In regard to classical Chinese architecture, "Its added purpose was to use symbols to impart meaning. . . . [S]ymbols, as employed in language, art and music, were used to express the deeper meanings of daily life. . . . In short, the Chinese world view was embodied in the symbolism of both architecture and site planning."[38]

What we want to suggest in this essay is that while the nature of that universe, that world, has changed, these interpretations remain sound. Under Mao, China constructed a world of communism, which was, until 1978, both literally and metaphorically largely cut off from another, "outside world." The socialist iconoclasm of Mao, breaking down the "forbidden" wall of feudalism, transforming the urban spaces of the imperial center, and turning China *inward*, did not however change Beijing's role as the capital city of socialist China. Indeed, the design of Tiananmen Square as the symbolic core of the "new" China served to underscore, ironically, the continuity of China's past and present.[39] In more recent years, China has opened out to, and become part of, another universe, one of global capitalism. Just as in the "traditional" Chinese city, each of these universes is represented by a different set of images, of symbolic architectures, of different spatial and building typologies, which represent, for those who live there, "a structured vision of the universe . . . an ordered whole."[40]

The way in which China has become part of this world of global capitalism is, in cities such as Beijing and Shanghai, for it to accept, and contribute to, the same urban symbolic language, to participate in the same symbolic economy, to speak in the same architectural and spatial terms, as exists elsewhere in that global economy, and especially in the United States. This is the logic, as we discussed above, behind the current project in Shanghai to construct "the world's tallest building."

The Return of Old Spatial Concepts and the Making of a New Regional Center

In an attempt to uncover the "power of place" of Tiananmen Square following the rise and the crackdown of the Chinese student movement in 1989, art historian Wu Hung reveals the form of Chinese political power as it is represented in imperial Beijing at various moments in Chinese history. Wu argues that the Chinese emperor maintained his power by keeping it secret behind the layers of walls that separated the "inner" from the "outer": "The emperor was invisible from the public space and [yet] he saw everything outside from his private space."[41] This specific political philosophy suggested a centrifugal absorption of powers from the "four quarters" of the middle kingdom.[42] The emperor sat in his chamber of command, overseeing the influx of tributes offered by the lesser centers overseas.[43] Seeing without being seen, the emperor absorbed powers and concentrated them in the middle kingdom revealing thereby an aura of the center vis-à-vis its neighbors within its tributary networks. This concept can be reworked to illustrate the present geopolitical and geocultural position of China in the world capitalist economy. While "exposing" itself to the outside world, China absorbs a major portion of the "free" flow of capitalism circulating in Asia and has increasingly outflanked its Asian neighbors to become the center of rapid capital accumulation.

Starting from the early 1980s, the territorially demarcated imagining of the nation under Mao's communist revolution was disrupted when Deng Xiaoping opened China and refocused the forces of global capitalism from its "overseas" to the mainland. Since then an influx of capital investments, just like "tributes," from the "four quarters" of the Middle Kingdom have transformed the coastal areas of China into the world's largest manufacturing centers. The network of Asian "global cities" has thus been extended, with major Chinese cities becoming the locus of foreign capital investment that would otherwise flow to other parts of Asia. The vast internal market and the virtually unlimited pool of workers comes into clear view after an extraordinary forty years of concealment from the global market. These resources, therefore, immediately become available. China has only to provide the infrastructures and modern urban space for foreign investments to pour in. The entry of China into the competition for investments in Asia and its transformation into a container for free-flowing capital has occurred at a crucial moment, as many of its neighbors experience the collapse of their "Asian miracle." Temporally ahead of China in the capitalist game, these "older" competitors in Southeast Asia had, by the mid-1990s, already realized that, in the words of their representative, Indonesian ex-President Suharto, they would "never enjoy again an economic growth such as [they had] experienced for more than a quarter of a century."[44]

It is within this web of *regional* competition and the national comparison of "development" that the recent construction of transnational architecture and cities in China might be understood. By bringing *inward* the transnational space of global cities, China attempts to strengthen its global position (vis-à-vis other Southeast Asian states), on one hand, and to increase the power of the nation-state, on the other. It is true that within the realm of global capitalism, the images of New York, Tokyo, and London are explicit points of reference for major cities in China. Yet these dominant urban centers also serve as a kind of ventriloquist's trope in which the "weakening" regional centers of Asia are addressed and challenged.

The construction of transnational space in China's major cities, however, is far from an attempt to drain China of its national heritage. It has, in fact, been accompanied by an "invention of tradition" in the form of heritage and preservation projects in many cities of China, from the ancient town of Suzhou to the capitalist city of Shenzhen.[45] What this suggests is a contradiction within capitalism between preserving the old (as in Suzhou) or reinventing it (such as the Song Palace Complex in Kaifeng) and expanding the "modern forms" driven by the market. It is with this embodiment of capitalism that the Forbidden City of Beijing retains its aura of power beyond mere commodification. No high-rise towers are allowed to be visible from the walled courtyards of the imperial palace.

Greater China, Regional Identity, and the Localization of Global Cultural Flows

This field of difference constructed within the narrative of global capitalism has also marked the "Greater China" debate initiated by economists in the 1980s, which put into visible use the category of "overseas Chinese" capital. "Greater China" was constituted around the idea of using the role of the ethnic Chinese outside China for the flexible accumulation of capital across the region of Asia and ultimately *into* China.[46] Its manifestation in space would comprise a linking of Guandong to Hongkong, Taiwan, and other Southeast Asian centers. In this cultural logic of capitalism, the overseas Chinese would contribute to the formation of "socialism with Chinese characteristics" in China (an official slogan promoted by Deng).[47] The combination of labor and market resources within China with the capital of the overseas

Chinese who control a major portion of capital networks in the region has brought China back into the role it played centuries ago as the destination of tributary flows. This "tributary" capitalist system demands the provision of transnational architecture and cities that both are sufficiently open to a capitalist order but that also adequately register the "Asian" characteristics of the greatest power in Asia.

The attempt of the Chinese government to mold capitalism into "socialism with Chinese characteristics" reveals to us an ambiguous space that contains two extreme visions—one of a world structured by the master narrative of capitalism and the other a vision of the state which aims to "localize" it. In this context of inventing traditions in order to imagine the present, the city that China desires as its model is not really New York, London, or Tokyo (though the images of these places are central to mark the entry of China into the web of capitalism in Asia) but rather Singapore—a tiny, authoritarian, and capitalistically developed state searching for an all-encompassing structure of feeling called "Asian communitarianism."[48] In his speech in Shenzhen in 1992, Deng Xiaoping explicitly identified China with Singapore, which had succeeded in maintaining "social order" on its way to becoming a "developed" country. He thought that "China could borrow from Singapore experience to do even better."[49] What we have here is a play of ambiguities in the very category of Chinese (post)modernity. Temporarily, China is behind the capitalist transformation of Asia, where it had to learn from its "little" brother of Singapore. Yet spatially, China is in a position of the "center," outdoing the other regional centers of Asia in their competition for investments from the United States, the European Community, Japan, and the overseas Chinese.

The point that we want to make here is that the "postmodernity" of China is not merely an effect of Chinese entry into the geopolitical and geocultural space of capitalism; it also results from an anxiety that China has in relation with the economic ups and downs experienced by its Asian neighbors, coping with the dream world and potential catastrophe of capitalism. Moreover, Chinese postmodernity is constituted less as an internal cultural attempt to overcome Mao's modernist project of the communist revolution than a synthesis of different claims, from Mao's idea of "socialism with national style" to the imperial ethics of Confucianism à la Singapore and Western concepts of growth.

The symbolic construction of "China" and the "Chinese" as both bounded and unbounded categories ruptures the spatial imagination of the nation-state. Being "China" and "Chinese" in the contemporary world is also "being in the (capitalist) world," an existence which also means participating in the same economic, political, and social practices, introducing the same kind of institutions, such as world trade centers, financial centers, international hotels, convention centers, and the spatial and architectural forms in which these are represented. The attempt of Chinese authorities to turn capitalism into "socialism with Chinese characteristics" runs in paradoxical conjunction with "transnationalizing" China, attracting foreign capital, establishing joint ventures, inviting transnational companies and the personnel that come with them. It also involves constructing the culturally appropriate spatial and architectural forms to ensure they feel at home.

Conclusion

In the *fin de siècle*, we find ourselves in the moment of transit where space and time cross to produce complex figures of difference and identity, past and present, inside and outside, inclusion and exclusion. —Homi Bhabha, *The Location of Culture*

Given the way we have discussed these contemporary developments in China, it is perhaps wiser to make two or three observations than attempt to draw "conclusions." The first of these relates to the question of whether a particular sign, namely, that of the spectacular skyscraper, invented in the United States at the end of the last century, can still claim to be a globally recognized, internationally acclaimed signifier of modernity. As we have argued elsewhere, the evidence suggests that it is not.[50] As far as Western notions of urban modernity are concerned, a range of paradigm shifts has taken place in recent years: gargantuan architectural icons of corporate capitalism have been replaced by environmental indicators that put ecological, energy, and health concerns as more appropriate signifiers of the modern city: clean air, public and private safety, quality of housing standards, environmental efficiency, steady traffic flows. On these criteria, among the world's hundred largest cities, Shanghai and Beijing rank forty-eighth and forty-ninth; New York, which they may see as a model, ranks no better than twenty-seventh. The city with the highest score is Melbourne, Australia, principally a vast, single-story suburb, with a modest high-rise core. This is not, of course, to say that such hyperrational arguments will deter any city, nation, organization, corporation, or individual from making spectacular architectural statements in the future.

If these architectural manifestations of modernity in China initially seem to be new, there are also, as we have discussed, ways of seeing them as part of a longer spatial tradition in which China is always "in the center." From this perspective, urban transformation in contemporary China has to be understood as one among many "multiple paths to modernization."[51] In contemporary Chinese political culture, "consciousness of the world as such"[52] is inseparable from the process of global capitalism that, on one hand, seems to produce a general pattern of global cultural homogenization and, on the other, the construction of a particular culture, the result of economic, social, political, and historical specificities. Cultural flows and influences never operate in an innocent or neutral way; they are invariably nuanced and affected by the conditions in which they occur, producing meanings that are dependent on the contexts.

The question remains as to how far this construction of transnational space in China contributes to the formation of either individual or collective subjectivities, and whether for local Chinese or others overseas. This essay can only suggest that although the transnational architecture and space may be intended primarily for overseas consumption, be it Chinese or Euro-American, the population at large, particularly those who live and move around the metropolis, are no doubt affected by their presence. Transnational space perhaps arrives at the local site in the terms of the advertisement: "Look, but don't touch." [53] People "consume" a production that they could not afford to own. Nevertheless, the presence of transnational space in China intertwines with the circulation of popular culture that is increasingly transnational. The spread of "overseas" TV programs, music, films, and media, largely from Hong Kong, Taiwan, and Southeast Asia, have contributed to the formation of transnational urban cultures in contemporary China. The increasing density clusters of unbounded images, sounds, and the visibility of practices of the built environment have generated a chain of cultural signification that contributes to a general "fascination with and a hunger to learn about the world outside of state borders." [54]

Mao's modernist project of nation building, by which all subjects embody the nation-state, has been displaced by these forces of transnationality. The built-environment innovations in Beijing, Shanghai, and other Chinese cities have created a new form of transnational space that necessarily contributes to the production of a detached Chinese national subject, "a different way to be Chinese" [55] away from the state. To what extent this disjunction of nation and state—as a result of transnationalization of China—contributes to the liberation of the historical subjects of China remains to be seen. What seems to be evident is that economic globalization tends to produce economic and social polarization in the so-called global city,[56] whether in relation to incomes, housing standards, or life chances. There would seem to be a case to consider here in the one-time "socialist" capital of Beijing.

Notes

1   Anthony D. King, "The Times and Spaces of Modernity (or Who Needs Postmodernism?)," in Global Modernities, ed. Mike Featherstone, Scott Lash, and Roland Robertson (London: Sage Publications, 1995), 108–23.

2   See Arif Dirlik and Xudong Zhang, introduction to this volume.

3   E.g., Marshall Berman, *All That Is Solid Melts into Air: The Experience of Modernity* (London: Verso, 1983).

4   Arjun Appadurai, *Modernity at Large: Cultural Dimensions of Globalization* (Minneapolis: University of Minnesota Press, 1996), 3.

5   Dirlik and Zhang, introduction.

6   Dirlik and Zhang, introduction.

7   Dirlik and Zhang, introduction.

8   Doreen Massey, "Imagining Globalization: Power-Geometries of Time-Space," in *Future Worlds: Migration, Environment and Globalization*, ed. A. Brah, M. J. Kickmann, and M. Mac An Ghaill (London: Macmillan, in press).

9   Mohammad Bamyeh, *Genealogies of Transnationalism: Profiles of Governmentality and Culture in the Global Era* (Minneapolis: University of Minnesota Press, forthcoming 2000).

10 *China Daily*, 14 Oct. 1997 (hereafter *CD*, which I cite parenthetically in the text).

11 Given that all of our examples come from the American edition of *China Daily*, this is, of course, not surprising.

12 This citation is from Wu Hung's article, discussed below (see note 20).

13 Anne Guerrian, "The Metropolis and the Capital," *Zone* 1, no. 2 (summer 1986): 219–22.

14 This section (including citations) is largely drawn from Anthony D. King, "Worlds in the City: Manhattan Transfer and the Rise of Spectacular Space," *Planning Perspectives* 11 (1996): 97–114.

15 See King, "Worlds in the City"; see also the tall, slim, and oversize book prompted by these developments, Judith Dupré, *Skyscrapers: A History of the World's Most Famous and Important Skyscrapers* (New York: Black Dog and Leventhal, 1996). The buildings in China are in Shanghai, Hong Kong, Shenzhen, and Guanzhou.

16 The figure of 460 meters reported here conflicts with that of 420 meters, which Dupré gives for the Jinmao Tower, still "under construction" when her book was published (see *Skyscrapers*, p. 120).

17 The international competition began, presumably, only in 1996, when the highest building outside the United States was constructed in Malaysia.

18 Mona Domosh, *Invented Cities: The Creation of Landscape in Nineteenth-Century New York and Boston* (New Haven, Conn.: Yale University Press, 1996), 76.

19 Spiro Kostof, *A History of Architecture: Settings and Rituals* (New York: Oxford University Press, 1995), 231.

20 Wu Hung, "Tiananmen Square: A political History of Monuments," *Representations* 35 (summer 1991): 84–117.

21 Dong Liming, "Beijing: The Development of a Socialist Capital," in *Chinese Cities: The Growth of the Metropolis since 1949*, ed. Victor F. S. Sit (Hong Kong: Oxford University Press, 1988), 67.

22 John Hancock, "The Apartment House in Urban America," in *Buildings and Society: Essays on the Social Development of the Built Environment*, ed. Anthony D. King (London: Routledge and Kegan Paul, 1980), 151–92, from which the first part of this section is taken.

23 Cited in Hancock, "The Apartment House," 152.

24 Cited in Hancock, "The Apartment House," 158.

25 Prices quoted for these new apartments were $1,200 to $1,500 per square meter. According to the report, prices had risen during 1997.

26 Beijing's Finance Street, designated in 1993, is 1,700 metres long and covers 88 acres, with a planned building area of 1.8 million square meters. "Though it is far from being a financial center like Wall Street in the United States," Finance Street brings together

the headquarters of China's top banks. It will also house the "most powerful institutions of the banking, securities, and insurance sectors, the China Securities Regulatory Commission as well as leading insurance companies." Among new developments are Corporate Square, "an imposing 17-story office building, jointly developed by major contractors based in Hong Kong, Malaysia and Singapore." At present, foreign banks are scattered throughout the commercial centers, close to their customers. According to the *China Daily* report, the development of Finance Street is being held up by limited business opportunities for banks, inadequate facilities, the lack of a business atmosphere, and inability to house stock and futures exchanges (CD, 8 Sept. 1997).

27 Fewer than half of the new developments have local Beijing names; examples of some that do are Hengfu Gardens, Huade Mansion, and Hua Yuan Apartments.

28 In August 1994, 53 of the world's top 100 multinational corporations, and 28 of the 50 largest American companies had opened offices in China. During January to June 1994, 402 foreign companies were given approval to open offices or branches in Beijing, bringing the total of foreign subsidiaries in the city to 3,700. Beijing expected to attract between 200 and 300 multinational companies in the next three to five years. See "Beijing becomes city of choice for multinationals," CD, 22 Aug. 1994, 7.

Three years later, according to the *China Daily*, China had approved 293,556 overseas-funded firms by the end of June 1997, 13,000 of them in Beijing and 16,580 in Shanghai. This information accompanies the information that "more and more investors have begun to show interest in ["service"] apartments as a result of surging demands for the new property product." Such apartments (developed, in this case, by Zeng Jiang Overseas Investment Groups, Australia, Ltd.) were usually 50–80 square meters in size and offered at between $70,000 and $80,000. "Highly ranking officials of such [overseas-funded] firms need such apartments, as do rich people in China" (CD, 13 Oct. 1997, 5).

29 See Anthony D. King, *Colonial Urban Development* (London: Routledge and Kegan Paul, 1976), chaps. 6, 7.

30 It might, in fact, be argued that the choice of these two residential types, currently being constructed in Beijing as the principal investment vehicle for "overseas buyers," has been carefully thought out as meeting the most widely accepted preferences of prospective occupants from the United States and Europe.

31 See Pierre de la Ruffinière du Prey, *John Soane: The Making of an Architect* (Chicago: University of Chicago Press, 1982).

32 As one English contemporary observed in 1753, "If one wished to see a coxcomb expose himself in the most effectual manner, one would advise him to build a villa, which is the *chef d'oeuvre* of modern impertinence." Cited by du Prey, *John Soane,* 381.

33 See Richard A. Walker, "A Theory of Suburbanization: Capitalism and the Construction of Urban Space in the United States," in *Urbanization and Urban Planning in Capitalist Society,* ed. Michael Dear and Alan J. Scott (London: Methuen, 1981), 383–430. For the diffusion of the villa in nineteenth-century United States, see the various works of architect A. J. Downing, e.g., *The Architecture of Country Houses* (New York: Dover Publications, 1969; originally published in 1850), including designs for cottages, farm houses, and villas.

34 For the internationalization of real estate and property consultants, see Nigel Thrift, "The Internationalization of Producer Services and the Integration of the Pacific Basin Property Market," in *Multinationals and the Restructuring of the World Economy,* ed. M. J. Taylor and N. J. Thrift (London: Croom Helm, 1986), 142–92; Thrift, "The Fixers: The Urban Geography of International Commercial Capital," in *Global Restructuring and Territorial Development,* ed. J. Henderson and M. Castells (London: Sage, 1987), 219–47.

35 L. G. Liu, *Chinese Architecture* (New York: Rizzoli, 1989).

36 Deyan Sudjic, *The 100 Mile City* (London: Andre Deutsch, 1992).

37 Villa development is not confined to Beijing. Dalian—the economic, trade, and financial center of northeast China, promoted to become "the Hong Kong of the north," with two hundred foreign-invested enterprises approved for property development—as part of its plan to attract additional foreign investment and "to further improve the living condition of foreign business people" decided to build the Overseas Chinese Villas, "the first and only villa zone . . . in the scenic area of Dalian. . . . [T]he zone, backed by green mountains and facing the sea, is a paradise with European- and American-style villas, under unique and beautiful surroundings." *CD*, 22 Aug. 1994.

38 L. G. Liu, *Chinese Architecture*, 34, 37, 39.

39 Marwyn S. Samuels and Carmencita Samuels, "Beijing and the Power of Place in Modern China," in *The Power of Place: Bringing Together Geographical and Sociological Imaginations*, ed. John Agnew and James Duncan (Boston: Unwin Hyman, 1989), 202–27.

40 Liu, *Chinese Architecture*.

41 Wu Hung, "Tiananmen Square," 87.

42 Paul Wheatley, *The Pivot of the Four Quarters* (Chicago: Aldine, 1971).

43 Takeshi Hamashita, "The Tribute Trade System and Modern Asia," *Tokyo: Memoirs of the Research Department of the Toyo Bunko*, no. 46 (1988).

44 Benedict Anderson, "From Miracle to Crash," *London Review of Books*, 16 April 1998, 3.

45 Ann Anagnost, "The Nationscape: Movement in the Field of Vision," *Positions* 1, no. 3 (fall 1993): 585–606.

46 Aihwa Ong, "A Momentary Glow of Fraternity: Narratives of Chinese Nationalism and Capitalism," *Identities* 3, no. 3 (fall 1997): 331–66.

47 Officially sanctioned for the twenty-first century in China at the Fifteenth Party Congress on 12 Sept. 1997. See *CD*, 23 Sept. 1997.

48 Beng-huat Chua, "Between Economy and Race: The Asianization of Singapore," in *Space, Culture, and Power: New Identities in Globalizing Cities*, ed. Ayse Oncu and Petra Wyland (London: Zed Books, 1997), 23–41.

49 Cited in Arif Dirlik, "Critical Reflections on 'Chinese Capitalism' as Paradigm," *Identities* 3, no. 3 (fall 1997): 317.

50 See King, "Worlds in the City."

51 Jan Nederveen Pieterse, "Globalization as Hybridization," in *Global Modernities*, ed. Mike Featherstone, Scott Lash, and Roland Robertson (London: Sage, 1995), 45–68.

52 Roland Robertson, *Globalization: Social Theory and Global Culture* (London: Sage, 1992).

53 Susan Buck-Morss, "Dreamworld of Mass Culture: Walter Benjamin's Theory of Modernity and the Dialectics of Seeing," in *Modernity and the Hegemony of Vision*, ed. David Michael Levin (Berkeley: University of California Press, 1993), 309–38.

54 Mayfair Mei-hui Yang, "Mass Media and Transnational Subjectivity in Shanghai: Notes on (Re)Cosmopolitanism in a Chinese Metropolis," in *Underground Empires: The Cultural Politics of Modern Chinese Transnationalism*, ed. Aihwa Ong and Donald M. Nonini (New York: Routledge, 1997), 296.

55 Yang, "Mass Media," 301.

56 See, for example, James W. White, "Old Wine, Cracked Bottle? Tokyo, Paris, and the Global City Hypothesis," and responses from Saskia Sassen and Michael Peter Smith, *Urban Affairs* 33, no. 4 (winter 1998): 451–77.

3   Postmodern Literary Discourse and Contemporary
Public Culture in Taiwan

With the increasing importance of Taiwan's role in the global economy and
since martial law was lifted in 1987, a number of literary critics have tried to
apply the term *postmodernism* to discussions of contemporary Taiwanese public culture. Often these critics singled out features that could be loosely defined as postmodern in terms of the fascinating, albeit unstable, mixture of
speedy economic and political change, consumerism and multinational capital flows, the feminist and gay rights movements, cyberspace and counterdis-
course, new occult imaginary and alternative medicine, satellite TV and the
transnational mediascape, call-in radio programs and semipublic spheres, interior design and the multiple layers of cultural bricolage, metafiction and
generic hybridity, architectural double-coding and the resurgence of traditional religious and moral beliefs, and the shifting identities in increasingly
plural, though at times polarized, arenas, et cetera.[1]

  While these aspects of transcultural imaginative appropriation have been
extensively studied largely by academics and bilingual intellectuals living on
the island or in the United States, there has been, regrettably, little attention

paid to the sociopolitical history of the double marginalization of Taiwan in the New World Order and its implications for the supposedly postmodern condition in Taiwan. In this essay, I argue that it is precisely this double marginalization of Taiwan since 1971 that helps produce the desire on the part of the Taiwanese, who have been almost universally abandoned, to engage with or to be entertained by current theoretical trends, and, moreover, that it is a peculiar global/local cultural dialectics that stresses the urgency to negotiate from the periphery, to deconstruct Chinese-Western grand narratives of ideological mapping.

The year 1987 is usually considered to be crucial with regard to Taiwan's democratization and push toward postmodernity, if we take that word to mean a life situation after and because of (*post*) the collapse of totalizing modes of historical understanding and philosophical description, a new condition of being that arises because of the "qualitative transformation" of a previous authority that lays bare the "simulacra of power" or brings in a sense of "subversive play."[2] Since the forty-year-old martial law was officially lifted on 15 July of that year, people have been able to speak and to move more freely, permitted not only to go back to the mainland to visit their relatives but also to openly criticize the government of Taiwan. During this pivotal year, Karl Marx's *Capital: A Critique of Political Economy* was among the best-selling books in Taiwan, according to a poll conducted by the *China Times* (*Chung-kuo shih-pao*); it is also the year that postmodernism was more systematically imported to Taiwan through institutional networks and agencies, among them the Aesthetics and Literary Studies Conference organized by National Tsinghua University, Taiwan, where Fredric Jameson discussed his own seminal essay "Postmodernism, or, The Cultural Logic of Late Capitalism" before a large audience in Taipei. With him was a small but diverse group of American university professors, including Yu-kung Kao, Masao Miyoshi, Louis Montrose, and Wai-lim Yip, who represented, in a peculiar way, different positions in lyric, phenomenological, Marxian, new historicist, and postmodern criticism.

In fact, before Jameson visited Taipei, the postmodernism craze in Taiwan had been manifested by the appearance of books and articles in local magazines on related topics. Between 1981 and 1984, William Tay, a professor of literature at the University of California, San Diego, and a one-time student of Jameson, published essays on the impact of poststructuralism and postmodernism on literary and cultural studies in the *Chung-wai Literary Monthly*. Tsai Yuan-huang, professor of English at National Taiwan University, published *Tang-ta wen-hsueh lun-chi*, an introduction to poststructuralism and postmodern fiction, one year before Jameson came to Taipei. *Con-temporary* (*Tangtai*), a literary monthly founded in May 1986, devoted several of its first issues to poststructuralist and postmodern cultural theories, even though the original idea of the magazine was to revive the spirit of the May Fourth Movement.

By 1987, the term *postmodernism* was by no means unfamiliar to Taiwanese art critics, as there were already performers and cultural workers who considered themselves postmodernists. However, it was mainly Jameson who provided Taiwanese scholars with a general survey of postmodernist culture; Xiaobing Tang's translation of his 1985 Beijing lectures appeared in consecutive issues, beginning with volume 14, of *Con-temporary* (June 1987), and it came out in book form one and a half years later, just in time for Jameson's second visit to Taipei in the summer of 1989, hosted again by National Tsinghua. Since 1987, dozens of Chinese-language books on postmodernism, including some by Hong Kong and mainland scholars, have been made available in Taiwan. Essays on the subject published in special issues of *Taipei p'ing-lun*, *Chung-kuo lun-tan*, *Hsiung-shih mei-shih*, and many other leading journals and news magazines—not to mention *Chung-wai Literary Monthly* and *Contemporary*—number in the hundreds. Between 1987 and 1992, not only did owners or designers of cafés and public buildings playfully demonstrate their spatial imagination in late- and postmodern styles but several studios devoted to "postmodern art and culture" were launched in major cities such as Taipei and Kaohsiung. In the field of literature, Chang T'a-chun, Chu Tien-wen, Chung Ming-te, Lin Yao-te, and Lou Ch'ing, among others, are celebrated postmodern writers who freely mix metafiction with journalism, romance with magic realism, literary discourse with post–identity politics, and localized pastiches with globalized ones. However, if the postmodernism craze in Taiwan sprang up like "bamboo shoots after the rain," it soon declined and virtually disappeared. In only a few years, postmodernism became outdated and was replaced by peculiarly "glocalized" versions of localism. In 1992, a beer house in Taipei frequented by artists and cultural workers was named Hou-hsien-tai Fen-ch'ang (Postmodern, or Postmodernism Graveyard). It was as if the age of post-postmodernism had arrived overnight—even before postmodernism took root in Taiwan.

Postcoloniality, Postmodernity, and Alternative Postmodernisms

The Taiwanese reception of postmodernism, and, to a certain extent, its postmodern condition (or, to be more precise, its postmodernity), is characterized by an intensity and a fluid energy, especially when speedy developments and cultural politics within the local context are taken into consideration. To people such as Jameson, Taiwan may appear to be in its late modern phase, moving toward the postmodern.[3] Perceived in this way, Taiwan is at least a decade behind Hong Kong, which is regularly featured in many postmodern architecture books as a fascinating city-colony where international or "hyphenational"—culturally mixed and always in transit—consumers walk through two- or three-story hyperreal arcades (*Passagen*) to move among street signs of cultural hybridity (Cantonese intermixed with Chinese and English), to hurry from one building to the next on "borrowed time and space." However, given the ambivalent and highly contested perspectives on postmodern anxieties (or "postcolonial liberal guilt") on the part of the postindustrial West in relation to the so-called Third World,[4] we could venture to examine public culture in present-day Taiwan, just as Robert Thornton does in his discussion of South Africa, in terms of "alternative postmodernisms," each one being "specific to a particular locale in the global culture-map."[5] In fact, compared to critics who have discussed South Africa or Latin America in terms of postmodernism, we may be in a better discursive situation to talk about the postmodern condition in Taiwan by stressing that Taiwan is a "non-national nation-state" (to borrow Jameson's phrase), or a fifty-two-year-old "transitory" government created by national disunity. Such disunity forces people to endure uncertainty—the worst kind of uncertainty—about virtually all elements of the social edge, from the state-created domains to the various aspects of everyday life, since almost all identities—cultural, ethnic, national, and so on—now not only cut across each other in multiple ways and through multiple sites but are also open to threat and renegotiation.[6] To quote a political scientist, "there is practically no place like Taiwan—great tradition, small island; conservative state, drastic change; cultural imperialism, committed Nationalism; localist sentiment, cosmopolitan sophistication."[7] Indeed, it is the oxymoronic and self-contested nature of that unnatural state of being that easily lends a "postmodern aura" to Taiwan.

Before moving on to describe the postmodern condition in Taiwan, let me briefly dwell on the topic of alternative postmodernisms. In his succinct introduction to *Postmodernism and Politics*, Jonathan Arac has summarized respective contributions and discursive positions of several leading thinkers on postmodernity, especially of Bell, Lyotard, Habermas, Jameson, and Rorty. He suggests that "it remains wholly unsettled whether the relation of the 'postmodern' to 'modern' is more a break or a continuity."[8] He cites different views on the question of art's autonomy and tentatively concludes that "a great deal of the controversy in this debate depends on misunderstandings, not at all surprising across so wide a range of disciplinary and national traditions, which obstruct significant direct engagement with the arguments, motives, and the various positions."[9] In fact, these unsettling "misunderstandings" have become exacerbated, as "American, French, and German emphases" have recently been challenged or made even more complex by Indian, African, Latin American, and Japanese inputs.[10] The most remarkable contributions to the debate are from critics in the field of multiculturalism and feminism, in which postmodernism is perceived to be not only a disguised form of minoritizing discourse but irrelevant or "of no use value in relation to the rest of the world."[11] To some scholars, postmodernism has indeed opened up new possibilities for rethinking ethnography and the intertwined relationships between anthropology and colonialism, but postmodernism has also been faulted for its quick dismissal of "localized questions of experience, identity, culture, and history" as if they were nothing but "reiterations of cultural 'essence' or unified, stable identity."[12] For a number of Third World feminists, postmodernist theory does not explain the relations of ruling and is nothing but a "white, middle-class" cultural discourse. Moreover, in its haste to dissociate itself from all forms of essentialism, postmodern theory "has generated a series of epistemological confusions regarding the interconnections between location, identity, and the construction of knowledge."[13] Similar comments have been made concerning postcolonial theory.[14]

In these sharp and pointedly persuasive critical accounts, however, there is a tendency to assume that postmodernism is a hegemonic and homogenized discourse that leaves no room for Third Worlds. In spite of the limitations of postmodernist theory, it can be appropriated as a discourse of palimpsestual reinscription that deepens our thinking about identity and even pluralized "postidentity" politics.[15] In the term *postcolonial*, as Linda Hutcheon reminds us, *post-* is a marker of dynamic complexity: "On the one hand, *post-* is taken to mean 'after,' 'because of,' and even unavoidably 'inclusive of' the colonial; on the other, it signifies more explicit resistance and opposition, the anticolonial."[16] This is also a strategy Achille Mbembe advocates in his important essay on postcolonial banal improvisation. What Mbembe suggests concerning the people's connivance and mobility in response to "the banality of power" in the postcolony is perhaps more true of the postmodern: "The postcolonial 'subject' mobilizes not just a single 'identity,' but several fluid identities which, by their very nature, must be constantly 'revised' in order to achieve maximum instrumentality and efficacy as and when required."[17] In addition to Hutcheon and Mbembe, several other people have enlightened us concerning the possibility of reinterpreting the meaning of coloniality and modernity in Third World contexts, so that postmodernist discourses may be rewritten or "renegotiated" to constitute tactics of survival in the global cultural economy.[18]

Teasing out the warring forces in Michel Foucault's concluding passages to *The Order of Things* on the "calm violence" of the birth of ethnology and psychoanalysis, Homi Bhabha calls attention to the ways in which philosophical discourses of modernity and postmodernity have been constituted by the ambivalent object of a colonized other, a "minus in the origin." By detailing the lapses created by differential temporalities and communalities, the splits between the project of modernity (pedagogy) and colonial sentiments or rhetorical execution (performativity) in relation to the "intimate enemy," Bhabha highlights the deconstructive and agonizing force of seemingly nonsensical mimicry and imaginative appropriation in the process of cultural translation. He suggests:

> It happens at a symptomatic moment when the representation of cultural difference attenuates the sense of History as the imbedding, domesticating "homeland" of the human sciences. For the finitude of History—its moment of doubling—participates in the conditionality of the contingent. An incommensurability ensues between History as the "homeland" of the human sciences—its cultural area, local chronologies, and specific geographical boundaries—and the claims of Historicism to a more universalist perspective.[19]

That is to say, the distant and damned other is constituted by and constitutive of the human sciences in the West. Problematic though that "conditionality of the contingent" may sound, Bhabha's notion of a disjunctive historical agency, of the historical being as much an internal as an external event, does raise the possibility of recognizing the margin of hybridity where the histories of the "metropolis" and the "peripheries" interrelate and become more mutually constituted than we normally think. In this regard, Catherine Hall's recent study of Edward John Eyre, who moved between London and the British colonies in the Pacific from 1845 to 1865, together with Paul Gilroy's revealing accounts of the black Atlantic world, enables us to reread modernity as part of a complex transcultural process, to produce a decentered and postmodern re-vision of earlier imperial grand narratives.[20]

Postmodernity is, of course, not the same thing as postcoloniality, although in many cases the two are helplessly intertwined, at least according to postcolonial critics such as Mbembe, or new area studies scholars such as Raymond Lee. Speaking of hedonism and the fascination with commodities in Pacific Asia, Lee writes: "Postmodernism as a postcolonial strategy of ludic inversion fragments and deflates the Western ego, but contrastingly provides a medium for renewed self-assertion among Third World individuals whose historicities are beginning to come into their own."[21] To some Australian writers, the term *postcolonial* covers attempts on the part of those "affected by the imperial process from the moment of colonization to the present day" to unsettle Enlightenment certainties and to foreground the tension with the foreign power.[22] Or, as Kwame Anthony Appiah asserts, it can be cynically referred to as "the condition of what we might ungenerously call a *compra-*

dor intelligentsia: a relatively small, Western-style, Western-trained group of writers and thinkers, who mediate the trade in cultural commodities of world capitalism at the periphery" ("Post-," 348). On the other hand, postmodernism can be seen as a "retheorization of the proliferation of distinctions that reflects the underlying dynamic of cultural modernity, the need to clear oneself a space" ("Post-," 346). However, after making the distinction between the postcolonial and the postmodern, Appiah also suggests that the postmodern may be able to be linked up productively with the postcolonial, a point several critics of postcolonial theory tend to dismiss all too quickly. He points out that the *post-* in *postmodern* and *postcolonial* is the "*post-* of the space-clearing gesture" ("Post-," 348). He actually sees in "postmodernism" a possibility of developing more inclusive and localizing strategies that serve to challenge earlier legitimating narratives and to fight neocolonial co-optation. He writes:

> Indeed, it might be said to be a mark of popular culture that its borrowings from international cultural forms are remarkably insensitive to, not so much dismissive of as blind to, the issue of neocolonialism or "cultural imperialism." This does not mean that theories of postmodernism are irrelevant to these forms of culture, for the internationalization of the market and the commodification of artworks are both central to them. But it does mean that these artworks are not understood by their producers or their consumers in terms of a postmodernism: there is no antecedent practice whose claim to exclusivity of vision is rejected through these artworks. What is called "syncretism" here is a consequence of the international exchange of commodities, but not of a space-clearing gesture. ("Post-," 348)

To Appiah, then, postmodernism as a "space-clearing" gesture is also a move toward re-evocation of transnational African identities based on local constituencies. Speaking of "African identities" in another context, he cautions us that it is not enough to point to the general instability, heterogeneity, and deconstructive character of identity categories. In other words, we need to analyze the concrete historical context and all sorts of forces—spatial, cultural, technological, material, and representational—that are intertwined in the "constantly shifting redefinition of 'tribal' identities to meet the economic and political exigencies of the modern world."[23] The idea is that we can certainly cherish the remarkable acts of imaginative appropriations worldwide but only with the limits of postmodern discursive strategies in mind.

As a consequence of these ongoing postmodern and postcolonial debates, it is now more difficult to reach an overlapping consensus concerning what postmodernism is to different cultures, especially when we confront the problem of incommensurability in transnational studies. More than ever, according to Arjun Appadurai, in the complex interactive and refractive processes of cultural transfer, individuals situated within specific national and social trajectories may bring their somewhat localized imagination to bear on the subject in question in various and often unpredictable ways.[24] However, we cannot be too careful about the power relations involved in the construction of agency in the transcultural nesting of imaginative appropriation. As Appadurai reminds us, "not all deterritorialization is global in its scope, and not all imagined lives span vast international panoramas. The world on the move affects even small geographical and cultural spaces."[25]

In the pages ahead, I will look at contemporary Taiwanese public culture in terms of what Appiah, Bhabha, Mbembe, and Thornton have outlined as a "space-clearing gesture," a "margin of hybridity," "everyday improvisation," and "alternative postmodernisms." First, I will give a brief description of Taiwan's postmodern predicament as seen in the rapid development of innovative information technology and social change, in the hybridized pastiche of foreign and local material in transnational satellite TV programs, in the chaotic political arenas and social incongruities, in the contingency and indeterminacy of identities, and in the grotesque resurgence of traditional beliefs such as *feng-shui*. Then, I will discuss the ways in which contemporary Taiwanese public culture is shaped by the political history of double marginalization. Finally, I will speculate on the implications of Taiwan's postmodernity for new area studies.

The Postmodern Condition in Taiwan

Although only 18 percent of the residents of its urban areas own at least one computer per family, Taiwan now produces the most innovative chips for notebook computers in the world, and it is ranked fourth in the world overall as a computer manufacturer, slightly behind America, Germany, and Japan. During the Gulf War, CNN reporters were said to have used a tiny, but technologically advanced, transmitter that was made in Taiwan. It is much easier to access the Internet in Taiwan than it is in Singapore or China, where networks and e-mail messages are constantly supervised by the government. Visit the BBS bulletin boards on practically any college network in Taiwan, and you will find the sophisticated homepages of the gay and lesbian community and the counterculture, in addition to a superabundant cyberspatial pastiche at various sites that link up glocally. Most striking is the playful and subversive deployment of neologisms and discourse strategies on those seemingly innocuous homepages. *Homepage* is transliterated, in one instance, as hung-pei-chi (literally, concubines who do the baking and cooking), which indicates the special buffer zone in which gender is heatedly debated. This sort of witty semantic innovation is often done by intermixing ethnic dialects that challenge kuo-yu (the national language, or Mandarin Chinese) by revitalizing other racial and cultural heritages that have been suppressed or persecuted to the edge of extinction by the KMT government.[26] Such innovations constitute one of the many ways of creating the younger generation's own political and cultural agendas, of organizing countermovements or social struggles against state domination, of actively engaging in or disengaging from shifting identities. This is, however, not simply a game for college students, as the use of computer-mediated representations and of cyborgs has become common in many contested arenas—the political protest, the labor union movement, and most notably, the new literature in hybrid languages.

By the seventies, Wang Wen-hsing, a novelist and professor of literature at National Taiwan University, had already produced his Kafkaesque-Joycean masterpiece Pei-hai te jen (Backed against the sea), in which he mixed Chinese with Taiwanese dialects. Quite different, however, is the work of the late city poet Lin Yang-te, who fuses literary imagination with technology by portraying the urban subjects as digitally simulated (and stimulated) bodies (bodies without organs) that move in and out of computer monitors, from one postmodern building to the next, with only the desire to desire "obscene" sex or consumerism (hsia-p'ing, literally, blind consuming passions). While mostly an imaginative appropriation of codes and images introduced by Baudrillard, Lyotard, Jameson, and even Haraway, Lin's Tu-shih-chung tuanchi (Terminals inside the city [1988]) is quite remarkable in terms of its linguistic and rhetorical experiment, which brings the problematics of technoscience in hypertext to the representation of the fluid, albeit fragmented (or disconnected), social field.[27] In their exploration of gay and lesbian sexuality in the Taiwanese context, other writers, such as Hung Ling, Ch'i Tawei, Chang Hsiao-hung, Chu Tien-wen, and Cheng Ying-shu, join Eve Kosofsky Sedgwick, Judith Butler, Michel Foucault, and many new Japanese and Latin American science fiction writers in the list of global forces of influence. These writers tend to transgress the boundary between literary and nonliterary discourses, constantly drawing on journalism, stock-market reports, fashion designs, diaries, popular songs, new religious cults, political propaganda, social-movement slogans, and all sorts of everyday public or private speech. Like their protagonists, who often have difficulty figuring out their sexual orientations—gay, lesbian, bisexual, transsexual, or transvestite—these authors themselves embody multiple and fluid identities: as professionals or academics, host(esses) of talk shows, newspaper columnists, leaders of ecofeminist or gay organizations, antiques dealers, stockholders, moderators of the 1996 vice presidential candidates' TV debates or of multiculturalism conferences, lovers, and so on.

Juxtaposed to the above, and politically incongruous with them, are oral narratives and full-length novels that concern themselves with rewriting Taiwanese national history. While the oral history projects are directed by a group of nativists such as Chang Yen-hsien and Chiang Wen-yu, the historical novels are by versatile authors such as Yeh Shih-t'ao and Li T'ao, who continue to write on colonial or postcolonial subjects in the nativist tradition. Unlike postmodern fiction by the yuppie generation, which is characterized by generic and linguistic hybridity, these oral narratives and historical novels are by people who have been affected by Japanese imperialism, by the February 28 Incident of 1947, when the KMT took over Taiwan, and by the following fifty years of internal colonization. In fact, most of the oral histories collected are narrated by women from different ethnic and cultural backgrounds who are now in their eighties or nineties. Some are illiterate aboriginal women who witnessed the dark side of modernization projects launched by the Japanese and KMT governments; others are mainland Chinese women who came with the KMT army and until now have remained silent about their diasporic experience. Still others are Taiwanese women of southern Fukien or Hakka origins who were daughters of local elites and who had married into powerful families who were unjustly purged by the KMT between 1945 and 1955.

Thus, in the field of literature, there is a large gap between postmodern fiction and realism (or the historical novel). Writers in both categories do relatively well, since they address different sociocultural issues that appeal to different groups of readers. Ideologically in conflict with each other, writers of both camps sometimes have no difficulty working together to push new social movements forward; they don't seem to be hampered by identity politics. However, none of them outshines Yang Chao (the pseudonym of Li Mingchuen), who has managed to blend postmodern gay fiction with conventional family romance in tracing the indigenous roots of quasi nationalism, local elitism, state violence, and the erotic behavior of grotesque social bodies. A successful novelist and a Ph.D. candidate at Harvard University, Yang Chao is also a spokesman for the Democratic Progressive Party (DPP), a popular media personality and cultural critic, a public intellectual, a social activist, a husband, an orator who delivers speeches islandwide, and a member of various committees that bestow literary awards. He epitomizes the postmodern literary discourse in Taiwan, and this is the image audiences of Fourth Cable TV tend to associate him with.

A recent survey conducted by a group of sociologists shows that more than two-thirds of households islandwide (68 percent in the Taipei area and 74 percent in other parts of Taiwan) now subscribe to the so-called Fourth Cable

TV company (ti-ssu t'ai), and thereby gain access to various kinds of information and entertainment—Chinese Star TV, TVBS, NHK, CNN, HBO, the Disney Channel, the Movie Channel, MTV, and dozens of local channels that carry the stock-market report, talk shows, programs on the occult or orthodox Buddhism, ethnic group or political party news, et cetera. Rather than operate under the rubric of a monopolistic syndicate or cartel, Fourth Cable TV is comprised of several decentered, but mutually competitive, companies that have ambivalent ties with political parties and local sectors. Fourth Cable TV literally transforms Taiwan into an information-saturated society. Chinese Star TV, for instance, brings news, movies, and sitcoms produced in Chinese-speaking communities around the world to audiences in Pacific Asia, from southern China to India to Australia. It frequently rebroadcasts popular programs so subscribers have a better chance of seeing them. Well-adapted to the tastes of local subscribers, the programs on Chinese Star TV serve to create a sense of difference and to generate a new cultural imaginary for the Chinese-speaking communities around the Pacific. Some of the most popular programs, ranging from soap operas to the traditional folktales of Judge Pao to Japanese sitcoms, take as their subjects themes that relate to the everyday life of these communities: transnational codes and fashions, the generation gap, value changes, consumerism, school experiences, pollution, and political corruption. Together with TVBS, which also is located in Hong Kong, Chinese Star TV has exposed Taiwan to all sorts of international and transnational news and entertainment.

TV and radio talk shows, which consist of a mixture of news reports and opinion, punctuated by the chatter of telephone callers from virtually all levels of society, have transformed the state of electoral politics from campaigning and vote buying to media wars and a fascination with visual culture and visuality. Instead of talking real politics, Wen-chien Chen, a spokeswoman for the DPP, took the island by storm during the 1993–1994 elections, when she deployed glamour and body politics instead of real politics on national TV. Since 1988, political parties have engaged each other through TV networks and underground radio programs (ti-hsia tien-t'ai chieh-mu). Candidates are not so much concerned with how well their TV commercials rate as with keeping track of campaign budgets. In a parody of a notorious Italian female politician, Hsiao-tan Hsu, a woman dancer, put up large billboards in which her nipples were shown to penetrate the national flag, an image that almost won her a seat in the Legislative Yuan in 1992. In the music industry, heavy-metal rock and roll mixed with Taiwanese vernacular tradition that addresses current political issues has been a commercial failure. But when Lin Ch'iang recorded his first CD in 1991, it sold fifty thousand copies in just one week. Nevertheless, most remarkable are the Taiwanese contributions to karaoke, which originated in Japan. In Taiwan, karaoke is performed in flashy buildings and wonderfully decorated audio rooms. As if in reciprocal assimilation of local tradition and exotic melodies, of social energy and personal touch, people act out the ritual of a heterogeneous, partially coordinated ensemble, cherishing the (ironically closeted) social experience of intergenerational music making by singing popular songs from various decades and of different national origins. They inevitably prefer, however, to end with a Taiwanese vernacular "quick-burst" song "Ai-pian-chia-ye-yiang" (Work hard to win).

The karaoke buildings in Taiwan, like other commercial buildings, are not postmodern in the true sense of the word; however, their interior decor and use makes them postmodern. William Tay has observed that even in the details of a seemingly premodern monumental building such as the Chiang K'ai-shek Memorial Hall, one can detect nuances of the postmodern.[28] His remarks are supported by several instances of use and abuse of the hall during the 1989–1991 student protests, in which the semisacred space—the hall is sometimes called "Chiang's Temple"—was turned into a "thirdspace" to oppose political leaders. The plaza in front of the hall, which is overlooked by a monumental and stern-looking statue of the generalissimo, was so packed with grotesque and incongruous objects—political caricatures, a wild lily statue, a funeral procession, a masked parade—that the atmosphere around "Chiang's Temple" was more like that of a circus or carnival. Indeed, with the exception of the Hung-kuo Building, designed by Li Tzu-yuan, and the Sheraton Plaza and the Hsin-kung Mitsukoshi Tower, both designed by multinational talents, few high-rises in Taiwan can boast a postmodern appearance. It is their interior design and the way in which global and local cultural icons, European baroque furniture and Chinese *feng-shui* are yoked together that make some buildings postmodern. The two Chiu-ch'ing-mien-mien (Remembrance of Things Past) cafés, for example, shock and amuse the consumer by juxtaposing a nostalgic atmosphere with futuristic spatial imagery, exposing ugly-looking pipes in the ceiling while displaying numerous photographs from the fifties on the wall. Several beer houses exhibit whimsical skeletons of dinosaurs, pastiches of traditional Chinese landscapes, and simulated multinational or multiethnic images and objects, not to mention (g)localized live rock-and-roll performances or karaoke equipment for group entertainment. Generally, the exterior and interior of these public spaces display a cultural logic of incongruity, the so-called *pu an p'ai-li ch'u-p'ai* (not playing the card according to the rules). As in the films *Eat Drink Man Woman* (directed by Ang Lee), and *Rebels of the Neon Gods* (directed by Ming-liang Tsai), the subjects of cuisine and people in cultural hybridity and in constant motion generate a sense of excessive exuberance, of disproportional expenditure, in which political uncertainty in everyday life is playfully and temporarily negated.

But there is something more to this sense of uncertainty that haunts the people on the island, especially in recent years, since President Teng-hui Lee took power and started the localization process under the rubric of communalism. In part a response to the threats posed by China, Lee's style of political improvisation can hardly be characterized as coherent or determinate. It is a "stylistic of connivance," in the sense developed by Mbembe, which is composed of myriad ways to "toy with power instead of confronting it directly."[29] The political drama, however, produces doubts and uncertainty in the psychosocial structure of identification. Not only does national identity become an unsettling issue but discourses of ethnic and gender difference threaten to subvert the grand narrative of cultural belonging, of a homogenizing and "harmonizing" totality. Consequently, identity turns into a plurality of contested arenas, as practically all the indigenous countertraditions and colonial legacies that were suppressed or marginalized are now being mobilized in the name of an alternative modernity or a postidentity politics. In reaction to the so-called Han-Chinese chauvinism that has ruled out other racial and cultural heritages on the island, for example, there have been many attempts made to call attention to the multiple layers and ways of appropriation and negotiation on the part of the peoples from the margin.

Taiwan since 1971: From Periphery to Marginality

As I have suggested, the rise of postmodern literary discourse in Taiwan has something to do with its double marginalization, that is, the traumatic shift in Taiwan's role, from the periphery of China to the margins of the world, in 1971, the year Chiang K'ai-shek decided to withdraw the Republic of China (ROC) from membership in the UN to protest the Shanghai Communique, which established relations between the United States and the People's Republic of China (PRC). The complex and difficult process of transformation since then can best be revealed in the Taiwanese people's efforts to survive the crisis of diplomatic and political isolation. Not only did the people learn to cope with the brutal reality of being almost universally abandoned but the government of Taiwan was gradually forced to come to terms with its marginality and to develop a multiple identity politics that recognizes the different lifestyles and temporalities that exist within local Taiwan communities in order to renegotiate its sociocultural positionality in relation to mainland China.

Historically, as far back as 1683 (the year the island was incorporated into China), many, including a Ch'ing emperor, regarded Taiwan as a barren and insignificant place on the *pien-tsui* (periphery). In his preface to *Taiwan t'ung-shih* (A general history of Taiwan), published posthumously in 1945, Lien Yia-t'ang wonders if Taiwan took its name from *tung-fan* (barbarians in the east), a derogatory phrase in the Fukien dialect that refers to the aborigines on the island. Throughout the book, Lien suggests that Taiwan was considered by Chinese officials to be *tao-yi hai-ke* (an isolated and primitive place to shelter pirates).[30] Chiang K'ai-shek must have felt as if he were in exile when he was pushed by Mao to escape to the island in 1949. This may, in part, account for the major streets in Taipei being renamed by him after cities on the mainland—for example, Peking Road, Nanking East Road, and Chungking South Road. Nixon's visit to China in 1972 was indeed a blow to Chiang, forcing him to come to the tragic realization that he could no longer legitimately claim to be a political outcast. The idea of *pien-yuan* (margin) and double marginalization likely occurred to him when he advocated the slogan "Tzu-pien pu-chin, chuang-chin chih-ch'iang" (Don't panic in times of danger; cultivate self-reliance) in response to almost global rejection. Before 1972, Chiang could entertain himself with the grand illusion of taking back the mainland, using Taiwan as a temporary bastion. However, after 1972, Chiang's faith was badly shaken, even though he desperately held on to it until his death. The situation changed when Vice President Yen Chia-kang succeeded Chiang in 1975, with Chiang's son Ching-kuo as premier. By the time Chiang Ching-kuo took over as president in 1978, he was ready to declare himself a "Taiwanese" and, unlike his father, gradually accepted the historical effects of Taiwan's relocation from China's *pien-tsui* to the world's *pien-yuan*, of a tiny island-state being twice removed from the global culture map.

As in the old Chinese saying, "The loss of a horse may not necessarily be bad fortune," the double marginalization of Taiwan has undoubtedly disabled the people on the island, but it has also enabled them to challenge the domestic authoritarian regime and to be strongly desirous of acquiring transnational codes and technologies. Indeed, tolerance to the expansion of the public sphere increased as attention shifted from politics to the economy. Soon after Taiwan severed diplomatic ties with the United States in 1978, students and political dissidents led a series of demonstrations. One major demonstration was held in Kaohsiung City in 1979, after which several members of the opposition were arrested, tried, and sentenced to ten to twenty years in prison. The Beautiful Formosa (*Meili Tao*) Incident, as it was called, captured the attention of the international media. In 1981, the remaining members of the opposition won approximately 30 percent of the vote in local elections and dramatically transformed the sociopolitical situation in Taiwan. As a result, in September 1986, the DPP was formed and constituted the first opposition party in Taiwanese or, for that matter, Chinese, history. In 1987,

Chiang Ching-kuo, who had witnessed these tumultuous changes, decided to lift martial law and all restrictions on newspapers. Upon Chiang's death in 1988, power was handed over to Lee Teng-hui, a Taiwanese, who eventually succeeded in giving voice to the locals and, by doing so, enabled the former president's project to take root in Taiwan. With the collapse of older totalitarian regimes, Taiwan emerged as a remarkably vibrant island-state of whimsical hybridity and chaotic fluidity, as a statesman turned sportsman in the tripartite parliament and as a salesman at international conventions.

One of the motivating forces behind these rapid political changes is, to be sure, the people's struggle against the double marginalization of Taiwan in the New World Order. During the seventies, the island was famous for "Cousin Lee," who single-handedly created an economic miracle by ingenuity and the ability to improvise. Not only were books pirated and disseminated but high-tech products and fashions were reproduced so cheaply that the copies outsold the originals, as the designers soon found out. In addition to the psychosocial need to imaginatively appropriate global products so as to win the nation's way back into the global cultural economy, there was also the people's desire to mobilize indigenous countertraditions in recognition of internal cultural dynamics. In my opinion, it is this twofold pull, or double articulation, that helps generate the postmodernism craze in Taiwan. But I will also point out that the recent trend is to go local, to renegotiate with the mainstream culture from the margin. To pay tribute to aboriginal culture, Chieh-shou Boulevard, in front of the presidential office, for example, was renamed two years ago by Taipei City Mayor Chen Shui-pien, a DPP member who defeated the KMT and New Party candidates in 1994.

Here, we need to make a distinction between *pien-tsui* and *pien-yuan*, the two problematic Chinese terms being discussed. In classical Chinese literature, *pien-tsui* always points to a wasteland far from the center, far from the metropolis or the imperial court of the Middle Kingdom. A synonym for *pien-chiang* (distant border), *pien-tsui* is often associated with uncivilized inhabitability and backwardness, and sometimes with banishment or exile.[31] On the other hand, *pien-yuan*, a relatively new concept, is used to denote something on the edge of being frivolous and insignificant, too marginal or even superficial to be worthy of any attention. So understood, *pien-tsui* connotes the peripheral in terms of spatial location, while *pien-yuan* connotes the marginal in terms of discursive position. Disadvantaged and distant, places in the *pien-tsui* symbolize desolation and deprivation; however, those in the *pien-yuan* may benefit from detachment and lack of attention, and may gain unmediated access to the global. It is in this sense that the two Chinese terms can be translated in a new light as "periphery" and "marginality." For in current cultural theory, the concept of "core-periphery" refers to an established hierarchy of human geography, with its systematic grouping of national or economic units from the Euro-American perspective, whereas the notion of marginality is celebrated for its ambivalence in terms of mobile positionalities that deploy tactics of a nomad or a chameleon, in order to move somewhat freely between peripheral and metropolitan spaces, to fashion multiple, albeit minimal, selves in relation to the ever changing ethnoscapes and to cross-cultural, disciplinary, or gender boundaries.[32]

In the field of "minor" literature, James Joyce, Franz Kafka, Wole Soyinka, Toni Morrison, and Salman Rushdie are but a few of the remarkable authors who have written about what the marginals can do to challenge or deconstruct the grand traditions.[33] Another example more relevant to this discussion is Hong Kong during the sixties through to the present day. While located at the periphery and considered to be marginal by the two polities on the Taiwan Strait, Hong Kong has served as an intermediary zone for China and Taiwan. Numerous books and films that are banned by the communists or nationalists have been produced in Hong Kong. However, with the July 1997 deadline for Hong Kong's return to China now realized, Taiwan seems the obvious alternative for taking over the roles once played by Hong Kong. Other examples of negotiation from the margin can now be found in the new social movements initiated by minority groups in Taiwan, among them feminists, gays and lesbians, the transnational labor force (mainly from the Philippines and Thailand), and those who are in the disordered spaces of difference—veterans and fishermen, for example. As new sites that offer "the possibility of radical perspectives from which to see and create, to imagine alternatives, new worlds," marginality can be understood as the position and place of resistance crucial not only for the oppressed, exploited, and colonized but for the subalterns who explore or appropriate the thirdspace to develop new cultural capital as well as new subjectivities.[34] This notion of marginality is, from time to time, evoked by the aborigines on the island in their efforts to revive mother tongues and traditions, and to claim their rights to protect their environment. But more often, it constitutes a vantage point and a discursive position that enables people to reconsider the identity of Taiwan in relation to the complex transnational network of cultural flows established in the processes of migration and colonialism over the span of a thousand years.

Thinking beyond the Posts?

With regard to transnational ethnoscapes, we should pause to reflect on the power and limitations of theoretical models currently available. Three schools of thought immediately come to mind in our current discussion of the ways in which a tiny island such as Taiwan, with such strong foreign currency reserves, a big national-capitalistic ego, and a fluid social energy, can be placed in the global cultural economy. The first dominant trend is that of the world capitalist system as proposed by Immanuel Wallerstein and other political economists.[35] As the notions of developmental logic and the nation-state are generally assumed in advocating the theory of a world-system, its structuring principle of the "core-periphery" (or First-, Second-, and Third-World) classification tends to be static and hence fails to consider the more complex and dynamic transactions across national borders among groups and communities other than the Common Market, the United States, and Japan. While a useful descriptive framework, a world-system cannot explain the various levels of migration, trade, and cultural flow and exchange that are normally not controlled by the states.

Arjun Appadurai's conception of the difference and disjuncture in the global cultural economy, Benedict Anderson's observation of multifarious forms of "long-distance nationalism," and Roland Robertson's view of the "global-local" may sound more nuanced and sensible in this regard.[36] Quite a few cultural studies professionals and anthropologists are enthusiastic proponents of the global-local dialectics, even though "glocal" phenomena are mostly found in the fields of architecture, telecommunications, fashion, advertising, and international corporation management. Often criticized for its premature optimism toward global culture, for its discursive complicity with transnational exploitation, and for taking local everyday resistance for granted, the model, in fact, cannot account for the reasons why some particular cultural, ethnic, or religious traditions are mobilized to consolidate the transnational communities that simply refuse to be integrated in ways either global or local (for example, Chinese immigrants in Indonesia; ethnic groups in the United States; and Jews, Muslims, and Roman Catholics all over the world).

A more appropriate model, in thinking beyond the postcolonial and in considering the pan-Chinese community in the world today, may be that of transnational exchange.[37] While maintaining its supposedly unique identity by disseminating the politically centralizing myth of the "middle kingdom" on the one hand and of the Han people's ability to incorporate other races or ethnic groups on the other, many dynasties in Chinese history have always already been involved in battles, trade, and cultural exchanges that transgress the territorial boundaries of the state. As a variation of what originally flourished in India, Chinese Buddhism, for example, was introduced to Japan by Japanese monks and scholars who visited the T'ang empire. And nowhere is Chinese Buddhism more obvious and complex than in the semic effects that the Japanese modernity project had on its neighbors and colonies—Manchuria, Korea, Taiwan, and many parts of China, among others. With Lee Teng-hui in power and the revival of Taiwan's indigenous traditions, the ambivalent colonial legacies of Japanese rule from 1895 to 1945 are now being mobilized and renegotiated in postcolonial hindsight. These legacies were, and indeed continue to be, intertwined with transnational cultural flows—for example, the Japanese baroque and the incomplete imperial project of South Asian studies in Taiwan, a set of new urban planning and interdisciplinary area-studies paradigms that were rejected by the Japanese government and then reintroduced to the island. Accepted ambivalently, these colonial legacies are being reassessed and incorporated into the localization processes.

A clear indicator of this kind of renegotiation is the Nan-chin (Moving South) Project, launched by the government in 1995, which is intended to make Taiwan the Asian Pacific hub. Unlike the Japanese imperial project, which was launched some seventy years ago to take over South Asia, Taiwan is remobilizing the effort to reduce the risk of economic dependence on, or direct confrontation with, China, and to shift Taiwan's identity from a Han-Chinese orientation to a multicultural and transnational one. The desire to renarrate the past or to remobilize these incomplete modernity (and coloniality) projects is even more apparent in the number of nonacademic or scholarly works that trace the development of an alternative modernism in Taiwan to the localization processes in relation to transnational cultural forces. Today, genealogies of Chinese immigrants and of the Taiwanese aborigines of Malayo-Polynesian origin are beginning to be detailed, and many supplementary reading (and audiovisual) materials that deal with indigenous traditions are available. Moreover, multinational research teams are now working together to unravel the colonial legacies left behind by Dutch, Japanese, and earlier immigrants.[38] Archaeologists and cultural anthropologists, not to mention literary critics and historians, are taking advantage of this new discursive situation and are exploring the complex network of ethnoscapes that contribute to the making of an alternative modernism in Taiwan.

To make sense of the complex multiplicity and relative autonomy of contemporary Taiwanese public culture, we may have to find a new way to theorize about it in terms of alternative postcolonialisms. In this respect, the postmodern condition in Taiwan is far from over. Given the wealth of information now available, Taiwanese people are only beginning to put together an alternative postmodernism puzzle.

Notes

This essay is part of a project under the aegis of the National Science Council, ROC. I am indebted to the arguments made by several scholars in Richard Werbner and Terence Ranger, eds., *Postcolonial Identities in Africa* (London: Zed, 1996).

1 See Chung Ming-te, *Tzai-hou-hsien-tai te cha-yin-chung* (Taipei: Bookman, 1989); Tsai Yuan-huang, *Ch'ung-lang-man-chu-yi tao-hou-hsien-tai-chu-yi* (Taipei: Tien-ya, 1991); Wai-lim Yip, *Kung-chien te su-wei* (Taipei: Tung-ta, 1992); and Chang Hsiao-hung, *Hou-hsien-tai/nu-ren: chuen-li yu-wang yu hsin-pie piao-yuen* (Taipei: Shih-pao Wen-hua, 1993), among others. To avoid confusion, I use the Wade-Giles system of romanization, rather than the pinyin system, as Wade-Giles is the standard system in Taiwan. For the sake of consistency, I also cite family names first.

2 See Jonathan Arac, introduction to *Postmodernism and Politics* (Minneapolis: University of Minnesota Press, 1986), xiii. He puts Daniel Bell, Jean-François Lyotard, and Richard Rorty in the same school that de-emphasizes " 'totalizing' modes of description and explanation." Here, I also draw on Kwame Anthony Appiah, "Is the Post- in Postmodernism the Post- in Postcolonial?" *Critical Inquiry* 17 (1991): 336–57; as well as Achille Mbembe, "The Banality of Power and the Aesthetics of Vulgarity in the Postcolony," *Public Culture* 4 (1992): 1–30; and Barry Smart, *Postmodernity* (London: Routledge, 1993). Hereafter, Appiah's essay is cited parenthetically as "Post-."

3 "It cannot be said that Taipei is a modern and Western-style city, in the same way that one could affirm this of Shanghai, for example," Jameson writes in his review of Edward Yang's *Terrorizer*. See *The Geopolitical Aesthetic: Cinema and Space in the World System* (Bloomington: Indiana University Press, 1992), 117. "Rather it is an example of some generally late-capitalist urbanization (which one hesitates, except to make the point, to call postmodern), of a now classic proliferation of the urban fabric that one finds everywhere in the First and Third Worlds alike," he continues. He made similar remarks in a conversation with me during the summer of 1987. However, it is now clear that Shanghai is not as "modern" as Taipei and that Taipei is in many ways different from other cities in the world in terms of what goes on inside those "late-modern" and occasionally "postmodern" buildings that look like their counterparts.

4 See Homi K. Bhabha, "Postcolonial Authority and Postmodern Guilt," in *Cultural Studies*, ed. Lawrence Grossberg, Cary Nelson, and Paula Treichler (New York: Routledge, 1992), 56–68; and Julie Ellison, "A Short History of Liberal Guilt," *Critical Inquiry* 22, no. 2 (1996): 344–71. Ellison mentions in passing that colonial critics seldom deal with the issue of "liberal guilt." Concerning the problematics of the term *Third World*, see Arturo Escobar, *Encountering Development: The Making and Unmaking of the Third World* (Princeton, N.J.: Princeton University Press, 1995).

5 Robert Thornton, "The Potentials of Boundaries in South Africa: Steps towards a Theory of the Social Edge," in *Postcolonial Identities in Africa*, 136–61.

6 Thornton, "Potentials of Boundaries in South Africa," 144.

7 Edwin A. Winckler, "Cultural Policy on Postwar Taiwan," in *Cultural Change in Postwar Taiwan*, ed. Stevan Harrell and Chun-chieh Huang (Boulder, Colo.: Westview, 1994), 22.

8 Arac, *Postmodernism and Politics*, xii.

9 Arac, *Postmodernism and Politics*, xiv.

10 Homi K. Bhabha, "Articulating the Archaic: Notes on Colonial Nonsense," in *Literary Theory Today*, ed. Peter Collier and Helga Geyer-Ryan (Ithaca, N.Y.: Cornell University Press, 1990), 203–18; Masao Miyoshi and H. D. Harootunian, eds., *Postmodernism and Japan* (Durham, N.C.: Duke University Press, 1989); John Beverley and José Oviedo, eds., *The Postmodernism Debate in Latin America* (Durham, N.C.: Duke University Press, 1993).

11 M. Jacqui Alexander and Chandra Talpade Mohanty, eds., *Feminist Genealogies, Colonial Legacies, Democratic Futures* (London: Routledge, 1997), xvii.

12 Talal Asad, "From the History of Colonial Anthropology to the Anthropology of Western

Hegemony," in *Colonial Situations: Essays on the Contextualization of Ethnographic Knowledge*, ed. George Stocking (Madison: University of Wisconsin Press, 1991), 314–23. Micaela di Leonardo, ed., *Gender at the Crossroads of Knowledge: Feminist Anthropology in the Postmodern Era* (Berkeley: University of California Press, 1991). Nicholas B. Dirks, ed., *Colonialism and Culture* (Ann Arbor: University of Michigan Press, 1992).

13 Alexander and Mohanty, *Feminist Genealogies*, xvii.

14 Benita Parry, "Current Problems in the Study of Colonial Discourse," *Oxford Literary Review* 9 (1987): 27–58, for example, sets the tone, followed by, among others, Arif Dirlik, "The Postcolonial Aura: Third World Criticism in the Age of Global Capitalism," *Critical Inquiry* 20 (1994): 328–56, and Aijaz Ahmad, "The Politics of Literary Postcoloniality," *Race and Class* 36 (1995): 1–20.

15 On the fluid structure of "postidentity politics," see Dan Anielsen and Karen Engle, eds., *After Identity: A Reader in Law and Literature* (New York: Routledge, 1995).

16 Linda Hutcheon, "Colonialism and the Postcolonial Condition: Complexities Abounding," *PMLA* 110, no. 1 (Jan. 1995): 10; see also Richard Werbner, "Introduction: Multiple Identities, Plural Arenas," in Werbner and Ranger, *Postcolonial Identities in Africa*, 4.

17 Mbembe, "The Banality of Power," 5.

18 A number of works illuminate this perspective, among them, Arjun Appadurai, *Modernity at Large: Cultural Dimensions of Globalization* (Minneapolis: University of Minnesota Press, 1996); Homi K. Bhabha, *The Location of Culture* (London: Routledge, 1994); P. Kaarsholm, ed., *From Post-Traditional to Post-Modern? Interpreting the Meaning of Modernity in Third World Urban Societies* (Roskilde, Denmark: IDS, 1995).

19 Homi K. Bhabha, "In a Spirit of Calm Violence," in *After Colonialism: Imperial Histories and Postcolonial Displacements*, ed. Gyan Prakash (Princeton, N.J.: Princeton University Press, 1995), 326. This essay is also included in Bhabha, *The Location of Culture*, under the title "Race, Time, and the Revision of Modernity," 236–56.

20 Catherine Hall, "Histories, Empire, and the Post-Colonial Moment," in *The Post-Colonial Question: Common Skies, Divided Horizons*, ed. Ian Chambers and Lidia Curti (London: Routledge, 1996), 65–77; Paul Gilroy, *The Black Atlantic: Modernity and Double Consciousness* (Cambridge, Mass.: Harvard University Press, 1993).

21 Raymond L. M. Lee, "Trend Report: Modernization, Postmodernism, and the Third World," *Current Sociology* 42 (1994): 4.

22 See Bill Ashcroft, Gareth Griffiths, and Helen Tiffin, *The Empire Writes Back: Theory and Practice in Post-Colonial Literatures* (New York: Routledge, 1989).

23 Kwame Anthony Appiah, "African Identities," in *Social Postmodernism: Beyond Identity Politics*, ed. Linda Nicholson and Steve Seidman (Cambridge: Cambridge University Press, 1995), 108.

24 Appadurai, *Modernity at Large*, 60–61.

25 Appadurai, *Modernity at Large*, 61.

26 Daiwie Fu discusses the rise of subversive Internet homepages in "The Waning of Taiwan's Social Movement," a paper delivered at a workshop entitled Culture, Media, and Society in Contemporary Taiwan, Harvard University, 10–15 June 1996. In the same workshop, Allen Chun gave a talk on two kinds of transnational media in Taiwan—the World Wide Web and International Community Radio Taiwan. The title of his presentation was "Cosmopolitanism and Countertalks in an Emerging Discursive Public."

27 I am referring to Haraway's earlier work on cyborgs but also to her recent book *ModestWitness@SecondMillennium.FemaleMan Meets OncoMouse: Feminism and Technoscience* (New York: Routledge, 1997).

28 William Tay, "Ideology, Identity, and Architecture: Modernism, Postmodernism, and Antiquarianism in Taiwan," *Humanities Bulletin* 4 (1995): 85–96.

29 Mbembe, "The Banality of Power," 22.

30 A more reliable account suggests that the name Taiwan may derive from a Fukienese phrase referring to a "big shelter" for fishermen.

31 A dictionary entry under *pien-tsui* in *Tzu-hai*, vol. 1 (Hong Kong: Chung-hua, 1965), traces the first use of the idiom to a foreign invasion across the border in approximately 650 B.C.E. *Pien-tsui* is used in this case as a synonym of *pien-chiang* (border, territory). *Pien-yuan*, on the other hand, is not listed among the entries, except as an adjective to indicate marginality in location, for example, *pien-yuan hai* (a marginal sea).

32 See Stuart Hall, "Minimal Selves," in *Black British Cultural Studies: A Reader*, ed. Houston A. Baker Jr., Manthia Diawara, and Ruth H. Lindeborg (Chicago: University of Chicago Press, 1996), 114–19.

33 Gilles Deleuze and Félix Guattari, *Kafka: Toward a Minor Literature*, trans. Dana Polan (Minneapolis: University of Minnesota Press, 1986).

34 The quotation is from bell hooks, *Yearning* (Boston: South End Press, 1990), 150–51. See also Edward W. Soja, *Thirdspace: Journey to Los Angeles and Other Real-and-Imagined Places* (Oxford: Blackwell, 1996), 96–105.

35 Immanuel Wallerstein, *The Capitalist World-Economy* (Cambridge: Cambridge University Press, 1979); and "Culture as the Ideological Battleground of the Modern World-System," in *Global Culture, Nationalism, Globalization, and Modernity*, ed. Mike Featherstone (London: Sage, 1990), 31–56.

36 In particular, see Roland Robertson, "Globalization Theory and Civilizational Analysis," *Comparative Civilizations Review* 17 (1987): 20–30. See also the essays collected in Rob Wilson and Wimal Dissanayake, eds., *Global/Local: Cultural Production and the Transnational Imaginary* (Durham, N.C.: Duke University Press, 1996).

37 To further his main arguments in *Rescuing History from the Nation: Questioning Narratives of Modern China* (Chicago: University of Chicago Press, 1995), Prasenjit Duara has written extensively on some important aspects of transnational moral and political agencies (or "redemptive transnationalism," as he calls them) in modern Asia. I would like to thank him for sharing his work in progress with me, particularly the essay entitled "Transnationalism and the Predicament of Sovereignty: China, 1900–1945."

38 See, for example, essays in Chang Yen-hsien et al., eds., *Taiwan-shih yu Taiwan shih-liao*, vols. 1 and 2 (Taipei: Wu San-lien Foundation Press, 1995); and in Li Hsien-wen, ed., *Chin-tai Taiwan mei-shu yu wen-hua ren-tung* (Taipei: Cultural Planning Council, forthcoming).

xiaoying wang

4 Hong Kong, China, and the Question of Postcoloniality

The change of sovereignty over Hong Kong in 1997 occasions deep reflections on the new world situation after colonialism. A region whose identity is bound up with the history of British colonialism, Hong Kong does not have a precolonial past to return to. More significantly, as a world trade center, a symbol of the free market in the age of transnational corporations, the place is too much at odds with the idea of the "nation-state" (let alone a "socialist" nation-state) to be incorporated without grudge within the boundaries of the Chinese national culture and identity. This, however, is not a situation faced by Hong Kong alone. Whatever the initial goals of anticolonial struggles may have been, it is clear, in the current global situation, that decolonization signifies neither the possibility of a return to the precolonial past nor the beginning of a new era that is not already conditioned by the economic order of capitalism. In this light, the unique historical circumstances of Hong Kong serve more to throw into sharp relief the general predicament of the "postcolonial" than to set the region apart from other former colonies. This essay addresses these issues through a detailed examination of aspects of colonial and postcolonial Hong Kong, followed by a close reading of how Hong Kong is represented in the discourse of "postcolonial studies."

Of all the former colonies, Hong Kong is perhaps the best place to observe how colonialism has won the heart of the colonized and how, subsequently, a multiculturalism that parades racial and ethnic difference in the wake of the colonial history is actually predicated on the attenuation of the indigenous cultures within the framework of the global market. Such an attenuation has its specific historical manifestations in Hong Kong, which I shall discuss below. But similar phenomena have been brought about in different contexts by the development of global capitalism. This gives one reason to think that pluralism on a global scale is more likely to occur through the perfection of the capitalist market than through the political efforts of "deconstruction" and liberal democracy. For better or for worse, the development of the global market has not only forced different racial and ethnic populations into an increasing homogeneous world of capitalism and in so doing created tensions among them, it has also eliminated or at least attenuated strong values associated with traditional ways of life, and thus offered a solution to the problem of its own creation (a solution that rests more on the gradual disappearance of cultural differences than on a real and substantive respect for differences). But this solution applies only to parts of the populations that have made it into the ranks of the bourgeoisie. Those stranded in the lower end of the social and economic scale continue to suffer from racism, a racism that is now more an "act of maintaining the existing international social structure" than a "neologism for racial discrimination."[1]

The colonial history of Hong Kong, to get down to the specific, has its unique characteristics. Compared with other former colonies, the history of Hong Kong is marked by a conspicuous lack of resistance against colonialism. Edward Said remarks in *Culture and Imperialism*: "Along with armed resistance in places as diverse as nineteenth-century Algeria, Ireland, and Indonesia, there also went considerable efforts in cultural resistance almost everywhere, the assertions of nationalist identities, and, in the political realm, the creation of associations and parties whose common goal was self-determination and national independence."[2] For a variety of reasons, this is not true of Hong Kong to anything like the same degree. Armed resistance and the assertion of a nationalist identity was hard to find in Hong Kong history. Unlike other former colonies, most of which were decolonized after World War II through armed rebellion inspired by nationalism, Hong Kong was decolonized because the lease of the territory came to a "natural" end in 1997. Indeed, the departure of the colonial government was greeted by very large numbers of Hong Kong people with more apprehension than joy. This attitude was not just a function of the material prosperity of Hong Kong, for which the colonial government was given a huge amount of credit. Nor did it merely reflect Hong Kong's apprehension of what the Beijing government might do to the free market that had made Hong Kong's material prosperity possible. Rather, it had to do with the lack of a fixed identity for the Hong Kong population, which has characterized the region since the mid-nineteenth century (especially after 1949, when the linguistic and cultural ties to Guangdong could no longer withstand the political and ideological conflicts between the region and the mainland).

Hong Kong was, first and foremost, an immigrant society. The population was a mere 5,000 in 1842 when British troops first landed. Then, thanks to the colonial appropriation of Hong Kong as a trading port and the subsequent emergence of a mercantile community in the region, the place began to attract immigrants from mainland China, the southern provinces in particular. By the time of the Japanese invasion, the population surpassed 1,500,000.[3] People came to Hong Kong, however, not to take root but to escape wars and political upheavals and, in the meantime, to make money, hopeful that one day they might go home enriched. They stayed in Hong Kong, but with a transient outlook, leaving their home culture behind or projecting it into the future. This made it difficult, indeed unnecessary, to construct an identity that would reach beyond contingent and mundane considerations. It preempted the possibility of resistance against a colonial power that violated an intransigent identity based on such abstract ideas as the "people" or the "nation." To be sure, at certain moments, sentimental attachment to traditions was converted into an identification with the Chinese as a people and China as a nation. The Hong Kong–Guangzhou strike of 1925–1926 in response to the massacres of May 30 in Shanghai and June 23 in Shameen was a case in point. But the nationalist tie between Hong Kong and the mainland remained tenuous throughout the history of the region, especially after the founding of the People's Republic of China in 1949. Partly because of the totalitarian policies of the Chinese Communist Party, which led to continual political and economic disasters in the mainland, not only did the propertied class flee to Hong Kong to find a safe haven for their businesses but also all those who for various reasons fell victims to the totalitarian government sought exile in Hong Kong if they were not able to emigrate to the United States, Canada, or Australia.

The alienation of Hong Kong from the mainland (which was political and ideological rather than cultural and ethnic) drove the population, especially the propertied class, to form a strategic identification with the colonial government. Unlike the bourgeoisie in other former colonies, which included among its ranks the founders of nationalism, the propertied class in Hong

Kong had a vested interest in siding with colonialism. Colonialism offered them protection against communism. It was thanks to China's defeat in the Opium War and the subsequent lease of Hong Kong to Britain that the propertied class had a place to flee to after 1949. This gave rise to a phenomenon that was rare in the history of colonization around the world. Anticolonial consciousness was often treated in Hong Kong not as the "spontaneous" consciousness of those who actually suffered colonization, but as the product of communist propaganda imported from the other side of the border. Those who wish to teach postcolonial studies in the University of Hong Kong—to use a recent example to illustrate the point—have to distinguish their position from the Chinese version of anticolonialism by invoking the current transformation of the Western academic canon under the influence of poststructuralism, telling their students that postcolonial studies is one of the most trendy disciplines in the United States.

Hong Kong's lack of a fixed identity, however, has not only given rise to its alienation from the mainland and its strategic identification with Britain. It has also paved the way for the emergence of a society that is ideal for the development of capitalism. If we leave aside Marx's focus on class exploitation and "surplus value" and Weber's emphasis on the Protestant ethic that exalts the diligent and rational seeking of profit, the crucial features of capitalism as an economic system can be well captured as "private disposal of the means of production, market and price mechanisms as means of coordination, and profit and utility maximization as the basic motivation in economic action," in the words of Peter Koslowski (a defender of capitalism).[4] Such a system is incompatible with any worldview that condemns moneymaking or assigns the activity of moneymaking to a low position in its scale of values. Insofar as profit maximization is the condition of survival in the marketplace, the zeal for moneymaking has to be made socially respectable, beyond being legally permissible. To put it in Albert Hirschman's terms, the conversion of "passions" into "interests" was a necessary condition for the initial development of capitalism in the West. It was only after the "demolition of the heroic ideal" (an ideal that was closely associated with the passions for "honor and glory") and the conversion of such passions into interests which "eventually came to be centered on economic advantage as its core meaning"[5] that it became possible for capitalism to gradually take the center stage. In the scale of medieval values, "commerce and other forms of money making . . . stood lower than a number of other activities, in particular the striving for glory."[6] Thus, with the downfall of the idea of glory, moneymaking became a respectable profession or "calling" in the Weberian sense.

As an exception that proves the rule, Hong Kong did not need to wait for the downfall of strong values (or passions) for the activities of moneymaking to become socially respectable. In fact, there were hardly any strong values in the history of Hong Kong that were incompatible with the economic imperative of profit maximization and that had to be demolished to make room for capitalism. Unlike the old imperial China (or Japan before Meiji Restoration for that matter), which had to go through a painful renunciation of its traditional values (or at least a fundamental transformation of such values) to be able to finally adjust itself to its position in the global market, Hong Kong was thrown into the framework of the global market with a population that, thanks to its lack of strong attachment to traditional values, was almost as ready-made for the development of capitalism as that of the Dutch Republic in the early seventeenth century.[7] I am not arguing, of course, that the immigrants came to Hong Kong without bringing any traditional values with them. The claim I make is a weaker one, namely, the economic motive of immigration had rendered traditional values marginal or instrumental.[8] What Ambrose King calls "imperial Confucianism" or "institutional Confucianism" (a "complex and sophisticated combination of state ideology as well as a set of strategic institutions, including the literati, the examination system, and, above all, the imperial bureaucracy") never truly developed in Hong Kong.[9] More completely than anywhere else in China, the imperial version of Confucianism had disappeared into the "folk religions of China that fully sanctioned the behavior of 'getting rich,' "[10] such that the mandarin highbrow aspirations for knowledge and virtues had given way to a more pragmatic worldview centered on the pursuit of material prosperity. "Unlike Imperial China, the most promising road to social eminence for the Chinese in Hong Kong is not by becoming officials and scholars, but through gaining wealth in the business world."[11] Instead of literati and high mandarins, shipping magnates and business tycoons were the real heroes of Hong Kong life.

Colonialism may have helped to bring about this phenomenon, but this is different from saying that it had caused it. As the political sector was closed to the Chinese in the colony, wealth might have indeed been "the only means by which a Chinese individual in Hong Kong could come to have any influence at all on community affairs, and the only means by which he could stand out in society as an important person."[12] Yet we can also address the issue the other way round, asking why the colonial regime was tolerated in the first place, or whether the fervor of moneymaking had channeled energies away from politics. Rey Chow has recently argued with great indignation against the view that "Hong Kong thrives economically only because it is lacking in political autonomy and self-determination."[13] She asks why Hong Kong's aspiration for material prosperity has to be read as a sign of "deficiency, degeneracy, abnormality, and hence basic inferiority,"[14] as "female sexuality" was believed to compensate for the missing penis. I agree with Chow (except on the alleged "negative equation of femininity and the city," [15] which is to my mind too much a product of pure speculation to serve any purpose to the issue at hand) that Hong Kong's material prosperity does not follow from the region's need to compensate for its lack of political autonomy and self-determination but is rather the core identity of the place. But I do not proceed, as Chow does, from Derrida's supplementary logic, assuming that we need to subvert the hierarchy of the "mind" (culture and politics) and the "body" (material prosperity) in Hong Kong. Rather, I am more concerned with the fundamental materialistic view of life, which was the basis of the identity of the region from the very beginning of its history. Being essentially a mercantile community in exile, the population of Hong Kong had little interest in issues that did not bear directly on economic advantage. Until the 1980s, "few fundamental ends of government were ever the subject of public debate," with "neither the arena for nor the interest in a public discourse on the rights and wrongs of social policies on fundamental principles." [16] Small wonder, then, that Hong Kong had produced throughout its history "no diplomat, no military general, no international civil servant, no ideology and therefore no ideologue." [17] This was not just because Hong Kong was a colony. Successful Hong Kong people only aspired to be what ranked the highest in their list of social hierarchy, namely, merchants and tycoons in East Asia. They were neither interested in, nor capable of, producing say, a Fanon or a Mandela.

The ideology of the market is therefore more or less superfluous in Hong Kong, except during the few years before the change of sovereignty, when the region was in a panic about the future of the free market. In the West, the long history of the Christian aspiration for the otherworldly made it necessary for the secular impulse toward profit maximization to express itself in an ideologically sublimated form [18] — the freedom to make money had to legitimize itself and to make itself morally acceptable or even commendable by keeping silent, on the level of ideology, about its economic content, and transforming itself into the lofty and empty idea of freedom as such. In Hong Kong, different historical conditions rendered this detour of ideological sublimation unnecessary. To a population that was already predisposed to the activity of profit-making, there was no need for a systematic ethical neutralization of the profit motive to remove moral barriers to legally permissible profit making. Nor was there the ideological impulse to abstract freedom from its economic context so as to make freedom out to be something of a moral value in its own right. Unlike the bourgeoisie in the West, the formation of the mercantile community in Hong Kong was not the result of religious secularization and desublimation. The population had no need to resort to the detour of ideological sublimation to make up for the loss of metaphysical meanings.

To be sure, the economic activities of the region were not left unmediated but structured around ideas that we may express in terms of "(native) freedom," "(formal) equality," and "procedural justice." But these ideas were not the objects of public contestation, any more than the presence of the colonial government that was responsible for the transportation of these ideas from England to Hong Kong in the first place.

Political apathy of this sort gave way to high waves of political enthusiasm only when the free market was under threat. In comparison with the conspicuous lack of anticolonial consciousness in its history, Hong Kong has been extremely active in defending human rights in the mainland since the Sino-British agreement for the change of sovereignty—some of which rights (e.g., political participation) Hong Kong had never demanded from the colonial government in the past. Hundreds of thousands people have taken part in an annual vigil since 1989 to mark the Tiananmen massacre, an occasion the likes of which Hong Kong had never witnessed, except during the General Strike of 1920s. Behind this political enthusiasm, however, was not only moral indignation against the brutality of the Chinese government, or the apprehension that Beijing might do to Hong Kong what it had done to students in Tiananmen Square. There was also a strong sentiment that jealously guarded Hong Kong's material prosperity and the free market order. For the majority of people in Hong Kong, freedom is synonymous with the free market, protected by the colonial government, while "unfreedom" is associated with the planned economy, controlled by the totalitarian regime in Beijing. The divide between the "we" (i.e., Hong Kong people) and the "they" (i.e., mainlanders) is constituted as much by different standards of living as by political and ideological conflicts. "We" are the people of comfort, luxury, and style. And "they" are the masses with their poverty, hardship, and dullness. This mundane impulse to protect the economic interests of Hong Kong had not been sufficiently sublimated so that there would emerge a chance for politics in Hong Kong to lead a relatively separate life from that of economy. But it had nevertheless been completely disavowed in the rhetoric of Hong Kong's politics, so much so that "freedom" was indeed pursued vigorously without cynicism. During the few years of heated debates about the future of freedom in Hong Kong, no distinction was drawn between the content and the form of freedom, let alone the distinction between a weaker defense of freedom and a stronger one.[19] All there was in the political consciousness of the region was an *abstract idea* of freedom, which, because of its very abstractness, served to articulate the economic interests of the population without this function being publicly acknowledged or even recognized.

Interestingly enough, the lack of strong values and the more or less unsublimated pursuit of economic interests are not just features specific to Hong

Kong that emerged under the unique historical circumstances of the region. They are now becoming general features of the global economic order. Capitalism cannot exist without "constantly revolutionizing the instruments of production, and thereby the relations of production, and with them the whole relations of society."[20] On the level of the superstructure of the system, this revolutionary tendency manifests itself as a subversive potential against all traditional values and metaphysical beliefs. The initial conversion of passions into interests that paved the way for the rise of capitalism eventually becomes an ongoing project, a perpetual movement of desublimation, serving to dissolve not only such medieval notions as honor and glory but also all ideas that stand in the way of the economic imperative of the market. "All fixed, fast-frozen relations, with their train of ancient and venerable prejudices and opinions, are swept away, all new-formed ones become antiquated before they can ossify. All that is solid melts into air, all that is holy is profaned, and man is at last compelled to face with sober senses his real conditions of life and his relations with his kind."[21]

This desublimating tendency of capitalism has the potential to transform and undermine all traditional values that do not give pride of place to material prosperity in the marketplace. As happened with the Enlightenment in the West, "reason" (instrumental reason as opposed to substantive) will triumph over "superstition," though in the case of the non-West this process takes place not so much through "enlightenment" as through colonization. "The cheap prices of its commodities are the heavy artillery with which it batters down all Chinese walls, with which it forces the barbarians' intensely obstinate hatred of foreigners to capitulate."[22] The "barbarians" do not even have to leave their homelands to forsake their gods and temples. Western civilization has come to destroy their traditions and customs amid themselves. The "Chinese walls" and the "barbarians' intensely obstinate hatred of foreigners" may have created some troubles for the expansion of the capitalist market in its initial stages. But they are old stories now. Nowadays, the flow of capital across the globe no longer meets with much resistance, if any. It is therefore no longer escorted by the military might of colonialism. Instead of armed soldiers, the colonized now receive from the colonizer the dreams of affluent living, accompanied by the import of Western consumer goods that make the realization of such dreams possible. Though only a minority of people in the world can actually benefit from the development of the global market—the capitalist mode of production always carries with it, wherever it goes, the class distinction as the condition of possibility of surplus value— ideological aspiration and the hope of affluent living in the Western style are shared by all.

To anticipate my discussion of multiculturalism in Hong Kong, I shall argue that, through the elimination or attenuation of traditional values (and through the removal of Marxism as the ideology of the former socialist states), global capitalism has achieved a "depoliticization" of the world (with the active participation of such former socialist states as China, which have given up their "socialist" politics and become increasingly incorporated into the global market) and in so doing created the possibility for different racial and ethnic populations to coexist peacefully, *within the framework of capitalism*. When the CEOs of multinational corporations brag of themselves as the "peacemongers" of the twentieth century, they are not just cracking jokes about capitalism. The flow of capital across the boundaries of the nation-states has created a "global factory" without geographical ties, along with a global "consumption community"—"a bond transcending race, geography, and tradition based on eating, drinking, smoking, wearing, and driving identical things." [23] To be sure, the members of the "planetary petty bourgeoisie" [24] who constitute the population of this global consumption community are always quite limited in number. The expansion of global capitalism "did not homogenize the world but, rather, created two new worlds of development and underdevelopment." [25] Yet this division of the world has not prevented global capitalism from achieving what Arif Dirlik calls "ideological homogenization"—a process through which "nations of the Second and Third Worlds alike assimilated the spatial and temporal assumptions of capitalism that were built into the very notion of development." [26] The introduction of Western consumer goods into non-Western countries has eroded traditional lifestyles along with the passions to defend them. Moreover, a similar process has taken place across the ideological divide between socialism and capitalism, resulting in the dissolution of the socialist ideology and the absorption of the former socialist states—including those that still call themselves socialist—into the orbit of the capitalist market order. Tom Friedman, a journalist for the *New York Times*, reports after his trip to the McDonald's headquarters in Chicago that there has never been a war between two countries that have McDonald's restaurants. Though presented in a jovial manner, Friedman's "golden arches" theory has indeed revealed something important about the trend of the world. The golden arches of McDonald's, which are a sign of the economic and cultural expansion of global capitalism, have become paradoxically the index of political and ideological toleration of the host countries, a toleration that is based on the attenuation of the indigenous cultures, on the conversion of the passions for the ideal of socialism into the zeal for economic development within the framework of capitalism. In proportion to the degree of their assimilation into the global market, people of different racial and ethnic origins have scaled down the importance of their indigenous cultures (while rejecting socialist ideology, if they live in the former socialist states) and become more tolerant of the West *and* of each other.

Different cultures do not therefore disappear, but are appropriated by the capitalist market as the means of capital's self-proliferation. To create the "world customer" for their products, multinational corporations cannot simply substitute the Western industrial civilization for the indigenous cultures. They have to make good use of the indigenous cultures so as to tailor their products to people of different habits and tastes. In fact, as Dirlik has noted, "multiculturalism" originates not so much from the "deconstruction" of Eurocentrism launched by the academic Left as from the economic imperative of multinational corporations:

> Transnationalism, and the management of transnational production, were very much in evidence in management studies by the late seventies. *Managing Cultural Differences* was the revealing title of a management text published in 1979, that addressed questions of "multiculturalism" or "polyculturalism" that managers faced with regard to organizational behavior, production and marketing in an age of multinationalism. The text argued for a new kind of training for managers that would enable them to operate more effectively in this new situation that demanded cultural flexibility. Such training would not only minimize the effects of "cultural shock" as they moved from one cultural realm to another, but would also prepare them for the newly required tasks of creating a "corporate culture" that was to be constituted "synergistically" out of a multiplicity of cultures.[27]

Having thus become the focus of the global market, however, cultural differences do not flourish but disappear into their own simulacra. The global market can allow different cultures to exist within its own framework only to the extent that these cultures no longer constitute *substantive* differences. The indigenous "gods" are welcome on the market only insofar as they no longer have the power to conjure up a whole train of traditions and customs that are fundamentally at odds with the economic imperative of profit maximization. Max Weber once lamented that the care for economic profit, which should have been the empty vessel for the expression of the Protestant ethic, had been unfortunately reified into the "iron cage" of industrial capitalism. The indigenous gods share the same fate with the Protestant ethic, albeit in an inverted fashion. Traditions are now the empty vessels for the expression of multinational capital. It is the self-proliferation of capital that provides the possibility for the survival of traditions, not the other way round.

This particular way for traditions to survive in the global market leads me back to my reading of Hong Kong. To view the history of Hong Kong against the background of a commercial culture that has hollowed the meaning of traditions and customs should not prevent us from seeing that, when the immigrants came to Hong Kong in the mid-nineteenth century, they indeed brought their traditions and customs, along with their aspiration for material prosperity. But we should also emphasize that traditions and customs were not the main reason for their immigration. People came to Hong Kong not because they were looking for a haven for some of the strong values that had become difficult to uphold in their homelands (as was the case, for example, with the passengers in the *Mayflower* sailing for America in the early seventeenth century). On the contrary, they came to Hong Kong primarily for economic reasons, for the opportunity of making a better living. In this regard, Hong Kong might be said to have anticipated the immigration pattern in the late twentieth century. Long before the flow of multinational capital sets in motion an international immigration wave, whose ebb and flow depends on the rate of economic profits at a given time, economic consideration was already the decisive factor in immigration in Hong Kong. Salaries in Hong Kong were higher than in mainland China and the adjacent South Asian countries, and that was a sufficient reason for immigration for most people, then and now.

Under these conditions, traditions and customs are left to live or die according to circumstances, or more precisely, according to their degree of affinity with the capitalist market. The fate of Confucianism is a case in point. Just as the May Fourth movement in 1919 passed Hong Kong by, leaving Confucianism unscathed in the region (notwithstanding the fact that what went by the name of Confucianism was only a *transformed* value orientation under the joined pressure of colonialism and the market), the recent reinvention of Confucianism as "one of the most prolific intellectual industries of the decade"[28] has not breathed much real life into the truncated version of Confucianism. Ambrose King argues, quite convincingly I think, that the Confucianism discussed by Weber never took root in Hong Kong. What goes by the name of Confucianism is actually a "rationalistic traditionalism," a cognitive and instrumental attitude toward traditions. He maintains that though many Hong Kong people still attach some importance to traditions, "traditions are not necessarily treasured affectively for their intrinsic goodness" but "selectively preserved mainly on their extrinsic usefulness in pursuing economic goals."[29] The practice of nepotism is a good example. It is common knowledge that the economic structure of Hong Kong is dominated by small factories, and that the owners of small factories often have their relatives in their workforce. But this does not indicate at all that kinship relationship is being cherished in Hong Kong as a value in itself. On the contrary, it is just a sign that the Chinese familistic system has been used as an instrumental mechanism to secure for employers a workforce they can trust. As King argues, "The Chinese traditional familistic system has been modified by Western business ideology and practical necessity, or by the functional prerequisites . . . of the industrial system. As such, it may have enhanced rather than undermined the economic performance of the small factories."[30] This pragmatic attitude toward tradition makes it unnecessary to launch, in the context of Hong Kong, a wholesale critique of traditions (if one wishes to modernize Chinese society) or to advocate a complete restoration of traditions (if one wants to resort to the past as the means of resisting the present). Confucianism will survive where it is conducive to the development of capitalism, and it will die a slow and barely noticeable death where it has been rendered irrelevant. Questions often raised in the debates about Neo-Confucianism—e.g., whether Confucianism is instrumental to the development of capitalism; whether the doctrine has a part to play in alleviating the problems of capitalism—may not have any basis in reality but stem from the institutional needs of the Chinese diaspora in the United States to reassert their cultural identities when such identities are becoming less and less relevant to the modern way of life.[31]

From the demise of traditions follows a peculiar multicultural characteristic of the population in the region that is predicated, paradoxically, on the lack of substantive cultural differences. In the public space of Hong Kong, people of different racial and ethnic origins—Chinese, Muslims, Indians, Europeans, and Americans—rub shoulders with one another less as Chinese, Muslims, Indians, Europeans, and Americans than as the residents of the cosmopolitan city who have, even if only temporarily, suspended their cultural specificity. The governing principle of this public sphere is, to allude to the ideal of John Rawls's political liberalism, the priority of the "right" over the "good." At the heart of this priority is the (formal) political and economic equality among people who, as citizens rather than as members of specific cultural communities, have suspended judgments rooted in their specific cultural contexts and have entered a relationship with one another as autonomous individuals. What distinguishes the reality of Hong Kong from John Rawls's ideal, however, is that the pluralism that is predicated on the priority of the "right" over the "good" is not achieved (as Rawls postulates) through "reason" but through the workings of market forces. Different "comprehensive doctrines" can peacefully coexist in Hong Kong (despite subtle or even open prejudice and discrimination directed at the non-Chinese populations, the Vietnamese and Filipinos in particular), not because people of different cultural origins have come to a common understanding of Western liberal ideals (the ideal of toleration first and foremost), but because the economic imperative of the capitalist market has sufficiently transformed different comprehensive doctrines so that there is not much cultural difference left as the object of liberal toleration.

In this regard, Samuel Johnson's remark on the innocuousness of money-making—"There are few ways in which a man can be more innocently employed than in getting money"—may deserve some attention. Making money may not be as innocent as Johnson believes, as the history of colonialism driven by the impetus of economic profits has abundantly shown. But the brutality of colonialism has a built-in tendency to reduce the need of its own existence—all thanks to the expansion of the capitalist market that has been changing the world of the colonized more and more into its own image and thus rendering military coercion less and less necessary. Driven by a passion that has no specific cultural content, moneymaking is an activity in which all can participate, provided that all who participate in it have gone through the same cultural transformation that is destined to result in the attenuation of cultural differences. At the entrance of the global market, all have to leave behind their own cultural specificity so as to trade for admission.

Different conceptions of the good, however, do not vanish upon being subsumed under the priority of the right. They are left in the private realm, or allowed to reenter the public realm through the commercial (rather than political) avenue. There is, in Hong Kong, a clear distinction between the public and the private in terms of how people deal with their cultural differences. People are left to pursue their own way of life according to their own cultural and ethnic traditions, as long as this does not stand in the way of the activities of the market. One never sees, for instance, the kind of violent cultural and ethnic conflicts that have occurred in places like Bosnia or Rwanda. Where different cultures do make their appearance in the public realm, they do so through commodification, which neither alters the overall structure of the market predicated upon the lack of subversive cultural differences nor upsets the political regime of liberalism in tune with the overall structure of the market.[32] Hong Kong has a splendid market of cultural goods, where "cultures" are commercial covers and "goods" are the substance. The consumption of these cultural goods is not a cultural activity that involves, among other things, the necessity of living according to traditions and customs; it is consumption par excellence. The best example of this is the consumption of exotic foods. There are few cities in the world that have such a variety of ethnic restaurants as one sees in Hong Kong. One can literally "taste" dozens different cultures—Chinese, Japanese, Korean, Indian, Indonesian, Arabian, Italian, Spanish, French, and so on—through a single trip to downtown restaurants without at the same time learning anything substantial about them. This commodification of cultures, through which commercial transactions take place precisely because the substance of cultures has been neutralized, is what defines cosmopolitanism in the twentieth century—not just the cosmopolitanism of Hong Kong but also the cosmopolitanism of other big cities such as Toronto and New York. Unlike the imperial version of multiculturalism in the histories of the multinational empires, where different racial and ethnic populations existed as they were, kept apart from each other by an imperial regime that was at an equal distance from all of them,[33] the contemporary version of multiculturalism is made possible by a market mechanism that is both predicated upon and contributive to the attenuation of cultural differences.

One should not be misled to think, by the colorful sight of the multicultural population, that racial discrimination in Hong Kong has become a thing of the past. Apart from the inconsistent treatment of Chinese and Westerners, which is still practiced subtly or flagrantly in the region,[34] racism has, recently, taken on a new *economic* form against the poor immigrants, Filipinas in particular. Since 1974, the Immigration Department has begun to formally accept application of overseas domestic servants to work in Hong Kong, and the number of Filipina servants employed in Hong Kong has increased annually. By the end of 1987, Hong Kong had 39,100 Filipinas in its population, the largest group among foreign residents in the region.[35] The Filipinas, however, do not enjoy equal access with other foreign residents to the comfort and luxury of the cosmopolitan life of Hong Kong. They are bound by their domestic duties to the flats and houses of well-to-do families and are released into the streets of Hong Kong only during weekends and holidays. Even this occasional appearance is barely tolerated by the city. The Central District, where Filipina servants gather during the weekends and holidays for the lack of a better venue of communication and entertainment, has become a problem area in the city since the eighties. Policemen patrol the area frequently to inspect the identity cards of Filipinas or those who look like Filipinas. Some buildings on the edge of the Central District have even intensified their security measures and installed "No entry" signs or rope barriers at entrances and staircases. "These notices are written in English and Tagalog. Obviously, they are meant for the Filipinas meeting thereby."[36]

Like everything else in Hong Kong, this economic turn of racism falls squarely within the framework of global capitalism. Filipinas have become the least privileged ethnic group in Hong Kong, not because their ethnic identity is least tolerated but because they are lower-class, standing on the lower end of the economic scale. What they experience is not racism as such, but a *racist manifestation* of class distinction and exploitation. This has to do, in the final analysis, with the uneven development of capitalism as a world system. Immanuel Wallerstein argues that "the accumulation of capital, the *leitmotiv* of capitalism, has been an uneven process both spatially and temporally. . . .

Spatially it has been uneven in that different kinds of economic activities have been located in different geographical loci, such that at any given time there exist concentrations of more highly capitalized, higher-wage, higher-profit activities in some places (core) and less capitalized, lower-wage, lower-profit activities in others (periphery)." [37] From this it follows that the development of the capital-labor relationship across the globe has been accompanied by "two processes of worldwide class-formation—proletarianization and bourgeoisification—the combination of which has had a worldwide polarizing effect on distribution over time." [38] On the one hand, the appropriation of surplus of the whole global economy by "core areas" enables a "redistribution of surplus-value to some groups (some workers in the core zones, and some bourgeois in the semiperiphery)." [39] On the other hand (and by the same token), the peripheral countries are kept underdeveloped, serving mainly as the sources of raw materials and cheap laborers for the core zones.

The immigration of Filipinas who work in Hong Kong as domestic servants and the unequal treatment they receive from other racial and ethnic groups in the region are results of this international polarization. Thanks to the colonization of the Philippines by Spain and by the United States and to the subsequent incorporation of the nation into the periphery of the global structure of capitalism, immigration to some "core zones" provide a better life prospect for people of the lower classes. What is worth remarking, however, is that this is not only the situation of Filipinas alone but is common to a large proportion of the lower classes in the former colonies. Not only do young Filipinas choose to work abroad and to endure more or less in silence the unequal treatment they receive (memories of worse living conditions and lower wages at home make the pain of racial discrimination somewhat easier to bear), the same is true across the globe as the polarizing tendency of global capital causes unending waves of immigration from the developing countries to the developed countries as cheap laborers. In New York, London, and Tokyo, to name just three cosmopolitan cities of the world, poor immigrants are "disproportionately concentrated in blue-collar and service jobs" in comparison with nonimmigrant population in the cities.[40] In New York in particular, immigrants from Asia and Latin America have formed a steady supply for low-wage jobs, along with inner-city blacks who have, as William Julius Wilson argues, benefited little from the civil rights movement and affirmative action.[41]

In this context, it is fitting to raise a couple of questions about the politics of the academic Left. Since the late sixties, it has become a commonplace for the academic Left to argue that it is symptomatic of colonialism and patriarchy to subsume race and gender under the rubric of class. Though this may have indeed broadened the political horizon of the academic Left, it has also bracketed class as *the* defining feature of the capitalist social relations. The survival of capitalism depends on the availability of surplus value, which in turn depends on the possibility of economic exploitation. This economic imperative makes class (rather than race and gender) the category underpinning capitalist social relations. Racial discrimination (along with gender inequality) may facilitate economic exploitation, in that it renders certain social groups particularly vulnerable to the mechanism of the labor market. Yet racial discrimination cannot, in the final analysis, substitute class distinction as the condition of possibility of surplus value, and hence the condition of possibility of the capitalist mode of production itself. Failing to recognize this may lead to a blindness to the political and economic needs of the "truly disadvantaged" (i.e., racial and ethnic minorities who have not made it into the ranks of the bourgeoisie) and hence to the promotion of the interests of racial and ethnic minorities within the bourgeois class, which "most frequently results simply in a shift in location of the privileged stratum."[42]

Along with this exclusive focus on race and ethnicity, the trend toward multiculturalism that is now all the rage on the university campuses in the United States also calls for some sober reevaluation. For one thing, we should realize that the fixed idea of the nation-state, which has increasingly been "deconstructed" by such figures as Homi Bhabha, is *not* a necessary condition of capitalism, at least it is *no longer so* in the age of multinational corporations. Even though the notion of the nation-state may not be able to survive beyond the era of national independence and decolonization, we still need to ask ourselves why it is at this particular historical moment that we choose to focus on the nation-state as the object of our critical analysis, a moment where even the raison d'être of the university (literature departments in particular) is called into question by the free flow of capital across the boundary of the nation-states, and by the subsequent declining significance of national cultures and literatures.[43]

Last but not least, we also need to reconsider the political significance of the fierce postmodern attack on the transcendental paradigm (in which postmodernism throws, quite indiscriminately, everything that contradicts the ephemeral and fragmented characteristics of life in the marketplace, ranging from Christian fundamentalism to Kant's transcendental consciousness). Again, like the fixed notion of the nation-state, transcendental or metaphysical values may not be worth keeping from the perspective of a thoroughgoing emancipatory politics. Yet we should not mistake what are only concomitant to, or at the most have a partial affinity with, capitalism for its necessary conditions.[44] Such a confusion may result in a politics that hastens the obsolescence of what the capitalist market itself is leaving behind. It would make the academic Left look as though it were urging the system, like "its great mentor Friedrich Nietzsche, to forget about its metaphysical foundations, acknowledge that God is dead and simply go relativist."[45] Capitalism has, as Marx maintains, "drowned the most heavenly ecstasies of religious fervor, of chivalrous enthusiasms, of philistine sentimentalism, in the icy water of egotistical calculation. It has resolved personal worth into exchange value, and in place of the numberless indefeasible chartered freedoms, has set up that single, unconscionable freedom—Free Trade."[46] In this light, the question the academic Left should ask is whether it makes any sense to focus more on the transcendental paradigm as the object of its critical analysis than on problems that emerge in the wake of the collapse of the transcendental.

With these questions in mind, I now turn to examine how Hong Kong is positioned in postcolonial theory (as part of the postmodern paradigm), and how postcolonial theory, through its positioning of Hong Kong, positions *itself* in relation to global capitalism. By "postcolonial theory" I refer to a particular way of writing the postcolonial under the influence of postmodernism, particularly in the U.S. academe. An exemplary case is Rey Chow's writing on Hong Kong, which shows both the kind of postcolonial theory I have in mind and the way such theory deals with cases like Hong Kong.

Chow defines the postcolonial by giving a new interpretation to the prefix "post" in the word "postcolonial." The "post," she argues, is not simply a matter of chronological time but includes in it "a notion of time that is not linear but constant, marked by events that may be technically finished but that can be fully understood only with consideration of the devastation they left behind."[47] That a culture has gone beyond colonialism does not mean that colonialism is no longer a part of its life. On the contrary, the "ideological legacies" and "cultural effects" of colonialism will remain at work long after the departure of territorial colonialism. These points are well taken. I made similar arguments at the beginning of this essay. What distinguishes her arguments from mine, however, is that under the heading of "colonialism" she introduces something we usually do not associate with that term. With a sudden and barely noticeable twist in her logic, Chow substitutes China for Britain as the main target of her postcolonial critique. "The most critical of these problems is that Hong Kong will not gain territorial independence at the end of British colonialism. This is due to the fact that a large part of Hong Kong (the Kowloon Peninsula and the New Territories) has been 'on lease' from China to Britain since the mid-nineteenth century, and, when the 99-year lease expires in 1997, Hong Kong will be 'returned' to China."[48] I am not taking issue with Chow's presentation of the facts but her interpretation of them. Through a sweeping generalization and a violent reduction of historical specificities, Chow conflates China's reclaiming sovereignty over Hong

Kong in 1997 with Britain's initial occupation of Hong Kong in 1842, without mentioning at all that the former is an act of *nationalism* against colonialism (in fact, a belated act under special circumstances) whereas the latter is colonialism par excellence: it is the beginning of the West's semicolonization of China after the Opium War. Quoting with approval a contemporary Hong Kong essayist, Ha Gong, Chow argues that Hong Kong is being "gang-raped" by China and Britain through the Sino-British Joint Declaration. "The Sino-British talks closely resemble two men gang-raping Hong Kong, with the victim being denied the right to scream or protest." [49] I find this an ill-chosen metaphor. It makes the kind of sense Chow wishes to make only if those who are now against China have been as vehemently against Britain in the past. But that has not been the case. Until fairly recently, that is, until China made its appearance as a new "colonizer," colonialism had not been much of an issue in Hong Kong (with the exception of the twenties and the sixties when communist fervor caught on across the border). The air began to vibrate with resistance to "colonialism" only when it became clear, through the Sino-British Joint Declaration, that the (poor and communist) Chinese were about to come and stay in the region. Britain is caught up in Hong Kong's resentment against China not because, as Chow gives one to understand, Britain will continue to exercise its colonial power but because it has decided to *give it up*. The "foster parent" has decided to return the "child" to the "biological mother," and the "child" protests against the decision, kicking and screaming.

The unthinking prejudice against China, however, is not all there is to Chow's argument. Behind the prejudice is a profound change in the definition of colonialism and hence the main problematic of postcoloniality. Once nationalism is conflated with colonialism (or more precisely, once nationalism substitutes colonialism as the main issue), the predicament of the "postcolonial" is no longer seen as the difficulty for the previously colonized to leave behind the ideological legacies of colonialism but begins to be viewed as the impossibility for ethnic and cultural "differences" to be represented within the framework of nationalism. Chow emphasizes that though there has never been a single case in the history of colonialism where the national identity of the colonized was achieved through "obligatory restoration," as has happened with Hong Kong, illusions of the possibility of reclaiming a "native" culture have remained the "strongest grounds for anticolonial resistance among previously colonized countries around the world." [50] The epistemological presupposition of anticolonial resistance has thus remained the binary opposition between the "native" and the "foreigner," with the result that struggles *within* the boundary of the native have never been appropriately addressed. This situation, Chow argues, calls for a new ethics of postcoloniality. The idea of "referentiality" should be problematized in postcoloniality as thoroughly as it has been elsewhere. The method of deconstruction that subverts the primordiality of the "self" by exposing its condition of possibility in the supplementarity of the "other" should be applied to the supplementarity of the other as well. The other should not become the harbor of essentialism. Instead, the ontological condition of possibility of the other has to be found in another other—the other of the other, so to speak—the suppression of which has made the binary opposition of the self and the other possible. But the discovery of the other of the other does not mean at all that we have finally put our finger on the ever-receding "origins" of the "native." On the contrary, the radical other is the opposite of origins. It has nothing to do with ethnic and cultural "essence" presupposed by old postcolonial politics. If there is anything that can capture the essence of the new other, it is the lack of origins, as indicated by such concepts as ethnic and cultural impurity, hybridity, or in-betweenness. To what degree this postcolonial politics is predicated on poststructuralism and postmodernism and hence on some of the structural features of capitalism is a topic I shall pick up at the end of the essay. In the meantime, I will simply try to follow through Chow's argument.

On the face of it, we are dealing with an epistemological issue. Chow gives one to understand that we are now leaving behind the concerns of the "old" postcolonial politics (e.g., territorial sovereignty, and sovereignty over ethnic and cultural history) because we have realized through the help of poststructuralism that the philosophical presupposition of these concerns (i.e., essentialism) is inadequate. But I would argue, following Arif Dirlik, that what occasions the repudiation of the old postcolonial politics is not the awareness of the epistemological groundlessness of racial and ethnic "essence" but the political undesirability of such an essence under changed circumstances produced by global capitalism. Radical struggles, Dirlik writes, whether in their anticolonialist or Third World expression or in the language of national liberation "did not presuppose an essentialist primordialism, but rather viewed cultural identity as a project that was very much part of the struggle for liberation that it informed. That this is ignored in postcolonialist representations of these struggles raises the question of whether the objection is indeed to the essentialism of past conceptualizations of the world, or to the aims those struggles promoted, which have become undesirable from a contemporary perspective." [51] At stake here are the material conditions under which postcolonial theory rejects the construction of national identities as part and parcel of the political aims of anticolonial struggles. Since the end of the Cold War and the subsequent triumph of capitalism over socialism (in ideology if not yet in "reality," as many Marxists contest), the world has witnessed a structural transformation of global relations and a remapping of the geography of the world economy. Capital, whose expansion was once escorted by territorial colonialism and resisted by various kinds of Marxist practices in the previously colonized countries, has now changed, thanks to the "demise" of Marxism, from liability to asset for most of the Third World countries. In fact, given that the divide between the First World and the Third World involved in the past an ideological antagonism between capitalism and socialism, we can hardly say that the divide is still there once the Cold War is over and the socialist block has dissolved. What has survived the ideological divide is the *economic* distinction between the developed countries and the developing ones, which boils down to different stages of the linear process of the capitalist development. As far as the developing countries are concerned, this means that the need for the construction of national identities decreases in proportion to the reduced political needs of resisting Western capital. Though, as Dirlik reminds us, "it is quite premature presently to declare the nation a thing of the past," [52] the changed ideological circumstances of the world and the more aggressive development of transnational corporations have indeed rendered the borders of the nation-state more porous than before. Partly due to the diminished resistance from the developing countries (which is in turn due to the diminished *means* of resistance), transnational corporations are now in the position to admit different cultures into the realm of capital—"but only to break them down and to remake them in accordance with the requirements of production and consumption, and even to reconstitute subjectivities across national boundaries to create producers and consumers more responsive to the operations of capital." [53] Those who come off the best from this process and thus feel the least need to resist it are, needless to say, the diasporic population working in the core zones of the developed countries (in the United States in particular), including the postcolonial division of the academic Left who theorize the diaspora. Unlike the real "margins"—namely, "those peoples or places that are not responsive to the needs (or demands) of capital, or are too far gone to respond 'efficiently' " and thus have to be kicked out of its pathway [54]—the postcolonial critics who proclaim themselves to be at the margin of the U.S. academe are actually at the center of the global power structure, enjoying, among other things, the status of cultural brokers between their places of origin and the U.S. academe where such origins disappear into cultural commodities. "Native historiography" or "national identity" are profoundly at odds with the experience of ethnic and cultural in-betweenness of this diasporic population, who are in a unique position to articulate what is postcoloniality. A new postcolonial politics has thus been invented, a big part of which is just to transform in-betweenness from a particular way of life in the privileged zones of global capitalism into a general condition of postcoloniality as such.

Now, to the extent that the construction of national identities does not presuppose a belief in essentialism, the disbelief in origins is not the result of an epistemological critique of essentialism. Instead, the epistemological critique needs to be explained with reference to the political positions of those who practice it. This brings me back to Chow's reading of Hong Kong and China. In order to view the return of Hong Kong to China as the beginning of another round of colonialization, Chow insists that Hong Kong is both linguistically and culturally different from the mainland. To enlist support for her argument from the "locals," she quotes from Leung Ping-kwan, a renowned Hong Kong author and critic:

> The identity of Hong Kong is more complex than that of any other place. . . . Vis-à-vis foreigners, Hong Kong people are of course Chinese, but vis-à-vis the Chinese from the mainland or Taiwan, they seem to have the imprints of the West. A Hong Kong person who came from China after 1949 is obviously an "outsider" or "someone coming south"; but to those who "came south" during the 1970s and 1980s, such a person is already a "local." A Hong Kong person may speak English or Putonghua, but it is not the language with which he is familiar since childhood; and yet what he knows best, Cantonese, is not convenient for writing. He recites the Chinese classics while at school, but in his eventual employment he would have to acquaint himself with forms of commercial correspondence or the brief and cute wordings of advertising. Such linguistic impurities are also a reflection of the impurities of Hong Kong's cultural identity.[55]

Chow does not mention, while evoking Leung as the "true" voice of Hong Kong, that Leung was educated in the United States and graduated with a Ph.D. in comparative literature from the University of California in the eighties when postmodernism was still on the rise. This gives one some reason to believe (if one takes into account the institutional framework of Leung's thought) that what one sees in Leung's writing is not so much the *self-presence* of the linguistic and cultural "impurity" of Hong Kong as the *representation* of such impurity in terms of the key concepts of postmodernism, chief among them hybridity. To put it in plain English, the site for the construction of the consciousness of the local is not Hong Kong in isolation but Hong Kong as part of the global structure with the United States at the center. This is not to "pretend," to borrow some expressions from Chow's criticism of someone else, "that there is some pristine, as-yet uncorrupted, ethnic 'raw material' on the other side of the Western world," or that "we should not and cannot read a Chinese text in the West at all."[56] The point is rather to make clear how the power relations in the current global structure work, and why there is no more ethnic raw material left on the other side of the Western world (if that is indeed the case).

But that is only a side issue, albeit an important one. The main issue is what Chow has made of Leung's writing. With the help of such concepts as impurity, which comes more from Leung's borrowing of the postmodern vocabulary than from his unmediated observation of Hong Kong life (if such an observation is possible), Chow creates an ethnic "essence" of Hong Kong as distinct from that of the mainland. She argues that Hong Kong is marked by a double impurity—the impurity of its past and the "vicissitudes of the 'native' language, which is also impure and multiple." [57] This double impurity makes Hong Kong an other to the "totalizing nativist vision of the Chinese folk." While " 'proper' Chinese cities such as Beijing and Nanjing are viewed with a reverent sense of their centrality in Chinese history," Hong Kong is viewed with "disdain by most mainland Chinese as a symbol of decadence, artificiality, and contamination." [58] To make sure that the reader will understand this distinction in unmistakably ethnic terms, Chow brings in Ranajit Guha's native historiography of India to pair with the totalizing nativist vision of the Chinese folk. Guha's project, she maintains, presupposes a belief in the presence of the British as an "*outside* colonizer in India." [59] This epistemological clarity between inside and outside entails a suppression of the knowledge of "struggles within India among the various ethnic languages and cultures," encouraging the idea that national history has a "single source in a particular ethnic group." [60] The point of Chow's comparison is quite clear: Hong Kong is to Beijing what the "various ethnic languages and cultures" of India are to the "throne of Delhi," except that what is suppressed in the native historiography of India comes to the fore in the case of Hong Kong. As Chow herself says in the voice of Hong Kong: "From the perspective of those living in Hong Kong . . . what is self-writing for China is definitely not self-writing for Hong Kong; the restoration of China's territorial propriety in/through Hong Kong does not amount to Hong Kong's repossession of its own cultural agency." [61]

No one will deny that the "self-writing of China is definitely not self-writing for Hong Kong." The annual vigil since 1989 is the best proof for that. What *is* doubtful, however, is whether Hong Kong's opposition to Beijing can be attributed to an *ethnic* conflict between the two places, or whether the alleged ethnic difference is an alibi for something else, as I will try to show. To my knowledge, neither the "impurity" of the region's past nor the "vicissitudes of the 'native' language" (which is also "impure and multiple" according to Chow) has anything to do with ethnicity. The impurity of Hong Kong's past is the legacy of British colonialism. It is the self-writing of Britain that has already been materialized, as opposed to the self-writing of China that is yet to take place. Chow has good reasons *not* to oppose the self-writing of Britain the way she opposes that of China, especially given what happened in Tiananmen Square in 1989. One may even agree if she insists that the colonial legacy of Britain has become an irreducible constituent of the Hong Kong identity. Yet I think it is crucial to distinguish an identity that has largely resulted from the self-writing of British colonialism from an identity that is ethnically based (as in the case of minority groups in India)—a distinction we need to maintain not in order to valorize ethnic essence but to clarify the issue at hand. The "vicissitudes of the 'native' language," which makes up the other half of the double impurity, is just another name for Cantonese. For different reasons, this native language cannot constitute an *ethnic* dimension of Hong Kong's identity either. As we know, Cantonese is not the ethnic language of Hong Kong but a regional dialect shared by Hong Kong and millions of Chinese in and around Canton (Guangzhou). What Leung describes as the linguistic in-betweeness—local dialect, on the one hand, and Mandarin, on the other— characterizes not only Hong Kong but many cities and regions in the mainland. Just think of Canton, or Shanghai for that matter. In both places there is a tremendous difference between the local dialect used for everyday conversation and Mandarin for radio and TV broadcast. We might say, with only a little exaggeration, that with the exception of those who were born and grew up in Beijing, the majority of the population of China is marked by linguistic impurity.

The point, however, is not to prove that Hong Kong is of the same ethnicity as much of China. Rather, my purpose is to show that, if impurity and in-betweenness are not cultural and linguistic features that can be traced back to Hong Kong's ethnic origins (or the lack thereof), then there is reason to believe that these alleged *ethnic* characteristics are actually political and ideological constructs that have been articulated in quasi-anthropological terms. Earlier I discussed how the political and ideological outmodedness of national identities under the new circumstances of the global capitalism is transformed in the discourse of postcolonial theory into the epistemological groundlessness of national essence or origins. What we see in Chow is the same traffic in the opposite direction. Such concepts as "impure origins" or "origins as impure" cannot even be criticized as being guilty of anti-essentialist essentialism, for they are merely neologisms with which Chow articulates, in philosophical terms, an ambivalent reluctance on the part of a sizable portion of the Hong Kong population to part with Britain in exchange for Beijing. To put it bluntly, the alleged cultural and linguistic difference between Hong Kong and Beijing is only an alibi for political and ideological antagonism of liberal democracy to communism, of the economically developed to the underdeveloped.

The power relations between the two places are completely misconstrued —thanks to Chow's culturalist or idealist approach. By "idealist" I do not mean the banal definition Chow gives this term in her *Ethics after Idealism*— "idealism operates as the tendency to idealize"; to "imagine the 'other' as essentially different, good, kind, enveloped in a halo."[62] Rather, I use the term in the Marxian sense to refer to a way of thinking that is incapable of addressing the material circumstances of its own existence. To be more precise, I have in mind the conspicuous silence of the postcolonial critics on the *material* conditions of their profession in the U.S. academe. They have been silent on this not because they have chosen an idealistic worldview, as Kant and Hegel did in the eighteenth and nineteenth centuries, but because they are unable or unwilling to see the complicity of their profession in the global division of labor under late capitalism. This kind of idealism has generated in the field of postcolonial studies a great many false problematics that are derivative of French poststructuralism and have little (if not none at all) to do with the real predicament of the postcolonial era. What Chow calls "ethics after idealism"—an ethics that is characterized by a relentless pursuit of "supplementary logic" or by a way of writing the postcolonial that privileges the diaspora over the Third World as the true margin or other—is a paradigmatic case of this idealism. It leads to the reification of deconstruction as the limiting term of analysis, and subsequently to the reduction of the complex relationship between Hong Kong and Beijing in the overall context of global capitalism to the predictable imperative of subverting the "primordial" with the "supplementary." Chow's own political sentiment aside, which compels her to side with the supplementary (Hong Kong) against the primordial (Beijing), the canonical practice of deconstruction in postcoloniality has made it almost an institutional mandate nowadays to subvert, for being the center, everything that has to do with national identities and national cultures. Many of those who find themselves on the wrong side of the divide are now in a great hurry to change allegiance, to such a degree that even Chow herself feels it necessary to fend off from the terrain of the margin those who do not belong there.[63] Few who are part of the scene seem to have realized that this reversal of the hierarchy of center and margin does not follow from the practice of deconstruction in postcoloniality, but results from the unobstructed development of transnational corporations across national boundaries (thanks to the dissolution of the socialist block and the assimilation of the Third World into the orbit of the developmental logic). As transnational diasporic populations move across the borders of the nation-states, driven by the dynamic of global capital, national allegiances cannot but give way to the celebration of impure origins as a new identity of the "planetary petty bourgeoisie." Hybridity and in-betweenness, once liabilities, cannot but "become assets that facilitate the transnational operations of global corporations."[64]

As far as the relationship between mainland China and Hong Kong is concerned, a similar reversal of hierarchy has also taken place. In a world where economic development is the ultimate point of reference for the international status of a country or place, China is no longer related to Hong Kong as the center to the margin. The power relations between the two places very often go the other way. "When Deng declared that he liked what he saw in Shenzhen and, by extension, Hong Kong (since Shenzhen is but an extension of Hong Kong, for all practical purposes), the urge became to reproduce Hong Kongs all over China so that, in the words of one cynical commentator, 'all of China could be turned into one big Hong Kong.'"[65] If these lines from Dirlik are not convincing for readers who do not share his Marxist point of view, a comment to the same effect from Ackbar Abbas—a "local" scholar who writes about Hong Kong from a postmodern perspective—may be more telling:

> As for China, administering the Hong Kong "special administrative region" after 1997 may be for the Chinese authorities a little like handling a gadget from the future. For example, one of the hiccups about the new airport, besides the huge cost, is anxiety on the Chinese side about whether they will be able to handle the extremely high-tech sophistication of the project. The historical ironies will only become more accentuated as China continues on its reformist course, as it looks likely to do, making the formula of "one country, two systems" so much more easy to dismantle: what we will find will not be two systems (socialist, capitalist) but one system at different stages of development—a difference in times and speeds.[66]

Whether or not China will *actually* be able to handle Hong Kong as "a gadget from the future" (a difficulty symbolized by the "extremely high-tech sophistication of the project" of the new airport, as Abbas points out), Abbas's *disbelief* in China's capacity tells us clearly how the power relations between the two places are conceived by a particular Hong Kong person and an influential scholar in the region. More importantly, Abbas is not alone in the region. The tide has turned. Along with other former socialist countries, China is no longer regarded as the center of the Third World as it was in the sixties, but is trying hard to move once again to the center—now defined in terms of global capital—from where Hong Kong beckons.

By way of a conclusion, I will tie up the various arguments I have made with a general comment on postcolonialism, especially on how postcolonialism is predicated on postmodernism and poststructuralism and hence on some of the structural features of capitalism. To that end, I need to clarify a distinction I have presupposed throughout this essay. By the word *postcolonialism* we can mean, as I have done here, two different things. We can mean a world situation after colonialism, where the possibilities of retrieving "native" cultures at the end of the colonial era emerge alongside the difficulties of articulating the autonomy of the local from within a structure that is always already global and that has indeed become more and more homogeneous since the end of the Cold War and the subsequent triumph of capitalism as an ideology. Alternatively, we can mean an academic discipline whose founding categories are virtually indistinguishable from those of postmodernism and poststructuralism. The postmodern polemic against the Enlightenment ideals of truth and freedom (which, as Terry Eagleton points out, has served to bridge capitalist ideology and its practice) is regurgitated in postcolonialism as the gospel of truth, with the sole difference that the "native" has substituted the Western self as the object of critical scrutiny.

To make the point clear, let me bring back my earlier reference to Derrida. If I am to capture the spirit of deconstruction in a few words, I would say that deconstruction is characterized by what Derrida calls "supplementary logic," the subversion of the primordial by the supplementary. Though this supplementary logic is, like Kant's synthetic a priori, presumably formal in the sense that it is content-neutral and can therefore be used to subvert any social order, the actual targets of supplementary logic in Derrida's writings are almost always those parts of the social order that have already been rendered obsolete or irrelevant by the development of the capitalist system. In other words, what is conceived by Derrida as the primordial and subsequently subjected to the subversion of the supplementary almost always turn out to consist of elements of the pre-Enlightenment (and hence precapitalist) transcendental paradigm, not least the concept of metaphysical truth that is grounded on the postulate of God.[67]

The same supplementary logic is at work in postcolonialism, *with the same effect.* Anthony Appiah asks whether the "post" in postcolonialism is the same as the "post" in postmodernism. The answer is clearly "yes," if by *postcolonialism* we mean the academic discipline that hosts such postcolonial celebrities as Edward Said, Gayatri Spivak, Homi Bhabha, and Rey Chow. The reason for this is not so much that postcolonialism has no other theoretical underpinning than French thought ranging from Lacan to Foucault to Derrida. More important than this theoretical lineage is how the problematics of both paradigms fit in with the structural features of capitalism. As Eagleton argues, postmodernism "scoops up something of the material logic of advanced capitalism and turns this aggressively against its spiritual foundation."[68] Postcolonialism does the same when it pits the achievement of capitalism on the level of its economic practice (i.e., the dissolution of national boundaries and identities through the workings of the free market) against its ideological rhetoric and beliefs (the "nation," the "people," etc.). As a result, the real predicament of the postcolonial as a world situation, the increasing assimilation of the previously colonized into the orbit of global capitalism, gets lost in the picture.

Admittedly, the attenuation of nationalism, whatever its cause, is not an unmitigated disaster for the previously colonized. For it makes it possible for indigenous peoples around the world to retrieve their identities, which have been subsumed under the category of the "nation." As the history of colonialism is drawing to an end, and with it the necessity of nationalism as a political project against colonialism, crucial dimensions of global relations that have been neglected in the era of colonialism (and nationalism) come to the fore.[69] Let me hasten to add, however, that it is one thing to address the interests of the local from the perspective of concrete local places, and quite another to proceed from some ready-made postmodern and poststructuralist categories, such as hybridity, and approach the local as concrete instances that serve to exemplify the universal significance of the "post" theory.

In the case of Hong Kong, the two distinct aspects of postcolonialism—as a world situation after colonialism and as an academic discipline—become each other's simulacrum. The reality of Hong Kong as a place of hybridity and impurity furnishes evidence for what postcolonial critics in the United States think postcoloniality is or ought to be—a paradigm beyond nationalism. Once the reality of Hong Kong is seen through the lens of postmodernism and poststructuralism, nothing appears important except the kind of linguistic and cultural hybridity that confirms the claims of postmodernism and poststructuralism. In this way, all those aspects of the postcolonial Hong Kong that shed light on the key elements of postcolonialism as a world situation (e.g., the attenuation of strong values, the depoliticization of public life, and the unsublimated pursuit of economic interests as the most important goal of life) are subsumed under the rubric of the supplementary logic,[70] if not consigned to oblivion altogether.

In making a distinction between postcolonialism as a world situation and as an academic discipline, I do not mean to argue that the former is an unmediated objective existence. I only wish to point out the limitation of postcolonial studies in the U.S. academe and where this limitation fits in with the structure of global capitalism. To be aware of this may not help much in reconstructing local cultures in concrete local places, but it can at least alert us to the danger of turning the local into the simulacrum of a particular trend of the global, be it postmodernism or postcolonialism.

Notes

1 Immanuel Wallerstein, *The Capitalist World-Economy* (Cambridge: Cambridge University Press, 1979), p. 180.

2 Edward Said, *Culture and Imperialism* (London: Chatto & Windus, 1993), p. xii.

3 Statistics are from David Faure, *A Documentary History of Hong Kong Society* (Hong Kong: Hong Kong University Press, 1997), p. 149.

4 Peter Koslowski, "The Ethics of Capitalism," in *Philosophical and Economic Foundations of Capitalism*, ed. Svetozar Pejovich (Lexington, Mass.: Lexington Books, 1983), p. 33.

5 Albert O. Hirschman, *The Passions and the Interests* (Princeton, N.J.: Princeton University Press, 1977), p. 32.

6 Hirschman, *The Passions and the Interests*, p. 9.

7 The Dutch Republic, an example of what Marx calls the "capitalist state par excellence," had a population in the early seventeenth century that had a very high percentage of immigrants. Though many of these immigrants held strong Protestants beliefs, which were instrumental to the development of capitalism at the time, the professions of these immigrants were essentially the same as those in Hong Kong, namely, merchants and traders.

8 It may be appropriate here to say a few words about the so-called merchant ethic, which, according to Yu Ying-shih, parallels the Protestant ethic in the West. Yu argues, or implies, that since Neo-Confucianism possesses features similar to those of the Protestant ethic (e.g., inner-worldly asceticism), China might have developed capitalism on its own if religions in China had been left to follow their own natural course without foreign interference. Even if this is indeed the case, the merchant ethic is (like the Protestant ethic) instrumental to the pursuit of material prosperity, and it cannot make the merchants a class of higher inspirations.

9 Ambrose King, "The Transformation of Confucianism in the Post-Confucian Era: The Emergence of Rationalistic Traditionalism in Hong Kong," in *The Triadic Chord: Confucian Ethics, Industrial East Asia, and Max Weber*, ed. Tu Wei-Ming (Honolulu: Institute of East Asian Philosophies, 1991), p. 216.

10 King, "The Transformation of Confucianism," p. 211.

11 King, "The Transformation of Confucianism," p. 212.

12 Stephen Boyden, Sheelagh Millar, Ken Newcombe, and Beverley O'Neil, *The Ecology of a City and Its People: The Case of Hong Kong*, ed. Stephen Boyden et al. (Canberra: Australian National University Press, 1981), p. 57.

13 Rey Chow, *Ethics after Idealism* (Bloomington: Indiana University Press, 1998), p. 170.

14 Chow, *Ethics after Idealism*, p. 171.

15 Chow, *Ethics after Idealism*, p. 171.

16 Faure, *A Documentary History*, p. 2.

17 Faure, *A Documentary History*, p. 11.

18 By *ideological sublimation* I mean a process through which the sheer economic impulse to profit maximization elevates itself into an ideological aspiration for something else. The practice of the market is transformed in people's minds into what Marx calls the "idealized expressions" of the practice. This ideological sublimation differs from what I shall call substantive sublimation, in that it does not change the object of pursuit. It only changes people's conception of it.

19 In his paper "Justice and the Moral Bounds of Capitalism," Jiwei Ci makes a subtle but important distinction between a weaker and a stronger defense of negative freedom.

"The weaker line of defense suggests, with a touch of modesty, that whatever may be the uses (self-regarding, other-regarding, or whatever) to which people put their negative liberty, it ought to be nobody's business to force them to do otherwise, because, as a matter of moral psychology, one cannot be forced to be good, and, as a matter of (liberal) politics, one should not be forced to do good (i.e., conform to some standard of goodness) beyond being law-abiding. According to this weaker line of defense, then, negative freedom is morally defensible . . . even when what is done with negative freedom is not itself morally defensible in a direct way, i.e., with reference to its content. . . . In contrast to this weaker line of defense, the stronger line of defense is more optimistic, or more ideologically loaded, in that it invites us to believe, if only in a vague or implicit sort of way, that people will actually put negative liberty to uses that themselves have a morally positive quality, or, failing that, that the very act of exercising negative freedom (within the law) has such a value" (Jiwei Ci, paper presented at the School of Social Science, Institute for Advanced Study, Princeton, April 1997).

20 Marx, *The Communist Manifesto*, p. 12.

21 Marx, *The Communist Manifesto*, p. 12.

22 Marx, *The Communist Manifesto*, p. 13.

23 Richard J. Barnet and Ronald E. Muller, *Global Reach: The Power of the Multinational Corporations* (New York: Simon and Schuster, 1974), p. 33.

24 Giorgio Agamben argues that, in consequence of the expansion of the global market, a single planetary petty bourgeoisie is about to replace different social classes. "If we had once again to conceive of the fortunes of humanity in terms of class, then today we would have to say that there are no longer social classes, but just a single planetary petty bourgeoisie, in which all the old social classes are dissolved: The petty bourgeoisie has inherited the world and is the form in which humanity has survived nihilism" (*The Coming Community*, trans. Michael Hardt [Minneapolis: University of Minnesota Press, 1993], p. 62).

25 Arif Dirlik, *After the Revolution: Waking to Global Capitalism* (Hanover, Conn.: Wesleyan University Press, 1994), p. 61.

26 Dirlik, *After the Revolution*, p. 61.

27 Dirlik, *The Postcolonial Aura* (Boulder, Colo.: Westview Press, 1997), p. 191.

28 Dirlik, "Confucius in the Borderlands: Global Capitalism and the Reinvention of Confucianism," *boundary 2* (fall 1995): 238.

29 King, "The Transformation of Confucianism," p. 209–10.

30 A. Y. C. King and P. Man, "The Role of the Small Factory in Economic Development," in *Hong Kong: Economic, Social and Political Studies in Development*, ed. Tzong-biau Ling (New York: M. E. Sharpe, 1979), p. 54.

31 For detailed discussions of this issue, see Dirlik, "Confucius in the Borderlands," pp. 254–71.

32 In this respect, both John Rawls's emphasis on the priority of the "right" over the "good" and Habermas's distinction between the "normative" and the "evaluative" are derivative of the actual features of life in the capitalist market.

33 Michael Walzer, *On Toleration* (New Haven, Conn.: Yale University Press, 1997), pp. 14–19.

34 All faculty members at the universities, for instance, are divided into two racially distinct categories, "locals" and "expatriates." "Locals" refers mainly to the Chinese, regardless of whether they were born and grew up in the region. "Expatriates" refers, primarily though not exclusively, to Westerners. Those who belong to the category of expatriates

enjoy many privileges which locals are not entitled to—for instance, university housing, education of children abroad, free trips to countries of origin, etc.

35 Faure, *A Documentary History*, p. 362.

36 Faure, *A Documentary History*, p. 363.

37 Immanuel Wallerstein, "Capitalism and the World Working Class: Some Premises and Some Issues for Research and Analysis," in *Labor in the World Social Structure*, ed. Immanuel Wallerstein (Beverly Hills, Calif.: Sage Publications, 1983), p. 17.

38 Wallerstein, "Capitalism and the World Working Class," p. 18.

39 Wallerstein, "Capitalism and the World Working Class," p. 18.

40 Saskia Sassen, *The Global City: New York, London, Tokyo* (Princeton, N.J.: Princeton University Press, 1991), p. 302.

41 See William Julius Williams, *The Truly Disadvantaged: The Inner City, the Underclass, and Public Policy* (Chicago: University of Chicago Press, 1987).

42 Wallerstein, *The Capitalist World-Economy*, p. 230.

43 For detailed argument in this regard, see Bill Readings, *University in Ruins* (Cambridge, Mass.: Harvard University Press, 1996), p. 2.

44 In his paper, "Justice and the Moral Bounds of Capitalism," Jiwei Ci makes a distinction between what the market merely allows and what it actively promotes as its own condition of possibility. He emphasizes that there is a difference between, say, moral virtues that, as supererogation, are made "formally" possible by negative autonomy and negative freedom and the actual practices of these moral virtues, which the "very nature of the market makes materially next to impossible in all areas of social life penetrated by the market." He also emphasizes that Kant's categorical imperative—which has been mistaken as the morality of capitalism both by the ideologues of capitalism and by some of the academic Left, postmodernism in particular—has only a partial affinity with capitalism, mostly in terms of its formal universality. "This partial affinity depends, moreover, on Kant's distinction between the sphere of Right and the sphere of virtue, between law and morality. Of these, only the sphere of Right (or law) has a potential affinity with the market, in that, as applied to the sphere of Right and to the market alike, the categorical imperative can translate, or be downgraded, into the formal principle of universal negative freedom (as the obverse of universal reciprocal coercion). It is no accident that those aspects of Kant's ethic that have no such affinity with the market—say, the formulation of the categorical imperative in terms of the Kingdom of Ends, the rejection of hedonism or eudaemonism as an ethical determinant, or indeed the very (formal) unconditionality of the categorical imperative—find no room in the market order."

45 Terry Eagleton, *The Illusions of Postmodernism* (Oxford: Blackwell, 1996), p. 133.

46 Marx, *The Communist Manifesto*, p. 11.

47 Chow, *Ethics after Idealism*, p. 151.

48 Chow, *Ethics after Idealism*, p. 151.

49 Quoted in Chow, *Ethics after Idealism*, p. 173.

50 Chow, *Ethics after Idealism*, p. 151.

51 Dirlik, *The Postcolonial Aura*, p. 15.

52 Dirlik, *The Postcolonial Aura*, p. 16.

53 Dirlik, *The Postcolonial Aura*, p. 72.

54 Dirlik, *The Postcolonial Aura*, p. 72.

55 Chow, *Ethics after Idealism*, p. 153.

56 Chow, *Primitive Passions* (New York: Columbia University Press, 1995), p. 86.

57 Chow, *Ethics after Idealism*, pp. 153–54.

58 Chow, *Ethics after Idealism*, p. 155.

59 Chow, *Ethics after Idealism*, p. 154.

60 Chow, *Ethics after Idealism*, p. 154.

61 Chow, *Ethics after Idealism*, p. 153.

62 Chow, *Ethics after Idealism*, p. xx.

63 Chow thus describes the reversal of the hierarchy of the "self" and the "other": "Toward the end of the twentieth century, as the aftermath of the grand imperialist eras brings about major physical migrations of populations around the globe, it is no longer a question of white people going to the colonies, but rather of formerly colonized peoples settling permanently in their former colonizers' territories. The visible presence of these formerly colonized peoples in the 'first world' leads to violent upheavals in 'Western thought.' The overriding preoccupation among first world intellectuals has now become: how to become 'other'? How to claim to be a minority—to claim to be black, Native American, Hispanic, or Asian, even if one has only 1/64th share of these 'other' origins? In other words, how to 'go native'?" (*Ethics after Idealism*, p. 31).

64 Dirlik, *The Postcolonial Aura*, p. 9.

65 Dirlik, "Looking Backward in the Age of Global Capital," in *In Pursuit of Contemporary East Asian Culture*, ed. Xiaobing Tang and Stephen Snyder (Boulder, Colo.: Westview Press, 1996), p. 196.

66 Ackbar Abbas, *Hong Kong, Culture, and the Politics of Disappearance* (Minneapolis: University of Minnesota Press, 1997), p. 6.

67 Here my argument has to do with the logic of capitalism, not its practice. On the level of practice, capitalism contains many features that are contradictory or irrelevant to its logic, chief among them metaphysical truth and God. This distinction is needed to take account of what Eagleton calls the "political ambivalence" of postmodernism in relation to capitalism. Insofar as "metaphysical truth" and God are still invoked by the ideology of capitalism as the spiritual foundations of the system, the postmodern attacks on these concepts can indeed be seen as politically oppositional to capitalism. Yet if by capitalism we mean not the avowed ideology of the system but its founding philosophy (represented, say, by Locke, Hume, Adam Smith, and part of Kant), and the principles of the free market that fit in with such philosophy, we will realize that the postmodern critique of metaphysical truth serves to remove what is incompatible with the logic of capitalism rather than to change the system in any fundamental way.

68 Eagleton, *Illusions of Postmodernism*, p. 133.

69 See, for instance, Arif Dirlik, "Narrativizing Revolution," *Modern China* 23, no. 4 (1 Oct. 1997): 363–97. Exemplifying an illuminating new way of "narrativizing" the Chinese revolution, it brings to light how the perspective of the local people differed from what has been treated in official historiography as the solely legitimate global perspective of the Chinese Communist Party and the Comintern.

70 Rey Chow, for instance, subsumes the phenomenon of unsublimated pursuit for material prosperity in Hong Kong under the rubric of deconstruction and equates it with "femininity" as one of the underprivileged signifiers in the paradigm of phallogocentrism. For details, see her *Ethics after Idealism*, pp. 170–73.

ii cultural politics

liu kang

5   Popular Culture and the Culture of the
Masses in Contemporary China

Popular culture is perhaps the best place to test the claim that "(capitalist) globalization is now an accepted reality," as the new world-space of cultural production and representation is inhabited by images and goods pertaining to the everyday life of the world population, that is, by images and goods that are manufactured by multinational corporations and circulated in a global market. China, the emergent economic giant of the 1990s, has caught on to the latest global cultural production and marketing trends at an astonishing pace. "Get on-line!" for instance, is a popular catchphrase among the millions of Chinese whiz kids who use the Internet. Such a rapid change defies the imagination not only of its Western analysts but also of die-hard Chinese ideologues of Western-style modernization and liberal democracy who were exiled overseas in the aftermath of the 1989 Tiananmen event and whose goals are purportedly nothing less than a prosperous, market-oriented economy and social plurality. Journalists, the proper "postmodern culture workers," on the other hand, have no time to ponder the probability of China's transformation. Two examples may help illustrate both the extent to which China is now assimilated into the global popular culture market and the character of its native and local peculiarities and legacies.

The first example, headlined "Wind of Christmas Sweeping Shanghai: Money Oriented," is based on a Reuters news report and comes from the 16 December 1996 issue of *China News Digest*, an Internet publication:

> Holiday commercial promotions in Shanghai department stores started earlier than ever this year, expecting a major kick-off with Christmas shopping season. . . . The stores, especially the joint-venture ones, are working hard to promote the idea of Christmas as a gift-sharing holiday among the young people in their 20s. Christmas decorations, trees, and cards can be seen everywhere in the stores. Some stores give out a ten percent gift certificate for every 500 yuan spent in the store to encourage spending. One young salesman told the reporter that he planned to spend 500 yuan on Christmas gifts and cards for friends. According to him, "we young people in Shanghai like to copy Western habits." The traditional holiday shopping season in China is during January and February before the Chinese New Year, which is still the case to most old people in Shanghai. Some stores reported a drastic rise in sales, ranging from 50–100% in December as compared with the sales volume in November, with Christmas as the contributing factor. However, as one salesman said, "There is no religious feeling. It is just commercial." [1]

Except for the reference to the Chinese New Year, which adds local flavor, the report is nearly identical to *U.S. News and World Report*'s account of the 1996 Christmas season in America. "Imagine a purer, less commercial, more spiritual Christmas," we are told, "but don't call it history." It is "more a product of our cultural imagination than of historical fact." Although many Americans now complain that Christmas has become too commercial (about 48 percent polled by *U.S. News and World Report* say gift giving detracts from the religious celebration), the holiday is still in essence "a grand festival of consumption." [2]

Amid the commercial blitz raging throughout China, there are not many different stories to tell, yet the ways in which these stories are told vary considerably. The second example I will cite is taken from Chinese reportage literature, a nonfiction genre popular in China since the 1930s known for its poignant exposure of social ills and its penchant for inciting political sentiment. " 'Armchairs' of the Summer Palace" relates the story of the construction of Nandaihe, a new beach resort, in the 1990s. The new resort is located next to Beidaihe, the well-known beach resort near Beijing that has served as the virtual summer palace for China's top political leaders since Mao's days, a place where many historically significant meetings that have changed China's course have been held. The new resort capitalizes on the political fame of its neighbor as it rushes to gain the advantage in the "third industry," namely, the service, sales, entertainment, and tourist industries. For the authors of this piece, and perhaps for the builders of the new resort as well, the construction of a tourist attraction is as much a noble political task as it is a great commercial adventure, and hence, we are led to see the scene as imbued with a passion and a zeal that is matched only by the revolutionary wars of Mao's era, in which military metaphors dominated every aspect of Chinese discourse and the cultural imaginary, from harvesting rice crops to giving birth:

> The Funing County Party Committee assigned Vice Party Secretary Hou, Vice County Governor Chen, and Director of the County Tourism Bureau Nie to be in charge of the construction project. Because of Secretary Hou's authority and popularity throughout the county, he coordinated efforts and ironed out troubles, making way for the smooth daily progress of the construction. Thus, a collective of passionate fighting spirit was formed. Confronting all kinds of interferences, they resolutely fought on, day and night, at the construction site. Yes, it's a battle, it's determination and will, it's pathos, it's rhythm and tempo, and it's dedication and adventurousness — there was nothing but the fiercest fighting on the battleground.[3]

The above passages report real events, and yet the texture of their discourse bears a certain effect of unreality, a sense of displacement or disjuncture, caused not so much by the events reported as by the discourse used in the reporting. When reading the first passage, one has the feeling that Christmas Eve in Shanghai in 1996 is no different from Christmas Eve in New York City; both cities are ablaze with the same desires and anxieties of the shopping spree. Its decontextualized composition results in a postmodern leveling off of differences. The second passage, in its overall seriousness, cannot be construed as a parody/travesty of bygone revolutionary discourse but must be grasped instead as something radically *other* than itself: the collective "fighting spirit" of Mao's era is transposed into an altogether unfamiliar locus whereby global capital celebrates its success hand-in-hand with the revolutionary soldiers-turned-managers.

To call this postmodern would probably not be off the mark. It seems certain that in China's popular culture arena, the infiltration of global cultural production (read Western capitalist commercial culture) is accelerated by historical reappropriations and displacements of older structures in the service of a qualitatively very different situation. However, the hybridity of those reappropriated, displaced, and heterogeneous segments that constitute the popular culture scene in China raises serious questions about the critical concepts and interpretive strategies available to us now. In what follows, I intend to address the correlation between and the contradictions in the practices and theories of commercial popular culture and the revolutionary culture of the masses. I begin by underscoring the political nature of popular culture and its interpretation. This is not simply to state the obvious once again; I want to argue that the very meaning of politics has undergone significant metamorphoses in this case. It is the practical and theoretical legacy of *qunzhong wenyi* (the culture of the masses) that needs to be reexamined as the radical *other* of China's popular culture. *Qunzhong wenyi*, a legacy of the revolutionary past and an essential component of the revolutionary hegemony, cannot be dismissed as merely residual and irrelevant today. Its aesthetic forms and structures are deeply ingrained in the Chinese cultural imaginary, constituting a significant dimension in the contradiction-ridden cultural arena. To understand this vibrant legacy in China today, one may view it against a complex set of historical practices and conceptual codes that addresses issues of both revolution and culture. I refer specifically to two critical models, namely the Frankfurt school's theory of mass culture and Gramsci's concept of hegemony. Furthermore, as the world-system of capitalism and globalization has inevitably shaped the reality of the world, at least in the realm of popular culture, postmodernity as a style of culture seems to have a universal appeal. Yet, to describe China's culture as postmodern tells only a half-truth, for the radical *other* of the postmodern global imaginary, namely the local, cannot be left unacknowledged. The local, as opposed to the global, in the present context may first refer to the geopolitical and cultural specificities of China, but it then may have to be narrowed to the more specific, to the more concrete social practices of particular locations and temporalities within China. Ultimately, the global postmodern has to return to the most fundamental question of the everyday. The everyday is not only both global and local (in the sense that it must encompass different temporalities, subjectivities, spaces, and public spheres); it may also serve as a site that unravels and critiques the contradictions and fallacies of the age. The following account of the contradictions in China's popular culture is by no means comprehensive; it only suggests the complexities of the overall contradictions in China's modernization process during the recent past.

The Politics of Popular Culture in China Today

One can discuss politics in the present Chinese context from at least three perspectives: (1) from the classical perspective of political economy; (2) from the perspective that the political and ideological struggles that have taken place in the cultural arena are part and parcel of Chinese tradition; and (3) from the perspective that politics today is a new configuration that has yet to be worked out—a "postpolitics" of some sort—which may address China's changing political functions and structures. Politics in the first two senses, however, is hardly straightforward. In an article entitled "China's Challenge to the United States and to the Earth," Lester Brown and Christopher Flavin claim that "as [China's] population of 1.2 billion people moves into modern houses, buys cars, refrigerators, and televisions, and shifts to a meat-based diet, the entire world will feel the effects."[4] The rapid marketization of the economy, bolstered by the enormous absorption of foreign investment and China's linking with the capitalist world-system (or, in Chinese idiom, *yu guoji jiegui* [joining the international track]), has significantly transformed Chinese social life. Its effect can be felt mostly at the level of everyday life, as Western consumer culture, or popular culture, has infiltrated the world's largest marketplace.

The effect of marketization on China's politics cannot be underestimated, especially at the grassroots level and in everyday life. However, China's politics, as portrayed by the mainstream Western media in headline news, has always assumed the familiar scenario of age-old ideological and political dissent and suppression. Such cold war horror stories of communist persecution and human rights violations are validated and substantiated by academic China specialists and native informants/dissidents, and are then circulated and finally regurgitated at the negotiation table, where officials from the U.S. State Department or the U.S. Department of Commerce and their Chinese counterparts use such tales as bargaining chips in matters such as (de)linking the trade with China from human rights issues. It becomes clear that tales of China's political repression and terror have more to do with the political, ideological, and commercial objectives of the Western media (and the national interests that lurk behind) than with what is really happening in China today. Yet, notwithstanding the very real political repression and human rights violations that *do* occur daily in China and that affect its cultural arena and intellectuals, politics now does assume a different function and meaning, which China specialists and the Western media fail to comprehend.

A different model is needed in order to analyze the political mechanism of manipulation, negotiation, diversion, and reconciliation. Chinese society is now replete with tensions and contradictions as a result of its modernization and marketization programs. It is well known that the phrase "socialism with Chinese characteristics" designates China's peculiar situation of the coexistence of incommensurable forces, of a market-oriented economy and a bureaucracy founded on the past command economy and Maoist ideology. The policy of the post-Mao leadership, headed by Deng Xiaoping, was simply to ban any public debate about issues of political ideology and revolutionary legacy. But silence can hardly dispel the specters of the past that are still very much alive, insofar as the bureaucratic institutions, and the ideological state apparatuses, still hold power. Consequently, post-Mao Chinese leadership has been entrenched in ideological crises ever since "reform and opening-up" campaigns were launched.[5]

In the mid-1990s, however, as the political transition from the post-Mao to the post-Deng eras has gotten well under way, the so-called third generation of post-Deng leaders, headed by Jiang Zemin, has gradually shifted its strategies to focus on the ideological and cultural arenas. By allowing and encouraging China's indigenous popular-culture products, such as state-sponsored MTV, karaoke concerts, TV soap operas, and kung fu fiction, to prosper and to compete with Western commercial popular culture, the government has effectively ameliorated the tension and conflicts that arise between an increasing mass demand and ideological control. Another powerful strategy is to invoke nationalism. This is achieved either by a revival of Confucian values and ethics, which are said to be beneficial to an East Asian model of modernization, or by a renewed call for patriotism that goes out whenever the Western powers, alarmed by China's rapid economic growth and its increased assertiveness in international affairs, begin to clamor for a new containment strategy in the face of the "Chinese threat." In official announcements and ceremonies, such as the Chinese Communist Party (CCP) 14th Central Committee's 6th Plenum Resolution on Socialist Spiritual Civilization, or the celebration of the sixtieth anniversary of the Long March, ideological slogans about Marxism and socialism still appear,[6] but the political agenda in cultural spheres has been shifted decidedly away from idealistic propaganda and toward pragmatic objectives for maintaining order and stability, or the status quo. With the death of Deng Xiaoping, the early days of his rule, when the ideological state apparatuses still had the power to sanctify all the pragmatic measures of reform in economic quarters, have quickly become a memory.

A kind of "postpolitics," with its ideological and idealistic core virtually discarded, is in order now. Chen Xiaoming, a Chinese postmodern critic, defines postpolitics in contemporary Chinese film as a condition in which "everything is political and nothing is political at one and the same time. Politics is everywhere, and yet it subverts itself at any moment."[7] It is no coincidence that Jiang Zemin, the CCP general secretary, when addressing the 6th National Congress of the Chinese Writers and Artists Association, made a comment on politics that is remarkably similar to Chen Xiaoming's: "Although we no longer hold that the arts are subject to politics, . . . as Comrade Deng Xiaoping says, 'We of course do not mean to say that politics and arts are separable. Arts and literature cannot be separated from politics.' Politics exists in concrete social life and in the minds and feelings of our culture workers."[8]

The similarity lies primarily in the ambiguity and slippage of the concept of politics itself. Chen Xiaoming sees postpolitics as a "symbolic act" and a largely subversive parody/travesty of the old revolutionary discourse, accomplished by ambiguously displacing political and aesthetic images. Jiang Zemin, on the other hand, while acknowledging the wisdom of relinquishing the political subjugation and policing of all cultural activities, is less ambiguous about the function of cultural politics under the current conditions of "Western economic and technological pressures and ideological penetrations."[9] Jiang, in fact, hardly worries about bourgeois liberalism and humanism, which were widely espoused by intellectuals in the 1980s. Western-style liberal humanism, being an old foe of the "anti–spiritual pollution" campaigns of 1983 and 1989, has now largely lost its political relevance as an oppositional rallying cry. The rise of commercial popular culture and the government's decree to ban political and ideological discussions have doubly undermined the status and credibility of the intellectual elite, who self-consciously served, in the heyday of the "Great Culture Debates" in the 1980s, as China's "social conscience" and as representatives of political reform. Of course, consumerism itself is discreetly tolerated, if not publicly encouraged, by the authorities to distract the public from political debates. In the 1990s, it is no longer a curious phenomenon that the so-called oppositional intellectual elite joins hands with the government in denouncing the "vulgarization" of culture and the "pollution and corruption of the young mind" by popular culture products. In the meantime, the liberal elite and the government are courting, in their different ways, multinational capitalism's "high" values of the global cultural imaginary, either new Confucianism or new versions of liberal humanism.[10]

Popular culture has become a new battleground—one bombarded by heavy artillery. But the battles are fought largely as symbolic acts to achieve maximum theatrical effect. Wang Shuo, arguably the most popular writer of fiction, film, and TV soap operas in China today, has staged commercial and political controversies about his works and about himself both inside and outside China. "The mocking tone and racy themes of 'hooligan literature' by author Wang Shuo have pushed the censor's limits and made him hugely popular," an Associated Press reporter wrote after a fall 1996 controversy over the author's economic dealings and his new TV scripts.[11] The Chinese liberal elite, who invoke either the Frankfurt school notion of reification or Confucian moral didacticism, also deplore Wang Shuo's lack of idealism and ethics. Writers and critics who show sympathy toward Wang Shuo and popular culture trends in general are labeled "amoral opportunists." Some critics, such as Zhang Yiwu and Chen Xiaoming, have alluded to postmodern and postcolonial theories in their writings and are therefore sharply rebuffed, along with their imported theories of postmodernism, by the guardians of high cultural values and idealism.[12] Yet, however intensely dramatic, the politics in China's popular culture arena does seem to bear certain postmodern features of decenteredness and indeterminacy, as various political and ideological forces and persuasions engage in a multidirectional war of positions with no ultimate authority or repercussions (the fact that Wang Shuo's fame has increased as a result of his offense to the government attests to the altered rules of the political game). "It all boils down to power struggles," declared a Chinese critic, "power struggles for obtaining symbolic capital."[13] In other words, the debates and controversies are now translated into fights for the ownership of discourse (zhengduo huayu quan) in the cultural and intellectual market. Postpolitics in the present context, according to Chinese critics, is a power struggle without revolutionary ideology as the central locus. It resembles a politics in the Foucauldian sense of having multiple and plural technologies of domination and control such as those that exist in advanced capitalist societies.

But it would be a gross overstatement to say that China has now fully merged with the world-system and thus that its cultural arena has become predominantly postmodern. What is left out in such sweepingly global and globalizing accounts is nothing less than China's own traditions and legacies. In the realm of popular culture, the revolutionary practice and theory of the "culture of the masses" have by no means disappeared. This indigenous tradition has been the cultural dominant, to borrow Raymond Williams's distinction of cultural layers, for nearly half a century. It is still alive and flourishing in terms of its forms, structures, and functions, not to mention its institutions, which remain largely in place. It is true that, on the one hand, the ideological core of revolution has ineluctably lost its grip on the Chinese population and become inexorably "residual."[14] But, on the other hand, deeply embedded in the Chinese political unconscious, revolutionary hegemony still plays a significant role in the overdetermined structural relationships, particularly at discursive and symbolic levels, by which the advocates and opponents of the revolutionary tradition have wrestled to articulate their positions vis-à-vis the revolutionary hegemony. Yet the crucial question remains: How do we interpret these complex layers and modes of cultural production and reproduction that are filled with tension and contradictions?

The Culture of the Masses: The Revolutionary Legacy and Its New Forms

In China today, few, except perhaps a small number of literary historians, are interested in the culture of the masses. Such an interest is, first, politically incorrect: Smacking of Maoist radicalism, the invocation of qunzhong wenyi is suspicious of recalling (if not exorcising) the specters of the Cultural Revolution. But the masses, or China's vast populace, have simply ignored the academic high fashion of political correctness by creatively embracing and transforming the revolutionary tradition and its national and nativist forms and structures. Here, I am referring not only to the popularity of Mao as a new folk icon in today's popular myths and superstitions among Chinese rural populations (and middle-aged or older lower-class urban residents). Insofar as popular culture is predominantly an urban youth cultural phenomenon, it is more instructive to see how, in the contemporary popular culture scene, creativity and imagination emanate from the old collective forms and structures.

Karaoke and the dance party, for instance, are two imported forms of modern popular entertainment—the former being imported from Japan and the latter from Western Europe and Soviet Russia—that were popular in Shanghai during the 1920s and in Yanan during the 1940s. Karaoke, or public "singalong," is a collective form of entertainment that is enjoyed throughout China today. Its collectivity has quickly assumed the social function of crossing the boundaries of official (*guanfang*)/unofficial (*minjian*), and public/private. Not only do teenagers, young lovers, and business partners entertain themselves at karaoke bars; it is also customary nowadays for local party committees (which are still the most important power brokers in China's social organizations), trade unions, women's unions, Communist Youth League groups, et cetera, to organize official or semi-official karaoke contests and concerts as holiday celebrations or special occasions.

Dance is another popular activity that merits thorough analysis, though the present essay cannot adequately address it here. Ballroom dance originated in the European aristocracy and became popular in bourgeois salons because of its elegant style and formalities. In China today, it has become perhaps the favorite leisure activity among ordinary citizens from diverse backgrounds: For the middle-aged and retired (the latter forming the morning teams that often number in the tens and hundreds), dancing at public parks, playgrounds, and other sports facilities is the best physical exercise, rivaled only by the classical martial arts form of *taijiquan* (*tai-chi*). Ballroom dance parties and sumptuous banquets often follow government-sponsored events, such as certain local and national holiday celebrations, school commencements, and the like, and promote comradeship, good-fellowship, and equality. In addition, these dance parties provide a form of light exercise, both aiding in digestion and encouraging fitness. Through dance parties, then, fun and romance are shared as a communal and collective experience. (However, some would link the increase in extramarital affairs, the divorce rate, and sex scandals to dance parties.)

The history of ballroom dance in China is ambiguous. It can be traced back to the Yan'an years of revolution in the 1940s. The communists, including Mao Zedong and Zhou Enlai, were avid Soviet-style ballroom dancers in Yan'an. After the revolution, the tradition continued in the cities and was made popular among the masses, mostly among young factory workers and college students. The large dance parties, organized by the Communist Youth League in the 1950s and early 1960s, always emphasized the collective spirit of the revolutionary years. During the Cultural Revolution, however, ballroom dances were replaced by large group dances that displayed loyalty to the Great Leader, and European and Soviet music that had accompanied the earlier dance parties disappeared altogether. These "loyalty dances" were eventually performed to the accompaniment of Yan'an folk dances called *yangge*, or rice-sprout songs, which were played by peasants to celebrate labor and the harvest. In addition to the revolutionary tradition, there is, of course, another side to the story of the dance party. When held in the dimly lit European-style pubs in Shanghai and accompanied by live dance bands, the well-dressed but by now gray-haired couples, long-retired employees of Western firms established in the 1940s, could indulge in nostalgia for the bygone days of Shanghai's colonial glory and decadence. Shanghai is the "authentic origin" of China's Western-style cultural life, and even Yan'an revolutionaries such as Mao could not help but submit to the alluring temptations of this style, which was embodied by none other than his mistress-turned-wife, Jiang Qing, who was a third-rate film star in Shanghai during the 1930s. Jiang Qing and other women like her, on arriving in Yan'an, the Holy Land of revolution, quickly found that Western bourgeois styles and pastimes such as ballroom dance could be readily modified and incorporated into the revolutionary culture, in the name of internationalism, following the Soviet models.

Revolution transformed the Chinese appropriation of Western bourgeois and aristocratic culture into popular forms but failed to resolve the historical ambiguities and contradictions. In the 1990s, collective and public forms of entertainment, such as karaoke and dance parties, have been rejuvenated. Although the new experience is generally devoid of any revolutionary spirit and is largely nurtured in the cultural ambience of consumerism, collectivity, at least as a formal feature, still imparts a cohesiveness to the population. To understand the persistence of the collective spirit not merely as a residual force but as something dynamic in China today, notwithstanding all the contradictions it entails, it is necessary to go back to the historical formation of the practice and theory of the culture of the masses.

Culture has been the core of the Chinese Revolution, which started in urban centers such as Shanghai and Beijing. Rather than being called forth by a powerful proletariat prompted by capitalist economic crises, as prescribed by the classical Marxist theory of revolution, the Chinese Revolution was first promulgated by the radical intelligentsia of the May Fourth period (1919–1927), who were inspired by Western ideas and by Marxism in particular. But the failure of communist urban insurgencies necessitated a decisive strategic shift from the cities to the rural areas as the site of revolution and resistance, and the key issue confronting the revolution, as Arif Dirlik points out, was how to translate Marxism, an urban-centered and Eurocentric theory of revolution, into native and vernacular strategies for everyday practice.[15] Drawing on Dirlik's indispensable insights into Mao's sinification or vernacularization of Marxism, I have further observed that central to Mao's project was an *aesthetic* concept of "national form": Mao's solution was to endow urban, cosmopolitan, and foreign thought—classical Marxism—with a national form bearing primarily aesthetic and artistic features.[16] In Mao's view, the "sinification of Marxism" entailed a replacement of "foreign stereotypes," "vacuous and abstract tunes," and "dogmatism" with "the refreshing, lively Chinese styles and tunes that are palatable to the tastes and ears of the common folks of China."[17] Mao's rhetoric about arts was not merely metaphorical. It can be argued that cultural and aesthetic forms and their transformation lay at the heart of Mao Zedong's revolutionary vision, in which the establishment of revolutionary hegemony was given the highest priority. In other words, the question of cultural and aesthetic formation (national form) was elevated to the center of Mao's revolutionary strategy for creating a Chinese Marxism that would instill in the peasants a revolutionary consciousness and mobilize them in the revolutionary struggle.

The concept of the culture of the masses was first conceived by Qu Qiubai, an early leader of the CCP and China's leading Marxist literary theorist. A major figure in the post–May Fourth urban New Culture Movement, which paved the way for the Chinese Communist Revolution, Qu sharply critiqued the Europeanizing and bourgeois tendencies of the May Fourth Movement. In the wake of the failed urban proletarian insurrections, for which he was directly responsible, Qu believed that the urban Marxist intellectuals and the peasantry would have to be brought together to form one revolutionary force. To accomplish this, Qu proposed to wage a "mass cultural revolution" (*dazhong wenhua geming*) as "the concrete task of seeking the leadership in cultural revolution."[18] After being ousted from the CCP leadership in 1931 as a result of the debacle of the urban communist uprisings, Qu first devoted his energy in Shanghai to the theoretical study of Marxism and, together with his closest friend, Lu Xun, China's modern literary giant, to the urban proletarian literary movement. Then, from 1933 to 1934, Qu Qiubai went to Jiangxi, the impoverished, backward, rural revolutionary base-area, where he launched the famous rural cultural revolution and education movement. The main objective of this movement was to create a popular national vernacular language by drawing on traditional aesthetic forms and literary discourses, such as the folk arts of storytelling, puppet theater, folklore, local operas, et cetera, which had been excluded from the canon of the national cultural tradition by the ruling classes and the aristocratic elite.[19]

During the Yan'an years of the 1940s, Mao finally set up the culture of the masses as an integral component of the Chinese Revolution and of Chinese Marxism. "Revolutionary culture is a powerful revolutionary weapon for the broad masses of the people," Mao proclaimed. "It prepares the ground ideologically before the revolution comes and is an important, indeed essential, fighting front in the general revolutionary front during the revolution."[20] "Revolutionary culture," or the "culture of the masses," was further codified in Mao's *Talks at the Yan'an Conference on Literature and Art* (1942). This canonical text defined the audience and subject matter of cultural representation as essentially the peasant population, while urban intellectuals and their pioneering work in the revolutionary hegemony were downgraded and even harshly denigrated. Consequently, the legacy of the urban cultural revolution, an essential component of the Chinese Revolution, became a negative element in Mao's new version of the culture of the masses, which was grounded on dichotomies between the rural masses and the urban bourgeois or petit-bourgeois intellectuals. Urban intellectuals were subjected to endless "thought reform" and "remolding" after the publication of the *Yan'an Talks*. After the CCP's seizure of state power, urban and cosmopolitan social reconstruction became the central task of the revolution. However, contrary to Mao's numerous promises and strategic blueprints for building a "new democratic culture," whereby a pluralistic amalgamation of diverse cultural forms would constitute a new social space or hegemony, Mao reasserted, and increasingly intensified, an instrumentalist and manipulative cultural policy that stifled, rather than encouraged, cultural diversity and plurality. Under these circumstances, the crude peasant and native folk cultural forms were valorized and elevated to the apex of revolutionary romanticism and revolutionary realism, and urban, cosmopolitan literary and aesthetic discourses, forms, and structures were subjected to incessant assaults as bourgeois, imperialist, and colonialist cultural remnants.

The Great Proletarian Cultural Revolution (1966–1976) was a paradoxical culmination of the Maoist populist mass democracy and mass culture movement and of widespread political repression and terrorism. On the one hand, one witnessed a collective, carnivalesque atmosphere of singing and dancing. Hundreds of millions of people of all ages danced loyalty dances to the Great Leader in public squares daily during the Cultural Revolution, and it is this atmosphere that is curiously recaptured in the present-day ballroom dances held in public parks and streets and in the karaoke parties and contests. But in "serious" representations of the era, this festive mood has all but disappeared, except in absolutely negative terms. Take, for example, the film *Blue Kite* (1993), directed by Tian Zhuangzhuang, a Fifth Generation director whose credits also include such international festival films as *Horse Thief*. The film's dominant metaphor is a solitary blue kite flying languidly against a gloomy sky, portraying symbolically the sullen banality and horror of everyday life, as viewed and narrated by the child protagonist. Even the more upbeat comedy *Yangguang canlan de rizi*, adapted from Wang Shuo's novel and directed by Jiang Wen, a much younger, Sixth Generation filmmaker, had to underplay its negative message in order to win Taiwan's Film Festival Awards.[21] The movie recaptures the libidinous impulses and merrymaking of a group of carefree adolescents and juvenile delinquents during the Cultural Revolution. But rather than translating the Chinese title more literally, as *Bright Sunny Days*, which would have been faithful to the texture of the film, the producers translated the title as *In the Heat of the Sun*, alluding obviously to the recent Oscar-winning Russian film *Burnt by the Sun*, which portrays Stalin's reign of terror through the eyes of a schoolboy. (It is no coincidence that a similar narrative perspective—of an innocent, docile child—is used by Tian Zhuangzhuang in *Blue Kite*.) The amusing experiences of the teenage protagonists in Jiang Wen's film become subtly transfigured in the English title into a suggestion of torment under the blazing heat of the sun.

The darker, more tragic aspects of the era, on the other hand, were also represented by the endless spectacles of parades, mass rallies, and presentations of the eight model revolutionary operas devised by Jiang Qing, the so-called great banner holder of the literary revolution. These revolutionary operas, which blended the styles and structures of traditional Peking opera with the European high-cultural forms of ballet and the symphony orchestra, were at once burlesquely avant-garde and anachronistically neoclassical. These contradictory features were well demonstrated in the recent restagings of these operas both in China and overseas. During a 1996 North American tour, the China Central Ballet repeatedly performed *The Red Detachment of Women* as its grand finale, which caused postmodern audiences in Los Angeles and New York to marvel at the opera's innovative multipositionality and hybridity, in which revolutionary ideologies, exotic nativist music and dances of the Li ethnic minority on Hainan Island, and high European styles and modalities coalesce in a neo-Wagnerian *Gesamtkunstwerk*. But the political references, embodied in the rigidly designated and stylized neoclassical types, which were once deeply ingrained in the social consciousness and practice of everyday life, have been almost completely effaced in the recent restagings of these operas for profit. However, their political rancor and deconstructive predilection can hardly be concealed or exonerated, even though the present entertainment industry may indeed be able to customize them so as to satisfy today's voracious market demand for cultural diversity. Above all, the contradictions shown in today's commercial popular culture have long been embedded in earlier forms of the culture of the masses and have only become more intensified at the present historical conjuncture.

The Culture Industry and Hegemony: Critical Models Revisited

To account for the transformations, as well as the persistence, of the revolutionary legacy of the culture of the masses, some methodological and epistemological difficulties have first to be considered. The critical models of the Frankfurt school's theory of culture industry and of Gramscian hegemony remain powerful despite the general tendency to discredit Marxism throughout the world. As capitalist globalization in the post–cold war era claims the end of history with self-complacency and self-assurance, the assumptions that Adorno made about the durability of modern capitalism seem more relevant than ever. The secret of the self-regeneration of capitalism, according to the Frankfurt school, rests on affluence and consumerism, and on effective forms of social control, which are imposed by the combined forces of state and civil society. The Gramscian notion of hegemony, on the other hand, offers a broader spectrum of spices and a more refined assortment of ingredients in the intellectual (and popular) kitchens of cultural diversity and multiculturalism. But the strategies of nonsystematic, nontotalizing post-Marxism, of micropolitics, identity politics, or politics of difference, are viable only by way of a double displacement of Gramsci's fundamental principles. First, Gramsci's tactic of socialist revolution, the core of his theoretical thinking, is displaced in much of contemporary cultural studies, which is obsessed with *discourses* on gender, race, and ethnicity, by issues related primarily to language and sexuality. Second, Gramsci's notion of the interregnum is now taken for granted, not as a transitional historical interlude but as a condition of existence with no foreseeable future of fundamental transformation, thus deferring or postponing indefinitely the agenda of social change.

However, it would be misleading to presume that popular culture in China falls seamlessly under the hegemony of global capitalism's cultural imaginary. As I have tried to demonstrate in this essay, in the domain of popular culture, the revolutionary legacy of the culture of the masses, together with the legacy of China's own folk traditions and customs, constitutes a distinctively different site and space, one whose position in the global geopolitical order or world-system has yet to be fully worked out. The dilemma of critical models of popular culture within the Western context is further complicated by China's legacies.

In view of China's rapid development as a society of affluence and commercialism, which is manifested in commercial popular cultural productions, Adorno's observation about the mechanism of capitalism at work in mass culture is probably closest to the truth: "The real secret of success . . . is the mere reflection of what one pays in the market for the product. The consumer is really worshipping the money that he himself has paid for the ticket to the Toscanini concert." [22] This classical concept of reification or commodity fetishism needs little qualification when used to describe what happens in China's popular culture market and, indeed, in the social consciousness of the country today, where money and capital were once denounced and nearly abolished during the height of the Cultural Revolution. One could argue, too, that reification occurs precisely in the formation of the dominant ideology as "false consciousness," which, ironically, in China's case, is nothing less than Deng Xiaoping's pragmatic "socialism with Chinese characteristics." "To get rich is glorious," Deng declared. In the wake of his death, his predecessors have been wrestling with the quite unpleasant, but compelling, problems of his legacy: the mounting tension and contradictions between the more affluent coastal urban areas and the still-impoverished vast rural hinterland; the widening economic and social gaps among the working class, the poor peasants, and the newly rich; and the rising gender and ethnic inequalities and conflicts.

Having in mind the historic dialectic of contemporary China in terms of both its rapid modernization and its social problems, one may better understand the curious twists and turns in the ideological formations at issue here. While Adorno sees deceptive individuality manufactured by a standardized process of production as the ideological hallmark of the culture industry, Chinese ideology valorizes the *collective*, rather than the individual, as the very locus of material affluence and prosperity. If, following Adorno's logic of argument but modifying his cultural elitism, there is a utopian moment to be recuperated in the reified capitalist mass culture, it would be, as Fredric Jameson puts it, a cultural production that "can draw on the collective experience of marginal pockets of the social life of the world-system, black literature and blues, British working-class rock, women's literature, . . . the literature of the Third World." [23] But Jameson immediately qualifies such a utopian cultural production by dictating that it "is possible only to the degree to which these forms of collective life or collective solidarity have not yet been fully penetrated by the market and by the commodity system." [24] However, as Jameson has repeatedly argued about the postmodern late capitalism and globalization that colonizes the last uncontaminated cultural experiences of the Third World, as well as the realms of the unconscious and the aesthetic, such a utopian possibility has become exceedingly remote.

But what if the *collective* experience itself, as the Chinese case indicates, is fully consistent with the logic of capitalism? What would happen when a collective, or, indeed, a *national*, will sets itself squarely on a trajectory toward a capitalist market and commodity system? In its lived experience of the regime's ideology of market socialism, with all its contradictoriness and inconsistencies, the collectivity may actually legitimize the current moves of the regime. But such an ideological legitimation cannot guarantee any coherence between market and socialism; rather, it only reveals the deep-seated problems inherent in China's course of revolution and modernity.

Mao's legacy was inherited and at the same time metamorphosed by Deng. The promises and failures of Mao, however, cannot be adequately comprehended without looking at his complex historical endeavor of creating an alternative modernity through political, ideological, and cultural revolutions. In this respect, the Gramscian model of hegemony can be very useful. I have discussed elsewhere the correlation of hegemony and cultural revolution by comparing Gramsci and the Chinese Marxists, from Qu Qiubai to Mao and Hu Feng.[25] Suffice it to say that the Chinese Revolution greatly resembles Gramsci's vision, especially in terms of constructing a socialist hegemony or a leadership in cultural spheres. The Chinese experience in both the revolutionary and postrevolutionary periods, on the other hand, problematizes hegemony and cultural revolution as strategies to oppose capitalist modernity or globalization.

An important lesson to learn in the present context of popular culture is how to rethink a cultural space in a postrevolutionary society, which is characterized by plurality and diversity of forms, structures, and institutions, rather than by monolithic state control and manipulation. What Gramsci envisioned in the fascist prison is *not* the bourgeois civil society in the advanced capitalist West as such, but a visionary and, indeed, utopian future of socialism, whereby the democratic civil society and the state interpenetrate and are interdependent. Gramsci remained ambivalent and often contradictory on the actual formation of such a future state, where the relationship between civil society and the revolutionary party and state is of central importance.

But in Mao's valorization of the rural, nativist, and national-popular culture of the masses, the urban culture was viewed as exclusively bourgeois and had to be completely rejected and transcended by incessant cultural revolutions. Mao adopted a hegemonic strategy that combined coercion and manipulation by the state with gaining the broadest consent of the masses through ideological self-study and thought reform. Mao's hegemony proved to be enormously effective during most of his reign, despite the fact that these coercive, manipulative, and instrumentalizing measures increasingly dominated China's cultural arena, and during the Cultural Revolution, the masses were largely manipulated by Mao and his radical cohorts, and the situation degenerated into a virtual reign of mob terror.

During the Cultural Revolution, the subaltern classes, or "the workers and poor peasants," in Mao's parlance, were mobilized precisely by the tactics and strategies that Gramsci and Mao envisioned. There were many examples of the flexible "wars of position," such as the Red Guards assaulting state cultural institutions and establishments. And there was no lack of subversive multipositionalities, such as the so-called worker-peasant-soldier college students who switched roles with professors and university administrators to educate, administer, and transform so-called bourgeois educational institutions. In literary discourse and the arts, discursive hybridities were glorified as the best accomplishments of the subaltern classes, who became the masters of experimental plays, poetry, dance, and painting, all of which blended native and ethnic arts, rural folklore, the European high-art forms of ballet, symphony, piano concerto, and oil painting, and the Stalinist neoclassical styles of pomposity and pretentiousness.

Again, these concrete, historical practices were built into the structures of the culture of the masses, giving rise to contradictory impulses and orientations. Mao's hegemony of the culture of the masses, however, always valorized culture and cultural revolution in his vision of an alternative modernity. When Mao's repressive hand was in firm control, these contradictions were overshadowed by the overarching theme of class struggle. But during Deng's era of reform, a Pandora's box was opened. Deng's socialism with Chinese characteristics bears all the contradictions of Mao's vision of alternative modernity, except for Mao's emphases on class struggle and cultural revolution. Hence, the contradictions inherent in Mao's hegemony of the culture of the masses exploded and sank into the newly risen commercial popular culture in Deng's market-driven economic reform and modernization campaigns. The question we must now ask is: What happens when the revolutionary hegemony is replaced by capitalist hegemony, namely the commercial popular culture of today?

The Issues of the Everyday: A Site of Critique and Reconstruction

Ultimately, we must return to the most basic level of everyday life to search for answers to those questions that have been conceived in the past primarily under the rubrics of metanarratives such as revolution, capitalism, and hegemony. The everyday is of critical significance insofar as popular culture, or the culture of the masses, deals precisely with the issues of the everyday life of the populace, not only in terms of their leisure activities, entertainment, and cultural life but in terms of the most elemental, the most minute routines in life, namely, eating, drinking, sleeping, working, traveling, resting, et cetera.

The everyday is crucially related to the larger issue of cultural and social criticism, particularly the global/local correlation, in contemporary capitalist cultural production. As Henri Lefebvre defines it, "the everyday is a product, the most general of products in an era where production engenders consumption, and where consumption is manipulated by producers. . . . The everyday is therefore the most universal and the most unique condition, the most social and the most individuated, the most obvious and the best hidden." [26] Lefebvre understands this, of course, to be a condition of existence in a capitalist society, and he goes on to say, "The everyday is covered by a surface: modernity." [27] I want to add that the everyday is not only both global and local (in the sense that it must encompass different temporalities, subjectivities, spaces, and public spheres); it may also serve as a site that critiques the contradictions and fallacies of the present, and that provides a space for imagining and practicing cultural transformation and reconstruction.

Conceived in this way, the everyday may unravel the promises and failures of Mao's culture of the masses. Mao's national form, or the culture of the masses, as we know, was conceived primarily at the everyday level, too, precisely as a counterhegemonic formation to Western bourgeois, imperialist, and colonialist hegemony. Mao's strategy was to emphasize the concrete, the material, and even the bodily functions, forms, and structures of the everyday, which were rooted in the textures, temporalities, and rhythms of Chinese peasant life, "the refreshing, lively Chinese styles and tunes that are palatable to the tastes and ears of the common folks of China."

The utopian vision and promises of Mao's culture of the masses were concrete, material ones that appealed to the sensuous desires of the populace. The vision, in its simplest and crudest form, was a promise of land to the tillers. Such an ideology of "land to the owners," however, was not intended to reproduce the idyllic harmony of the precapitalist, agrarian mode of production. On the contrary, it was formulated as a more advanced, progressive stage that transcended not only the agrarian, "feudalist" mode of production but also the modern capitalist mode of production. It is true that such a utopianism is still deeply ingrained in the teleological thinking about modernization and modernity that is epitomized by Marxism. But Mao's utopianism succeeded because of his ability to translate the teleological concepts of history and utopian future into concrete scenes and images of the everyday (the images of the happy life on a Soviet collective farm portrayed by the Russian media contributed in no small part to such a utopian vision for the Chinese peasant population).[28]

But where Mao succeeded is also where his vision blurred. This is not to say that Mao failed to deliver on his promises after the revolution was won; the peasants *did* get their share of land, and millions of Chinese people were encouraged by Mao's plan for social and economic reconstruction, and were dedicated to the course of transforming China into a materially and economically prosperous society with justice, equality, and democracy.

However, after the city (rather than the countryside) again became the locus of social life after the establishment of the revolutionary regime, the vision of the everyday in Mao's culture of the masses failed to provide a stabilizing and enduring point of reference for "everydayness," that is, the tangible, the concrete, and the countless individual routine activities—eating, dressing, sleeping, working, lovemaking, et cetera—in a vastly complicated and diverse urban environment. Instead, the everyday was constantly transformed into spectacles of the noneveryday—stories of violence, death, catastrophe, revolutionary martyrs, and counterrevolutionary villains and enemies abounded. In other words, the ideological state apparatuses projected, or interpellated, in Althusserian parlance, the subjectivities of ordinary citizens by way of noneveryday political and social events, in the aesthetic forms and styles of the political sublime. The everyday was deprived of its everydayness. The failure of the culture of the masses, in sum, lay in its political instrumentalization and manipulation, which imposed on the populace from above social meanings, normality, and conformity, but these cultural products could barely meet their needs and desires.

In contrast to Mao's culture of the masses, the contemporary culture industry, or the commercial popular culture, succeeds precisely by affirming the social relevance of everyday life despite its overt objectives of making profit or inspiring commodity fetishism. Commercial popular culture today is, by and large, a "joint venture" between the products of the culture industries and everyday life. According to Michel de Certeau, popular culture is the art of making do with what the system provides.[29] The "system" refers to the social space in contemporary capitalist societies in which the populace has enough room and the ability to creatively maneuver the cultural products in order to satisfy their everyday needs and pleasures.

It seems that the contemporary Chinese culture of the everyday has increasingly become the site of dialogical contention of a variety of forces, among which the culture industry, or the commercial popular culture, and China's local and national forms and styles, including the revolutionary legacy of the culture of the masses, intersect and interpenetrate. The sudden emergence of attractive shopping malls, the giant commercial posters of multinational corporations such as Sony and Nike, karaoke, MTV, and ballroom dance parties, along with imported (or pirated) Hollywood big-budget action movies, and

CDs, all seem to validate Certeau's overly optimistic, and populist, hypothesis of "making do" with diverse cultural products within the system. However, everyday life under such circumstances may reveal the degree to which the human psyche bears the irrationality and contradictions of a crazed "gold rush with Chinese characteristics" in the age of global capitalism. The specificities of the Chinese everyday and its "systems," particularly the tension and contradictions inherent in China's popular culture domain, have to be fully analyzed in order to begin a much needed project of cultural reconstruction.

Such a project of reconstruction cannot, however, build on the fantastic spectacle provided by the global cultural imaginary of transnational capitalism, for the libidinous wish fulfillment underlying such a spectacle functions as a displacement of the genuine satisfaction of the everyday with the glamorous but illusory vision of fortune making, or *fa cai*. As the global cultural imaginary and its local and nativist incarnations of the "Asia-Pacific Age of Fortunes" sweep across Asia, East Asia, China, and the whole world, popular culture and the everyday must bring the dual function of critique and reconstruction to bear on their material practices as well as their theoretical inquiries. The historical dialectics and contradictions in the Chinese legacy of the culture of the masses will not lose their relevance in the foreseeable future. What remains to be seen is whether the dialectics of history can turn these cultural contradictions into something constructive and creative; failing that, history itself will be a casualty of a cultural situation that offers no alternative to a reified pleasure principle.

Notes

Unless otherwise noted, all translations are mine.

1   Wu Fang and Ray Zhang, "Wind of Christmas Sweeping Shanghai: Money Oriented," *China News Digest* (16 Dec. 1996), http://www.cnd.org:8009/CND-Global/CND-Global.96.4th/CND-Global.96-12-15.html.

2   Jeffery Sheler, "In Search of Christmas," *U.S. News and World Report*, 23 December 1996, 56, 58, 62.

3   Yi He and Li Zongpu, "Xiadu pang de 'quanyi' " ("Armchairs" of the summer palace), *Zhongguo zuojia* (Chinese writers) 4 (1996): 145.

4   Lester Brown and Christopher Flavin, "China's Challenge to the United States and to the Earth," *World Watch*, September/October 1996, 10. The magazine is published by the U.S. environmental watchdog organization World Watch Institute in Washington, D.C.

5   For a discussion of the ideological conflicts in contemporary China, see Liu Kang, "Is There an Alternative to (Capitalist) Globalization? The Debate about Modernity in China," *boundary 2* 23, no. 3 (1995): 193–218.

6   See "Zhonggong Zhongyang guanyu jiaqiang shehuizhuyi jingshen wenming jianshe ruogan zhongyao wenti de jueyi" (CCP Central Committee's resolution on strengthening the construction of socialist spiritual civilization), *Renmin ribao* (People's daily), 14 October

1996, overseas edition. See also the front-page report on the celebration of the sixtieth anniversary of the Long March in *Renmin ribao*, 22 October 1996. Of note in this otherwise routine Chinese-media coverage, which focuses on official celebrations, meetings, and conferences, is the accompanying photo of an art event in the Great Hall of the People, in which gigantic portraits of the three leaders, Mao, Deng, and Jiang, were projected on a huge background screen. The event signaled the complete takeover of Jiang as the third generation political leader.

7   See Chen Xiaoming, "The Mysterious Other: Postpolitics in Chinese Film," in this issue of *boundary 2*, 124.

8   Jiang Zemin, "Zai zhongguo wenlian zhongguo zuoxie di 5/6 ci quanguo daibiao dahui shang de jianghua" (Speech given at the 5th/6th National Congress of Writers and Artists), *Renmin ribao*, 17 December 1996, 4.

9   Jiang Zemin, "Zai zhongguo," 4.

10 See Liu, "Is There an Alternative to (Capitalist) Globalization?"

11 Associated Press news wire, 27 November 1996. The Voice of America (VOA) also covered the Wang Shuo controversy and related events several times. I was invited by the VOA Chinese program to discuss recent events in contemporary Chinese culture, media, and public opinions, including Wang Shuo's works and their reception in China. The discussion was held 4 November and 1 December 1996. See the VOA Chinese program transcripts, © U.S. Information Agency.

12 See, for instance, recent discussions about postmodernism in China in the Hong Kong journal, *Ershiyi shiji* (Twenty-first century) 27 (Feb. 1995), in which largely liberal critics from China and overseas attack postmodern critics as ultraconservatives who are complicit with the Chinese communist regime.

13 Tao Dongfeng, "Cong wenhua ziben de zhengduo kan zhishi fenzi de fenhua" (Seeing the dissolution of Chinese intellectuals through their contests for cultural capital), *Dongfang* (Orient) 4 (1996): 92.

14 For the distinctions between "dominant," "emergent," and "residual" cultures, see Raymond Williams, *Marxism and Literature* (Oxford: Oxford University Press, 1977).

15 See Arif Dirlik, "Mao Zedong and 'Chinese Marxism,'" in *The Companion Encyclopedia of Asian Philosophy*, ed. Brian Carr and Indira Mahalingam (London: Routledge, 1997), 593–619.

16 For further discussion, see Liu Kang, *Aesthetics and Marxism: Chinese Marxists and Their Western Contemporaries* (Durham, N.C.: Duke University Press, 2000).

17 Mao Zedong, "Lun xin jieduan" (On the new period), in *Mao Zedong ji* (Collected works of Mao Zedong), ed. Takeuchi Minoru, vol. 6 (Hong Kong: Po Wen Book Co., 1976), 260–61. For an English translation of the text (in a different, heavily edited version), see *The Selected Works of Mao Tse-tung*, vol. 2 (Peking: Foreign Language Press, 1970), 209–10.

18 Editorial Committee of the Collected Works of Qu Qiubai, *Qu Qiubai wenji* (Collected essays of Qu Qiubai), vol. 2 (Beijing: Renmin Chubanshe, 1955), 880.

19 See *Qu Qiubai wenji*, 913. For a study of the cultural popularization movement in modern China, see Chang-tai Hung, *Going to the People: Chinese Intellectuals and Folk Literature, 1918–1937* (Cambridge, Mass.: Council on East Asian Studies, Harvard University, 1985).

20 *The Selected Works of Mao Tse-tung*, vol. 1 (Peking: Foreign Languages Press, 1965), 308.

21 Associated Press news wire, 22 December 1996.

22 Theodor Adorno, *The Culture Industry* (London: Routledge, 1991), 34.

23 Fredric Jameson, *Signatures of the Visible* (London: Routledge, 1990), 23.

24 Jameson, *Signatures of the Visible*, 24.

25 Liu Kang, "Hegemony and Cultural Revolution," *New Literary History* 28, no. 7 (1997): 69–86. For earlier discussions of the relationship between Gramsci and Mao, see Arif Dirlik, "The Predicament of Marxist Revolutionary Consciousness: Mao Zedong, Antonio Gramsci, and the Reformulation of Marxist Revolutionary Theory," *Modern China* 9, no. 2 (Apr. 1983): 182–211. Also see Nigel Todd, "Ideological Superstructure in Gramsci and Mao Tse-tung," *Journal of the History of Ideas* 35 (Jan./Mar. 1974).

26 Henri Lefebvre, "The Everyday and Everydayness," *Yale French Studies* 73 (1987): 9.

27 Lefebvre, "The Everyday and Everydayness," 10.

28 For a discussion of Mao's utopianism, see Maurice Meisner, *Marxism, Maoism, and Utopianism* (Madison: University of Wisconsin Press, 1982).

29 See Michel de Certeau, *The Practice of Everyday Life* (Berkeley: University of California Press, 1984). For a "liberal-populist" view of popular culture that draws on Certeau, see John Fiske, *Understanding Popular Culture* (London: Routledge: 1989). For a critique of such views, see Ien Ang, "Culture and Communication: Towards an Ethnographic Critique of Media Consumption in the Transnational Media System," in *What Is Cultural Studies?* ed. John Storey (London: Arnold, 1996), 237–54.

6   Global POSTmodernIZATION: The Intellectual,
the Artist, and China's Condition

1

We are blessed to have the rare opportunity in our lifetime to witness and live
through two historical endings: the ending of both a century and a millennium, according to the Gregorian calendar. Yet, as the twenty-first century
and the third Christian millennium approach, our thoughts seem to be singu-
larly unprepared for a new beginning. We live in the aftermath and aftershocks
of the foundational events of past centuries. Rather than preparing for the
dawning of a new era, we are immobilized, unable to step out of the impasse
of "post-" thought. Indeed, one may say that the last decade of the twentieth
century and of the second millennium is the age of global "post-ization."

   Globalization in the 1990s is at one and the same time the *postmodernization*
of the globe. There is no society in the world today that is completely untouched by transnational capital and postmodern culture. Having said this,
one must also hasten to add that the cultural logic of postmodernism in a
Third World country is also significantly different from that in an advanced
Western society such as the United States. "Postmodernism is what you have

when the modernization process is complete and nature is gone for good,"
writes Fredric Jameson in the introduction to his book *Postmodernism, or, The
Cultural Logic of Late Capitalism*, which is by now an artifact of Euro-American
postmodernism.[1] Yet, when speaking of postmodernism in a non-Western
context such as China, we must revise this statement. Nature might be gone
for good, but the modernization process is far from complete, and modernity is still an incomplete project. One cannot periodize historical processes
so neatly in the Chinese case, and there is no clear temporal pattern of the
supersession of the ancient world, modernity, and postmodernity as in the
West. Contemporary China consists of the superimposition of multiple temporalities; the premodern, the modern, and the postmodern coexist in the
same space and at the same moment. Paradoxically, postmodernism in China
is even more spatial and more postmodern than its original Western model.
Spatial coextension, rather than temporal succession, defines non-Western
postmodernity. Hybridity, unevenness, nonsynchronicity, and pastiche are
the main features of Chinese postmodern culture.[2] A consideration of recent non-Western experiences thus allows us to make a modification of the
unilinear Euro-American paradigm and envision alternative postmodernities.
Postmodernity on a global scale, then, is necessarily a hybrid postmodernity:
a palimpsest of nonsynchronous, emergent, and residual formations, a mixture of various space-times, and an overlap of different modes of production.

While modernity seems to be indefinitely deferred, postmodern formations
have also arrived on the Chinese scene. It is the belated, yet premature, arrival
of postmodernity in China in the 1990s that has caused a radical reconceptualization of the role of the intellectual among critical circles. In the socioeconomic realm, China is experiencing both the throes and the euphoria of
a transition to a capitalist market economy, or what is officially called a "socialist market economy." To a large extent, China, like many other developing
countries, is an integral, inseparable part of a post-Fordist global economy
and operates in accordance with the mechanisms of transnational production, subcontracting, marketing, and consumption.[3] However, economic liberalization does not necessarily bring about political liberalization, and a
capitalist economy does not change the socialist character of the state. At the
same time, there is a general depoliticization and de-ideologization of everyday life. The state has adopted a pragmatic orientation quite unlike Mao's
heavy-handed political and cultural/culturalist approach to governance. In the
cultural realm itself, genres of popular culture are on the rise, and cultural
production is undergoing unprecedented commercialization. Commercialization and commodification have loosened the control of the state, on the
one hand, but have also put cultural workers at the mercy of another equally
merciless factor—capital—on the other hand. This disjuncture of realms in

postsocialist, postrevolutionary China is the cause of the severe social and cultural disorientation of Chinese intellectuals. The urgent task for them is their *repositioning*, the remapping of new kinds of spatiotemporal coordinates in the social landscape.

Indeed, the crisis that envelops anyone who still has the courage to regard himself/herself as an intellectual endangers the category of *intellectual*. The Chinese or Third World intellectual is no longer the *other* of the First World intellectual, as Jameson rightly described in the mid-eighties. Commenting on the stories of Lu Xun, considered the greatest Chinese writer of the generation of the May Fourth Movement of 1919, Jameson writes that "in the third-world situation the intellectual is always in one way or another a political intellectual. No third-world lesson is more timely or more urgent for us today, among whom the very term 'intellectual' has withered away, as though it were the name for an extinct species." [4] Today, Chinese intellectuals experience the same danger of extinction, but with more anguish. First, the political intellectual has been forcefully silenced as a result of the events in Tiananmen Square in May and June of 1989. Second, and no less important, a rampant market economy is redefining social classes and their function. The development of capitalism and the process of modernization have created a sharper division of labor and skills, transforming intellectuals into technical and professional specialists. Borrowing a heuristic distinction from Michel Foucault, we may describe this change in the function of Chinese intellectuals at the fin de siècle as a shift from the universal intellectual to the specific intellectual. Today, there are more professionals than intellectuals.

From the May Fourth Movement until the 1980s, Chinese intellectuals consciously searched for a new social role in the modern tradition and positioned themselves at the forefront of enlightenment and national salvation. Intellectuals aspired to speak for their own class, the people, and the entire nation. They were often called on to represent the conscience of the people. There existed an organic, unbreakable relation between Chinese intellectuals and the modern Chinese nation-state. Even in the late seventies and through the late eighties, one can still cite a long list of public, universal intellectuals.[5] At the present time, because of either the intolerance of the state or the omnipresence of capital, or both, there seems to be no place for the political intellectual in the public arena. Post-1989 China witnesses the professionalization of formerly "organic" intellectuals, their retreat into the academy, and their (self-)imposed exile overseas. Given the impossibility of raising political questions, who can be said to represent the conscience/consciousness of the Chinese people as a whole today?

It is no surprise, then, that the major debates in contemporary Chinese humanities, or "cultural studies," all turn centrally around the theme of the position of the intellectual in society. Broadly speaking, one may notice several prominent types of critical discourse and cultural criticism in post-1989 China: the debate on the humanistic spirit (*renwen jingshen*), the theory of "post-ism" (*houxue*), Chinese national studies (*guoxue*), and notions of Asian modernity (e.g., Asian values [*yazhou jiazhi*], New Confucianism [*xin ruxue*], and so on).

Chinese humanists—teachers in higher education, editors, journalists, and writers—have been engaged in a nationwide debate on the nature, function, and possibility of existence of what they call the "humanistic spirit,"[6] a term rooted in both the philosophic tradition of humanism and the academic disciplines of the humanities in China (literature, history, and philosophy [*wen shi zhe*]). The occasion for such a debate is the loss and downfall (*shiluo*) of humanism, as well as the decentering of the humanities in an increasingly commercialized environment. Participants question whether Chinese humanists can still assume the role of the vanguard of enlightenment and culture; whether a transhistorical, transcendent, universal humanist spirit can be found in the classical Chinese world, the ancient West, and the modern world; and whether humanism is still possible both as an ethical imperative and as a real social practice in the 1990s. Given the trend of academicization and commercialization, there is a strong nostalgia for the figure of the organic modern Chinese intellectual who was exemplified by the May Fourth tradition and who resurfaced all too briefly in the 1980s. Wang Yuechuan, a leading Chinese scholar of postmodernism and the author of *Houxiandai zhuyi wenhua yanjiu* (A study of postmodernist culture), argues that one may accept the critical, negating character of postmodernism and its multidirectional cultural orientation on the conceptual level; but one must reject postmodernism for its "nihilistic" notion of life and art, and its lack of humanistic spirit on the axiological level.[7]

In sharp contrast to the pursuit and reconstruction of the subject in Chinese humanism is the discourse of what is called "post-ism" in China. Chinese post-ism finds its source of inspiration in Western "post-theory" (poststructuralism, postcolonialism, and, most important, postmodernism) and takes the cultural condition of the "post–New Period" (*hou xin shiqi*), or post-1989 China, as its object of investigation. The "post-masters" (*houxue dashi*) deliver the latest fashions in critical theory from the West and apply them to the local Chinese situation. (For instance, Zhang Yiwu and Chen Xiaoming, two of the chief practitioners of postmodern theory, have been given the unofficial, honorary/sarcastic titles of Post-master Zhang [*Zhang houzhu*] and Post-master Chen [*Chen houzhu*].) Post-ism radically historicizes Chinese humanism and dismisses it as the "last myth."[8] The humanistic spirit is regarded as yet another universalizing, essentializing discourse that is hollow and bankrupt in light of global capitalism, which is part of contemporary China. Post-ism does not take China as an isolated object of interpretation but endeavors to situate it in the historical context of globalization in the late twentieth century. China has become a new market for world trade and another locus in the network of transnational capital. Popular culture and mass media are therefore important phenomena to study. The return to a pristine humanist discourse unaffected by global changes is but an illusion.

The post-ism debate itself has turned into a transnational debate waged not only by academics based in China but also by transnationals—overseas Chinese based in American and European institutions of higher education. The Chinese-language journal Ershiyi shiji (Twenty-first century), a bimonthly published in Hong Kong—the middle ground between China and the West—has been the site of the debate for the last two years. There have been several rounds of exchanges and confrontations between post-ist advocates from the PRC and their opponents in the Chinese diaspora. The debate in the transnational context began in early 1995, when the journal featured two articles critical of the Chinese appropriation of postmodernism and postcolonialism by Zhao Yiheng (Henry Zhao) and Xu Ben, two academics who were born in mainland China, received academic training in the West, and now teach at Western universities (in London and California, respectively).[9] Since then, the journal has featured articles that follow up on the debate. Zhao, Xu, and others like them criticize post-ism for being just another form of conservatism in China. For them, Chinese postmodernism eclipses the critical, negating function of independent intellectuals, subjects them to the reign of popular culture, and ultimately dissolves the unfulfilled problematic of modernity (freedom, democracy, human rights, etc.). The Chinese appropriation of the critique of postcoloniality/orientalism sets up an opposition between an oppressed East and a hegemonic West but displaces the real sources of domestic oppression. What might be an initially progressive discourse in the Western context is turned into an expression of Chinese nationalism. Here is an interesting case of global intellectuals in the Chinese diaspora versus local intellectuals in China proper. While indigenous Chinese critics attempt to reexamine the object of China through the critical lens of recent Western theory (its various post-isms), overseas Chinese academics hold on to an earlier mode of humanism.

The backlash against post-ism is also evident in another academic discourse, that is, Chinese national studies. This is an inward turn to Chinese tradition, a complete withdrawal into the academy in response to the unbridled commercialization of cultural activities. Advocates of Chinese national studies promote independent scholarship in the "ivory tower" and advise scholars to return to the legacy of great modern masters such as Wang

Kuowei and Chen Yingke. Independent, autonomous scholarship is thus a response to the decline of the humanistic spirit and the onslaught of commodification.[10]

The problematic relation between globalization and Chineseness in postcoloniality comes to theoretical expression in yet another type of discourse—the revival of Confucianism and Asian values. The debates regarding the relationship between Confucianism and Asian modernity are not limited to the mainland but extend to overseas Chinese communities, the Chinese diaspora, and Asian countries with a history of Chinese influence. A major event worth mentioning is the founding of the International Confucian Association (ICA) in October 1994. The association consists of constituencies from mainland China, Taiwan, Hong Kong, Singapore, Korea, Japan, the United States, and other countries and regions.[11] The ICA Bulletin regularly reports the latest activities in Confucian studies. The endless reports, symposia, and publications foreground the question of Asian identity in global cultural awareness. Are there distinct Asian values at work in the enduring Confucian tradition, as well as in the strong performance of Asian economies in the contemporary world? The debate on Asian values versus global values is an attempt to revise and mediate the universal claims of Western Enlightenment values (individualism, freedom, democracy, human rights, etc.). Putatively communitarian, Confucian, East Asian values are called on to redress the excesses of Western values and account for the economic success of East Asia. Confucianism is seen no longer as an obstacle to modernization in Asian societies as was formerly thought, but rather as its driving force. The revival of Confucianism, then, is the occasion for the reassertion of Chinese cultural identity and the resistance to the Eurocentric conception of modernity and modernization.[12] It is no surprise that, in 1996, one of the most popular books in China was the Chinese translation of *Megatrends Asia: Eight Asian Megatrends That Are Reshaping Our World* by the futurologist John Naisbitt.[13] In his book, Naisbitt makes the prediction that the twenty-first century will be Asia's century, a prediction that pleases readers all over the Chinese-speaking world. This is just another telling example of Chinese contemporaries being validated by foreign works on "tradition."

The types of critical discourse discussed above are symptomatic of the loss of intellectual orientation among Chinese cultural workers. The debates are all attempts to formulate a new intellectual identity. Specialization, academicization, and professionalization—the processes that have characterized the decline of the public, independent intellectual in the West since the 1960s—have befallen the Chinese today.[14] What might become of the intellectual in China? As Bruce Robbins puts it, "We must consider the intellectual as a character in search of a narrative."[15] The Chinese situation is further aggravated by the combined pressure of restrictions enforced by the state and the flow of transnational capital after the end of the cold war. Does the advent of postmodernism and postmodernity imply a "universal abandon," an abandonment of certain Enlightenment universals that are still not fully realized in China? In the United States, postmodernist politics has been posed as a politics of difference and a critique of universalism, "wherein many of the voices of color, gender, and sexual orientation, newly liberated from the margins, have found representation."[16] The relation between postmodernism and politics is also lucidly stated by Jonathan Arac: "The crucial contemporary agenda is elaborating the relations that join the nexus of classroom, discipline, and profession to such political areas as those of gender, race, as well as nation."[17]

Chinese intellectuals face a similar, and yet different, set of domestic historical conditions. It is natural, then, that they must formulate their own agendas of critical intervention. Their response is as varied as it is mutually contradictory, but several features seem evident. First, Chinese postmodernist politics, in several expressions (humanistic spirit, national studies, etc.), involves a critique of capital and commodification, and such a critique is part of the Chinese rethinking of the modernity project. Second, Chinese postmodernist politics may also be described as a relation of universality and difference. The humanist reconstruction of subjectivity, as exemplified in the debate on the humanistic spirit and the critique of post-ism, aims for the realization of the still unfulfilled Enlightenment universals on Chinese soil. *Humanism* is, in part, a code word for the long awaited advent of Western values (human rights, democracy, freedom, individualism, etc.). However, this longing for universality must be imbued with a Chinese difference. The postmodern politics of difference, or identity politics, as another way of saying it, can be summarized as the question of cultural identity—the question of Chineseness in relation to the Eurocentric narrative of history, modernization, and capital. The Confucian revival in the Chinese/Asian world is an important case here, not because of the substance of its discussion but because of the kind of issues it raises. It is an attempt to rewrite and overwrite the narrative of world capitalism.[18] The centers of modernity and capital are no longer confined to the metropolises of the West but extend to formerly peripheral Asian countries. Traditional Asian values become a "cure" for the one-sided Enlightenment universals emanating from the West. Asian modernity is not a derivative, simulated modernity but an alternative modernity in its own right. In such a critical maneuver, Asian societies are no longer the passive recipients and imitators but the *subjects* and *agents* of capitalism, modernization, and change in contemporary world history.

My discussion above is a brief outline of a major shift in the self-knowledge of intellectuals in contemporary mainland China. What about praxis? Given the significance of cognitive *mapping* in postmodernist politics, the question of *siting* is also fundamentally important in the struggle of Chinese intellectuals. What does it mean to move out of a compartmentalized, commodified existence, to extend the political into all domains and practices of everyday life in the Chinese condition? Is there a public space for carrying out such activities? With the infiltration of public culture by the forces of the state and the market, is there any room for a relatively independent, critical space for the debate and dissemination of social and cultural issues? To be sure, there is no ideal public sphere that is completely detached from any political, social, or economic constraints. Yet, it seems necessary to explore possible and actual shapes of the public sphere(s) in contemporary China. As we recall, the issue becomes especially pertinent among scholars after the fall of the former socialist states at the end of the cold war and in the wake of the tragedy in Tiananmen Square in 1989. Tracing the possible origins and historical transformations of civil society and the public sphere in late imperial China and modern China, and comparing the findings with their Western counterparts were the focus of much critical scrutiny.[19]

First, there is the space of commercialized popular culture and mass media (cinema, television, audio cassettes, magazines, advertisements, billboards, etc.). This is made possible by the new forms and technologies of twentieth-century mass communication. Popular culture as such simultaneously expands and constricts the public sphere.[20] It brings the logic, principles, and values of the market into the realm of culture and, in doing so, threatens to subjugate the space for critical thinking to the forces of the market. At the same time, the socialist market economy introduces a new space for cultural activities and in effect loosens the grip of the state. It has also become clear that the state has moved quickly to adapt forms of popular culture such as music, TV dramas, and film to its own purposes. To a certain extent, the state has successfully appropriated elements of popular culture to legitimize its rule. Both the state and the market, then, contend for control of the public sphere.

Second, it is equally important to recognize the relatively autonomous critical public spaces in contemporary China that are constituted by critical journals, avant-garde literary works, art exhibits, academic symposia, and the classroom in some institutions of higher education. This is the terrain occupied by intellectuals (academics, humanists), and their goal is to preserve an enclave of free thinking under drastically changed social, economic, and cultural circumstances.

It has been argued that "there have been two or three moments in the past century when a nascent public sphere began to emerge in China—1880–1917,

1930s, and the mid-1980s—each time to be crushed."[21] The "protopublic" space that evolved in the course of the twentieth century includes bookstores, publishing houses, study circles, salons, teahouses, coffeehouses, and theaters. Today, there seems to be a strong resurgence of a critical public space, however small, limited, and fragile it may be. That space is widened by transnational crossings in the age of global capitalism, by the flows of ideas, images, people, and capital between China and the West, between China and overseas Chinese communities, and between the three constituents of Greater China (the mainland, Taiwan, and Hong Kong).

With the realization that intellectuals "have gone to the margins of society" for the first time in Chinese history, it then becomes a question of how one should operate from within the margins vis-à-vis the twin centers of consumer culture and the state. As many critics believe, the "cultural mission" of intellectuals is to stay in the academy, to perform "pure criticism," and to oppose the utilitarian mainstream culture. In this prescription for the role of the intellectual, the critical public sphere has shrunk to the academy.[22]

Like it or not, specialization and academicization are the fate of Chinese intellectuals in the 1990s. Yet, if one believes, along with Antonio Gramsci, that it is desirable and possible to be an "organic intellectual" in one's society, the urgent task at hand is to discover how one can make a difference from within the academy. "All men are intellectuals, one could therefore say: but not all men have in society the function of intellectuals."[23] An intellectual must possess the ability to be the organizing and directive force of his or her own class and profession, and the capacity to effect new modes of thinking.

It is strategically advantageous for Chinese humanists to hold on to the territory of the academy, where they can perform important pedagogic, didactic, and critical functions. Currently, "critical negation" is necessarily a main practice.[24] But Chinese humanists should also, not unlike the state and the market, find ways to use the space created by the mass media and popular culture for their own ends. There should be an effort to mediate the space of the intellectuals and the space of the populace. Chinese intellectuals could act and struggle from their own specific, situated locales, as well as intervene in the global postmodern space.

In closing this section, I would like to mention the concluding passage from Jonathan Arac's introduction to *Postmodernism and Politics*. What he writes about the plight of American academic life is also relevant to the situation of Chinese intellectuals:

Mass culture is our element, neither a sudden and welcome liberation from a worn-out high culture, nor the threat to corrupt all that we most treasure. Since we come late enough not to confuse ourselves with the modernists, we can accept our condition as postmodern. . . . Finding ourselves, as if from birth, in the academy, we can work there without the shame of ivory-tower isolation or the euphoria of being at the nerve center of a brave new world. We will not transform American life today, or tomorrow, but what we do to change our academic habits and disciplines, the questions we dare to ask or allow our students to pursue, these are political and make a difference, too, for the academy itself is in the world.[25]

The Chinese academy is also in the world, and Chinese academics can make a difference in their continuous struggle for suitable identities and new ways of raising questions.

2

What is the position of the avant-garde artist in contemporary China? What kind of Chinese art can adequately react and respond to the conditions of globalization, commodification, and depoliticization in the 1990s? Concomitant with the severe intellectual disorientation, the issue of representation in contemporary Chinese avant-garde art is exacerbated. Arriving at new spatial-temporal coordinates and coming up with effective strategies of *mapping* and *siting* have been the main preoccupation of artists in the post-1989 period. In terms of international reception, the appearance and blossoming of post-modern art in post–New China have gone through two phases. The first phase has been called "political pop" (*zhengzhi bopu*). The oil paintings of this genre are a combination of American pop art and Chinese politics (icons of Mao, etc.) The juxtaposition of "ontologically different worlds" on a depthless surface (e.g., commercial billboards next to or on top of images of revolutionary workers, peasants, and soldiers) is a trademark of postmodern art in Chinese style.[26] In appropriating the strategy and style of American pop artists such as Andy Warhol, Chinese artists foreground the pervasive commodity fetishism in the everyday life of postsocialist and postrevolutionary China as well as reexamine the legacy of the revolutionary Maoist past. As an underground, unofficial art in the People's Republic, political pop is both a critique and a travesty of mainstream art and official ideology. It has become an internationally recognized genre since the first major exhibition was held in Hong Kong in early 1993, organized by the Hanart T Z Gallery.[27] Political pop artwork has been sold to collectors and is frequently exhibited in galleries and museums all over the world. Promoted by the international media and bolstered by the art market, some of the pop masters (*bopu dashi*) have become China's new millionaires. (What began as a critique of commodification has turned into a commodity itself.)

Critics and opponents of political pop assert that it has gained international visibility mainly for political rather than artistic reasons. Its success is built on a residual cold war ideological antagonism between the East and the West that is still prevalent in the international news media and the art world.[28] Political pop art and the New Chinese Cinema (films by Zhang Yimou, Chen Kaige, etc.) are often compared, as both are censored in their home country but are immensely popular in the international cultural arena. Domestic and global politics have, in part, provided the condition for their popular appeal outside China. Thus, the local is admitted into the global because of the peculiar cultural and political dynamics of the transnational art market.

The second phase of post-1989 avant-garde art includes installation, performance, body, video, and mixed-media art. Practitioners, critics, and advocates of such art claim that political pop represents only a small segment of the contemporary Chinese art scene and is, in fact, already a thing of the past. They proclaim that they will not "play the political card" as they say the political pop artists did and attempt, instead, to create an international postmodern art that is independent of nationality and ethnicity. Their art aims for innovation in ideas, media, and artistic language, as they explore the very status of art, the interrelations of various media and materials, and the nexus between art and life. In the indefinitely expanding field of avant-garde art, anything is possible for Chinese artists. While distancing themselves from the artistic strategies of political pop, their desire for international recognition is no less strong.

It should be emphasized that experimental Chinese art of the post-1989 period has been labeled—quite appropriately, I think—*avant-garde* art. Such art is iconoclastic, subversive, and antiestablishment, and ought to be taken as a political gesture, regardless of content, by virtue of its being denied official recognition in China. Most exhibitions have been organized either as underground events inside China or in legitimate venues outside China. For instance, the only public space for avant-garde exhibitions in Beijing for some time was the small exhibition hall of Capital Normal University, although authorities exercised far less control in other parts of China. It should also be noted that installation art, unlike the oil paintings of political pop, is uncollectible, noncommercial, and not very lucrative. Many avant-garde artists have no institutional affiliation, and they constitute one of the most marginal, displaced classes in Chinese society.

The Chinese avant-garde consists of artists who live and work in China as well as artists who were born in China but who now reside in the Chinese diaspora (North America, Europe, etc.).[29] Some (Gu Dexin and Wang Jianwei, for example) are more interested in matters concerning the exploration of the human condition and in the artistic language of the international avant-garde than in signifying China. Others, especially overseas artists, tend to confront cross-cultural dilemmas, reflect on their Chineseness, and search for the relation between China's past and its insertion in contemporary global culture. In discussing U.S. and European postminimalist art in the postmodern era, Irving Sandler writes in a recent study: "Postminimalists dematerialized the object (process art); spread it out into its surroundings (process art and earth art); formulated an idea and presented that as a work of art (conceptual art); and employed their own bodies in performance (body art). Ephemeral 'situations' in actual space and real time struck the art world as radical because they dispensed with art-as-precious-object." [30]

What Sandler describes here is similar to what is happening in the Chinese art scene today. The radical expansion of the field of art in turn raises the question of what constitutes art in China. In my opinion, the Chinese avant-garde is *postmodern* because it shares the assumptions and strategies of international postmodern art.

For video and mixed-media artists such as Zhang Peili and Wang Jianwei; members of the former New Measurement group (*xin jiexi xiaozu*), including Wang Luyan, Gu Dexin, and Chen Shaoping; and many other Chinese practitioners of "conceptual" art, art is a process of depersonalization and deaestheticization. They strive for the discovery of a new structure of perception, meaning, and the world. The interrelations of various materials and media to each other, the status and function of art, the nature of representation and signification, and the relation between the social and the natural and between humanity and ecology are among the themes of their art. The postmodern turn, evident in the work of these Chinese artists, may also be described again in the words of Jameson: "Indeed, we may speak of spatialization here as the process whereby the traditional fine arts are *mediatized*: that is, they now come to consciousness of themselves as various media within a mediatic system in which their own internal production also constitutes a symbolic message and the taking of a position on the status of the medium in question." [31] Their techniques and experiments belong to a global avant-garde, postmodern art.

The body-art performances of Zhang Huan provoke the audience to think about the condition of life and art in China. His *65 Kilograms* (June 1994) (Figure 1) referred to his own body weight. The artist was naked and bound to a horizontal bar with ten iron chains three meters above the ground. Beneath the horizontal bar, and placed on a stack of white mattresses, an electric stove heated an iron plate. A doctor drew 250 mls of blood from the artist. The blood was then slowly dripped onto the heated plate. It burned immediately, and the room filled with a strong, pungent smell. This performance of self-abuse lasted for an hour and a half. The body of the artist/performer became the material of art. The audience was involved in the situation of the performance and experienced the theatricality of this enactment of postminimalist,

Figure 1   Zhang Huan. *65 Kilograms*. Performance. 1994. Courtesy of Huang Du.

Figure 2   Wang Luyan. *Bicycle*. Installation. Courtesy of Wang Luyan.

postmodern art in real time. It is up to the viewers of this kind of art to de-cide whether they want to push the "representational" potential of art to such an extreme. That is, is it possible to force national allegory into the perfor-mance, and is the theatrical, in this instance, symptomatic and symbiotic of the postmodern stage of the Chinese nation?

Wang Luyan's various installations and mechanical devices play with logic or antilogic and interrogate the ingrained patterns of thought in people's minds. His famous installation *Bicycle* (Figure 2) has been exhibited outside China on several occasions. Wang changed the mechanism of a bicycle by add-ing two small freewheels to the rear wheel so that if pedaled forward, the bi-cycle moved backward. The work creates a tension between human beings and machines, and gives rise to doubt and confusion concerning past experience and common sense. Wang's tampering with the mechanisms of machines, in what seems to be the common artistic language of the international avant-garde, may yet have a distinct Chinese character, for it is well-known that China is the "country of bicycles." Riding a bicycle is not a leisurely, recre-ational, or sport event in China as in the United States; rather, it is one of the most basic means of transportation for the average Chinese household. Wang's work brings out in sharp relief the conflict between humanity and technology in contemporary China.

Yin Xiuzhen's 1995 installation/performance *Washing the River* (*Xi he*) represented the act of cleaning the heavily polluted environment. The artist used four plastic buckets, brushes, and clean water. She took ten cubic meters of water from the polluted Funan River in Chengdu, froze the water into large blocks of ice, and then had people brush and clean them. Yin attempted to raise the spectator's awareness of the conflicting relation between the social and the natural in China's ever escalating modernization and industrialization project. In another 1995 installation, *Sowing and Planting* (*Zhongzhi*) (Figure 3), Yin used balloons, socks, clothes hangers, and flowerpots to represent the interrelations of nature, culture, and ecology. Her summer 1996 installation, *Ruined Capital* (*Feidu*) (Figures 4 and 5), was an assemblage and a collage of fragmentary materials that brought back memories of the past. The long stretch of gray tiles, cement, and pieces of furniture (a table, a dresser, a wardrobe, a bed, several chairs, a mirror, and a washing basin) were indexes of the material objects that made up and were sought after by the average Chinese household in the heyday of socialist construction during the Mao era of the 1950s and 1960s. The private, interior space of the family in a bygone era was turned inside out for public gaze in the exhibition hall of Capital Normal University. Amid the shattered, decomposed, strewn fragments of the past, the dream and promise of the wholeness of the modern Chinese family was also broken. This re-collection of the familiar familial objects of the past recalled an ultimate object, the "sublime object of ideology": "modern China."

Zhang Peili's 1995 installation *Divided Space* (*Xiangdui de kongjian*) (Figure 6), at Centro d'Art Santa Monica, Barcelona, Spain, immediately evoked a claustrophobic ambiance for the viewer. An area was divided into two boxlike, tiny rooms. The activities in one room could be observed at all times from another room through a surveillance monitor that was placed in the middle wall between the two rooms. Viewers moving through such an enclosed space were severely restricted. (The cinematic counterpart to Zhang Peili's simple, compact installation would be Bernardo Bertolucci's extravagant, nearly three-hour-long production *The Last Emperor*, or Zhang Yimou's glamorous feature *Raise the Red Lantern*. In both films, walled-in human space threatens to annul temporality. The imprisonment of the inhabitants in physical space is a national allegory and alludes to the situation of the "iron house" described by writer Lu Xun.) As these examples show, postmodern Chinese art opens up for us the question of possible political intervention.

A reflection on traditional Chinese culture and aesthetics was expressed in Qiu Zhijie's installation/performance *Copying the "Orchid Pavilion Preface" a Thousand Times* (*Shuxie yiqianbian Lantingxu*) (1992–1995) (Figure 7). The "Orchid Pavilion Preface" was written by Wang Xizhi (fourth century A.D.), one of China's most famous calligraphers, and has been considered for centuries a rare masterpiece of calligraphy. Practicing calligraphy by imitating the style

Figure 3   Yin Xiuzhen. *Sowing and Planting*. Installation. 1995. Courtesy of Yin Xiuzhen.

Figures 4 and 5   Yin Xiuzhen. *Ruined Capital*. Installation. 1996. Courtesy of Yin Xiuzhen.

Figure 6   Zhang Peili. *Divided Space*. Installation. 1995. Courtesy of Huang Du.

Figure 7   Qiu Zhijie. *Copying the "Orchid Pavilion Preface" a Thousand Times.* Installation/Performance. 1992–1995. Courtesy of Hanart T Z Gallery, Hong Kong.

of an ancient master such as Wang has always been regarded as an important self-cultivation project, a spiritual process, and an awakening experience. One's calligraphic style is considered a mark of one's personality and individuality. Yet, in Qiu's work, copying the same text as many as a thousand times on the same piece of rice paper made the text illegible, thus defeating the very purpose and meaning of calligraphy. The solemn practice of calligraphy was transformed into a meaningless postmodern game, an absurd play of signifiers without signification. Indeed, the repetitive, mechanical nature of Qiu's work allowed the viewer to question the cherished rituals and procedures of traditional Chinese art and culture. Yet on another level, after endless copying, the paper was turned into a multilayered, richly textured, painterly surface, which seemed to become a new kind of material and medium for artistic experimentation.

In the work of overseas Chinese artists, the focus is not so much on the search for some common language of the international avant-garde but on the cultural politics of alterity. Cultural identity in the postmodern and postcolonial world becomes the main theme. The artist functions as an ethnographer. In this role, his or her field of experimentation is the ethnic and cultural other. Yet, since the artist is an ethnic Chinese who resides in the West, he or she plays the double role of native informant as well as ethnographer. Diasporic art, then, is self-ethnography and self-othering.[32]

The ethnography paradigm informs the recent work of such artists as Zhu Jinshi and Xu Bing. As a Chinese artist residing in Germany, Zhu travels between Berlin and Beijing, and both places are sites of his creation. In his site-specific installation works created in Beijing, such as *Water of Lake Houhai* (*Houhai hushui*) (1995) (Figure 8), in which the artist placed bamboo baskets, rice paper, cement, paint, and water along the shore of Lake Houhai; *Water Clock* (*Shuizhong*) (1995), in which he also used bamboo baskets, cement, paint, and water; *Boulders and Rice Paper* (*Jushi/xuanzhi*) (1994), at Eight Kings' Tombs in the northern suburbs of Beijing; *Rice Paper Pile* (*Xuanzhi dui*) (1994); *Stone Wall with Rice Paper* (*Shiqiang/xuanzhi*) (1994), at Baiwang Mountain; *Rice Paper Floating in a Small Stream* (*Xiaoxi/xuanzhi*) (1994), at Dajue Temple; and *Sunflower with Rice Paper* (*Xiangrikui/xuanzhi*) (1994), at Liyuan Garden, Zhu explored the delicate balance between artistic media and the environment, and the relation between nature and culture. Rice paper, the very medium of traditional Chinese art (painting, calligraphy), was the object, material, and medium of representation. His works exhibited traces of Italian *arte povera*, minimalist features, and the postminimalist genealogy. As simple and minimal as his materials and art objects were, they enticed the viewer to experience something like a sudden awakening, a grasp of the gestalt of the "worldhood" of the world. This was not the "objecthood" of some precious minimalist artwork but the

Figure 8   Zhu Jinshi. *Water of Lake Houhai*. Installation. 1995. Courtesy of Zhu Jinshi.

pattern and nature of the inner relationships of the situation and the surrounding, the worldhood of a world made up of the spatial arrangements of bamboo baskets, water, cement, stone, and rice paper, a world whose materiality and spirituality can come to human understanding not through some disinterested contemplation but only by way of pacing back and forth around the artwork through time. In a work such as *Water of Lake Houhai*, social labor, nature, art, earth, water, and the sky were brought to an order of meaningful coextension.

It was difficult for the viewer not to be affected by what seemed to be an underlying Chinese Chan (Zen) aesthetic. The site-specific installations conveyed an aura of tradition, tranquillity, and Chineseness, and are intended to induce some form of spiritual enlightenment. In his Berlin installations, such as *Impermanence (Wuchang)* (1995), a sculpture installation that used iron plates, a pine tree, and stone, at the Ruine der Kunste, and *The Word of Chan: Puzzle (Chanyu/huo)* (1995), which used a copper plate, trees, and chairs, at Kauzchensteig 10, traditional Chinese aesthetics was brought into contact and cohabitation with a European environment. In poeticizing and orientalizing the ruins of Berlin, these artworks purported to materialize an aesthetic fusion between East and West, and between tradition and modernity. They also posed the questions of how to grasp permanence within impermanence, and how to understand change amid the ruins and fluctuations of time, a theme recurrent in traditional Chinese thought. At the same time, the title *Impermanence* was a self-referential comment on the nature of site-specific installations, which are, by definition, ephemeral, being quickly dismantled after exhibition, and which rarely make their way to becoming part of a permanent collection.

Zhu's art achieved its purest and clearest expression in his two-part, Berlin-China, 1996 exhibition of *Impermanence*. In the exhibition hall of Capital Normal University, from 29 June through 4 July, Zhu piled fifty thousand pieces of rice paper (1500 × 1500 × 300 cm), creating a gigantic visual spectacle. Zhu first wrinkled all the pieces of rice paper, and then straightened them out and stacked them in the hall (Figure 9). From an aerial view, these fifty thousand pieces of rice paper looked like a huge square. A narrow passageway allowed the viewer to walk through the installation. At the end of the exhibition, Zhu splattered water and ink on the paper and then transported the exhibit to a field where it was burned. The same procedure was repeated in the second leg of the exhibition in the Georg Kolbe Museum in Berlin in September of the same year. Through such an artistic practice, Zhu interrogates traditional Chinese art, its institution, language, and mode of expression.

Qin Yufen (Zhu's wife), another transnational Chinese artist, mediates between China and the West in a similar fashion. In the 1994 two-part installa-

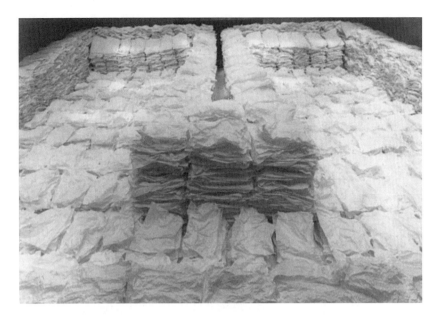

Figure 9   Zhu Jinshi. *Impermanence*. Installation. 1996. Courtesy of Zhu Jinshi.

tion *Lotus in Wind* (*Feng he*) (Figure 10), she spread and "planted" ten thousand Chinese lotus fans, as symbols of withered lotuses, in Kunming Lake at the imperial Summer Palace in the suburbs of Beijing and planned to do the same in the lake at Charlottenburg Palace in Berlin. Through the mechanism of postmodern installation art, the aesthetics of the traditional Chinese garden is intended to conjoin with the classical European past. In such postmodern spectacles, Qin invites the spectator to think about questions concerning the relation between high art and low art, between East and West, and between tradition and modernity.

The most widely known and discussed Chinese avant-garde artist in the United States undoubtedly is Xu Bing, who now lives in New York City's East Village. Xu first shocked the art world with his massive installation *A Book from the Sky* (1987–1991). He carved some four thousand handsome pseudo-Chinese characters, printed them on Chinese paper, and bound them in the traditional book format. The gigantic installation, which filled the exhibition hall, was a play of signifiers without signifieds and referentiality. Whereas some viewers appreciated Xu's masterful craftsmanship, others felt that this most solemn, meticulous exercise in absurdity amounted to a devastating deconstruction of Chinese language, culture, tradition, and indeed meaning itself.[33] While continuing the exploration of questions of language and communication, Xu's latest work has taken a *cross-cultural* turn. Cultural identity

地点:颐和园　　　　　　　　　　1994 年　　　　　　　　　　秦玉芬

Figure 10　Qin Yufen. *Lotus in Wind*. Installation. 1994. Courtesy of Qin Yufen.

and intercultural relations between East and West were brought to the forefront in such works as *Post Testament* (1992–1993), *A Case Study of Transference* (1994), and *Square Words: New English Calligraphy for Beginners* (1994–1996). In the installation/performance *A Case Study of Transference* (also known as *Cultural Animals*) (Figure 11), a male and a female pig in their high breeding season were enclosed in a pen, in which books were scattered. While unreadable English words were printed all over the body of the male pig, nonsensical Chinese characters were printed on the body of the female pig. After a period of courtship, the two mated in the exhibition area, which was surrounded by spectators. The original title, which was later abandoned, was *Rape or Adultery?* While the Beijing audience in this underground exhibition was both amused and embarrassed as they observed the mating of these two "cultural animals," Xu Bing provoked the spectator to ponder the nature of the relationship between China and the West, and to observe the patterns of power imbalance, violence, and complicity involved in any "cultural transference."

In the ambitious project *Square Words* (Figure 12), Xu matched each letter in the English alphabet with a Chinese word radical, designed a system of correspondences between Chinese and English, and thus completely converted English words into Chinese characters. For the inexperienced, Xu gave comprehensive guidelines for practicing this new English calligraphy in traditional Chinese style. Spectators were then able to practice this Chinese style of writing on a "red-line tracing book" (*miaohong*) provided for them and thus be-

Figure 11   Xu Bing. *A Case Study of Transference* (also know as *Cultural Animals*).
Installation/Performance. 1994. Courtesy of Xu Bing.

came active participants in a kind of "cultural transference." The exhibition
halls in Copenhagen, Uppsala (Sweden), and Munich were turned into study
rooms where the visitors could sit at desks, practice Xu's new English calligraphy, and be immersed in a different, unfamiliar sign system. In handling
the brush and ink and tracing Chinese/English characters on soft-textured
rice paper, the Western audience went through an experience of self-othering
and self-exoticization within Xu's creation. Xu is currently collaborating with
computer specialists to produce software and a database in order to market
his invention. In addition, Xu will make available more textbooks and training
sessions to spectators. He has compared his enterprise to the mass literacy

Figure 12   Xu Bing. *Square Words: New English Calligraphy for Beginners*. Mixed Media. 1994–1996. Courtesy of Xu Bing.

campaigns organized in the 1950s in China to educate illiterate peasants and workers, and he reports that his audience has always consisted of enthusiastic learners.[34]

The works of Zhu Jinshi and Xu Bing engage the audience and invite them to meditate on and mediate the cultural interface between China and the West, the relation between globalization and localism, and the synergies of nature and art. An aura of traditional Chinese aesthetics implicit in their works is nevertheless reconfigured and recomposed through the media and technologies of the late twentieth century. In representing the paradoxes and enigmas of communication, signification, and transference, their art strikes one as both familiar and strange, traditional and postmodern. They approach the task of resolving the tensions brought about by globalization and commodification by rethinking and redeploying the traditional. In their art, one catches a glimpse of something on the order of "utopianism after the end of utopia."[35] Their flight from the contemporary is at the same time the most powerful entry into and critique of our postmodern present.

My foregoing discussion of the Chinese situation includes fragments of centennial and, at an even more basic level, *millennial* thought. They aim to illustrate the larger picture, that is, to pinpoint a crucial change in the function of the intellectual and the artist in what was formerly called the Third World in the age of post-Fordist, transnational capitalism, and to forecast future configurations of the local, the national, and the global as the twentieth century comes to an end and the third Christian millennium approaches. Throughout the twentieth century, and up until the last decade, Third World intellectuals and artists were very much national intellectuals and artists, for they were more or less anchored in an organic relation with the nation-state. Although they may have been dissatisfied with, or even persecuted by, the nation-state, it was still the nation-state that provided them with a sense of identity and a platform for expression. With the advent of globalization and commercialization at the fin de siècle, the nation-state is no longer the principal site of activity for Third World intellectuals and artists. As we have seen, Chinese intellectuals have retreated into "subnational" institutions, such as the academy, as a way of opting out of domestic politics. In the meantime, they participate in critical activities and academic politics in transnational settings, thus skipping the link of the nation. Chinese artists seem to have made similar choices as intellectuals. Third World artists step directly onto the supranational scene and operate in the global art market, and more so in the Chinese case since avant-garde art is still largely not tolerated in the nation's public arena. Yet paradoxically, their international credibility rests on an indigenous appeal, a cultural localism, a certain Chineseness. This double orientation of the local and the global that besets intellectuals and artists, with all its contradictions, points to a condition of postmodern transnationalism. What we observe in the last years of this century, and perhaps also at the beginning of the next millennium, is the continual fading of the primacy of the national and the increasing importance of the transnational and the local in cultural, artistic, and intellectual spheres, as well as in economic realms. It remains to be seen if what I call *transnational postmodernity* will persist into the next millennium, or if we will move beyond the deadlock of "post-" thought and wake to an unspeakable, sublime new beginning, a veritable "Second Coming."

In his poem "The Second Coming," W. B. Yeats wrote,

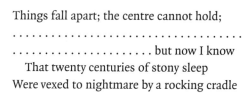

> Things fall apart; the centre cannot hold;
> . . . .
> . . . . but now I know
>   That twenty centuries of stony sleep
> Were vexed to nightmare by a rocking cradle

The poem evokes the disintegration of grand metanarratives in the early twentieth century and renders a terrifying apocalyptic vision. Yet, as an exemplary high-modernist poet, Yeats believed in the redemptive power of such things as art and nationalism (loyalty to Ireland). As the bond between art and the nation erodes, my final question is this: Will there be anything left besides global capital in the next century and the next millennium?

Notes

I thank Arif Dirlik and Jonathan Arac for reading an earlier draft of this essay and offering incisive comments for revision. I am also grateful to Lin Xiaoping, Huang Du, and Anne T. Ciecko for many happy conversations on art and for updating me on current developments in the Chinese and international art scenes. I learned a great deal about their art in my conversations during the summer of 1996 with the following Chinese artists: Wang Luyan, Gu Dexin, Wang Jianwei, Xu Bing, Zhu Jinshi, Yin Xiuzhen, and Zhang Peili. Part of this essay was presented at the annual meeting of the Modern Language Association in Washington, D.C., in December 1996. I benefited from the challenging questions raised by members of the audience. I also owe Meg Havran a note of thanks for editing the manuscript.

1   Fredric Jameson, *Postmodernism, or, The Cultural Logic of Late Capitalism* (Durham, N.C.: Duke University Press, 1991), ix.

2   For my earlier explorations of the postmodern in the Chinese context, see "Postmodernity, Popular Culture, and the Intellectual: A Report on Post-Tiananmen China," *boundary 2* 23, no. 2 (summer 1996): 139–69; and "Art, Culture, and Cultural Criticism in Post–New China," *New Literary History* 28, no. 1 (winter 1997): 111–33.

3   For a description of the transition from Fordism to flexible accumulation, see David Harvey, *The Condition of Postmodernity: An Inquiry into the Origins of Cultural Change* (Cambridge, Mass.: Blackwell, 1990), esp. pt. 2, 119–97.

4   Fredric Jameson, "Third-World Literature in the Era of Multinational Capitalism," *Social Text* 15 (fall 1986): 74.

5   For instance, the astrophysicist Fang Lizhi, nicknamed "China's Sakharov," who spoke for the democratic aspirations of Chinese students; or the reportage writer Liu Bingyan, whose work stood for the people's battle cry against corruption; or the writer Zhang Xianliang, whose stories written in the mid-eighties were testimony to the indestructible spirit of the Chinese intellectual under state oppression. (It is also helpful to think about the fate of these formerly well-known intellectuals in the 1990s. Zhang Xianliang became a businessman in China, Fang Lizhi took the position of professor of physics at the University of Arizona, and Liu Bingyan was forced into exile at Princeton University.)

6   See Wang Xiaoming, ed., *Renwen jingshen xunsi lu* (In pursuit of the humanistic spirit) (Shanghai: Wenhui Chubanshe, 1996).

7   Wang Yuechuan, *Houxiandai zhuyi wenhua yanjiu* (A study of postmodernist culture) (Beijing: Beijing University Press, 1992), 405 and passim.

8   See, for instance, Zhang Yiwu, "Renwen jingshen: Zuihou de shenhua" (The humanistic spirit: The last myth), in Wang Xiaoming, ed., *Renwen jingshen*, 137–41.

9   Zhao Yiheng (Henry Zhao), " 'Houxue' yu Zhongguo xin baoshou zhuyi" ("Post-ism" and Chinese neoconservatism), *Ershiyi shiji* (Twenty-first century) (Feb. 1995): 4–15; Xu Ben, "Disan shijie piping zai dangjin Zhongguo de chujing" (The situation of Third World criticism in contemporary China), *Ershiyi shiji* (Feb. 1995): 16–27.

10   For an overview of this academic discourse, see Chen Lai, "Jiushi niandai bulü weijian de 'guoxue yanjiu' " (The difficult steps of "national studies" in the 1990s), *Dongfang* (Orient) 2 (1995): 24–28.

11 This transnational academic organization has Singapore's former Prime Minister Lee Kuan Yew as honorary president, former Chinese Vice Prime Minister Gu Mu as president, and Hong Kong business tycoons such as Li Ka Shing among its funders, and disparate scholars such as Tu Wei-ming, Tang Yijie, and Li Zehou on its executive board.

12 For the kinds of issues under discussion, see *International Confucian Association Bulletin (ICA Bulletin)* 1 (Mar. 1995), 2 (July 1995), 3 (Nov. 1995), 4 (Dec. 1995), 5 (Mar. 1996), and 6 (June 1996).

13 John Naisbitt, *Megatrends Asia: Eight Asian Megatrends That Are Reshaping Our World* (New York: Simon and Schuster, 1996); for the Chinese edition, see Yuehan Naisibite (John Naisbitt), *Yazhou da qushi*, trans. Wei Wen (Beijing: Waiwen Chubanshe, 1996).

14 For a discussion of these problems and a rethinking of the role of the intellectual in the West, see Bruce Robbins, *Secular Vocations: Intellectuals, Professionalism, Culture* (New York: Verso, 1993).

15 Bruce Robbins, ed., *Intellectuals: Aesthetics Politics Academics* (Minneapolis: University of Minnesota Press, 1990), xxv.

16 Andrew Ross, ed., *Universal Abandon? The Politics of Postmodernism* (Minneapolis: University of Minnesota Press, 1988), xvi.

17 Jonathan Arac, ed., *Postmodernism and Politics* (Minneapolis: University of Minnesota Press, 1986), xxx.

18 For a perceptive critique of the Confucian revival, see Arif Dirlik, "Confucius in the Borderlands: Global Capitalism and the Reinvention of Confucianism," *boundary 2* 22, no. 3 (fall 1995): 229–73.

19 Many symposia were held on the topic. For publications, see William T. Rowe, "The Public Sphere in Modern China," *Modern China* 16, no. 3 (1990): 309–29; *Modern China* 19, no. 2 (Apr. 1993), a special issue on the public sphere/civil society in late imperial and early modern China, which features contributions by Frederic Wakeman Jr., William T. Rowe, Mary Backus Rankin, Richard Madsen, Heath B. Chamberlain, and Philip C. C. Huang; Benjamin Lee, "Going Public," *Public Culture* 5 (1993): 165–78; and Wang Hui and Leo Oufan Lee with Michael M. J. Fischer, "Is the Public Sphere Unspeakable in Chinese? Can Public Spaces (*gonggong kongjian*) Lead to Public Spheres?" *Public Culture* 6, no. 3 (spring 1994): 598–605.

20 In revising his earlier one-sided account of mass media and consumer culture in *The Structural Transformation of the Public Sphere*, Jürgen Habermas states: "In fine, my diagnosis of a unilinear development from a politically active public to one withdrawn into a bad privacy, from a 'culture-debating to a culture-consuming public,' is too simplistic." See Habermas, "Further Reflections on the Public Sphere," in *Habermas and the Public Sphere*, ed. Craig Calhoun (Cambridge, Mass.: MIT Press, 1992), 438. The role of mass culture on the public sphere in China seems to be double-edged.

21 Wang and Lee with Fischer, "Is the Public Sphere Unspeakable in Chinese?" 598.

22 See Zhao Yiheng (Henry Zhao), "Zou xiang bianyuan" (Going to the margin), *Dushu* (Reading) (Jan. 1994): 36–42.

23 Antonio Gramsci, *Selections from the Prison Notebooks*, ed. and trans. Quintin Hoare and Geoffrey Nowell Smith (New York: International Publishers, 1971), 9.

24 See Paul Bové, *Intellectuals in Power: A Genealogy of Critical Humanism* (New York: Columbia University Press, 1986), esp. chap. 6, "Critical Negation: The Function of Criticism at the Present Time," 239–310.

25 Arac, *Postmodernism and Politics*, xxxix. For discussions of problems facing the academy,

faculty work, and career development in our present age of transnational capital, see *Profession 1996* (New York: Modern Language Association of America, 1996).

26 David Harvey takes the "superimposition of different ontological worlds" as a major postmodern characteristic of advertisements as well as paintings by artists such as David Salle. See Harvey, *The Condition of Postmodernity*, 50, 64.

27 For a survey of this new wave of art, see *China's New Art, Post-1989* (Hong Kong: Hanart T Z Gallery, 1993), exhibition catalog. For a critical study, see my "Art, Culture, and Cultural Criticism in Post–New China."

28 For an expression of such sentiment, in English, see Hou Hanru, "Towards an 'Unofficial Art': De-ideologicalisation of China's Contemporary Art in the 1990s," *Third Text* 34 (spring 1996): 37–52.

29 For an overview of the Chinese avant-garde, see Huang Du, "Xin jiaobu" (New step), *Jiangsu huakan* (Jiangsu art monthly) 172, no. 4 (1995): 3–14. I was given the following limited, personal copies of exhibition catalogs, among many other useful and informative materials, by Chinese artists and critics: *Mund auf, Augen zu: Beijing-Berlin* (Open your mouth, close your eyes: Beijing-Berlin), the German and Chinese bilingual catalog of an exhibition held in the exhibition hall of Capital Normal University in Beijing, 10–14 November 1995 (Berlin: Oktoberdruck, 1996); *New Asia Art Show—1995, China, Korea, Japan*, the catalog of an exhibition held in Osaka, Japan, 20 July–3 August 1995 (Tokyo: Committee of International Contemporary Art, 1995); the catalog of Zhu Jinshi's exhibition *Impermanence (Wuchang)* held in Beijing, 29 June–4 July 1996, and in Berlin, September 1996 (Berlin: Georg Kolbe Museum, 1996).

30 Irving Sandler, *Art of the Postmodern Era: From the Late 1960s to the Early 1990s* (New York: HarperCollins, 1996), 11.

31 Jameson, *Postmodernism*, 162.

32 For a discussion of the "ethnography paradigm," see Hal Foster, *The Return of the Real: The Avant-Garde at the End of the Century* (Cambridge, Mass.: MIT Press, 1996), chap. 6, "The Artist as Ethnographer," 171–204.

33 Much has been published in English and Chinese regarding Xu Bing's work. See, for instance, Janelle S. Taylor, "Non-Sense in Context: Xu Bing's Art and Its Publics," *Public Culture* 5, no. 2 (winter 1993): 316–27; and Charles Stone, "Xu Bing and the Printed Word," Wu Hung, "A 'Ghost Rebellion': Notes on Xu Bing's 'Nonsense Writing' and Other Works," and Tamara Hamlish, "Prestidigitation: A Reply to Charles Stone," *Public Culture* 6, no. 2 (winter 1994): 407–10, 411–18, and 419–23.

34 See Feng Boyi, "Dangdai yishu xitong chule shenmo wenti: Yishujia Xu Bing fangtan lu" (What went wrong with the contemporary art system: An interview with artist Xu Bing) *Dongfang* (Orient) 5 (1996): 65–68.

35 See Jameson, "Utopianism After the End of Utopia," in *Postmodernism*, chap. 6, 154–80.

s e b a s t i a n h s i e n - h a o l i a o

7 Becoming Cyborgian: Postmodernism and
Nationalism in Contemporary Taiwan

Discovering Liminality

The year 1985 was a significant one for Taiwanese culture because in that year
the advent of postmodernism was "announced" by a poet named Luo Qing.
The announcement did not inaugurate the production of cultural formations
in Taiwan that could be described as "postmodern" or "postmodernist" (as
some have thought), but it did articulate the fact that a postmodern(ist) cultural tendency was already in the making in Taiwanese society. These events
lead us to ponder why and how postmodernism was actively introduced one
way or another into Taiwan around this time and why and how it was subsequently transformed. In thinking about the phenomenon of postmodernism
in this way, however, we realize that the early eighties also witnessed the first
wave of intense Taiwanese nationalism. In fact, Taiwanese postmodernism
and Taiwanese nationalism have been the two most important cultural tendencies of the island since the early eighties; together they have defined the
outlook of Taiwanese society up to the very present. Indeed, their curious
coexistence invites the question as to what kinds of interactions and negotiations have been taking place between the two tendencies.

Given Taiwan's past colonial experience and its present besieged political status, Taiwanese nationalism seems to have been an inevitable product of history; the question remains why the second tendency, postmodernism, could play an important cultural role in Taiwan. A thorough explanation will need to take us back to where it all began: the fact that the two tendencies developed at the same time means that they both were attempts to deal with the same historical situation, as part of a process of transformation that Taiwan has been undergoing since the mid-eighties and that is still at work. In the process, Taiwan has been rendered into a liminal space in which little that was once taken for granted has been left untouched by a deconstructing thrust coming from the country's increasingly uncertain political status, recently registered cultural hybridity, and newly occupied and informatically strategic location. The initial symptom of this liminality was an islandwide restless, anxious atmosphere. The most ready antidote to this sense of uncertainty was Taiwanese nationalism.

The seeds of Taiwanese nationalism were sown as early as the February 28 Incident in 1947. But a more recent catalyst was the banning of the *Free China* magazine in 1960, an event that eliminated *waisheng* liberals from the dissident movement and facilitated the communalization of political dissidence.[1] *Bensheng* Taiwanese, who bear a deep sense of being victimized by the repeated colonization of the island by different powers, have an emotional reason for investing in communal sentiments. More recently, in the intensification of anti-Chinese nationalist sentiments, the Taiwanese nationalist project represents a resistance against the political as well as the cultural hegemony of the People's Republic of China (PRC). However, even though there may be a general "national(ist)" feeling shared by all Taiwanese, an articulation of this feeling in the nationalist format immediately sets up an imaginary "national" boundary between pro-independence people and others on the island.[2] Worse still, a unity based on the imaginary extrapolation of Japanese colonial temporality,[3] though having the instantaneous political effect of temporarily suppressing the hegemonic Chinese temporality, not only entails being vulnerable to Western bourgeois modernity but crudely tailors the unlimited liminality for limited and sometimes reactionary use. Thus, the politics of nationalism, or what Haraway calls the politics of "unity through domination," is banalized and unable to cope with the increasingly complex and fluid cultural-political situation of contemporary Taiwanese society.[4]

Being curiously both a "nonplace" (neither nation nor province, neither Chinese nor non-Chinese, neither island nor mainland, etc.) and a nodal point for "all places" (having recently registered the hybrid nature of its culture, in which Malayo-Polynesian, Chinese, Japanese, Dutch, Spanish, American, and other cultural legacies have intermixed, and having found itself a focal point for communication technologies and information exchange), contemporary Taiwan indeed deserves a better interpretation to sound out fully the potential inherent in this liminality. This is where postmodernism comes in.

Postmodernism represents a new attempt to articulate the sensibility that was forming at the intersection of postindustrial cultural complexity and fluidity, on the one hand, and an identity crisis, on the other, in contemporary Taiwan—a job for which the nationalist (Chinese or Taiwanese) framework seemed inadequate. Unrelated as they may at first seem to the Taiwanese cultural milieu, some forms of radical postmodernist thinking in fact could best serve this purpose not only by helping to sort out the convoluted and contradictory cultural and political situation but also by pointing toward future possibilities.

To articulate the new sensibility as well as make good use of the material reality underlying it would involve a two-pronged approach: to come to terms with the internal cultural hybridity and to deal with the pressure from China. Whatever theoretical framework (such as the seemingly progressive notion of a "common historical experience") Taiwanese nationalists claim to found their project upon, they invariably choose to totalize this internal hybridity in order to compete with China in being a "natural" cultural entity and identity, believing this could bring about a completed modernity germane to the new global age.[5] The strategy, however, has proven to be of limited effect, degenerating inevitably into a communal politics. This competition for being natural, for being human, in fact not only stifles the potentiality inherent in the liminality of contemporary Taiwan but undermines both the resistance toward PRC political and cultural hegemony and the project of occupying a strategic position in the global remapping. While it seems uninspiring to say that a commonly held postmodernist contention for identity, on the contrary, deconstructs the essentialist myth of the new Taiwanese identity in order fully to reveal liminality as a reservoir of potentiality, this is precisely what Taiwan needs to do but has postponed doing until very recently. To take full advantage of this liminality, a strategy has to be worked out for tapping it in terms of both coordinating internal hybridity and negotiating cross strait relations. And indeed since the late eighties, a practice—shared by several groups of people and manifested in various seemingly dissimilar forms, that could roughly be described as "cyborgian"—has gradually emerged in response to this need, amidst the sometimes unanchored postmodernist celebration of difference.

Calling this practice cyborgian brings into play not just Donna Haraway's theory but also other radical contemporary theories, such as those of Baudrillard, Deleuze, Bhabha, Judith Butler, Stuart Hall, Benjamin, Lacan, and

Derrida, that could be articulated with hers. For this postmodernist practice to be anchored, in other words, it has to be interpreted as well as carried out strategically and syncretically.

According to Haraway, the cyborg is a "condensed image of both imagination and material reality, the two joined centres structuring any possibility of historical transformation."[6] While making full use of complex material reality, the cyborgian move also enables the imagination to take off from this reality. Having come to terms with its status as an "illegitimate offspring," the cyborg is "resolutely committed to partiality, irony, intimacy, and perversity"[7] and "not afraid of partial identity and contradictory standpoints."[8] For the cyborg comes out of a postcolonial situation where the "disorderly polyphony"[9] no longer has use for a politics based on "natural identification" but instead requires a postmodernist politics that could produce identity that "marks out a self-consciously constructed space that cannot affirm the capacity to act on the basis of natural identification, but only on the basis of conscious coalition, of affinity, of political kinship."[10]

This theoretical account evokes very much the practice I just mentioned and seems to address squarely the material reality of postmartial law in Taiwan. In other words, cyborgian politics emphasizes the necessity of hybridizing, of acting out of a processual subjectivity. This brings us to Baudrillard's theory of seduction and fatal strategies. For a society like Taiwan, which faces at once a postcolonial uncertainty of identity and a postindustrial saturation of information and commodity, Baudrillard's theories further elaborate the usefulness of the cyborgian principle of coupling and hybridizing. A constant reapplication of the fatal strategies toward the explosion and implosion of meaning, that is, an unflagging willingness to be seduced by the meaningless "pure object," is precisely what could deliver us from a lack of meaning derived from uncertainty.[11] To be seduced involves a going beyond what things appear to be. In so doing, fatal strategies reveal the "pure and empty form" of naturalized reality and meanings and grasp the truth of liminality as the void underneath them.[12] More specifically, to outsmart the twin antihistorical principles of postindustrial societies—ecstasy (acceleration) and inertia (deceleration)—fatal strategies raise every trait "to the superlative power"[13] in two ways, each tackling one of the twin principles: faster than fast and slower than slow.[14] Fatal strategies thus applied push things beyond the critical point and result in a reversal that enables one to see the void.[15]

To put it in Bhabha's terms, Taiwan can see her interests best served, not by enforcing a pedagogical austerity on her liminal status, but by negotiating momentary performativity in and through liminality.[16] The increasingly fluid and diversified sociocultural energy needs to be coordinated not by fixed channels but by a highly flexible system of mapping and remapping so that internal differences could be made a major source of creativity. Only after we have managed to negotiate the internal other and disperse the fantasy of impurity (for example, unificationists or *waisheng* Taiwanese as the threat of China from within) can we deal with that external other and the fantasized hyperpurity that is China. If Taiwan's being contaminated by China were no longer considered a problem, China would not be perceived as a monolith. Then, and only then, could (the threat of) "China" be "dissolved" (to use a term from Haraway) through constructive cross-strait dialogues on the basis of a recognition of the multiple temporalities inherent in all socioscapes.[17]

A cyborgian interpretation of contemporary Taiwan then would take away the "noun" of Taiwan to reveal its status as a "verb," [18] and pay special attention to how cultural and social practices operate in and through liminality, which is the truth of contemporary Taiwan, while acknowledging the input from Taiwanese nationalism, which serves, if nothing else, to anchor Taiwanese postmodernism.

In the following sections, I first delineate how Taiwanese postmodernism has developed in a dialogic relationship with nationalist discourses and then examine how their interaction has given rise to a cyborgian practice that is currently being adopted by cultural workers as well as by political figures. In the final section, I use two texts to illustrate how the cyborgian principle points to radical possibilities for the future of Taiwan.

Postmodernism as Alternative Vision

Beginning in the early seventies, Taiwan underwent a series of transformations that eventually brought about a new culture. These cultural revitalization movements can be conveniently subsumed under the rubric of a nativist impulse. Curiously, it was an attempt both to wrest a native "Chinese" voice from the Western domination in cultural production and to reorient the latter from the mainland-centered official ideology. Thus, the nativist reorientation was not meant to challenge the dominant Chinese nationalist outlook apparently espoused by the government. If anything, it was originally carried out with a view toward flushing out and exorcising the bad conscience of a government kowtowing to the West in the disguise of Chinese nationalism as well as reinstating a "genuine" Chinese nationalism. The momentum of this attempt was so powerful that all the seventies and the first half of the eighties saw consecutive waves of revitalizing cultural movements in most areas of cultural production.[19] Despite their slightly different time frame and ideological underpinnings, all these cultural revitalization attempts were underlain by a common drive, one that sought to assert a new identity, not necessarily in opposition to the Chinese identity, but definitely rooted in the Taiwan experiential field.[20] The nature of this identity is captured in a famous phrase that appeared in a manifesto put out by one of the literary groups involved in this islandwide sweep of cultural revitalization: "the China in front of us." That is, a new Chinese identity premised on local Taiwanese experience.[21] The nativist momentum persisted into the mid-eighties, with the New Cinema movement marking its last wave of high tide even as the first signs of an ironic turn in the nativist movement were already making themselves felt in the late seventies, a turn that eventually grew into the nativization movement, which, in a patricidal gesture, substituted Taiwan for China as the "native soil" and ushered in a new cultural orientation.

The demand by the nativist movement to pay more attention to the "China in front of us" was eventually transformed into a radical call for desinicization by the nativizationists.[22] For the first time in post-1949 Taiwan, explicit attacks on the "Chinese consciousness" appeared, reaching a peak during 1983–1984 in the prolonged debate between the independentists and the unificationists and in which the first stirrings of a Taiwanese cultural (as well as political) nationalism were unmistakably registered.[23] The upsurge of Taiwanese nationalism within the dissident movement seemed indeed overwhelming to the political and cultural establishment. It actually took over the proto-opposition and made significant forays into the cultural arena. Some of the most active nativist younger writers switched sides and became zealous advocates of Taiwanese nationalism.[24]

It is against this background that the rise of postmodernism in Taiwan should first be understood. In other words, from the very beginning, postmodernism in Taiwan was defined against nationalist discourses (Chinese and Taiwanese). The two tendencies developed side by side with some intermingling, though a certain uneasiness existed between them.[25]

The earlier form of Taiwanese postmodernism, however, developed only in reaction to the overpoliticizing dimension of nationalist discourses and was on the whole apolitical. Given the strain imposed on creative imagination by literary nativism during the years 1972–1979, the cultural arena was already witnessing a turning away from politics. The nativization movement further aggravated this strain by carrying out a politicization along populist lines and thus appearing to have stronger coercive potential.[26] This resulting politics-weary cultural atmosphere provided fertile ground for an apolitical postmodern culture to take root. Despite the fact that the unintended cooperation between the highly politicizing cultural Taiwanization by literary nativism and the government's political Taiwanization begun at about the same time had indeed succeeded in shifting cultural focus to the local, society at large became rather blasé about overtly politicized cultural trends and therefore did not receive with open arms this new form of nationalism, which apparently celebrated the same "Taiwan."[27]

On the other hand, postmodernism was also a legacy of the literary nativist period. Having developed under the influence of (literary) nativism a much more decentered notion of "China," which construes Taiwan as Chinese as any other place in China, the majority in this society seemed to have adopted an eclectic outlook on culture and society and remained unwilling to become involved in the ideological struggle between the independentists and the unificationists.

The second consideration for understanding the rise of postmodernism in Taiwan is a commercial one. By the time the literary nativist phase ended in 1979, Western and Japanese culture and capital were, ironically, celebrating their latest triumph in Taiwan. While Western capital and cultural influence became more entrenched, the long-warded-off Japanese cultural influence made a full comeback that had been anticipated for years by the infiltration of Japanese capital.[28] Indeed, the popular domain was permeated by American and Japanese influences that were commercially postmodern (or postindustrial) to a high degree. The emergence of the eastern district of Taipei, which replaced the western district as the center of consumer culture, for instance, is evidence of the morphology of the new cultural trend brought about by commercial postmodernism.

Third, the emergence of a competitive local entrepreneurial class and an affluent middle class drastically transformed Taiwanese society (at least in the north) into a largely postindustrial consumer culture. Meanwhile, the growing influence of the media and the advertising profession was also helping to disseminate the commodifying power of consumerism. The resultant "aestheticization of everyday life" readily diffused politicizing pressures, whether they came from the government or from cultural critics immersed in an ideology of hard-and-fast binary opposition.[29]

Fourth, during the years after the literary nativist movement ended (1979) and before martial law was lifted (1987), social control steadily loosened up. This was due in large part to the proto-opposition, but the acceleration of information flow was also conducive to this change. Indeed a carnivalesque cultural atmosphere developed, eager for more new ideas to keep opening up new horizons.

These four factors account for the emergence of a distinct manifestation of the postmodern culture in Taiwan. What we have been witnessing is a differential mixture of the postmodernist aesthetic and the nationalist thematic in cultural products.

On the popular level, the result has been a rather commercialized appropriation of the nativist thematic in which "loving Taiwan as China" becomes "loving Taiwan as Taiwan/non-China." On the surface, this appropriation evokes a sense of local pride, but its eclectic form has brought it closer to postmodernism than to Taiwanese nationalism in that, necessarily fore-grounding the hybrid nature of Taiwanese culture, it both upholds and under-mines Taiwan-centeredness, unlike the nationalist discourse that was de-veloping around the same time, which prided itself on a purist, totalized conception of Taiwaneseness. Nevertheless, in popular culture, the differ-ence between commercial postmodernism and Taiwanese nationalism was not emphasized. Under the commercial logic, both this particular postmod-ern tendency (i.e., nonpolitical eclectic aesthetic) and the germinal Taiwanese nationalist sentiments (i.e., passion for local culture) were accommodated.[30]

In the intellectual cultural arena, however, things were different. The writ-ers were roughly divided into two groups, one associated with Taiwanese nationalism, and the other avoiding politics. The latter of course contained some conservative elements, but there was a young group that was begin-ning to think in proto-postmodern terms. Satiated by quantities of mostly aesthetically impoverished and politically straitlaced nativist writing, these young writers turned away from the so-called indigenous themes much glori-fied by both the nativists and the nativizationists and looked actively for in-spiration from other sources.[31] The fact that the years immediately after the end of the literary nativist movement witnessed a gradual retreat of govern-ment monitoring from general cultural affairs, coupled with an increasingly lively cultural atmosphere, opened the newly liberalized cultural arena to new ideas that could stir up the stagnant cultural production.

The emergence of urban literature and women's writing at this juncture ranked among the most important new developments that responded to the urge for the new. But the ultimate inspiration had to come from avant-garde aesthetics, that which was most distant from the politicized realist aesthetics that had reigned for a while. Thus, while the flourishing of urban literature and women's literature represented a seemingly overdetermined development in the sense that it bespoke a postindustrial cultural logic that Taiwanese society had come under, the drive for the change of aesthetic paradigm came from elsewhere.[32] The most radical departure from nativist/nationalist think-ing, therefore, was directly linked to postmodern cultural expressions that were often avant-garde in form and considered by some to be a repetition of the historical avant-garde.[33]

While the outburst of energy in the theater, ordinarily referred to as the "Little Theater movement" (xiaojuchang), was probably the most visible evi-dence of the appeal of the avant-garde,[34] urban literature and women's writ-ing were also engaged in a more substantial transformation of the literary scene into a postmodernist landscape. It was the poets Luo Qing and Lin Yaode who first presented a postmodernist project, in 1985. The fact that the manifesto of postmodernism by Luo Qing, once a devotee to nativist literature, was printed in the poetry broadside *Grassroots* bears witness to the double status of this manifesto both as beginning—announcing the advent of the postmodern era—and end—marking the completion of a long process of breaking with the nativist/nativization's legacy of overpoliticization.[35] Granted that the understanding of postmodernism by either the Little Theater movement or these poets was rather superficial and thus denuded postmodernism of most of its politics, it fulfilled the need of the times. To the extent that it was initially a reaction to the prolonged politicization of the cultural sphere in general, then, postmodernism was introduced in the guise of yet another apolitical avant-garde aesthetic, serving as an "alternative vision" in much the same way as the modernist aesthetic in the fifties and sixties.[36]

Emergence of Cyborgian Practice

The next eight years (1987–1995) were among the most tumultuous as well as productive years in postwar Taiwan. The revocation of martial law, the lifting of the ban on political parties and the formation of the first opposition party, the easing up of restrictions on newspaper licenses as well as number of pages newspapers could print, the legalization of travel to mainland China, the emergence of all kinds of social movements—all these indicated that the society was opening up and entering into a new and "enlightened" era. On the one hand, the newly released social energy was reshaping Taiwanese society into a highly fluid, pluralist, and sometimes chaotic cultural sphere from which new and exciting social and cultural formations were emerging. On the other hand, now that the beliefs and values that once held the island together were unraveling owing to the greatly increased information flow, Taiwan was also bracing up for a growing sense of uncertainty, of which the vexing dispute over identity was a major manifestation.[37]

Both the excitement over the liberation of the public sphere and the concern over the lack of certainty should be seen against the backdrop of a further consumerization of the society, an invincible trend that swept through Taiwan in larger and faster waves than ever in this period, thanks to more advanced communication methods and the fast expanding influence of the mass media. The powerful deterritorialization process of capital sped up a homogenizing process that diminished the differences between the urban and the rural areas and between the different communities while proffering new possibilities for developing cultural diversity and resistance strategies taking advantage of this diversity.

Obviously, then, both postmodernism and Taiwanese nationalism had larger roles to play in this period, with the former seizing on to the increasingly diversified social reality and the latter trying to overcome the sense of uncertainty. But, as both were trying to expand their spheres of influence, the tension between them grew in proportion to their respective efforts and eventually developed into open discursive skirmishes.

In the years immediately following the end of martial law, Taiwanese nationalism under the name of the nativization movement enjoyed a dramatic increase in popularity. Hoisting the banner of "Taiwan," a word that was made a potent symbol of rebelliousness by the government's prolonged wariness of it, was the first opposition party, the Democratic Progressive Party (DPP), formed in 1987 and based on Taiwanese nationalism. For a while it seemed to be just marching into Kuomintang (KMT) territories without encountering much resistance. Even the opening up toward mainland China, which at first sight seemed to diminish Taiwanese nationalism, was eventually turned to its advantage.[38] The sudden unleashing of social energy manifested in all the social movements in the making was especially conducive to a further expansion of Taiwanese nationalism.[39] Alongside the fast accumulated political clout of the DPP, there appeared a spate of cultural initiatives that worked toward a new and exclusionary Taiwanese identity.[40] The most important breakthrough for Taiwanese nationalism was certainly the formal incorporation of the article of Taiwan independence into the party platform of the DPP in 1990.

Meanwhile, as global trends enjoyed a much higher profile in and exerted a more profound impact on Taiwanese society, postmodernism became a major source for cultural inspiration, and its influences expanded to all areas and levels of cultural production. While in the popular domain commercial postmodernism was infiltrating all areas from advertising, fashion, sports, popular literature, popular music, entertainment, to business management,[41] the postmodernization of literary and artistic creativity was no less phenomenal. The number of works with a postmodernist slant increased dramatically. And some of the best postmodernist writers (such as Xia Yu, Chen Kehua, Lin Yaode, Zhang Dachun, and Zhu Tianxin), artists (such as Wu Mali and Qu Deyi), and performing groups (such as Pingfeng and Hezuoan) began to carve out their own niches. Possessing a more sophisticated understanding of postmodernism and enjoying a liberated cultural sphere, the postmodernists were soon able to make use of the micropolitical insights of Western critical postmodernism and went beyond the stage of postmodernism merely as aesthetic rebellion.

The repoliticization of postmodernism was most evident in the Little Theater's well-publicized plunging into social activism around the agitating mid-eighties. However, the engagement of postmodernist writers in postmodern political themes utilizing postmodernist textual strategies might have left a more enduring legacy.[42] Although this critical postmodernist literature covered a whole range of contemporary progressive issues (not least among them the feminist issue, as in the well-known, highly suggestive poem "The Hidden Queen and Her Invisible City" (1985) by Xia Yu, which ridicules patriarchal grand narratives through the queen's point of view, in a language that beautifully accentuates linguistic materiality), much of it was directed toward statism/Chinese nationalism. Another oft cited poem, "Traffic Problem" ("Jiaotong wenti") (1986), from Lin Yaode's pioneering postmodernist poetry repertoire, combines the highly politicized street names of Taipei and ordinary traffic terms to satirize the government's political repressiveness and inanity during the martial law years. In the novel *The Big Liar* (1989), while juggling various postmodernist techniques in creating a circus of mixing fact and fiction, life and art, Zhang Dachun was able to put such postmodernist strategies to profound political use: criticizing both the deep-rooted essentializing tendencies in the Taiwanese/Chinese society on the macropolitical level and the various corrupt political and social practices on the micropolitical level.

Cultural criticism, which became a major cultural practice in this period, was a distinct postmodernist contribution. Although this new type of cultural criticism, having been inspired by contemporary (mainly postmodern and neo-Marxist) thinking,[43] was trying to move beyond the old type which was based on traditional Marxism and practiced by the nativists, it did not in its earlier phase completely break with the terms set up by the nativists. For example, even though (Taiwanese) culture was construed by the postmodernists as decentered, the limits of nationalism were left relatively untouched, lest the universalist quest for democracy get caught up in the psychological warfare between the independentists and the unificationists and degenerate into communal struggles for power. For a while, this type of middle-of-the-road discourse (literary as well as nonliterary) had some currency. Even many of the would-be supporters of Taiwanese nationalism were still hanging on to nativist beliefs and formed an unwitting alliance with the postmodernists.[44] Given that during the mid-eighties Taiwanese society had reached an unprecedented level of affluence and confidence, it seemed that there was a possibility of achieving a synthesis between these two cultural tendencies, which in a sense would be an extension of a positive aspect of the nativist legacy: a decentered, relatively loose notion of culture and society.

But as we moved toward the end of the eighties, cultural criticism was gradually radicalized and divided into two: pro–Taiwanese nationalism, on the one hand, and the criticism of all totalizing discourses, including nationalism, on the other. Accordingly, the Taiwanese public sphere was more or less divided into two, with each side dominated by one form of cultural criticism and hostile to the other. The eventual split of the public sphere indicates that in negotiating cultural transactions in Taiwan, one has to come to terms with a built-in factor, which is Taiwanese nationalism. For postmodernism in Taiwan, then, this comes down to the following questions: How should postmodern thinking negotiate with nationalist concerns? How should postmodernism be anchored? Is there a possibility of working out a way to reconcile or integrate these two trends?

And yet the turn of the decade saw more than just this demoralizing cultural change; other events included the drastic decline of social movements, the closing up of several important cultural publications, the appointment of a military figure as premier, and the government's flirting with the entrepreneurs and local political kingpins. But probably nothing was as discouraging as the apparent tilting of the government under president Li Denghui, who was once considered a reformer within the KMT, toward Taiwanese nationalism, a move seen as an attempt to divert attention from Li's growing populist and neo-authoritarian tendencies. The fact that he was soon applauded and revered as a hero of "national liberation" by the nationalists confirms this suspicion. For Taiwanese society, which had just come out of authoritarian rule, this came as an unexpected shock.

Having received a huge boost from Li, the Taiwanese nationalist movement seemed to be gaining ground at a faster pace. Terms like "Chinese pigs" (referring to the *waisheng* Taiwanese) and "alien regime" (referring to the whole KMT regime, minus Li Denghui) were churned out one after another by nationalist groups and became standard usage among hard-core nationalists.[45] Li himself has adopted a more self-assertive policy toward cross-straits relations since he assumed presidency in 1988 after the death of Chiang Ching-kuo, causing the pressure from the People's Republic of China to mount to an unprecedented level. The urgency of creating a new Taiwanese identity had never been so arduously advertised by earlier Taiwanese nationalists, but now they reasoned that a solidified new identity would help cement the society and unite it against the ubiquitous political pressure from the PRC. Even though forging an identity in opposition to "China" seemed, in the banal imagination, to be the only way out available to Taiwan, the postmodernists were obviously not convinced. Thus, while critical postmodernist arts and literature in this period continued to engage in a multipronged oppositional project aiming at contesting the establishment of the complex of patriarchy-heterosexuality-nationalism-statism-capitalism, the nationalist factor in this complex came to contest Taiwanese nationalism as well, now that it seemed to be in the process of becoming the new official ideology.

New trends in the realm of literature and arts in the early nineties bear witness to this change of perception. Postmodernist writers who used to interrogate statism/Chinese nationalism as complicitous with patriarchy and heterosexuality now were equally if not more concerned about the increasingly totalizing and exclusionary tendency of Taiwanese nationalism. This concern was manifested in two strands of postmodernist writing that had political implications. One strand was represented by novelists such as Zhang Dachun, Zhu Tianxin, Ping Lu, Lin Yaode, and others, who radicalized the critique of essentializing and totalizing tendencies that they had initiated in the late eighties with various postmodernist techniques, whereas the other strand included novelists such as Zhu Tianwen, Hong Ling, Ji Dawei, Cheng Yingshu, and Qiu Miaojin, who were engaged in the kind of gender-conscious erotic writing whose sociopolitical criticism, though not always overt, was nevertheless fundamental. Of the postmodernist works produced around this time, Lin Yaode's *Lilium Formosanum 1947* (1990), Zhu Tianxin's *Remembering My Brothers in the Military Village* (1992), and Zhang Dachun's *The Lying Disciple* (1995) stand out as both politically insightful and aesthetically accomplished. In *Lilium Formosanum 1947*, Lin examines the February 28 Incident from perspectives other than the standard nationalist one, thereby exposing the inadequacy of this event as the foundation for a nationalism, as well as highlighting the hybridized cultural reality covered over by nationalist fervor. Zhu Tianxin's project in her novella is to provide a sympathetic as well as deconstructive understanding of the people from the "military villages," [46] which Taiwanese nationalism believes to be "anti-Taiwanese" strongholds, so that the Taiwanese identity could be opened up to include them. Coming out a few days before the presidential election, *The Lying Disciple* by Zhang Dachun was actually meant to intervene in the election by exploring yet again the interpenetration of fact and fiction by caricaturing the incumbent Li Denghui as a coward who consistently tried to hide his true history.[47]

Of all the developments in critical postmodernism in this period, the most significant was probably the formation of the radical group Isle Margin. Based on a cyborgian-Gramscian principle of resistance, this group attracted people involved in all kinds of social and intellectual movements including feminists, gay and lesbian activists, labor activists, Lacanians, postnationalists, culture critics, avant-garde artists, neo-Marxists, aboriginal rights activists, and so on and had since become the very core of an aggressive critical postmodernism. When this group first appeared on the cultural scene, it encountered considerable sarcasm over its potential as a driving motor of social movements, which it defined itself to be. What mainly evoked such doubt about the group was the postmodernist textual strategies it employed profusely in the magazine it published under the same name, *Isle Margin*. These posttextual or parodic strategies, albeit a common feature of postmodern cultural expressions, were rarely, if at all, found in other "serious" public publications until the mid-nineties.[48] Completely destabilizing the conventions of critical writing, this seemingly self-deconstructing practice was immediately held to be frivolous and unlikely to generate any genuine social change. But as a matter of fact, the magazine's postmodernist practice was precisely what drew attention to its existence as well as its content.

Unlike previous social and intellectual movements, Isle Margin was not mobilized around a centralized guiding philosophy but welcomed interested parties to bring their own beliefs to bear on the movement and thereby to make cyborgian coalitions and couplings.[49] Having recruited the most radical figures in most of the social and intellectual movements in Taiwan, thus representing a broad spectrum of concerns, and having latched onto the current social sentiments by utilizing postmodernist textual and political strategies, Isle Margin, founded in 1991, was soon able to exert wide-ranging influence, especially among students and young intellectuals. Indeed, it would not be exaggerating to say that Isle Margin was the main driving force in cultural politics in the first half of the nineties.[50]

Rallying around a mixture of postmodern theories (Deleuzian, Gramscian, and cyborgian, as well as other radical theories), Isle Margin actively sought to confront the power complex of patriarchy-heterosexuality-nationalism-statism-capitalism that was little affected by the end of martial law. But, as Taiwanese nationalism seemed to be joining forces with statism, the urgency of countering this expansion argues a good case for Isle Margin. Under the leadership of Isle Margin, cultural criticism in the postmodern vein began directly critiquing this trend in 1993 with a special issue entitled "Bogus Taiwanese," in which the importance of heterogeneity, including not least the "improper" elements in it, is thematized with Deleuzian and cyborgian theoretical support.

The challenges presented by critiques of this nature as well as other well-received postmodernist literary works, which often relentlessly thematized the antiessentialist and antitotalizing drift,[51] were finally taken up around this time by Taiwanese nationalists. One of the pioneering works was Xiang Yang's article "The Taiwanese and the Taipeinese: A Preliminary Inquiry into the Differences between Modern Literature of the Urban and Rural Areas." In this article, Xiang Yang sets out to undermine the legitimacy of Isle Margin's postmodernist literary practice by construing it as politically suspicious (i.e., pro-Chinese and anti-Taiwanese) or simply superficial.[52] Even though his understanding of postmodernism is seriously flawed, since his realist taste not only leaves no room for most postmodern insights but also ignores all that was added to early straightforward anticolonialism by postcolonial theories, his strategy of misreading has since become the standard way in which Taiwanese nationalism appropriates postmodernism, the former's self-professed mission being straightforward anticolonialism.

Even as the contestation between Taiwanese nationalism and postmodernism was getting increasingly vociferous, an initial effort toward reconciling them had already unfolded in a most unlikely sector by a most unlikely person—President Li Denghui. As mentioned earlier, the development of Taiwanese nationalism entered a new stage after Li consolidated his power within the ruling party around the turn of the decade. Under the leadership of Li, the KMT regime actively sought to coopt Taiwanese nationalism, which until then had been the asset as well as debt of the opposition DPP. With his status both as the first *bensheng* Taiwanese president and the chairman of the old-guard party, KMT, it was relatively easy for him to adopt an ambiguous political attitude by walking the tightrope between independence and unification. Manipulating this Janus ambiguity, Li Denghui, on the one hand, almost completely neutralized the DPP's status as opposition because the latter was convinced that Li was actually working toward the same goal of Taiwan independence as they were, and, on the other hand, considerably heightened nationalist sentiments all over the island and led to a split in the KMT.[53]

This further Taiwanization of the KMT under Li Denghui, made possible by his mystifying performance, was one of the two central events in cultural politics in the nineties, the other being the formation of Isle Margin. Li's contribution to post–martial law Taiwan has been given contradictory evaluations by scholars and critics. Whether or not his behavior or thinking could be interpreted in a coherent manner will remain something of a mystery, but his apparent incoherence is perhaps all the more important for our understanding of Taiwan in this period as well as for our imagining of its future possibilities. Although probably all parties involved in the evaluation of Li and the examination of this period would agree that Li personally engineered the rapid spread of Taiwanese nationalism, which the DPP with its more radical populist strategies would not have been able to achieve in such a short time, few recognized that Li's performance, by transcending differences and effecting coalitions, actually bodies forth a creative ambiguity that is very postmodernist or cyborgian.[54]

In fact, Li himself is a cyborg. His tendency to equivocate, his public touting of his identity as an "illegitimate offspring,"[55] his political resiliency, his quickness to make new coalitions and couplings—all these make him a near perfect cyborg, or what Haraway alternately calls a "chimeric monster," by whose performance the whole island is mesmerized.[56] By manipulating these cyborgian strategies, Li has been able to reinvigorate the senile KMT, withstand intraparty insurrection, neutralize parliamentary opposition, democratize Taiwanese politics, diffuse the radicalism of Taiwanese nationalism, and last but not least make the cyborgian potential of Taiwan as a whole more visible than before.[57]

Toward Living Together: The Rising People *and* Good-bye, Formosa

The first popular presidential election in 1995 in which Li Denghui was re-elected marked a new era in Taiwan. Most people see Li's reelection as yet another high tide of Taiwanese nationalism, but few are able to see the effect of this carnival, in which communal tension was diffused through the highly symbolic act of popularly electing a *bensheng* Taiwanese as president. In the same year that Li the cyborg reached another high point of his potent cyborgian operation, a project that was "dangerous" to both Taiwanese nationalism as well as PRC hegemony, the cyborgian group Isle Margin broke up.[58] This indicates that the tension between Taiwanese nationalism and postmodernism was so profound that even a radical group such as Isle Margin, which professed to be inclusive à la Gramsci, proved unable to be exempt from it. Isle Margin began its onslaught on the Taiwan cultural scene with an untested yet highly successful strategy—parodic frivolousness—but in the end it was exactly the uncomfortable feelings on the part of some of its members toward further frivolization that tore the group apart.[59]

But the end of Isle Margin did not mean the end of the tension between Taiwanese nationalism and postmodernism. In fact, Taiwanese nationalist attacks on and appropriations of postmodernism in the terms set up by Xiang Yang (that is, undermining the legitimacy of the postmodernist practice by construing it as either politically suspicious or simply superficial) continued unabated.[60] Even the realm of spatial arts, which produced a much less coherent postmodernist movement and little direct critique of Taiwanese nationalism, also witnessed a prolonged debate launched by Taiwanese nationalists between the two camps.[61] Belonging with a larger maneuver by influential nationalist-minded scholars to establish a *bensheng*- or, more precisely, Minnan-centered interpretation of history, these attacks and appropriations entail dire consequences. Not only is the so-called hybrid nature of culture paid just lip service to by these self-proclaimed postcolonial scholars,[62] but, even more seriously, the "me-too-ism" on the part of the nationalists, which confounds the different degrees of urgency pertaining to the different types of "(post)coloniality" in Taiwan, results in the usurpation by *bensheng* Taiwanese of the aborigines' status as the colonized and therefore severely affects the reinstitution of justice.[63]

In the face of these powerful misconstruals of postmodernism in the service of exclusionary nationalist purposes, radical postmodernist practice has kept up a queering endeavor to ensure openings for Deleuzian flights and sites for cyborgian couplings.[64] More importantly, instead of indicating an end to cyborgian politics, the disbanding of Isle Margin actually signifies that a cyborgization of the society as a whole, including Taiwanese nationalism, was under way. It means that the postmodernist thematics and strategies that Isle Margin consistently adopted have been to a certain degree assimilated into the mainstream way of life and can no longer provide the "shock" experience that avant-garde gestures are supposed to produce. This banalization would seem to have domesticated the postmodernist impact, but a careful examination helps us to detect hopeful signs, especially in the postmodernization of Taiwanese nationalism. While the recent spectaclization of DPP's self-presentation seems a more conspicuous form of postmodernization, our attention, however, is drawn to a less spectacular form, one that embodies an attitudinal change, of which the book *The Rising People* (*Xinxing minzu*), edited by Xu Xinliang, a former political exile who was twice elected chairman of DPP, is representative.[65]

The book initiated the "Rising People" movement, a concerted effort to reform Taiwanese nationalism. The movement was bolstered by the pledge of Shi Mingde, a longtime political prisoner who had also been chairman of DPP, to work toward a national reconciliation, as well as Xu's call for reforming the party outlook, and it represented the boldest attempt ever to open up Taiwanese nationalism.[66] Collectively written by a group of mostly nonpartisan young intellectuals with Xu as the mastermind, this book amounts to a manifesto of an open-ended nationalism, which has little in common with the exclusionary Taiwanese nationalism currently in vogue. The basis of this new "nationalism," according to Xu, is a restless always-on-the-move spirit with which the Taiwanese, being descendants of settlers, have been endowed and which underlies all past civilizations that re-set the course of history. To formulate this nationalism therefore is to call upon the Taiwanese to accept the invitation of destiny to create new history at this crucial moment in the history of Taiwan as well as in the process of global transformation. To make sure this happens, the book constantly evokes that desire to go beyond to where the seduction of adventures calls: "In a settlers' society, the idea of boundary is not fixed; it can be altered any time. At any moment, there's someone who is imagining whether or not there is a new and rich land beyond the boundary."[67] The book emphasizes the settler "is not crazy about purity, nor is he afraid of hybridity."[68] Hence, his extraordinary mobility. And for new economic prospects, he is willing to cross that treacherous Black Ditch (the Taiwan Strait) again back to China, "the last and largest market."[69] Even though the book is mainly focused on the theme of securing political viability by means of economic expansion into China, the open-ended strategic thinking it elaborates can be applied to culture as well.

While Li Denghui is adept at negotiating internal differences through his equivocating, mystifying performance,[70] Xu complements Li's cyborgian operation while developing Taiwan's cyborgian potential with a well-articulated project to forge solidarity within the island and to negotiate with Taiwan's most significant external other which is China. Albeit a bit Faustian in its tone and definitely ethnic Han–centered in its formulation of the "Taiwanese spirit,"[71] the book's exhortation to take advantage of uncertainty and to "move on fast and undauntedly" into the unknown somehow echoes the necessity proposed by Baudrillard of being constantly seduced, of being "faster than fast" in order to outdo the multiplication of the hyperreal. When, in trying to appease the sense of uncertainty, Taiwanese nationalism gets caught up in the hyperreality of exclusionary nationalist identity,[72] the usefulness of the strategy of moving "faster than fast" becomes obvious: it exposes the antiquatedness of Taiwanese nationalism's "fastness" and stretches Taiwan beyond the confining limits of nationalism.[73]

While the postmodernization of Taiwanese nationalism brought about a decentered nationalist vision of Taiwan, the novel Good-bye, Formosa (1998) by Dong Nian represents a more anchored postmodern vision of Taiwan from a vantage point of "slowness."[74] The story is about the battle between Zheng Chenggong and the Dutch in southern Taiwan in 1661, in which Zheng took over Taiwan from the Dutch. Narrated by a Dutch ex-Jesuit in the form of letters written during the siege that Zheng laid to the fortress where he is staying, the novel describes the relations between the aborigines, ethnic Han Chinese, and the Dutch in a very calm and plain language, as if the Dutchman were indeed an onlooker. The triangle relationship among the three is a metaphor for the deep structure of Taiwanese society where there are layers and layers of sediments of different cultures. In reclaiming this part of the history of the aborigines, whom he calls "our maternal ancestors," Dong Nian does two things: on the one hand, with materials culled from the Dutch archives, he has gone three hundred years further back in time than the Japanese historians of the colonial period, who have accumulated a large amount of research on Taiwanese aborigines and presumably have made a considerable definitive contribution to our understanding of early aboriginal society, thus symbolically killing the newer Father—the Japanese—which Taiwanese nationalism had found for the Taiwanese.[75] On the other, however, since these cultures are represented in both their positive and negative aspects, none of them seems to be able to serve as an absolute origin for Taiwan, a fact that deconstructs the myth of origin and rediscovers the truth of Taiwan as the Void, the liminality where everything can begin again.

The calm and plain tone of the story suggests an unperturbed, pacifist attitude toward the chaotic wartime life, which is a symbol for contemporary Taiwan where psychological warfare over independence and unification is almost daily rehearsed. The narrator seems to have a premonition as to what will happen eventually: when all this stampede is over, when our fixated desires and deep-rooted prejudices are removed, we will set sail out to the sea where we can be reborn as free human beings:

> I certainly can't see any of God's spirit on the water. I can only feel an energy that can move winds and rains, ocean currents, and stars, and effect the transformation of the myriad of things. Such a divinity is certainly not transcendent to the world; for the human being, it certainly resides within his own body or spirit. A person with such a consciousness would not harp on what kind of life he could have led; nor would he worry about what kind of existence he would have in the future. I can only see my own spirit moving on the water. If in this darkness I want to have light in my heart, then there is light. I see that light is good, then I separate light and darkness.[76]

Compared with the fastness of *The Rising People*, this calmness represents a completely different, though equally intelligent, way of dealing with uncertainty. Its profundity is best demonstrated when it is put side by side with the "strategy of inertia" that Taiwanese nationalism adopts as a defense against uncertainty: the fatal strategy of "becoming slower than slow" could help resuscitate our sense of the real, which, however, is always discovered to be the Void, the liminal, where potentiality rather than chaos prevails.

The two books each propose from their respective unique angles a rather postmodern vision of Taiwan as a seafaring culture, a culture that always seeks to open up new horizons. Whereas Xu sees fast moving commercial fleets crossing the Black Ditch, Dong Nian contemplates all by himself the darkness on the water with light in his heart. Taiwan as a cyborg certainly needs both visions to keep up a viable existence in the new century.

Notes

1 As a publication with a consistently outspoken, dissenting voice, *Free China* was almost the most exasperating thorn in the government's side during the fifties. It was eventually banned when the publisher of the magazine, dissident Lei Zhen, took the initiative to form the Chinese Democratic Party. The people who came together to organize the abortive Chinese Democratic Party included the most prominent *waisheng* (post-1949 settlers from all over mainland China and their descendants) liberals and *bensheng* (descendants of Chinese settlers who came before the Japanese colonization of Taiwan, mostly from the Fujian and Guangdong provinces) dissidents. After *Free China* was banned, almost all

of the most vocal *waisheng* critics of the government were put into prison and the *waisheng* dissident voice was completely hushed. While most of the *bensheng* dissidents involved in this event were spared in this crackdown, they've since developed a populist strategy for survival, one that resorts to "regionalist sentiments" to bolster their struggle for democracy. The strategy was quite successful in accelerating the pace of democratization, but it also sowed the first seeds of anti-Chinese Taiwanese nationalism.

2 For a discussion of this effect of "nation-dividing," see Hsien-hao Liao, "A Tale of Two Identities: The Second Generation *Waisheng* Writers' Re-negotiation of Identity," paper presented to the 49th annual meeting of the Association for Asian Studies, Chicago, 14–18 Mar. 1997.

3 Taiwanese nationalism often ascribes its origin to the occupation of Taiwan by Japan, because it cut off Taiwan from China and brought about Taiwan's modernization. See for instance Wang Yude, *Taiwan, Kumen de lishi* (Taiwan, a dejected history) (Taipei: Zili Wanbao, 1993).

4 Donna J. Haraway, *Simians, Cyborgs, and Women: The Reinvention of Nature* (New York: Routledge, 1991), 157.

5 See for instance Zhang Maogui, "Shengji wenti yu minzu zhuyi" (The problem of provincial identity and nationalism) in *Shengji wenti yu guojia rentong* (Communal relations and national identity), ed. Zhang Maogui (Taipei: Yeqiang, 1993), 233–78; and Chen Fangming, "Zhimin lishi yu Taiwan wenxue yanjiu" (Colonial history and the study of Taiwanese literature), *Literature Chinese and Foreign* 23, no. 12 (1995): 110–19.

6 Haraway, *Simians, Cyborgs, and Women*, 150.

7 Haraway, *Simians, Cyborgs, and Women*, 151.

8 Haraway, *Simians, Cyborgs, and Women*, 154.

9 Haraway, *Simians, Cyborgs, and Women*, 156.

10 Haraway, *Simians, Cyborgs, and Women*, 156.

11 A "pure object" is one that does not signify and therefore contains a secret, whence comes its seductive power. See for instance Jean Baudrillard, *Fatal Strategies*, trans. Philip Beitchman and W. G. J. Niesluchowski, ed. Jim Fleming (New York: Semiotext(e), 1990), 111–16.

12 In positing the hyperreal, Jean Baudrillard admits that we always already live in a world replete with pure and empty forms, but he also argues that only when we *recognize* this fact by being seduced by these forms can we grasp the truth behind them as void. This recognition is also the source of power. Such moments of recognition come from the experience of "seizure," which reveals to us "that 'reality' is nothing but a staged world." See Baudrillard, *Seduction*, trans. Brian Singer (Basingstoke, England: Macmillan, 1990), 62–66.

13 Baudrillard, *Fatal Strategies*, 9. For a discussion of ecstasy and inertia, the twin principles that are canceling out history, see *Fatal Strategies*, 7–27; see also Jean Baudrillard, *The Illusion of the End*, trans. Chris Turner (Cambridge, England: Polity, 1994), 1–9.

14 For a discussion of the two forms that fatal strategies take to tackle these twin phenomena, see Baudrillard, *The Illusion of the End*, 89–100, 110–23.

15 Baudrillard, *Seduction*, 64.

16 See Homi Bhabha, "DissemiNation: Time, Narrative, and the Margins of Modern Nation," in *Nation and Narration*, ed. Homi Bhabha (London: Routledge, 1990), 291–322.

17 Haraway suggests that the way to "dissolve the West" lies in a politics in which the formerly "othered" admits to the impossibility of a unified subjectivity because it at the same time exposes the impossibility of the West as a unified subjectivity. This strategy I

believe can also be applied to the work of "dissolving China" that contemporary Taiwan is presented with. See Haraway, *Simians, Cyborgs, and Women*, 156.

18 Haraway, *Simians, Cyborgs, and Women*, 155.

19 These cultural revitalization movements included a literary movement disseminated under the name of nativist literature (1972), a modern dance movement launched by the Cloud Gate (Yunmen) dance group (1972), a popular music movement inspired by the Modern Chinese Folk Song (Zhongguo Xiandai Minge) initiative (1975), a theater movement begun with the Lanling theater group (1979), and a cinema movement pioneered by directors such as Xiaoxian Hou (Hsiao-hsien Hou), Dechang Yang (Edward Yang), and others under the name of New Cinema (1983).

20 All these cultural movements share approximately the same qualities with the first one— literary nativism. That is, not only were there no apparent anti-Chinese sentiments in these movements but China and Taiwan were always considered one and the same by all parties involved until the emergence of the nativization movement toward the end of the seventies.

21 Chen Fangming, "Xinyidai de jingshen" (The spirit of the new generation) in *Xiandaishi daodu* (Introduction to modern poetry), vol. 4, ed. Zhang Hanliang and Xiaoxiao (Taipei: Guxiang, 1979), 437–47.

22 The transformation of the nativist thematic in the literary field was a, if not the, most curious phenomenon in the cultural history of Taiwan. The literary nativist movement was initiated by a group of left-leaning Chinese nationalists. But as the literary nativist phase approached its end, the whole momentum, through strange twists and turns, was diverted into the hands of the middle-class-oriented and pro-independence nativizationists. The result was a decisive defeat for the unificationists (mainly those associated with the nativist movement) within the opposition by the upstart independentists (mainly those supporting the nativization movement). For the reasons of this dramatic change, see my article "From Central Kingdom to Orphan of Asia: The Transformation of Identity in Modern Taiwanese Literature in the Five Major Literary Debates," *Literature East and West* 28 (1995):117–20.

23 For a general idea of the modality of these attacks, see Shi Minhui, ed., *Taiwan yishi lunzhan xuanji: Taiwanjie yu Zhongguojie de zong jiesuan* (Selected essays about the debate on Taiwanese consciousness: Settling the scores between Chinese complex and Taiwanese complex) (Taipei: Qianwei, 1988).

24 Among others, Song Zelai, Lin Shuangbu, and Chen Fangming were the best-known figures. They represent a larger trend in which young intellectuals reneged on their earlier Chinese nationalist stance to pursue a new career as Taiwanese nationalists. The proselytizing of Chen Fangming, one of the younger-generation standard bearers of nativism, is especially indicative of the extent to which the nativist movement hemorrhaged.

25 The apparent incompatibility between postmodernism and Taiwanese nationalism is basically derived from the different emphasis they put on the democratic (*minzhu*) impulse and the nationalist (*minzu*) impulse. The two cultural trends are thus not necessarily mutually exclusive, but the uneasiness between them existed throughout the eighties and intensified in the nineties. See Hsien-hao Liao, "Lisan yu jujiao zhijian: Bashi niandai de bentu shi yu houxiandai shi" (Between deterritorialization and reterritorialization: Neo-nativist poetry and postmodern poetry in the eighties) in *Taiwan xiandai shishi lun* (Essays on the history of modern taiwan Poetry), ed. Editorial Board of *Wenxun* magazine, (Taipei: Wenxun, 1996), 437–50.

26 Literature, for example, was often divided by the nationalists into just two categories:

Taiwanese/pro-Taiwanese or non-/anti-Taiwanese. See for instance Chen Fangming's classic essay, "Xianjieduan Taiwan wenxue bentuhua de wenti" ("The problems concerning the current stage of the localization of Taiwan literature"), in *Fangdan wenzhang pinmingju* (Writing boldly and drinking wildly) (Taipei: Linbai, 1984), 93–134.

27   The expulsion of Taiwan from the United Nations compelled the ruling KMT to reconsider its relationship with Taiwan; the result of this rethinking was the policy of political Taiwanization, in which the government recruited and promoted a large number of *bensheng* Taiwanese to high government positions. This political process was paralleled by two major spontaneous intellectual reform movements: the left-wing nativist movement and the liberal Reform to Preserve Taiwan (Gexin baotai) movement.

28   Although the Taiwanese economy had been controlled by the Japanese through various joint ventures ever since the retreat of the KMT government to Taiwan, Japanese cultural products were excluded by official policies in order to eradicate remaining Japanese influences. During the period under discussion, Japanese influence began to seep through a more relaxed government monitoring. While American popular culture, especially pop music and sports, enjoyed overall predominance in Taiwan, Japanese comic books, TV programs, pop music, workplace etiquette, 24-hour grocery stores, teen fashions, etc., became widespread, rivaled only by the cultural hegemony consolidated during the 1960s and 1970s by American popular culture.

29   For a discussion of how aestheticization softens bourgeois rigidity toward the Other, see Mike Featherstone, "Postmodernism and the Aestheticizaiton of Everyday Life," in *Modernity and Identity*, ed. Scott Lash and Jonathan Friedman (Oxford: Blackwell, 1992), 265–87, esp. 282–87.

30   The best examples of this eclectic, neo-nativist popular aesthetic are the teahouses and places like the restaurant–coffee house Jiuqingmianmian. Teahouses, one of the most salient indigenous cultural products in contemporary Taiwanese culture, appeared all over Taipei in this period. The cultural characteristics of most teahouses are a combination of traditional Chinese, local Taiwanese, Japanese, and Western cultural elements. Even though the first few (such as Zitenglu) had political intent built into them, the spreading of the trend was mainly due to a successful commodification of nativist motifs.

31   To be fair, not all nativist writing was aesthetically lacking. The realist art of authors such as Huang Chunming and Wang Zhenhe has achieved a high level of sophistication.

32   The urban turn in modern Taiwan literature overlapped to a considerable extent the postmodern turn, while women's writing heralded the era of feminist writing. But the decisive step toward the next stage in each case was taken after the introduction of postmodernism.

33   Charles Russell, *Poets, Prophets, Revolutionaries: The Literary Avant-Garde from Rimbaud through Postmodernism* (New York: Oxford University Press, 1985), 237.

34   The origin of the Little Theater movement is traced back to the Lanling Drama House, founded in 1979, which conceived of their project in the nativist vein, as an "integration of East and West" achieved by bringing together ideas and techniques from both contemporary Western avant-garde theater and traditional Chinese theater. Its eclectic aesthetic, however, made it readily amenable to a postmodern outlook. In the years that led up to the mid-eighties, the Little Theater movement transformed Taiwanese theater from an art form whose creativity was completely weighed down by realist conventions into an experimental theater that was among the most important "postmodern" cultural phenomena. See Zhong Mingde, "Lanling jufang de chubu shiyan he xiaojuchang yudong" (The initial experiments of the Lanling Drama House) in *Taiwan xiandai juchang yantaohui*

lunwenji (Proceedings of the conference on modern Taiwan theater) (Taipei: Committee on Cultural Construction, Administrative Yuan, 1996), 35–69.

35 Luo Qing, "The Second Manifesto of *Grassroots*," *Grassroots* (new ed.) (1985): 2.

36 At the earlier stage of its transmission to Taiwan, postmodernism was quite similar in its function to modernism, popular in Taiwan back in the 1950s and 1960s: it represented a reaction to an overpoliticized reigning ideology, an attempt to break away from the straitjacket imposed by political ideologies on artistic creativity, and a fascination with macro issues, issues that purported to look into the general "human condition."

37 The sense of uncertainty was publicly acknowledged right before the end of martial law by the late president Chiang Ching-kuo, when he announced that he himself was also Taiwanese.

38 The introduction of cultural products and information from mainland China after the end of martial law was so enthusiastically received that some even argued there was in fact a "mainland fever" going around. While a widened knowledge of contemporary (mainland) Chinese society afforded new and less opinionated perspectives on the PRC, this process of relearning eventually did more to foreground the distinctness of Taiwanese culture.

39 Initially the flourishing of social movements (including the peasant rights movement, the aboriginal rights movement, the Hakka rights association, the labor movement, the overhauling of the feminist movement, etc.) seemed to proceed in lockstep with the expansion of the DPP. As the standard bearer of Taiwanese nationalism, however, the DPP was interested less in promoting the causes of these movements than in capitalizing on them by means of subordinating them to its own cause of priority: "national liberation." The opposition's success in doing so through populist strategies resulted in the split of most of the movements into at least two factions or, more often than not, two different organizations, with one pro-DPP (and therefore proindependence) and the other either nonnationalist or prounification, thus leaving most of them considerably enervated. A most conspicuous example is the labor movement.

40 These include among other things the promulgation of a new Taiwanese identity based on the notion of "all Taiwanese as one living organism" (*shengming gongtong ti*) and the attempt to create a script for the Taiwanese Minnan dialect in order to build a literary tradition thereon. The attempt to put Minnan or southern Hokkien, by far the largest Chinese dialect spoken in Taiwan and the widely accepted symbol for the suppressed Taiwanese culture, into writing was one of the most conspicuous acts of self-assertion by the *bensheng* Taiwanese of Minnan descent. Owing to its Minnan-centered outlook, however, it has been met with tremendous resistance even among the nationalists themselves and remains as yet a cultural gesture rather than a cultural praxis.

41 In the area of advertising, for example, the so-called ideology advertisement (*yishixing-tai guanggao*) was a typical "end-of-ideology" postmodernist advertisement, in which an inclination toward (lighthearted) nonmeaning is emphasized.

42 For a discussion of the Little Theater's involvement in social activism, see Li Shimin, "Xiaojuchang yu shehui yundong—Taiwan, 1979–1992" (The Little Theater and social movements—Taiwan, 1979–1992) in *Taiwan xiandai juchang yantaohui lunwenji* (Proceedings of the conference on modern Taiwan theater) (Taipei: Committee on Cultural Construction, Administrative Yuan, 1996), 76–100.

43 While considering the ongoing competition between Taiwanese nationalism and postmodernism, we should note that postmodernism in Taiwan owed much of its repoliticization to interactions with the revival in the second half of the eighties of leftist thoughts

and activism, another intellectual trend that was then competing with Taiwanese nation-alism. Although the leftist trend was very soon either drowned out or assimilated by Taiwanese nationalism along with the social movements, this short revival left indelible marks in Taiwanese culture, of which one was its contribution to the rise of postmodern-ist cultural criticism in Taiwan by helping to facilitate the repoliticization of postmod-ernism.

44 Many of the articles and essays in journals such as *The South* and *China Tribune*, for instance, represented this trend.

45 Derogatory and hostile terms such as "the Chinese" and "alien regime" are regularly used by the hard-core Taiwanese nationalist groups such as the Jianguo (Nation-building) Party and Taiwan Association of University Professors, both of which are made up of mainly *bensheng* Taiwanese and a few token *waisheng* Taiwanese. "Chinese pigs" is a lay-man variation on "the Chinese."

46 The term "military villages," or to be more precise, "villages of the families of military personnel" (*juancun*) refers to enclaves near military bases all over Taiwan, where military families live.

47 Zhang's novel was immediately criticized by Taiwanese nationalists as unsympathetic with the past history of Taiwan. Although nationalists often too hastily suspect *waisheng* criticism of Taiwanese nationalism of having ulterior motives, the criticism may have a grain of truth. See, for instance, Chen Fangming, "Dang houzhimin yudao houxiandai: Wudu Zhang Dachun *Sahuang de xintu*" (When the Postcolonial Meets the Postmodern: Misreading Zhang Duchun's *The Lying Disciple*), *Literature Chinese and Foreign* 25, no. 4 (1996): 149–54.

48 The success of Isle Margin contributed to a whole new trend of utilizing postmodern textual strategies for political satirizing. Give Me News/Hugs (Geiwo Baobao), a troupe that produces textual satire as well as theatrical performance, and *The Journalist*, the most respected journalistic magazine in Taiwan, have taken advantage of these strategies but in a much milder way. The former even won the important Golden Bell award from the government for its innovative ways of doing social and political satire.

49 The extent to which Isle Margin embraced the cyborgian principle can be conveniently corroborated by a metaphor they consistently employed in describing themselves — a half-human and half-mechinic robot they called "war machine" — a legacy bequeathed to them by the radical group War Machine on the basis of which Isle Margin was formed.

50 The group itself was not particularly large, but each of the members, being a leading figure in his/her own field, was able to create a ripple effect, which this group did set out to achieve and which its detractors did not in the least expect. Even the relatively marginalized Independent Labor union (Zizhu Gonglian), led by Isle Margin members, could have its own voice heard when it came to labor issues. The feminist and queer movements especially developed side by side with the growth of Isle Margin.

51 The special issue "Bogus Taiwanese" (July 1993) was followed by two other issues with antinationalist themes; one is entitled "Women/Nation/Family/Identity" (Oct. 1993) and the other "Queer" (Jan. 1994). Both of the later issues, however, were directed against nationalism in general as a chain in the power complex of patriarchy-heterosexuality-nationalism-statism-capitalism, rather than Taiwanese nationalism. And in June 1994, in association with the journal *Taiwan: A Radical Quarterly in Social Studies*, Isle Margin mem-bers organized a conference entitled "Critiquing the Discourse of the Southward Push," which took to task a special feature section in *China Times*, a major newspaper in Taiwan, that, according to Isle Margin, argued for the government's economic quasi-imperialism

toward Southeast Asia. And the nationalist camp responded by a conference on Taiwanese nationalism, in which some of the papers refuted directly the idea of "postnation," which the nationalists believed to be the central tenet of Isle Margin and other postmodernists.

52 Xiang Yang's article has two main arguments. First, there is a difference between the "Taiwanese spirit" and the "Taipeinese spirit," as manifested in contemporary Taiwanese literature: the former puts up a stalwart resistance to Chinese cultural hegemony, and the latter is complicitous with it. Second, the Taiwanese spirit represents a true understanding of postmodernism, as opposed to the frivolous Taipeinese appropriation of postmodernism. In other words, Xiang Yang appropriates postmodernism by means of what he believes to be the "postcolonial dimension" of postmodernism in order to counter the dominance of "false" postmodernism. See Xiang Yang, " 'Taibeide' yu 'Taiwan de': Chulun Taiwan xiandaiwenxue zhong de chengxiang chaju" (The Taipeinese and the Taiwanese: A preliminary inquiry into the difference between the urban and the rural in modern Taiwanese literature), in *Dangdai Taiwan dushi wenxue lun* (On contemporary Taiwan urban literature), ed. Zheng Mingli (Taipei: Shibao Wenhua, 1995), 39–58.

53 Li's project to Taiwanize and rejuvenate the KMT led to a fierce power struggle within the party and eventually resulted in the forming of the splinter New Party.

54 According to Haraway, "The cyborg politics is a struggle for language and a struggle against perfect communication," because incomplete communication interferes with and subverts the totalizing attempts coming from (reactionary) hegemonic forces. See Haraway, *Simians, Cyborgs, and Women*, 176.

55 The fact that Li Denghui was educated mainly during the Japanese colonial period and often unabashedly foregrounds this cultural heritage relieved many *bensheng* Taiwanese of their guilt for being "impure Chinese." Besides, being reminiscent of the legendary Zheng Chenggong—who was of mixed Chinese and Japanese parentage, the first ethnic Chinese to rule Taiwan, and a well-known symbol for the hybridized cultural heritage of Taiwan—this public touting of a hybridized background gives Li additional symbolic capital.

56 See Haraway, *Simians, Cyborgs, and Women*, 175.

57 Despite his contributions, however, some of Li's actions, such as flirting with entrepreneurs and local political kingpins with shady backgrounds, remain to be accounted for.

58 By "dangerous" Haraway means "subversive of totalizing attempts." See Haraway, *Simians, Cyborgs, and Women*, 154.

59 To be sure, the increasing importance of the cultural roles of many of its members and the diminishing of distance between some members and the mainstream (among other things) also reduced the activist drive and therefore the significance of Isle Margin as a group. But internal disagreement might also have played a crucial role. The constant "queering" of their journal since the special issue "Bogus Taiwanese" alienated those who were not ready for further frivolities (especially those who were not as disenchanted with Taiwanese nationalism) and an open anti-(Taiwanese) nationalist stance and led to its final disbanding in 1996.

60 For this type of criticism of postmodernism, see for instance Chen Fangming, "Houxiandai huo houzhimin: Zhanhou Taiwan wenxueshi de yige jieshi" (Postcolonial or postmodern: An interpretation of the postwar history of Taiwanese literature), paper presented at the conference "Writing Taiwan: Strategies of Representation," Columbia University, New York, 30 Apr.–2 May 1998; Liao Pinghui, "Taiwan: Houxiandai huo houzhimin?"

(Taiwan: Postmodern or postcolonial?) in *Liang'an houxiandai wenxue yantaohui luwenji*, ed. Lin Shuifu (Proceedings of the Conference on postmodern literature from both sides of the strait) (Taipei: College of Foreign Languages, Fujen University, 1998), 107–25.

61 The spatial arts, despite having produced a less coherent postmodern movement and little direct critique of (Taiwanese) nationalism, also witnessed a prolonged debate between the two camps, launched by Taiwanese nationalists. For details, see Ye Yujing, ed., *Taiwan meishu zhong de Taiwanyishi* (The Taiwanese consciousness in Taiwanese art) (Taipei: Xiongshi, 1994).

62 Even though the pronationalist scholars who claim expertise in postcolonial theories are perfectly aware of the postcolonial call for recognizing the hybrid nature of culture, most of them tend to suspect difference of being potentially subversive of the Taiwanese nationalist project when it comes to practice and are often stuck on the following formula: loving Taiwan = identifying with Taiwan = identifying with the need of Taiwan independence = identifying with the nationalist project of Taiwan independence. For examples of this unwillingness to go "postcolonial" all the way, see the essays written by some of the scholars who joined the debate on identity in *Literature Chinese and Foreign* during 1995–1996. For a preliminary inquiry into this phenomenon, see my article "Chaoyue guozu: Weishenme yao tan rentong" (Beyond nationalism: Why do we talk about identity?) *Literature Chinese and Foreign* 24, no. 4 (1995): 61–76.

63 The term *me-too-ism*, though used by Diana Brydon to serve as a red herring in defending her own position on postcoloniality, is used here to refer precisely to the kind of phenomenon that her notion of postcoloniality may very well entail and that Linda Hutcheon and Ella Shohat criticizes: the scrambling for a postcolonial status by former settlers' colonies, which blurs the distinctions between the different kinds of "(post)coloniality" at the expense of the already underprivileged aborigines. Taiwan presents a similar case. By collapsing *bensheng* Taiwanese (the colonizers) and aborigines (the colonized) into the same category of "the colonized of Chinese imperialism," the "me-too-ism" of *bensheng* Taiwanese completely erases the historical fact that the colonization of the Taiwanese aborigines was largely carried out by the settlers themselves, rather than by the imperial government, which was reluctant to extend administration to Taiwan. On the other hand, the power struggle between earlier and post-1949 ethnic Han settlers could be considered a form of "colonization," only in a very stretched and hyperbolic sense. The latter form of "colonization" however is the only one that ever commands attention, because the aborigines, being a very small minority, wield little political influence. For the original context in which the notion of me-too-ism was presented by Diana Brydon, see her "The White Inuit Speaks," in *Past the Last Post: Theorizing Post-Colonialism and Post-Modernism*, ed. Ian Adam and Helen Tiffin (New York: Harvester Wheatsheaf, 1991), 194–95. For critiques of me-too-ism, see Ella Shohat, "Notes on the Post-Colonial," in *Contemporary Postcolonial Theory: A Reader*, ed. Padmini Mongia (London: Arnold, 1996), 322–35, especially 324–25; and Linda Hutcheon, "Circling the Downspout of Empire," *Ariel* 20, no. 4 (1989): 154–59. For the consequences of rampant "me-too-ism" in Taiwan, see Hsien-hao Liao, "Ping 'Taiwan: Houxiandai huo houzhimin?" (Commentary on "Taiwan: Postmodern or postcolonial?") in *Liang'an houxiandai wenxue yantaohui luwenji* (Proceedings of the conference on postmodern literature from both sides of the strait), 126–33. See also my "Mimike yu mingnizu: Xiandaixing, houzhiminxing yu Taiwan xiandai xiaoshuo" (Of mimicry and manes: Modernity, postcoloniality, and modern Taiwanese fiction), paper presented at the conference "The History of Taiwan Fiction," United Daily, Dec. 24–26, 1997; and "Don't go gentle into that *Han* night: The new cultural discourse of the Tai-

wanese aborigines," paper presented at the 50th annual meeting of the Association for Asian Studies, Washington, D.C., 24–28 Mar. 1998.

64 In the area of critical discourse and social activism, one new and powerful postmodernist practice comes from the group Center for the Study of Sexualities, formed by some of the former members of Isle Margin toward the end of 1995, whereas in the literary field Zhu Tianxin's novella *The Ancient Capital* (1998) opened up another front, where the issue of the myth of modernity in which the nationalists are heavily invested is examined from the point of view of postcolonial historiography.

65 Xu Xingliang, *Xinxing minzu* (The rising people) (Taipei: Yuanliu, 1995).

66 The "great reconciliation" (*dahejie*) move taken toward the end of 1995 by Shi Mingde was an attempt to diffuse the communal tensions heightened by the Taipei mayoral election, whereas in the intraparty debate of April 1996, the younger DPP leaders, concerned about the party's inability to gain popular support, argued for an overhaul of the party ideology by replacing its older generation's "fascist" and communally based nationalism with a democratized and civil rights oriented nationalism.

67 Xu, *Xinxing minzu*, 179.

68 Xu, *Xinxing minzu*, 187.

69 Xu, *Xinxing minzu*, 353–54.

70 Li Denghui's latest feat, during the recent mayoral election of Taipei, was to mobilize support for his party candidate, Ma Yingjiu, beating the DPP incumbent, Chen Shuibian, without, however, undermining DPP's faith in his secret comradeship. The concept of "New Taiwanese" that Li used during the campaign to bolster the legitimacy of Ma Yingjiu (a *waisheng* Taiwanese) as also a "native son" has had profound reverberations. Despite the fact that notions of a new identity that can transcend linguistic and ethnic differences and reintegrate the increasingly politically divided society have been postulated by various parties since the eighties, none of the formulations was as inclusive and flexible as this one, which enlisted only such loose criteria as "willing to work hard for Taiwan" and "caring about Taiwan." While the elimination of regionalist/communalist bigotry was a major reason for its success in the campaign, its being posited by Li, the first president of *bensheng* Taiwanese descent, was presumably crucial in making it appealing to a significant portion of the *bensheng* population.

71 Although Xu's project is not without its limitations, due to his basically Han-centered social vision, which gives precedence to the "pioneer's spirit" of the "settlers," and his economic determinism, which believes that cultural creativity comes from economic prosperity, it nevertheless has a potential openness that would allow a further queering of nationalism. See my article "Namuo, qing'ai nide diren: Yu Liao Chaoyang tanqing shuo'ai" (Please love your enemy: A conversation with Liao Chaoyang on "emotion" and "love") *Literature Chinese and Foreign* 24, no. 7 (1995): 107, n. 1.

72 Timothy W. Luke observes that "the multiplication of nation-states" is just a "replaying of codes of hyperreality," since most or all nation-states are simulations of the model (in the Baudrillardian sense) of the nation-state. See his "New World Order or Neo-World Orders: Power, Politics, and Ideology in Informationalizing Glocalities," in *Global Modernities*, ed. Mike Featherstone, Scott Lash, and Roland Robertson (London: Sage, 1995), 97.

73 The Rising People movement, however, has been harshly criticized by hard-core Taiwanese nationalists in and outside of the DPP as tantamount to high treason. Nevertheless, Chen Wenqian, one of the central figures in the think tank of Xu Xinliang expressed full confidence in the eventual prevalence of this approach in an interview I had with her, a prediction that seemed to have been verified in the defeat of the DPP incumbent, a hard-

core nationalist, in the Taipei mayoral election in December 1998 and in the ensuing discussion within the DPP of how to soften the party's nationalist stance to widen popular support, a discussion that revolved around the issue of whether or not there is a need to modify the "article of independence" in the party platform. For Chen's elaboration of the position of the Rising People movement, see Hsien-hao Liao, "Rentong qiuzhu rongyi; Shuiruo yili gongjian: zhuanfang Chen Wenqian tan rentong" (Identity as opening up: A conversation with Wenqian Chen on identity), *Literature Chinese and Foreign* 27, no. 3 (1998): 109–23.

74 Dong Nian, Zaijian, Fuermosa (Goodbye, Formosa) (Taipei: Lianhe Wenxue, 1998).

75 This is also suggested in the preface to the novel, where he expresses incredulity toward some nationalist historians' attempts both to substitute Japan for China as the originary moment in the history of Taiwan and to exclude the aborigines from this history. He argues that, as a *bensheng* Taiwanese, he believes that those aborigines who had disappeared in history might very well have been the "maternal ancestors" of a majority of *bensheng* Taiwanese and deserve a fuller historical account. See his preface to *Zaijian, Fuermosa*, 6–8.

76 Dong Nian, Zaijian, Fuermosa, 138.

iii cultural studies

8 Imagined Nostalgia

Translated by Judy T. H. Chen

Fashion and Remembrance

In 1996, the first issue of the journal Hua *cheng* displayed on its cover a series
of Guo Runwen's oil paintings entitled The *Memory Locked Away* (or, perhaps
more accurately, The *Eternal Remembrance*), which depict scenes from a bygone
era. Under the shadowy and barely lit ceiling lamp, a young girl is fast asleep
and sprawled over an old-fashioned sewing machine. The sewing machine
seems to emerge from an uneven, decrepit, and defaced mud wall. On another
spot-stained, ancient wall, curled and torn used envelopes serve as wallpaper.
In front of the sewing machine, in the foreground, is an extinguished red
candle. In progress at the sewing machine is an almost finished handmade
infant suit. In this set of paintings, which evokes seemingly familiar but elusive memories, the minuteness and material expressiveness stand out: the
young girl's faded, coarsely knit wool vest; her long, trailing skirt hem; the
old paint-stripped sewing machine without a speck of dust; the long-since-
threadbare rag tied to the machine; the red candle and wax on the overturned
coarse ceramic bowl.

Hua cheng accompanied this set of paintings with a short essay by Xiao Yen, entitled "The Right to Nostalgia," in which the author writes:

> Nostalgia is not only a kind of remembrance, but a kind of right. We all have a longing for the past—lingering over some mundane objects because these mundane objects have become the memorial to the trajectory of one's own life, allowing us, without a doubt, to construct a human archive. While he [Guo Runwen] sees the expressive materiality of these objects of personal memorial as the magnificent radiance of life, I look at this magnificent radiance as resistance against the desolate experience of alienation from human nature. Whenever one sees the reflection of stainless steel and glass walls cruelly swallowing up all traces of human life, whenever one unwittingly hails a taxi cab with a cloud of exhaust trailing behind, slowly and resolutely advancing on the cold, hard, paved concrete surface, the meaning of modern "progress" truly depends on the expressive materiality of memory to sustain its equilibrium.[1]

Xiao Yen's short essay seems to attribute to or highlight in Guo's paintings the following notions: remembrance, right, individual, human nature, and the struggle for balance in "modern 'progress.'" If we consider these two works as mutually reflective texts, then some symptoms of contemporary Chinese culture may emerge: on the one hand, modernist or Enlightenment discourse—in terms of the individual, the individual's right, and the human archive, the achievement of all of which depends, as a matter of course, on the progress of Chinese society; on the other hand, the persistent doubt of modern progress inherent in the critique and repulsion of stainless steel, glass walls, industrial pollution, et cetera.

From a certain point of view, it is precisely within a social discourse, seemingly fraught with fragmentation, that Chinese cities of the 1990s unassumingly mobilize the ambience of nostalgia. As one of the most important cultural realities of contemporary China, rather than as a trend of thought or as an undercurrent that resists the systematic progress of modernization and commercialization, nostalgia functions more prevalently as a fashion. Rather than originating from the writings of intellectual elites, it is more a pulse of the not inelegant urban noise; the trappings of nostalgia become perfectly suited as alluring commercial packaging, as a fashionable culture. If, by the writings of the intellectual elites, we mean the passing on of a glimmer of regard, full of contradiction and discontent, then nostalgia as fashion, like the anxiety infused with the feverish exuberance of the last half of the 1980s, veils a self-congratulatory and festive joy. The Chinese, who could hardly wait to "burst through Gateway 2000," are suddenly seized by a nostalgic languor, as if bearing witness to the result of progress. If, however, the sentiment of nostalgia is still accompanied by the desire to "catch up," then the Chinese nostalgic sentiment's invisible correspondence with the world (that is, with the industrial nations') phenomenon of nostalgic reflection becomes a testimony to cultural catching up. Facing a finite closure—taking leave of the eventful twentieth century—the sentiment of nostalgia arrives in an untimely manner at the century's end; for the China that marches in step with the rest of the world, this is a tacit ineluctability. The prevalence of cultural policing supports a posture of discontented backward gazing. Nevertheless, a closer inspection shows that submerged within the nostalgic sentiment of Chinese urban and contemporary culture is not necessarily the inevitable manifestation of a kind of fin de siècle mood. In fact, the imposed calendrical mode that equates China's age with that of anno Domini (setting aside for the moment the incursion of Western thinking into China's long history) has never been the calendar with which the Chinese people, in their hearts, reckoned time; therefore, it is difficult for Chinese to understand and experience the catastrophic connotation of the end of the millennium for Christian culture. For an entire century, in an interesting irony, we have surpassed the present, anticipating the golden future, and have gone past the end, looking forward to new horizons. Thus, in contemporary rhetoric, the voyage of hope in crossing over the century replaces the tragic lingering of the fin de siècle. If, during the conquest of the 1980s and 1990s, one of Chinese culture's ongoing internal efforts is to consciously construct and strengthen a mesmerizing mirror of the West while at the same time relentlessly fabricating Oriental mythology in front of this magical mirror, then the "fashion" of nostalgic sentiment becomes one application of such a construction, as well as a necessary misreading and explication of the construction. No nostalgic writing can be considered a "re-creation of the original scene." Different from a written record that calls up memories of yesterday, nostalgia, as the fashion of contemporary China, uses the construction and embellishment of remembrance to assuage the present.

The Need for Nostalgia

From the mid-1980s to the 1990s, the process of Chinese society's systematic progress toward modernization and commercialization has been accompanied by large-scale urbanization, or urban modernization. Not only have new cities, such as Shenzhen, Haikou, Zhuhai, and Shekou, sprouted from what had been villages and small towns; large cities have also undergone extensive renovation. Along with the foundational structures of the ancient cities, a certain destructiveness of construction work shoulders the burden of the ancient cities' space of history and remembrance; and day after day, high-rise buildings, luxury mansions, commercial centers, shopping complexes, writing galleries, and fitness gyms replace the ripped-open spaces of the new cities, the metropolises encroaching endlessly like greedy monsters toward their surrounding townships. Thus, a fascinating picture typical of Chinese cities in the 1990s is the ubiquitous construction site, similar to images depicting postwar reconstruction: Amid the airborne dust, the towering cranes, and the chorus of the humming concrete mixers, a new city emerges. The old cities—for example, Shanghai, which is a few hundred years old, or Beijing and Suzhou, which are thousands of years old—quietly recede into oblivion in the explosive transformation. If the spaces of old remain the milestones of individual remembrance and of regional history, and if the decay of the space, and the space of decay, is unique in Chinese history—if not its sole explication and trace—then the prosperous, cosmopolitan, anonymous big city already truncates its enduring visible history, truncates the prodigal son's road home.[2] If history reveals its own footsteps in the process of a continuous flattening out of space, then contemporary Chinese people are fortunate to encounter history and to witness this process of revelation.

From a certain point of view, this process of the giddy and aggressively rapid urbanization of the 1990s embodies the most contradictory sentiment of contemporary Chinese people, especially contemporary Chinese intellectual elites. On the one hand, the ideology of progress is undergoing the materializing process of identification and verification, which consequently brings the joy and excitement of discovery; on the other hand, even a "home-grown" Chinese is suddenly stripped of hometown, homeland, and home country and abandoned to the beautiful new world. The feeling of family is no longer conveyed by a *hutong* (small lane, Mongolian in origin), a courtyard, a street corner, a city, but by the increasing retreat and confinement to the sleeping quarters, which consist of an apartment's entryway and its four walls. If during the period between the 1970s and the 1980s modernization is still the coveted golden horizon, much like the secret password to Ali Baba's treasure cave, then in the social realities of the 1980s and the 1990s people discover, not without anguish and disillusion, that the cave that is opened by "open sesame" is not only a Pandora's box but a labyrinthine palace and a dangerous wilderness constructed out of concrete, stainless steel, and glass enclosures. The closer one gets to the facile, universal embodiment of modernization—that wealthy and friendly, healthy and rational, democratic and free horizon—the more it seems like the "hope" left behind in the box.

On another level, if one of the most transformative changes of the 1980s and the 1990s is the replacement of the 1980s collective dream of nationalism with the 1990s individualist dream of wealth, then between 1994 and 1995, the vicissitudes and destructiveness of the dream for gold, at least for the intellectual elites, is more swift and poignant than the fragmentation of the nationalist dream. From the point of view of the intellectuals, who struggled with both repression and debilitation, nostalgia is a strategic need, a necessary spiritual space for imagining and for consolation. That is not all. The anguish of the 1980s and the repression of the 1990s and the rapid reorganization and transformation of society caused the Chinese people to experience the most chaotic identity crisis in many decades. In the 1990s, a "continuous loss of language"—except for a certain Wang Shuo stylistic, or the comedy television series Bianjibu de gushi (The story of the editorial section), Feihua (Useless babble), and Wo ai wo jia (I love my family)—effectively produces a tragicomic effect by the transposition, manipulation, and "misuse" of language. The intellectual collective is mostly immobilized by the taboo and ineffectiveness of discourse (in fact, it is the intellectual genealogy that loses touch with reality). As much as Wang and his group strongly disown the grand narrative of the 1980s, they are, however, the sole group to effectively communicate modernist language; it is they, and not the spiritual thinker or the reformer, who have no reservations about embracing modernization or about embracing the era of gold worship and individualism. As for other intellectual circles, the 1990s reality is fraught with conflicts and contradictions, and is filled with suffering, pain, and superficiality. Therefore, while the important cultural event of 1995, the debate on Renwen jingshen (humanistic spirit),[3] undoubtedly has memorable and concrete motivations and arguments, and undoubtedly analyzes and reorganizes the cultural divisions and camps of the 1990s, it nevertheless resembles more a war of signifiers, targeting the foundational ideas and views shared by both discursively warring parties, while, through adroit manipulation of ideological jargon, forcibly producing very disparate views, expressions, and principles. In fact, the ideological support of "progress" and the rush toward modernization forces Chinese intellectuals to drastically promote analytical thinking about modernism; nonetheless, modernization, with its flow of cash and material worship, creates pressure, anxiety, and anguish. What the Chinese people refuse to see is that the "human archive" is "built" on "humanity"—the history of Western civilization has always coexisted with industrial pollution and forests of steel and concrete.

The emergence of nostalgia answers a cultural need. It attempts to provide not only an imagined haven in the face of a reality of weariness and toil, but also, more importantly, a positive construction—according to Xiao Yen, a reliance on the resistance of remembrance's "expressive materiality" to ensure the "meaning of modern 'progress.'" Resembling, while distancing itself from, the 1980s, the construction of historicist historical narration becomes the vehicle of 1990s Chinese culture. Nostalgic representation here is indeed the best substitute for historical consciousness. Even though what the Chinese intellectual culture attempts to resist is the ubiquitous commodity craze, elegant nostalgia quickly becomes precisely one of the most marketable cultural commodities. Thus, whether it is the searching for roots, the homecoming fever, the inauguration of various student group organizations,[4] or the publication of folio-size illustrated journals on "old-style homes";[5] whether it is the popularity in China of the American best-seller *The Bridges of Madison County*[6] or the unrelenting popularity of its film adaptation at the Chinese movie theaters;[7] whether it is the sentimental meditation of Chen Yifei's films *Haishang jiumeng* (The old dream at sea) and *Renyue huanghun* (The twilight rendezvous), or the novels of Su Tong and Xu Lan, or Wang Anyi's *Changhen ge* (The ballad of eternal remorse),[8] Zhang Yimou's *Yao-a-yao, yao dao waipo qiao* (Shanghai triad), Li Shaohong's *Hongfen* (Rouge), Chen Kaige's *Fengyue* (Temptress moon), or Li Jun's *Shanghai wangshi* (Once upon a time in Shanghai), which gives expression to the delicate texture of the wilderness, to the fragile beauty of the old south, and to the mesmerizing yet corrupt Shanghai; whether it is the appearance of *gudian re* (classics fever) and the *Huaijiu shuxi* (Nostalgia book series)[9] in the so-called publishing market; whether it is the popularity of regional folk songs of Hong Kong and Taiwan, such as "Qianshou" (Holding hands) by Su Rei, "Zai huishou" (Look back again) by Jiang Yuheng, or the ephemeral trend of intimate lyrics in Chinese campus folk songs, such as "Tongzhuo de ni" (Classmate) by Lao Lang, "Tuanzhibu shuji" (Communist youth secretary) by Wang Lei, "Lutian dianyingyuan" (At the drive-in theater) by Yu Dong (not to mention the nostalgic atmosphere and nostalgic representation that has, in fact, become a trend of 1990s MTV); whether it is the high ratings of television's nostalgic melodramatic soap operas *Fengyu liren* (The belle of misfortune), *Nian lun* (The annal), and *Zaoyu zuotian* (Encounter yesterday), or the various appearances of confessional talk-show television programs—together they create a culture, a fashion, a cultural, psychological, and consumerist need and wish fulfillment. Similarly, in Liu Yan's *Yuanqule, Fadaier* (Going far away, Fadaier), an expensive, exquisite antique rattan chair and a bunch of carnations evoke for the heroine a hitherto unknown feeling of languor and an austere, yet elegant vision of a bygone age;[10] in Guo Runwen's oil painting, even though the mud wall, the paint-stripped sewing machine, the old-fashioned stationary, the red candle and wax, and the infant suit infer a common childhood remembrance, the long skirt of the young girl, the old-fashioned frosted-glass lightbulb, and the technical realism of the painting's portrayal imply a Western classical ambience that would be difficult to usher into any Chinese historical period.

In 1990, in his film *Xin xiang* (The fragrant heart), the Fifth Generation director Sun Zhou transforms, for the first time, the history-forsaking forward gaze and posture of the Fifth Generation into a posture of regarding history and embracing historical culture; he is also the first director to infuse a similar figuration of warm-hearted nostalgia into a successful advertisement. The advertisement, for Black Sesame Beverage of the South, which he wrote and produced for the advertisement firm 999, featured the warm glow of a red candle foregrounded in a dull-colored setting; a grandmother's old, yet graceful and kind, face; an adorable, traditionally clad little boy with a greedy expression; and some old-fashioned bamboo pails. Nostalgic atmosphere, in embellishing the vacuum of memory and in creating personal identities within the span of historical imagination, simultaneously accomplishes a representation of consumerism as well as a consumerism of representation.

The Harborless Ship of Nostalgia

When the shocking events in Tiananmen Square at the end of the 1980s created a mediated view of the golden horizon, and when the resurgence of a materialist trend after 1993 once again predicted a fragmentation of the realm of experience, the energetically mobilized nostalgic trend faced a historical memory that had no place in the collective remembrance. The arduous periods of revolution and war obstructed the Chinese people's memories of a seemingly authentic "Chinese history." Even for the group of retrospective intellectual elites, the parameter of their visibility still consisted of the steel and iron of war machinery and of blood and anguish. Within the debate of the so-called *jingshen jiayuan* (spiritual homeland) of the 1990s, there exists an ambivalence toward an emergent home for memories to which one can return and whose images one can evoke. An Italian poet can sing, "Those who have not lived in the age before revolution cannot comprehend the sweetness of living." [11] But the Chinese people, hailed by the ship of nostalgia in these days of increasingly shrinking space and rapid passage of time, discover that they possess only memories of revolution, before which is the bloodstained story of the dynastic empire. When Chen attempts to construct a memory of an ethnic society, the resistance that he encounters far exceeds the identification that he forges. We remember the history of the revolution, we possess the history of revolution—but the memory of the early revolutionary period of the 1950s and the 1960s is already made into a space for reminiscence. The legacy of the 1970s and the 1980s is once again reframed as "the golden age of spirit"; however, this history cannot provide us with the torment and decay that are necessary for feelings of nostalgia.

An extremely interesting cultural phenomenon in urban China in 1994 and 1995 was the sudden popularity of an American best-selling novel, *The Bridges of Madison County*, which sold millions of copies (not including the incalculable distribution of pirated copies) in China. In addition, the 1996 film adaptation of the book prolonged this wave of popularity. The 1990s novel was popular in the United States because it rewrites a couple's love affair from the 1960s—a revolutionary period in American history—and because it resolves the desolate, isolated, postmodernist space with the imaginary of "true love" among people. (Similar rewriting can also be seen in the Hollywood blockbuster film Forrest Gump, which was also well received in China, and in Robert J. Waller's second novel, Slow Waltz in Cedar Bend, which is slated for publication in China.) But The Bridges of Madison County was popular in China because, besides acknowledging a cultural identification in the process of globalization, it moreover (if not more importantly) indicates a space, a destination, for the contemporary Chinese urbanite's harborless ship of nostalgia, a resting place for the individual's remembrances. It is an uncompromising story of a torrid love affair. Therefore, when individual remembrance emerges through retrospection from the broken debris that was lost in the cracks of memory, at the same time it sexually romanticizes both revolutionary history and remembrance. There are no heroic lovers caught in the vicissitudes of history, no scene of blood and war; instead, we have the aesthetic music of romance. In fact, if we examine another best-selling novel of the 1990s in China, Manhadun de Zhongguo nüren (A Chinese woman of Manhattan), we find a similar strategy at work.[12] Although this novel, which sold hundreds of thousands of copies in China, focuses on a "real" American dream, the most moving part of the book is not how the character Zhou Li conquers Manhattan and moves into an apartment overlooking Central Park, or the various war stories that authorize the "hidden" personal narrative. The most emotionally satisfying chapters in the book are "Young Girl's First Love" and "The Small House in the Wild North." Here, the various segments of childhood narratives are pieced together into a private love story that effectively erases the emotionally and politically rife, cruel historical backdrop.

If the sexual romanticization of the memory of revolution effectively compensates for the vacuum left by the loss of the grand stage and the failure of the grand narrative, then its own historical narration is also fragmented by the conflictual, disparate authorizing languages and thus is full of blind spots. The representation of history, infused with nostalgic sentiments and revisions, once again regains harmony and continuity in the name of the individual, or consumerism. Among the numerous television commercials for Confucius Family Liquor, the following is a prime example: A background scene stylized into a faded yellow, like that of an old photograph, is accompanied by the words, "That's when I recognized 'home'; that's when I left home; that's when we protected our home." Appearing respectively is an image of a carefree pupil, of a progressive youth leaving home to join the revolution and to resist American intervention, and finally of a family reunion meal depicted in bright technicolor, voiced-over by the commercial jingle, "Confucius Family Liquor makes one think of home." In this nostalgic representation aimed at consumerism, mutually conflicting languages combine to yield a complete, effective historical narrative.

Nostalgic Feelings and the Construction of the Individual

Similar cultural movements existed before the juncture of the 1980s and 1990s. The sexual romanticizing of memories of the revolution accompanied by consumer strategies couched in personal values together constitute the many-faceted expressions of nostalgia in the 1990s. Although for the generation of writers born in the 1960s, including Han Dong, Bi Feiyu, and others, the portrait of childhood through the remembrance of the cultural revolution has an entirely different significance (they are more inclined to think of the carefree soberness in "Classmate," "The Bureaucrat's Chronicle," and "At the Drive-in Theater"). Representing another generation, Liu Heng's *Xiaoyao song* (Ode to the carefree) resembles more a fable in the style of William Golding's *Lord of the Flies* (*Yingwang*). At least in Tie Ning's *Meigui men* (The gate of roses), Wang Shuo's *Dongwu xiongmeng* (Ferocious animals), and Mang Ke's *Yeshi* (Primitive things), the memory of the Cultural Revolution is written as a story of sexual romance, a personalized history.[13] It becomes a space accessible to retrospection because of the intervention of the point of view of the self. Wang Shuo's story opens with the tone of an extremely anguished, nostalgic narrator:

> I envy those people who come from the countryside. In their memory exists an infinitely recollectable hometown. Even though this hometown may in reality be a destitute and unpoetic shelter, if they want, they can imagine that certain things that they thought to have lost may still be safely kept in that innocent hometown, and thereby restore their self-esteem and comfort their sorrow.
>
> I left home for this big city when I was very young, and I have never left here since. I consider this city to be my hometown. Everything in this city is changing rapidly—houses, streets, and people's dress and conversation—everything has changed, becoming a brand new city that keeps up our standard of fashion.
>
> Not a lingering trace of what came before. Everything is stripped clean.[14]

This is the anguish of an urbanite without a hometown, or of one robbed of a hometown. But at the end of the story, the narrator has undoubtedly found in the emotional reminiscence of a youthful romance a space, a haven for remembrance, and a harbor for the ship of nostalgia. If in Wang Shuo an impressionistic expression of the memory of youth filled with emotional turmoil allows another picture of the Cultural Revolution to emerge in an individualized vision, then for younger-generation, first-time film director Jiang Wen, the Cultural Revolution instinctively becomes an "age of magnificent sunlight": "Back then, the sky was more blue, the clouds whiter, the sunlight was warmer. It seems as if it never rained—that there was no rainy season. No matter what was done then, the remembrance is still attractive, still beautiful." [15] The salience of Wang Shuo's and Jiang Wen's work consists not only of sexually romanticizing the remembrance of revolution and individualizing the writing of history, but, more importantly, it embodies the "self" and the expression of self. This is manifestly different from the self of the 1980s vocabulary of historical narratives, which is not only encumbered with a certain grand narrative but more closely resembles the embodiment of a newly born or suddenly emerging collectivity.

More interestingly, although the intellectual elites and literatures of the 1980s contributed substantially to the theorizing of 1990s society, the infusion of mass culture from Hong Kong and Taiwan since the 1980s has been more effective in creating and expanding the cultural and psychological space for the self.[16] Undoubtedly, Wang Xiaobo's novella series Huangjin shidai (The golden age) is far more successful in carrying out a cultural-political strategy: The grand narrative of revolution is replaced by an absurd dialectic of abuse and being abused, of loyalty and betrayal, of chastity and promiscuity. What his works offer is not so much nostalgia as deconstruction and parody.[17] In the 1990s, if the sexual romanticization of the era of revolution or the recasting of the Cultural Revolution through the evocation of childhood powerfully rewrites the memory of history and of the individual, and eliminates paralysis and anguish, thus making it possible to transform that historical era into a representation of nostalgia and of material desire, then in the 1990s mass media, the expression of self and of nostalgia points to an even more interesting phenomenon. Since Kewang (Aspiration, 1990), television soap opera (or television melodrama) has become the most powerful and successful form of narrative of the masses. The immensely popular 1992 soap opera Guoba yin (Joys of living), directed by Zhao Baogang, the 1995 film Yongshi wo ai (My love eternally lost), directed by Feng Xiaogang, and the 1996 soap opera Dongbian richu xibian yu (Eastern sunrise, western rain), directed by Zhao Baogang, all exhibit the important symptom of this form—the metaphor of nostalgia. A product of the popular "Wang Shuo clan," these works successfully transpose the space of nostalgia from the rural countryside of the 1980s to the anonymous metropolis of the 1990s; they effectively open up an individualist space, while at the same time concretely reconstructing moral values, a work ethic, and a value system within the metaphor of nostalgic sensibility and nostalgic aura. In *Guoba yin*, the disjunctive combination of Wang Shuo's three novels (and in its chronological reversal of the novels), an oppositional cultural effort is at work vis-à-vis the 1980s; the various cultural and social roles that Wang Shuo and his clan played during the 1980s and 1990s emerge from the interstices. Interestingly, the attraction of these three stories comes not so much from their romanticization of contemporary urban life as from their ambience of a discontented nostalgia fashioned by the editor. Although these stories effectively generate and shape a representation of the anonymous metropolis, they all return their protagonists to a final destination of a space of the self that is an escape from the urban city: In *Guoba yin*, the male and female protagonists, Fang Yan and Du Mei, ultimately abandon their apartment and return to an old, semicolonial-styled classroom. When Fang Yan joyfully slips toward death in Du Mei's embrace, the camera lyrically sweeps up to a word, written in chalk in childlike handwriting on the blackboard: *love* is shaped into a close-up. Similarly, the protagonists of both *Yongshi wo ai* and *Dongbian richu xibian yu* live in a small cabin outside the city. Although in *Yongshi wo ai* the rural refuge is near a freeway, it is located nevertheless at the margin of the city; in *Dongbian richu xibian yu* the cabin is located in an unnamed forest. The final moments of *Yongshi wo ai* are a representation of the joy and harmony of the nuclear family: As the camera pulls up and away from the scene, the dying central male character's ardent voice can be heard—"My dearest ones, I love you. I will wait for you in heaven." In *Dongbian richu xibian yu*, the male protagonist watches in anguish, in the early light of morning, as a police car speeds away with his beloved. Thus, the bourgeois or pettybourgeois pretentions and sentimentalism create a metaphorical mood for nostalgia. While successfully transcending the survival realities of contemporary urban life, the film producer, the dream weaver, creates not only an effective portrayal of an urban protagonist—the individual—but also a timespace metaphor through the feelings of anguish and nostalgia, thus enabling him to bypass the filthy, chaotic reality and to call forth a Chinese middle class to reconstruct a work ethic, a morality, and a value theory that corresponds to a consumer market society.

The Emergence of the South

As mentioned previously, the most intense and ubiquitous nostalgic trend of the 1990s is the emergence of the south in novels and films. If the social function of the sudden wave of representation of nostalgia is to successfully overcome the fragmentation of language in order to rebuild or reconcile the narratives of history and reality, then the south, remembered or imagined, becomes an integral cultural touchstone. Representations in literature and art of the 1980s are saturated with the north (or, more precisely, the northwest and the northeast): whether it is *xungen* fiction, *zhiqing* literature, Fifth Generation films, or television documentary, what stand out are the decadent glamour, the dry and desolate yellow earth, and the relentlessly rolling Yellow River. If the entire cultural effort of the 1980s is to wholeheartedly construct and disseminate a portrait of the rupturing of Chinese history, then the north, or the figure of the yellow earth, becomes the materialization of this portrait. To quote a saying with wide currency in the 1980s, "Let history tell the future." In the narrative space of the 1980s, the north seems to be the figurative reminder of Chinese history, while the south (particularly the Yangzi delta region and the deep south, brought into prominence by the emergence of Shenzhen) seems to have become the signifier of the future. However, as much of the 1990s is in fact an extension of the development and cultural logic of the 1980s, this period brings about a reversal in terms of cultural representations. If we view the intellectual elite culture of the 1980s as a beautiful painting, then 1990s culture — mass or intellectual elite — is the flip side of the painting, the coarse fabric of the canvas. If 1980s cultural efforts clamorously delineate historical stages and depict the rupture of history, then the 1990s inscribes the continuity of history in a posture of discontented glancing backward. In other words, it is inscribing the flow of life within the narrative of self and destiny.

As part of the reversal of cultural representation, the spatial embodiment of historical China is representationally shifted from the north to the south. The north, with the route of the Yellow River as its nucleus, embodies a spatialized history that has ended or must be bid farewell, while the south imbues history again with the dimensions of time and life. At the end of the 1980s, the south first appears in the works of New Wave writers. Then, between Su Tong's white fields and the decadent glamour, there still exists a tacit complicity with mass consumption. Beginning with the novels *Wo de diwang shengya* (My life as an emperor), *Huozhe* (To live), and *Bianyuan* (The margins), stories that concern the individual and fate emerge from the south.[18] Authors begin to write of the lost ship of life that navigates through the brutality of history, the shifting of powers, and human catastrophes. In the 1980s historical reflection, or saga, a narrative tone of misery, melancholy, and torment imbues with a certain nostalgic look and reminiscent flavor the cold, inhumane spectacle of Chinese history. Quietly entering the 1990s scene, the young writer Xu Lan adds a bleak, yet somewhat sentimental, story to the historical perspective with her unique characterization of a vulnerable, indeterminate individual drifting through a series of catastrophes: that flashing moment of "as if," that moment of an absolutely private "indolence."[19] Changing course once again after *Jishi yu xugou* (Facts and fictions), another lengthy work, *Changhen ge* (The ballad of eternal remorse), by Wang Anyi shows the transformation and symptoms of this culture. The grand narrative is replaced by rumors and whispers.[20] The protagonist is an inconspicuous woman, subsisting on the margins of history. Like the spectral and wandering individuals of Xu Lan's novels, Wang Anyi's Wang Qiyao slips through historical upheavals in an evasive and illicit manner, like an outdated, forgotten, and therefore clandestinely kept bunch of dry, dead flowers.

Putting aside the specific factors of politics and the cultural market, the wave of long novels written in the 1990s can be seen as a revival of real-time duration in the temporality of narratives. The Chinese attempt once again to grasp time, to grasp the history that extends through time, rather than adopt a certain model, posture, or scene. If the culture of the 1980s identifies Chinese history with the desolate, arid ground of the northwest and places the future of China in Shenzhen, Zhuhai, Haikou, and other newly developed cities, then the seemingly overlooked cities of the south, including Jiangnan and Shanghai, are suddenly "discovered" and lionized by the culture of the 1990s, and are used for writing history and for bearing nostalgic anguish and languor. Obviously, the cultural emergence of Jiangnan and Shanghai is undoubtedly related to the boom in Shanghai's economy during the 1980s and 1990s, and to the prosperous growth in the economy of the Yangzi delta. This cultural emergence is, without a doubt, a result of the fulfillment of regional economic prosperity and the corresponding demand for regional culture. Shanghai, Nanjing, and Guangzhou coincidentally have become the gradually formed multicenters in the process of economic and cultural pluralization. However, as a focal point of 1990s national cultural consumerism, the emergence of the south displays a nostalgic penchant/tendency that is extraterritorial and transregional. In fact, in the 1990s, even without the benefit of cultural criticism, people can already sense, through the commercial malls, freeways, fast-food restaurants, designer boutiques, television commercials, billboard advertisements, and computer networks, the change in contemporary Chinese society wrought by an ineluctable global process. A profound identity crisis threatens to intrude on the contemporary Chinese, on various levels and in varying degrees: survival needs versus desires; self versus race, community, or region; China versus "the world." The wave of nostalgia here is undoubtedly an expression of identity construction, one of the many ways of gaining cultural identity. Thus, Shanghai becomes today's important "immigration" city and yesterday's "premier port of the East," "Ten Miles of Foreign Goods," and "Adventurer's Paradise." It becomes the unconscious of contemporary Chinese history—a place in history that must gain its writing through forgetting, that must transform itself into an appropriate and necessary discovery. As a specific historical and existing real space, Shanghai reflects the historical period that includes the beginning of China's belonging to the world. In addition, with its success in the past (or perhaps today or in the future) in setting trends, finding opportunities, and witnessing miracles, Shanghai provides a somewhat infectiously decadent, but alluring, background and setting. In the 1990s cultural reversal, Shanghai suppresses and foreshadows imperialism, semicolonialization, the profound wounding of the race, the uncanny phenomenon of money, and the picture of globalization. Shanghai possesses the history of revolution, as well as the history before revolution. Intellectual elites or the mass public may either accept or reject a narrative of ethnic, cultural paradise, and they may either reject and denounce an ancient obsolete city, but they have never explicitly rejected the historical representation and narrative of Shanghai and Jiangnan. In the imagined nostalgic scenario, the historical Shanghai and Jiangnan succeed in becoming a cultural springboard that allows us to leap unscathed across cultural experiences and to express new freedom.

Private book vendors, who peddle the most commercialized cultural commodity of the 1990s, report that, in addition to literature and art, the culture of the south has become a small-scale best-seller: from the prominence of the Jing Pai (Beijing School) and the Hai Pai (Shanghai School); to the publication and republication of Chengshi jifeng (The seasonal wind of the city);[21] to the encouragement of "reconstructing the humanism of southern China" and the fever of Eileen Chang; to the popularity of the disciplinary study of the city of Shanghai; to the Qian Zhongshu craze, a part of the classical craze, which spread from campuses to the book market to the black market. In terms of cinematic expressions, this sudden surge of southern vistas is in fact more variegated and chaotically pluralistic. However, in the pioneering works—for example, Chen Yifei's Haishang jiumeng and its sequel Renyue huanghun, Li Shaohong's Hongfen, Zhang Yimou's Yao-a-yao, yao dao waipo qiao (which was originally translated as Shanghai Story), Chen Kaige's Fengyue, the commercial films of the Sixth Generation (or the "New Generation"), or Li Jun's Shanghai wangshi—the one outstanding common feature is the construction of a representation of nostalgia and the southward move of the narrative space of history. Although in Chen Yifei's film it is a specter-like presence briefly passed over by the gaze of the wanderer, the images of bygone times are represented by MTV-style collage; what courses through the films is a nostalgic person's unmediated anguish. Fengyue is the retelling and collapse of a historical fable. In Hongfen, Renyue huanghun, and Yao-a-yao, yao dao waipo qiao, the "old tale" is valued as much as any other emotional entanglement in the aura of nostalgia. On an implicit level, instead of seeing the sudden surge of nostalgic tendency and its representation as a historical sense of lack or need, it is better to see it as testimony to the real and profound anxiety over the aggressively speedy process of modernization; instead of seeing it as a self-conscious cultural rebellion, it is better to see it as another effective process of legitimization. If one of the cultural functions of the 1980s reflection on historical culture is to identify, through a new cultural "enlightenment," as absent the presence of certain so-called historical, political, and cultural catalysts (in other words, we may see the 1980s culture as an instance of "clearing the arena," or cultural exile), then we, in the 1990s, must construct a narrative about the rupture of history in order to promote new historical progress. But the modernization of the 1990s, or the globalizing burst of progress, causes people to panic, as if they are teetering on the edge of the abyss. The wave of nostalgia brings new representations of history, making history the "presence in absentia" that emits a ray of hope on the Chinese people's confused and frenzied reality. A kind of familiar yet strange representation of history, a long repressed memory emerging from the horizon of history, through the repeated identification of contemporary Chinese history, allows people to receive consolation and gain a holistic, imagined picture of modernized China. In this picture, modernization is no longer the miracle of the 1979 reform of an old China in decline but an always integral part of the history of China. The difficulty of life is undoubtedly an incontrovertible fact, as is the impossibility of annihilating the pressures or the inner anxieties of reality. Nevertheless, the mesmerizing allure of this picture is that it rebuilds a kind of imagined link between the individual and society, between history and the present reality, in order to provide a rationale for our contemporary struggle and to impart to us some sense of comfort and stability.

The painting *New Literati Painting* (*Xin wenren hua*) by the young Nanjing painter Xu Lei perhaps provides a new perspective and insight. In this exquisite painting, the skillful old-style brushwork recaptures the body of a stallion.[22] Instead of a nostalgia for an elegant bygone antique, or a postmodern collage, what is exposed by the incompatibility of this beauty is the disintegration of history's representation in its emergence and restoration. While the painting transmits a certain Oriental secret, it also exudes a certain uncanniness, or even an omen. It is a kind of cultural memory that is more profoundly eternal than *The Memory Locked Away*, a kind of memory that can capture its representation but never again evoke its spiritual aura. What we can capture is merely an imagination; what we are able to achieve is merely a kind of writing. If, by borrowing the springboard of nostalgia, we are trying painstakingly to piece together a narration of history, spattered with the miscellany of language and crisscrossed with scars from its rupture, then whether it is an enigmatic sentiment of nostalgia or a consumption of such nostalgic representation, all will swiftly go the way of oblivion. The first example is Zhou Xiaowen, adroit in depicting urban cities and in writing about the anxiety of contemporary people, filming the historical epic Qin song (1996) with a capital of 40 million yuan. Even though the gravity, the authentic old style, and the concise conceptualization of the film all successfully evoke an imagined Qin dynasty–Han dynasty ambience, the anxiety of contemporary male intellectuals is still prevalent throughout. Surpassing Chen Kaige's epic film Ci Qin (Assassination of the Qin emperor) with its impressively grand cinematic setting, which was slated to open later as a theme park called Zhonghua Riyue Cheng, the film's budget reached 120 million yuan.[23] This transnational capitalization is in itself a more precious windfall. The film's exhorbitant capital investment far exceeds any possible return from the as yet unformed Chinese cultural and film market. If the 1990s nostalgia movement has not yet been able to provide an integral, globalized picture of China because of its instability, then the emergence of the representation of a history further back in time will mobilize the gigantic and anonymous economic machine behind the scenes to complete the scenario.

Another city of mirrors and lenses, another alienation closing in on the center.

Notes

1   See Hua cheng 1 (1996). Guo Runwen's paintings appear on both the front and back cover. Xiao Yen's short essay appears on the back cover.
2   Chinese people living overseas lament the changes in, or disappearance altogether, of their hometowns. Gu Xiaoyang once wrote in an American Chinese-language journal: "I used to be afflicted by a profound case of homesickness after coming to the U.S." But one day when going to see the film Beijing nizao (Good morning, Beijing), directed by Zhang Nuanxin, he discovered that the Beijing in which he grew up was no longer recognizable. He deeply regrets the demise of his hometown.
3   See Ding Dong and Sun Min, eds., Shiji zhijiao de chongzhuang: Wang Meng xianxiang zhengming lu (The turn-of-the-century clash: Essays on the Wang Meng phenomenon) (Beijing: Guangming Ribao Chubanshe, 1996).
4   See "Huaijiu qingchao" (The sentimental tide of nostalgia), Quanqiu qingnian (Global youth), no. 1 (1996): 1.
5   Several volumes of black-and-white photograph collections of ancient houses and streets from different places have been published under the title Lao fangzi (Old houses) (Nanjing: Jiangsu Meishu Chubanshe, 1995).
6   Robert J. Waller, Lanqiao yimeng (The bridges of Madison County), trans. Mei Jia, 1st ed., 1st printing (Beijing: Waiguo Wenxue Chubanshe, 1996). Several editions were subsequently published. Sales were still strong in 1996.
7   See "Liu wan ziji de lei, zou hui ziji de jia" (Returning home with tears), Beijing qingnianbao (Beijing youth daily), 24 Apr. 1996, 1–2, 5, 8.

8   See Su Tong, *Wenji* (Works) (Nanjing: Jiangsu Wenyi Chubanshe, 1994); *Xu Lan xiao-shu xuan* (Selected writings of Xu Lan) (Shanghai: Shanghai Wenyi Chubanshe, 1995); and Wang Anyi, *Changhen ge* (The ballad of eternal remorse) (Beijing: Zuojia Chubanshe, 1996).

9   Cai Maoyou and Shan Yuanyang, eds., *Huaijiu shuxi* (Nostalgia book series), 6 vols., 1st ed. (Beijing: Huaxia Chubanshe, 1995).

10 See Liu Yan, "Yuanqule, Fadaier" (Going far away, Fadaier), *Xiaoshuojie* (Fiction world), no. 1 (1996), 56–81.

11 Quoted in Ulrich Gallagher, *Shijie dianying shi* (A history of world cinema) (Beijing: Zhong-kuo Dianying Chubanshe, 1987), pt. 1, 110.

12 Zhou Li, *Manhadun de Zhongguo nüren* (A Chinese woman of Manhattan) (Beijing: Guang-ming Ribao Chubanshe, 1992).

13 Liu Heng, *Xiaoyao song* (Ode to the carefree) (Changsha: Hunan Wenyi Chubanshe, 1993); Tie Ning, *Meigui men* (The gate of roses) (Beijing: Zuojia Chubanshe, 1989); Wang Shuo, *Dongwu xiongmeng* (Ferocious animals), in *Wangshuo wenji* (Literary works of Wang Shuo) (Beijing: Huayi Chubanshe, 1992), 1:406–93; and Mang Ke, *Yeshi* (Primitive things) (Changsha: Hunan Wenyi Chubanshe, 1994).

14 Wang Shuo, *Dongwu xiongmeng*, 1:406.

15 See "Jiang Wen zhishu xiongyi," *Dienying gushi* (Cinema stories) no. 1 (1994): 7.

16 See Li Tuo, Song Weijie, and He Li, "Si ren tan" (A panel of four critics), *Zhongshan* (Purple mountain) no. 5 (1996): 187, in which Song Weijie mentioned and described this phe-nomenon.

17 See Wang Xiaobo, *Huangjin shidai* (The golden age) (Beijing: Huaxia Chubanshe, 1994). Of particular relevance are *Geming shiqi de aiqing* (Love in the revolutionary era), 3–190; and *Wo de yinyang liang jie* (My yin and yang worlds), 191–352.

18 Su Tong, *Wo de diwang shengya* (My life as an emperor), in *Su Tong wenji: Hou gong* (Literary works of Su Tong: The royal backyard) (Nanjing: Jiangsu Wenyi Chubanshe), 3–154; Yu Hua, *Huozhe* (To live) (Beijing: Renmin Wenxue Chubanshe, 1993); and Ge Fei, *Bianyuan* (The margins), in *Ge Fei wenji: Jijing de shengyin* (Literary works of Ge Fei: The silent sound) (Nanjing: Jiansu Wenyi Chubanshe, 1996).

19 See Xu Lan, *Fangfo* (As if), *Xianqing* (Indolence), and *Hong louban* (Red floor), in *Xu Lan xiaoshuo xuan* (Selected writings of Xu Lan), 1–48, 223–60, and 94–183, respectively.

20 *Rumors* is the title of a famous collection of essays by Eileen Chang, who wrote in Shang-hai during the 1940s. In *Changhen ge* (The ballad of eternal remorse), Wang Anyi writes about "rumors" in old Shanghai in a style reminiscent of Chang's.

21 Yang Dongping, *Chengshi jifeng: Beijing yu Shanghai de wenhua jingshen* (The seasonal wind of the city: On the cultural spirit of Beijing and Shanghai) (Beijing: Dongfang Chubanshe, 1994).

22 Xu Lei, "The Mystery of Absence," in *Selected Works of Xu Lei* (Hong Kong: Asian Fine Arts, 1994), 17.

23 See the special issue on Ci Qin, *Xiju dianying bao* (Theater and film weekly), 10 May 1996, 4.

chen xiaoming

9 The Mysterious Other: Postpolitics in Chinese Film
Translated by Liu Kang and Anbin Shi

In an interview with French TV, the production crew of the film *To Live* placed an empty chair on the set for Zhang Yimou, the director, to symbolize the presence of politics in his absence. As a mysterious signifier, the chair can be seen as a historical subtext in Chinese films. In fact, politics plays a decisive role in contemporary Chinese motion pictures—not only in the ideologically oriented orthodoxy but also in Fifth Generation films that deviate from the mainstream. In the tight fists of the revolutionary discourse, the Chinese film industry is characterized by a fully developed and omnipotent code of politics. However, in the Fifth Generation oeuvres that aim at artistic experimentation and internationalization, the political codes are divorced from the ideological practices of the state and are transformed into motifs, signs of cultural identity or superimposed sociohistorical backgrounds. Politics becomes a highly stylized, stereotyped, complicated, and ambiguous symbol, a hallmark of Chinese cinematic narratology. The multifarious functions of political codes constitute a peculiar narratological ambience in which Chinese film is produced, circulated, watched, and interpreted. Such a manipulation of political codes can be labeled "postpolitics" in Chinese film, where everything is political and nothing is political at one and the same time. Politics is everywhere, and yet it subverts itself at any moment.

In the 1990s, Chinese film is marching aggressively toward the world market. Therefore, postpolitics in Chinese film not only animates native cultural production but also manages to dance to the tunes set forth by the Western cultural imaginary about China. As such, concepts such as *postmodernity* or *postcolonialism* cannot adequately describe the complexity and ambiguity of this power relationship. The purpose of this essay is to unravel the means by which the omnipresent politics is mysteriously transformed into the revolutionary narrative, and to see how politics constitutes a symbolic act, replete with paradoxes, in contemporary Chinese film.

1. Rewriting and Reconfiguring History: The Abstraction of Politics

The 1950s and 1960s witnessed the apex of the revolutionary discourse in China. An edifice of the revolutionary myth of history was erected, under which literature and the arts served as the Communist panacea for the enlightenment and unification of the people and as a lethal weapon to eradicate the "capitalist influence." Under such circumstances, the Chinese film industry, like any other form of cultural production, "undertook the task of providing visual representations of the orthodox historical discourse, and, in turn, those historical representations were entitled to an important position in the mainstream ideology." [1] Films directed by Xie Jin epitomized this ideological function of Chinese cinema during this period. Despite the incessant ideological campaigns aimed at the realm of culture that assaulted "anti-Party" tendencies among artists, few Chinese writers and artists publicly espoused political dissent during those years.

In the wake of the Cultural Revolution, historical narratives that exposed the previous dark decade took on the twofold objective of redefining the relationship between the arts and politics and of resurrecting humanism as the core of literature and the arts. The political interests of writers and artists had by no means diminished. Instead, the anti–Cultural Revolution historical narrative served to reinforce political passion by providing an aesthetic representation of the ideological emancipation movement of the New Era of the late 1970s and early 1980s. Films produced during this period bear a close relationship to the political campaigns of the time. One of the then highly acclaimed feature films, The Legend of Mount Tianyun (Xie Jin, 1980), for instance, tried to express its political theme through the love affairs of its male and female protagonists. Its goal was to attenuate political concerns by promulgating humane feelings and sensitivity and by extolling romantic love and beauty. However, the reconstitution of the intellectuals' loyalty to the Communist Party was the film's unmistakable thesis, no matter how the producer tried to romanticize it. Obviously, the film's high romantic sentiment and humanism were in line with the official political orientation. Love and humanism were indeed the true desires of intellectuals, who wanted to break away from the domination of ultraleftist policies; therefore, romanticism and humanism were integrated into the practices of the prevalent ideology, constituting an imaginary commonwealth in which the Party and the intellectuals reached a consensus and a mutual understanding.

The political campaign of ideological emancipation came to an end in the mid-1980s. At that time, the happy ideological marriage between the Party and the intellectuals began to break down, as shown by the increasing schism between the discourse of the political power and that of the intellectuals. The earlier, anti–Cultural Revolution historical narrative that promoted "Marxist humanism" gave way to theories of alienation under socialism, literary and philosophical (and, indeed, existential) subjectivities, and holistic antitraditionalism or iconoclasm. In the arena of literature and the arts, the inevitable rise of modernism gradually eroded the revolutionary discourse. The impassioned enthusiasm for artistic innovation and aesthetic novelty ultimately pushed the revolutionary discourse to its limit. As a result, the revolutionary discourse was deeply entrenched in an irresolvable dilemma: On the one hand, it still policed all cultural activities with its institutional power; on the other hand, it lacked an effective system of ideology and representation that could accommodate itself to the new sociohistorical developments. Motivated by the call for innovation and novelty, writers and artists then plunged into bold adventures charted by modernism. Modernism furnished the generation of the 1980s not only with new artistic concepts and ideas but also with new ways of expression and representation. Largely inspired by the modernist aesthetics of innovation, this generation of Chinese artists was able to detach itself from authority and, as such, succeeded in distinguishing itself from its predecessors.

Challenging the orthodox aesthetic principles of "revolutionary realism," the emergence of the Fifth Generation filmmakers effected an imaginary act of rebellion rather than an aesthetic revolution. This was the moment when the dominant ideology, on which earlier films were dependent, ran aground. Any experiment, however limited in its scope, was viewed as a violation of the aesthetic principles of revolutionary realism. Such a rigid cultural hegemony could not adapt to, nor would accept, any new artistic forms and expressions. It could only exercise its institutional power of control and restrictions. In this context, the Fifth Generation films have a twofold significance: They differ fundamentally from earlier, ideologically centered films, and they also threaten to subvert the ideological authority and its discourse. Therefore, the Fifth Generation filmmakers reluctantly took on the role of rebels on the periphery of the dominant ideology.

The One and the Eight (Zhang Junzhao, 1984), the Fifth Generation's debut, shocked audiences with its overwhelmingly subjective camera perspectives and arbitrary long shots. One may wonder why Zhang Junzhao went to such great lengths to reiterate the revolutionary myth of the Anti-Japanese War. It perhaps embodied "the social order of the late 1970s and early 1980s, which restored the collectivity of fathers and served in the meantime as a self-defense for the 'deviant' Fifth Generation artists who were viewed as aberrant." [2] However, it is difficult to identify any specific political reference in the film's revolutionary myth. In this film, one no longer sees the kind of heroism and absolute loyalty to the revolution that was seen in earlier revolutionary realist films. The historical circumstances narrated in the film are evasive and indeterminate. But still, since revolutionary myth as subject matter legitimizes avant-garde experimentation within the framework of the revolutionary discourse, it is a strategic choice. On the other hand, the film employs a plethora of unconventional techniques, such as fragmented narration, abrupt long shots that intersect close-ups, and long scenes with muffled off-camera sound effects that generate a bizarre sense of repression and repulsiveness. The film capitalizes on the unique circumstances of hardship and the violence of war as a space for the repressive narrative and for technological and formal experimentation, but it also distorts this revolutionary myth beyond recognition. Since technical and stylistic innovation outweighs subject matter, revolutionary history and politics recede into the negligible background. Just as revolutionary discourse is replaced by a long interlude of silence, political codes of revolution become abstract and are transformed into striking graphic and narrative designs bereft of any specific meaning. In other words, the seemingly canonical legend of revolution is reduced to a by-product of the artistic experimentation, through which Fifth Generation filmmakers call the authoritative revolutionary discourse into question. By the same token, repeated queries about loyalty, misunderstanding, wrongdoing, and morality in *The One and the Eight* severely undermine the legitimacy of the revolutionary myth.

Such a reinterpretation of the revolutionary myth is echoed in *Yellow Earth* (Chen Kaige, 1984). As a film that recounts the revolutionary history, it maximizes the abstraction of the revolutionary myth by turning the center of the film (revolutionary legend) into a lonely symbolic figure. Because the camera is placed on the broad vista of the yellow earth, where the revolutionary myth originated, the revolution also becomes a narrative perspective. Only a land of extreme poverty and hardship could generate the revolutionary myth, as well as the unadorned folklore of the peasants. What does Chen Kaige want to find? Is it the "human relationship," as he put it?[3] What is the ideal humanity, human understanding, and friendship? Chen once acknowledged that his goal for the film was to explore the "humane" relationships between a revolutionary soldier, a stubborn peasant, and the peasant's daughter. Scenes that try to capture humane moments—such as when Gu Qing, the soldier, Cuiqiao, the peasant girl, and Cuiqiao's father are sitting around the peasants' hut, and Cuiqiao gives her father the shoes she made for him—are intended to demonstrate the authenticity of the origin of the myth, as pure and simple as native folklore. However, history hindered and altered the trajectory of revolution. In the end, the soldier fails to save the girl from the coercive marriage arranged by her father and the village matchmaker. The helpless girl vanishes from the scene like an unrecognizable tiny dot fading on a gigantic canvas. Something went wrong in the origin of this revolutionary myth. Humane understanding and compassion are limited and transient, while nonchalance and misunderstanding seem permanent. In the highly acclaimed scene of "praying for rain," Gu Qing, the soldier, returns. But none of the local folks recognizes him, and no one seems to pay any attention to the stranger. The peasants are busy worshiping the God of Rain instead of the God of Revolution. Gu Qing, the very symbol of revolution, appears superfluous and alienated under these circumstances. He is an arbitrarily superimposed signifier, completely out of context.

Of course, it would be an exaggeration to say that Chen Kaige intentionally rewrote the revolutionary myth. Actually, the meaning of the film is rather confused and contradictory. The question is not what he wanted to express— Chen Kaige didn't seem to intend to express any meaning. To him, a soldier, the yellow earth, the Yellow River, and the caves were sufficient in themselves. The film can be described in Taoist aesthetic terms as a "grand image without a form" or as a "grand sound without a tone." It presents an immense physical space with a vast and low horizon, as well as a boundless yellow earth. These grand images are the objects frozen by tedious long shots. And an aphasic crowd in these silent, frozen scenes further underscores the enormity and physicality of the long shots of scenery. This is a world in which physical objects overwhelm human subjects. In this world of yellow earth composed by history and culture (or of history and culture composed by yellow earth), the destinies of human beings are long predetermined. The locus of the film is obviously not the story, which the revolutionary myth prescribes; rather, it is the aesthetic form itself. The form compresses the revolutionary myth to the most abstract level and rewrites it through the formalist language of the camera.

The Fifth Generation filmmakers were defined by this bold experimentation with artistic form on the ideological margins. Formal experiment endowed their work with a certain historical legitimacy. Formal experiment then became a symbolic act, an imaginary resolution of the real contradictions.[4] It appears now rather arbitrary and contrived, but it gathered the real contradictions and offered some resolutions. The act of rewriting the revolutionary myth became a way to escape being manipulated by the orthodox political discourse. As a result, the revolutionary myth was transformed into stereotyped political codes, which provided the camera with infinite possibilities for maneuvering between the nuances of politics and literature. What was important was not *what* to tell but *how* to tell, and such a formalist motto was faithfully observed by the Fifth Generation. "How to tell" emerged as the primary aesthetic question to be tackled. As Zheng Dongtian put it, "Film must be made like a film first."[5] Politics, in this process of artistic renovation, was relegated to the periphery. However, this is not to say that the Fifth Generation was apolitical. Its politics lay in the very act of seemingly apolitical, formal, and aesthetic experimentation. In the Fifth Generation films dominated by the repugnance for the ideological mainstream, anything apolitical was thus turned political, and vice versa.

2. The Dislocated Imagination: Politics and Cultural Identity

The Fifth Generation filmmakers have amputated and encapsulated the orthodox political discourse in a reservoir of mythologies, a cultural resource that can be manipulated, in order to subjugate the stereotypical discourse of politics to artistic experimentation. When "culture" became the central motif of the Fifth Generation, politics was turned into culture's supplement. A good case in point is *Red Sorghum* (Zhang Yimou, 1987), a film, based on Mo Yan's novel, that again introduces the revolutionary myth of the Anti-Japanese War. Rather than offering a conventional eulogy of the Communist leadership during that time, *Red Sorghum* resorts to a naturalistic expression of the nation's vital power by means of a legendary love-and-death story. As a disguised political code, the revolutionary historical legend merely serves to bring to dramatic climax the romance between the narrator's "grandpa and grandma" and their heroic ambush of Japanese invaders. Expressions of primitive passion, the joys of lovemaking, and the slaughter in the sorghum fields all lead to the climax of the film, which reflects nothing less than the tenacity of the nation's existence.

Such a national character, or cultural essence, constituted the very spiritual basis of Chinese society in the late 1980s. The philosophical debates about antitraditionalism were then ironically transformed into a discussion about the global issue of cultural identity, by the involvement of the overseas "new Confucianism" movement. Under the banner of "root searching," a cultural fad in the late 1980s, writers who were "educated youth" (or former Red Guards) found an excuse to retreat from modernism and triumphantly proclaimed their retreat a grand march in search of national roots and origins. The problems of contemporary China that could not be dealt with in the antitradition debate, which was a thinly disguised critique of the present, could now be solved in the ambiguities of root searching. The answer in Mo Yan's novel (and in the film) lies in the primitive passion of the nation, embodied in the grandpa's way of living, which reveals the ideological dilemma—the individual can refuse to accept any preordained concept or grand ideology. *Red Sorghum*, then, by the end of the 1980s, became a symbol of the moment when culture was rewritten as something that existed above and beyond politics. But culture was, at the same time, construed as a counterculture phenomenon of the "way of life," an instinctual behavior driven by repressed libido. It signified nothing less than the subversion of the social power structure. Politics was thus turned upside down, to become again a historical subtext of the film.

As a film that strays from the ideological mainstream, *Red Sorghum* gives full expression to the zeitgeist of casting off sociopolitical and cultural yokes. In some sense, the critical praise it won both at home and abroad was proof that the omnipotence of political codes had almost ceased to exist, except in name. Far from the orthodox ideological discourse, the carnival of life depicted in the film was intended to provide an emotional catharsis and cause a spectacular sensation. *Red Sorghum* marks both an end and a beginning. When ideology can no longer sustain its intellectual and rational grip on society, and can only assert itself through emotional relief that provides society with nothing more than a momentary spectacle, the demise of the orthodox ideological practice becomes imminent.

Politics never has the final say in the films of the Fifth Generation; instead, politics is subjugated by culture and deconstructed in the name of artistic experimentation. Politics becomes a style that only resembles the politics in canonical revolutionary films in a formal sense. In terms of meaning and substance, however, it is ambiguous and indeterminate. But this does not mean that politics is not important to the Fifth Generation. On the contrary, their films are sustained by revolutionary discourse. Politics serves as the very identity of Chinese oeuvres in the international film market by virtue of the fact that politics is the most effective means and raw material for the artistic expressions of Fifth Generation Chinese cinema. Of course, Zhang Yimou certainly wants to avoid politics and tries to downplay the importance of politics in most of his films. But once his films enter the world film market, politics inevitably captures the spotlight. Hence, in the eyes of a Western beholder, Zhang Yimou's *Judou* (1991) is interpreted as an innuendo against the gerontocracy, and *Raise the Red Lantern* (1992) is seen as a political power struggle. Political readings of these Chinese films are not necessarily far-fetched misreadings insofar as the cultural imaginary of Oriental culture has always already inculcated an invisible, but omnipresent, nexus of absolute power and totalitarianism, which overshadows Zhang Yimou's, and others', films. It does not matter whether such a power nexus refers to ancient feudalism or despotism, or to the "proletariat dictatorship" of modern China, for the cultural imaginary of Oriental culture is fundamentally timeless—the present is all but a reappearance of the past. Politics is thus a determinant situation in the cultural imaginary of China. In the Foucauldian view, sexuality and politics are two sides of the same coin. Augmented by sexual themes, Chinese politics can only become more interesting to the Western audience.

Fredric Jameson's insight into the relationship between Third World politics and art—"the narratives about personal destiny contain a national fable in which mass culture and society encounter tremendous challenges" [6]—best illustrates what took place in the Chinese cultural arena during the mid-1980s. However, the late 1980s saw the decentralization of the orthodox ideology and a split between the public and the private, between poetics and politics, between sexuality, the subconscious, and the secular world characterized by class, economy, and political power.[7]

In the 1990s, Chinese artists have in effect strayed from political and ideological practices and have become increasingly individualistic in their expressions. In contrast, the films that "go out into the world" are more emphatically political and have national allegorical themes. Films chronicling the lives of human beings all tend to reinforce the national and collective identity of China. *Farewell My Concubine* (Chen Kaige, 1992) can be seen as a chronicle of the modern Chinese revolution. Personal biographies are embedded in the twentieth-century Chinese history of the republican revolution, the civil war between warlords, the Anti-Japanese War, the civil war between the Communists and the Guomindang, the socialist reform, and the Cultural Revolution. The historical vicissitudes that people endured have added a significant complexity and enrichment to the stories of their lives. The image of China in this film is not characterized by the Peking opera or by the homosexual relationship between the male protagonists but rather by the diachronic political catastrophes in modern Chinese history. Only the political events can properly delineate the contours of a modern China in the global cultural imaginary. If in Zhang Yimou's *Red Sorghum*, the revolutionary myth is subjugated under the culture myth, serving only as a marginal discourse, then in *Farewell My Concubine*, culture is displaced by politics, which constitutes the dominant discourse of the film.

The trials and tribulations of Cheng Dieyi, the hero of the film, are inextricably intertwined with China's modern revolutionary history. Even his sexual orientation is political, insofar as his intimacy with his "brother" is fostered not so much by pure brotherhood as it is by his fear of the imperial eunuch and the warlords. Homosexuality is thereby endowed with a political message, one that reveals the political history by which personal preferences and lifestyles have been fatalistically circumscribed. Predetermined by political history, Cheng Dieyi's personal fate becomes, to a large extent, a symbol of modern history, manipulatable by revolutionary movements. Political conflicts dominate the second half of the film. Obviously, such an abusive use of politics diminishes the exploration of the human psyche. However, as Ping-hui Liao puts it, "to reconstruct large historical events through collective memories may provide Westerners with a bird's-eye view of modern Chinese history and may satisfy their curiosity about the Orient."[8] Chen Kaige's adroit manipulation of political codes won him international acclaim, including first prize at Cannes and an Oscar nomination.

Chen Kaige's film version of modern Chinese history is divorced from the ideological mainstream and caters primarily to the West's cultural imaginary about China, in which politics not only constitutes the dominant narrative situation but also serves as an indispensable essential constituent of China's history and culture. But what is the "authentic" cultural identity of China? Is it the poverty depicted in Old Well (Wu Tianming, 1987)? The primitive rituals in Red Sorghum? The incest in Judou? The power struggle among the concubines in Raise the Red Lantern? The Peking opera in Farewell My Concubine? The shadow puppet play in To Live (Zhang Yimou, 1994)? In all these films, politics serves as the very identity of China, without which all the stories about human beings would lose their exotic appeal as representing an absolute Other. It is not surprising that even in 1994, Tian Zhuangzhuang produced Blue Kite, a film that rehearses the political hardships during the Antirightist Campaign and the Cultural Revolution in the 1950s and 1960s. The film reiterates the thematics of the "scar literature" of the late 1970s, which portrays political persecution and fear. To be sure, this particular historical period may have left an indelible impression in Tian's mind, and his film indeed serves as a reminder of that unforgettable era. However, Tian's reconstruction of the outmoded Fourth Generation films yields little more than a well-conceived reproduction of the "China image" in the Western cultural imaginary.

Politics in Fifth Generation films became an effective narrative strategy that integrated politics, ethnography, and sexuality, and was thus conducive to the mass production of an exotic Other in the transnational film market. Following their frustrated honeymoon with modernism, Fifth Generation filmmakers resorted to the mystification of political codes as their dominant narrative strategy in the globalized cultural context. Endowed with certain traits of postmodernism and postcolonialism, their films created an unprecedented spectacle characterized by recurrent political persecutions and omnipresent totalitarianism, a politics that is the legacy of the ancient dynasties and that has culminated in the history of revolution. It is no coincidence that the recurrence of this history serves as a metaphorical innuendo to today's sociopolitical situation. In some sense, the present, always absent in the Fifth Generation's reverie about the past, is the historical subtext, always already embedded in personal stories. What is important is not the time of the story but the time of telling the story. Telling the story of the past in the present, when intertwined with the story per se, creates a peculiar effect of the "real" that otherwise irrelevant political symbols have all but displaced.

3. Subversion and Reappropriation: The Dialectics of Aesthetics

When Fifth Generation filmmakers arrived on the scene for the first time, they still had to rely on the revolutionary hegemony and draw on the revolutionary myth for their raw materials. They reinterpreted the canonical revolutionary myth in their own artistic symbolic act. However, when they determined to pursue the international film market, they severed politics from China's social and historical practices and turned the former into a cultural fountain to quench the Western thirst for a mystified China. Without politics as the inexhaustible theme and primary cultural background, Fifth Generation films would have received little international attention. However, it would be equally wrong to view politics as the only obstacle to Chinese cinema. The question is: How does one appropriate the political as a cultural resource? When employed as a narrative mechanism rather than as an oversimplified cultural label, political symbols create powerful aesthetic effects.

Zhang Yimou's To Live is a good example of such a creative appropriation of political symbols. Throughout the film, Zhang attaches great significance to politics, which is the trademark of China's cultural identity in the international film market. Personal lives again bear all the traces of a political history of revolution, from civil war to the incessant political campaigns after the establishment of New China. The protagonist Fu Gui's personal odyssey to survive recurrent political hardships gives full expression to the basic life philosophy of the Chinese people—"to live is good." Its tragic dimension is revealed by the revolutionary history, which makes even the most fundamental needs of life unattainable luxuries. Which one—the political ebb and flow, or the will of Heaven—has the final say in human fortunes? Zhang Yimou apparently remains ambivalent on this issue (an ambivalence he may owe to the decidedly apolitical Yu Hua, the author of the novel from which the film is adapted). Despite all the ambiguities, politics still directly determines the lives of individuals, not through specific political cadres (such as the district governor, Chunsheng, who is a nice man but also a victim) but through the invisible political network that overshadows the everyday life of each human being.

The film is split into two halves with incongruous styles. The first half is characterized by its linear chronology that blends political history with cultural history, deliberately setting the stage to conform to the Western image of China. This part of the narrative bears Zhang Yimou's distinctive style — repressive, closed, linear, and orientalist. The second half, however, turns out to be a political parody with a hybridized narrative style that constantly shifts modes and perspectives. In the first half, politics is included simply to appeal to the Western audience; but in the second half, political events become incorporated into the texture of the narrative in order to arouse and reverse simultaneously the imagination of the audience. Such a narrative smuggles in the classic technique of suspense film, in which the occurrence of events is always abrupt and unexpected.

To Live's wedding scene is a good example of this technique. When Fu Gui and his wife are shopping for the occasion, a neighbor hurries to inform them of an unexpected crowd in their yard. They rush back home, thinking that some disaster looms. Breathless, they arrive only to find that their would-be son-in-law and his friends are painting a gigantic mural of the Great Helmsman on the front wall of their yard in preparation for the wedding. In another long shot that appears rather abruptly, a throng of Red Guards parades with a deafening roar, shouting revolutionary slogans and waving red banners and giant posters. This scene of demonstration is reminiscent of everyday life during the Cultural Revolution, which was suffused with fear and terror. Rather than a much expected scene of violence, what follows is a tender moment when the parents (Fu Gui and his wife) feel genuinely touched by their crippled son-in-law, who has come with all his friends and fellow workers to greet the bride, their mute daughter. As soon as the audience's expectations and curiosity are aroused, a comic reversal occurs. This has become a pattern that, in the end, fulfills expectations that nevertheless draw heavily on the narrative's peculiar historical situation — the tragicomic ambience of the Cultural Revolution. Permeated with aesthetic dialectics in the era of posttragedy, the unexpected turns and developments of the much consecrated Cultural Revolution and of secular pursuits of happiness result in a drama that blends tragic and comic elements.

As I have indicated, the stereotyped politics is conducive to the construction of the internal and/or external symbolic act in contemporary Chinese film. Jiang Wen, a much younger, Sixth Generation actor-director in China, recaptures the sexual pursuits and merrymaking of juvenile delinquents during the Cultural Revolution in his film debut, In the Heat of the Sun (1996)—or, more accurately, Bright Sunny Days, as Liu Kang points out.[9] Wang Shuo's novel Ferocious Animals, from which the film is adapted, focuses on the sex lives, sexual fantasies, and revelry of the adolescent protagonists. It is a collective account, with no apparent animosity for its own historical context. Jiang Wen, however, rewrites the title as Bright Sunny Days in order to convey a different experience. Activities such as sexual fantasies, girl chasing, fisticuffs, and partying show a very different side of the Cultural Revolution. By all standard accounts, the Cultural Revolution was a destructive and catastrophic national disaster, as depicted in Fourth and Fifth Generation films. But in Jiang Wen's narrative, "it becomes a dream of the young and the restless, of a bunch of brazen, adventurous youngsters ablaze with the passions of love and hate."[10] Obviously, Jiang Wen has a bittersweet nostalgia for that period, which he reveals in great detail through private memories. The adolescent libido, rather than political codes, dominates Jiang's sentimental narrative, which eludes any possible association with the politically oriented national allegory. It no longer projects an epic vision of power struggles and politics but draws a portrait of private lives in their naked and natural forms. Free from direct repression by the political power, the protagonists are a carefree, reckless gang who experience the Cultural Revolution only as playful, carnivalesque "bright sunny days," not as gloomy, disastrous nightmares. The personal histories, the personal predicaments encountered in sexual awakening, and the difficulties of being accepted by the group are all imbued with Kafkaesque bizarreness and jocundity. As the dominant theme, sex guarantees the successful evasion of political allegory. The concentration on sex also casts doubt on the plausibility of the historical events narrated in the film. For instance, Ma Xiaojun's skepticism of Mi Lan's real existence and the incommensurability of the portrait of the young girl and Mi Lan the real person seem to reinforce the suspicion of the reliability of all the classic accounts of the era. Jiang Wen uses color to express the "bright sunny days" of the Cultural Revolution, but he uses black and white to express the present, which he tends to reject. Even a fool in the film curses the flashy Cadillac and the Napoleon X.O. cognac, status symbols of the newly rich of the 1990s, as "fucking stupid." However, Jiang Wen's nostalgia for the Cultural Revolution cannot be said to come at the expense of the present. He states, "Although the fire was put out, there are still flickers amid the ashes. Who says all the passion is gone forever?"[11] Of course, to Jiang Wen, the reality of the present, which is anything but "bright sunny days" and banal, adolescent passion, must be relentlessly castigated. And it is clear that his memory of adolescent passion is entirely different from the standard version of the time.

The adolescent fervor of the 1960s that has resurfaced in recent years has, in fact, very little to do with the ideological practices of contemporary China. The sentimentality of private nostalgia has significantly diluted the political colors of the Cultural Revolution. Ironically, however, the Sixth Generation's infatuation with libidinal impulses is inevitably embedded in the sociopolitical subtext. Jiang Wen capitalizes on the historical context of the Cultural Revolution in his film to make it appear nonconformist. The more he pays attention to issues of libidinal wish fulfillment, the more his narrative is entangled in the political current of canon rewriting. In the Heat of the Sun (or Bright Sunny Days), for instance, won international acclaim for its repudiation of the traditional political codes—the cultural identity of China. In some sense, politics, as the external subtext and internal context, maintains its mysterious omnipotence in Chinese film.

4. The Insurmountable Obstacle and the New Narratology

Politics, as I have pointed out, has been the determining factor in the reconstruction of the image of "China" in the West. Without the strategic employment of political codes, Chinese film would lose its cultural identity and consequently be denied international recognition. But Zhang Yimou, the reputed enfant gâté of international film festivals, experienced a crushing rejection with Shanghai Triad (1995), a direct, if not heavy-handed, imitation of a Hollywood film noir. The failure of the film was due to its cultural ambivalence, and this ambivalence was the direct result of its apolitical narrative strategy. For the sake of producing a commercial movie for the domestic market, Zhang Yimou broke from the Western cultural imaginary of China, which had been a trademark of his films. In Shanghai Triad, Zhang Yimou wanted, above all, to redefine his own style. But the film went too far and had too many facets, no obvious political identity, and no clear goal, wavering between entertainment and serious art. For example, Zhang Yimou shows the swinging legs of go-go dancers amid the hubbub of urban existence, but he also implies a nostalgia for the idyllic, rural life: The Chinese title, which translates literally as "Row to Grandma's bridge," comes from a popular children's swinging song and can easily be interpreted as evoking a pastoral scene in the Chinese context. But it would be superficial to see this as Zhang making a simple contrast between the values and lifestyles of city and countryside. In fact, the film aims at a serious exploration of the social and cultural origin of Chinese modernity— one of the blind spots in the study of modern Chinese history.

In Zhang's film, Chinese modernity is inevitably interwoven with the patriarchal clan system. Setting foot in such a modern metropolis as Shanghai, the rural bullies and landlords immediately form Mafia-like gangs for their clandestine and illegal business. Although they are engaged in modern forms of trade and commerce such as banking and savings and loans, the ways in which their businesses operate are entirely determined by the traditional clan system. In the very process of modernization, those who show any truly modern spirit will ultimately be banished by the clan, which determines and steers the course of modernity. The hero and heroine's quest for modernity—which includes a love affair, plans for a wedding in Paris, and a modern education—is considered an act of disobedience by the clan authority. The couple's individualistic pursuits and strategies for reforming tradition all fail, and they are sentenced to death, to be buried alive.

In some sense, Zhang intended to reveal a tragic paradox: Modernization in China had to be accomplished in traditional ways. Despite the ambiguities and ambivalence, his reflection on China's way to modernity was quite provocative. However, few paid attention to this serious examination of the fate of modernity in China because of its radical change in style, from an exotic and ethnographic depiction of folk tradition to something very much like the early Hollywood musical or second-rate gangster movie. When the English title of the film became *Shanghai Triad*, it inevitably alluded to the generic features of Hollywood musicals and westerns. In short, this film, because of its lack of distinctive political codes and features of oriental despotism, fails to be identified in the Western cultural imaginary about China. Zhang Yimou tried to create a new narrative style to portray the complex origins of history and the dense textures of everyday life, but stereotyped politics had become an insurmountable obstacle for contemporary Chinese cinema, an obstacle even Zhang Yimou could not overcome.

Arriving on the heels of the controversial Fifth Generation, the ambitious Sixth Generation filmmakers based their work on individualism and market-oriented opportunism. Their films sever all connections with the revolutionary discourse and/or the artistic experimentation advocated by their predecessors. The appearance of the Sixth Generation is not the result of artistic renovation but rather the outcome of the market-driven opportunism that permeates today's cultural arena. These filmmakers act self-consciously as fearless iconoclasts and, accordingly, push the limit in whatever they do, hoping the public accepts their work as artistically revolutionary. Despite complaints about political constraints and the lack of political freedom, the Sixth Generation never uses politics as their main motif. They have no interest in politics, for few remember the days when politics was everything. Wary of any political interference with their films, they undertake an artistic vaudeville with the purpose of subverting the existing conventions. Black-and-white frames, simultaneous sound tracks, shabby studios, and maladroit, yet true-to-life, performances by amateur actors and actresses distinguish the Sixth Generation as a group of rebels and misfits.

Beijing Bastards (Zhang Yuan, 1991) portrays the reckless lifestyle of Chinese rock-and-roll singers. Deeply rooted in their antipathy toward institutionalized power structures—political, social, and artistic—they indulge themselves in making money, having sex, and producing unconventional artwork. Time and again, however, libidinal wish fulfillment is inevitably implicated in a political myth of counterrepression. The unconventional pastiche of black-and-white shots and close-ups insinuates the anti-institutional stance of these self-styled unconventional artists. The title *Beijing Bastards*, with "the eggs under the red flag" (the title of a popular song by the rock star Cui Jian) as a sociological marker of the post-1949 generations, sheds light on the Sixth Generation's manipulation of the connection between politics and commercialism.

The Sixth Generation was perhaps born at the right time. On the one hand, they do not have to bear the immediate pressure of revolutionary discourse, which is on the brink of collapse. On the other hand, they still can take advantage of the discourse, using it as the context to give their film a political aura. In this sense, the Sixth Generation achieves a postmodern effect by using history as a dispensable background. In the 1990s, their strategy is to play the cards of both politics and commercialism in order to join the international film market. The Sixth Generation has a very strong sense of contemporary social life. Their impudent pastiche of the superficial phenomena of social life is in keeping with their instinctual refusal to bow to politics per se—they simply have no interest in political issues, and they use politics only as an empty signifier. Perhaps someday they may find a new narrative strategy.

The contemporary Chinese cinema has ineluctably turned away from the ideological and political center. Even in ideological, keynote films, ideological discourse appears extremely contrived and self-contradictory, because political life in China today has radically degenerated. Institutionally speaking, revolutionary discourse still maintains a certain degree of control, but it can no longer provide any intellectual or artistic substance to cultural production. The tension between the existing institutional power and the dysfunctional representational framework within the revolutionary discourse has created a great deal of contradiction in the cultural arena. A vicious circle occurs amid the constant displacement and deconstruction of the correlations between purpose and effect, signifier and signified, subject and object, and imagination and reality. Under such circumstances, the much inflated political discourse in film constructs only an illusory politics that sustains itself by reproducing, over and over, its imagined reality as a hyperreality. Such a hyperreality, however, has become effective insofar as it has become encoded by the global cultural imaginary, which produces and reproduces an imagined and an imagining China as a political entity both in history and in the contemporary world. As Baudrillard puts it, "the real is not only what can be reproduced, but that which is always already reproduced—the hyperreal."[12] This "always already reproduced" political reality has become the backbone of Chinese cultural production, from which contemporary cinema draws its vital sustenance. In the past, art served politics. But today, politics serves art. The stereotyped politics provides effective resources as well as necessary contexts for film. This is what I call the "postpolitics" in Chinese film today, where the dual aesthetic and cultural function of politics is essential.

Postmodernism, therefore, has incorporated the dazzling Chinese political, economic, and cultural environment into its own symbolic existence. Chinese postmodernism displays all the complexities and contradictions, and is caught between the odd correlations of cultural production and the revolutionary discourse. The parasitical/disobedient relationship between the domestic cultural production and the revolutionary discourse, and the subordinate/resistant relationship between the native and the global cultural imaginary have arbitrarily imposed a postmodern condition on China's cultural arena, a result of the massive historical displacements of social phenomena—lifestyles, values, concepts, and behavior patterns of vastly different cultural spaces and temporalities coexisting, intersecting, and jockeying for their legitimate positions in China today. The monolithic power center and its subsystems have all but crumbled, resulting in the paradoxically simultaneous dependence on and destruction of its foundations.

The incredible hybridization and heterogeneity of cultural and symbolic production have inevitably yielded a series of displacements: name/substance; purpose/effect; true/false; serious/playful; real/unreal; authority/clown; spirit/material; politics/economy; culture/commerce; tragedy/comedy; ritual/parody; love/lust; construction/deconstruction; dedication/deprivation; development/degeneration; progressive/conservative; and left/right; among others. The constant displacements and separations of these binary oppositions have produced a strange social and cultural ecosystem in which the real events always take place amid the cracks and fissures of the social order, disregarding the pompous and grandiose ideological myth and symbolism that still legitimize the very order and system. Under such an ecosystem, noble idealism and heroism are completely replaced by a real sense of comedy, manifested in a rhetoric of parody-travesty, irony, and black humor. Postmodernism thus emerges in Chinese social life as well as in cultural and cinematic productions and artistic experiments, not so much as a cultural construct of the artists, critics, and theorists, as is the case in the West, but as an enormous social text produced by the historical process of Chinese modernity in the age of globalization.

In the 1990s, the extent to which China has been integrated into the process of globalization and into its cultural imaginary is historically unprecedented. China stands at the historical conjuncture that, however uncertain and over-determined, seems to have inevitably moved toward the final "end of history," or the ultimate triumph of global capitalism. The "progress of" world history, according to such a deterministic teleology, will leave only some residual imagination to contemporary Chinese culture. And cultural products cannot be anything but the residual by-products of globalization and its cultural imaginary. The postpolitical strategy of Chinese film today may continue to provide aesthetic resources and contexts for producing the image of the exotic Other for the world, as long as China continues to prosper on its way to modernity. But the question remains: Shall we lament China's failure to go beyond its historical limits, or shall we compliment its success in the global cultural market today?

Notes

1. Li Yiming, "Xie Jin dianying zai Zhongguo dianying shi shang de diwei" (Xie Jin's films in the history of Chinese cinema), *Dianying yishu* (Cinema art) 2 (1990): 9.
2. Dai Jinhua, "Duanqiao, ci yidai de yishu" (Broken bridge: The art of the next generation), *Dianying yishu* (Cinema art) 2 (1990): 139–40.
3. See Tony Rayns, *Video, New Chinese Cinema, Director* (London: Routledge, 1988).
4. See Fredric Jameson, *The Political Unconscious: Narrative as a Socially Symbolic Act* (Ithaca, N.Y.: Cornell University Press, 1981).
5. See Rayns, *Video, New Chinese Cinema, Director*, 6.
6. Fredric Jameson, "Third-World Literature in the Era of Multinational Capitalism," *Social Text* 15 (fall 1986): 65–88.
7. Chen Xiaoming, "Zhuti yu huanxiang zhi wu—xin shiqi wenxue de yishi xingtai tuilun shijian" (Subjectivity and the imaginary—The ideological practices of the literature in the new era), *Zhongshan* 1 (1993): 57–72.
8. Ping-hui Liao, "Shi kong yu xingbie de cuoluan: Lun bawang bie ji" (The displacements of time, space, and sexuality: A Reading of *Farewell My Concubine*), *Chung-wai Literary Monthly* 22, no. 1 (1993): 10.
9. See Liu Kang's article, "Popular Culture and the Culture of the Masses in Contemporary China" in this special issue of *boundary 2*, 99–122.
10. Jiang Wen, "Ranshao de qingchun meng" (The burning dreams of the young), *Dangdai dianying* (Contemporary cinema) 1 (1996): 59.
11. Jiang, "Ranshao," 59.
12. Jean Baudrillard, *Simulations* (New York: Semiotext[e], 1983), 146.

10 "Let Him Fucking See the Green Smoke Beneath
My Groin": The Mythology of Chinese Rock

The fact that we cannot manage to achieve more than an unstable grasp of reality doubtless gives the measure of our present alienation: we constantly drift between the object and its demystification, powerless to render its wholeness. —Roland Barthes, *Mythologies*, 1957

Positioning Rock

"What's the 1990s gonna bring?" wondered rock singer Xie Chenqiang at the beginning of this decade.[1] He might have been disappointed, because although rock has become an established music genre on the mainland, the nineties certainly did not bring a spectacular rise of Chinese rock. Neither did the critical debate on Chinese culture that characterized both intellectual and artistic discourses of the 1980s continue. Especially after Deng Xiaoping's visits to southern China in 1992, the ideological vacuum that emerged in the wake of the 1989 crackdown of the student protests apparently shrank as further economic reforms were enacted by Deng. The immediate and easy answer to Xie Chenqiang's question would be "a boundless celebration of consumerism." However, the commercialization of Chinese culture triggered many complex processes that profoundly changed the everyday life of Chinese citizens, processes that certainly cannot be summarized in just one word, *consumerism*. Chinese society has experienced another Cultural Revolution over the last decade, a revolution that has *post-* as its signifier: postrevolutionary, postsocialist, and postmodern.[2] It is marked by "dizzying change and bewildering fragmentation [that] not only undermine inherited narratives but call into question the very possibility of encapsulation within a coherent narrative of the past, the present and the future."[3] The postmodern functions as a site of ongoing struggles between the legacies of the past, the contradictions of the present, and the uncertainties of the future. Not the intellectual domain, nor the political arena, but rather the cultural sphere serves as the most important battleground for these struggles. A wide array of aesthetic forms, ranging from the movies of Zhang Yimou or, especially, Zhang Yuan to the novels from Wang Shuo or Wang Xiaobo and soap operas such as *Eastern Sunrise, Western Rain* (*Dongbian richu xibian yu*), along with popular music such as Cantopop from Hong Kong and rock from Beijing, can be interpreted in relation to "Chinese" postmodernism.[4] According to the mainland academic Chen Xiaoming, in contemporary China, "The real events always take place amid the cracks and fissures of the social order, disregarding the pompous and grandiose ideological myth and symbolism that still legitimize the very order and system. Under such an ecosystem, noble idealism and heroism are completely replaced by a real sense of comedy, manifested in a rhetoric of parody-travesty, irony, and black humor."[5] The adjective "real" is problematic, since it suggests one can separate "the real" from "the unreal" (for example, what is an "unreal event"?), but Chen rightly points to the importance of a new cultural space that appears to be very remote from the grand socialist narratives of the past.

Although market reforms go hand in hand with gradual depoliticization in China (in the sense of a certain withdrawal of the state from the public sphere), this does not imply an absolute absence of politics in these public spaces. The market reforms and its cultural manifestations did not create a public sphere in which people privately could debate societal change.[6] As Foucault reminds us, power is everywhere (this seemingly hollow statement points to the impossibility of clearly separating the political from the nonpolitical), and rather than localizing spaces that are presumably far removed from Chinese political realities, we might do better to rethink the complex relationships among politics, popular culture, and the everyday life. This essay presents a modest attempt to deal with this cultural landscape by singling out the rock culture and unraveling the complex negotiations among past, present, and future; among China, Greater China, and the West; and among production of the music, the rock musicians, and reception of the music by its audiences. As one commentator notes, "In the postmodern condition, production and culture mingle with one another through a dialectical third: commodification and consumption."[7] Chinese politics remains pervasive in all these domains.

Chinese rock can be considered one of the new cultural domains that emerged during the 1980s, when it appeared along with other cultural products such as the TV documentary *River Elegy* and shared with them a sharp cultural critique. It reached its peak on the waves of commodification and commercialization in the 1990s. A critical intervention of the dominant narrative on Chinese rock as it appears in both academic and journalistic discourses inside and outside the mainland might open up spaces to grasp the broader dynamics in which this subculture could emerge, as well as direct us to the meanings negotiated by the music.

Strike a Pose

More than ten years have passed since Cui Jian's "Nothing to My Name" marked the rise of a spectacular youth subculture in China. The old Mao suits—signifying conformity to Party rule—were replaced by leather jackets; communist revolutionary classics were transformed into punk. Music was turned into a site of political struggle. It is not a coincidence that documentaries over the Beijing rock scene always include images of the 1989 June 4 crackdown.[8] The provocative poses struck by the artists were warmly welcomed as first signs of China's path to democracy. The anger of a government official who in 1987, after hearing Cui Jian's cover of the revolutionary classic "Southern Muddy Bay" (*Nanniwan*), banned his performances and thus forced Cui Jian to perform underground,[9] strengthened the impression that rock symbolizes the struggle to free oneself from the communist burden, toward a free, democratic society. Cui Jian was the first of many rock singers who daringly challenged dominant culture. His ban in 1987 was to be followed by many other incidents. In spring 1989, singer He Yong expressed his anger while performing on the streets of Beijing. He screamed (from "Garbage Dump"):

> The world we are living in
> Is like a garbage dump
> People are just like worms
> Fighting and grabbing
> What they eat is conscience
> What they shit are thoughts

> Is there hope   is there hope
> Is there hope   is there hope

His radical, sarcastic nihilism is politically subversive in a country where one is supposed to support the construction of a socialist, healthy society. That these lyrics passed censorship in 1994 is still considered a miracle by the record company.[10] That the accompanying video clip, depicting He Yong caught in a cage, desperately trying to escape, was banned in China was no surprise at all.

The tanks that violently ended the student protests did not crush the rock culture. On the contrary, the first part of the 1990s showed a rapid growth of Chinese rock, a growth that was accompanied by conflicts and repression. After bursting into tears while reporting the June 4 massacre, China's Central Television reporter Wei Hua was fired and became China's first female rock singer. A stadium tour by Cui Jian was cut short in 1991 after government officials got scared by the enthusiastic response of the audience. Bands constantly censor their lyrics in order to get approval from the Ministry of Culture. At the end of 1996, after making fun of the communist model worker Li Suli, He Yong was not allowed to perform for three years. From these examples, randomly selected from the subversive history of Chinese rock, the singers emerge as true heroes, fighting for a free, democratic China, disturbing Party bureaucrats with their electric guitars. It is hardly surprising that the official Chinese media condemn the local rock culture: it is considered "unacceptable for Chinese society,"[11] it is seen as a sign of unhealthy spiritual pollution from the West and as a cultural form that by its very nature remains incompatible with Chinese culture.[12] Deng Xiaoping had already warned that "capitalist living styles should not run wild in our country; it is intolerable to corrupt the younger generation with the declining culture from the West."[13] In October 1997 the Party launched a new set of regulations to strengthen their control on artistic performances, in order "to advance the construction of our socialist spiritual culture . . . and improve the excellent culture of our nation and enrich the people's spiritual life."[14] The new regulations further limited the freedom of the rock musicians.

It goes without saying that not only the musical content but also the imagery and lifestyles of the rockers are considered by the Party as decidedly not an enrichment of the spiritual life of the common people. The red dyed hair of punk singer Gao Wei, the drug use of female star Luo Qi, the mysterious death of Tang Dynasty's guitar player Zhang Ju are all miles away from the idealized lifestyle of the famous communist model soldier, Lei Feng. From the fringe of society, Chinese rock challenges, subverts, disturbs, and maybe even changes contemporary Chinese culture. The dissonant voices stirred up the tranquil waters of Chinese politics in the 1990s. To quote China's controversial writer Wang Shuo: "What didn't happen through June 4th will happen through Rock."[15]

This highly selective, romantic reading of Chinese rock corresponds with popular notions of rock as a countercultural movement. It suits our desire to see dominant ideologies subverted. It strengthens the stereotypical image (among other stereotypes) of China as a severely repressive society with a cruel political regime, and by doing so it indirectly celebrates liberal Western society. It is a product of what I call the rock mythology.[16] It is this mythology, as I will argue, that functions as the glue that binds producers, musicians, and audiences together; it is the basis of the production of the rock culture. In this essay I aim to analyze this mythology and search for different readings of the rock culture. In doing so, I employ an eclectic approach in which I combine theories of subculture and popular music studies with Chinese writings—both popular and academic—on rock music, as well as my own observations from Beijing.

The Rock Mythology

Chinese rock can easily be read as genuinely subversive and oppositional. Consider, for example, these remarks: "Since its release, the wide availability of this music of anger and frustration has continued to empower opposition to the regime. Yaogun yinyue's [Chinese rock] role as an objectivation of anti-government feeling—as a resource for use in political opposition—has intensified."[17] Chinese rock is said to subvert Chinese politics, just as rock from communist countries is said to have resulted in the collapse of communism.[18] Václav Havel, former president of Czechoslovakia, even claimed that the revolution began in the rock scene.[19] The rock mythology, as it appears in both academic and journalistic discourses, apart from being a projection of the researcher's romantic desire to see ideologies subverted, is based on several assumptions.

First, "rock culture" is seen as a monolithic whole. In fact, the opposite is more the case. A bias in theories of subcultures toward the deviant, countercultural, and masculine is also prevalent in accounts of the Beijing rock culture.[20] I consider it a highly fragmented subculture, with multiple relations to its wider cultural milieu, and with constantly shifting, permeable boundaries. It is a fragmented cultural practice, with regard both to music style as well as the degree of commitment of musicians and audiences. Styles range from folk music to heavy metal, and some bands address wider social issues, while others are very introspective. It is a fluid cultural practice, and personal as well as collective identities are constantly being negotiated.

Second, Chinese politics is interpreted as ideologically uniform, as absolutely totalitarian.[21] But in fact the complex Chinese political landscape is characterized by factional struggles within the Party. One can distinguish progressive factions (those who desire further modernization of the political system), conservative factions (with a strong nostalgia for "real" communism), and liberal factions (with a strong focus on economic growth).[22] Party hegemony is therefore by no means homogeneous and internally uncontested.

Third, censorship is, like Chinese politics, too easily considered total and consistent, whereas in practice it is constantly being contested and negotiated by artists, producers, and publishers.[23]

Fourth, rock is seen as incompatible with communism by definition. But there are no reasons to believe it is so. Rather than criticizing communism, rock often challenges broader societal norms. According to Pekacz, in Eastern Europe the state actually succeeded in domesticating rock, and relations between the state and rock were more often symbiotic than hostile.[24] There is no state funding in China for rock, nor do presidents express their appreciation (as did Gorbachev). But state officials are not by definition hostile toward rock. Cui Jian toured to raise money for the Asian Games, the rock band Hei Bao was allowed to perform in Tibet,[25] musicians are allowed to leave the country for performances, and a rock music school is even allowed to operate in Beijing.

Fifth, Chinese rock is sometimes interpreted and valued in relation to the dichotomy of high culture versus low culture. Partly because of its strong links with other cultural practices, such as avant-garde art and modern literature, rock is often conceived as belonging to the "high arts," the "liberating," "enlightening" high arts, as opposed to the "oppressing" low arts such as Cantopop (commercial pop music from Hong Kong and Taiwan). This is a pertinacious, yet false approach, based on outdated theories of the Frankfurt school.[26] Cantopop is too often reduced to an overtly commercial, noncreative expression, an analysis that ignores its musical and textual complexities, its diversity, the reception of audiences, and the contradictory dynamics of commodification.

Closely related to this last point is the issue of authenticity. Artists are often considered gifted, highly talented persons who are always ready to express their authentic emotions. From this perspective, rock, in contrast to pop, is generally considered an authentic expression of personal feelings, a musician's testimony to his or her anger, sufferings, and personal struggles. However, as Howard S. Becker observed, "works of art . . . are not the products of individual makers, 'artists' who possess a rare and special gift. They are, rather, joint products of all the people who cooperate via an art world's characteristic conventions to bring works like that into existence."[27]

The reception and use of the music by the audience is also usually ignored. Audiences are too often seen as uniform. But texts are polysemic, and seemingly controversial lyrics might be "read" in a different way, just as Party propaganda can be and is being read in a subversive way.[28] Finally, the tendency to politicize rock is even more pronounced for China, as both modern China studies and the media coverage of China show a strong bias for the political. Chinese society is frequently restricted to politics.

There is a need to dismantle rock mythology, to go beyond unidirectional interpretations. One should not focus solely on the tensions between the musicians and the state.[29] To quote Richard Kraus, "A stark dichotomy between virtuous artists and an oppressive state no longer goes very far in explaining the multiple stresses to which China's artists must respond."[30] Instead I opt for a fluid, dynamic, and most probably contradictory analysis of this cultural practice, an analysis that constantly questions dichotomies such as East–West, local–global, communism–capitalism, high–low, and art–commercialism. The challenged does not lie in a complete deconstruction and rationalization of rock as a commodity; this would too easily guide us to a Marxist interpretation in which rock, as part of commercial mass culture, is viewed as yet another product to stupefy and silence the masses. Rather, the challenge lies in illuminating the complex and contradictory processes at work in the production, creation, and reception of rock music while at the same time grasping, and thus doing justice to, the feelings being expressed and shared with audiences.

Deconstructing Boundaries: Rock contra Pop

The perceived dichotomy pop versus rock is worth further analysis since it dominates both academic and journalistic discourses on Chinese rock and is a crucial identity marker for both musicians and audiences. Within Chinese pop, one can distinguish Cantopop, Cantonese songs produced predominantly in Hong Kong; Mandapop, Mandarin songs produced predominantly in Taiwan; and pop from mainland China (tongsu yinyue). Cantonese songs are most popular in southern parts of China, while Mandarin songs are most popular in northern China.[31] Whereas Beijing can be considered the center of Chinese rock music, Hong Kong and Taiwan can be considered the center of Chinese pop music for the Greater China region. As I will show in this essay, this locality, like the music genres, turns out to be of crucial importance for the articulation of the identity of both musicians as well as audiences. The popularity of pop music can hardly be overestimated and by far surpasses that of Chinese rock in the Greater China region.[32] In earlier descriptions of Chinese pop, the musicians, the music style, the lyrical contents as well as the production of the music were all considered to be essentially different from rock.[33] Closer analysis shows it is hard to essentialize differences, as strict typologies ignore the fluidity and diversity of both music worlds, which in fact frequently overlap. For example, imagery of the artist is, for both pop and rock artists, a crucial promotion strategy. But rockers tend to wear leather and tough styles of clothes that signify a self-made subcultural identity, whereas pop stars dress according to the latest fashions, that is, hip, sexy, and often extravagant. The stardom of pop singers, unlike that of rock musicians, is usually not restricted to music alone—for example, Cantopop singer Faye Wong acted in *Chunking Express* from Wong Kar-wai, and Cantopop star Leon Lai traveled in October 1998 to Brazil as an ambassador of UNICEF while being busy at the same time with the shooting of his new movie.[34] Pop music is usually considered to be more melodic than rock music, and its lyrics are said to deal more prominently with love, whereas rock lyrics are believed to be more diverse.

Pop music is eclectic in style: over the years, dance music and hip hop have been incorporated in the music. Not only the West, but also Japan serves as a major source of inspiration for Chinese pop. A typical Chinese pop album would consist of predominantly love ballads with one or two often upbeat songs about life in general. The recordings are technically sophisticated. There is usually a strict division of labor in the production of the music: someone composes the music, after which a lyricist writes the lyrics. The record company identifies in advance what they expect from the song.[35] The singer is often not involved in the actual writing of the music and/or the lyrics. These characterizations of the production of pop music are broadly true, though they tend to misrepresent the diversity. Faye Wong, for instance, often writes her own songs and lyrics,[36] and some singers communicate directly with both the composers and the lyric writers. What at first sight appears to be a music assembly line (and is often characterized as such by the rock singers) turns out to be a complex creative process. To simply label the music as "easy listening"[37] dismisses both the musical complexity and diversity of Chinese pop. There are great differences between, for example, the avant-garde pop from the now disbanded Cantopop band Tatming (which might be considered the Chinese equivalent of the Pet Shop Boys) and the more "mainstream" Cantopop of Jacky Cheung.[38] The highly commercialized and commodified cosmopolitan aesthetics of pop are full of pastiche, decadence, and play, the MTV videos often depict surreal urban landscapes, the karaoke culture that emerged around pop and that destabilizes boundaries between stardom and everyday life as well as between production and consumption. Pop—especially pop from Hong Kong and Taiwan—can thus be considered an important cultural site for the articulation of postmodernity.[39] Pop music from the mainland is less popular than pop from either Hong Kong or Taiwan, but still reaches a large audience on the mainland. Pop singers in China usually belong to a working unit (*danwei*); they are thus part of the formal structures of Chinese society. Both the production as well as the music style and the musicians of mainland pop are comparable with those from Hong Kong and Taiwan, although pop from the mainland is, especially in Hong Kong and Taiwan, usually considered of lower quality, being rather old fashioned, in composition, lyrics, and imagery of the artists, and in being too much affected by communist ideology. It is worth noting that pop musicians from Hong Kong and Taiwan, apart from dealing with the local regulations, also have to deal with censorship and strict regulations on the mainland, like the rock singers from Beijing.[40]

The dichotomy between rock and pop can also be found in discourses on Western popular music, especially around the 1960s. Simon Frith distinguishes three music worlds: art (or bourgeois), folk, and commercial (or pop).[41] In contrast to pop, he notes, "the assumption is that rock music is good music only when it is not mass culture, when it is an art form or a folk sound."[42] Rock lyrics therefore mattered more than pop lyrics; rock verse was said to be poetry.[43] With the rapid differentiation into different music scenes in the West the distinction seems to have lost its value, but rock's underlying legitimizing narrative still prevails in Western journalistic discourses. Rock is said to be sincere and authentic. The desperate screams of Kurt Cobain signify a truly tormented soul, whereas the sweet voice of Mariah Carey conveys a mass-produced product. Frith opts for a reverse of this narrative: "If, for example, the standard line of rock 'n' roll history is that an authentic (that is, folk) sound is continually corrupted by commerce, it could equally well be argued that what the history actually reveals is a commercial musical form continually being recuperated in the name of art and subculture."[44] These processes of commodification are not restricted to rock; on the contrary, all sorts of music are being commodified. Frith therefore concludes that "a comparative sociology reveals far less clear distinctions between music worlds than their discursive values imply."[45] The value distinctions made between "commercial" and "authentic" are debatable. There are no reasons to believe that the emotional impact of a song is reduced by its commodification, nor that a song considered "authentic" automatically leads to a stronger reception by the listener.

In the two major publications on Chinese rock from Andrew Jones and Andreas Steen,[46] a typology from Ray Pratt is used to identify different functions or uses of the music by audiences:[47]

(1) The conservative, hegemonic use, strengthening the existing status quo and supporting those in power.
(2) A negotiated use, in which the music functions as a safety valve. According to Pratt, "instead of taking action to change fundamentally

the repressive existence of daily life, one is offered a substitute world of music, a 'negotiated' form of consciousness."[48]

(3) The emancipatory use, in which music functions as a tool to emancipate suppressed people.

This typology is highly problematic. It leads to unidirectional interpretations of the meanings of music. It has inspired both Jones and Steen to consider rock emancipatory as long as it is not yet commodified. As I have shown, this assertion is part of the rock mythology and ignores the contradictory processes at work. Whereas rock can be emancipatory, pop music is, if not part of the hegemonic structure, at most a safety valve for Chinese youth, according to Steen.[49] Jones argues for a more positive reading for negotiated uses, by stressing the struggle in production, linked to larger struggles in society. But "the outcome of these negotiations, because of their imbrication with the apparatus of [pop] music production and dissemination, are by definition never emancipatory."[50] Also for Jones, it is only rock that can be emancipatory. Thus the typology of Pratt that has been so crucial in previous writings on Chinese rock music, a typology that resembles Hall's typology for different forms of reception (i.e., preferred, negotiated, and oppositional),[51] classifies rather than clarifies. It strengthens the dichotomy rock versus pop, ignores the fluidity of musical meanings, and reinforces the rock mythology.

The difference between rock and pop is underlined by Asian record producers to position rock advantageously. In their marketing, rock is labeled as authentic music, in contrast to commodified, "canned" music, especially the kind produced in Hong Kong and Taiwan. Rock mythology is thus crucial for, and strengthened by, the professional marketing of the rock culture.[52] Ayse Caglar made a similar point for Turkish hip-hop in Germany, which also positions itself strongly vis-à-vis pop: "Within the context of valorized discourses of marginality and diaspora the image of being the 'authentic' voice of the subversive ethnic minority might work as a successful marketing strategy."[53]

Deconstructing boundaries does not equal denying differences. I have already pointed to the perceived differences between pop and rock. To point out these differences is interesting, but more significant is the question why one chooses to fixate and essentialize the dichotomy. What is relevant is the ideology behind the dichotomy, the way in which it invents rock as a specific music world that is considered essentially different from pop.

Behind the Scenes

Until now commentators have described the Chinese rock culture chronologically.[54] Instead, I opt for an overview based on different scenes that I distinguish within the rock culture, since this subculture has by now become too fragmented to invent a neat chronology. With subcultures, boundaries are only momentarily fixed and scenes frequently overlap. In my opinion, the idea of a music scene corresponds closely with Johannes Fabian's interpretation of a genre: "A concept like genre can help us better understand the role popular culture may play in situations where power meets with resistance. . . . [It] allows us to conceptualize the process that produces, through differentiation of forms, a particular domain of popular culture and to locate, as it were, sites where struggle with and for power take place. Nevertheless . . . genre remains a concept so much associated with classifying that it is easy to forget its kinship with generating." [55] Genre channels creativity and generates markers of distinction, and thus facilitates the construction of identities.

What interests me is not a neat classification of the rock culture, to create an order that provides us with an illusionary understanding, to create yet another typology, but rather the processes that produce different scenes, and the related articulation of identities. As such it might reveal both moments of struggle and compliance with the cultural, economic, and political realities of China, and thus do justice to the fragmented, fluid nature of the rock subculture. To illustrate this, I will closely analyze two of these scenes, namely alternative bands and hard rock bands.[56] I will elaborate on the position of both scenes in the cultural arena of China and discuss how place (mainland China) is being negotiated by both scenes, how the notion of authenticity is articulated, and which aesthetics can be distinguished. Ethnographic observations guide me to theoretical interventions. In my view, interpretation of "field data" implies a critical, theoretical interrogation of ethnographic reports.

THE ALTERNATIVE BANDS

Summer 1997, Beijing. The serene sounds of the *guzheng*, a traditional Chinese string instrument, fill the room. Zu Zhou, the twenty-six-year-old singer of the band NO, is playing his demo tape. But soon the listener starts to wonder; something is different. The string sounds are full of disturbing dissonances, far from the tranquillity the ancient instrument is reputed to exude. Zu Zhou sees the surprise in my eyes and stops the tape. He starts playing the *guzheng*, this time in the familiar way. Now I recognize the peaceful sound, a sound used by classical musicians and also by other rockers in Beijing such as Cui Jian and Wang Yong. "You know, I can play the instrument in a classical way, like they do. But what's the point? It makes no sense!" [57] Then he puts a pair of scissors between the strings and starts to pull them more violently. The sound transforms; gone is the myth of the peaceful, deep Chinese traditional culture. What remains is a disturbing noise in which anger competes with confusion.

Singer Feng Jiangzhou from the punk-noise band The Fly is also fascinated by "characteristic" Chinese sounds, which he aims to combine with computer samples and sounds from electric drills: "I am most interested in using Chinese instruments as well as revolutionary songs. . . . But I would definitely refuse to make them sound beautiful; I would try to make them sound uncomfortable. I like uncomfortable things."

This conscious distortion of musical expressions considered "traditionally Chinese" forms one important marker of difference used by alternative bands such as NO and The Fly. The transformation of sounds considered stereotypically Chinese alters rather than completely subverts the connotations attached to them. These connotations are, in the case of the *guzheng*, mainly quietness, deepness, signifying China's long history, and in the case of the communist songs, the heroic revolutionary past. Zu Zhou's refusal to use traditional music instruments in a classical way sets him apart from other scenes, where the traditional sound is used to construct an "authentic" Chineseness. However, in both cases, the use of traditional instruments can be said to prove that this is indeed *Chinese* rock. This perspective is rooted in a rigid local versus global dichotomy. What distinguishes Chinese rock from, say, Western rock or even rock from Taiwan, is indeed its locality, the mainland. This does not imply that one can or should discover its locality in specific sounds, words, or images. Its locality also encompasses the global, as both are intertwined categories rather than mutually exclusive ones. According to Fabian, "The local is the global under the conditions of globalization that obtain at this moment in history." [58]

The negotiation of the past, either by a conventional or a "distorted" way of using traditional instruments, can be interpreted as an act of self-orientalizing. The dissonant sounds of Zu Zhou's *guzheng* might not create the tranquil, peaceful, mysterious China that is evoked by rock musician Wang Yong, yet they still mark a difference from "the West." It can be considered an act of "othering" done by the "other" himself, albeit unconsciously, thus constructing an essentialized Chinese identity.[59] The articulation of "Chineseness" corresponds with two dominant images of China, namely *antique China* and *communist China*. Not only in their music but also the clothing styles of rock musicians often stress this Chineseness: the Mao cap of Cui Jian and the communist youth league shawls that singers were wearing during a punk performance I attended are just two examples. Here, one can see links between the rock culture and the avant-garde painters, among whom the Mao suit has been tremendously popular (not to speak of the imagery used in the paintings themselves, often closely linked to the style of communist propoganda art). Thus rock employs sounds, words, and imagery that construct the music as being specifically Chinese. At the same time, however, other symbols are used to stress its international, cosmopolitan character. Bands refer frequently to their inspiration sources, such as the Beatles and U2. The use of English for band names (e.g., The Fly and NO) and the titles of albums (such as Cui Jian's latest release *The Power of the Powerless*) tends to give an international aura to the CDs. Through these seemingly contradictory dynamics, place is being negotiated, a place that is both local and global, and, depending on the moment, either one of them will be articulated. The Western journalist is happy to find traditional sounds in the music, the Chinese youngster is attracted by the sense of cosmopolitanism the music provides him with. For audiences in Hong Kong and Taiwan, both markers of sameness (the shared Chinese tradition) as well as markers of difference (the communist past) are employed. The negotiation of place does not equal the construction of the local. Rather, as Ang Ien says, place needs to be interpreted as "a borderland, a crossroads—that is, a space where the boundaries between inside and outside are blurred, a space characterized by a multiplicity of crisscrossing forces rather than by some singular and unique, internally originated 'local' identity." [60]

Apart from being a musician, NO singer Zu Zhou is a writer, poet, and painter and has participated in several performance art activities. His girlfriend is an internationally acclaimed painter. He can afford his marginal lifestyle because of her and her parents' money. Whereas funding from relatives or friends to engage in a rock lifestyle is common in the Beijing rock scene, links with other "art worlds" are obvious, especially in the alternative scene. Feng Jiangzhou from The Fly is also an avant-garde painter and currently makes a living by selling kitsch paintings to tourists. His CD was released in 1997 by a small Taiwanese label and cannot be bought in the official circuit on the mainland because of its controversial jacket design—depicting copulating couples and naked men—as well as its contents, with song titles such as "I Don't Like You Cummin' a Lot" and "Educated from Ugly Life." [61] A mainland critic concluded after listening to the CD: "Chinese avant-garde art is usually impotent art. Chinese rock is usually hollow. What kind of chemical reaction will happen if we put these two things together? . . . The Fly has set new standards for Chinese rock and made us realize how hypocritic and senseless the so called avant-garde rock music was. . . . Grunge, punk, and noise are really the best ways to express avant-garde art because they are extreme. The lyrics of this album are controversial; they tried hard to use filthy words to enhance their dirty, noisy, and bad aesthetics." [62] Being the avant-garde of the rock culture, the alternative bands have close ties with the cultural avant-garde of China.[63] The review just quoted also underlines the paradox that despite government control, CDs will find their way to music critics who are able to publish their reviews nationwide, thus indirectly promoting CDs that are supposed to be banned by the government. Party hegemony, it seems, is far from absolute and uncontested. The review also shows how critical the Chinese discourse on rock can be. Assessments are based on comparisons over time (with references to the Chinese rock classics) or over place. Reviews of new Chinese releases appear along with reviews of the latest CD of the Chemical Brothers or Beck.[64] The reviews of Chinese rock are based on comparisons with Western rock, a comparison that more often than not turns out in favor of the latter.

For Zu Zhou and Feng Jiangzhou, music functions as a site to negotiate feelings of anger and frustration, feelings young people are hardly allowed to express in Chinese culture. Both Confucian and Party ideology stress the importance of conformity, of obedience to parents, educators, and bosses. Feng Jiangzhou's response to these pressures is divided: "I am actually very angry about a lot of things in China, like disrespect among people, the whole political system, but I do not have the courage to confront people directly, so when I write I can be very angry and aggressive." Dick Hebdige puts it, "The subcultural response . . . [is] a declaration of independence, of otherness, of alien intent, a refusal of anonymity, of subordinate status. It is an insubordination."[65] The danger is that by focusing on and thereby stabilizing the subcultural identity one overlooks or ignores other forms of identities that are being explored in other spheres of life by the musicians. The rock mythology, by romanticizing the provocative poses, ignores the more mundane aspects of a musician's life.

Besides the negotiation of expressions considered "Chinese," and the strong ties with other cultural domains such as the visual arts, alternative musicians are vocal in their critique of contemporary Chinese society. In an article on the post–Cui Jian generation, Chinese academic He Li quotes from rock critic Kong: "Zu Zhou's uniquely penetrating tenor, like a knife stained with blood and sperm, tears up everything. . . . His purely despondent bass divulges the loneliness toward the future and the destruction of the will to live. Their simple and weird minor-scale progressions embed anxiety and emptiness. It is not only a musical language but also a spiritual wandering guided by some old, instinctive language. Their irregular and airy sound texture constructs a kind of imaginary space."[66] "NO is like a group of sadists coming from hell," according to He Li.[67] Zu Zhou (the lead singer of NO) gives a more radical denial of meaning in contemporary Chinese society: "I am disgusted by Marxism. In my opinion, it has cheated me. . . . This is a senseless age, maybe the true age hasn't come yet." He expresses his alienation and fatalism in his song "Let Me See the Doctor Once More":

Let this rickshaw take me to the home of the surgeon
Let him fucking see the green smoke beneath my groin
Let me see you once more—doctor
I want to recover my
Left thigh, left rib, left hand, left lung, and my right-wing dad

This song is, in its reference to the singer's lost "right-wing dad," obviously political, but at the same time alienating and confusing, the listener wonders what is meant by "the green smoke beneath my groin." The elements that characterize Zu Zhou's music and lyrics are basically dadaistic.

These dadaist aesthetics are similar to those we hear in the music of The Fly. In a Taiwanese review, The Fly's music was compared to the guerrilla tactics of Chairman Mao: instead of launching a frontal attack, the critic pointed out, The Fly was employing sideways movements to oppose dominant culture. The Fly's singer Feng Jiangzhou prefers to write about sex rather than politics. Sex—another topic difficult to discuss in China—also signifies the political, but, as becomes clear in my interview with him, Feng's critique goes beyond politics:

> What would be considered beautiful by a lot of people is just a very popular notion of beauty. I don't think my lyrics are dirty at all, I want people to rethink what is beautiful and what is dirty. . . . The other reason why I choose sex as the subject matter is as a reaction to the pop music of China. The government seems to if not encourage at least condone pop music, whereas it puts so many problems on rock 'n' roll. I find pop music so superficial, but it represents its own vulgar aesthetics. It would be very difficult for me to write very sophisticated lyrics as its critique. The only way to do so is to find another subject matter which could be as vulgar for the general people, and sex seems to be very appropriate to counter Chinese pop music. . . . Everything [in China] is just so covered up. In the past there have been extremely erotic books, pornographic materials, but people would hide them and present themselves as gentlemen. We have a song entitled "Gentleman." In China, everyone would like to be that gentleman, and I would like them to tear off that mask. Because if you are always wearing a mask, you don't exist; people should be real.

In Feng Jiangzhou's statement, some aspects of rock mythology emerge in a sophisticated way. He aims to subvert the ideology of pop by using provocative, vulgar lyrics. The implied accusation that pop is superficial and in line with dominant ideology remains important for his positioning as a rock musician. Also the idea of tearing away the masks people wear, in order to reveal their true, authentic identity, is closely linked to the belief that his music—in being open about sex—is an example of authenticity. The promotion materials of The Fly point out that the recording is done in low fidelity. The underlying assumption is that technology is falsifying. Thus, not only the contents of the music but also the recording techniques negotiate notions of authenticity. Like The Fly, NO would stress its preference for low-fi; their demotape has consciously been recorded on a Walkman.[68] The mirror The Fly offers the audience is far from comforting. The lyrics are characterized by directness and absurdity, as this fragment from their song "Nirvana" shows:

> Because there is no electric light in this village hut
> Because today is not the day of the full moon
> Because tonight I cannot fall asleep
> Because tonight I want to play with myself
>
> .   .   .
>
> Under my bottom shines the first ray of sun
> I want to bring with me this entire hut of the fragrance of shit
> I am in Nirvana
> In Nirvana

I interpret the dadaistic and vulgar aesthetics of Zu Zhou and The Fly as tactics of *symbolic inversion*, which can be defined as an aesthetic "negation of the negative." [69] This aesthetic negation confronts the audience with the lineaments of Chinese culture. It questions the normal in its focus on what is considered abnormal. It destabilizes the illusory symbolic order. "Such 'creative negations,' " notes Barbara Babcock "remind us of the need to reinvest the clean with the filthy. . . . The *modus inversus* does more than simply mock our desire to live according to our usual orders and norms; it reinvests life with a vigor and a *Spielraum* attainable (it would seem) in no other way." [70] Mainland rock critic He Li, in a text written as part of the promotional material of The Fly, points to the significance of these tactics of symbolic inversion: "Flies are not lovely creatures. Their connotations in our language are negative: multiple-eyed, dirty, sickness-spreading, full of pus . . . and we are expecting a more hygienic, more civilized, more elegant, more orderly time of money-making. The flies and us are enemies! In major cities of China, punk, I am afraid, only enjoys very limited audience, because we are all the time concerned about hygiene, neat clothes, civilization, politeness. But it is also because of this that flies bear special meaning to our life."

The alternative bands were all formed around 1993, shortly after Deng Xiaoping argued for an almost total release of market forces. NO has recently negotiated a contract with a Hong Kong-based company. The Fly gradually gains popularity; they performed in Hong Kong on October 3, 1998. The alternative bands, whether they agree or not, enter the stage of commodification, and, in line with the rock mythology, question this process. According to He Li, the fear of NO is that whatever is expressed is destined to be consumed by the greedy commercialization and the mediocre modern man.[71] He quotes Zu Zhou, who stated: "We want to be famous. But then one day, when we are indeed famous, when our music becomes popular, that implies we are so bad" (interview, Hong Kong, 8 August 1994). Based on the debatable perception that only noncommercial music can be sincere, authentic, and thus good music, Zu Zhou says he feels caught in the paradox of both desiring and condemning fame. Ironically, what he fears to lose are precisely the unique selling points used by record companies to promote rock. The dialectics of commodification, grounded in the rock mythology, constantly reinvent rock as a specific music world.

After the release of the recording by The Fly in 1997, reviews spoke of a rebirth of Chinese rock. Their discontent with the mainstream rock culture is found also among the bands. In the words of Feng Jianghzou: "In China, from 1986 to 1996, for ten years, Chinese rock remained quite the same. It is basically hard rock. So I believe that from 1997 there should be something new. But I can't jump too far, otherwise there would be a displacement. What I am trying to do is to create something that is just beyond the existing rock 'n' roll, to create the avant-garde in China."

Other markers of difference are the bands' (already mentioned) subversive use of traditional Chinese instruments, their articulate criticisms of Chinese culture, for which tactics of inversion are used, their strong ties with other art worlds, and the articulation of authenticity through direct lyrics and low-fi recording techniques. These are crucial markers of difference that have generated (to put it tautologically) a specific genre in the rock culture. Both NO and The Fly are banned from the Chinese market and thus forced into a marginal position. However, as He Li points out, "What is socially peripheral is often symbolically central, and if we ignore or minimize inversion and other forms of cultural negation we often fail to understand the dynamics of symbolic processes generally."[72]

In their lyrics, their sounds, and their imagery, the bands generate moments of opposition. As I have shown, their aesthetics are indirect and encompass more than just the political. In their music they express an anger and dissatisfaction with contemporary Chinese society, feelings they can hardly express in other ways. At the same time I question the construction of "Chineseness" in the music and imagery, the "othering" vis-à-vis the non-Chinese world (that is, nonmainland). The use of Chinese instruments, and maybe even their provocative poses, not only corresponds with Western perceptions of Chinese rock, but also strengthens the illusion of a fixed cultural identity. It accommodates rather than challenges the dominant notion, namely the uniqueness of China, currently very much *en vogue* in the Chinese political arena. These contradictions become even more apparent if we look at the hard rock bands.

HARD ROCK

Ding Wu, born in 1962, used to play with rock band Hei Bao. Unable to express there his interest in heavy metal, he left the band and formed, in late 1988, together with Zhang Ju and two American-Chinese students (among whom was Kaiser Kuo), the band Tang Dynasty. The name expresses the band's longing for a China at its most glorious. During the Tang Dynasty (618–907), Chinese art and culture reached, according to popular notions, its highest point. As the record company Magic Stone describes it in their promotional material:[73] "While Western Europe struggled through the hardships of the Middle Ages, Chinese culture flourished during the Tang Dynasty as the center of world trade and the highest point of the world civilization." In its marketing, the record company transfers the richness of that past onto this musical product.[74] In a comparison with the West, the record company states (also in the promotional material): "The most important thing is, here you will hear the self confidence of the Chinese, because they have done what you thought only Westerners could have done."

But another reading is even more obvious: in its imagery and music, as well as in the lyrics, a strong longing for the past is expressed. This celebration of the past and its related criticisms of the present forms the leading philosophy of Tang Dynasty. In their songs, they express their solitude in modern time, their despair and search for a better world. A music critic comments on the band: "In their music, they express their true feelings toward life and their understanding of the world. . . . They express in their own way a longing for a strong and influential China: a return to the Tang Dynasty."[75]

In line with rock mythology, their criticisms on modern time are considered authentic. After being contracted by Magic Stone they became successful overnight; their CD is said to have sold more than one million copies, and, within a few months of its release, more than ten pirated versions were on the market.[76] But in real life, the search for a different life has been far from unproblematic. Unable to cope with their instant success, they floundered. Band members became addicted to drugs for years, and in May 1995 guitarist Zhang Ju died in a motorcycle accident. They split with Magic Stone, who, according to the band, did not support them during their hard times. Only in 1997 did the band start again, with manager Dickson Dee from Hong Kong. American-born Kaiser Kuo, who had left the band in 1989, returned to replace Zhang Ju on guitar. His return was severely criticized by other rock musicians. Whereas Zhang Ju played the guitar in a Chinese way, Kaiser is said to play it in an American way, unsuitable for Chinese rock. Besides, he is said to be a bad guitar player. This hostility toward foreign elements is illustrative of the attempt to make rock with "Chinese" characteristics. It is ironic that a band who excels in a celebration of Chinese culture is faced with these criticisms.

The importance of Tang Dynasty for the Chinese rock culture can hardly be overestimated. They introduced heavy metal to China; the piercing, high voice of Ding Wu could be heard in the streets all over China in the winter of 1993. With their long hair, naked upper bodies in the MTV videos, motorcycles, and leather jackets, they conform closely to the stereotypical rock image from the West. Boys are impressed by their masculine poses. The archaic language of their lyrics further strengthens the chivalric pose, a pose that corresponds to the tradition of Chinese swordsman novels (wuxia xiaoshuo). Added to their masculine poses and archaic lyrics are powerful compositions, some almost military in tone, with strong melodies and unexpected twists. Through these chivalric aesthetics, authenticity is negotiated, authenticity that is constructed around notions of the real, tough man who dares to express loudly his discontent with modern society. The sophisticated recordings (hi-fi, not low-fi) as well as the poetic lyrics (indirect rather than direct) further articulate a changed notion of the authenticity of the music.

Aware of its market potential, Tang Dynasty looked carefully for a record company and wanted to set up its own company, according to Kaiser Kuo:[77] "The company should have an art director, a manager, and the members of Tang Dynasty. It is financially advantageous for Tang Dynasty to have a corporate identity, to define priorities." Rock musicians consciously position themselves within the discourse of commercialism. In line with the rock mythology, this relationship is more often than not hostile. Tang Dynasty is an exception. It shows that "production" and "text" are closely intertwined rather than being two separate stages of the "communication process."

In a reflection on the symbolism of Tang Dynasty, Gregory Lee states that "through the recuperation of national symbols and spaces rock both recovers or challenges nationalism. There is both irony and a recuperation of popular nationalism."[78] The symbolism in the music and the videoclips of Tang Dynasty, full of references to the past, express a pervasive sense of cultural loss. Andrew Jones quotes Lao Wu, at that time bass player for Tang Dynasty:[79] "Rock is based on the blues, and we can never play the blues as well as an American. It's just not in our blood. We can imitate it, but eventually we'll have to go back to the music we grew up with, to traditional music, to folk music."[80] The irony is that his dogmatic, essentialist approach in fact resembles Western discourses, in which rock is also frequently linked to folk music in order to differentiate it from commercial pop music. According to singer Ding Wu, the band indeed feels a longing for the old China, for the cultural richness of the past. But, he continued, this does not reflect a discontent with the present, it is just a longing. This longing is expressed in their song "A Dream Return to the Tang Dynasty":[81]

Wind—cannot blow away our grievances
Flowers—cannot color over our longing for home
Snow—cannot reflect the mountain stream
Moon—cannot fulfill the ancient dream
Following the patterns on my palm
Branded there by fate
Following fate I fall into a trance
In dream I return to the Tang Dynasty

Kaiser Kuo stresses that they do not want to oppose politics. According to him: "We are not rebellious at all, we are actually pro the present administration. Because of the open door policy we can exist. China is such a huge country that it needs a strong leadership." He agrees that they are in a way actually patriots. Kaiser basically sees their music as a kind of safety valve, as a way for youngsters to release their emotions and energies, as a way to rediscover the Chinese culture, to be proud to be Chinese. In his celebration of Chinese culture he draws a comparison with Japan: "[Japanese history] is going to be dwarfed by China. . . . Chinese culture is a mine, there is so much to do. There are people who go crazy for these Japanese samurai stories, but there is so little in it; there is such a well in China." The philosophy of the band strongly resembles nationalist ideology as expressed by the Party.[82] Kaiser Kuo believes the band to be proestablishment. He, as well as the record company in their promotion, voices popular notions when he talks of the supremacy of Chinese culture above Japanese culture. More than the alternative bands, Tang Dynasty's music is an attempt to essentialize cultural differences. It not only accommodates but also celebrates the dominant notion, supported by the Party, of the uniqueness of China. The act of "othering" can also be considered a commercial strategy. In Jones's words, "The band is an avowedly commercial venture, and in this light, its nativism . . . is perhaps less an ideological stance than a marketing device."[83] The affiliation between Tang Dynasty and both political and economic realities is, however, not solely characterized by compliance. The power of the music, the archaic, mysterious lyrics, the saintlike charisma of vocalist Ding Wu, the critique on modern culture—all these elements create a music world that challenges the current celebration of economic progress and rapid modernization in China. The music world of Tang Dynasty forms a contradictory space; it both challenges and accommodates today's political realities. As such, it shows that rock culture can never be interpreted as solely oppositional or solely in compliance with dominant culture. To accuse the band of naive nationalism is a truth as well as a lie, just as viewing them as authentic rebels is both true and false.

Audiences Re-searched

Tang Dynasty, how are you? I have become increasingly fascinated [by your music]. I can even listen to your tape more than a dozen times a day. I have come to know the meaning of heavy metal and understand that this is what I longed for for so long. . . . Last February I resigned from my job. My mother could not understand. I felt very annoyed. —Letter to Tang Dynasty from Li Junjun, a male fan, July 1997

The day before yesterday a very, very big event happened, Deng Xiaoping died. I feel very sad because I feel as if I have lost someone to depend on, Deng is a very important character in Chinese history. I think I will only use the word "great" to describe him. Mao Zedong was also an outstanding man. He was talented and brave and did a lot for the founding of new China, but he had been a myth, too far away from us. . . . [Deng Xiaoping] was charming and had his own principles. He knew how to grasp the chances and did not overdo things. I feel a sense of awe, of sadness and of loss in my heart. —Letter to folk-rock star Zhang Chu from Xu Li, an eighteen-year-old female student, 1997

These extracts from letters from fans to Tang Dynasty and Zhang Chu indicate how differently rock music can be used.[84] The boy felt strengthened by the music and dared to quit his job. It might be fair to say that rock (or, more precisely, the chivalric aesthetics of Tang Dynasty) helped him to resist the dominant value of remaining loyal to one's boss. The girl shared her feelings of loss after the death of Deng Xiaoping. In her case, the rock star is treated as a close, personal friend with whom one discusses personal feelings.[85] In her narrative, the personal is intertwined with the political, but remains far removed from the counterpolitical. Later in the same letter, she writes how Zhang Chu's songs helped her to pass her exams ("When I took the examination, the melody echoed in my ears") and how the lyrics made her think of "things I have never thought of." The musician is transformed into a friend out of reach; the sounds are used to survive hard times; the words inspire retrospection. It shows that audiences are actively involved in incorporating the music into their personal life scripts. Music is one cultural product used by people to construct their identity. The importance assigned to music differs among people, as the involvement in the music differs. Does rock mythology produce a prefabricated, rebellious identity for the fans to pick up? Reality turns out to be more complex, as these two extracts show. Although fans use the music in various ways, in their narratives rock mythology frequently appears, especially the pop-rock division and related discourses of authenticity and honesty. Consider, for example, a poem by a fifteen-year-old boy, Zhang Yu, dedicated to the heavy-metal band Overload:

Overload, you are the light in my heart that never dims
You are the embodiment of my ascestors from a long time ago
You are the herald of power and courage
You bring me the courage to be a man
You teach me the truth of this world

The music is used by the fan to articulate his gender identity and, in line with rock mythology, he sees it as telling "the truth of this world." An eighteen-year-old fan, Xie Wei, also stresses his male identity in a letter to Overload by stating he is a *rock man*. The pop-rock distinction also appears: "[My class-mates] indulge themselves in their pure love for Hong Kong and Taiwan pop music. What pure love? It is only musical rubbish, catering to ignorant young-sters. Anyway, there are some young people like me who are trying hard to find the essence of music and to find the source of life."

Inspired by rock mythology and related discourses of authenticity, rock music is used as an identity marker, as a way to distinguish oneself from other classmates, and at the same time, to link up with other fans and the musi-cians. An "authentic" relationship—the shared sense of being—is articulated between artist and audience.[86] Another fan, Wang Yan, points to this authen-ticity in his letter to the record company Red Star: "I am a pure rock fan. I like Chinese rock musicians—they express their true feelings in their lyrics. I appreciate their frankness. However, besides me, no one else in my class loves rock music."

A predominantly male, imagined community emerges outside the realm of parents, teachers, and politicians, a community that positions itself vis-à-vis pop. And pop at the same time symbolizes Hong Kong and Taiwan: "We have to admit that Chinese recording techniques are much better than those from Hong Kong or Taiwan. . . . Your emergence is the new starting point of Chi-nese and Asian culture. It is a great comfort to us that rock music saved us from the suffocating sea of pop music from Hong Kong and Taiwan" (Zhou Zhou, a fifteen-year-old male student, in a letter to Overload). In this case, a global sound is used to articulate a sense of belonging. Like the singers, the audience uses the music to negotiate place (mainland China) and gender (predominantly male) but also including some females, as the quote from the female fan Xu Li at the beginning of this section shows.

Different meanings are negotiated by different audiences. Genre certainly plays a role in this process, but to construct essentialized differences by clas-sifying gendered audiences to specific genres is questionable. We may say that the chivalric aesthetics of hard rock are more open for male identifications,

Table 1. Music Preference of Young Chinese Males and Females

Music Preference	% of total (N = 650)	Males (%)	Females (%)
Chinese pop	36	39	61
Chinese rock	21	64	36
See no difference	23	49	51
No preference	20	55	45

just as the folk aesthetics of Zhang Chu cater more to female identifications. But to what level do genres produce specific audiences? In order to answer that question, I want to focus on the division that appears to be most crucial: pop versus rock. How important is the pop-rock division for those who are less committed to music than fans who write letters to their idols?

In October 1997, I conducted a survey among 650 Chinese youngsters, ranging in age from fifteen to twenty-five.[87] The sample is representative for the real population on the variables age, sex, and education.[88] The survey shows that for 43 percent of the listeners the pop-rock division is not important: either they don't hear any difference, or they don't have a preference. This finding leads me to ask if music for this group is less important than it is for those who do show a preference for either pop or rock. The survey in fact supports the assumption that those who show no clear preference are less involved in music in general. In the case of this 43 percent, music is not considered an important part of one's identity. The group who showed a preference for either pop or rock agreed significantly more with the statements "Music reflects my personality" and "Music is more important than TV." If we single out the group with a preference for either rock or pop, what are the differences between them? In answering this question I would like to focus on the following factors: gender, importance of music, and opinions about life.

GENDER

Table 1 presents the gender differences between different audiences. Significantly more males than females show a preference for Chinese rock. As suggested earlier, genre differences do make a difference. Whereas folk-rock singer Zheng Jun is equally popular among young men and women, rock singer Cui Jian and the band Tang Dynasty mainly attract a male audience. Folk-rock singers cross the boundary between pop and rock, thus the male dominance decreases. Pop stars such as Jacky Cheung and Leon Lai appeal significantly more to a female audience. Crossovers from pop singers to rock, such as Faye Wong, do result in an increase of popularity among the male audience: both men and women like her. The male bias of the rock subculture, which has been criticized by authors such as Angela McRobbie,[89] does also apply for Chinese audiences. The aesthetics of rock are predominantly male aesthetics. Consequently, it reasserts rather than subverts the regulation of gender roles.

IMPORTANCE OF MUSIC

The picture that emerged from the fan letters is one of strong involvement in the music and the musician. Is rock more important for the articulation of one's identity than pop? This seems to be only partly the case. The rock audience listens on average to more music than the pop audience (77 minutes and 63 minutes a day respectively). The audiences who see no difference or show no preference both listen 59 minutes a day to music, slightly less than the pop audience. If we compare the pop with the rock audience, it is the rock audience that mainly believes music to be more important than TV. Both pop and rock fans agree on the statement that music reflects one's personality (75 percent). Value judgments on the genres differ: the rock audience believes pop to be superficial and rock lyrics to be more important than pop lyrics. Mainly the pop audience believes Chinese rock to be a copy of Western rock. Thus the notion of "authenticity" is being contested, with the pop audience accusing rock of being inauthentic, and vice versa.

OPINIONS ABOUT LIFE

My short analysis of the fan letters already indicates that the rock mythology does not produce a prefabricated identity. According to Andreas Steen, it is highly unlikely that rock fans can also appreciate pop.[90] In his opinion, rebellious rock fans are not supposed to be fooled by the hegemonic pop music. But how rebellious are rock fans? Table 2 presents the response of the different audiences to several statements. The statements are loosely grouped under "conformity," "attitude and aspirations," and "gender and sexuality." The audiences who see no difference between pop and rock or show no preference have been lumped together in one group, as a "neutral" audience. Statements with a significant difference are marked with two asterisks.

Significant differences exist predominantly between the rock audience, on the one hand, and the pop and neutral audiences, on the other. The rock audience is more accepting of sex before marriage but is as hostile toward homosexuality as the pop audience. The acceptance by both the rock audience and the neutral audience of the statement that university is more important for boys points to the conservative attitude of the predominantly male rock audience and contradicts the progressiveness implied by rock mythology. All groups get along well with their parents, although the generational conflict seems to be stronger for the rock audience, which admits to disagreeing more

Table 2. Opinions of Pop, Rock, and Neutral Audiences
(% in agreement; N = 650)

Statement	Pop audience (36% of total)	Rock audience (21% of total)	Neutral audience (43% of total)	Significance
Conformity				
I get along well with my parents	90	86	91	(0.33)
I usually have the same opinions as my parents	31	20	32	(0.03)**
Rules are necessary	87	84	81	(0.20)
Attitude and Aspirations				
I want a happy family life	97	96	95	(0.46)
Money is the best indicator of one's achievement	35	45	42	(0.10)
Helping other people is very important in life	81	70	84	(0.01)**
I am proud to be Chinese	97	96	93	(0.13)
I currently lead a happy life	80	71	80	(0.09)
Gender and Sexuality				
Sex before marriage is acceptable	48	63	54	(0.03)**
Love is more important than money	80	75	73	(0.19)
Homosexuality is acceptable	24	27	26	(0.86)
University education is more important for a boy	22	32	33	(0.03)**

Note: The significance was calculated by the chi-square test, based on a 95 percent confidence interval.

often with the opinions of their parents. However, this is not translated into a more critical stance toward the importance of rules: all groups strongly believe rules to be necessary, but interestingly enough, the musically neutral audience tends to value the importance of rules less. The rock audience seems to be more self-centered, as the respondents agree less often with the statement that helping others is important. Mainly the rock audience shows dissatisfaction toward life: they more often agree that they are unhappy, although the difference is not significant.

In another question, the respondents were asked to choose five out of eleven qualities that they believed children should be encouraged to learn at home.[91] Differences turned out to be minor: the rock audience would more often say that imagination is important, whereas the pop audience values tolerance and respect for other people significantly more. This strengthens the idea of the rock audience as being more self-centered (or, to put it in a more positive light, more self-conscious). The general picture that emerges from these statistics is not that of a conservative, obedient pop audience and a progressive, rebellious rock audience. Despite more conflicts with parents, the rock audience does not seem to be less obedient. Their more liberal stance toward (hetero-)sexuality goes hand in hand with a conservative attitude toward women. Their self-consciousness seems to be merely reflected in caring less for others, rather than in a more critical positioning of the self vis-à-vis broader issues such as nationalism or family values. And, more importantly, on most issues, the rock audience has the same opinions as both the pop audience and the audience who does not show a clear music preference.[92] The rock mythology creates an imagined community that, if we look more carefully to its characteristics, seems to be less rebellious, subversive, and provocative, than is suggested not only by the participants of this subculture but also by journalists and academics.

It is not my aim here to essentialize differences between audiences, but rather to destabilize assumptions about the rock audience in search for a more subtle approach, in which reception of rock is interpreted as a moment of cultural struggle, "an ongoing struggle over meaning and pleasure which is central to the fabric(ation) of everyday life."[93] The analysis apparently leads us to the truism that different audiences read different cultural texts in different contexts in a different way. The audience as unit of analysis has been decentred, leaving nothing but an analytical vacuum that too often has been camouflaged by an uncritical celebration of notions of difference and possible subversive readings. Analysts eagerly trace subversive decodings from cultural texts by the audience.[94] What remains problematic is how to link these subversive readings to broader political struggles. According to Anglen, "What matters is not the certainty of knowledge about audiences, but an ongoing critical and intellectual engagement with the multivarious ways in which we constitute ourselves through media consumption."[95] My doubts remain, unfortunately, since her description seems to mystify rather than clarify the aim of audience studies. Audience studies is at a crossroads; the crux of the current crisis lies in the question how to link knowledge on how audiences negotiate texts with broader cultural processes.[96] Mark Liechty argues that it makes no sense to think of audiences in association with particular media, "since various mass media . . . as well as other commodities, mix together and resonate with each other in a sphere of mutually referencing, mutually reinforcing ideas and images."[97] The next step could well be to abandon the concept of audiences—and thus audience research—entirely. This seems the easiest way out, but I would rather argue for further theorization on how audiences are constituted through media consumption, and when, where, and how this binds them together, and integrate this analysis into a broader framework that includes the music, the musicians, and the production of the music. According to Lawrence Grossberg's analysis of American rock, the power of rock "lies in its ability not only to construct maps of everyday life, but also to deconstruct such maps as well. Rock can celebrate insecurity and instability even as it constructs secure spaces."[98] The aesthetics of Chinese rock challenges everyday life in China, as I have outlined in this essay. The tactics of symbolic inversion negates what is considered normal; the chivalric aesthetics of hard rock challenge modern Chinese society. An alternative reality, new maps of everyday life emerge. It is there where we can locate the rock audience. For this imagined community, the rock mythology serves as the unifying narrative; it articulates differences based on, to name the few I have outlined in this essay, gender (male), place (mainland China), and shared notions of authenticity/honesty. However, closer analysis destabilizes the supposed cohesion of the rock audience. A considerable part of the audience—43 percent—either does not see a difference between rock and pop, or simply has no preference. The ideological difference between pop and rock, fueled by the rock mythology, seems partly to lose its value at the moment of reception. Furthermore, differences between the audiences that indicate a preference for either pop or rock, or that did not discern a difference or have a clear preference, do not show an emancipated rock audience and an obedient pop audience. On most value statements, the different audiences shared the same opinions. Chinese audiences seem to subvert genre differences that are often considered crucial by politicians, producers, musicians, journalists, and academics.

By Way of Conclusion

The "music world" of rock consists of producers, musicians, audiences, and a fourth group, of academics, journalists, and politicians. The fourth group is particularly relevant for Chinese rock, but each of them plays a part in the construction of the rock culture. The underlying rock mythology, as outlined in this essay, functions as the glue that binds the world together. If we aim to grasp the meanings of Chinese rock music, or rather rock music in China, there is a need to think beyond rock mythology and search for a more subtle analysis in which we trace the moments of both opposition against and compliance with the political, social, and economic system. Such an analysis needs to question fixed dichotomies such as pop–rock, high–low, commercial–alternative, East–West, local–global, in favor of a more fluid approach. This implies stepping beyond the dominant subcultural paradigm, in which subcultures are "read" vis-à-vis a certain dominant culture and their "symbolism" is solely interpreted within that paradigm. The red scarf of Cui Jian can be read as an ironic, symbolic act of resistance. This interpretation is valid, but it dismisses broader processes at work. Chinese rock emerged in a rapidly globalizing world. Thus the context in which it emerged includes not only the mainland, but also the region ("Greater China") and the world, in particular the West. Place is being negotiated, a place that is both local in its focus on Chineseness, as well as global in its adaptation of a global sound and cosmopolitan imagery. This construction of place is problematic; the self-orientalizing practices traced in this essay resemble Party politics of the 1990s, in which nationalism played a dominant role. I have shown that this does not imply that rock carries no critique at all. I outline different aesthetics used by the bands — dadaist, vulgar, or chivalric — that can be considered challenging to dominant cultural and political values. But rather than celebrating these subverting practices, I believe it necessary both to point to the other side of the coin — the moments of compliance — and to avoid romanticizing rock at the expense of pop. The aesthetics of rock articulate, as I have shown in this essay, notions of authenticity that strongly link the bands with the audiences. A shared sense of being emerges within genre-specific conventions.

Including the audience in the analysis further destabilizes the rock mythology. We are not only left with the contradictory narrative that rock both accommodates and resists dominant culture but also discover that this narrative creates imagined communities, which, after close analysis, prove to be at most momentarily fixed. Rock can at best be considered a cultural space through which audiences move in and out, in which differences are being articulated yet rapidly evaporate. If we are to grasp the politics of rock in China, we need to further investigate these contradictions, rather than covering them under the comforting blanket of a consistent theoretical narrative.

Postscript

In 1988, the Beijing writer Liu Yiran published a short story entitled "Rocking Tiananmen." He writes about the universal power of "rock":[99] "How ya doin', Michael Jackson? Blood brother across the seas, you really turn us on. The second I flick on the tape, the music, that totally universal music, comes just rock-'n'-rollin' out over the room. The choreographer and party bosses don't even have time to take a breath. Sorry, folks, today I'm gonna party. Outrageous? Yeah, it's a fuckin' rebellion all right." Under the gray Dutch clouds, gazing out over a tidy, boring university garden, caught in the predictabilities of everyday life, I wonder whether I am simply jealous, snobbish, or critical when the first thought that strikes my mind after reading these words is "Keep on dreaming, keep on dreaming . . ."

Notes

I am deeply indebted to Chow Yiufai for the continuous inspiration and support. His comments on my earlier writings revealed an idealized reading of Chinese rock and forced me to search for alternative interpretations. Throughout the writing of this article, his critical readings proved to be an indispensable source of inspiration. All translations are mine.

1 Geremie Barmé and Linda Jaivin, eds., *New Ghosts, Old Dreams: Chinese Rebel Voices* (New York: Times Books, 1992), 471.

2 Arif Dirlik and Xudong Zhang, introduction to this volume.

3 Dirlik and Zhang, introduction.

4 Chinese intellectuals argue that one can speak of *Chinese* postmodernism (Ning Wang, "The Mapping of Chinese Postmodernity," in this volume). Such a claim on authenticity contradicts the discourse of postmodernism itself, which questions the idea of authenticity. According to Dirlik and Zhang, "Postmodernism [functions] as a concept with which to grasp and make sense of a complex reality that does not lend itself to comprehension through categories marked by the spatial and temporal teleologies of modernity" (introduction). Rey Chow argues strongly against localizing theories, *in casu* cultural studies: "If one of the major tasks of cultural studies is that of bringing the entire notion of 'culture' into crisis rather than simply that of assembling different cultures for their mutual admiration, then a localist and nationalist strategy as such, which returns culture to the status of some origin, property or set of attributes—such as 'Chinese,' 'French,' 'American'—that everyone owns prior to language and discourse, would precisely put an end to the critical impetus of cultural studies" (Chow, *Ethics after Idealism: Theory, Culture, Ethnicity, Reading* [Bloomington: Indiana University Press, 1998], 9–10).

5 Chen Xiaoming, "The Mysterious Other: Postpolitics in Chinese Film," in this volume.

6 Deborah S. Davis, "Introduction: Urban China," in *Urban Spaces in Contemporary China: The Potential for Autonomy and Community in Post-Mao China*, ed. Deborah S. Daves, Richard Kraus, Barry Naughton, and Elizabeth J. Perry (New York: Cambridge University Press, 1995), 7.

7 Dirlik and Zhang, introduction.

8 BBC, *Voices of the World: Cui Jian* (London: BBC, 1992); Peter Sackman, *Beijing: Rock Buiten Western* (Hilversum: VPRO TV, 1997); Peter Sackman, *Uit De Schaduw* (Hilversum: IKON TV, 1992).

9 Andrew F. Jones, *Like a Knife: Ideology and Genre in Contemporary Chinese Popular Music*, Cornell East Asia Series (Cornell: Cornell University Press, 1992), 94.

10 According to Niu Jiawei, manager of the Beijing office of record company Magic Stone.

11 Chen Zhi Ang, "MTV zai Zhongguo boran xingqi" (MTV thrives in China), *Renmin yinyue* (People's music), (1994): 14–18.

12 Song Xiao, "Zhongguo yaogunyue yao xiang hefang?" (Where will Chinese rock music rock to?), *Zhongguo yinxiang* (China audio visual monthly), no. 5 (1997): 13.

13 In Chen Zhi Ang, "MTV zai Zhongguo boran xingqi."

14 "Yingyexin yanchu guanli tiao li" (New regulations for performances), *Renmin ribao* (People's daily), 21 Aug. 1997, p. 5.

15 In M. Eckhardt, "Ich haben nichts, wir haben nichts," in *Yaogun Yinyue: Jugend-, Subkultur und Rockmusik in China, Politische und gesellschäftliche Hintergrunde eines neuen Phänomes*, ed. T. Heberer (Hamburg: 1994), 119.

16 By using the term *mythology* I do not wish to suggest the existence of a "reality" that lurks

behind the mythology. I believe rock mythology to be an important discourse that produces rock culture as a music world. The aim in deconstructing the mythology does not lie in revealing a "truth" about the rock culture as such, but rather in analyzing how rock culture is constructed. I aim to develop a different perspective on this cultural practice in which frequently overlooked discussions are included.

17 Tim Brace and Paul Friedlander, "Rock and Roll on the New Long March: Popular Music, Cultural Identity, and Political Opposition in the People's Republic of China," in *Rockin' the Boat: Mass Music and Mass Movements*, ed. Reebee Garofalo (Boston: South End Press, 1992), 127.

18 Timothy W. Ryback, *Rock around the Bloc: A History of Rock Music in Eastern Europe and the Soviet Union* (Oxford: Oxford University Press, 1990).

19 Sabrina Petra Ramet, "Rock: The Music of Revolution (and Political Conformity)," in *Rocking the State: Rock Music and Politics in Eastern Europe and Russia*, ed. Sabrina Petra Ramet (Oxford: Westview Press, 1994), 1. Between 1989 and 1992 Havel presided over a government that had a heavy representation of rock musicians (Ramet, "Rock," 55). During Havel's 1998 visit to President Clinton, the rock singer Lou Reed was invited to perform at Havel's request (*NRC Handelsblad*, September 17, 1998). While this shows how rock in the West has moved from the fringe of society to its political center, it may be equally accurate to say that the perception of rock in the West as being at the fringe of society in its early days has always been a myth.

20 Dick Hebdige (*Subculture: The Meaning of Style* [London: Methuen and Co., 1979]) deconstructed in his work oppositional styles (like punk) that challenged dominant culture. In later works (*Hiding in the Light* [London: Routledge, 1988]) he questioned his previous assumption that subcultures intentionally challenged dominant culture and developed a more nuanced approach by adopting Foucault's ideas of power and surveillance. The idea of surveillance is useful in emphasizing that Chinese youngsters have to respond to multiple stresses: they are expected to be good sons or daughters, hardworking, obedient students, and model citizens. According to Angela McRobbie (*Feminism and Youth Culture: From "Jacky" to "Just Seventeen"* [London: Macmillan, 1991], 33), "The classic subculture does provide its members with a sense of oppositional sociality, an unambiguous pleasure in style, a disruptive identity and a set of collective fantasies." It is crucial to trace and analyze the moments in which this happens, while searching for its reverse, e.g., the moment in which rock does support today's political realities in China.

21 Jolanta Pekacz ("Did Rock Smash the Wall? The Role of Rock in Political Transition," *Popular Music* 13, no. 1 [1994]: 42) makes a similar point for Eastern Europe.

22 For an analysis of the political landscape of China, see Andrew Nathan, *China's Crisis: Dilemmas of Reform and Prospects for Democracy* (New York: Columbia University Press, 1990).

23 To give three different tactics used by record companies to circumvent censorship: (1) the lyrics of Cui Jian's song "Like a Knife" were not published on the jacket, but the song was included on the tape; (2) the printed lyrics from The Fly's "Gun or Bullet" were changed, controversial words were replaced by homophones, "sex" (*xing*) was turned into "heart" (*xin*), "making love" (*zuo ai*) was changed into "loving wrongly" (*cuo ai*); the same tactic was used for Wang Yong: while the printed lyrics run "Shall I marry you soon?" (*Wo jiu qu ni ma?*), he actually sings "I will fuck you" (*Wo jiu qu ni made*); (3) controversial images on the jacket of Zhou Ren's album—such as a portrait of Chairman Mao—were covered on the mainland version (but not in Hong Kong and Taiwan).

24 Pekacz, "Did Rock Smash the Wall?" 44.

25 Liang Liang, "Zai shijie wuji shang juxing de yaogunyue" (Rock concert on the ridge of the roof of the world) *Zhongguo Yinxiang* (China Audio-Visual Monthly), no. 9 (1995): 8.

26 Theodor W. Adorno, *Einleitung in die Musiksoziologie: Zwölf theoretische Vorlesungen* (Frankfurt: Suhrkamp Verlag, 1962).

27 Howard S. Becker, *Art Worlds* (Berkeley: University of California Press, 1992), 35.

28 Edward Friedman, "The Oppositional Decoding of China's Leninist Media," in *China's Media, Media's China*, ed. Chin-Chuan Lee (Boulder, Colo.: Westview Press, 1994), 132; and Stuart Hall, "Encoding-Decoding," in *Culture, Media, Language*, ed. S. Hall, D. Hobson, A. Lowe, and P. Willis (London: Hutchinson, 1980), 157–62.

29 Tensions between music cultures and the state are of course not restricted to China. Illustrative is the enactment by the English parliament of the Criminal Justice Law (1995) that restricted the playing of loud music with a repetitive beat and banned gatherings of more than ten persons at unsuitable places (with the aim of preventing "techno" parties). Consequently, a new genre emerged, labeled *Chemical Beats* (named after the band the Chemical Brothers). The music is even more psychedelic, aggressive, and provocative than "common" techno, yet the beat is less repetitive" (Hester Carvalho, "Niet te verbieden ritmes," NRC Handelsblad, 18 April 1997).

30 Richard Kraus, "China's Artists between Plan and Market," in *Urban Spaces in Contemporary China: The Potential for Autonomy and Community in Post-Mao China*, ed. Deborah S. Davis, Richard Kraus, Barry Naughton, and Elizabeth J. Perry (New York: Cambridge University Press, 1995), 190.

31 It is worth noting that the methods used to classify music are by no means consistent. Whereas on the mainland, rock tapes would usually be grouped together and separated from pop, the HMV music store in Hong Kong simply uses one classification: male vs. female. Rock bands—which are predominantly male—are here grouped under male, together with pop singers. Another popular classification is rooted in China's feudalist past: the four most popular male "Cantopop" stars (Leon Lai, Jacky Cheung, Aaron Kwok, and Andy Lam) are often referred to by the popular press as the "heavenly four emperors" (*tianwang*), Faye Wong as "the princess" (*wangfei*), and Sammi Cheng as the "heavenly empress" (*tianhou*). The older Cantopop stars are referred to as the "song gods" (*gesheng*).

32 "Greater China" is a problematic concept; it remains disputed whether, for example, Singapore or other overseas Chinese communities ought to be included. The concept is predominantly used to analyze economic interdependencies. A study of the global circulation of Cantopop would deepen our understanding of what constitutes "Greater China." Cantopop is a crucial part of a global Chinese popular culture, and Cantopop stars frequently tour all over the world to perform for overseas Chinese. See *Greater China: The Next Superpower?*, ed. David Shambaugh (Oxford: Oxford University Press, 1995).

33 Jones, *Like a Knife*.

34 These two artists also provide an interesting example of the inconsistencies and blunt simplifications of categorization. They are contracted by Hong Kong record companies and are usually considered Cantopop stars. However, both were born in Beijing and only later moved to Hong Kong. Faye Wong still resides in both Hong Kong and Beijing. Furthermore, both singers sing in Cantonese as well as in Mandarin.

35 For example, to tie in with a forthcoming concert, the lyrics should be on the warm relationship with the fans, or if the image of the singer is on the sexy side, the lyrics could be more sensual or even explicitly seductive.

36 She might be inspired by her boyfriend, Dou Wei, who is one of China's major rock singers. Faye Wong has also been working together with the Cockteau Twins, one of the rare examples of cooperation between Western and Chinese artists.

37 Brace and Friedlander, "Rock and Roll on the New Long March," 117.

38 Jacky Cheung can be considered *the* pop star in the Greater China region. His image (down-to-earth, funny, and friendly) is open for multiple identifications. He participated—along with cellist Yo-Yo Ma—in a performance of avant-garde Chinese composer Tan Dun's *Symphony 1997* during the Hong Kong handover. When I attended the performance, I felt that a certain electricity suddenly filled the space with his appearance on stage; everyone started whispering. It was clear he was not just a singer but rather *the* celebrity of Hong Kong.

39 It goes beyond the scope of this essay to elaborate on the aesthetics of Chinese pop. Not only do these aesthetics inspire further reflections on notions such as postmodernity and decadence, they might also lead to (related) discussions on gender and sexuality. The aesthetics of, for example, Leon Lai, negotiate notions of Asian masculinity that, from a Western perspective, are very gay. So far, Chinese pop has been largely neglected by academics. A few examples in English are Joanna Ching-Yun Lee, "All For Freedom: The Rise of Patriotic/Pro-Democratic Popular Music in Hong Kong in Response to the Chinese Student Movement," in *Rockin' the Boat: Mass Music and Mass Movements*, ed. Reebee Garofalo (Boston: South End Press, 1992), 129–47; and Larry Witzleben, "Cantopop and Mandapop in Pre-Postcolonial Hong Kong: Identity Negotiations in the Performances of Anita Mui Yim-Fong," *Popular Music* 18, no. 2 (1999): 241–58. For an overview of pop music in Hong Kong with a focus on the lyrics, see Yiu Wai Chu, *Xiang Gang Liuxing Geci Yanjiu* (A Study of Pop Lyrics in Hong Kong) (Hong Kong: Joint Publishing Co., 1998).

40 For example, the tour of Anita Mui in 1995 was cut short in Guangzhou after she insisted on performing one of her banned songs, "Bad Girl," which was considered too obscene by mainland authorities. In Witzleben, "Cantopop and Mandopop."

41 Simon Frith, *Performing Rites: On the Value of Popular Music* (Oxford: Oxford University Press, 1996), 42. The concept "worlds" comes from Howard Becker (*Art Worlds* [Berkeley: University of California, 1992]), who describes the art world in a tautological way as consisting "of all the people whose activities are necessary to the production of the characteristic works which that world, and perhaps others as well, define as art. Members of art worlds coordinate the activities by which work is produced by referring to a body of conventional understandings embodied in common practice and in frequently used artifacts" (p. 34). The vagueness of the concept provides space for multiple interpretations, yet inherent in the idea of a "world" are its boundaries, and it tends to ignore the processes at work. The advantage of the idea of a "music world" is that its connotations include both producers and well as audiences, whereas *subculture* mainly refers to the musicians and their fans.

42 Simon Frith, *Sound Effects: Youth, Leisure, and the Politics of Rock 'n' Roll* (London: Constable, 1982), 41.

43 Frith, *Sound Effects*, 34.

44 Frith, *Performing Rites*, 42.

45 Frith, *Performing Rites*, 43.

46 Jones, *Like a Knife*; Andreas Steen, *Der lange Marsch des Rock 'n' Roll: Pop und Rockmusik in der Volksrepublik China*, Berliner China-Studien, no. 32 (Hamburg: LIT Verlag, 1996).

47 Ray Pratt, *Rhythm and Resistance: Explorations in the Political Uses of Popular Music* (New York: Praeger, 1990), 9–14.

48 Pratt, *Rhythm and Resistance*, 12.

49 Steen, *Der lange Marsch*, 14.

50 Jones, *Like a Knife*, 42.

51 Hall, "Encoding-Decoding," 157–62.

52 Also, the marketing slogan of Taiwan-based record company Magic Stone indicates the strong ties between the rock mythology and the marketing of the music: "The worst times, the best music" (*zui huaide shidai, zui haode yinyue*), as if rock automatically emerges in a repressive society.

53 Ayse S. Caglar, "Popular Culture, Marginality and Institutional Incorporation: German-Turkish Rap and Turkish Pop in Berlin," paper presented at the conference "Globalization and Ethnicity," Amsterdam, 1997 (sponsored by the Netherlands Foundation for the Advancement of Tropical Research, with the Research Center for Religion and Society, University of Amsterdam).

54 For example, in Jones, *Like a Knife*, and Steen, *Der lange Marsch*.

55 Johannes Fabian, *Moments of Freedom: Anthropology and Popular Culture* (Charlottesville: University Press of Virginia, 1998), 68–70.

56 For a comprehensive encyclopedia of Chinese popular music, see *Shi nian Zhongguo liuxing yinyue 1986–1996* (Chronicles of ten years of Chinese pop music, 1986–1996), ed. Liaoyuan Huang (Beijing: Zhongguo Dianying Chubanshe, 1997). For a detailed account of the early history of Chinese rock and the first bands, see Steen, *Der lange Marsch*. For a brief overview of contemporary bands, including music fragments, see *http://www.geocities.com/SunsetStrip/Studio/2418/cubl.html*.

57 Unless otherwise indicated, quotations from singers are drawn from my interviews with them in the fall of 1997.

58 Fabian, *Moments of Freedom*, 84.

59 An interesting case in point is the music of Sister Drum (DaDaWa). Her "world music," presumably strongly influenced by Tibetan folk songs, is one of the rare examples of Chinese voices that succeed in entering the Western market. Its popularity outside China (both in East and South-East Asia as well as in the West) can partly be explained by its strong exotic flavour, which corresponds well with stereotypical images of Tibet as a mythical place with a long and rich history. Both the music as well as the imagery, with a jacket depicting a veiled, mysterious woman, construct an exotic place, far away from modern world. The following critical review, which appeared in China, is interesting: "The singer does not express the spirit and philosophy successfully. . . . This music copies a lot from Tibet folk music in an unnatural way. In some songs, the background vocals are more unstable than mysterious. The electronic instruments merely belong to superficial and snobbish modern culture" (Dai Cheng. "Miandui Xinling" [Face the heart], *Zhongguo Yinxiang* [China audio-visual monthly], no. 12 [1995]: 12). Instead of questioning the exoticism in the music, this critic refers to the incompatibility of folk songs and pop music. Of course the adjectives he used to describe modern culture and the related mystification and celebration of either the past or other ("traditional") places are not unfamiliar. Instead of following his accusation of Sister Drum's cheap cultural adaptation, I rather refer to Sister Drum as a self-orientalizing musical act that is part of a carefully planned commercial strategy.

60 Ang Ien. "Doing Cultural Studies at the Crossroads: Local/Global Negotiations," *European Journal of Cultural Studies* 1, no. 1 (1998): 24.

61 Both The Fly and NO could not release their albums on the mainland at the time of writing (1998). However, the Beijing-based record company Modern Sky has released both

albums in 1999 on the mainland market. The jacket of The Fly as well as the printed lyrics have been greatly modified to make this release possible.

62 An Ning. "Review of CD *The Fly*," *Zhongguo Bailaohui* (Chinese Broadway), 1997, p. 42.

63 The same applies to their Western counterparts such as the German industrial band Einstürzende Neubauten, who also participates in other cultural fields such as theater. Both NO and The Fly admit to having been strongly influenced by Einstürzende Neubauten.

64 For example, the magazines *China Broadway* and *Music Heaven*, both belonging to the popular press, which functions relatively independently from the state press, always include reviews from recent releases in the West, releases one can actually not buy in China. The latter magazine includes a compilation tape with Western music, for example, presenting the history of house music from Kraftwerk in the seventies until today's Orb. This magazine seems to be mainly popular among students.

65 Hebdige, *Hiding in the Light*, 35.

66 Kong Bu, in He Li, "Yaogun 'guer" (Rock 'n' roll orphans), *Jinri xianreng* (Today's avant-garde), no. 5 (1997): 88.

67 He Li, "Yaogun 'guer," 88. He Li also quotes critic Sun Mengpu, who describes the music of NO thus: "A soul is bleeding in the butchery. A man, cursing the cultural garbage, cruelly exposes his anger, his tears and his despair. Rock and roll is music beyond limits. I see, in the darkness of fear, a pair of eyes, stunned, and a heart, floating in the air, dying."

68 Also, Western musicians claim technology to be falsifying, a notion that can be traced back to the romantic critique of industrial capitalism in the nineteenth century. For a concise overview on this critique, see Keith Negus, *Producing Pop: Culture and Conflict in the Popular Music Industry* (London: Edward Arnold, 1992), 27–37. The popularity of MTV's *Unplugged* series in the 1990s can be seen in this light, and might be considered a reaction on the ultimate technologized aesthetics of house music.

69 Barbara B. Babcock, introduction to *The Reversible World: Symbolic Inversion in Art and Society*, ed. Barbara B. Babcock (London: Cornell University Press, 1978), 19.

70 Babcock, introduction, 32.

71 He Li, "Yaogun 'guer."

72 Babcock, introduction, 32.

73 In Steen, *Der lange Marsch*, 165.

74 Steen, *Der lange Marsch*, 165.

75 Dao Zui, "Wuyue huainian Zhang Ju" (Remember Zhang Ju in May) *Dangdai getan* (Modern music field), 1997, 27.

76 Interview with Niu Jiawei, manager of the Beijing office of Magic Stone, September 1997.

77 Kaiser Kuo left the band in June 1999 after a personal conflict with vocalist Ding Wu. According to rumors in the rock culture, NATO's bombing of the Chinese embassy in Belgrade in May 1999, during the Kosovo war, sparked the conflict. Apparently, the nationalist sentiments of the band turned against its American-born guitar player.

78 Gregory B. Lee, *Troubadours, Trumpeters, Troubled Makers: Lyricism, Nationalism and Hybridity in China and Its Others* (London: Hurst, 1996), 158.

79 Jones, who has been the first to analyze the complicity of rock with CCP politics, refers to an article in *China Youth News* (1991), which stated that the government should tolerate rock to oppose the dominance of Cantopop. "There is not just a little irony here: an oppositional subculture based on an Anglo-American musical form that originally sprang from a repudiation of traditional Chinese culture is nationalistically invoked in

the official press as a domestic alternative to foreign products." In Andrew F. Jones, "The Politics of Popular Music in Post-Tiananmen China," in *Popular Protest and Political Culture in Modern China*, 2d ed., ed. Elizabeth J. Perry and Jeffrey N. Wasserstrom (Oxford: Westview Press, 1994), 161.

80 Jones, "Politics of Popular Music," 159.

81 Jones, "Politics of Popular Music," 160.

82 Jones ("Politics of Popular Music," 160) quotes Lao Wu, who left the band after conflicts with vocalist Ding Wu, in his critique on Western society: "I've been westernized almost my whole life. I spent twenty years absorbing anything Western that I could get my hands on. I never knew anything about my own tradition. And now I really hate anything from the West. I resent its influence. . . . Modern Chinese culture has never lived up to the tradition because it's been ruined by all the Western influence. We have to get back to our roots, . . . that's what the mission of [Chinese rock] should be all about."

83 Jones, "Politics of Popular Music," 161.

84 Two major record companies of Chinese rock, Magic Stone and Red Star, agreed to my request to read letters of fans. At the end sixty-two letters, all from 1997, were included in the analysis.

85 That she writes to a folk-rock singer shows how different genres produce different (gendered) audiences. Ideally, in folk music, "there is no separation of art and life" (Frith, *Performing Rites*, 39). In folk, stardom and glamour are consciously avoided; the musician is merely "the boy next door." The folk aesthetics produce a discourse of authenticity that is based on notions of equality and normality. Consequently, this female fan writes about her personal worries rather than about her admiration for Zhang Chu.

86 Keith Negus, *Producing Pop: Culture and Conflict in the Popular Music Industry* (London: Edward Arnold, 1992), 77.

87 The survey has been funded by Philips Sound and Vision and was implemented in close cooperation with Diamond Consultancy, Beijing.

88 Figures from the real population are from the *China Population Statistics Yearbook 1995* (regarding age) and were calculated by the Beijing Bureau for Statistics for this survey (regarding education). Figures from the sample differ at most 5 percent from official figures. The survey was conducted in five different districts in Beijing; thus different neighborhoods are represented. The ten research assistants worked with a quota while selecting their respondents.

89 McRobbie, *Feminism and Youth Culture*.

90 Steen, *Der lange Marsch*, 154.

91 The options were good manners, independence, hard work, feeling of responsibility, imagination, tolerance and respect for other people, thrift and saving money, determination and perseverance, religious faith, unselfishness, and obedience.

92 There were no significant differences for eleven out of the sixteen statements, and only on two out of the listed eleven qualities were differences significant.

93 Ang Ien, *Living Room Wars: Rethinking Media Audiences for a Postmodern World* (London: Routledge, 1996), 43.

94 Henry Jenkins, "Television Fans, Poachers, Nomads," in *The Subcultures Reader*, ed. Ken Gelder and Sarah Thornton, 506–22 (London: Routledge, 1997); and Paul Willis, *Common Culture: Symbolic Work at Play in the Everyday Cultures of the Young* (Buckingham, England: Open University Press, 1990).

95 Ang, *Living Room Wars*, 52.

96 For a discussion on this crisis, see Sonia Livingstone, "Audience Research at the Crossroads: The 'Implied Audience' in Media and Cultural Theory," *European Journal of Cultural Studies* 1, no. 2 (1998): 193–218.

97 Mark Liechty, "Fashioning Modernity in Kathmandu: Mass Media, Consumer Culture, and the Middle Class in Nepal" (Ph.D. diss., University of Pennsylvania, 1994), 475.

98 Lawrence Grossberg, "The Framing of Rock: Rock and the New Conservatism," in *Rock and Popular Music: Politics, Policies, Institutions,* ed. Tony Bennett, Simon Frith, Lawrence Grossberg, John Shepherd, and Graeme Turner (London: Routledge, 1993), 207. Influenced by Lefebvre, Grossberg interprets the everyday life as "an historically produced plane of existence which is built upon principles of repetition, redundancy, recurrence (and ultimately, boredom). . . . It is, in a sense, a structure of discipline by which people's daily practices are subjected to the demands of a comfortable predictability and routinization" (204).

99 In Barmé and Jaivin, *New Ghosts, Old Dreams,* 11.

chao-yang liao

11 Borrowed Modernity:
History and the Subject in *A Borrowed Life*

1

Although it has become an "industry standard" to speak of postmodernism in terms of poststructuralist tenets such as difference, playful randomness, liberating fragmentation, incredulity toward metanarratives, and loss of reality, there are signs that the favorite themes of earlier debates are being replaced by a new set of problems and some new solutions. I am not referring to that "new breed of radical anti-postmodernists" who, as Edward W. Soja warns us, homogenizes the entire movement as reactionary and forecloses "the very possibility of radical postmodernism"; nor will I be concerned with the kind of "neo-modernism" in social theory that, in Jeffrey C. Alexander's words, specializes in "post-postmodern theorizing."[1] What I will try to indicate in what follows is the reemergence of depth and the real as major concerns for radical postmodernism and its relevance to the cultural and political conditions in contemporary Taiwan. Specifically, I will use Wu Nianzhen's feature film *A Borrowed Life* (1994) as an exemplary, albeit third-worldly, case that illustrates the stakes involved in this new turn.

What is, then, this reemergence of depth and the real? How is it not a regression to pre-postmodern, "naïve" accounts of what is important in the world? This is not the place to give an elaborate assessment of the state of the art theorization of postmodernity. With regard to visual art, Hal Foster has provided a useful outline of what I have in mind. Referring to Lacan's conception of the gaze as located in the object and as having the effect of threatening the subject (the seeing eye) with a feeling of being observed, or looked back at, "from all sides," Foster proceeds to explain why, in Lacan's schematic representation of vision as two superimposed cones, the image also appears as a screen shielding the subject from direct exposure to the gaze. For Foster, this screen is "the cultural reserve," the codes and conventions of visuality, that "mediates the object-gaze for the subject," protecting the latter from being captured by the assimilating gaze of the world. Without this screen, the subject would be "blinded by the gaze or touched by the real" and would not even be able to see.[2] While postmodernism, in general, registers an awareness of this shielding effect of the symbolic reserve and a desire to disrupt or reach beyond the screen, various strategies for coming to terms with this awareness are possible, and, in the 1990s, Foster observes a shift in much postmodernist art from an earlier concern with problematizing the image-screen to a new tendency to retrieve the object-gaze as an "event of trauma," an ambivalently abjected excess, and to allow it to recalibrate experience without the mediation of the symbolic.[3]

Here we must carefully distinguish this concern with abjection and trauma from the Lyotardian privileging of the postmodern sublime as the ecstatic contemplation of the unpresentable in presentation. Although the Lyotardian sublime insists on "allusions" to the unpresentable, such allusions are not meant to point to anywhere beyond the image-screen: "The conceivable which cannot be presented" is still conceivable and therefore cannot be thought of as existing on a different plane from that of the conceivable which *can* be presented. These allusions provide, rather, occasions to invent new "rules of the game," to replace old categories with new ones, all in the name of a "war on totality," a disillusioned soberness about the terror of fantasized reality.[4] The point, then, is to experiment with effects of representation (the conceivable), to shake up the cultural reserve or the artistic repertoire in the hope of turning up new possibilities or at least prevent the rigidification of old conventions. Although it is reasonable to expect such experimentation to open up the cultural apparatus and make the general conditions more congenial to a return of the abjected other as a meaningful presence in public consciousness, no rationale is provided for the necessity or even desirability of such a return. In fact, the constant vigilance against totalization cannot exempt the very abjected alterity from its list of possible sources of totalizing terror.

Alterity must be alluded to but not granted too much proximity lest it turn into another maker of oppressive metanarratives. Thus there is nothing, in this conception, to prevent alterity from being trapped perennially in the limbo of the unpresentable, lost in the abstract structure of mere allusiveness. The possibility of any real return is obviated.

Nor is the problem solved by Scott Lasch's return to an earlier Lyotard to reformulate postmodernism as "de-differentiation." Lasch acknowledges that Lyotardian postmodernity, in its insistence on the constant questioning of foundationalism, retains too much of the modernist drive for cultural differentiation and suggests that Lyotard's contribution lies in the elaboration of an aesthetics based on the nondiscursive ("figural"), immediate discharge of psychic energy.[5] Although this formulation defines the postmodern in terms of its refusal to problematize representation, to "lay bare the device," the observed countermove (or proposed alternative) to problematize reality amounts to much the same thing, since the signifier and the referent, or the real, have been de-differentiated. If "the 'real' that the [cinematic] spectator has been drawn into is revealed as artifice," then such postmodernity still instances an imperative to level distinctions and eliminate depth, and eventually abjected alterity would still be allowed the semblance of a return only under a "more ambivalent and less fixed positioning of subjectivity," produced and reflexively justified all without leaving the image-screen, the procedural construction of fictive/real representation.[6]

Foster's proposal, on the other hand, is to find a shift "from reality as an effect of representation to the real as a thing of trauma."[7] The idea of trauma introduces a dimension of temporality that gives depth to the layered and split structure of representation. It does not matter whether the real can or cannot be absolutely differentiated from its representation, since the point now lies elsewhere—in the retroactive construction of trauma and the layered differentiations of time lags. There is de-differentiation in representation, but there is also the temporal embeddedness of experience pointing to the constant sedimentation of excesses generated by symbolic ordering. Thus, we may postulate two levels of the real: an ultimately hypothetical "presymbolic real" and a real returned from the symbolic, "characterized by impasses and impossibilities [that are] due to the relations among the elements of the symbolic order itself."[8] If an earlier postmodernism universalizes everything as it "abandons all sense of historical continuity and memory, while simultaneously developing an incredible ability to plunder history and absorb whatever it finds there as some aspect of the present,"[9] then the shift toward traumatic embeddedness reintroduces difference as a principle of particularistic memory. This is not a return to the mastery of unitary, closed narrativity but the mobilization of a force that, in a different cultural context, enabled the

Buddhist principle of emptiness to solve the opposition between unity and fragmentation by acknowledging the "circuminsessional interpenetration" of all things.[10] The crucial move for Foster's new phase of postmodernity, therefore, is to recognize the deepening of reciprocal difference effected by traumatic temporality. When the real is defined as lack, ambivalence, or embedded antagonism in both the subject and its other, a new particularism emerges that is at the same time an opening onto the universality of shared lack: "Only insofar as I experience my own particular position as fundamentally deficient does the universal dimension involved in (and obfuscated by) it appear as such."[11]

A good example of the issues involved here is provided by a brief scene from Trinh T. Minh-ha's documentary film *Surname Viet Given Name Nam* (1989). A candidate of the Miss Vietnam 1988 pageant is asked about "what characteristics of Vietnamese culture we should preserve in American society." She replies: "I think that, as far as women are concerned, we should preserve our Vietnamese heritage and the four virtues Cong Dung Ngon Hanh."[12] How do we read this strange scene, which at the same time appears to be nothing extraordinary? Laura Mulvey, in an interview with the director, summarizes a possible reading of the scene as exemplifying the "commodification" of traditional Vietnamese culture: "What I thought was very interesting was the way that the question of women came out as taking a different form in each country—the way in which I thought it was important to show the Miss Vietnam pageant, in the U.S., so you could see the Vietnamese community and traditions becoming Americanized, as well as becoming kitsch."[13] While Mulvey's comments are, in general, quite sensitive to cultural differences (instanced here by the very reference to contextual variations of "the question of women"), the point about the Vietnamese community becoming Americanized and Vietnamese tradition turning into kitsch evokes the familiar postmodernist catechism about the loss of historical continuity and the purposeless plundering of history, thus throwing up the question of whether Mulvey is hiding a universalizing agenda behind a pluralist facade, of whether it is more appropriate to speak of the reification of packaged theory than of the Americanization of the patriarchal straitjacket of the "four virtues."

The difficulties involved in dealing with cultural particularity are, of course, a much debated problem in recent feminist theory. But how does Trinh respond? A few exchanges later, she returns to the beauty pageant scene in a general statement about the kind of criticism she wanted to present in the film. She begins with the more complicated case of a Vietnamese doctor who seems to have internalized her position as a submissive wife and then proceeds to the generalization:

The difficulty in that case [the case of the doctor] was, I was not simply criticizing. Because I think it would be very abusive in such a case to be merely critical. The challenge was to present the plight critically without condemning. For someone who is in that kind of situation, it seems important to be caring at the same time as one is critical. That's something I find most difficult in working on this film. The same applies for many of the scenes of the Vietnamese community in the U.S., of which the Miss Vietnam pageant event that you mentioned is an example. How can a critique also be a compliment without being any less of a critique? [14]

The critique must coexist with a different level, where "compliment" is appropriate; obviously Trinh is concerned about not losing sight of depth in dealing with particularity. In other words, when the candidate of the beauty pageant speaks of the necessity to preserve the patriarchal heritage, she cannot be construed as being merely insincere in an attempt to enhance her marketability in some way. That is a possibility, but there is also always a "beyond" to that possibility involving the cleaving points to the binding force of some traumatic "real," which must be kept in view and respected because, in a sense and if nothing else, it is shared by all. As Trinh warns us, people laugh at traditional feminine "virtues" only because "the higher we climb, the more multiply sophisticated the forms of oppression prove to be"; and that is why "one cannot criticize here without getting caught in the criticism itself." [15]

Here, Trinh touches on the fine differences between paying homage to patriarchy and paying homage to suffering under patriarchy. The "question of women" varies when one heritage interacts with another not because of some essentialized incompatibility between cultural formations but because there are time lags separating more from less "sophisticated" forms of oppression. The cleaving to an oppressive heritage deserves compliment not because it possesses any intrinsic value but because the heritage, having been displaced by cultural migration or modernization from the immediate presence of real oppression, sedimented, as it were, into deeper layers of memory, assumes a different meaning and comes to take the place of a surplus testifying, through its own persistent evoking of defunct functionality, to the nullity of the more "sophisticated" forms of oppression in the new context. Such a surplus of (non-)meaning may appear to be a laughable, idiotic fixation or a lowly object of commodification, but precisely through the nullification of its own meaning and substance, it acquires a psychic depth, a different sort of meaning and substance in the real. Paradoxically, when oppression is displaced into traumatic memory and revealed as built on its own nullity, it turns into a placeholder for its opposite, a constraining closure pinpointing a place where the suffering particularity yields to and enables an openness now universalizable through shared lack. To criticize such cleaving to an oppressive past would reproduce the very same oppression (the criticism would cannibalize itself), unless one also conceives the cleaving as an act of "choosing the margin," [16] of forgoing solipsistic cynicism and accepting the shared limits of human existence, of "saying yes to the inevitably fictional nature of identity and the otherness of the self." [17] This is by no means an obvious option for theoretical analysis, and very often we resort to empathy or "caring" to account for the intuitively perceived need for a more nuanced approach to suffering. But further analysis of this need is justified by the fact that such analysis would reconnect us with the reemergence of the real as a general concern in contemporary culture and is therefore of some significance for the theorizing of postmodernity.

2

A Borrowed Life is veteran scriptwriter Wu Nianzhen's debut work as a director and a memorial homage based on Wu's recollections about his dosan (father). At first glance, this is mainly a work of nostalgia steeped in the by now familiar "new wave" tradition typified by Hou Hsiao-hsien's early works. This belatedness seems to have caused local critics to maintain a respectful distance from the film. When not criticizing it for participating in the elitist aestheticism found responsible for failing box-office figures faced by the industry,[18] commentaries usually describe the film as a dutifully realistic representation of a certain type of Taiwanese man whose character has some touching qualities that are particularly captivating for a certain segment of the population but whose fixations belong, in any case, to a bygone age that should now be forgotten by a healthier generation.[19] Serious critical attention is, therefore, more often focused on other works of the same period that are considered to be more innovative.[20]

The present reading will, however, take this very critical silence as symptomatic of a perceptual gap created by the divisive confrontation with the historical real made possible by the film. Such confrontation is divisive because the film, though not explicitly political, takes something away from the sinicized perceptual order that has continued to reign even after four decades of martial law in Taiwan ended in 1987. In terms of reception, this division is signaled by the fact that the film failed to win a major award at the 1994 Golden Horse Film Festival but was designated the Audience Choice of Best Feature Film. Although this was clearly unusual (the audience choices in both 1993 and 1995 — The Wedding Banquet and Summer Snow, respectively — both confirmed the official Best Feature Film awards), it would be unwise to exaggerate the significance of such a discrepancy. But there are other indications that the reception of this film was polarized. Wu not only used his neighbors to play themselves as well as to help in other ways,[21] but he had his own way of bypassing public discourse and getting direct feedback from radio and cable TV audience calls, which appeared to be quite enthusiastic and led him to speak in an interview about how cinema could "heal" and "cause resonance."[22]

This, being entirely incompatible with market rationalization and the normativity of "implied" readership, is by no means an indication of commercial success. Rather, the appeal to the full presence of particular audience sensibilities highlights the folding of concrete experience into cultural production, pointing to resistance against the leveling pedagogy of conformist perception. Filmmaking, in this sense, becomes a way to achieve the gathering of concrete memories and particular people, to give them an imaginary place of appearance, a variation of the "bounded place-form" that, in Frank Frampton's account of critical regionalism, is the precondition of resistance to world capitalism.[23] Resistance, of course, is accompanied by divisiveness, and it is a divisive structure of meaning in the text that should prevent us from reading the story as simply an expression of cohesion and forgetting.[24] Paradoxically, such divisiveness, by disrupting the imaginary screen of false social harmony and by insisting on history and the real, radicalizes reciprocal difference and offers the vision of an alternative postmodern particularism as a way to counter ideological conflict and ethnic antagonism.

Let us look more closely at the film. Bbungian, who represents Wu in the film, recounts a chronological series of episodes from the life of Seiga, his father.[25] The minutiae of autobiographical narration are shaped into a few major themes, and we will be concerned mainly with one, perhaps the most conspicuous: Seiga's identification with and admiration for Japanese culture and industry. This identification, of course, has larger implications for older Taiwanese people who lived through both the Japanese occupation and the Chinese takeover of Taiwan, and is readable as part of a national allegory.[26] But more interesting is the parallel with the situation of the women in *Surname Viet Given Name Nam* discussed above. Seiga, too, is an oppressed subject, an economically disadvantaged miner who cleaves to an identity internalized from the earlier presence of Japanese colonialism. He listens to Japanese radio, frequents geisha houses while they still exist, idealizes Japanese products and athletic performances, and makes it his lifelong wish to visit Japan and "see the royal palace and Mt. Fuji." At the same time, this loyalty also turns into defunct sedimentation in a drastically altered ideological field within which even his children (especially Bbungian's younger brother and younger sister), who are educated in the new Chinese worldview, enjoy calling him an unreasonable maniac, a traitor to the Chinese people, and a "running dog" for Japan.

However, just as *Surname Viet Given Name Nam* refuses to denigrate suffering, there is never any possibility that *A Borrowed Life* would lower itself to a "condemnation" of either this fossilized subject of the Japanese empire or the children alienated from him by a more up-to-date indoctrination. The issues involved here are articulated in a way that preserves both ideological and narratological resistance to unitary closure and that manages to problematize transparent openness as well. Let us begin with the formalistic side of this articulation. The split between the diegetic presentation of Seiga's life (predominantly carried out in the Minnan language) and the first-person voice-over supposedly spoken (in Mandarin Chinese) by Bbungian creates a divisive focalization, and Seiga's position in this structure of divided vision is not at all a negative one. This structure is established by the opening episode and is confirmed again by a late scene that concludes Seiga's life with an explicit allusion to the main point of the divisive structure of meaning. Such accentuation indicates an attempt to give some coherence to an otherwise free-ranging thematic field and is an important key to any interpretation of the film.

The opening episode portrays Siega's visit to a geisha house. Bbungian, then six years old, is sent by his mother to keep an eye on Siega and his usual gang but is left alone in a movie theater, having been led to believe that a telephone call has summoned his father to visit a hospitalized friend. The child feels lonely and bored by the Japanese movie being shown on the screen, described in the script as an "endlessly talking literary drama." [27] The scene contains a loving reconstruction of early (1950s) cinematic practice in Taiwan, featuring an "orator" who serves simultaneously as interpreter, narrator, pager, maintainer of peace and order during the show, and announcer of the arrival of new merchandise at the snack bar downstairs. Bbungian's feeling about the predictable narrative of the movie sets up a pattern of boring continuity accompanied by teleological progress: Later, when queried by his mother, he describes the movie as nothing but hugging and kissing and the tragic death of a woman at the end. This pattern will be enlarged and inflected as the general drift of Bbungian's later life; what is observed will come to be embodied in the observer. We see Bbungian grow up, leave home to study in the city, become employed, get married, and so on. There are subdued references to the larger movements of history: the general urbanization of Taiwan, the economic boom and improvement of living standards, the depletion of natural resources signaled by the desertion of the mining town; but we see no interiority, no uniqueness, no life project. Bbungian's life is like a flattened image-screen, constituted by the stabilized grids of modernization but exhibiting features of general de-differentiation. In conspicuous contradistinction to the "absence of a powerful and dominating patriarchy" observed in (but not limited to) some of Hou Hsiao-hsien's works,[28] therefore, A Borrowed Life highlights the absence of a Bildung of the son into power and knowledge, the failure, one is tempted to say, of real initiation into "filiarchy."

This is not simply the result of Bbungian's role as a passive narrator of the course of his father's life. From the very beginning, the uneventful surface of this normalized life is contrasted with and presented as attracted to Seiga's transgressive world: Sometime after the movie is over, Bbungian is rescued from boredom and loneliness by a woman sent by his father to take him to the geisha house, and a later scene shows him peeping voyeuristically through a curtained door at the men's merriment on the other side. This is not really a third-person narrator; he has every opportunity to organize the story into his own initiation but does not do so. Many years and events later, at the end of a failing struggle with silicosis, Seiga jumps out of the window of an intensive care ward and kills himself. At this point in the film, the voice-over returns us to the traumatic scene at the movie theater:

> As he lay there in front of our eyes, smeared with dirt and grass and surrounded by hospital staff who were dutifully making the last attempt to save his life, I was frightened and helpless, not knowing what story I could make up to tell my mother who was waiting for word at home. All of a sudden, I recalled the time when I was a little kid and was abandoned by dosan, left alone in the movie theater. In a trance, I imagined that dosan has played his trick again and stood me up. I was again thrown into a void filled with subdued sobbing, and he went away to a place that was strange, mysterious, and beyond my understanding, to have a good time with his old buddies.

This is followed by a shot that visually echoes the first episode and shows Seiga combing his hair in a darkened room, all dressed up for an evening out. He turns and grins to the camera, then strides out of the room and toward the light at the other end of the hall, fading to white.

The imaginary transgressiveness of Seiga's world is tempered with failures and ambiguity. Seiga is an incompetent father who does not get along with his family, who gambles, and who is typically misogynist in his behavior. He stops his good friend Acan from running away with his lover, Akiko, forcing the latter to accept an arranged marriage, which eventually leads to Acan's suicide. He borrows a watch for a family reunion to show everyone at home how well he has been doing as a gold miner but is forced to give it away when his younger brother asks for it as a memento. In a local election, he arranges for everyone living out of town to return for the occasion, enthusiastically coordinates the vote "to show solidarity," and, when it turns out that there is one missing vote, clamors for the disclosure of the deserter's identity, only to be embarrassed when it is revealed that it is he himself who, preoccupied with mobilizing the other voters, has forgotten to cast his own ballot. These are not "human touches" that serve to neutralize paternal authority, for there is really no paternal authority to neutralize. Rather, within the structure of divisive focalization, all these failures, as well as the anachronistic allegiance to things Japanese, are transformed into evocations of an enigmatic power to veer away from the routine normality of everyday life, to have a good time at some secret place unknown to the son. There is no doubt that Seiga is a postmodern "anal" father: a father who does not live up to his symbolic function (as paternal metaphor) but who knows certain secrets and has the power to transgress and enjoy, that is, an "obscene-knowing father."[29]

There are two sides to this traumatic paternal relation in Bbungian's experience. On the one hand, the licentious side of the father is viewed from a respectful distance that accepts the aberrant behavior of the father as necessitated by external circumstances and that tolerates it as something beyond understanding but not congruent with symbolic correctness. Thus, after Seiga dies, Bbungian dutifully takes a photograph of him to Japan to carry out his wish to "see the royal palace and Mt. Fuji," a wish now normalized by the time lag into an ancestral demand, a symbolic responsibility placed on the son without requiring him to understand its meaning. This is the point of closure for Bbungian's side of the focalization, the point where he has paid his homage, done his filial duty, and given final shape to this part of his life. On the other hand, within the structure of divided meaning, this closure is revealed as superficial and perfunctory, the mere result of orderly symbolic narration, as uninteresting as the literary drama in Bbungian's memory. This is why the movement of the narrative must counter this flatness with a "strange, mysterious" place, a room not one's own, a space of possibilities on the other side of the divisive gap in focalization. Thus, Bbungian's recollection of the evening at the movie theater introduces lack into his otherwise untroubled subjectivity and provides a vantage point from which the lack in Seiga's world will turn into fullness and virility, his failures into daring attempts to go beyond imposed symbolic correctness and to preserve autonomy and agency.

The narrative is not lacking in indications that reveal such reversals as necessarily part of its production of meaning. Seiga's final decision to kill himself is a gesture of refusal made on learning that the only medical resort left to him would be "inserting tubes" into his body. Again, this points to repetition in traumatic time. Just as Bbungian's recollections start with being abandoned by his father in a movie theater, his retelling of Seiga's life harks back to instances of the man refusing the "insertion" of external will into his world:

After a bad quarrel with his stepmother, Seiga, then a teenager, left home to become an apprentice in traditional medicine; after the 1947 massacre, he was forced to leave again for the far end of the island and to become a miner there because he had had the audacity to flout the authority of the new rulers by performing mourning rites in public to honor local victims slaughtered by Chinese soldiers. These are also failures, but such failures exceed rather than fall short of the ordering of the symbolic mandate. In light of such reversals of lack into plenitude, Seiga's admiration for Japanese culture takes on new dimensions of meaning. In the last scene of the film, Bbungian's mother, conversing with Bbungian about the passing away of the old Japanese emperor and the enthronement of his son, presents her own reading of Seiga's love of Japan: "They [the emperors], father and son, have the fortune to be employed in the same business—not long after you were born, your *dosan* said that the greatest wish in his life was that his children should never have to work underground again. He was half buried even when he was young. His children should be free from that."

Seiga's valorization of Japanese identity, therefore, is read not as a simple act of submission to imperial power but as a borrowing of that power to achieve something else, a way to confirm the presence of a subjectivity that undermines the very hierarchy of imperial rule by conceiving the difference between royalty and miners as one between more and less fortunate occupations. Such subjectivity is itself expressed as a lack, as a yearning for a better life, a hole to be plugged by borrowed substance: The imaginary compatibility of this subjectivity with royal power inevitably fails to materialize into observable transgression. But the very failure reasserts the abyss, the void, that prevents colonial power from closing once and for all the symbolic pact of unproblematic oppression. This is the void of "modern-age subjectivity,"[30] and Seiga's cleaving to borrowed identity, an idiotic, pathological fixation built on the carcass of a dead ideology, must be read as a reminder that any nonpathological symbolic totalization in this context is a forgetting of the presence of oppression and ambiguity in real history.

Precisely because this cleaving is experienced as pathological, "as fundamentally *deficient*," it is not a regression to the narcissistic power of the modern individual but a development of shared lack and universality: "The surplus Particular embodies the Universal *in the form of its opposite*, it comes in excess precisely insofar as it fills out the *lack* of the Particular with regard to the Universal."[31] This paradoxical, excessive "Particular" is what motivates the divisive focalization of *A Borrowed Life*: On the one hand, there is Bbungian, the normalized subject, the standardized product of modernization in post-1947 Taiwan, "the sacrifice of all 'pathological' content for the Cause [which] is the alienation in the signifier (in the symbolic mandate)"; on the other hand, there is Seiga, fixated on an obsolete project of colonial modernization but taking over its voidness to constitute his own agency and desire—"the sacrifice of this mandate itself involves a gesture of separation, of gaining a distance from the symbolic order."[32] The very differentiation of these two phases, of subjectivity from subjectivization, marks the proximity of the film to the problematic of the postmodern, for this differentiation pinpoints a new way of dealing with the "pathological content" or "the Thing" and a new relation to the real that, by refusing to conceal the abyss of "modern-age subjectivity," distinguishes postmodernism from modernism:

> Within modernism, the Thing assumes either the form of "remnants of the past," of the inertia of prejudices to be cast away, or the form of the repressed life power to be unchained (as in the naive psychoanalytical ideology of the liberation of drive potentials from the constraints of social repression); we enter postmodernism when our relationship to the Thing becomes *antagonistic*: we abjure and disown the Thing, yet it exerts an irresistible attraction on us; its proximity exposes us to a mortal danger, yet it is simultaneously a source of power.[33]

The crucial point here is that, for the subaltern subject, one cannot be related to the subjectivizing other except as an "antagonistic" subject opposed to that other. For the subaltern subject, by definition, has never been anything but the subject as void, as a deficient opening in the order of things, in need of an identity borrowed from the subjectivizing other. Inevitably, the status of this borrowed identity creates a split in the subject, a depth laid bare by the unconcealed violence of oppression, a time lag instanced in Seiga's inability to update his subjectivity when the Japanese empire collapsed and the identity on loan became unclaimed baggage. At the same time, this split in the subject is paralleled by a corresponding destabilization of the other, which in turn is split into, on the one hand, the possibility of symbolic ordering and, on the other, a particular actualization of that possibility.[34] Thus, not only does the logic of subjectivization require that Seiga's incompetence be projected as the failure of Japanese superiority to live up to its name, but, through the mediation of the same logic, the apparently successful assimilation of Bbungian's generation to official Chinese identity is also revealed as highly problematic: By placing Bbungian on the side of subjectivization in symbolic correctness, the divisive focalization of the film effects an implicit criticism of the modernization of Taiwan as epitomized in its blind economic development and its ruthless suppression of historically rooted subjectivity to protect imposed Chinese identity. At the same time, the articulation of Bbungian's world with Seiga's transgressiveness points to a way out, a new cultural sensibility that will expose the poverty of the defense mechanism of subjectivization and, by "gaining a distance from the symbolic order," become fully cognizant of the powers of antagonistic subjectivity.[35]

3

A Borrowed Life, therefore, can also be read as an allegory about the quest for understanding, for a way to deal with the dividing lines of identity and fixation created by concrete historical experience. Such understanding will be achieved neither by the mere celebration of antagonism and voidness nor by another turn of the screw of sublimation driving toward increasingly more tolerant and more correct forms of harmony and integration. What precludes this simple choice between deconstructive resignation and benign totalization is precisely the return of memory and traumatic time, which, by legitimizing a more radical divisiveness, cut through the dividing lines of narcissistic possessiveness to behold a new middle ground on which a viable national culture could become possible.

This point is brought home by a recent television commercial claiming that the usually proindependence newspaper Liberty Times has won first place in national readership statistics. The commercial features a middle-aged man indulging in a patriotic song about the Chinese people being masters of the "beautiful land" of China. He is interrupted by a voice announcing the new number one newspaper of the island nation, which leads him to perform various comic acts expressing disbelief. At one point, he is shown wearing undershorts in contrast to a rather formal jacket. Being convinced by the voice, he is about to sink into his chair in dismay when the renewed song pumps new strength into him and literally forces him into a march. The target of the satire (mainstream media dreaming of unification with "great" China) is obvious,[36] but the effect can be divisive. Although there is nothing in the commercial explicitly indicative of any ethnic grouping, at least one Usenet poster condemns it as promoting ethnic hatred against "provincial aliens." [37] What is remarkable, on the other hand, is how this divisiveness is accepted with a certain imperturbable calmness. The Usenet poster's criticism is replied to with a few calls for restraint, and the thread is soon buried under the daily influx of postings. This robust resilience in the face of divisive fixation (on the part of the man in the commercial, the makers of the commercial, and the Usenet poster) should not be mistaken as a form of tolerant coexistence. In fact, the politics newsgroup in which the posting in question appears is, predictably, filled with venomous denunciations and hate messages every day, but these are, in principle, symbolic wars, wars fought between differing opinions and conflicting political symbols. Passions generated from such wars usually keep to their embeddedness in the symbolic order; they are not inflated into universalizing fantasies. When fixations emerge, people may criticize, but most will not condemn. The difference becomes obvious when one considers the fact that, a few decades ago, people making reference to "redness" without taking proper measures to guard themselves would risk the suspicion of communist conspiracy.

In one sense, Wu Nianzhen's *dosan* is like the strange man in the commercial, the defender of imagined ethnic harmony on Usenet, and the makers of the commercial who, obviously, are not unbiased satirists. All these people can be judged, even ridiculed, for the correctness or incorrectness of their behavior and beliefs, but none should lose all their particularism and be thought of as having become one with the defunct ideologies to which they hold. This is the position taken by the benign critical silence mentioned above.[38] In another sense, however, Wu's film and the *Liberty Times* commercial go one step further in that their insistence lies not only in irreducible particularism but also in the need to explain and justify how divisive particularism can be transformed into a ground for shared experience so that the assertion of particularism will not stop at mere pluralist tolerance. This is done in the film through building the particular into the broken historical continuity, so that what are usually taken to be "fixations" become foregrounded in the real and retreat to the background of the symbolic. Thus, the fixtures become a connection between the two orders, namely, the historical and the symbolic. What is achieved in the commercial is admittedly more elusive but involves a dimension of disarming self-parody that reveals its claim for the newspaper as subject to the same kind of delusions as its satirical target (few would really believe that the mainstream newspapers have ceased to dominate), all the time using this parodic doubling ("borrowing") of private dreams to sustain a pragmatic hold on the objective of the genre: to sell. In both cases, divisive cleaving is affirmed nonoppressively by locating that cleaving, not in self-righteous possessiveness (sacred territoriality, regulatory harmony) but in shared want (want for a better life, want for better news media). When this sharedness prevails in the perception and interpretation of historical experience, a new dimension emerges in the common material life of the "imagined" community, out of which a collective subjectivity will take shape and a national public culture will evolve.

In the real world, of course, sharedness sometimes fails to penetrate defenses and to become bidirectional. Inevitably, the path to national understanding and public culture has been conceived of by many as part and parcel of a new national myth created to prevent unification and to preserve Taiwan's independence from China. Although such embeddedness in concrete politics cannot be denied, it must be pointed out that there is a more fundamental realm of shared cultural affect and subjectivity that, without being in any sense free from retroactive overdetermination, should be maintained as a separate source of desiring interiority and a determining ground of meaning and motivation in any practical solution to the political future of Taiwan. Without the separation of this realm of subjectivity from symbolic subjectivization, whether the latter assumes the form of a new Taiwanese state or some version of a reunified China, any future will remain a captive of modernist objectivity and, in a complicitous repetition of the colonial history of the island, lead to nothing but unfruitful oppression.

To date, Western theories of postmodernity have not been very helpful in pointing to possible ways to break such historical circularity. Most local practitioners of cultural criticism still subscribe to a postmodernism informed by the entrenched poststructuralist hostility toward identity and the autonomous subject. In recent debates about ethnicity and nationhood, it is typical for participants who assume more "progressive" postures to conflate ethnic or national identity with political nationalism (usually rephrased as "state-nationalism"), which tends to slide further toward fascism or imperialism.[39] In this critique, nationalism is usually denounced as the pathological cleaving to invented or imagined (read "fabricated") identity, a totalizing repression of deviance, a cause of intolerance and animosity (at the expense of those it still believes to be "provincial aliens"), a deceptive alibi for promised decolonization, and a barrier to the liberation of all oppressed groups.[40] There are, obviously, unresolved tensions between this defense of particularism and those modernist theories of nationalism that reject it in the name of social and cultural globalization,[41] but fine theoretical differences are lost in the rush to forestall any political change that may cause the perceived dangers of nationalist violence to materialize, and the universalizing schemes of modernist rationality are frequently used in support of presumably postmodernist positions.

There have been some indications that the situation might be changing. In a recent attack on "voodoo nationalism," amid the fiery discharges of intellectual libido, Zhao Gang displays some awareness of the real problems involved: He explicitly distances himself from the postmodernist "politics of difference," proposing, instead, to reclaim the critical thrust of an older "universalist dialogics" so that a normative ground may be constructed for the "radical democracy" of a "democratic nation."[42] This should be welcomed as a timely attempt to go beyond the vagueness of an imported "postmodernist" discursive apparatus and to come to terms with the local situation. Nevertheless, beyond general pleas for the "reconciliation" of particularity and universality and for the reciprocation between the local and the global, Zhao's sketchy account has failed to present an adequate explanation of what a democratic nation is and how such a conception of nationhood can be expected to stay clear of traps that are said to have plagued all varieties of nationalism.

It is in the further elaboration of the possibility of reintroducing critical modernity and participatory democracy into the problematic of postmodernity that *A Borrowed Life* may provide valuable insight. It has been said that "a radical democratic approach views the common good as a 'vanishing point,' something to which we must constantly refer when we are acting as citizens, but that can never be reached." [43] This splitting of normativity into a "vanishing point" and its imperfect approximations is the only way to maintain a divisive, "antagonistic" relationship with symbolic ordering and to prevent "reconciliation" from collapsing into indifferentiation. At the same time, such fissuring of the objective order also implies a constitutive lack in subjectivizing power, and hence the constant need to draw its subjects into renewing the process of identification.[44] Without this need for repetition, there would not be any possibility for the same subjects to rework the "performativity" of symbolic identity.[45] In this light, *A Borrowed Life* may be said to have articulated some profound principles of how to deal with identity and subjectivity. Most importantly, it refrains from presenting Seiga's admiration for Japanese culture as the result of some simple mechanism of deception or mental contamination but conceives of it as being underlaid by a void, an open network of connections (a psychoanalytic version of "circuminsessional interpenetration") that enables lack and failure to circulate between power and its desiring subjects, bringing about the possibilities of subversion and freedom. Without acknowledging this structure of lack in identity and identification and its embeddedness in the real, in the impossibility of symbolic pedagogy to subsume everything and totalize itself, advocacy of radical democracy will not lead to fruitful intervention either in postmodern culture or in the settling of political conflicts in Taiwan.

Notes

Unless otherwise noted, all translations are mine.

1   See Edward W. Soja, *Thirdspace: Journeys to Los Angeles and Other Real-and-Imagined Places* (Oxford: Blackwell, 1996), 93f.; Jeffrey C. Alexander, *Fin de Siècle Social Theory: Relativism, Reduction, and the Problem of Reason* (London: Verso, 1995), 42.

2   Hal Foster, *The Return of the Real: The Avant-Garde at the End of the Century* (Cambridge, Mass.: MIT Press, 1996), 138ff. As Foster points out, Lacan explains this threatening gaze as symbolizing the "central lack expressed in the phenomenon of castration." See Jacques Lacan, *The Four Fundamental Concepts of Psychoanalysis*, trans. Alan Sheridan (New York: Norton, 1977), 77.

3   Foster, *Return of the Real*, 165–68.

4   Jean-François Lyotard, "Answering the Question: What Is Postmodernism?" trans. Régis Durand, in *The Postmodern Condition: A Report on Knowledge*, trans. Geoff Bennington and Brian Massumi (Manchester, England: Manchester University Press, 1984), 79–82.

5   Scott Lasch, *Sociology of Postmodernism* (London: Routledge, 1990), 172–80. This reading draws mainly on Lyotard's *Driftworks* (New York: Semiotext[e], 1984).

6   See Lasch, *Sociology of Postmodernism*, 21, 191f., 198. This part of Lasch's discussion appropriately ends with an invocation of "de-differentiated representation" to foster the kind of subject positioning that will help further "political-cultural tolerance" (198).

7   Foster, *Return of the Real*, 146.

8   Bruce Fink, *The Lacanian Subject: Between Language and Jouissance* (Princeton, N.J.: Princeton University Press, 1995), 27. The two levels must not be conceived of as in some sense fixed, since there is a constant exchange of positions between them. This is why it is said that the real is "*progressively symbolized in the course of a child's life*" (26; Fink's emphasis).

9   David Harvey, *The Condition of Postmodernity: An Enquiry into the Origins of Cultural Change* (Oxford: Basil Blackwell, 1989), 54.

10 For an exposition on "circuminsessional interpenetration," see Keiji Nishitani, *Religion and Nothingness*, trans. Jan Van Bragt (Berkeley: University of California Press, 1982).

11 Slavoj Žižek, *The Indivisible Remainder: An Essay on Schelling and Related Matters* (London: Verso, 1996), 216.

12 See the film script, reprinted in Trinh T. Minh-ha, *Framer Framed* (London: Routledge, 1992), 83.

13 Trinh T. Minh-ha, " 'Who Is Speaking?' Of Nation, Community, and First-Person Interviews," interview with Issac Julien and Laura Mulvey, in Trinh, *Framer Framed*, 197. This passage obviously harks back to an earlier comment on Trinh's own point about the commodification of Vietnamese culture in the United States (see 196), so that the Americanization mentioned in the present passage has to be construed as another reference to the commodification of sexuality in American culture, this time materialized in a beauty pageant that is Vietnamese only in name.

14 Trinh, " 'Who Is Speaking?' " 200.

15 Trinh, " 'Who Is Speaking?' " 201.

16 bell hooks, "Choosing the Margin as a Space of Radical Openness," in *Yearning: Race, Gender, and Cultural Politics* (Boston: South End, 1990), 145–53.

17 James Donald, "The Citizen and the Man about Town," in Stuart Hall and Paul Du Gay, eds., *Questions of Cultural Identity* (London: Sage, 1996), 186.

18 A typical example of such criticism is Huang Yingfen, "Changpai yunjing zhi hou: Yige dangdai Taiwan dianying meixue qushi de bianzheng" (After the long shot: A dialectical view of aesthetic trends in contemporary Taiwanese cinema), *Dangdai* (Con-temporary monthly) 116 (1995): 72–97.

19 See, for example, Huang Ren, "Wu Nianzhen de dianying meng he *Dosan* de qingjie" (Wu Nianzhen's dream of filmmaking and the fixations of *A Borrowed Life*), *Shijie dianying* (World screen) 309 (1994): 102f.; Du Wenjing, "Ziwo zhuisi de jiejing" (The essence of self-remembrance), *Zili zaobao* (Independent morning news), 29 Aug. 1994; Huang Jianye, "Wo fuqin daren yu guangyin suxiang" (A monument for my father and for time), *Lianhebao* (United daily news), 6 Aug. 1994.

20 The otherwise insightful analysis of Ye Yueyu, "Cong minzu zhuyi dao houxiandai xing" (From nationalism to postmodernity), *Dianying xinshang* (Film appreciation) 77 (1995): 44–57, for example, makes no reference to *A Borrowed Life*, although the latter is relevant to its topic in more than one way.

21 Lu Huiwen, "Dosan," *Yingxiang* (Imagekeeper monthly) 46 (1994): 98.

22 Xie Renchang, "Ningshi nayidai de nanren: Wu Nianzhen tan *Dosan* ji qita" (Gazing at men of another generation: Wu Nianzhen on *A Borrowed Life* and other matters), *Dianying xinshang* (Film appreciation) 71 (1994): 56. Wu's description of audience enthusiasm is partially corroborated by the fact that as late as 1997, isolated praise can still be found in the local Usenet movie group (which is usually dominated by Hollywood); see the thread started by Xian Sanke <ckro327@ms13.hinet.net>, "Huainian de qishiniandai: Dosan zhebu pianzi shifou gei ni huo ni de gandong" (Remembering the 70s: Have you been moved by the movie *A Borrowed Life*?), 27 Mar. 1997, <tw.bbs.rec.movie> (7 Apr. 1997).

23 Frank Frampton, "Towards a Critical Regionalism: Six Points for an Architecture of Resistance," in *Postmodern Culture*, ed. Hal Foster (London: Pluto, 1985), 24f.

24 At least one review praises the film for its affirmation of filial piety and family values. See Huang Ren, "Wu Nianzhen de *Dosan*" (Wu Nianzhen's *A Borrowed Life*), *Dachengbao* (The great news), 3 Aug. 1994.

25 Most of the names as well as the dialogues in the film are pronounced in either (creolized) Japanese or Minnan dialect. *Seiga* is derived from *Seika*, Japanese for the Minnan name, *Cingko*. I refer to characters' names in the form in which each is pronounced most characteristically in the film. Except for tone indications, "Minnan fangyan pinyin fang'an" (A romanization plan for the Minnan dialect), as given in *Putonghua Minnanyu cidian* (A Chinese-Minnan dictionary), Taiwan ed. (Taipei: Taili, 1993), is followed in the romanization of Minnan names.

26 The published synopsis gives some explanations for Seiga's belief in the excellence of Japanese culture, based on his experience in a primary school administered by the Japanese. See Wu Nianzhen, *Dosan: Wu Nianzhen dianying juben* (A Borrowed Life: A film script by Wu Nianzhen) (Taipei: Maitian, 1994), 67, 72. See also Wu, *Dosan*, 182f. Such explanations may easily provoke debates about the factual basis of the perceived indebtedness of Taiwan's modernization to Japanese colonial rule, which will not be pursued here.

27 Wu, *Dosan*, 90.

28 See William Tay, "The Ideology of Initiation: The Films of Hou Hsiao-hsien," in Nick Browne et al., eds., *New Chinese Cinemas: Forms, Identities, Politics* (Cambridge: Cambridge University Press, 1994), 151–59.

29 See Slavoj Žižek, *Enjoy Your Symptom!: Jacques Lacan in Hollywood and Out* (London: Routledge, 1992), 158ff. Žižek defines the "postmodern shift" as one from modernism, which focuses on "enjoyments which elude the Father's grasp" and undermine his authority, to postmodernism, which focuses on the "anal" father as the living example of obscene enjoyment (124).

30 Žižek, *Enjoy Your Symptom!* 167.

31 Slavoj Žižek, *For They Know Not What They Do: Enjoyment as a Political Factor* (London: Verso, 1991), 47.

32 See Žižek, *Enjoy Your Symptom!* 168. For useful expositions on alienation and separation in Lacanian psychoanalysis, see Fink, *Lacanian Subject*, 49–68, as well as Eric Laurent, "Alienation and Separation" (I, II), and Colette Soler, "The Subject and the Other" (I, II), in *Reading Seminar XI: Lacan's Four Fundamental Concepts of Psychoanalysis*, ed. Richard Feldstein, Bruce Fink, and Maire Jaanus (Albany: State University of New York Press, 1995), 19–38, 39–53, respectively.

33 Žižek, *Enjoy Your Symptom!* 123.

34 See Ernesto Laclau and Lilian Zac, "Minding the Gap: The Subject of Politics," in *The Making of Political Identities*, ed. Ernesto Laclau (London: Verso, 1994), 13f.

35 For the need to acknowledge the antagonistic relationship between subjectivity and subjectivization, see Žižek, *Enjoy Your Symptom!* 186.

36 See the thread started by Dataoke <Ankh.bbs@csie.nctu.edu.tw>, "Shei kandedong zhege guanggao?" (Who got the point of this commercial?), 1 Apr. 1997, <tw.bbs.rec.tv> (5 Apr. 1997).

37 Jingcai Jueyan <model.bbs@csie.nctu.edu.tw>, "Ziyou shibao jihua shengji qingjie, jiduan elie" (*Liberty Times* plays up ethnic animosity and is totally reprehensible), 1 Feb. 1997, <tw.bbs.soc.politics> (3 Feb. 1997). "Provincial aliens" refers to people whose families moved from the provinces of mainland China to the island in 1949, when the nationalist regime collapsed and retreated to Taiwan. Some people would imagine (or imagine others imagining) them to be hard-liners who would do anything to ensure the eventual unification of Taiwan with China.

38 Wu Nianzhen himself has been criticized for failing to honor "national dignity" in his excessive evocation of Japanese culture in some commercials he made for Japanese beer. See the thread started by Bihai Lantian <chuchen.bbs@csie.nctu.edu.tw>, "Taiwan Nianzhen qing: Wo zui xihuan de yige jiemu" (*Thinking of Taiwan with Nianzhen: My favorite program*), 24 Mar. 1997, <tw.bbs.rec.tv> (5 Apr. 1997). Like the attack on the *Liberty Times* commercial, the complaint (a follow-up in this thread) is countered immediately by several defenses of Wu and is not pursued further.

39 For relevant debates and position statements, see recent issues of *Zhongwai wenxue* (Chung-wai literary monthly), *Daoyu bianyuan* (Isle margin), and *Taiwan shehui yanjiu jikan* (Taiwan: A radical quarterly in social studies). See also Zhao Gang, *Xiaoxin guojiazu* (Watch out for the state-nation) (Taipei: Tangshan, 1994).

40 For some of these points, see Chen Guangxing, "Guozu zhuyi yu quzhimin" (State-nationalism and decolonization), *Daoyu bianyuan* 14 (1995): 26ff.

41 For a critique of these modernist theories, see Anthony D. Smith, *Nations and Nationalism in a Global Era* (Cambridge: Polity, 1995), 29–50.

42 See Zhao Gang, "Xinde minzu zhuyi, haishi jiude?" (New nationalism or old?) *Taiwan shehui yanjiu jikan* 21 (1996): 62ff.

43 Chantal Mouffe, "Feminism, Citizenship, and Radical Democratic Politics," in *Social Postmodernism: Beyond Identity Politics*, ed. Linda Nicholson and Steven Seidman (Cambridge: Cambridge University Press, 1995), 326.

44 See Laclau and Zac, "Minding the Gap," 23.

45 For the concept of performativity, see Judith Butler, *Bodies That Matter: On the Discursive Limits of "Sex"* (London: Routledge, 1993), 220ff. Butler misses the point that the "impossible real" may be precisely the motor of destabilization for this resignifiable performativity, conceiving it rather as inseparably bonded to social stigma and abjection from the symbolic; see her "Gender as Performance," an interview with Peter Osborne and Lynne Segal, in *A Critical Sense: Interviews with Intellectuals*, ed. Peter Osborne (London: Routledge, 1996), 119f.

12 Postmodernism and Hong Kong Cinema

Victoria Harbour
by *Ho Fook Yan*

The day the Queen arrived
my five-year-old niece decided
to christen her fish tank
Victoria Harbour.

The same day she took
the cross-harbour ferry
for the first time. From a distance
she noticed the ever rising buildings
of Whampoa, where she was born,
was actually a floating mass
of blocks in which people
work and study.

On the promenade of
Tsimshatsui East are

people constantly on the move
—for what, nobody knows.
Boats big and small come and go,
leaving the seagulls
swinging airily above the water
and her hair blown unkempt
by the rugged air. Dad was holding
her tightly to shield her
from catching a cold. She asked:
Do you really take the same ferry
to work everyday? Do you really see
the same place everyday?

After christening the tank,
she christened the fish.
Dad has been kept busy
getting fish food, replenishing the water,
keeping it at the optimum temperature,
and nursing the sick in solitary confinement.
The incurable ones, Dad told her,
are those who have swum
into distant oceans.

For sure years later, my niece
will have seen oceans that are real,
that'll make Victoria Harbour
a mere fish tank—
an insignificant strait
that doesn't make it to an atlas,
that warrants no one's attention
to either its body temperature,
or its oxygen content.
So be it! Isn't it a family business
to sail over the rough sea
in blistering wind?
We'll make it! And there'll always be
something beguiling
to keep her interested.[1]

As Hong Kong's anticlimactic 1997 decolonization came and went, the British (post)colony experienced a tumultuous decade—it was discovered by the international media, by Hollywood, and finally by the postmodernists. A question that might be put by a contemporary academic Sepulveda to a latter-day Bartholomew de las Casas would be "Are they True Postmodernists?" or "Are they True Postcolonialists?" If there is any doubt that the project of the Enlightenment, or secular rationalism, is still very much with us, the publication of this book testifies to the universalizing Western intellect's mandate to name and classify. As we approach the new millennium, the knowledge-power regime(s) that Hong Kong (and China) seem already enmeshed in are apparently as inescapable and indispensable as the cyberculture.

The Modernist zeitgeist, according to Jürgen Habermas, is marked by the passage of utopian thought into historical consciousness. Since the French Revolution, Western utopian thinking has armed itself with methodology and become aligned with history. "Utopia," as Ho Fook Yan observes, has become "a legitimate medium for depicting alternative life possibilities that are seen as inherent in the historical process. . . . [A] utopian perspective is inscribed within politically active historical consciousness itself." [2] As Immanuel Wallerstein in a succinct formulation describes it, the Enlightenment constitutes "a belief in the identity of the modernity of technology and the modernity of liberation." [3] We can see how Enlightenment beliefs, through the imperialist expansion of the West, get translated into the parlance of the May Fourth movement that erupted in China in 1919. Apparently the persecution of the first generation of Chinese intellectuals in this century is still haunting China at the century's end. The May Fourth crowd was looking for guidance from Mr. D (democracy—the modernity of liberation) and Mr. S (science—the modernity of technology). However, even at the time of the French Revolution, the parting of ways between Mr. D and Mr. S became inevitable in terms of realpolitik. The ruling class quickly noticed that Mr. D and Mr. S don't really share an agenda. Invariably, those who embrace Mr. S were often appalled by Mr. D and had the means to cut the latter down. Today, observers can enter points to rate the presence and absence of Mr. D and Mr. S in Hong Kong, Taiwan, China, and even Singapore to chart the venture of modernity in Chinese civilization.

Whatever merits a theory of postmodernism may have, to declare the total bankruptcy of the Enlightenment project, of which the idea of universal human emancipation is a key component, seems a bit of a joke for Hong Kong and China. We have seen powerful arguments developed by Foucault and the Frankfurt school that unmask the unfreedom of people in the post-Enlightenment West. We can certainly appreciate the inadequacy of formal freedom when economic inequalities and other tricky micropolitics are built into the everyday life of civil society. However, Hong Kong is a place where the promise of democracy has been deferred again and again—from its colonial era to the postcolonial present, where the persistent official myth is that Hongkongers are simply moneymaking machines who are antipathetic to politics. Yet, in May of 1989, a quarter of its (6.5 million) population took to the street in support of the demonstrating students in Tiananmen Square; and in May of 1998, about the same number of people showed up at the first postcolonial polls to cast their votes for the window-dressing seats (twenty out of sixty) that are open to direct elections. It is hard not to agree with Habermas that modernity—its emancipatory premises—remains an unfinished project here.

The past decade also witnessed intermittent, bruising battles over the U.S. renewal of China's most-favored-nation status. Undoubtedly there are racist undertones in the American Right's pounding of the human rights situation in China, when they can be tight-lipped about Israel, for example. Still, it would be easier for the two thousand plus prisoners of conscience in China to accept U.S. foreign policy as pragmatic and calculating than to swallow the theory that universal human rights is a mere Western prejudice. An unwitting intellectual irony has been spawned by the existential-structuralist debate since the rhetoric of cultural relativism—of respect for "differences" as expounded by Lévi-Strauss—was co-opted by Third World authoritarian governments. The lobby for American business in China has begun attacking the imposition of alien values in that country with its longstanding, presumably inviolable customs.

Meanwhile, Confucianism, which was once furiously condemned as an impediment to China's modernization, has recaptured some of its lost luster. It has been drafted, along with Far East dragons, into the narrative of capitalist development under the rubric of "Asian Values." [4] A chief advocate of this concept is none other than Singapore strongman Lee Kuan Yew, an acknowledged idol of Hong Kong's new, Beijing-appointed executive chief, Tung Chee-hwa. In my recent documentary film, *Journey to Beijing*, Hong Kong's democratic leader, Martin Lee, and political commentator Philip Bowring both call the bluff on these "Asian values," which extol a politically apathetic populace in a condition of Confucian submissiveness who achieve unprecedented economic success. For the flip side of Asian values—nepotism and corruption— is apparently at the heart of the region's recent economic crisis. What this setback will mean to the neo-Confucian revival remains to be seen.

Despite postmodernism's growing currency, one can still find wholesale dismissal of its conceptualization. Ellen Meiksins Wood recently described the condition of postmodernity as "not so much a *historical* condition corresponding to a period of capitalism but as a psychological condition corresponding to a period in the biography of the Western left intelligentsia." [5] But the odds are stacked against her. Terry Eagleton, who harbors a deep revulsion against postmodernism, laments that "part of postmodernism's power is the fact that it exists."[6] And Wallerstein castigates postmodernism as a confusing explanatory concept, while conceding that it is a prescient "annunciatory doctrine." "For we are indeed moving in the direction of another historical system," he says. "The modern-world system is coming to an end."[7]

Via Taiwan auteur Edward Yang's *The Terroriser*, Fredric Jameson notices that both modernism and postmodernism arrive "in the field of production of [Third World cinema] with a certain chronological simultaneity in full post-war modernization" because Third World films emerge from "traditions in which neither modernist nor post-modern impulses are internally generated."[8] I think Jameson's observation can be extended to the realms of culture and politics in much of the Third World in general. One can sense the wound caused by the incompleteness of the utopian modernist project while the postmodern present seems inalienably here—if by "postmodern" we mean the meshing of high and low cultures, as well as the interpenetration of multicultural experience in the contemporary metropolis.

Recently, I took an Italian TV producer up the Central Escalator (reputedly the longest escalator in the world) on Hong Kong (HK) island in order to show him the dizzying mix of HK's urban semiotics—a Chinese temple next to a blues club, a mosque at a stone's throw from the Jewish community center. We can find Nepalese, Vietnamese, Scandinavian, and Portuguese restaurants on a street where Indian immigrants and Tibetan monks saunter past a cluster of Chinese paper offerings to be burnt for the imminent Ghost Festival. That moment is, well, postmodern—as recognizably so as Auden's experience at a passport control point was, as he defined it, Kafkaesque.

Such Baudrillardean total eclecticism may just be icing on this drab cake of a Chinese city. The escalator area has been considered a hangout for the elites of international expatriates and Hong Kong yuppies, and not typical of the city. Jameson has no qualm in dubbing yuppies the agents of postmodernism.[9] It makes sense. Who else are more in tune with the cultural ideology of transnational capitalism that orchestrates the condition of our postmodernity? While one can polemicize endlessly against postmodernism, Jameson seems right when he argues that "ideological judgment on postmodernism today necessarily implies . . . a judgment on ourselves."[10] All these questions, can be distilled to one: In our context, how should postmodern Hong Kong be evaluated?

An apartment right by the Central Escalator is, as it happens, one of the main sets for Wong Kar-wai's *Chungking Express*, the movie that was one of Hong Kong's breakthroughs in the international art houses. One can't overlook *Chungking*'s postmodern pastiche stylistics, which are part MTV affectation and part retro fantasy. Quite a number of people I know dismiss the first half of the movie as little more than HK action flick with a chic twist. Yet it is in this segment (starring Brigitte Lin as a gun moll) that I saw something both indicative and symptomatic of Hong Kong's postmodern visibility.

In a new essay, Gina Marchetti describes Lin's outlandish imaging in *Chungking* as follows: "[with] blond tresses framing an Asian face, dark glasses, and raincoat . . . 'disguised' as a Marilyn Monroe 'look alike,' this drug dealer . . . forms the visual foundation for the film's bricolage of American pop culture, British colonialism, and Asian commerce."[11] For Marchetti and other critics, the Chinese gun moll is fighting—150 years later—an opium war of her own.

Whatever the categorical significance of the story—in my opinion, the 1997 subtext in most Hong Kong films is more often an afterthought than an integral part of the creative intent—the *Chungking* gun moll embodies intrepid playfulness and self-assurance. She proclaims the moment of Asian/Chinese/ Hong Kong ascendancy. The re-presentation of a white pop icon is no longer an exclusive white prerogative—Brigitte Lin has as much a right to vampirize the Monroe image as Madonna. Lin's semiotic significance in *Chungking Express*, in my mind, forges a powerful link to that of Bruce Willis's in *Pulp Fiction*, directed by Quentin Tarantino, *Chungking*'s hip sponsor in America. In *Chungking*, Lin finally guns down her enemies, who include a Caucasian heroin supplier and an array of brown-skinned South Asian runners. In *Pulp Fiction*, Willis saves his ass and avenges a viciously sodomized black gangster boss by wielding a *Japanese* sword—a weapon of choice among seemingly more deadly gear—to finish off some sadistic homo sickos. The axis formed by Lin (the white Asian woman) and Willis (the Asianized, straight, white male) may signal a new, and not exactly innocent, alliance politics in this postmodern hour of global (image) politics.

So Hong Kong films—an awkward subset within Chinese-language films —have arrived. And my pairing of Lin/Willis points to what might be an unconscious Orientalist logic, that is, a feminizing of the ethnic Other, still at work in this stage of cultural encounters. I am struck by the high percentage of works with a homosexual theme among the notable award-winning Chinese-language films of the past decade: *Farewell My Concubine* (China), *The Wedding Banquet* (Taiwan), *The River* (Taiwan), and *Happy Together* (Hong Kong). And the first historic documentary about Chinese cinema with any international visibility is by another Hong Kong auteur—Stanley Kwan's *Yin ± Yang: Gender in Chinese Cinema*, the Chinese entry in a British Film Institute–commissioned series to celebrate the centennial of cinema. While extremely interesting, *Yin ± Yang* favors a gay reading of Chinese cinema that tends to edge out other equally valid interpretations. For example, the famous butterfly lovers legend, which tells of a Chinese Yentl who cross-dresses as a man to attend school and falls in love with a schoolmate, is viewed completely as a repressed gay romance—at the expense of its profoundly feminist implications.

Hence, to some extent Hong Kong/Taiwan/Chinese cinema gains respect-ability through the back door of postmodern culture's sexuality agenda. While Eagleton's complaint about sophisticates who know "little about the bourgeoisie but a good deal about buggery" seems cantankerous and homophobic, his observation isn't exactly off-base.[12] The advancement of the sexuality agenda in our times may be a result of the postmodern, triumphalist pleasure principle, backed by a maturing market of gay consumers, as well as by urbanites' fascination with playfulness, artificiality, and alternative lifestyles. While no one denies that the progress of gay rights is an important matter, still, a more tradition-bound class-based politics has seemingly gotten short shrift. Tony Kushner, whose gay play *Angels in America* is our fin-de-siècle theatri-cal tour de force, laments that "nobody can talk about economics anymore. Nobody can talk about capitalism. Nobody can talk about that workers have rights, or that maybe the rich aren't entitled to maximum profit to the moon. . . . It's much easier now to write a play saying 'I'm gay and I'm proud,' than to say 'I'm a socialist and I'm proud.' " There may be some truth in Kushner's claim that "the Right has stolen" these issues.[13] But greater and more abstract forces seem to be at work at the moment. On the cultural front, both Habermas and Baudrillard have brought us news about the supercession of the sphere of production and the exhaustion of labor-based utopian energy.

The gay minority is not the only microgroup that postmodernism promotes. This celebration of popular culture in a multiracial context has given HK cinema, for a while, a global niche. According to David Chute,

> The high profile enjoyed by Hong Kong cinema in the West over the last few years is a unique cross-cultural phenomenon. . . . The critics and the festival programmers who embraced HK movies in the mid-'80s were not the ones who created the current market for them in rep houses and video stores. The grass-roots fans did that, by passing muddy bootleg tapes from hand to hand, by bending the ear of anybody who would listen, by launching fanzines and web sites devoted to the new religion. . . . And embracing the high-octane Hong Kong films of the mid-1980s as purveyors of pure sensation gave us a way to respond to them unselfconsciously, in a more direct and forthright fashion than is often possible with foreign films. No mediating cultural analysis was required to enjoy them, at least on this superficial level.[14]

Chut's description confirms the gut-level appeal of Hong Kong cinema to Western in-the-know-postmod audiences. No doubt there's the component of "camp" taste, (defined by Susan Sontag as "dandyism in the age of mass culture") in this group of thrill-seeking grassroots fans. One may even venture to guess that the kind of sensibility that discovered Ed Wood—"the ultimate Camp statement: It is good *because* it is awful" [15] —would be the one that helped discover Hong Kong films, which were held in low esteem for a long time for the simple reason that they were mostly written off as "purveyors of pure sensation." Yet the moment of official anointment arrived a decade ago when the New York Film Festival presented Jackie Chan's *The Police Story* with much fanfare. Having made a couple of U.S.-distributed English-language films that were dismissed as stinkers by the press, Chan was suddenly being compared to Buster Keaton. Overnight big-budget mainstream Hong Kong movies such as Chan's and John Woo's gained their ambiguous status as Third World art films. The rest, as they say, is history.

For much of the past two decades, the Hong Kong film industry, never encumbered by a high-modernist tradition, has borrowed right and left from Hollywood movies to keep up its frenzied output. In that respect, postmodern pastiche aesthetics has been practiced from the very beginning. However, an Eastern visual sensibility and martial-arts-fed action pyrotechnics have given Hong Kong cinema its unique edge. Movies that have achieved cult status in the West include *Naked Killer*, a copycat *Basic Instinct* that focuses on a group of lesbian warriors, and the gorgeously lyrical *A Chinese Ghost Story*, which incorporates special effects reminiscent of *Poltergeist*.

Yet, in the early nineties, the *nostalgia mode*, a key feature of postmodernism highlighted by Jameson, arrived in Hong Kong cinema mostly in the form of postmodern farces.[16] Hong Kong cinema discovered its own tradition—by plagiarizing and satirizing it. A film like 92: *The Legendary La Rose Noir*, putatively remaking an old movie about a cat-woman Robin Hood, is a freewheeling spoof of Cantonese genre films from the sixties. At the lower end of this aesthetic, we find Stephen Chiau, the biggest-grossing star of the nineties, cranking out dumb and dumber comedies that can, in the case of *From Beijing with Love*, spoof Cantonese melodramas, Bond movies, and *Barton Fink* at one stroke. At the higher end we encounter Stanley Kwan's *Rouge*, juxtaposing Hong Kong's past and present sexual mores, and Wong Kar-wai, who freely borrows the Chinese titles of *Rebel without a Cause* and *Blow Up* for his *Days of Being Wild* and *Happy Together* respectively.

It's an irony that Hong Kong cinema's growing international prominence, thanks to its grassroots fans in the West, has fizzled out like a star shooting across our murky postmodern sky. Almost before one can make a wish, it's gone. I still remember how in the late eighties, HK was celebrated by some Western film cognoscenti as a model of ethnic cinematic culture that stood its ground against the onslaught of Hollywood, motor of our postmod cultural industry. Maybe HK cinema has flown too close to the sun. (Interestingly enough, HK cinema's final fireworks were kindled by Brigitte Lin's stunning embodiment of "the Invincible East," in her role as a postmod sex-changed villain in a series of martial art films by Tsui Hark.) Ellen Wood took the post-modernists to task for their retreat from examining the logic of the Euro-American capitalist system, which finally became "mature," that is, global-ized, from the seventies on. Postmodernism does signal the maturing of the capitalist logic—its relentless ability to absorb different native cultures. The film products of HK, from Bruce Lee onward, have bequeathed Hollywood with a tremendous file of software—remake possibilities like Stephen Chiau's *The God of Cookery*, which Twentieth Century Fox is planning to turn into a Jim Carrey vehicle following the success of *The Truman Show*.

Hong Kong, known as the Hollywood of the East, was probably in some way ready to be, so to speak, bought out. The "takeover/merger" finally happened, with HK directors, led by John Woo, trooping to L.A. I sincerely hope that Hong Kong screen idols like Jackie Chan, Jet Li, and Chow Yun-fat can travel far. However, the Orientalist scheme doesn't bode well for them—a case in point is Stephen Chiau being asked to direct but not to star in the Hollywood remake of *The God of Cookery*—though maybe it'll bode well for Michelle Yeoh, the postmodern Bond-girl-cum-ethnic-Charlie's-Angel.

The postmodern concomitant to the privatization of culture (in which one immerses oneself in a miniature world made up of VCRs, PCs, video compact discs [VCDs], and digital video discs [DVDs]) has favored blockbusters like *Titanic* and *Jurassic Park*, which are big enough to draw crowds of teenagers and adults from their home-cocoons. Such Hollywood films are less and less dependent on the U.S. markets. (Admission to *Titanic* was $4.00 in China—an exorbitant sum considering the wage level there.) The East Asian mar-kets beckon, and the consequences to the HK film industry have been dire. Together with digital reproduction (also known as piracy), the penalizing, Hollywoodized global setup of sourcing, financing, producing, and market-ing is the primary force that delivered the coup de grace to ethnic film indus-tries, including that of HK's. The decline of the HK film industry is stupen-dous—from a few hundred made every year during its heyday to just dozens being made now. And the industry may decline further. In the past, the Chi-nese New Year slot in HK was reserved for high-profile local productions with big stars fighting it out at the box office. The Chinese New Year of 1998 saw two postlocal stars vying at the box office in their Hollywood debuts: Chow Yun-fat and Michelle Yeoh, the former in *Replacement Killers*, and the latter in *Tomorrow Never Dies*. Even the Disney cartoon, *Mulan*, based on a Chinese folk tale, opened in traditional Cantonese cinema chains. The homegrown Hong Kong pastiche is no match for the upscale Hollywood version for a local audi-ence with increasing middle-class pretensions. (According to a news report, before the pedestrian Star Wars prequel, *Phantom Menace*, opened, one of the fans camping out for tickets in New York claimed that he had flown in specially from Bombay to attend the opening.[17] Such is the power of Hollywood hype and the imagistic seduction of North Atlantic affluence over a Third World middle class that refuses to be left out.) With celeb culture becoming the new opium of the masses in a global auditorium without borders, one can only watch in silence the biggest real-life, sci-fi horror coproduction of the decade: the saga of Hollywood's star-snatching, mind-tapping, bone-crunching digestion of the HK film industry.

Hong Kong's postmodern visibility, while a confluence of several narratives, was no doubt catalyzed by the 1997 colonization cutoff date. So far, Hong Kong looks like the Cinderella who never made it—after midnight of 30 June 1997, everything comes crashing down—with Rolls Royces reverting to pumpkins during a ferocious economic downturn, and the brand-new, most-expensive-ever, $16.5 billion airport itself being the biggest crash. The repressive censorship measures of British colonial rule were resurrected by the Special Autonomous Regional (SAR) administration, at least on the books. And the Hong Kong film industry was cannibalized by Hollywood. Probably the fact that the British handover of Hong Kong to China now seems so anticlimactic should be viewed through the postmod grid of global capitalism. The doomsday scenario—heavy-handed intervention by China—hasn't really happened. China's more or less hands-off approach should probably be interpreted as an index of its entrenchment in the forward march of developmentalism, to which a threat to Hong Kong might be too serious a disruption to contemplate, yet. And after all the pomp and circumstance, one wakes up to the revelation that the age of imperialism is long gone. Hong Kong was just one of the few remaining anomalous lights to go off in a world that has been engulfed by neocolonialism and globalism.

There is a paradox in talking about Hong Kong's visibility, which after all, is equally marked by its invisibility. Rarely is Hong Kong seen as a social-political entity with any semblance of a collective will. Always trapped in the vise of superpower politics or macro cultural discourse, Hong Kong is like a tabula rasa, an empty signifier that always drifts into narratives not of its own making. (After all, HK's population is the size of many smaller nations, such as Belgium and Switzerland, its GNP surpassing that of Britain—though bear in mind that HK remains a place with one of the starkest income inequalities in the world, the majority of its people being far from affluent.) For example, To Liv(e), my first feature film, was prompted by Liv Ullmann's visit to Hong Kong in 1990, when she condemned the repatriation of Vietnamese refugees from the colony. The context of her pronouncements was that Vietnam was relentlessly evil. American-led economic sanctions against the impoverished country that it had ravaged were not addressed in her complaint. Hong Kong's effort to accommodate the refugees, spending in excess of $100 million—

supposed to be but never reimbursed by the United Nations—on humanitarian support for more than two decades was also overlooked. Hong Kong, which was still reeling from the shock of the Tiananmen massacre six months before, found itself being condemned as the shame of humanity by a talented European actress/filmmaker, who was acting no doubt out of strong liberal instincts. (In the postmod era's continual focus on catastrophe, after Somalia, Rwanda, Sarajevo, Indonesia, and Kosovo, few people know that Vietnamese boat people, now confirmed economic migrants, are still arriving in Hong Kong every year. As recently as June of 1999, riots broke out in a Vietnamese refugee camp among the 1,470 refugees who, unwanted by any country, had been left in limbo there for a decade. Hong Kong seems poised to give them residency.)

At times, even with sympathetic commentators, Hong Kong itself is still curiously absent from discussions supposed to be about it. Take a look at Rey Chow's recent paper, "King Kong in Hong Kong," which is in the main a very useful analysis of the dynamic behind U.S.-British political discourse, as well as the Western media's coverage of the handover.[18] Castigating the double standard of the United States and the United Kingdom when both countries fail to meet the democratic ideals that they apply to China, Chow says,

> All the [Anglo-American] criticisms of the P.R.C. are made from the vantage point of an inherited, well-seasoned, condescending perspective that exempts itself from judgment and which, moreover, refuses to acknowledge China's sovereignty even when it has been officially reestablished over Chinese soil. Instead, sovereignty . . . continues to be imagined and handled as exclusively Western. Sovereignty and proprietorship here are not only about the ownership of land or rule but also about ideological self-ownership, that is, about the legitimating terms that allow a people to be.[19]

Make no mistake about the "people" that Chow is talking about. She means the people of China, not the people of Hong Kong. In a sweeping formulation, she declares that for "Chinese people all over the world . . . regardless of differences in political loyalties . . . the symbolic closure of the historic British aggression against China . . . accounted for the unprecedentedly overwhelming expression of jubilation . . . at the lowering of the British flag in Hong Kong." [20] It sounds like what Iran's beating America in the 1998 World Cup might mean to the Muslim world. All's well, except that Chow overlooks the reaction of Hong Kong itself. If Hong Kong was born out of the ignominious Opium Wars, its postwar growth has been fueled by an immigrant population fleeing the communist regime. The handover itself, exacerbated by the 1989 Tiananmen horror, has triggered some of the most astounding spread of Chinese diaspora of recent times. Presently, close to half of Hong Kong's population have foreign residences—what locals call their "fire exit"—a fact that should be taken into account when one talks about "the overwhelming expression of jubilation throughout the Chinese-speaking world."

In a polemical spirit, Chow draws a parallel between democracy, as pushed by Britain and America on China, and the opium trade of the last century, "with implications that recall . . . Westerners' demands for trading rights, missionary privileges, and extraterritoriality." [21] Few would mistake Britain's eleventh-hour endeavour to introduce democracy in Hong Kong as anything less than a face-saving, hypocritical, and cynical measure. However, Chow sees it as part of a consistent British decolonizing strategy, intended to de-stabilize and create a source of conflicts in the decolonized state. After bash-ing Western-imposed democracy and speaking up for China, Chow suddenly finds herself "in anguish," because, after all, she is "whole-heartedly sup-portive" of the Chinese *democratic* movement in Hong Kong.[22] What about China's "ideological ownership . . . the legitimating terms that allow a people to be" that Chow is so convinced of? Doesn't she consider China's ideo-logical hostility toward democracy part of those "legitimating terms"? Ap-parently, Chow's reading of Chinese history is selective and reactive. The search for Mr. D(emocracy) began long before the communist takeover and wasn't planted by colonizers. What is the source of Chow's anguish, if not the "the wound caused by the incompleteness of the utopian Modernist project" I mentioned earlier? It is a lot easier to hate gunboat diplomacy than the ideals of the Enlightenment, which, unfortunately, are automatically sus-pect in a postmodern perspective by virtue of being universalist—indicted by Jean-François Lyotard's (in)famous dictum of "incredulity toward metanar-ratives." [23]

Chow has painted herself into a corner in her zeal to combat the vicious demagogy of Western imperialism and neocolonialism. Consequently, Hong Kong fits uneasily into her discursive scheme because it is close to being just a pawn in her narrative about the contest of nations and the struggle of cultural hegemony. And she elides China's authoritarianism and repressive-ness. The irony is that China, instead of being King Kong, "the spectacularly primitive monster" [24] in Western representation, becomes in Chow's scheme of things, a "hysteric"—is that a postmodern Deleuzean promotion?—in its understandable but not defensible "autocratic reaction" toward the West.[25] In the final analysis, China is not exactly a country that many overseas Chinese, even when they are supportive of the Hong Kong handover because it vindi-cates a shameful chapter of modern Chinese history, are willing to return to and live in as ordinary citizens.

If Hong Kong has such a ghostly presence in Rey Chow's discursive space, it is almost an embarrassing inconvenience in *The Chinese Box*, which purports to be a mainstream epic film about the 1997 changeover by Wayne Wang, who is, like Chow, an American of Hong Kong origin. With a corny plot and heavy-handed symbolism, *The Chinese Box* is a far cry from *Life Is Cheap*, Wang's smart film about the post–Tiananmen Massacre colony. The Anglo-American prejudice that Chow lashes out at is palpable in *The Chinese Box*, such as the transition itself being presented not by the lowering of the British flag, but by the ominous-looking stationing of the People's Liberation Army in Hong Kong—an entirely legal move on the part of the Chinese government, here shown as an "armed occupation" of its own territory.

The film has two fictional scenes of student suicide in protest of the imminent Chinese rule—one shoots himself in front of a roomful of merry 1997 New Year's Eve party goers; another sets himself on fire in what is presented as a TV news item in the movie. Because of the film's use of authentic news footage and "docudramatic" trappings, the two suicide scenes are problematic, if not outright exploitive, because nothing remotely resembling them ever happened. (The real altercation occurring on the handover night was more comic-tragic: protesters were ushered into a corner far removed from the ceremonial venue, their cries for democracy and the release of Chinese dissidents drowned out by the police's amplified broadcast of Beethoven's *Fifth* in the rain-drenched streets.) And China, instead of being King Kong–like, undergoes another familiar Hollywood metamorphosis: a Chinese whore, a latter-day Suzie Wong (played by the fabulous Gong Li of *Raise the Red Lantern*) who wants to become the respectable wife of a boring Chinese businessman. She is finally saved, at least psychologically, by the love of a white man, Jeremy Irons. He is a British journalist with a heart of gold, a huge designer's wardrobe, and a terminal illness; and he also dies on July 1, 1997 (the day of the handover of Hong Kong from Britain to China), or shortly after that, in the probably true fashion of Empire.

Squeezed uncomfortably between the marquee value of the British leading man and the superstar from PRC is Maggie Cheung, a remarkable Hong Kong actress who delivers a truly captivating performance in an otherwise undistinguished film. That she has to play a scarface with an unrequited love for a Briton who doesn't even remember her is the best joke that Wang plays on Hong Kong, or on his own film. Hong Kong, a mutilated presence, glimpsed only through a subplot, appears to Wang as an extremely inconvenient political subject—to be surmounted by sensationalistic melodrama, paranoic agit-prop, and combined British and Chinese star power in a poster that shows Irons and Gong in an intimate embrace, in which the HK actress is nowhere to be seen. Hong Kong, traditionally known as a borrowed place living on borrowed time finally slipped briefly through the radar screen of international media on the borrowed fame of 1997. Such is Hong Kong's visibleness and invisibleness at this postmodern, postcolonial hour.

Hong Kong is a distinct place, and history has not passed entirely unnoticed. Its 1997 fame has triggered a growing scholarship about its predicament, past and future. In some mechanical readings, Hong Kong identity has its origin in the 1984 Joint Sino-British Declaration that inaugurated the decolonization schema, or was precipitated by the 1989 Tiananmen massacre. But in more recent studies, the kind of urban, capitalist, laissez-faire identity that Hong Kong is known for has been more convincingly traced back to the riots of 1967, during which labor disputes and colonial repression resulted in the arrest of more than 1,300 unionists, strikers, and protesters, and in police killings of seven civilians. With the Cultural Revolution raging in China, Red Guards assaulted the British Embassy in Beijing in retaliation, and enraged Chinese soldiers marched across the border to kill five HK cops. But the defining moment of the 1967 experience occurred when pro-China leftists murdered a popular pro-Kuomingtang radio personality in a terrorist ambush, against the backdrop of HK streets lined with their random homemade bombs. This traumatic phase nurtured strong anticommunist/China and (one can argue) quasi-separatist, identity-formation sentiments in the psychological make-up of Hongkongers. The post-1967 city of Hong Kong marched forward with government campaigns like the Hong Kong Festival to create "a sense of belonging" for the local populace. Industrialization kicked in, and the colonial rulers responded by implementing basic, but still benign, public education, housing, and health care policies—in its way, the HK health care system can be considered one of the most generous in the world—which paved the way for HK's advancement, along with global capitalism.[26]

One important law-enforcement office that the colonial government instituted in the seventies has become the envy of mainland Chinese. It is the Independent Commission against Corruption (ICAC), with which the HK government was able to clean up the police force and the social body by using a crucial provision—discrepancy between personal wealth and income—as a basis for investigation. The legend of the ICAC survives, for example, in a pioneering TV miniseries in the late seventies, Family: A Metamorphosis, penned by the gifted TV and screenwriter Joyce Chan. This phenomenally successful soap opera tells of the aftershocks of a bigamous patriarch's flight from Hong Kong following an ICAC indictment. His family business is to be taken over either by the dandyish gay son of his first wife—the rightful heir—or the enterprising daughter of the second wife/mistress. The daughter's bold attempt to step into her father's shoes and her search for professional and romantic fulfillment riveted the whole community. Half of Hong Kong stayed home to follow one episode after another for weeks. A tremendous chord had been struck—probably by the story's feminist outlook and its affirming message of the birth of meritocracy out of Hong Kong's corrupt, patriarchal past. Almost a decade later, when I was traveling through the Chinese mainland in the spring of 1989, completely unaware of the catastrophe to come, many of the Chinese citizens I encountered invariably named two things outside of China that they were most impressed by: Watergate and ICAC. Both stand, for them, for the rule of law that remained elusive in China, with its capitalist reforms that ushered in abysmal corruption within the party, which in turn precipitated the democratic uprising.

The Tiananmen crackdown was, of course, a shattering experience. It meant for Hong Kong a nightmarish chronicle of bloody disaster foretold. I, for one, was driven to filmmaking after that watershed event—when HK, which I have taken for granted for years while living both there and abroad, seemed mortally threatened. However, I remember my excitement as a film critic in witnessing the birth of the short-lived Hong Kong New Wave cinema in the early eighties. A whole generation of HK-born and raised and, in some cases, foreign-educated filmmakers like Ann Hui, Tsui Hark, and Yim Ho were tackling the various facets of Hong Kong reality—from anarchistic fury at the colonial past in Tsui's *Dangerous Encounter of the First Kind* to either cheeky celebration or pessimistic rumination on a (Chinese) tradition-bound society in Hui's *The Spooky Bunch* and *The Secret*. I think Hong Kong woke to itself then, as a distinct place with its hopes, dreams, and memories. That happened before the 1984 Joint Declaration, and unquestionably the June 4 bloodbath of 1989 made Hong Kong take stock of its achievement as a "successful" colony more intensely than ever. The two poems that I selected to accompany this essay both show a sense of urgency for survival ("Victoria Harbour") and for recovery from a national trauma ("Elegy VII"), either in the poet's persona as a protective elder of the community or as a poet legislating language and consciousness.

If I said earlier that the 1997 subtext in most Hong Kong films is more often an afterthought than an integral part of their creative intent, it doesn't mean that 1997 doesn't cast a long shadow over pre-handover Hong Kong cinema. Snippets of current events have inevitably found their way into many movies. For example, even a shoddy film like *Underground Express* is about the gangster conduit to help dissidents out of China in the aftermath of the 1989 clampdown. But direct emotional experiences are often couched in coded signals. I remember a scene from John Woo's breakout movie *A Better Tomorrow* (1986), in which Mark, a Hong Kong folk hero character that propelled Chow Yun-fat to superstardom, stands on a hilltop to survey the glittering shards of Hong Kong's nighttime neons. He exclaims: "How beautiful! And we're going to lose all that. How unfair!" No doubt 1997, as much as Hollywood's summoning, finally pulled John Woo out of Hong Kong. But the exit path that served Woo so well has been a bumpy ride for Tsui Hark, the producer of *A Better Tomorrow*. More than his presumably more artsy, serious colleagues such as Ann Hui, Stanley Kwan, and Wong Kar Wai, Tsui is probably the Hong Kong filmmaker who has consistently woven the 1997 angst into his forty plus movies.

If Tsui is known mainly as a filmmaker of high camp, genre action flicks, Hong Kong is always the hidden Signified in his movies. At the end of his early, romantic-period comedy, *Shanghai Blues*, made in 1984 but before the Joint Declaration, we see the protagonist trying to catch a train to Hong Kong —obviously the new land of opportunity, the rightful successor to Shanghai as the next modern Chinese metropolis. When Tsui directed *A Better Tomorrow III* in 1989, again the protagonist flees to Hong Kong, but from the last days of the South Vietnamese regime. The allegorical foreshadowing of Hong Kong's worst-case scenario is lurking in this, yet another, prequel to the disappearing colony. As a postmodern pop auteur, a hyperkinetic producer-director, a Vietnamese Chinese who spent some time in the United States before hitting his stride in Hong Kong, Tsui seems desperately conscious of, and probably grateful for, his unexpected luck, hence his sense of urgency to race against time—in *Dragon Inn* (1992), a pair of warrior lovers ponder the life-and-death impasse lying ahead of them; in *The Wicked City* (1992), a sci-fi film that is a postquel about a decolonized Hong Kong invaded by half-human demons, a gigantic clock (Time) chases the hero furiously.

Critic Stephen Teo described Tsui's celebrated series *Once upon a Time in China* as his "vision of a mythical China, where heroic citizens possess extraordinary powers and self-sufficiency. . . . [It] is based on the realization that it is a country the potential strength of which remains curbed by tradition and the refusal of talented individuals to come to terms with a new world."[27] I would say that this series presents Tsui's imaginative fashioning of a "mythical Hongkonger" in the person of Huang Fei Hung (played by Jet Li). Assisted by his disciples and a savvy, Westernized girlfriend in a frilly Victorian dress, Huang is a wise, open-minded healer-cum-warrior who smartly negotiates his way to save the community from both rapacious white adventurers and obnoxious officials of China's ancient regime. This Cantonese-speaking southern corner of a "mythical China" is essentially an idealized Hong Kong, a de facto city-state with "extraordinary powers and self sufficiency," which could revitalize China if the mother country would adopt it as a model of success. For the potentials of talented individuals have a chance of realization here. And haven't Hong Kongers come to terms with a new (colonial) world with flying colors?

But even this mythical haven is not immune to the 1997 angst. In the series's sixth installment, "Once upon a Time in China and America" (1997) Huang Fei Hung becomes a nineteenth-century Chinese immigrant in Texas, allying with native Indians to fight white scum. A year after the film's release, Jet Li landed a role in Lethal Weapon 4 and kicked off his Hollywood career. (His persona swiftly morphed from that of the mythical intellectual-warrior to a latter-day, devilish, Fu-Man-Chuesque Chinatown gangster, who keeps muttering under his breath about his do-gooder white enemies in this Promised Land: "You'd be dead if you were in Hong Kong.") Tsui's angst-ridden take on Hong Kong may be right after all, though for the wrong reason. His momentous output was possible only in that golden era of pre-handover cinema before it got ruined, not by mainland politics but the Hollywood takeover. His first Hollywood film, Double Team, was both a critical and a box office flop, and his second outing, Knock Off, fared even worse. However, the much-maligned, English-dubbed Black Mask, starring Jet Li and produced by Tsui, was the fifth best-selling film on the chart during its opening weekend. While Tsui's Hollywood career is not exceptionally promising, it is too soon to write its obituary yet. The one Hong Kong director with staying power in Hollywood remains John Woo, whose visual flair and fantastical vision of male bonding and romantic heroes seem to have travelled/emigrated best.

At the end of Hong Kong Cinema, Stephen Teo reaches the conclusion that "Hong Kong cinema . . . is now set to return to the fold of the industry on the Mainland and perhaps to be brought back to the cradle of Shanghai, the original Hollywood of the East." [28] Some vague political alarmism underlies this observation. It would be very good news if Shanghai could rebuild itself to counteract Hollywood. But my inability to envision that possibility may indicate the paralyzing, homogenizing effect of transgressive global capitalism. What seems shocking is the fact that Teo's doomsday speech appears in the first comprehensive treatment of the subject in the English language. Indeed, while trying to decipher the cryptic codes of some Tsui Hark films, I already have the feeling that I'm an archaeologist going through the fractured blocks of a ruined, monumental edifice. Once upon a time in pre-handover Hong Kong . . .

While mourning the imminent passing of Hong Kong cinema, one shouldn't forget that Hong Kong Cantonese cinema was driven out of existence in the mid-sixties by Mandarin-language movies. In the early seventies, Hong Kong cinema rebounded, thanks to the powerful kicks of Bruce Lee, now an enduring icon of twentieth-century pop culture. One witnessed a curious reversal at that juncture: Lee resurrected Hong Kong cinema because of his frustration, as an Asian actor, with the American entertainment industry. He was too far ahead of his time to be coopted by Hollywood. But the kung fu film tradition that he revived became the backbone of the HK (Cantonese) film industry. (Lee also sent Mandarin-language productions, meant for a northern Chinese audience, into permanent exile.) It is not the purpose of this essay to examine the evolution of the kung fu film aesthetics through the innovative transformation of Lee, King Hu, Tsui Hark, and Jackie Chan. Yet it may be a reminder that the strength of ethnic cinema is frequently sustained by the vitality of a distinct genre film tradition. Think of the vibrant Indian film industry, and one can't help thinking about the Indian song-and-dance genre films. From such a perspective, as Hong Kong cinema heads toward a cul-de-sac, the three decades of kung fu film tradition inaugurated by Bruce Lee seems to have also been exhausted in the hands of Tsui Hark.

Well, not exactly. The first major hit in post-handover Hong Kong turned out to be a kung fu film—*The Stormriders*, based on a popular cartoon series, *Wind and Cloud*, and starring rock artists Cheng Ekin and Aaron Mok. While the directorial credit goes to Andrew Lau, also sharing top creative billing is the Centro Group, a special-effect postproduction house. The summer hit as well as the biggest-grossing HK film of 1998, *The Stormriders* emerges as, for better or worse, Hong Kong's first *digital* kung fu film. In the summer of 1999, the same team came out with the highly successful *A Man Called Hero*, a successor to *Stormriders*, which also starred Cheng Ekin. Digital pyrotechnics seem to be mainstream HK industry's answer to Hollywood, as borne out by the success of *GenX Cops*, a digital, contemporary-action film with a glitzy line-up of teenage idols, which features a sequence of blowing up the Convention Centre, Hong Kong's counterpart to New York's Empire State Building.

Yet these successes are oases in a desert. Their costliness has raised the bar for the industry as a whole, since not only Hong Kong itself but also the traditional overseas markets for HK films in Malaysia, Korea, and other overseas Chinese ethnic communities have already collapsed or been eviscerated by piracy. What has transpired in the aesthetics of HK action films has finally found, ironically, formal recognition in Hollywood, which credits Yuen Wo Ping as the "kung fu *choreographer*" for his outstanding contribution to *The Matrix*, a pretentious sci-fi thriller with a mishmash of kitsch New-Agey, Orientalist philosophies, *but* also a stunning postmod design and high-octane impact. That action sequence can be a form of choreography like ice-skating is a long overdue recognition of HK kung fu film's unique contribution to film aesthetics. I suppose one choreographs with people—no matter how illusory in a filmic sense—which up to the moment of John Woo and Tsui Hark, is still the time-honored, established approach for the Bruce Lee tradition. With *Stormriders*, kung fu cinema has lost, so to speak, its *innocence*. Human actions in such films have become subordinate to digital special effects. It's not so much that the techno-orientation of Hollywood's *Mummies* and *Godzillas* has swept the plate than the simple triumph of the digital revolution on a global scale. What has been lost to cybernetics is physicality, distance, and geography.

On top of that, one should be reminded that kung fu maestros like Jackie Chan, Jet Li, and Sammo Hung are truly a dying breed. The severe childhood upbringing, meant for grooming Beijing opera performers, that shaped their physical prowess may be gone forever. If revived, such a child-rearing program would today be considered child abuse rather than special education, if not in all of China, certainly in Hong Kong. The ultimate Hong Kong motto of self-reliance, which found one of its most powerful expressions in the astonishing martial arts skill displayed on screen for three decades, might have already seen its day.

Around the time of the first anniversary of the handover, the chief secretary of Hong Kong, Anson Chan (a colonial-groomed bureaucrat who was able to keep her job as the top civil servant through the changeover), said in a speech while visiting Washington that "the real transition is about identity and not sovereignty." Then she described how touched she was by the hoisting of the PRC red flag for the first national day (October 1) celebration in Hong Kong.[29] Her remarks provoked much joking and cynicism and disdain in the ex-colony. Understandably, identity remains a touchy, tickly issue in Hong Kong. And I must say a unitary, totalized identity doesn't interest me as a filmmaker. One issue among the controversies generated by To Liv(e) concerns the nature of the postcolonial subject. I was somewhat shocked by some of my critics' definite notions of what it should be like. One critic said the imaginary letters in the film—sent by Rubie, the film's protagonist, to Liv Ullmann—shouldn't be in English because Hong Kong is a Chinese city—despite the presence of high-profile English media and the fact that speeches in the pre-1997 legislative chambers were routinely made in English by Chinese lawmakers. Another critic decided that it's okay for the postcolonial subject to speak English, but Rubie has to speak with an accent to prove her Hongkongness.

In the flux of life and history, one naturally looks for constants and certainties. However, unexamined certainties of and about the self, subjectivity, and identity often create a hotbed for smugness and intolerance. It is true that the Hong Kong subject(s) of my three films are fairly mobile, if not wholly diasporic. They are either poised to flight (To Liv(e)), in New York already (Crossings), or journeying through China (Journey to Beijing). In Crossings, my second feature, a Hong Kong woman is threatened in the New York subway first by a deranged white man, then a black man, who insists that she's Japanese. And looking at the range of possible identities at her disposal: Hongkonger, Chinese, British colonial subject, and American new immigrant, this woman sadly realizes that none of them offers her any solace in terms of security. In

Journey, my documentary about the handover, I followed a group of philanthropic walkers from Hong Kong to Beijing on the eve of the historic transition. Their four-month walk passed through a number of meaning-heavy locales: Yellow River (supposedly the cradle of Chinese civilization), Mao's birthplace, Tiananmen Square, and the Great Wall. By juxtaposing the walkers' perspective with mini-essays about Hong Kong's dilemma, one of my aims was to affirm and reflect on and question the pull of (Chinese) identity for the people of Hong Kong, whose lives have been such a cultural and political hybrid.

On the global level, identity politics appears to be a disconcerting outcome of postmodernity, as Terry Eagleton so eloquently summarized:

> As the capitalist system evolves, however—as it colonizes new peoples, imports new ethnic groups into its labor markets, spurs on the division of labor, finds itself constrained to extend its freedoms to new constituents—it begins inevitably to undermine its own universalist rationality. For it is hard not to recognize that there are now a whole range of competing cultures, idioms and ways of doing things, which the hybridizing, transgressive, promiscuous nature of capitalism has itself helped to bring into being. . . . The system is accordingly confronted with a choice: either to continue insisting on the universal nature of its rationality, in the teeth of mounting evidence, or to throw in the towel and go relativist. . . . If the former strategy is increasingly implausible, the latter is certainly perilous.[30]

No wonder ethnic strife has become one of the predominant features of contemporary post–cold war existence. Our postmodern era is probably akin to that of late antiquity in the Western world—after Alexander the Great's victory in the Persian Wars and the Roman conquest, Hellenism dissolved the borders between the Egyptians, the Babylonians, the Syrians, and the Persians. Competing cultures collided in a stretch of polyglot world and, as a result, "Late Antiquity was generally characterized by religious doubts, cultural dissolution, and pessimism. It was said that 'the world has grown old.' "[31]

Well, our century is old, but postmodernism seems still fairly young, and postcolonial Hong Kong is a mere infant. But this age does induce profound pessimism. Thoughts, politics, and history are all being commodified and processed by the all-embracing media in the periodic artificial excitement of fashion and consumerism. Jameson, the leading theorist of postmodernism, announced that "there has never been a moment in the history of capitalism when this last enjoyed greater elbow-room and space for manoeuvre: all the threatening forces it generated against itself in the past—labor movements and insurgencies, mass socialist parties, even socialist states themselves—

seem today in full disarray when not in one way or another effectively neutralized." [32]

For a theorist like Virilio, there seems to be both an epistemological and existential crisis brought on by the new technologies in telecommunications and cybernetics, as "world time and a single present [has replaced] the past and the present. . . . This is an annihilation and extermination of world-space—a relative, local planet—and of a time—local time—to the benefit of another space and another time." [33] Welcome to the cine-, tele-, and cyber-city—our globalized city of relentless media control. Or is Virilio too much of a pessimist? Doesn't the immediacy of cyber time also offer freedom of escape and resistance?

In this time of tremendous political and ecological flux, probably identity—the only unapologetically immediate, instantaneously available entity—is the only concrete, manageable, but of course dangerously egotistical and also easily manipulated, politics one can grasp at the moment. In that sense, I think Eagleton has belittled the gains of postmodernism, which have firmly placed the issues of gender, sexuality, and ethnicity on the map of cultural discourse. He labels such identity as "nothing more than a *substitute* for more classical forms of radical politics, which dealt in class, state, ideology, revolution, material modes of production." [34] It will be a substitute only if it is allowed to be so. After the stunning collapse of the Second World, time—we don't know how long—is needed for new strategies to emerge and new political consciousness to push back the dominion of the numbing force of transnational capital, of which China is deeply entangled today, with Hong Kong a delicate piece in an evolving puzzle. (Three months after the handover and right before the regional crisis, Hong Kong hosted the World Bank and International Monetary Fund meeting, an arrangement that clearly represented China's assertion of its new-found (though problem-ridden) economic power on the global stage. Hong Kong, in which China has become a major investor, seems obliged to demonstrate its continued financial strength and capability to help further China's transformation.

Had Hong Kong been given a choice, it probably would have chosen independence. Racial and cultural affiliation are not enough ground for territorial annexation, or else we might see Quebec and Austria part of France and Germany today. Taiwan is a case in point. The reunification with China (recovery of the mainland) rhetoric has essentially been drained of its content. If there hadn't been threats of military invasion from PRC, Taiwan's nativist government might have declared independence already. With independence a lost dream, will Hong Kong—now a rectified accident of history—survive its marginalization and absorption into China under the "one country, two systems" arrangement on the one hand, and the ruthless class domination intensified by global capital with the acquiescence of the Chinese communist bureaucracy on the other? An important fact has emerged since the hand-over: No matter how much Beijing curtailed the first post-1997 legislative election, the Hong Kong democrats formed the first legalized minority opposition on China's political soil. And almost two years into the SAR regime, 70,000 people showed up on 4 June 1999 to commemorate the tenth anniversary of the Tiananmen crackdown—the only place in China where such public mourning has been possible.

Such seemingly "good" news has to be weighed against the defanging of the ICAC—no indictment was returned against Sally Aw, a media magnate who was named by the ICAC as being implicated in her company's financial misdeeds—and more importantly the outflanking of Hong Kong's Court of Final Appeal on an immigration case involving the right of mainland children (with HK parents) to reside in the territory. When the HK court's ruling, which granted right of abode to all children of Hong Kong's permanent residents, turned out to be unpalatable to the SAR administration, it immediately invited Beijing's Standing Committee to reinterpret the Basic Laws so as to overturn the ruling. Such political intervention threatens the independence of the judiciary, which is the cornerstone of a system that's distinct from China's and seemingly worthy of the much-touted "one country, two system" formula for reunification. While there's never any question that the future of postcolonial Hong Kong is completely tied up with that of post-Socialist China, many have harbored the belief that the two entities's mutual influence will be subtle and dialectical, with the possibility that Hong Kong may be able to gain the upper hand in terms of political culture, that is, set an example of a civil society for all of China to follow.

These hopes will have to be seriously qualified now. What seems to be undermining Hong Kong on a practical day-to-day level looks awfully familiar: what I described in the beginning of this essay as "the flipside of Asian values"—cronyism and nepotism. The failure to prosecute Sally Aw is almost as blatant as the awarding of a billion-dollar Cyberport project to the son of Li Ka-shing, the biggest developer in town, without competitive bidding. And Leung Chun-ying, a prominent real estate agent with business connections all over China, was made head of the Executive Council, Hong Kong's highest decision-making body.

The tentacles of the business elite, driven desperately by the regional economic downturn, are tightening their embrace mercilessly around Hong Kong's social body. As one local saying goes: "It's no longer Hong Kong people ruling Hong Kong, it's just the Hong Kong tycoons ruling Hong Kong." The inept and slippery leadership of Tung Chee-hwa is corroding Hong Kong's viability on every level by spreading an authoritarian political culture marked by secrecy and intolerance. The specter of patriotism is often invoked to counter, if not to mute, criticisms. Now, overseas Chinese dissidents are denied visas to enter Hong Kong. "Troublesome" Hong Kong politicians are barred from boarding planes to fly into the mainland. And legislators are complaining that visiting Chinese leaders such as President Jiang Zemin and Vice President Hu Jintao won't bother to meet with the partially elected legislature. "Even in the past colonial regime, British top officials met us to discuss issues concerning Hong Kong," lamented Democrat Lee Wing-tat.[35]

At least there's still freedom of expression—the strongest example being the "virtual" conversation between dissident Wang Dan and his mother via speaker relay at the 1999 Tiananmen vigil. Exiled former student leader Wang Dan couldn't get into Hong Kong, but he could call from the United States; it was not so easy for his mother, Wang Lingyun, when phone after phone was cut off in Beijing, but she managed to find a cellular phone at last. Via the speakers in Hong Kong, they could talk briefly and rather surreally for the crowd at Victoria Park, which suddenly rediscovered that the air(waves) they breathed and heard were indeed *free*.

Concomittantly, press freedom still exists, though marred by self-censorship (or deliberate downplaying) of sensitive political news. Full-blown sensationalism in the form of gory front-page pictures of auto accidents, gang fights, suicides, and gruesome murders is blamed on the public's apathy toward politics and pessimism about the future. But what else except commercial cynicism has killed off one cultural page after another from the local papers? For example, the Hong Kong Film Critics Society used to have review columns in a couple of dailies, but they were discontinued. Now the critics can only review films on-line, which automatically limits their readers to the 300,000 Internet-users in Hong Kong.

Despite the few digital successes mentioned earlier, Hong Kong films went belly-up at the box office one after another—from run-of-the-mill cheap horror flicks to Ann Hui's serious-minded political film, *Ordinary Heroes*, or Yu Wai Lick's *Love Will Tear Us Apart*, which competed in Cannes. The moment the bottom seemed to have fallen out of Hong Kong's film industry, an alternative filmmaking movement emerged, aided by the newly set-up Arts Development Council, which has provided either seed money to support the relatively high-budget *Love Will Tear Us Apart*, or the bulk of the funding for low-budget works like Lawrence Wong's black comedy *Cross Harbour Tunnel*, Bryant Chang's tale of adolescent woes *After the Crescent*, and my documentary *Journey to Beijing*.

I've made three movies about Hong Kong and its people. They're considered somewhat political, even interventionist, but neither mainstream nor quite avant-garde, straddled between Hong Kong and some vague Western cultural space, yet irrelevant to either. As an independent filmmaker fluctuating between Hong Kong and New York, I would hope, with the risk of sounding pretentious here, that the horizon of my films touches upon what Foucault called, at the end of his illustrious career, "the process of subjectification." One should perhaps try, beyond the rules of border, knowledge, and power, to become, if anything, the subject of one's own invention, rather than a conforming item in a collective, prescripted Identity—whether it is Hong Kong, Chinese, postcolonial Hong Kong Chinese, or transnational Chinese. We're talking about a unique, at times unbearable, kind of freedom that is available to postmodern men and women who have become dwellers in a virtual global village, or a veritable cyber Tower of Babel where consumption seems to be the only form of anarchy and communication—maybe it's the kind of freedom that Eagleton likened, in a burst of contempt, to that of "a particle of dust dancing in the sun."[36] For some of us, it's a troubling but genuine freedom.

Elegy VII
by *Huang Canran*

I

Motherland was hit like a grain of rice by a bullet.
Surrendering its golden crown to the emperor of Night,
the oak tree uprooted itself and became resigned to
the grand chorus of the storm looting its homestead,
tearing its bamboo fence, wrecking the stone table
and the ricing sieve. Tribes of crickets began
their migration, as did the ants
that were crawling beneath a wall
through fallen leaves, which, when raked over,
would reveal the complete decay of Fall.
If someone bothered to unfold
his palm of memory, he would see
the collapse of a nation's hills and rivers.
As the grass let out a scream,
horses' hoofs were stampeding over
green porcelain tiles.

If those tiny onions of childhood were, indeed,
nourishment, then memories of Father
might be easily erased
by a faraway exile. Yet an exile can't erase
memories of homeland, as long as Mother

remains an embedded image of a wound.
Hard-earned experiences aren't
garbage. Let grain-eaters be rendered
unto dust and those who feed on the fluid
of the Chinese language be doomed
to a life cast adrift.
In Fate there supposedly
resides secrets; unraveling them
turns out to be our unique fate
—like trying to distill a thicker variety of Blood,
or of Water that hurts the eyes.
And Motherland was like a grain of rice targeted by a bullet.
The mountain of May, the crowds of June,
were all steering their sobering gaze
into a world in retrogression.
When an eye fell to the ground,
or an arm got suspended in mid-air,
someone was mixing poetry
with politics. And the Fall rose, soundlessly,
like an oak tree that's been lost
—with its tonic aroma of rebirth.
Rebirth then, Memory! Let the Soul
be awakened by the stagnant pool
of the brain's dead matter.

II

Standing at the pier at dawn,
I am a lonely herder of Night.
Let Day be my homeland,
then my departure casts a much longer shadow
than that of my return.
Standing in the morning light
I realize how Dusk gets chewed up by Dawn.
Always, I take off from here and return
from somewhere else, forging a link
between the mountain wind
and the roaring tides.
In the heart of the financial district
I hide in my ear the floral mystery
of Motherland. On buses,
subway trains, or steady-going ferries,

I cast my alien glance on glassy landscapes,
poker faces and equally indifferent towns.
On a hilltop at daybreak,
in a satellite of morning light,
day for night, I am what they call
a lyric poet—shooting semen and egg cells
from highways into villages and hick towns,
driving shrinking shadows back into
the Womb. Under the surveillance
of Technology, in a metropolis of minds
and hearts besieged by a cyclone of images,
how can I care if a greater wreckage
is awaiting my diminished soul, or that
the starry firmament is tightening its net?
I'm also indifferent as to whether
my skin of knowledge is withering
or regenerating, growing calluses
or being bored shitless.
Amidst the city's blood-oozing nerves,
I am riding, back and forth,
the loveless buses and trams,
the secretively ominous subway,
leading a life as stable as cement, loitering
like an autumn leaf.
Everyday, coming in and out
of the entrances to Good Luck House,
and the National Splendour Building,
I've been thinking, dreaming,
gaining and losing
something.
What do I care?

III

No nihilism here, my friend.
Mere animalistic reality!
And aren't we the most animalistic
of animals that dwell
in the most mundane plane of reality,
which some call a dream
or dreamy Reality?
I have said that I don't care, perhaps.

Perhaps the only honor there is
is the honor of poetry;
and the only delight
the whispering of words.
Above the character "Dream"
my spirit soars. My shadow of happiness
is sweeping across my homestead,
which is nowhere but the very first word
I learned and copied.
I feel like a fish in the water
under the postcolonial sun, I have
my way of life.
I've learned what I've already learned,
yet I am still trying to be magnanimous
in my ragged boat, in a high-risk voyage,
across this treacherous flood of history.
Ahead are glimpses of the beasts of the age,
poison ivy, the torturing of high-tech,
and the third degree
of Freedom,
as I loiter like an autumn leaf,
recalling sunrise at the estuary of Evening.
With rhymes in my ear, I see
words shining through the spectrum
of politics, in the singing throat of the Pacific.
Still the only honor there is
is the honor of poetry.
Tear off the mask of *survivalism*
even though behind it
your face might have been long lost.
Hell is not the other,
it's yourself
in an age without heroes,
as a poet can't help but risk
his perishment in order to resurrect
himself in a poem.
And it seems easy—
secrets in hand, write down
the first word of a new poem
that transports you back to the Home
of language, where women

are seen scattering their fate
like flowers
on the streets of Heaven.[37]

Notes

My special thanks for the support, comments, and encouragement of John Charles, Arif Dirlik, Russell Freedman, Marina Heung, Linda Lai, Law Kwai-Cheung, Eva Man, Gina Marchetti, Tony Rayns, and Hector Rodriguez.

1   Ho Fook Yan, *Had It Not Been an Apple That Fell on Newton's Head*, trans. Evans Chan (Hong Kong: Su Yeh Publications, 1995), 178–81.
2   Jürgen Habermas, *The New Conservatism* (Cambridge: MIT Press 1989), 50.
3   Immanuel Wallerstein, *After Liberalism* (New York: New Press, 1995), 129.
4   Arif Dirlik, "The Postcolonial Aura: Third World Criticism in the Age of Global Capitalism," *Critical Enquiry* 20 (winter 1994): 341.
5   Ellen Meiksins Wood, "Modernity, Postmodernity or Capitalism?" in *Capitalism and the Information Age*, ed. Robert W. McChesney, Ellen Meiksins Wood, and John Bellamy Foster (New York: Monthly Review Press, 1998), 40.
6   Terry Eagleton, *The Illusions of Postmodernism* (Malden: Blackwell Publishers, 1996), ix.
7   Wallerstein, "After Liberalism," 144.
8   Fredric Jameson, *The Geopolitical Aesthetic: Cinema and Space in the World System* (Bloomington: Indiana University Press, 1995), 151.
9   Fredric Jameson, *The Cultural Turn: Selected Writings on the Postmodern* (New York: Verso, 1998), 45.
10 Fredric Jameson, *Postmodernism, or the Cultural Logic of Late Capitalism* (Durham: Duke University Press, 1991), 62.
11 Gina Marchetti, "Buying America, Consuming Hong Kong: Cultural Commerce, Fantasies of Identity, and the Cinema," paper presented at the meeting of the Asian Cinema Studies Society, April 1998.
12 Eagleton, *The Illusions of Postmodernism*, 4.
13 Robert Vorlicky, ed., *Tony Kushner in Conversation* (Ann Arbor: University of Michigan Press, 1998), 203.
14 David Chute, "Film Comment" (May–June 1998).
15 Susan Sontag, *Against Interpretation* (New York: Farrar Straus Giroux, 1986), 289, 292.
16 Jameson, *The Cultural Turn*, 7.
17 "New 'Star Wars' Trilogy—Episode I: The Wait for Tickets," *New York Times*, 13 May 1999.
18 Rey Chow, "King Kong in Hong Kong: Watching the 'Handover' from the U.S.A.," *Social Text* 55 (summer 1998): 93–108.
19 Chow, "King Kong in Hong Kong," 98.
20 Chow, "King Kong in Hong Kong," 97.
21 Chow, "King Kong in Hong Kong," 101.
22 Chow, "King Kong in Hong Kong," 101.
23 Jean-François Lyotard, *The Postmodern Condition: A Report on Knowledge*, trans. Geoff Bennington and Brian Massumi (Minneapolis: University of Minnesota Press, 1984), xxiv.
24 Chow, "King Kong in Hong Kong," 94.
25 Chow, "King Kong in Hong Kong," 101.
26 See various essays in *Whose City? Civic Culture and Political Discourse in Post-war Hong Kong*,

ed. Lo Wing-sang (Hong Kong: Oxford University Press [China], 1997). The 1967 data is compiled by Hung Ho Fung in his essay "Discourse on 1967," included in the volume.

27 Stephen Teo, *Hong Kong Cinema: The Extra Dimensions* (London: British Film Institute, 1997), 169.

28 Teo, *Hong Kong Cinema*, 254.

29 See "Searching for Identity in Hong Kong," *Washington Post*, 30 June 1998.

30 Eagleton, *The Illusions of Postmodernity*, 39.

31 Jostein Gaarder, *Sophie's World*, trans. Paulette Moller (London: Phoenix House, 1995), 100.

32 Jameson, *The Cultural Turn*, 48.

33 Paul Virilio, *Politics of the Very Worst* (New York: Semiotext(e), 1999), 81–82.

34 Eagleton, *The Illusions of Postmodernity*, 22.

35 *The Hongkong Standard*, 12 July 1999.

36 Eagleton, *The Illusions of Postmodernity*, 42.

37 Huang Canran, *Selected Poems (1985–1995)*, trans. Huang Canran and Evans Chan (Hong Kong: Su Yeh Publications, 1997), 207-10.

iv literary interventions

zhang yiwu

13   Postmodernism and Chinese Novels of the Nineties
Translated by Michael Berry

1

China is in the midst of unprecedented, widespread development. While the speed with which this development has taken place has altered the country's structures of space, the course of globalization and marketization has also infiltrated Chinese lives. Because the culture of the nineties is already completely different from the culture of the New Era (*xin shiqi*), we have begun to use the term *post–New Era* (*hou xin shiqi*) to deepen our analysis of the culture of the nineties.[1] I would like to begin my exploration into this culture of the nineties with excerpts from recent works by two authors who have emerged as the most lively and energetic young writers of the decade, Xu Kun and Liu Xinglong, and that clearly reveal the emergence and growth of a new social and cultural space.

In Xu Kun's novella *Hot Dog* (*Re gou*), a scholar, Chen Weigao, sees this sudden emergence of a new space in and around his place of work, a once illustrious research institution in Beijing, near Jianguo Gate:

To the east, the Chocolate Tower is dripping brown creamed honey. The greediness of the people makes them want to kick themselves for not being able to climb up and have a lick.

Toward the north, the Asian Pacific Building both day and night emits the smell of Indian sandalwood. The wretched stench makes those around it wish they were dead.

Across the way, at the Customs Building, those two lively clocklike pieces of construction that dwell on either side of the road sit face-to-face as if in competition. The sharp men in uniform, spirited and lively, in and out they come and go, expressing the ugliness and narrow-mindedness that lies beneath the coffinlike shell of their *diqueliang* uniforms.

To the west, the magnificent revolving restaurant at the International Hotel manages to eclipse the Science Research Building, arrogantly spinning round and round, providing a perfect birds-eye view of the research building below.

And it's only been a few days, all in the blink of an eye.

Going a bit further you have the Kai Cai, the Jianguo, the Prince's Palace, the Crown . . . one after another, these megahotels are, at an unprecedented speed, racing toward completion.[2]

What is interesting here is the powerful phrase "unprecedented speed" (*kan bu jian de shudu*, literally, invisible speed), which is used to describe the pace by which the structure of space is changing. Once the focal point of the city, the center of the city's soul and the center of conversation, the Science Research Building has been broken apart, scattered, and now floats amid the new space. What was *central* is now *multicentral* (*duo zhongxin*), the result of consumption (*xiaofei hua*) and product commodification (*shangpin hua*). The power of knowledge and discourse has, in the realm of space, become exceedingly self-enclosed and narrow. Moreover, all that the masses took to be sacred and holy has been drowned by the enchanting aura. A modernist view of space has been destroyed, lost in the labyrinth of postmodernism.

In Liu Xinglong's novella *Sharing Hardship* (*Fenxiang jiannan*), the secretary of the town Party committee, Kong Taiping, heads out to an aquatic nursery owned by a township entrepreneur, Hong Tashan. The speed with which the aquatic nursery has developed is extraordinary:

The aquatic nursery takes up over a hundred *mu*. The dozen or so large and small cement pools are almost all devoted to the raising of soft-shelled turtles. It is said that this is the single largest turtle nursery in the province. It used to be very small-scale. Back then, you could only buy turtles from individuals. Then, only after two or three years of naturally feeding and raising them, would they grow to weigh more than a kilogram. So the aquatic turtle nursery was always losing money. Then along came Hong Tashan. The first year, he built a winter incubation house for the turtles. By preventing them from going into hibernation, a baby soft-shelled turtle could weigh over one kilogram in only a year, bringing a hefty profit to the aquatic nursery. Next, Hong Tashan went to work on expanding the scale of the nursery. Moreover, he constructed that loud and attractive sign, West River Township Aquatic Nursery Inc.[3]

Here, the rapid development of the aquatic nursery causes a space once unknown to the public to be transformed into the center of this rural town, altering its social structure forever. This kind of dramatic transformation—from aquatic nursery to incorporated company—in this secluded, small town is precisely what Xu Kun depicts in his description of the transformation of the Beijing metropolis. And so it seems that at the same moment, in every corner of China, history is running its course, albeit with various fashions and styles.

Xu Kun and Liu Xinglong seem to have discovered two startlingly similar, yet very different, spaces. We have at once the superinternational metropolis and the backwater, rural town; the center of global capital and information exchange and the remote town that relies on agricultural products in order to find opportunities; the transnational global image (the Asian Pacific Building, the International Hotel, and the Customs Building) and the aquatic nursery brimming with developmental worries and misgivings. However, these two spaces, although seemingly filled with discontinuities (*duanlie xing*), are, without a doubt, of a homogeneous nature (*tongzhi*). Both are drawn into and caught up in the high tide of globalization and marketization, and resist the new cultural experience brought on by this tremendous speed. The "unprecedented speed" of which Xu Kun writes determines and controls a space overwhelmed by the shock (*chongdong*) experienced by a Third World society when it enters a global system. Xu Kun and Liu Xinglong have sketched a "map" of their time, a map that identifies a new domain, a new coordinate, and a new self-imagination (*ziwo xiangxiang*). Within the pastiche (*pintie*) of these two different locales, it is still possible to recognize China itself, enveloped in this speed.

In the works of Xu Kun and Liu Xinglong, speed is understood not only as a concept related to movement but as a symbol of native space (*bendi kongjian*) engaged in major transformation. China's rapid development in the nineties mercilessly proclaimed the death of that radical illusion of the eighties called modernism. In a manner that was previously inconceivable, China seemed to achieve a kind of economic, social, and cultural change, but one that is contrary to the utopian illusions of socialism. This development created a new relationship between the state, the society, and the individual. No longer a society managed from top to bottom in a unidirectional manner by the state, China is a multidirectional, "mixed" (hunza) society. This kind of complexity often surprises people in both China and the West. The postmodernist condition, which has been so astutely expressed by the literature of the nineties, is unique. The great glass tower of modernism has been shattered. Speed has brought not a romantic but a chaotic world, leaving us helpless to make decisions and render judgments. Reactions to this speed are the source of creativity for current mainland Chinese literature.

2

Currently, one of the most popular genres of contemporary Chinese literature is antiallegorical (fan yuyan) literature, which solidly and imaginatively reflects on and investigates the nation-state (minzu guojia) and individual subjects (geren zhuti) since the May Fourth Movement. This genre has not only gained historical legitimacy but has also become a narration of history. Employing allegorical-style narration, antiallegorical literature can be said to be both a deconstruction of mythological coding (shenhua shi de bianma) and an attempt at an allegorical style of writing with a "higher" meaning. Antiallegorical novels have fully adopted the basic ideographic tactics of national allegory (minzu yuyan), but in the process, the form has changed: Satire and rewrites in the pursuit of a legitimate investigation of national allegory have led to its parody (huaji mofang). Through this rewriting, antiallegorical literature has reexamined allegorical literature itself by using exaggerated deformation and the playful and farcical and by freely crossing the norms set up by old boundaries and hierarchical structures, which provide a new style of narration that is removed from allegorization (yuyan hua).

To find the origin of antiallegorical writing, we must go back to 1989 and the publication of Wang Shuo's novel Whatever You Do, Don't Treat Me as a Person (Qianwan bie ba wo dang ren). In this novel, an absurd narration, China's current cultural condition is woven into the story of the Boxer Uprising, transforming what could have been read as allegory into bizarre mockery and turning the text into a carnival of extravagant language. This is a wildly imaginative story that centers around a group of vague figures organized to search for a boxer who can win glory for their country. After they find the successor to the "Great Dream Boxer" (the boxer's title itself is also satirical), Tang Yuanbao, they attempt to foster him into a living symbol (literally code) of their nation's spirit. But the development of the story takes on a farcical or comedic aspect (*naoju shi*), particularly when Tang Yuanbao undergoes his initiation into the culture of food (*yinshi wenhua*):

> "This dish is composed of three walnuts and one meatball. It's called 'When I walk along with two others, they may serve as my teacher.' The meatball is called the lion's head."
>
> "Ya—!"
>
> "This dish is composed of shredded tripe and potatoes cooked with thirty-six different kinds of seasonings. It's called 'All is considered lowly —only scholarly pursuits are of a higher nature (*wan ban jie xia pin, wei you dushu gao*).'" . . .
>
> "This dish is composed of bear paws and fish cooked together in the same pot. After it's ready you take the bear paws out and serve the fish. It's called 'Fish and bear paws, you can't have them both.'"
>
> "Oh—"
>
> "This is elbow stew. You cook it until all the meat has fallen off the bone, and the bone is all that is left. It's called 'The soft may freely roam all under heaven, the hard take inch-long steps on their difficult journey (*ruanruo zuobian tianxia, gangqiang cunbu nanxing*).'"
>
> "Yi—"
>
> "This one is made up of deep-fried scorpions and worms. It's called 'After seeing the strange a few times, it no longer seems strange, and eventually the strange disappears (*jianguai bu guai, qi guai zibai*).'"
>
> "Oh—"[4]

Indeed, this use of Chinese homophonics and metaphor linking classical maxims and cooked dishes is a very strange practice. This is Wang Shuo's imagination running wild, but also a deconstruction of the national allegory. Throughout the novel, the ruthless destruction of the great narration of the recent past is carried out, in carnival-like merriment. The death of the allegory is declared. The passage above contains one of the special qualities of the allegory. Hiding classical maxims within the names of the dishes is one way of writing about culture in an allegorical way. However, in Wang Shuo's hands, this scene becomes both absurd and humorous. This type of language game makes any recovery of the allegory an impossibility. Furthermore, this story itself is a cold mockery of Western subjectivity (*zhuti*). It is the deconstruction of the allegory that created the imaginary relationship between China and the West. It satirizes extreme nationalism, as it does the fantasy of world harmony (*shijie datong*).

The deliberate reversal of the pattern of allegorical writing to deconstruct allegory can also be found in numerous other novels, including Liu Zhenyun's *Legend of Living Together in Hometown* (*Guxiang xiangchu liuchuan*), Liu Heng's *Day-*

dream of the Vast River (Canghe bairimeng), and Wang Meng's Season of Love (Lianai de jijie), all of which demonstrate that post–New Era literature is a strong and healthy trend in current Chinese fiction.[5] Liu Zhenyun's novel is one clear example of a "new realist" writer taking on the antiallegorical style. In this text, different periods of Chinese history are described by Cao Cao, Yuan Shao, and other figures of the Three States Period as they travel through time and chronicle their individual experiences as well as the chaos of their own time and space. Liu's vivid imagination in Legend of Living Together in Hometown rivals Lu Xun's in Old Stories Retold (Gushi xinbian),[6] but unlike the latter, in which allegory is used to bring a modern meaning to narratives composed by the ancients, Liu deconstructs meaning. Legend of Living Together in Hometown breaks down the barriers of past and present, and of East and West, and creates a kind of cultural code, intermixing the Qing dynasty with people and objects of the modern day ("foreigners" and cruise missiles). This is also an intentional subversion of the old standard of discourse, making a carnival-like mockery of allegorical-style cultural introspection.

In Liu Heng's novel Ode to the Carefree (Xiaoyao song), a powerful antiallegorical force is again expressed.[7] The bizarre narration of a Red Guard who occupies an abandoned building provides both a farcical and a satirical commentary on allegory. Even more antiallegorical is Daydream of the Vast River, a novel about a one-hundred-year-old man who witnesses the opening of a match factory by an intellectual who returns from the West. The intellectual uses violence to alter the world, but in the end, he accomplishes nothing. In both his public and private life, the intellectual is a complete failure. He is ultimately murdered, and his corpse floats down the vast river (the "vast river" [canghe] is metaphoric of Chinese history). At the end of the novel, the old man says to the narrator:

> I'm terribly upset
> My plane's out of fuel
> Child!
> My plane's out of fuel
> No—fuel—!
> No—ah!

This is the end of the old man's life, and it can also be seen as the end of the grand narrative of modernism. This novel is, in the sharpest way, a satire of macrohistory (da lishi).

Wang Meng's Season of Love serves as a parodic rewrite of his well-known novel from the fifties Long Live Youth (Qingchun wansui), which calls into question the legitimacy of the old discourse, mixing personal experience with free imagination.[8] The novel is filled with antiallegorical devices, such as the character Zhao Lin, who delivers a lecture on the invention of a new animal in Russia.

From the above examples, it is clear that antiallegorical writing has already taken over an important role in the literature of the post–New Era. As a new trend of the post–New Era, it conveys the characteristics of post–New Era culture. The emergence of antiallegorical literature makes it clear that allegory as a characteristic symbol of Third World modernism has already been exhausted.

Antiallegorical literature is marked by the following characteristics: First, one implication of antiallegorical writing is the end of allegorical writing, which positions itself at the intersection of time and space. It no longer strengthens the mythic image of China created by temporal hysteresis and the specificity of space but freely surpasses time and space, bringing what is Chinese and foreign, past and present, into its own field of vision. The role of the author is not necessarily the focal point, and his or her role is continuously changing, crossing different types of cultural and linguistic barriers to create a satire of the allegory. China is no longer restricted to the place of the Western other; however, it is also unable to define the end result of the operation of multiple reiteration (*duo chongfu*). Here, the modernist particularity of China's place as the other adds to the satire. The story of Tang Yuanbao in *Whatever You Do, Don't Treat Me as a Person* and of the abandoned building in *Ode to the Carefree* both express the destruction of the relationship with the old imagination.

Second, antiallegorical literature indicates a kind of "carnivalization" (*kuanghuan hua*) of the old styles of borrowing and imitating; it reverses the discourse of old and punctures the illusion of homogeneity. This type of parody has become a kind of collage (*pincou*), an inorganic, completely unconnected construction, clearly expressed by comedy. As in *Whatever You Do, Don't Treat Me as a Person* or *Legend of Living Together in Hometown*, these texts possess a very strange comedic nature, and it is this comedic or farcical (*naoju*) aspect that breaks through the many layers of cultural barriers. Moreover, the mark of this comedic or farcical aspect is the unlimited ability of language to be mixed and changed (*duozhong yanci de wuxian de hunza*). Slang, cryptology, political jargon, and the elegant classical language are, in random order, placed within the same pastiche. For example, in *Whatever You Do, Don't Treat Me as a Person*, a scene depicting the taking of an oath is a very interesting example of heteroglossia (*zhongsheng xuanhua*). Here, we have such political sayings as "From this day forth, I shall have no relations besides those I have with the organization" and "Let my head be split, let my blood flow," along with such common sayings as "Endure pain without flinching one's brow," and even such commercial phraseology as "All rights reserved, no illegal reproductions" and "If one party breaches the contract, all losses to the other party are to be compensated."[9] When they are read in the context of an oath or pledge, a sense of dislocation and absurdity is created. On the one hand, this method of writing has penetrated the sacred aspect of allegorical writing; on the other hand, it makes fun of our desires and our unconscious, thus presenting a new state of affairs.

This leads to another important literary trend of the Post–New Era—the "new state of affairs" novels. The definition of *state of affairs* (*zhuangtai*) in Chinese is "the form in which people or objects are expressed";[10] *new state of affairs* fiction, then, is a new writing trend that uses different forms of expression. By means of the author's impressions, experiences, and reflections, and the new method of signification created by numerous characterizations within the cultural context, new state of affairs literature surpasses allegorical writing, directly cutting into the state of the present. This powerful new literary genre lashes out and shocks, and because of this, it has already caught people's attention.[11] It includes the latest works by authors who, during the New Era, were already very influential, such as Liu Xinwu and Wang Anyi, as well as an emerging breed of writers, such as He Dun, Han Dong, Zhang Min, Diao Dou, Shu Ping, Chen Ran, and Lin Bai, among others.

New state of affairs literature and the postmodernist context have an inseparable relationship. The mass media determine a new cultural space wherein the consumer is given the central position. The destruction of the old totality (*zhengti xing*) has caused authors to be unable to reflect, observe, or explore outside their own culture, so they must stand fast amid the cultural surge. The author is a component of this state, and writing is no longer a search for the grand narration of the allegory but a direct reflection of language and existence. This new writer's identity is expressed by Wang Anyi in the preface to her work *Records and Fictions* (*Jishi yu xugou*, literally, reportage and fabrications): "As a writer, she feels herself to be in a terrible situation. Her position is far from encouraging. In the realm of time, she has no past, only the present; in the realm of space, she has only herself and no others. . . . Slowly, her ambitions become vague and unclear, the presence of a story or lack thereof no longer seems that important. Her attention has shifted to another question, which is: To children existing in this world, what is the role of time, and what is the role of space? Indeed, this sounds very mysterious and obtuse, but actually it is essential. To put it another way, how did she come into this world and what is the condition of her relationships with the objects around her."[12] This narration seemingly depicts the characteristics of new state of affairs literature very clearly. A reflection of culture based on the author's relationship with language and existence, new state of affairs literature is apparently the most outstanding characterization of China's present post–New Era context. It is precisely this type of experiential narration that has enabled the current era to form a new image. The "new state of affairs" can be said to have cut us off from every and any relationship with allegorical writing. This new mode of representation has placed itself within the reaction of the current situation and has no inclination to comment on the reliability of the position of the intersection of time and space. It is an impromptu grab at everything around, including itself.

In *Living Is Not a Crime* (*Shenghuo wuzui*), *I Don't Think about Things* (*Wo bu xiang shi*), *Hello Little Brother* (*Didi nihao*), and other texts, He Dun provides us with a cityscape that is brilliant and superficial, dazzling and exceedingly boring, a picture of the post–New Era as a disorderly extravagance.[13] This picture is as evasive and indeterminate as MTV. Like a bizarre dream, with no beginning and no end, it is also, like the work of Andy Warhol, extremely lifelike, providing a space forcibly thrown together that is lifelike and brimming with subjective style. *Living Is Not a Crime* is the story of man's transition to mediocrity. The narrator, "I," an aspiring painter, is awestruck by the luxuries he sees in the home of his friend Qu Gang, which include an "elegant light crimson floorboard," "a Toshiba color television set," "a Lion Dragon stereo system," and a "lambskin sofa." The narrator attempts to make money by trying everything from scalping movie tickets, to making repairs, to becoming the director of an affluent company. This big-city nobody gradually abandons yesterday's mythic illusions as he becomes more and more enthralled with money. The once aspiring intellectual, the man who had hoped to become a painter, finally confesses: "A half year ago I was determined to become a painter, but for this goal I've become ruthless and ruined myself. Now I realize the childishness of this spiritual mainstay. Like a baby seedling amid a forest, it is inevitably to be stepped on." It is in this way that the quasi intellectual gives up the pursuit of yesterday's goals, and, vowing never to turn back, walks into a different world, a world constructed of money, violence, and bewitching allure. The narrator emerges as the embodiment of the present state and not as allegorical introspection or a tranquil view.

Lin Bai's *One Person's War* (*Yigeren de zhanzheng*) is an individualistic, autobiographical novel. But it is not a summary of experience or a look back; it is a projection of the state of one's own life experience. After the main character, Duo Mi, is deserted by a man named N, she sets out looking for N with a camera: "Duo Mi quickly went for the bag and began to go through it. N's face suddenly turned a deathly pale, and he unconsciously backed himself into the wall. He had no idea if this crazy woman was going to pull out a bomb or a dagger, but he had no doubt that today was the day he was to die. But all Duo Mi pulled out of the bag was a camera. She grabbed the camera and snapped a shot capturing N's malicious expression. No matter what, she said,

I want a souvenir. I can't be left with nothing."[14] The photograph is not a representation of the reality of the past but a souvenir left by the past for the present state. By taking the present state as the center, this novel itself also freely intersects the present and the past. The past is not the past, but only one part of the present. In Chen Ran's *Private Life* (Siren shenghuo), *Drinking with the Past* (Yu wangshi ganbei), and other texts, we also see this type of narrative expression.

New state of affairs literature has several characteristics worth noting. First, it indicates the change from an external focal point to an internal focal point; observation and reflection have been exchanged for the appearance of an individualistic and contextual state. The mythic subjectivity (zhuti) of yesterday has given way to an infinitely symbolic individual (geti). The subjectivity of the author has already given way, giving precedence to experience and projecting a demonstration of the individual's experience of the outside world. The works of these authors are unable to maintain any abstract allegorical self-searches. The authors are not the bearers of enlightenment "overlooking" China, as they have not been entrusted by the masses to be the spokespersons for the people. They are expressionists in an equivocal position amid this state.

Second, new state of affairs literature has expressed a tendency for mixing photographic realism with abstract expressionism. In these novels, the sequence of time is not clear, but the state within is very real. However, this true-to-life expression is only as real as the photo in *One Person's War*, which is not reality itself but a reflection of multiple mirror images. Or, we could say that it is like the appearance of innumerable reflections of light on a realist oil painting. This is the result of the interaction between, flash back to, and overlap of sustained superrealism and the fleeting, instantaneous moment. It is MTV. It is the jumbling of a montage (mengtaiqi de mengtaiqihua). This type of narration is an unlimited projection toward a new space brought on by the incoherence of time and the loss of the solid subjectivity.

Third, new state of affairs literature has broken down the barrier between the popular (tongsu) and the refined (gaoya). Authors tend to use the resources of popular culture to provide a new form of expression. Symptoms of life in the postmodern metropolis, such as kleptomania (lian wu) and the supermoral (chao daode) life, are worked into the fiction, lending a highly readable quality to these works, which cannot be determined by the barriers of old.

Fourth, new state of affairs literature rejects profundity. These novels present a boundless narration of "state," rejecting the method of depth and meaning brought on by allegory. For example, in He Dun's *Hello Little Brother*, the relationship between the little brother and his Honda King motorcycle serves as an example of the disappearance of the deep and profound. The little brother is so infatuated with his motorcycle that it leads to the death of his lover. In He Dun's world, all things happen by chance, making all conjectures and explanations impossible. In his stories, we are unable to find a single example of the deeply introspective intellectual, of the intellectual who decries social injustice and the hardships of the people or who makes a thorough inquiry into the nature of existence. What He Dun has given us is a fundamentally anti-interpretive story (*fan jieshi de gushi*), a novel with no root or source, a novel that oversteps the bounds of the modern.

Antiallegorical and new state of affairs literature, the main literary trends of mainland Chinese fiction in the nineties, are expressions of the unique cultural imagination of a globalized and marketized China. They project onto a Chinese context the difficult situation facing culture today: On the one hand, China's economic growth and information exchange have brought new opportunities and possibilities; on the other hand, China faces an unprecedented culture shock. In the midst of this upheaval, Chinese writers have responded with their interpretations of the resulting instability and awkwardness of the time. Since the May Fourth Movement, the myth of Chinese modernism has been duly challenged. It is precisely this tension that has established Chinese postmodernism.

Notes

Unless otherwise noted, all translations are mine.

1 For a more thorough discussion of the post–New Era (*hou xin shiqi*), see Xie Mian and Zhang Yiwu, *Da zhuanxing: Hou xin shiqi wenhua yanjiu* (The great paradigmatic shift: Post–New Era cultural studies) (Harbin: Heilongjiang Jiaoyu Chubanshe, 1995).

2 Xu Kun, *Re gou* (Hot dog), in *Xianfeng* (Avant-garde: Selected writings of Xu Kun) (Taiyuan: Beiyue Wenyi Chubanshe, 1995), 205–6.

3 Liu Xinglong, *Fenxiang jiannan* (Sharing hardship), in *Xiaoshuo yuebao* (Fiction monthly) (Tianjin), no. 3 (1996): 40.

4 Wang Shuo, *Qianwan bie ba wo dang ren* (Whatever you do, don't treat me as a person), in *Wang Shuo wenji* (Literary works of Wang Shuo), vol. 4 (Beijing: Huayi Chubanshe, 1992), 334.

5 See Liu Zhenyun, *Guxiang xiangchu liuchuan* (Legend of living together in hometown) (Beijing: Huayi Chubanshe, 1993); Liu Heng, *Canghe bairimeng* (Daydream of the vast river), in *Liu Heng zixuanji* (The self-selected works of Liu Heng), vol. 2 (Beijing: Zuojia Chubanshe, 1993); and Wang Meng, *Lianai de jijie* (Season of love), *Huacheng* (Flower city) (Guangzhou), no. 5 (1992): 4–94; and no. 6 (1992): 101–208.

6 Lu Xun, *Gushi xinbian* (Old stories retold), in *Lu Xun quanji* (Collected works), vol. 2 (Beijing: Renmin Wenxue Chubanshe, 1981), 341–481.

7 Liu Heng, *Xiaoyao song* (Ode to the carefree), in *Liu Heng zixuanji* (The self-selected works of Liu Heng), vol. 1 (Beijing: Zuojia Chubanshe, 1995), 167–475.

8 Wang Meng, *Qingchun wansui* (Long live youth) (Beijing: Renmin Wenxue Chubanshe, 1978).

9   Wang Shuo, *Whatever You Do*, 321.

10 *Xiandai Hanyu Cidian* (Dictionary of modern Chinese), ed. The Chinese Institute of Social Science, Chinese Language Research Institute, Department of Dictionary Editing (Beijing: Shangwu Yinshu Guan, 1996).

11 The journals *Wenyi zhengming* (no. 3, 1994) and *Zhong shan* 1 (no. 4, 1994) published special issues discussing new state of affairs literature, which led to extensive discussions about mainland Chinese culture and literature.

12 Wang Anyi, *Jishi yu xugou* (Records and fictions) (Beijing: Renmin Wenxue Chubanshe, 1996), 5.

13 See especially He Dun, *Shenghuo wuzui* (Living is not a crime), *Shouhuo* (Harvest), no. 1 (1993): 24–54; and *Didi nihao* (Hello little brother), *Shouhuo*, no. 6 (1993): 42–85.

14 Lin Bai, *Yigeren de zhanzheng* (One person's war), *Huacheng* 2 (1994): 4–80.

14   Women and the Discourse of Desire in Postrevolutionary
China: The Awkward Postmodernism of Chen Ran

Feminism in Contemporary China

Since the death of Mao in 1976, feminism in China has worked in four ways.
The first way is in the practice of advocacy, engagement, and change characterized by the socialist approach to gender problems under Mao. This continuing legacy, which is aimed toward eliminating inequalities in social life,
focuses on assuring girls' and women's educational opportunities, providing
economic security, eradicating prostitution, and modifying other forms of
sexual oppression. Under Deng Xiaoping's capitalist reforms, gains made in
these areas from the 1950s through the late 1970s are under attack, and commentators have called attention to the reappearance of prostitution, the increasing sale of women and infant girls through organized gangs, and female
infanticide, which is changing the gender balance of the population. Problems in job security and education have also appeared. Culturally, the gender
similarities in dress styles and social roles promoted by Maoism are being
eroded by a discourse of difference in fashion, speech, and behavior that
highlights femininity and forms the basis of a new retail boom. Films, tele-

vision shows, bars, and other entertainment outlets are capitalizing on the new market freedom by offering women for sale in a flourishing sex trade. Coming into direct conflict with these for-profit ventures, feminist social reforms have nonetheless maintained a strong presence and are supported by the state through laws and women's organizations at all levels.[1]

Second, academic feminism has thrived and resulted in the establishment of a number of feminist university programs. One well-known example is at Zhengzhou University, where Li Xiaojiang has collaborated with other professors to initiate a series of publications on feminism and women. These books have straddled the earlier politics of engagement and the new demand for a more theoretical understanding of feminism, and they have opened the door to a strong academic feminist dialogue both nationally and internationally. As in the West, feminist academics have reevaluated mainstream Chinese history, literature, and the textual traditions that situate women within discursive frameworks of meaning, criticized patriarchal practices and logic, and recouped disregarded histories of women's writings and activities. They have also worked globally, translating and introducing articles and theories from abroad, attending and presenting at international conferences, and inviting scholars to visit China. Actively jumping into contemporary discussions about women, feminist academics have challenged leading male intellectuals and put forth their own theories about misogyny in Chinese film, literature, and popular or elite cultural practices.[2]

Third, a strong interest in women has emerged in popular culture books. Often straddling feminist critique and prurient voyeurism, these books examine the constricted situation of women in traditional China; the social meaning of taboos; sexual politics and morality (including the requirement of chastity); the reputedly universal concepts of female essence and desire in women; the love between young women and young men; and psychology. Some books are collections of older writings, and others are new publications. While the subject matter of these books ranges from popular, but explicitly feminist, concerns about power and control to more sexually suggestive topics, many of them focus on social or psychological eccentricities that supposedly are part of women's experience.[3]

The fourth area of feminist activity is the creative involvement of elite artists, filmmakers, and writers with gender concepts. One example of this is the continuing efforts of those working from the basis of Marxist social engagement. Typical of the immediate post-Mao era, these novels, films, and stories investigate social inequalities in education and jobs, sexual oppression through unfair practices, and traditional concepts of female inferiority that continue to function subtly and insistently despite laws to protect women. They also point a finger at socialist society under Mao and as it presently exists, and expose the rhetoric of equality that often hides discriminatory practices. Whereas the techniques used by these artists, writers, and filmmakers may not coincide completely with the socialist realism or the later revolutionary romanticism of the Maoist era, or even with the modified critical realism of the more recent past, like earlier writers, they position themselves within the Marxist framework of art as ideology and social engagement that works on behalf of the oppressed.[4]

These earlier practices of feminist engagement have now been joined by a postrevolutionary sensibility that appropriates the discourse of desire that has characterized postmodern culture in the West and provides a ready juncture where feminism and postmodernism meet. In this discourse, personal desire and sexuality have emerged as the counterpoint to revolutionary action and practice. Writers and others have rewritten the past in two ways. One approach defines Maoist politicism as the inversion of personal erotic passion, as a time when both political ideology and its directing of emotional life suppressed "true" feelings and sexuality. This era of sexual suppression and repression must be overcome, the narratives imply, in order for the reinvigorated Chinese subject—who is generally, but not exclusively, male—to move into the future. Such narrative configurations can be found in fiction by Zhang Xianliang, Su Tong, and others, and appear as visually powerful, internationally influential presentations in film adaptations by Zhang Yimou. Women directors such as Hu Mei have also portrayed the power and strength of erotic attraction against the more rigid and stultifying demands of the state.

The second approach reinterprets past revolutionary ideology, recasting it as sensual, erotic, and interesting. Here the Cultural Revolution stands not so much as a political ideal but as a decade of passion and devotion, symbolized by the Red Guards, whose unbridled forays around the countryside and violent attacks on all forms of authority become the most provocatively sensual liberation. Jiang Wen's 1995 film *Yangguang canlan de rizi* (Those brilliant days), for example, depicts a gang of youth in Beijing whose parents have been sent to the countryside. Freed from the demands of school and work, the youths indulge themselves in food, sex, and violence, and create a sense of sensual immediacy that contrasts sharply with their later, middle-aged entrepreneurial selves, who ride around in limousines and drink foreign whiskey. This reforming of the Maoist past is represented in elite culture but also appears in the reworking of Cultural Revolution songs and images—in particular, those of Mao—into icons and other forms of popular culture. Both reinscriptions give primacy to erotic expression as a means of understanding the past, the present, and the future, and situate Chinese culture within an established global—Western—context of sexualized stories and images, and in a more generalized foregrounding of desire.

If all of these erotic writings and films contain implicitly or explicitly gendered meanings and can be analyzed within a cultural system of gendered hierarchies, however, not all of them are concerned with feminism. Feminist critics in China have attacked many of these works as projecting a misogynist worldview that pulls people into a conventional approach to dominant/subordinate sexual relations and places women in a specularized, secondary, and eroticized position.[5] Feminism's progressive, equality-based demands, even as they were enveloped within the statist politics of Maoism, critics argue, were completely displaced onto eroticized images, contexts, and tales that reordered reality, from high art to the popular realm of fashion, onto a typically oppressive relationship, especially for women. Furthermore, in their hostile rejection of a sinicized Marxist materialist tradition, these films and fictions have been mocked for buying wholesale into Western paradigms of personal fulfillment and capitalist commodification, all within a gendered hierarchy. Works using this approach thus have come under sharp rebuke for selling out China to the wealthy and influential West, and for furthering the cultural imperialism of Western aesthetic paradigms.

The strong feminist expressions that are part of the Western discourse of desire—the glorification of female erotic subjectivity, or *jouissance*, and the construction of a theory of the body that reworks it as the ultimate site of resistance, pleasure, and in more general terms, reality—have also appeared in China. Less often in critical texts but more frequently in fiction by women writers, including the later works of Wang Anyi and the stories by Chen Ran and Shen Qiaosheng, as well as others, the discourse of desire and its representation has paralleled what exists in film and popular culture. This fiction is in a different position than that of its Western counterpart, however, and its existence brings up some interesting questions about the relationship between postmodernism and feminism in a postrevolutionary non-Western country. A feminist postmodern discourse of desire popping up in a culture so long engaged in Marxist materialist practice and analysis could be nothing more than the culture of capitalism as it expands and spreads out to encompass every possible site, along the way obliterating the truly local, hiding ideology within culture, and substituting an obfuscating politics of desire for one based on evaluating and changing relationships that emerge out of material inequalities. Perhaps Maoism, so easily constructed as both the essence of suppressed desire and the flowering of excessive passion, has just made China riper for this transformation.

Some elite fiction, however, presents other perspectives. In its reworking of the past into a memory of a memory, or a residual trace, in its juncture between the female subject and contemporary sensibility, and in its gentle but insistent call for a recognition of the new meanings of national borders and a recognition of the Chinese intelligentsia's diasporic situation, Chen Ran's fiction speaks to an alternative experience of postmodernity.

Women, Feminism, and Postmodernism

Since the mid-1980s, when "cultural fever" (*wenhua re*) settled in on the Chinese intellectual scene and authoritatively displaced Maoist cultural politics, a dizzying pace of replacements has determined what resides in the hottest spot. Restaurants where the schedules follow the needs of workers, not customers (a focus on production, not consumption)—the bell rings and chairs go up on top of the tables to allow for floor cleaning precisely at 8 P.M.—are disappearing and are being replaced by the all-night disco or karaoke bar. In film, the Fourth Generation, trained in Maoist film academies, was quickly replaced by the aesthetically advanced, internationally funded, viewed, and awarded Fifth Generation, which now has been challenged by the local, popular culture–based Sixth Generation. The audience for Marxist/Maoist analysis dwindled as interest in cultural studies expanded and was accompanied by the translation of nonrealist writers such as Kafka, theorists such as Derrida, Lacan, and Kristeva, and neo-Marxists such as Jameson. At the same time as Mao's power as a social ideologue faded, his image gained power as a popular icon. In literature, political poetry lost its clout with the emergence of the modernist Misty poets. A renewed interest in fiction followed, along with the development of a "roots" narrative of constructed mythologies that virtually replaced the previous literature of social engagement, which continues to exist today but gets less and less attention. After the roots writers came the experimentalists, or the avant-garde, a movement that now has been attacked as conservatively reproducing the national allegory form that existed since the early twentieth century. Finally, a postmodern literature of experience and sensation, of sexuality and instantaneous perception, and of realism mixed with abstractionism has developed.

Chen Ran (b. 1962) is one of the newly acclaimed women writers.[6] Many of Chen's stories, which are not linked as a novel but often feature the same characters showing up here and there, read like caricatures of the idea of a postmodern narrative. The characters, especially the ubiquitous and seemingly autobiographical Ms. Dai Er, are challenged by a confusing and complex sexual identity, incomprehensible and unplumbable psychological sensations that threaten to overwhelm them, a murky but dispassionate past, and the inability to locate a real and conceptual homeland, although they still recall and ponder this concept. Part of an urban elite, they smoke, drink, and have sex with those of the same and the opposite sex, and they work to exorcise demons from their subconscious minds. In terms of work or ideals, their pas-

sions are limited. Some of them zip around the globe, get involved with foreigners, and hang out in the intellectual milieu of Western university towns.

Two introductions to Chen's work show the available interpretive poles of
post-Mao Chinese culture with regard to women and contemporary writing.
Repeating an idea that has been common since the late May Fourth period
and before, former Minister of Culture Wang Meng, a professional writer
himself, begins his description with, "Women and literature seem to have a
natural link."[7] Connecting Chen Ran with a series of modern women writers
that begins in the early 1920s with Bing Xin, Lu Yin, and Ding Ling, Wang
Meng favorably compares women writers to their male counterparts: "Their
feelings and points of contact are more delicate and sharp. Their sense of
human emotions is more obvious. They possess less pronounced falseness,
grandiosity, and emptiness" ("Hong yingsu," 1). Because, according to Wang,
women writers are more sensitive and less politicized, he also blames fewer of
them for driving literature and writers into the "death fields" of the Cultural
Revolution, implicitly claiming that revolutionary discourse and its excesses
are masculinist ("Hong yingsu," 1–2).

Wang Meng is not discussing the recent so-called postmodern women
writers so much as he is claiming certain characteristics for all twentieth-
century women writers. It is as a counteraction against the masculine death
fields, more generally construed as excessive revolutionary zeal and the veiled
search for fame, glory, and power that present-day critics believe it always
contained, that the new literature of sexualized subjectivity appears as radically feminine. Poised against the large range of male corruption and power
abuses exposed after the death of Mao, the small scope of bodily desires
becomes a viable alternative that reduces the extent of action, implying a
smaller, more manageable space, consisting of personal emotions and the
inner world, that can resist totalizing state narratives of domination and control. Furthermore, because this space privileges the feminine, Wang Meng
associates it with heightened sensitivity, a quality that also can subdue the violence and urge toward mastery that he considers to lie behind Cultural Revolution excesses. The new women writers, inasmuch as they reject the overtly
political and maintain an element of lyricization, establish a new position
vis-à-vis the revolutionary past, which Wang Meng configures as male.

For Wang Meng, Chen Ran's somewhat sexualized and psychologized narratives fit right in with women's so-called natural literary tendencies and are
only extending a lyrical skill that belongs to women. One aspect of this skill
under present conditions is that women writers "clearly acknowledge that
they are women, themselves proclaim that they are women, and have their
own special issues and impressions" ("Hong yingsu," 3). Seventy years before, Zhou Zuoren asked women to express all of the things that men had been

unable to approach in their fiction, and now they appear to be fulfilling this demand.[8] Wang Meng states, "They have a lot of things to say," and he credits women writers with being more forthcoming than men writers in unrestrainedly exposing the inner mental, emotional, and physical life, in attacking male prerogative, and in general making people uncomfortable with their uncompromised explorations ("Hong yingsu," 3). If we want to see things as they really are, Wang Meng explains, we will have to look at the works of women writers. While not directly materialist in his approach, Wang Meng's position clearly comes out of a socialist theoretical stance, a perspective of finding and exposing the truth of things or the heart of the matter. At the same time, women writers are valuable because they appear to exist outside the experience of Chinese modernity—revolution and political jockeying for power— and therefore offer another alternative.

Wang Meng's account of modern historical continuity is counterbalanced by Beijing University Professor Zhang Yiwu's insertion of Chen Ran into the context of postmodern discourse.[9] Whereas Wang implicitly views the work of Chen and other women writers as the flowering of a suppressed but long-standing female aesthetic and ideological stance, Zhang includes her in a significant cultural change that dates from the 1990s. In this new era, where the contradictory but simultaneous co-optation and support of the masses has resulted in a reign of consumerism, pluralism, and utilitarianism, the narrative changes that avant-garde writers such as Yu Hua, Ge Fei, and Su Tong initiated—which were built on nontraditional and un-Maoist notions of personhood, the subject, history, and reality—have been abandoned. In particular, the national allegory that continued the century-long centering of China as the gazed-on object, a focus instigated through cultural imperialism, and the position of being watched that it forced onto China and other non-Western countries, has been rejected and replaced with what Zhang calls "situational fiction," a type of writing that directly expresses contemporary reality ("Hou yuyan," 7–8). In rebuffing this inherently unequal relationship and escaping from its determining power, Zhang implies, writers have entered a more fragmented, but ultimately more positive, postmodern sphere of representation. Gone are a number of approaches from the past, including the attempt to deal with social problems through art, the search for a unified lyrical self, and the quest for roots in non-Confucian or minority cultural life and attitudes. The socialist imposition of an overarching direction, aesthetic form, and large meaning of life has been replaced by a cynical belief that totalizing social theories have a basis in totalitarian control.

Chen Ran's contribution to this postmodern character, according to Zhang, lies in her expression of a new perception based on the combination of a daily-life sensibility and a transcendental nature that exists not in Hong Kong or abroad but unavoidably right in Chinese urban space ("Hou yuyan," 8). Through various mixtures of narcissistic personal experience and objective social description, and through an emphasis on sexuality, Zhang argues, Chen produces a new discourse of feeling ("Hou yuyan," 9). This novel perception and expression is not concocted out of thin air, however, but is a true representation of urban youth who live under the contradictions of advanced capitalism and is an accurate portrayal of their commodified lives. This fact qualifies Chen's work to be considered truly postmodern, Zhang claims. Although Zhang may recognize a gendered focus on sexuality and female subjectivity, his positioning of Chen Ran's work in the larger context of social, economic, and cultural change is only secondarily a gendered analysis and is even farther removed from feminist concerns of gender equality in the social realms of work, education, economics in general, and physical well-being.

Although not directly in a one-to-one correspondence, the interpretations of Wang Meng and Zhang Yiwu can be added to the debate over Marxist materialist analysis and the postmodernist discourse of desire. For Wang Meng, what is significant about Chen Ran's writing is not that she alters the reader's consciousness or produces a new structure of feeling but that she succeeds, where male writers fail, in exposing the way things are; she implicitly rejects the masculinist world of violence, corruption, manipulative power, and fame; and she continues a tradition of female excellence in writing. Furthermore, she links up historically with women writers from the early twentieth century, an interpretation that posits not a structural break but a renewed cultural continuity broken only by the death fields of the Cultural Revolution, turning Maoism into an aberration and implicitly claiming that the Chinese experience of the modern lies elsewhere. For Zhang Yiwu, however, Chen is representative of a radical change from modernist or socialist apprehensions to postmodern discourse. Within this paradigm, Chen's construction of an inner and an outer world of desire and sexuality is the significant feature of her work, and her floating characters are very different from the famous sexualized Sophia of Ding Ling's 1927 short story, "Ms. Sophia's Diary" (Shafei nüshi de riji).[10]

From one Marxist point of view, postmodernist criticism is a transhistorical, linguistically based discourse that elides and suppresses labor and class difference in favor of a theory of desire, where the important concept of difference—an idea that is most compelling when used to refer to a material difference in wealth—is abstracted and changed into an issue of identity.[11] In these "individual regimes of purposeless pleasure" promoted by Michel Foucault, Judith Butler, Gayatri Spivak, and many others, the trope of desire becomes a substitute for a class-based theory of materiality (LFA, 30–32, 40).[12] In postmodern theory, desire is the base of the real, but in Marxist theory, the real is the poverty and need that are endlessly produced by the capitalist extraction of surplus labor.

While it would be easy to claim that Zhang Yiwu promotes this postmodern "dance of desire"—the title of the book he has edited on postmodern fiction—and that Wang Meng stands by a materialist Marxist analysis, what does it mean when this apparent opposition appears in a culture where Marxism, in the form of Maoism, has ruled intellectual circles for the last fifty years? In urban China, economic and cultural changes similar to those in the West are taking place; large transnational corporations are emerging, technology is altering daily life, and economic forces function behind many personal transactions. It would not be accurate to claim, therefore, that postmodern conditions do not exist in China at all or that any expression of postmodern consciousness is an imitation. But the word *postmodernism* has only recently been used to describe the Chinese situation from within, and it has been adopted from the outside, a situation that has caused scholars such as Zhang Yiwu to reject it and to formulate new terms such as *situational*.

As Jing Wang has succinctly pointed out, reference to postmodernism is a "faddish current" in contemporary Chinese criticism.[13] But to identify postmodernism in non-Western cultures demands that we recognize that this faddishness is unavoidable and that it is inherent in China's situation and perhaps in the conditions of postmodernism within most or all non-Western cultures. Postmodern economic and cultural changes occur in the West within the context of globalism, or within a necessary orientation of the West—with its multinational corporations and worldwide entertainment technologies— where the cutting edge of style is a necessary component. The notion of a simulacrum, which contrasts with ideas such as the original and the authentic, seems to be a perfect trope for the postmodernity of non-Western cultures. Forced to constantly and consciously modernize and now postmodernize according to a model that struggles to keep ahead, Chinese culture still finds itself trapped in interpretations that impose on it older ideas of cultural essence and authenticity.[14] Maintaining other cultures as fully embodied traditions while positioning itself at a distant advantage, postmodernist culture at once dictates a prototype and makes it unattainable. Yet, following a precedent is not the same as producing only a simulacrum, because there always exists the possibility that the follower will "surpass" what is being followed. Jing Wang believes that China's participation in Western/global economies and cultures is indeed predicated on this notion: "China does not subjugate itself to the Other, but only to the seduction of a future that promises the coming of the Pacific century in which it will loom large in a new set of power relations with the West."[15] However, Prasenjit Duara, Gregory Jusdanis, and others have argued that "belatedly" modern cultures cannot establish a radically different scenario but must negotiate with what goes before and, to some extent, accept the patterns laid out for them.[16] Democracy, human rights, capitalism, gender equality, and so on—the political and cultural forms of modernity—dictate a direction.

The fact of precedence, which establishes distance between the model and what comes after, produces a gap between the "original," ever evolving toward the future, and the belated and behind. Because of this distance, modernisms and postmodernisms in non-Western cultures express a different "structure of feeling" than what went before.[17] Chen Ran's work, hailed by Zhang Yiwu as postmodern, certainly does not lead its readers toward a materialist analysis. Yet, her fiction is only awkwardly postmodern, as if it is aware of the imported nature of the term; Chen's stories project both a naive interest in the global cool and a cynical recognition of its distance from something else: the consciousness that results from life in China. They parade before us semiparodic references to the contexts and paradigms of postmodernity, often to the point of absurdity. The natural ease that we expect from a literary work has disappeared, replaced by a number of nearly embarrassing references to dances with wolves, scary phallic hypodermic needles, and the joy of sex.[18] Gliding between psychological probing, first- and third-person shifts, changing points of view, odd or imagined dialogue, lists of "favorite" words, and semihistorical reflection, Chen's fiction tells us about desire and mocks its revelations at the same time.

Postmodernism's seminal trope of desire and its infinite and purposeless play of the body has been criticized as the obfuscating ideology that displaces knowledge of unequal social relations. Teresa L. Ebert's *Ludic Feminism and After: Postmodernism, Desire, and Labor in Late Capitalism* is an impassioned critique of the way in which critical theory, in particular feminism, has "lost the revolutionary knowledges of historical materialism so necessary to understand the exploitative relations of labor and production and to transform them" (LFA, xi).[19] Ebert blames a number of recent feminist approaches, or ludic postmodernism, for this problem and suggests that they be replaced by resistance postmodernism, which views postmodernism as a contradictory historical condition. Ludic postmodern feminism, according to Ebert, has constructed a theory of desire to stand in for ideology; the theory appears under different names depending on the scholar (cyborg, performativity, citationality, remetaphorization, sexuality, sublime, difference, hyperreal, speculum, queer) but always represents an "impasse of apolitical invention" (LFA, 6) or the "panhistorical site of unencumbered freedom of the subject" (LFA, 5). Only by rejecting theories that depend on the autonomy or semiautonomy of the cultural—theories of desire—and by insisting on recognizing postmodernity itself as "articulations on the level of the *superstructure* of changes in the social, cultural, political" that result from new deployments of capital around the world can feminists historicize and understand the tropes of difference and desire that structure postmodern theory and cultural expression (LFA, 130).

Ebert's critique focuses on academic critics whose work on feminist theory has embraced tropes of the body and desire. The same interpretation could extend to literature, film, advertisements, and other areas of elite and popular culture, where desires are produced and desire itself is represented as the context and the goal of expression and reality.[20] In these spheres, China is a particularly interesting case to use in evaluating the discourse of desire and its global unfolding. Because China's recent past has demanded revolutionary zest from the state down to the person, the positing of desire as foundational to the will of the *person* rather than of the *state*, desire's radically antistatist refusal of ideological explanation, and desire's privileging of the body—specifically the female body—as a site of pleasure and resistance appear in a postrevolutionary context to be even more powerful as provocative and liberatory propositions. But because postmodernity in China unfolds under the aegis of a largely discredited political socialism and a rapidly developing economic capitalism, it would be difficult for Chinese writers and critics to counter this theory of desire with a Marxist materialist response, as Ebert argues we all must do; such a stance would be too close to that of the recently disavowed Maoist ideology.

Chen Ran's work can function as an example of what happens when theories of desire enter postrevolutionary China. It is undeniable that, in a way similar to what Ebert critiques, Chen Ran's stories establish desire as a basic trope of experience and reality, and that this expression is linked to capitalist cultural imperialism. Yet, desire in her stories possesses no naturalness; it is a sexualized and gendered stance of awkward postmodernism. This atomized, disembodied desire references the postmodern discourse of desire, yet simultaneously speaks to the distance between China and the postmodern West. Chen Ran's characters know of the revolutionary past and wistfully acknowledge its presence, but in their lives, its power becomes a residual trace.

Chen Ran and the Discourse of Desire

In the following three areas, Chen Ran's stories posit disembodied desire as foundational to reconstructing postrevolutionary consciousness:

1. Unlike the Maoist focus on the depth of revolutionary fervor and its translation into the passion of love that occurred in the immediate post–Cultural Revolution era, Chen's fiction transforms depth in romantic human rela-

tions—whether revolutionary or personal—into surface. This kind of transformation, from depth to surface, is typical in the postmodern sensibility but here marks the erasing of a full desire as a basis for action. In the story I use as an example, the symbol of this change is the switch in emphasis from the *diary* to the *datebook*.

2. Desire is not, as it is in Western postmodern expression, a basic stance from which all can be theorized and which is not subject to analysis or interpretation. Rather, desire is unrooted, vague, variable, and cannot really be called desire at all; it is mildly robotic, manipulated, and functional to the extent that it enacts itself to promote itself. The symbol of this constant reproduction of a recurring state of disembodied consciousness is the *prostitute* as opposed to the *lover*, and the delineation of a "prostitute mentality" takes as its basis for departure the fully humanistic lover depicted during the immediate post-Mao years.

3. Chen marks women as the particular example of this ungrounded consciousness. Only women are able to escape the national identification that global China demands of men, to float freely as a symbol of sexuality without desire, and, although they must work, to avoid identification by the world of work. What was once seen as women's marginalization here allows them to accurately represent the historical gutting of Chinese national modern culture, or revolutionary ideology, that globalism now accomplishes.

The short story I use for this essay is "The Sound of Another Ear Knocking" (*Ling yizhi erduo de qiaoji sheng*).[21] The main protagonist of the story is Ms. Dai Er, a character who appears in many other fictional pieces by Chen Ran. The other characters are Dai Er's mother, a female friend named Yin Duoren, and a male friend nicknamed Big Branch (*Da Shuzhi*). Dai Er's mother wants, above all, to make sure her live-at-home daughter remains a "good girl"—uninvolved in the seductive play of social affairs and sexual relations for fun—even though she is already over thirty and divorced. While remaining loyal to her mother in sentiment, Dai Er resists this old-fashioned control and has a sexual relationship with Big Branch, as well as an ambiguous attraction to Yin, and notes her liaisons in her datebook.

When Dai Er becomes friends with Yin, it threatens her deep, but somewhat antagonistic, relationship with her mother, who would rather have Dai Er involved with a man but who also relies on Dai Er's presence at home to give her a sense of well-being. Dai Er's mother discovers her daughter's dalliance with Yin not through the traditional spying technique of reading a diary but by stealing her datebook. The diary, which has been a symbol of obsessive

349 WENDY LARSON

involvement throughout the early and post-Mao twentieth century, often appears in semiautobiographical stories by Bing Xin, Lu Yin, Ding Ling, and also in the works of male writers such as Yu Dafu.[22] In its most famous example, Ding Ling's "The Diary of Ms. Sophia," the diary is a tool of deep psychological probing and examination, exposing for the reader Sophia's contradictory, yet intensely sexual, longings and desires. In the 1980 post-Mao short story "Love Must Not Be Forgotten" (Aiqing shi buneng wangji de), which swept the country as an expression of antipolitical fervor and as a statement in favor of elevating the value of human emotions, Zhang Jie uses the diary to elaborate on a hidden but profound romantic love, as well as to criticize the Maoist suppression of feelings.

In "The Sound of Another Ear Knocking," however, Chen Ran anchors Dai Er's identity not to the diary but to the datebook. Rather than indicating deep and obsessive desire, the datebook represents Dai Er's rejection of conventional values, as demanded by her mother, and a flitting sense of important but incidental associations. Dai Er's relationships are emotionally profound but make no sense; they inform her consciousness, but there is no direct or clear-cut expression of feeling, either in what she says or in what she writes. Compared with Sophia's confused fantasies of stolen kisses from a handsome young man from Singapore, Dai Er's sexuality is bland and without passion. Her relationships also indicate the transgressive world of female-female friendships, which threatens the intense and overbearing relationship between Dai Er and her mother as well as the relationship between Dai Er and Yin Duoren. Like Zhang Jie's "Love Must Not Be Forgotten," the structure of "The Sound of Another Ear Knocking" features a mother-daughter association wherein the daughter evaluates the mother's attitudes toward love and romance that are part of the legacy of the past. In "Love Must Not Be Forgotten," the legacy is socialist ideology under Mao, and the story suggests that personal relations under this sign are constructed on a basis of falseness. Maoism, in other words, has suppressed love, and this fact extends itself into social life at large, engendering the sham of revolutionary loyalty that is played out through daily personal and public acts. By the time "The Sound of Another Ear Knocking" is written, however, the possibility that love will replace revolution no longer exists. Dai Er's mother married, but not out of the deep desire that motivated the unfulfilled mother in Zhang Jie's story. Rather, "she once loved someone because she could not bear the bitterness of loneliness" ("Erduo," 27). After her last divorce ten years before, Dai Er's mother refused all offers and "resolutely left the company of men" ("Erduo," 27). Dai Er calls her mother a "widow" and herself "the latest generation of young widows," and the charmed distance of both from the usual expressions of regret or sorrow is indicated in a list of idiosyncracies, including wearing odd clothing, enjoying ruins, and liking a number of words, which are listed one by one ("Erduo," 27–28).

Far from the motivating, repressed, yet powerful and subtly invigorating desire of Sophia or the mother in "Love Must Not Be Forgotten," the desire of Dai Er and her mother is detached and without a possible object. Women, in the form of Dai Er for her mother and Yin Duoren for Dai Er, are a disembodied reference to a possible but problematic and socially difficult object for this un-desire. The listing of its qualities, in the form of eccentric quirks of personality and language, is a fitting expression of a calm but slightly blank state of mind. It would be a mistake, however, to read Chen Ran's construction of this internalized urban world as a critique along humanist lines. Although Dai Er rejects the fullness of a consciousness based on love and emotional clarity, and has some qualms about her life and goals, her own sense of things is far from a desperate cry for change.

Chen Ran identifies this floating mentality as typical of the younger generation. Even though Dai Er's mother was unable to put into effect a vision of love, Dai Er believes that her mother's generation, when young, "had possessed some firm beliefs and missions," whereas she "feels as if she has never lived" ("Erduo," 33). In order to get some sense of purpose and a work mission, Dai Er sneaks in among some mentally ill patients and records what she sees.[23] Boring as it is, Dai Er's "work," she claims, is as interesting as anything else. It is the "arrangement of people by time," which provided revolutionary meaning to her mother's generation, that allows Dai Er to be more alienated and detached than her mother ("Erduo," 33). Furthermore, because society does not demand that a woman excel in work, this consciousness is more available to women than to men. Women may be as dependent as men on work for a livelihood, but they have greater leeway in deciding how it will define their personalities and thoughts, Chen implies.

Dai Er's datebook finally falls into the hands of Yin Duoren, a woman who originally appeared in her dreams and for whom she searched for years ("Erduo," 53). In her monologue, Yin identifies Dai Er as a force inside herself linked to her inability to act, and when the two women eventually get together, Dai Er refuses to speak ("Erduo," 54). Yin insists that Dai Er should be with her: " 'I'll tell you, Dai Er, no man would want you, because in your heart you are like me, just as strong and powerful as they are. They are afraid of us, and avoid us out of this fear. If we are not together, you will always be lonely, you will never have anyone' " ("Erduo," 61). Yin's words imply a common feminist stance: that sexual involvement with men results in inferiority for women, who are forced to take a weaker position against which men produce themselves as stronger. As if to reinforce this idea that a relationship with a man demeans a woman, when she is making love to Big Branch, Dai Er persistently refers to herself as a prostitute. And when the narrative switches to Big Branch's mind, he claims that he does not want to be with an intelligent woman but simply with a prostitute. Chen implies that the prostitute mentality, which is no longer a moral issue, is not just an aspect of Dai Er's mind but is pervasively social and common.

Yin Duoren is far more than just a feminist lure that allows Dai Er to transgress sexual mores, however. Because Dai Er is part of Yin's past inability to act, Yin's tale and relationship to Dai Er is an integral aspect of Chen Ran's antidesire construction and a link to the space the postmodern model creates between itself and what comes after:

> Ms. Dai Er is like a prisoner, she is trapped in her own ideas and in a certain kind of lack. Lack is a ray of light, shining unusually brightly into the rooms of her thoughts. For so many years she left the seething outer world, and this simply means a hidden slow suicide, a plan for a limitless cutting off of the self from existence. This serious pathology of isolationist tendencies had completely destroyed her for too long. . . . I don't know if this world still has any kind of goodness at which we still have not arrived. She doesn't want to know. I don't seek clarity, and have no interest at all in concerning myself with the kind of difficult situation of the ordinary person. Those useless theories are nothing but the moon reflected in water and flowers in the mirror. . . . "Let life be full of valuable actions," is my saying. To realize an action is to get something meaningful. I too have traveled the twisted internal roads Dai Er is traversing. Once my hand as if shocked touched her tears, her emaciated shoulder trembled in agitation in my arms. At that moment I felt that my life finally had grasped onto something. I must hold her, I can't let go even for a second. Holding her is clasping myself, it is clasping the god that flows in my veins. I need her. She is nothing but the desire and ability to act that I lost so many years ago. ("Erduo," 53–54)

Written in the words of an omniscient narrator with added monologues by each character, the story tells of each person's sense of loss and betrayal. Rarely, however, is the feeling of loss accompanied by emotional upheaval or trauma. Although Dai Er regards herself as lost, drifting, and cheap, she does not struggle against that condition. The author expresses Dai Er's condition by idiosyncratic word lists and difficult-to-understand sentences.

In the immediate post-Mao protest against ideological excess that characterized much of the literature from 1978 to 1985, the lover emerged as a sign of new, exciting, and utopic emotional fullness. A number of stories and novels depicted people in the cities and countryside who were overwhelmed by strong emotions of love and who struggled against social restrictions that masqueraded as revolutionary or "feudal" ideology. The post-Mao lover was dedicated to the loved one and to the emotion of love to the point of death, promoting a self that was unified in thought, emotion, and action. Chen Ran's frequent references to the prostitute, which is not what Dai Er actually is but what she imagines herself to be and to want, marks the infusion of this profound and logical desire with suspension and a drifting sense of functionality. Not only has Dai Er lost the focus of resistance, as have the characters and narratives in works by avant-garde writers, but she also responds to her thoughts and feelings in a quirky, unfathomable manner.[24]

Dai Er is both trapped and liberated. She has set her body free from old morality, playing with men as if they were toys and denying that she wants to get married. The author shows her, however, as still snared within feminine behaviors of longing and musing. Unlike Ding Ling's Sophia, Dai Er is not inflamed by passion, nor does she wish to love someone. The only direct emotional connection available to her is her problematic link to her mother and her narcissistic, homoerotic tie with Yin Duoren as part of herself. The post-Mao humanistic vision of love and its infusion of strong, directed feelings into the lover, who replaces revolutionary passion and direction with this force, have disappeared and remain only as a fantasy and weak memory for Dai Er of her mother's generation and its failures.

Dai Er claims that she and Yin Duoren are, after all and in the same way, women ("Erduo," 58). This postrevolutionary consciousness is highly gendered and fixes women, not men, in the representative position. In this way, Chen's work is in contrast to the fiction of the avant-garde, or experimental, writers such as Ge Fei, Su Tong, and Yu Hua, in whose stories the troubled and troubling protagonist always is male.[25] More than these aestheticized male characters, Chen's Ms. Dai Er is a composite that interests us through both her state of mind and her urban lifestyle. Ms. Dai Er is also different from the largely male protagonists of Wang Shuo's pizi (hooligan) literature, whose consciousness stems almost entirely from their alienated and purposefully meaningless endeavors.

Chen unifies the feminist import of her writing with the national situation through the theme of the lost homeland, which is undeveloped throughout the story but framed in initial and final references. The protagonist Dai Er appears alternately in London and in China, with the flickering datebook and its on-again, off-again assignations and betrayals in China and across the globe also acting as a trope of an "exhausted memory" that characterizes Dai Er's diasporic state of mind ("Erduo," 20). "I have no homeland in my heart," she claims, and further, "my body is my homeland," which shows how the homeland is no more embodied with passion and desire than is the body ("Erduo," 20). Narrative time becomes homogeneous in the story, with the past, present, and future melding into a bland, uniform moment. At the end of the story, Dai Er, in London, claims that she "will never have a home again," and that "the fog hanging over all of Europe has infiltrated my eyes" ("Erduo," 77). Dai Er's body, and by implication the contemporary Chinese female body, has taken on the postmodern quality of surface, but what is indicated is not the ahistorical privileging of desire or the obfuscating problematics of the body.

Because of its ideological Maoist past, China's situation cannot fit into the dichotomy of the "discourse of the desiring body" versus a "materialist ideology." The omnipresent globe-trotter Dai Er no longer acts overtly on behalf of China, for such action is not possible without cultural gutting in the name of future economic power. At the same time, her existence is structured or framed by the covert knowledge that the old China, unified by revolutionary or humanist purpose, is no longer a homeland.

Jing Wang's recent discussion in *High Culture Fever* of the roots and avant-garde writers provides some clues about Chen Ran's experiment. As Wang describes, roots writers of the mid-1980s portrayed a male individual subject who was earnestly engaged in self-construction and critique: "The body is culturally inscribed but the heart and mind are free" (HCF, 216). This "self-enclosed subject" delves into culture yet simultaneously locates a way to transcend its limitations; he—it is almost always a male—thus can speak to China, the world at large, and the future (HCF, 215–16). Roots writers' delving into the peripheries of Confucian culture, Daoist experience and aesthetics, and minority life is, Wang explains, a "nativist romanticization about the cultural subject as a fixed space of its own" that reconstructs a more essential and authentic China (HCF, 212).

Jing Wang believes that the roots writers' emphasis on writing as a discursive (linguistic) practice rather than as an ideological practice is a precursor to the avant-garde writers' confident and "transcolonial subject," the "self-possessed subject position" that refuses to recognize the old "power versus resistance" logic coded within literary texts. Chen Ran's writing posits an entirely different posture for her female protagonist (HCF, 101). The experimentalists' conclusion that the subject is nothing more than a mere effect of language has its echo in Dai Er's datebook, but her vulnerable and semilyrical nature contradicts the arrogance of this position.

Chen Ran offers three representative aspects of the Chinese experience of postmodernity and some significant intersections between feminism and postmodernism in China. First, although the conditions of postmodernity exist in some aspects of urban society and although the style of postmodern culture—in this case, the discourse of desire—is available to China as it is to the West, the distance between Western and Chinese cultures will be expressed in cultural texts. A model that overuses the concepts of imitation, belatedness, and catching up does not recognize this gap and the consciousness of its existence that is illustrated in Chen's fiction, as well as in other works. Second, the Chinese diaspora is part of the postmodern condition of China, but its existence no longer is a cause for nationalistic anguish—the call to "return"—or gut-wrenching concern over what it means to be Chinese. The diaspora and its implications for national culture are recognized and accepted, not ignored or displaced; at the same time, local culture, consciousness, and experience is brought out and presented as equal to or more significant than the global context. Third, the socialist past, which, despite its problems, is acknowledged as a once full and impassioned form of Chinese modernity, shrinks in significance and becomes a residual trace in the mind of the contemporary subject. Along with it goes the central revolutionary demand to resist—capitalism, imperialist running dogs, or anything else.

For feminist critique, it is significant that Chen Ran links all of the above with being female. The Chinese male subject, she implies, is overdetermined by a revolutionary consciousness, a nationalistic feeling and duty, and a responsibility for explaining and discrediting the past. Unlike men, women can float, or refuse to be symbolically fixed by meanings of the past in the present. Chen's vision for women does indeed liberate them from many restrictive structures of sexuality, familial definition, and gendered labor. Yet, it is negative in many ways, very limited in scope, and gives us only a tiny picture of urban feminist sensibility in contemporary China. Chen's portrayal of Ms. Dai Er is important for its removal of the Chinese female subject from the overarching concern with any kind of determining meaning—revolutionary passion, humanistic love, lust for the new and different—outside of what she can gain from her own daily life.

Notes

Unless otherwise noted, all translations are mine.

1   For a description of socialist society under Deng, see Maurice Meisner, *The Deng Xiaoping Era: An Inquiry into the Fate of Chinese Socialism, 1978–1994* (New York: Hill and Wang, 1994).

2   See books in the series *Funü yanjiu zongshu* (Research series on women), ed. Li Xiaojiang, which includes individual volumes such as *Nüxing guannian de yanbian* (Evolution of concepts on women), by Du Fangqin (1988); *Funü yanjiu zai Zhongguo* (Women's studies in China), ed. Li Xiaojiang and Tan Shen (1988); and *Fengsao yu yanqing: Zhongguo gudian shici de nüxing yanjiu* (Coyness and amorous feelings: Studies on women in classical Chinese poetry), by Kang Zhengguo (1988), all published by Henan Renmin Chubanshe. See also historical works such as Wang Menglong, *Zhongguo funü yundong lishi ziliao* (Materials from the history of the women's movement in China) (Beijing: Zhongguo Funü Chubanshe, 1991). Literary histories include Qiao Yigang, *Zhongguo nüxing de wenxue shijie* (The literary

world of Chinese women) (Wuhan: Hubei Jiaoyu Chubanshe, 1993); and Sheng Ying, ed., *Ershi shiji Zhongguo nüxing wenxue shi* (The history of twentieth-century Chinese women's literature), vols. 1 and 2 (Tianjin: Tianjin Renmin Chubanshe, 1995).

3   See, for example, Li Jianyong, *Nüren shi shui* (Women are water) (Beijing: Zhongguo Hua-qiao Chubanshe, 1993), a collection of essays about women's psychology, social control, love, and other topics; Guo Jinfu, *Zhongguo nüxing jinji* (Taboos concerning Chinese women) (Shijiazhuang: Hebei Renmin Chubanshe, 1991), a scholarly study of social restrictions including footbinding; Fu Guilu, *Jiefu* (Chaste women) (Beijing: Qunzhong Chubanshe, 1994), a collection of twentieth-century stories about women and marriage; and Hua Shan, ed., *Dangdai nanxing bidu congshu* (A series of necessary reading for contemporary men) (Beijing: Zhongyang Minzu Xueyuan Chubanshe, 1993), which includes individual volumes such as *Nüren yu yu* (Women and desire), *Nüren de xin* (The hearts of women), *Nüren de ku* (The misery of women), *Nüren yu e* (Women and evil), and *Shijie buneng meiyou nüren* (The world cannot be without women).

4   See, for example, the films directed by Fourth Generation director Xie Fei, *Xiang nü xiao-xiao* (Girl from Hunan [1990]) and *Xiang hun nü* (Women from the lake of scented souls [1993]), which both emphasize the discriminatory conditions under which women live and work.

5   Many articles by Beijing University professor Dai Jinhua have focused on the sexism of literature and film in contemporary China.

6   Chen Ran was born in Beijing and studied music as a child. She received an M.A. in literature in 1987, has taught at universities in China, and has worked as a reporter and as an editor. Chen has published several collections of short stories and is a member of the Chinese Writers Association.

7   See " 'Hong yingsu congshu' xu" (Introduction to the Red poppy series), in Chen Ran, *Qianxing yishi* (Hidden natures, lost affairs) (Shijiazhuang: Hebei Jiaoyu Chubanshe, 1995), 1. Wang Meng's short text appears to be an introduction to the series and thus his words apply not only to Chen Ran but to all of the writers included. Hereafter, Wang Meng's introduction is cited parenthetically as "Hong yingsu."

8   Zhou Zuoren, "Nüzi yu wenxue" (Women and literature), *Funü zazhi* (The ladies journal) 8, no. 8 (Aug. 1921).

9   Zhang Yiwu, " 'Hou yuyan' xiezuo yu xin zhuangtai xiaoshuo" ("Postallegorical" writing and new situational fiction), in *Yuwang de wudao: Xin zhuangtai xiaoshuo* (Dance of desire: New situational fiction), ed. Zhang Yiwu (Lanzhou: Dunhuang Wenyi Chubanshe, 1994), 1–12. Hereafter, this work is cited parenthetically as "Hou yuyan."

10 "Ms. Sophia's Diary" stunned the literary world when it came out in 1927. Ding Ling's portrayal of Sophia, a young Chinese woman with a Western — and thus modern — name, was widely discussed as a representation of the "modern girl," a new entity whose frank sexual desires, convoluted inner mind, psychologized interior, and disregard for traditional feminine values seemed to indicate the direction of the future for Chinese women and more generally for Chinese culture at large. When leftist literary ideology took the lead in the 1930s, the story was criticized for its bourgeois sensibility, lack of social concern, and sexual bent. During the 1957 Anti-Rightist Movement, and as late as the Cultural Revolution in the 1960s and 1970s, Ding Ling was under attack for the story and for promoting antirevolutionary, "Sophia-like" ideas and values.

11 See Teresa L. Ebert, *Ludic Feminism and After: Postmodernism, Desire, and Labor in Late Capitalism* (Ann Arbor: University of Michigan Press, 1996). Hereafter, this work is cited parenthetically as LFA.

12 The inclusion of Spivak may strike some readers as odd. Ebert points out Spivak's interpretation of Marx's concept of value as a "catachresis or pun," thus turning what originally was the exploitation of contradictions in production into a linguistic pun and a play of textual differences (LFA, 40). While Ebert gives Spivak credit for her deconstruction of imperialist politics in Western representations of the subaltern, she finds that in her recommendations for First World intellectual work, Spivak substitutes a discursive, textualizing politics for the labor relations inherent in representations, reducing "imperialism to a ludic semiosis," in the process reinscribing the autonomous individual who possesses "a coherent, self-identical subjectivity outside the history of labor" (LFA, 291–92).

13 Jing Wang, "The Mirage of Chinese Postmodernism: Ge Fei, Self-Positioning, and the Avant-garde Showcase," Positions: East Asia Cultures Critique 1, no. 2 (fall 1993): 360. Wang's essay is an incisive critique of strategies used by Ge Fei and Yu Hua, and through a brief but winding reading of Chen Yingzhen's work argues that a "Chinese position, despite its ambiguous implication in Western discourse, can emerge and establish itself as the self-conscious center of a critical practice" (350).

14 For examples of the insistent interpretation of Chinese films as embodying a Chinese essence, see the discussion of Chen Kaige's Farewell My Concubine in "Film-Makers Baptized in Fire—An Interview with Chen Kaige," Financial Times, 8 January 1994; Brian D. Johnson, "The Red and the Restless, MacLeans, 15 November 1993, 9; David Ansen with Deirdre Nickerson and Marcus Mabry, "The Real Cultural Revolution," Newsweek, 1 November 1993, 74; Vincent Canby, "Top Prize at Cannes is Shared," New York Times, 25 May 1993, C13. A discussion of Western critics' tendency to universalize American films but see cultural characteristics in the films of other cultures has also been pointed out by Rey Chow throughout Primitive Passions: Visuality, Sexuality, Ethnography, and Contemporary Chinese Cinema (New York: Columbia University Press, 1995).

15 Wang, "The Mirage of Chinese Postmodernism," 381.

16 Prasenjit Duara, Rescuing History from the Nation: Questioning Narratives of Modern China (Chicago: University of Chicago Press, 1995). See also Gregory Jusdanis, Belated Modernity and Aesthetic Culture: Inventing National Literature (Minneapolis: University of Minnesota Press, 1991) for a similar argument concerning Greece.

17 See Fredric Jameson, "Remapping Taipei," in New Chinese Cinemas: Forms, Identities, Politics, ed. Nick Browne, Paul G. Pickowicz, Vivian Sobchack, and Esther Yau (New York: Cambridge University Press, 1994), 119. Jameson analyzes Edward Yang's (Yang Dechang) film The Terrorizers (Kongbu fenzi) as typical of postmodern culture outside of the center in that because the experience of capitalism is more recent in the periphery, the periphery's cultural products are more intense, expressive, and symptomatic (150). However, it is significant that Yang's film did not become well known in the West, whereas films that more readily indicate an exotic and erotic "Chinese culture," such as Zhang Yimou's Red Sorghum (Hong gaoliang) or Judou, did. In other words, no matter how symptomatic the expression of capitalist experience is, in the West it will not be as powerful as an expression of a vulnerable, attractive, and easily identifiable traditional culture.

18 The influence of Western literary traditions in China during the course of the twentieth century could be described as causing Chinese literature to lose any sense of ease it may have produced in the minds of its readers. Certainly the semirealist stories of Lu Xun, the psychologized and sexualized narratives of Yu Dafu and the early Ding Ling, the changes demanded by socialist realism, and the modernist or experimental works of the post-Mao era all are departures, many radical, from the past. Yet, I would argue that Chen

Ran's work goes a step further in producing an intense awkwardness that captures the sense of dislocation common among educated urban youth that critics such as Zhang Yiwu find in the postmodern sensibility.

19 For other critiques of the ideas associated with the postmodern discourse of desire, see Alex Callinicos, *Against Postmodernism: A Marxist Critique* (New York: St. Martin's Press, 1989); see also David Harvey, *The Condition of Postmodernity* (Oxford: Basil Blackwell, 1989). Callinicos argues against the idea that a "post-industrial society" exists (121); Harvey consistently links postmodern change to the development of labor relations under capitalism. Ebert discusses the work of Nobel Prize winner Rigoberta Menchú, who, in her autobiographical text *I, Rigoberta Menchú: An Indian Woman in Guatemala*, ed. Elisabeth Burgos-Debray, trans. Ann Wright (London: Verso, 1984), bases her analysis on a materialist critique of labor (295–96).

20 One of the problems with Ebert's work is that she does not adequately theorize the pervasive development of desire as an antimaterial stance that is promoted at all levels of society. In Ebert's analysis, academic critics become mere followers who reproduce the discourse of desire at the level of theory.

21 "Ling yizhi erduo de qiaoji sheng" (The sound of another ear knocking) is included in Chen, *Qianxing yishi*, 20–77. The title could be a reference to the famous Zen koan, "What is the sound of one hand clapping?" According to the note at the end of the story, it was written in London in 1994. Hereafter, this work is cited parenthetically as "Erduo."

22 See a critical discussion of the diary and women writers in the late 1920s and early 1930s in He Yubo, *Zhongguo xiandai nüzuojia* (Modern Chinese women writers) (Shanghai: Fuxing Shuju, 1935), 48–49.

23 Contrast this presentation of mental illness with that of the modern Lu Xun, in his early "Kuangren riji" (Diary of a madman), and the contemporary Can Xue, in *Huangni jie* (Yellow mud street). Although Lu Xun is a May Fourth writer and Can Xue is an avant-garde experimentalist, they both imply that madness has infected specifically Chinese society and caused the aberrant behavior that constitutes daily life. Chen Ran, however, locates society firmly within the domain of the sane.

24 See Jing Wang, *High Culture Fever: Politics, Aesthetics, and Ideology in Deng's China* (Berkeley: University of California Press, 1996), esp. chap. 5, "Romancing the Subject: Utopian Moments in the Chinese Aesthetics of the 1980s," 195–232, for the idea that what makes the experimentalists truly unacceptable to Chinese authorities is their refusal to posit a point of resistance. Hereafter, this work is cited parenthetically as *HCF*.

25 This is not true in the stories of Can Xue, however, where we find many examples of troubled female characters.

15   Melancholy against the Grain: Approaching
Postmodernity in Wang Anyi's Tales of Sorrow

1. "The easily spotted triggers of my despair"

A postmodern challenge, remarks Julia Kristeva at the end of her 1987 book
Black Sun: Depression and Melancholia, now confronts the "world of unsettling,
infectious ill-being" that Marguerite Duras so determinedly creates in her fiction. Underlying the novelist's imagination is a silence or nothingness that
insists on being spoken as the ultimate expression of suffering and that often
"carries us to the dangerous, furthermost bounds of our psychic life." Yet,
what the irreverent postmodern abandon finds in a Durasian malady of grief,
laments Kristeva, is "only one moment of the *narrative synthesis* capable of
sweeping along in its complex whirlwind philosophical meditations as well as
erotic protections or entertaining pleasures. The postmodern is closer to the
human comedy than to the abyssal discontent." Postmodernity erects an "artifice of seeming" and offers the "heartrending distraction of parody," both
of which promise to act as antidepressants for a literary obsession with the
illness of modernity.[1]

At this point, Kristeva, the renowned semiotician of desire, seems to suggest that a modernist seriousness and a postmodernist parody form successive phases of the "eternal return of historical and intellectual cycles" (BS, 259). This pattern of recurrence, however, is not so much a temporal process as a temperamental one, through which our experience in and of historical time becomes affected and eventually representable. "Thus moods are *inscriptions*," she declares earlier in the book. "They lead us toward a modality of significance that . . . insures the preconditions for (or manifests the disintegration of) the imaginary and the symbolic" (BS, 22). Relying on this thesis, Kristeva is able to conclude her somber study of melancholia and literature on a reassuring note: "Does not the wonderment of psychic life after all stem from those alternations of protections and downfalls, smiles and tears, sunshine and melancholia?" (BS, 259). The challenge of the postmodern, therefore, lies not necessarily in the threat that the malady of grief would be rendered passé and obsolete at one stroke but rather in recognizing the dialectics, the dynamic alternations that bring forth a postmodern lightheartedness in the first place. It is the capacity of our inner emotional existence that is being put to the test.

In fact, this is the stated motivation for Kristeva's journey into the dark interior of depression and melancholia. At the beginning of *Black Sun*, she writes, "For those who are racked by melancholia, writing about it would have meaning only if writing sprang out of that very melancholia. I am trying to address an abyss of sorrow, a noncommunicable grief " (BS, 3). Her first question is then a direct inquiry about the origins of her ravaging melancholia: "Where does this black sun come from?" (BS, 3). The main body of the book, in which she reads not only clinical cases of feminine depression but also literary texts by Dostoyevsky and Duras, therefore registers a double movement. It records Kristeva's broad effort to reinterpret melancholia from a psycholinguistic perspective; yet it is also a text that answers her own glaring and inescapable depression. Her writing about melancholia combats her devitalized existence by helping her name and dissect the abyssal and unnameable suffering that overpowers her. In other words, hers is a self-reflective text, produced with a narrator's full knowledge of the postmodern challenge to come at the end.

The immediate reason why the Kristeva of *Black Sun* is introduced here in an essay purportedly about Wang Anyi, the prominent contemporary Chinese writer, is that both writers at one point describe a similar onset of unspeakable sorrow. The accounts of their encounters with melancholy reveal a shared logic, although Kristeva's musings have the appearance of either psychoanalysis or literary theory, and Wang Anyi's narration is strictly fictional. In addition, while what Kristeva studies includes clinical melancholia, Wang Anyi's literary works deal mostly with melancholy as a subjective mood.[2] Nonetheless, more substantive reasons for making this initial comparison will become obvious in this discussion of some of Wang Anyi's recent stories, which may be called, as suggested by the writer herself in *Sadness for the Pacific*, tales of sorrow. The most vital linkage, on an abstract level, may lie in the similar response that both writers choose to mount to the postmodern challenge, namely, a melancholy subjectivity.

To begin answering her own question about the origins of melancholia, Kristeva ponders a series of possibilities. "The wound I have just suffered, some setback or other in my love life or my profession, some sorrow or bereavement affecting my relationship with close relatives—such are often the easily spotted triggers of my despair." As if this list is not enough, she goes on to enumerate a second, more severe group of likely causes: "a betrayal, a fatal illness, some accident or handicap that abruptly wrests me away from what seemed to me the normal category of normal people. . . . What more could I mention? An infinite number of misfortunes weighs us down every day" (BS, 3–4).

When the confessional, presumably male, first-person narrator in Wang Anyi's 1990 novella *Our Uncle's Story* announces his decision to tell a story, he apparently suffers from a setback in his love life and experiences the consequent interruption of everyday normalcy.[3] His sudden discovery, which comes to him one day as a result of some "extremely personal incident," is an unsettling insight about himself: "I've always thought that I was a happy child, but now I realize I am actually not" (*Shushu*, 2). This new realization dawns on him as an "elegant sadness," which prompts his desire to tell a story (*Shushu*, 2). Yet, this young writer-narrator does not wish to disclose the personal affair that triggers his new self-conception because it has something to do with love and sentiment. His therapeutic device, then, is to tell a story about another, more established writer, whom the narrator refers to as "our uncle" and whose awkward fate in the whirlwind of contemporary life gives rise to great ambivalence on the part of the narrator. This ambivalence is so intense that, toward the end, the storyteller concedes that this is the first story that has ever had such a personal impact on him. All his previous stories deal solely with other people and involve less investment. The uncle's life story, however, parallels the narrator's own "personal incident," which appears utterly trivial and frivolous when compared to the grand drama of the former. Nevertheless, the narrator feels that his recent experience allows him a better psychological interpretation of the events in the uncle's life. Therefore he is compelled to tell this story, and his conclusions are: "The outcome of our uncle's story is that he will no longer be happy. After I finish telling the story of our uncle, I will never tell a happy story again" (*Shushu*, 77).

In the end, we never find out what the "extremely personal incident" is that causes the narration of an unhappy story, although numerous hints are planted that "an individual inflicted an acutely painful experience" on the narrator (Shushu, 23). Nor do we get a closer look at the narrator himself except for a general intellectual portrait of a young, fashionable, and self-confident writer (of the same age as Wang Anyi herself) who is now stricken by an elegant sadness and absorbed in sober introspection. Yet, the narrator's temperament, poignant comments, and reflections frame the entire story, which proves to be as much a narrative about the political and erotic vicissitudes in the uncle's life as it is an analytical account of the historical constitution of his own melancholic mood. His altered perspective on reality and on his profession affects him to such a degree that he has no other story to tell but this fateful one. "Put differently, if I do not finish telling this story, I will not be able to tell any other stories. What's more, I am astonished by the fact that I should have already told so many stories before this one; all of those stories would have a different appearance if they were to be told after this one" (Shushu, 1–2).

What emerges from the beginning of his narrative is the almost standard structure of metafiction, in which a potentially infinite mirror game of writing a story about story writing is set to unfold. Yet, the refreshing spin of *Our Uncle's Story*, according to literary critics, comes from the productive tension that Wang Anyi maintains between the two levels of narration. Instead of ossifying the metafictional operation into a stiff technique or purpose, she adroitly keeps the encasing narration itself open to interpretation. For this reason, Wang Anyi's story is considered more successful than other works in contemporary experimental fiction.[4] For the critic Li Jiefei, the writing of *Our Uncle's Story* marks a definite turning point in the novelist's conception of the art of storytelling. It ushers in a new logic of literary creation, the premise of which is no longer referential experience or reality but the independent technique of crafting fiction. This transformation makes Wang Anyi a pioneering "novelistic technician," whose later stories should therefore be taken as part of a larger myth-creating project.[5]

While it is highly debatable whether, in the 1990s, one could label Wang Anyi as a freshly converted and purist "technician" bent on conjuring up a mythic world of her own, there is little doubt that *Our Uncle's Story* initiated a new mode of writing for the writer herself. She continues her well-known productivity and still excels at putting together intriguing stories buttressed by realistic character sketches.[6] Yet, more and more, her writings seem concentrated on capturing and gauging a mood, a persistent sentiment or emotional state that, because of its profoundly ambivalent nature, becomes intensified rather than diffused through narration. A central pathos is maintained and developed into an expressive affect, such as longing, sorrow, and nostalgia. *The Utopian Chapters* (1991), for example, is an evidently autobiographical narrative about longing as an authentic passion that promises a transcendental happiness, and that is in itself a comfort and an ideal.[7] In *Love and Sentiment in Hong Kong* (1993), Wang Anyi's story about the possibilities for emotional attachment in a consumerist metropolis, constant grief for the present as already past underlies an uneventful world.[8] Readily observable in these narratives is a reflective sorrow and mournfulness.

In retrospect, the narrator of *Our Uncle's Story* is telling a prophetic truth about Wang Anyi's writings when he declares that there will be no more happy narratives afterward. Or he happens to be the mouthpiece through which the author verbalizes her own melancholic mood. More revealing is the writer-narrator's observation that many of his earlier stories would have a different outlook if they were told now. This proves to be the case with Wang Anyi's critically acclaimed novella *Sadness for the Pacific* (1993), which is an imaginative rewriting of an earlier, much simpler short story. What motivates the rewriting, as the new title indicates, is an irresolvable sadness, a global desolation that, as I will show below, lies at the heart of Wang Anyi's melancholy imagination. But before we examine *Sadness for the Pacific*, let us return to *Our Uncle's Story* for clues about the origins of a disconsolate period. The trigger of ensuing unhappiness may well be the sudden crumbling of a presumed reality.

2. "And yet we have no courage to live a deep life"

All things considered, *Our Uncle's Story* is among the few truly complex and challenging works in contemporary Chinese literature. It is a profoundly unsettling story, in which the author methodically undermines established narrative paradigms, mocks aesthetic pretensions, and offers biting criticisms of ideological constructs. An occasional satirical tone aside, it is also a full-fledged allegory about the inescapable burden of one's own past, about suffering as constitutive of an individual's self-consciousness. Its circular structure of a double narrative, moreover, enables a parodic commentary on a society that rapidly outpaces itself and, in the process, yields little legitimacy to any hyperextended narratives of historical progress. We can even say this felicitous, irony-driven form effects the same "heartrending distraction of parody" that Julia Kristeva detects in a postmodern playfulness.[9] What comes through is indeed a heartrending ambivalence, directed toward a disorienting age that disavows genuine passion or heroic possibilities.

The story of "our uncle" is a tragicomic one, inextricably interwoven with the course of political and cultural life in China during the second half of this century. The nameless uncle, explains the narrator, is not a relative or even a friend, but rather a representative member of the older generation who were put into political exile as politically subversive "rightists" in the late

1950s, only to return as triumphant heroes to the center stage of society some twenty years later. About this generation's wasted youth and talents there are numerous movies, memoirs, and stories, including the uncle's own successful writings, widely assumed to be autobiographical. As a result of his story about the suffering of a young rightist, the uncle wins instant fame, becomes a full-time writer, and is relocated from the remote village where he has lived in exile to the provincial capital. This is where we find the uncle at the beginning of the narrative. In a matter-of-fact tone, the narrator undoes the popular image of rightists as romantic young men who invariably bade tearful farewells to their loves and, in eternal darkness, embarked on cold, snowy journeys to the forsaken western frontier. The truth is that the uncle was too young to fall in love then and was quietly sent home to his obscure native town rather than to remote Qinghai. He was first assigned to menial labor at the local school and later started teaching. Only after he had developed a following as a writer, quips the narrator, did tales of his trek to Qinghai get concocted and circulated.

From the outset, the uncle's story is told to debunk recent cultural myths and to reveal the gap between representation and lived experiences. When he describes the uncle's marriage to one of his students, for instance, the narrator realizes that there exists a wide range of narrative conventions for such an event.

> Many inspiring tales can be spun about a female student from a small town falling in love with her teacher, who happens to be from the city and an ex-rightist. There is the love relationship between a simple person of nature and a cultured person of society; there is the attachment between a free person and an exile, just as in the story of a Decembrist of old Russia and his wife; there is also the attraction between a person from an entrenched family and a rootless stranger. With these three relationships blended together, one can probe deep into human nature and capture a broad social background, bringing together a specific reality and a permanent humanity. Such a story our Uncle did write, in fact more than once. (*Shushu*, 8)

Eventually, all these elements seem to find their way into the uncle's stories and combine to make the misery of his youth appear soulful, heroically tragic, even sublime, a suffering that becomes an object of envy to the younger generation. The task of demythologization that the narrator sets himself, therefore, has to start with a recounting of the uncle's life in the small town. It is, in fact, an uneventful life, although two key events, comments the narrator, take place the spring after the uncle's marriage. The first is the birth of their son Dabao, which disappoints the uncle deeply because he wishes to have a daughter. The second incident, rather "petty and frivolous" (Shushu, 11), happens one spring evening. Accused of frolicking with one of his current students and subjected to brutal communal humiliation, the uncle has to be rescued by his wife, who then turns the tables by verbally attacking, for three long days and nights, the younger woman in public.

This demoralizing incident, according to the narrator, provides a credible motive for the development of the uncle's story, even though it may be altogether fabrication. Perhaps the uncle never talks or writes about what actually happened, further speculates the narrator, because the incident would compromise the heroic narratives of his noble suffering. But this sordid affair has the effect of "nailing suffering into one's body" (Shushu, 11), of rendering anguish into a memory of complicity. It does not help the husband love his wife any better, either, for that would be yet another hackneyed story. Instead, the narrator sees the growing resentment that the uncle harbors against his protective wife and the binding institution of marriage. "He felt that marriage did not lessen the humiliation and misery inflicted upon him, as it was supposed to. On the contrary, it intensified the humiliation and misery by giving it a lasting shell, now impossible to forget" (Shushu, 23). To numb his faculty of memory, the uncle indulges in sensual pleasures, starts drinking and smoking, beats his wife during the day, and demands sexual favors at night. He readily banishes his own soul and perseveres in an instinctual existence "like an animal" (Shushu, 26). Suicide as protest or for the sake of personal integrity is the remotest idea from his deadened mind.

Through his testimonial narratives in the wake of the discredited Cultural Revolution, however, the uncle manages to turn his personal ignominy into noble political suffering. He now reconstructs his life in a fictional world, where "all past experiences can be amended, the beautiful and the sublime preserved, the ugly and the base completely eliminated, and the destroyed given a new life" (Shushu, 28). His desire to shed his former self provides the psychological motivation for his seminal story, in which a young rightist departs this dismal world by inhaling poisonous gas. Symbolically, "our uncle's new life began with the death of a young rightist" (Shushu, 29). Not surprisingly, the same need to forget a painful past, analyzes the narrator, lies behind the uncle's widely publicized divorce, although the public tends to believe that another woman is the direct cause. At this point, the narrator details the uncle's romantic adventures after he moves to the city as an intellectual celebrity. First, there are simultaneously an older woman he visits regularly for platonic consolation and a young one, about the age of his imaginary daughter, whom he summons for more physical satisfaction. Then, in an effort to convince himself of his unflagging vitality, he sets out to conquer even younger women, easily winning them over with his paternal charm and rich experience. One inevitable exception, the narrator infers, occurs when the uncle visits Germany with a delegation of Chinese writers and mistakenly concludes that his attractive blonde interpreter must welcome his amorous groping.

The blunt slap on the face that the uncle receives from the German woman, as the narrator continually reminds us, is mandated by his logical inference. He has to rely on conjectures and reasonings in order to lead his story to its known ending, which is the uncle's final insight into his own unhappy fate. This reconstruction, therefore, becomes an opportunity that allows the narrator to compare and comment on two succeeding generations of writers. The term *generation* in the text now connotes undeniable cultural and psychological differentiations. While his analysis of the uncle's generation is penetrating but sympathetic, his assessment of his own generation conveys as much self-content as self-doubt. It is at this juncture that the narrator directly participates in the story and voices his ambivalence toward a contemporary world where either generation's self-image often turns into a burlesque.

The main distinction between these two generations of writers, summarizes the narrator, is that the older one already has its belief system in place when the normal course of life is derailed, whereas the younger generation encounters great social transformation before it has time to form any coherent ideals or worldviews. A constant source of anxiety for the uncle's generation, therefore, is whether to accept or reject a new idea or reality. Driven by the need for a systematic faith, this generation always seeks meaning and causality among things; with classical romanticism as its cultivated aesthetic sensibility, it is perpetually perplexed by the divergence between reason and emotion. "When [our uncle] lost one faith he had to look for another; when he accepted one principle of action he had to enthrone it as faith and then went on to witness yet another war for the same throne" (*Shushu*, 51). The younger generation, however, appears to have completely rid itself of any global romantic aspirations and possesses the prerequisites for playing pragmatic games, albeit under nihilistic pretenses.

> We grew up in an age of cultural desolation and then came into a most open time. One hundred years' worth of ideas, the most sophisticated as well as the crudest, from the end of the last century to the present, rushed in to swamp us overnight. What we ended up picking had much to do with our endowments and luck, but on the surface, we gave the impression of being innovative from day to day, always leading the newest trend of our time. . . .
>
> The latest philosophy urged us to believe in the significance of the moment, telling us that history is made up of instants and that every

instant is real. All we need do is enjoy to the fullest the pleasure and revelation of the moment. (*Shushu*, 29, 62)

These contrastive profiles bring into view two antithetical generations, and their difference is pointedly projected as one between an older, depth-obsessed modernist and a younger, postmodernized cosmopolitan. In neither case does the metafictional structure of *Our Uncle's Story* allow the narrator to invest a stable, positive value.[10] While the postmodernist playfulness pre-cludes any genuine passion or commitment, the grave modernist faith is re-vealed to be a compensatory myth. To adopt Julia Kristeva's characterization, the young generation misses an abyssal "winter of discontent," but the vain and all-too-human uncle can hardly resist the seduction of a shimmering postmodern "artifice of seeming" either. In a hurry to postmodernize him-self, the uncle rushes through two conceptual thresholds and plunges himself into the contemporary whirlwind, mistaking the shrinking of experience for new discoveries. "At first, fiction was for him an imaginary world in which our uncle could satisfy certain psychological needs of his; now it was reality that was transformed into a fictitious world, which supplied evidence and material for his novels." Inhabiting a real world that he took as a mere extension of his fiction, the uncle "no longer worried that an ordinary life could harm him and consequently showed greater than usual readiness to be vulgar" (*Shushu*, 48).

What undercuts this postmodern elusiveness and dismantles the artifice of seeming in *Our Uncle's Story* is the return of the repressed past, not neces-sarily through the memory of a redemptive mission but rather in the form of its unspeakable failure. Forgotten pain returns when Dabao, the uncle's frail and inarticulate son, shows up one day as an adult stranger and asks his father to find him an office job in the city. The father's resentment of his own past leads to an icy indifference, which quickly breeds a murderous hatred in the son. In the end, wielding a kitchen knife, Dabao steals into his father's bedroom, only to be overpowered by his outraged and stronger father. The father wins the battle, but sees in his opponent's despicable face a reflection of himself. In the pathetic weeping of the beaten, he cannot but hear his own life story bitterly recounted. "Overnight, our uncle's hair turned completely gray. He realized that he was not to be happy anymore" (*Shushu*, 75).

Thus, the uncle's victory is also his defeat. The final scene of the tragi-comedy of his life, which the young narrator and his associates appreciate as if it were directly from a Shakespearean play, restages his life as inescap-able suffering. He is now compelled to mourn the virtual death of his own son, whom he regards with a classical psychoanalytic ambivalence of love and hatred. Grief for the loss of a loved person or the loss of some abstraction, according to Freud, may be the cause for both mourning and melancholia.

"The loss of a love-object," furthermore, "constitutes an excellent opportunity for the ambivalence in love-relationships to make itself felt and come to the fore." A Freudian explanation of melancholia depicts a mental economy wherein "countless single conflicts in which love and hate wrestle together are fought for the object."[11] The loss of his child is precisely such a traumatic experience that foregrounds the uncle's ambivalence toward the failure of his life, which becomes the origin of his sorrow and his melancholy grasp of truth. The same ambivalence also affects the narrator, who, through an "extremely personal incident," comes to the same revelation as the uncle in his grander drama. The failure of history, as the narrator now realizes, is ultimately a failure of human will, because enormous pain comes from living in historical truth. It is this revelation that puts in critical perspective his own postmodernist predilections: "We always seek depth and detest shallowness, and yet we have no courage to live a deep life. A deep life is too serious and too momentous for us; we simply cannot stand it" (Shushu, 77).

3. "The same sharp sorrow suddenly arose from the vast ocean"

To draw a not entirely improbable comparison, Our Uncle's Story, in Wang Anyi's literary imagination, may occupy the same position as The Origin of the German Play of Mourning does in Walter Benjamin's historical thinking. In his study of the seventeenth-century baroque Trauerspiel as a historical structure of feeling, Benjamin develops his messianic hermeneutics and asserts that a theory of Trauer can only be secured "in the description of the world which emerges under the gaze of the melancholic."[12] By reconstructing this mournful gaze, in the words of Max Pensky, Benjamin delineates a "melancholy subjectivity" that dialectically unifies insight and despair and thrives on a symbiotic connection between a contemplative subject and the desacralized world of objects.[13] Central to this form of critical subjectivity is the resurrected notion of heroic melancholy, to which I will return at the end of this essay. With the completion of Our Uncle's Story, Wang Anyi seems to have discovered a passage to historical depth by way of sadness or melancholy. The unhappy tales that have ensued are intensely subjective and are often centered on intriguing anamnestic images. If Our Uncle's Story offers a self-conscious narrative of the origin of her melancholy writing, in her 1993 novella Sadness for the Pacific, Wang Anyi gives a global expression to melancholy subjectivity through revisiting a family history of sadness.

Not so much a story about the genesis of melancholia, Sadness for the Pacific is instead an emotional exploration, set against a contemporary landscape of postmodernity, of the melancholy truth of the passion incited by modernity. It has the structure of retracing a family tree over time and space, and the first-person narrator, who now seeks to empathize with her ancestors, participates in the narrative by projecting a subjective mood of sorrow over past events and retrieved memories. Nostalgia, as both the motivation for, and the mode of, historical remembrance, grips the narrator, and her journey into the past becomes an encounter with varying degrees and occasions of the same lament and mourning. The melancholy mood, as Kristeva would say, is inscribed here as the originary language, as the modality of significance that precedes any meaningful articulation. In the text, this melancholy is specifically associated with a contemplating individual who is stricken by the sublime eternity of a vast ocean.

At the beginning of the story, we find the narrator aboard a ship in the sun-scorched Strait of Malacca on her way to the Malaysian island city of Binang. This ancient passageway brings to her mind the adventures of Zheng He, the Chinese navigator of the fifteenth century who sailed the same reflecting waters; the surrounding tropical geography excites in her no small curiosity, either, with its exotic names suggesting a strange mixture of exuberance and desolation. This initial free association already sets up the structure of the narrative as one of a contemporary traveler's looking for signs of historical depth and relevance. As her destination emerges from the distant horizon, she suddenly realizes that her father must have had the same view half a century ago, when he and his theater group were approaching Binang. Such an imaginary identification with her father transfers the narrator back to the past and enlivens that earlier moment with a tangible immediacy. With the apparition of her father as a young boy over the Pacific Ocean, the narrator enters a space of spectrality in which the past as ghost always returns for a revelatory first time.[14]

> Back then, my father was nineteen years old, obsessed with theater and national salvation. He had followed the opera troupe from Singapore, traveled across the Malay Peninsula, and was going to Binang as the final stop. All the way, the group sang songs dedicated to the cause of fighting the Japanese. It was also the mid-summer season of southern monsoons, and the tropical sun had tanned my father dark as coal. A sunburned teenager in short pants appeared in my view. With his appearance, a sharp sorrow unexpectedly arose from inside me. The same sharp sorrow suddenly arose from the vast ocean, expanding and penetrating. Even the sun turned into a source of excruciating pain.[15]

This visceral experience of sadness in the middle of a timeless ocean strikes a keynote, and the rest of the narrative flows as if in an unstoppable search for the connection between this intense sorrow and the vivid image of an inspired teenage boy, who, as "my father," stands for an ineluctable destiny. Encoded in the anamnestic image is also the narrator's origin and sense of belonging, which she now must know. In order to fully account for this image and its inexplicable, but enveloping, melancholy, the narrator will have to relive time and space as lived by the bygone generations of her family. This root-seeking search will lead her southward through the Pacific as she retraces her fore-fathers' footsteps over Southeast Asia and through Singapore's gradual emergence as an independent modern nation. In the end, a melancholy perspective on the rootlessness of humanity on a global scale takes hold. The solidity of dry land dissolves, and the ocean asserts itself as the ultimate background and limit to human existence: "A world map shows us that even continents are drifting islands. . . . The ocean may well be the last home for humanity, the dead end of human migration. Herein lies all the sadness for the Pacific" (*Shangxin*, 383).

The hypertrophy of melancholy subjectivity in *Sadness for the Pacific* is most striking when we compare this 1993 narrative with Wang Anyi's 1985 short story "My Origins." The earlier account is also given from the perspective of a first-person narrator (whose name is Wang Anyi, no less), but in a markedly realistic style, and is broken into two separate components: The first is about her search for her mother's old Hangzhou home; the second focuses on her father's family overseas, mostly on the amused observations of her cousin, who is visiting from Singapore in the early 1980s.[16] This second part records many significant details that will reappear in the later, longer story: for example, the colorful confetti at the outset of the father's voyage to mainland China when he was twenty-one, and his not knowing how to use a blanket efficiently on arriving in a chilly Shanghai. However, no clear picture of either family emerges; the best that the confused narrator can visualize about her great-grandmother is a tiny boat drifting into the misty ocean. Everything about that ancient Fujianese woman "was too unspeakably vague, remote, and strange for me to feel related to it," sighs the narrator. More news about her relatives across the ocean started coming in later, "but because of the barrier of language and the lapse of time, or for other reasons, I always felt alienated from them. As a result, I was convinced I had a muddled origin."[17] Nonetheless, she regards herself as Chinese as everyone else around her, although the question of her true historical origin remains, especially after her Singaporean cousin sends over a photograph of the tomb where her grandparents and great-grandmother are buried. This question proved to be so haunting in reality that Wang Anyi felt compelled to confront it again in a two-part book with the scientific-sounding title *Patrilineal and Matrilineal Myths*, in which *Sadness for the Pacific* constitutes the first, patrilineal part.[18]

The pathos of the 1993 "patrilineal myth" seems to have drawn on two narrative modes that best define Chinese literature of the 1980s. One is the earlier and widely influential movement of cultural root seeking, which helped establish an anthropological concept of tradition and naturalistic vitality as critical antidotes to turbulent state politics as well as to the ills of modernization. The other development, loosely called either experimental, or even avant-garde, is one in which writers such as Mo Yan and Su Tong, by pursuing family genealogy as a personal and often redemptive project, push further the same intellectual and emotional concern with historical representation that underlies root-seeking literature. To these literary movements Wang Anyi has been an attentive and contributing contemporary.[19] In *Our Uncle's Story*, the narrator makes a point of presenting the root-seeking movement as an intellectual watershed between the uncle's generation and that of younger, more cosmopolitan writers (*Shushu*, 38–39). On another occasion, Wang Anyi singles out Su Tong's novella *Nineteen Thirty-Four Escapes* (1988) as a pivotal text in the experiment of fictionalizing family genealogy. The title alone is fascinating enough, she writes, for the word *escapes* already evokes a concrete mode of existence and suggests a perennial human condition of fleeing flood, war, and famine.[20] This fascination with desperate flight leads Wang Anyi to rediscover her family genealogy in light of the turn-of-the-century Chinese diaspora over the South Pacific. A broadened cultural geography in her narrative consequently helps reveal the historicity of such formations as the nation-state and national identity.

In *Sadness for the Pacific*, however, it is the stark discrepancy, from a contemporary perspective, between this perennial human restlessness and individual heroic efforts that seizes the narrator and engulfs her in a global melancholy. A woeful sense of loss and inconsequentiality, if not outright futility, now filters her vision of the youthful enthusiasm of her father's generation. At the same time, what renders her sorrow so visceral and unappeasable is an anxiety over the absence of comparable passion in her own life and the bustling world she inhabits. To compensate for the perceived lack, the narrating subject indulges in intense nostalgia, which, by widening the gap between a vividly remembered past world and an increasingly standardized present life, serves to defamiliarize the present as having failed its own historical potential. Such is the dialectical structure of the discourse of melancholy, which underlies the narrator's awestruck gaze at her father's specter on the Pacific Ocean and her prolonged stay in front of her ancestors' grave, now overgrown by robust tropical vegetation.

Moved by the imagined scene from her father's idealistic youth, the narrator looks back at herself and realizes that in her origins, "there were actually traces of the tropics" (*Shangxin*, 306). Now finding herself in Singapore for the first time at age thirty-seven, she discovers that a tropical island demonstrates its history through a changing human physiognomy. There, old people, wearing the grave expression of a tightly knit frown, all appear dark, angular, and achingly doleful. "Young people, however, have grown paler thanks to the incubation of modern air-conditioning. They no longer bear a regional distinction in their facial features and instead appear increasingly internationalized" (*Shangxin*, 306). Walking down the quiet side streets in Chinatown, the narrator sees in every old person the shadow of her own wearied and sorrow-laden grandparents. Although their pictures have always been in the family photo album, she never really recognizes them until she visits their grave, which is the first thing she does after arriving in Singapore. On approaching the cemetery, she feels her growing grief being compounded by the brutal heat. "An endless sorrow welled up inside me, and I wondered, how could the dead rest in peace in such sweltering heat?" (*Shangxin*, 306). Etched in the tombstone is a picture of her grandparents, looking as plaintive as ever. She also finds her own name engraved in the stone. "Not until then did I realize the fateful connection between myself and the old couple permanently asleep underneath the ground. I felt a deep pain for them, one that bound our hearts and bodies together" (*Shangxin*, 307).

Later, the narrator will observe that in her search for family roots in this "cosmopolitan nation-state" (*Shangxin*, 330) that too quickly buries its past, she reaps only two things: the oppressive heat and a deep sorrow. The clean and orderly city streets offer no consolation, nor do the impressive high-rises. The constant tropical temperature allows her to relate to her grandparents and to fathom what they must have endured when they, as first-generation immigrants, fought various hardships and each other in their struggle to settle in the new land. It also lends itself to a textured background against which the narrator can picture her father's unhappy childhood. In days dominated by the same tropical heat, a reticent, sunburned child would watch the ocean all by himself, nurturing his first fantasies about the mainland. "A sad child gazing into the sea: This was a melancholy, heartbreaking picture" (*Shangxin*, 316).

Nonetheless, her father is now recalled as a most representative modern youth. Born a full century after the British East India Company merchant Sir Stamford Raffles first landed in Singapore in 1819, as the narrator continues to infer from the historical context, her father comes of age in a time still charged by the revolutionary ethos of May Fourth literature. As an impressionable boy, he must have paid homage to Yu Dafu, the outspoken sufferer of modern romantic melancholy, who came to Singapore in 1940 and excited the imaginations of many an aspiring literary youth.[21] Based on an imaginary meeting between her father and Yu Dafu, the narrator goes on to portray a young generation of ethnic Chinese who, influenced by May Fourth liberal humanism, consciously practiced a modern way of living, longed for the mainland as their spiritual homeland, and readily identified with the cause of national salvation during the Japanese invasion of China. What the narrator reassembles, from the unfamiliar tropical landscape, is the same central bildungsroman of the generation of Chinese who, as the spiritual offspring of the May Fourth era, turned into the revolutionaries of the 1940s. It has the universal modern plot of an individual actively seeking to participate in a greater national historical enterprise. Her father's passionate longing for the mainland is first expressed as the indefatigable enthusiasm with which he joins the Malay Chinese theater troupe and its tour of the peninsula to promote the cause of the Resistance. Eventually, it will lead him to Shanghai and, after many self-doubts and trepidations, to the Communist base in southern Jiangsu. By then, he has consciously overcome his initial uneasiness with a crude communal life and matures into a "true soldier" (*Shangxin*, 371). He welcomes and enjoys the trip to the barren hinterland as a peaceful return to the warm interior of a maternal body.

At the same moment her father penetrates the mainland and claims his Chinese identity, her second uncle and his comrades are mobilizing to defend Singapore against the Japanese, who cross the Johor Strait on 8 February 1942. Such striking synchronicity of two distinct moments is the narrator's basic compositional strategy, by means of which she manages to include numerous historical figures, events, anecdotes, and legends as integral to her family history. From British colonialism to Lee Kuan-yew's successful rule in postcolonial Singapore, from the modern rubber industry to the worldwide Great Depression, from the course of World War II to the Comintern's determination to prevent the Japanese from attacking the Soviet Union, her multifocal narrative explores the tension between textbook knowledge on the one hand and concrete images and personal stories on the other. The ever deepening gap between a conceptual history and anamnestic concentrations makes unavoidable the question of historical failure and success, which proves to be a determining question for a melancholy subjectivity.

Of all the characters and family members, Second Uncle is portrayed with the greatest love and empathy. While Father deserts his parents to devote his life to drama and revolution, First Uncle is an avid gambler, who in his old age turns out to be a good citizen of contemporary Singapore, with the pride of "a well-mannered child brought up by Lee Kuan-yew" (*Shangxin*, 378). Unlike his two older, self-absorbed brothers, the youngest brother, Second Uncle, "an unusually tender and kind boy" (*Shangxin*, 331), is much more grounded, sensitive, and compassionate toward the people around him. He may share a similar abstract longing for the mainland, but he never leaves Singapore to pursue another path to self-realization. The narrator imagines his body to be slender and nimble, almost effeminate, and his soul to be that of a resolute hero. He quietly joins the Resistance during the war and, at age eighteen, is tortured to death by the Japanese police. After his death, "his soul soared into the sky and looked down. Only then did he find his island so gorgeously green that it made his heart ache. Floating in its radiant translucence, the island drifted with the ocean waves. At this he broke into tears" (*Shangxin*, 383). Both Father and Second Uncle, in contrast to Lee Kuan-yew, the most prominent Singaporean of the same generation, are "hot-blooded and passionate" young men, and both are vulnerable to a "drifting sensation" that is inseparable from their life on a small island (*Shangxin*, 333, 334). Father, in the end, returns to the mainland to escape that anxiety over rootlessness and successfully integrates himself into the maternal body of collective history. The pragmatic Lee Kuan-yew, with no idealistic pretensions, institutes a postcolonial order and helps "produce a new people" (*Shangxin*, 377) on the island for the modern world. Almost paradoxically, as the narrator comments, "the day when Singapore finally gained independence was also the moment when my father was exiled for real" (*Shangxin*, 378). For as a romantic revolutionary and determined expatriate, Father can no longer claim any affinity to his rapidly modernizing country of birth.

Such personalized perspectives give the narrator a chance to ponder the implications of a Singaporean-style prosperity. Ambivalence once again surfaces when she realizes that the stern rationalization necessary for Lee Kuan-yew's success, which seems to underline the contemporary horizon of expectation, has little room for her father's idealistic passion and aspirations.[22] Keenly aware of a cityscape shaped by global capital and culture, she finds herself haunted by thoughts of Second Uncle, whose untimely death creates a permanent lack and source of sadness for generations in the family. His memory, just like the granite war memorial, casts a gray, melancholy shadow over the present routine and insists on outlining history as a sorry experience of fragments and incompleteness. By inserting itself to prevent the present from coalescing into a seamless contemporaneity, this shadow comes alive as a haunting spirit that embodies other visions.

> The war memorial was a building endowed with the richest sentiment in this cosmopolitan nation-state. It projected a gentle and sorrowful shadow in front of us; it was the one consolation that I could find on this island, offering solace for the sadness that Second Uncle caused my grandparents. I left the war memorial and walked toward the bustling and colorful Bugis Street. Underneath my footsteps was a city street that was built over the ruins of the past two hundred years. The sun was shining. Who knows how many shadows and images were flying in the luminous sunlight, crisscrossing, up and down, and through my body and

soul. All I could do was to approach and try to comfort my second uncle in the formless and weightless air. This caused such a bone-crushing ache! (*Shangxin*, 330)

4. *"Les Mélancolies historiques, les sympathies à travers siècles"*

In *Sadness for the Pacific*, the narrator's immense sorrow over a past moment that is at once intimate and yet unapproachable, in the end, stems from a simultaneous longing for, and fear of, the genuine passion that she witnesses in the youth of her father and Second Uncle. This conflict translates into a deep historical ambivalence, which, expressed in the form of melancholy subjectivity, is in fact a complex response to another mass reaction to utopian visions. Her melancholy occurs at a moment when the modern project of collectively determining human destiny seems to be universally disavowed and when capital claims a global hegemony. Yet, "haunting belongs to the structure of every hegemony."[23] Amid the spreading postmodern euphoria, melancholy alone reveals negativity as indispensable to dialectical truth. When the high tide of entrepreneurial individualism rises across the land to sweep away egalitarian conformity, so reflects Wang Anyi in 1993, there ought to be solitary souls whose reaction is more contemplative than instinctive or spontaneous. Now is the time for writers to understand that "the independence we so desperately fought for does not entirely consist in happiness. Suffering is its essence."[24]

It may be helpful to recall that we began our discussion of Wang Anyi's writing of melancholy by way of Kristeva's description of the ravaging effect of melancholia. To the crushing experience of melancholic depression, writes Kristeva, "I owe a supreme, metaphysical lucidity. . . . My pain is the hidden side of my philosophy, its mute sister" (BS, 3–4). What Kristeva goes on to state in semiotic terms, along with her feminist concerns, is largely the European Renaissance concept of a "heroic melancholy," which views the moody temperament as a blessed curse, a humoral source of insight and creativity.[25] A consistent fascination accompanies the symptomatology of melancholia and depression from Hippocratic times to the twentieth century, although each historical age has offered a different etiology. Throughout the centuries, especially in the wake of great social upheaval, continual heroic encounters with melancholia have generated different legends, memories, and images.[26] More often than not, the melancholy figure emerges as the mournful and profound, bitter but compassionate individual endowed with an artist's sensitivity and imagination. For with the onset of melancholia, not unlike in the liminal experience of madness, insight and darkness are fused together, and the afflicted individual gains access to the ultimate truth only to compound his or her incapacitating sadness and pain. This brings about such an intensely private suffering that any effort to ease it through externalization is bound to result in ever greater despair. Hence the "abyss of sorrow," the "noncommunicable grief" that constitutes Kristeva's melancholia.

The ideal of *melancolia illa heroica* proved instrumental to Walter Benjamin in his study of the baroque *Trauerspiel*. Later, in Baudelaire, he would again find its perfect embodiment for Europe's modernizing nineteenth century. Through its heroic form, as Max Pensky points out when explicating Benjamin's "melancholy dialectics," the discourse of melancholy secures "the truest and most powerful historical image of its dialectical structure." [27] If such a discourse yields a dialectic of the emotive and the cognitive, heroic melancholy then strives to elevate this affective experience to a new form of subjectivity, albeit a precarious one. What helps keep this heightened subjectivity grounded and expressive, consequently, is bound to be melancholy as content rather than as form. Underneath Duras's inconsolable grief, explains Kristeva, lies the modern, silencing "malady of death" violently exposed by Auschwitz and Hiroshima, which now "informs our most concealed inner recesses" (BS, 221). Similarly, at the heart of Baudelaire's poetic rage lies the very inability to experience. The lyrical poet in the age of commodity capitalism, in the words of Benjamin, holds in his hands only "the scattered fragments of genuine historical experience. . . . To his horror, the melancholy man sees the earth revert to a mere state of nature. No breath of prehistory surrounds it: there is no aura." [28] It is this loss of aura, just as it is the loss of voice in the case of Duras, that dialectically marks Baudelaire's melancholy vision with historical specificity.

Historical melancholy, as I have tried to show here, is the origin and content of Wang Anyi's recent tales of sorrow. It expresses the profound ambivalence that the writer, conscious of the approaching end of a century, sustains toward the course of twentieth-century Chinese history, in particular its human dimension. Utopian longings, generated by grand historical visions that are brought into focus at moments of collective action, inevitably turn into traumatic experiences for the individual, but the rapid dissipation of idealistic passion in a postrevolutionary contemporary world also seems vastly depressing. The loss of genuine excitement, therefore, becomes the historical moment in which Wang Anyi, through a discourse of melancholy, examines the dialectics of success and failure. This structure of feeling generates the central plot of her late genealogical "myths": a melancholic individual in the contemporary world trying to recall and reconcile herself with historical failures as human triumphs.

For this reason, my claim that Wang Anyi's recent fiction articulates a "postmodern melancholy" does not mean that melancholy itself becomes a postmodernist sentiment. Rather, it acknowledges the postmodern condition that Wang Anyi's melancholic writings critically reveal and even interrupt. We may even conclude that her melancholy, in which the longing for a modern longing causes the deepest sorrow and ambivalence, gathers its historical content and relevance only in an age that deems itself "post" and beyond all ideologies of the modern. In other words, Wang Anyi's postmodern melancholy may be read as a critique of a transnational postmodernism that, in the words of Ross Chambers, is nonmelancholic, "a kind of modernism without its pathos of lack." [29] Melancholy against the grain: This may explain why in contemporary Chinese literature there is an increasingly pronounced mood of sorrow, particularly among a new generation of women writers.[30] This latest development raises complicated issues of gender, aesthetics, and subjectivity that ought to be engaged at greater length. It also adds renewed urgency to a famous question, posed by Gustave Flaubert in 1853, about historical necessity: "Whence come these fits of historical melancholia, these affinities from century to century, etc.?" [31] To begin answering this inquiry, we will have to enter the mournful and searching gaze that a melancholic directs at the world.

Notes

All translations are mine. In this essay, I have referred to Wang Anyi's recent works by their English titles, even though all of these works have been published in Chinese and, with the exception of the stories in *Baotown* (1986), do not yet have English translations.

1 Julia Kristeva, *Black Sun: Depression and Melancholia*, trans. Leon S. Roudiez (New York: Columbia University Press, 1989), 258–59. Hereafter, this work is cited parenthetically as BS.

2 For a discussion of the changing implications of these related terms, see Jennifer Radden, "Melancholy and Melancholia," in *Pathologies of the Modern Self: Postmodern Studies on Narcissism, Schizophrenia, and Depression*, ed. David Michael Levin (New York: New York University Press, 1987), 231–50.

3 Wang Anyi, *Shushu de gushi* (Our uncle's story), in *Xianggang de qing yu ai* (Love and sentiment in Hong Kong) (Beijing: Zuojia Chubanshe, 1996), 1–2. Hereafter, this work is cited parenthetically as *Shushu*.

4 See the comments made by Zhang Xinying and Gao Yuanbao in Chen Sihe, Wang Anyi, Gao Yuanbao, Zhang Xinying, and Yan Feng, "Dangjin wenxue chuangzuo zhong de 'qing' yu 'zhong'—wenxue duihua lu" (The "light" and "heavy" in contemporary literary works: Dialogues on literature), *Dangdai zuojia pinglun* (Review of contemporary writers) 5 (1993): 14–23, esp. 17–18.

5 Li Jiefei, "Wang Anyi de xin shenhua—yige lilun tantao" (Wang Anyi's new mythology: A theoretical investigation), *Dangdai zuojia pinglun* 5 (1993): 4–8.

6 See, for example, the stories *"Wenge" yishi* (Anecdotes from the "cultural revolution") and *Beitong zhi di* (The land of sorrow), in Wang, *Xianggang de qing yu ai*, 425–501, 124–59.

7 See Wang Anyi, "Wutuobang shipian" (The utopian chapters), in Wang, *Xianggang de qing yu ai*, 257–304.

8   See my discussion of this story, "Xianggang de qing yu ai" (Love and sentiment in Hong Kong), in "New Urban Culture and the Anxiety of Everyday Life in Contemporary China," in *In Pursuit of Contemporary East Asian Culture*, ed. Xiaobing Tang and Stephen Snyder (Boulder, Colo.: Westview Press, 1996), 107–22. The story appears in Wang, *Xianggang de qing yu ai*, 502–77.

9   According to Linda Hutcheon, the theoretician of postmodern poetics, parody is a central trope of postmodern fiction and art, because, "through a double process of installing and ironizing, parody signals how present representations come from past ones and what ideological consequences derive from both continuity and difference." See *The Politics of Postmodernism* (London: Routledge, 1989), 93–117.

10 This absence of positive terms, a necessary condition for signification, according to Saussurian structural linguistics, apparently causes discomfort in one commentator, who complains that the novella fails to provide a positive, uplifting attitude toward life. See Yan Shu, " 'Shushu' de kunhe—tan 'shushu de gushi' " (The confusion of "our uncle": On *Our Uncle's Story*), *Zuoping yu zhengming* (Works and controversies) 128 (Aug. 1991): 79–80.

11 Sigmund Freud, "Mourning and Melancholia," *Collected Papers*, vol. 4 (New York: Basic Books, 1959), 161, 168.

12 Walter Benjamin, *The Origin of the German Play of Mourning*, quoted in Max Pensky, *Melancholy Dialectics: Walter Benjamin and the Play of Mourning* (Amherst: University of Massachusetts Press, 1993), 90.

13 Pensky, *Melancholy Dialectics*, 107; see chap. 2, "Trauerspiel and Melancholy Subjectivity," 60–107.

14 The notion of the specter as "repetition *and* first time" comes from Jacques Derrida, *Specters of Marx: The State of the Debt, the Work of Mourning, and the New International*, trans. Peggy Kamuf (New York: Routledge, 1994), which, among other things, offers a complex discussion of the relationship between spectrality and mourning, and is profoundly pertinent to the investigation of contemporary melancholy.

15 Wang Anyi, *Shangxin Taipingyang* (Sadness for the Pacific), in Wang, *Xianggang de qing yu ai*, 306. I translate *shangtong* as "sharp sorrow." The Chinese conveys both a physical sensation and a mental state, evoking what Freud once described as *Schmerz-unlust* in his essay "Mourning and Melancholia." Hereafter, this work is cited parenthetically as *Shangxin*.

16 Wang Anyi, "Wo de laili" (My origins), in *Xiao Baozhuang* (Baotown) (Shanghai: Shanghai Wenyi Chubanshe, 1986), 100–30. Wang Anyi has another loving portrait of her father in the essay "Huashuo fuqin Wang Xiaoping" (About my father Wang Xiaoping), in *Pugongying* (Dandelions) (Shanghai: Shanghai Wenyi Chubanshe, 1988), 78–86.

17 Wang, "Wo de laili," 121–22.

18 See Wang Anyi, *Fuxi yu muxi de shenhua* (Patrilineal and matrilineal myths) (Hangzhou: Zhejiang Wenyi Chubanshe, 1994). Both parts of this book, *Sadness for the Pacific* and *Jishi yu xugou* (Records and fictions), were first published separately in the journal *Shouhuo* (Harvest) in 1993. An unabridged version of *Records and Fictions* was also published as an independent novel in 1993 (see note 20).

19 Wang's 1985 story "Baotown," for example, is often regarded as a representative work in the mode of critical root seeking. See "Xiao Baozhuang" (Baotown), in Wang, *Xiao Baozhuang*, 243–339. An English translation of this story is available in Wang Anyi, *Baotown*, trans. Martha Avery (New York: Penguin, 1989).

20 See Wang Anyi, *Jishi yu xugou—chuangzao shijie fangfa zhi yizhong* (Records and fictions: One method of creating the world) (Beijing: Renmin Wenxue Chubanshe, 1993), 413. Chapter 9 (367–413) of this obviously autobiographical novel may be read as a self-analysis

of Wang Anyi's literary career. An English translation of Su Tong's novella *Yijiusansi nian de taowang* is available in Su Tong, *Raise the Red Lantern*, trans. Michael Duke (New York: William Morrow, 1993), 101–78.

21   Here is one instance, out of several in the text, where the need for melancholy imagination is satisfied at the expense of historical accuracy. The narrative suggests that his meeting with Yu Dafu inspired the father to join the opera troupe in 1938, but in fact, Yu Dafu did not arrive in Singapore until 1940. See *Shangxin*, 317–18.

22   In this light, Wang Anyi's text can be read as a complex response to the growing desire among Chinese theoreticians as well as policymakers to emulate the Singapore model of modernization, which is promoted as an effective combination of the Confucian tradition and modern Western technology, although it is also obvious that Singapore does not enter the story because of an established analysis on the writer's part. To grasp the global concern of the narrative fully, we need to accept that Singapore, as part of the postmodern transnational landscape, signifies modernity at large.

23   Derrida, *Specters of Marx*, 37.

24   Wang Anyi, "Kexi bushi nongchaoren" (Sorry, but we are not surfers), *Dangdai zuojia pinglun* 5 (1993): 27–28.

25   This notion was most concentratedly developed by Marsilio Ficino (1433–1499), a Florentine humanist, who in turn took the idea from the Greek text *Problemata Physica* (attributed to Aristotle). See Stanley W. Jackson, *Melancholia and Depression: From Hippocratic Times to Modern Times* (New Haven, Conn.: Yale University Press, 1986), 100–101.

26   See Jackson, *Melancholia and Depression*, 29–246.

27   Pensky, *Melancholy Dialectics*, 32.

28   Walter Benjamin, "On Some Motifs in Baudelaire," in *Illuminations*, trans. Harry Zohn (New York: Schocken Books, 1968), 183–84.

29   See Ross Chambers, *The Writing of Melancholy: Modes of Opposition in Early French Modernism*, trans. Mary Seidman Trouille (Chicago: University of Chicago Press, 1993), 208.

30   For instance, see the following recent essays: Xie Youshun, "Youshang er bu juewang de xiezuo—wo du Chi Zijian de xiaoshuo" (A writing that is melancholy but not despairing: My reading of Chi Zijian's fiction), *Dangdai zuojia pinglun* 1 (1996): 66–71; and Meng Fanhua, "Youyu de huangyuan: Nüxing piaopo de xinlu mishi—Chen Ran xiaoshuo de yizhong jiedu" (Melancholy wilderness—the psychological history of female homelessness: An interpretation of Chen Ran's fiction), *Dangdai zuojia pinglun* 3 (1996): 57–62.

31   Quoted in Chambers, *The Writing of Melancholy*, vii.

16   Whence and Whither the Postmodern/Post–Mao-Deng:
Historical Subjectivity and Literary Subjectivity
in Modern China

If, for Chinese intellectuals, to be modern means to emulate (materially) advanced and/or (spiritually) progressive civilizations (either communism or
capitalism), the concept of modernity in twentieth-century Chinese literature
is naturally related to the intellectual concern for such issues as enlightenment, individual/national emancipation, and historical progress. Since the
beginning of this century, the paradigm of modern Chinese literature has
been saturated with the idea of History, which postulates a teleological order
of linear progress, a homogeneous, predestined temporality. Historical telos
became the primary idea, appealing strongly to Chinese intellectuals, who
were obsessed with the revival of the declining nation. C. T. Hsia's famous
characterization of modern Chinese fiction as an "obsession with China"
could well be rephrased more specifically as "obsession with the redemption
of China." The "major" modern Chinese writers are usually those who identify themselves with the imaginary Historical Subject by placing themselves
in a superior position from which History can be envisioned via totalistic representation.

Modernity, Emancipation, and Subjectivity

Liang Qichao's proposal at the beginning of the century to "first renovate [the nation's] fiction" in order to "renovate the people of a nation"[1] presaged what would become the dominant standard of modern Chinese literature for the following eight decades: its practical function. It is surprising today to realize that the literary ideas of writers from disparate factions (Guo Moruo, Mao Dun, or Xu Zhimo, for example) are all associated with social (r)evolution and as such not so distant from one another.[2] Lu Xun, in his famous autobiographical essay "Nahan Zixu" [Preface to Call to Arms], explains that he embarked on a literary career because he was convinced that literature is essential to the change of the national character. In a later article he writes, "As for why I wrote fiction, I still uphold the principle of 'enlightenment' that I did more than a decade ago. I think it must 'serve life' and furthermore reform life. . . . Thus my subjects were often taken from the unfortunate people in this sick society; my aim was to expose the disease so as to draw attention to its cure."[3] Anyone familiar with the canonical works of modern Chinese literature would have the impression that their ultimate aim is to transmit the meaning constructed by the authorial subject.[4] Transcendental subjectivity is embraced, consciously or unconsciously, according to the Enlightenment discourse that sanctions the maximum power of humans in their endeavor to achieve knowledge and emancipation. (Theoretically, this self-sufficient subjectivism is derived from Descartes, whom Hegel hails "as the Christopher Columbus of the philosophical modernity.")[5]

The Enlightenment motif that haunted the intellectuals and writers in the May Fourth period is part of this modern discourse of *emancipation*. Naturally, it quickly develops into other themes such as social (r)evolution, national salvation, and liberation of the lower classes. In any case, the intellectual subject has full responsibility for responding to the historical imperative by distributing grand historical messages with representational subjectivism. In other words, the historical subject must be realized in the formation of the representational subject. Historical subjectivity and representational subjectivity are the two major aspects of the discourse of Chinese modernity.

The paradigm of modern Chinese literature can be viewed as an effort to provide a transparent picture from which the reader can easily perceive, if not comprehend, the intended meaning. Such a literature is, manifestly or covertly, *liable to narratorial intervention or manipulation*.[6] The author occupies a historically sovereign position so as to formulate a redemptory or emancipatory subject, which arranges the homogeneous order of the (hi)story.

Such a superior subject appeared in the May Fourth era, in many cases, as an intellectual voice to transcend reality. In Lu Xun's "Zhufu" (New year's sacrifice), for example, the position of Xianglin's wife as a lower-class, secondary-gender object of observation (and hopefully, of redemption) is highlighted in a narratorial description that reveals her misery: "Her shallow, dark-tinged face that looked as if it had been carved out of wood was fearfully wasted and had lost the grief-stricken expression it had borne before."[7] This is a picture that calls not merely for pity but, more significantly, for a desire to deliver the pitiable from that state by the self-elevated historical subject.

Has Lu Xun presented a self-critical or self-suspicious subject? The intellectual "I" in Lu Xun's "New Year's Sacrifice" has been viewed as a self-critical or self-skeptical subject who is unable to redeem the lower-class woman (Xianglin's wife) from distress and misfortune. Marston Anderson has astutely noted that Lu Xun exposes the protagonist's "intellectual poverty and, more profoundly, his moral cowardice."[8] On the other hand, such an impotent historical subject (the role played by the character "I") is also what the confident narratorial subject attempts to critique and negate by establishing a critical distance between them. The reader would not miss the narratorial voice that repeatedly characterizes the "I's" responses to Xianglin's wife with such words as "falteringly" or "faltered," and describes the feeling of the "I" with such phrases as "preying on my mind," "taking fright," "feeling thoroughly disconcerted," or "remained uneasy."[9] By representing an inferior or unsuccessful historical subject, by distancing himself not only from the character to be redeemed but also from the character who fails to perform redemption (the "I"), the authorial/narratorial subject secures its *own* status as *the* modern historical subject. In other words, although the intellectual "I" in the story fails to function as a historical subject, Lu Xun establishes another narratorial voice that formulates a transcendental subject elevated from all the imperfect, "premodern" historical roles. The self-critical perspective ultimately yields to another arbitrary voice.

The arbitrary and tendentious narrative subjectivity that constructs national/historical modernity is not only a literary/aesthetic phenomenon but also a sociopolitical one. In terms of discourse, the modern modes of both literary and political representations were intended to map out a distinct and definite historical scenario. The interdependence between literature and politics is one of the most distinctive characteristics in contemporary China. Maoism, in particular, relies on a literary/aesthetic subjectivity. The function of Maoist discourse lies in its aesthetic magic, which absolutizes the grand narrative by enforcing a subjectively established significative construction. The same mode of narration—telling instead of showing—in Mao's writings is another example of the power of representational subjectivity in modern Chinese literature in establishing the historical subject. In his article "In Memory of Norman Bethune," Mao, despite the fact that he and "Comrade

Bethune . . . met only once," confidently characterizes Bethune's personality in highly subjective approving terms: "his utter devotion to others without any thought of self," "his great sense of responsibility in his work and his great warm-heartedness towards all comrades and the people," "true communist spirit," "the spirit of absolute selflessness," etc.[10] Before the reader is able to decide whether one can be "without *any* thought of self," whether there is such thing as "absolute selflessness," or what the "*true* communist spirit" really is, the representational signification has been positively prescribed without any latitude for hesitation or suspicion, even though the significative link may well be fictitious and illusory.

In those literary passages, Mao's narrative mode evidently corresponds to the canonical paradigm of representation in modern Chinese literature. In "Yugong yishan" (The foolish old man who removed mountains), another of his "three primal articles," Mao retells a parable from *Lie Zi* and ends with his conclusion: "Having refuted the Wise Old Man's wrong view, he went on digging every day, unshaken in his conviction."[11] In the original text of *Lie Zi*, the authorial tendency in the description of this event is reduced to a minimum: "Mister Simple of North Mountain [i.e., the Foolish Old Man] breathed a long sigh. . . . Old Wiseacre of River Bend [i.e., the Wise Old Man] was at a loss for an answer."[12] In Mao, however, the objective narration is intruded on by such words as "refute," "wrong," "unshaken," each strongly imposing a subjective judgment upon what is being represented. This is the typical symptom of the discourse of modernity. In both cases, Mao attempts to establish a grand historical subject whose position he is supposed to occupy at the time.

To Mao, the Foolish Old Man, whom he has imbued with a heroically "unshaken" image as opposed to the "wrong," "refuted" Wise Old Man, symbolizes the historical power that Mao assumes himself to represent. Only by dichotomizing and absolutizing the characterization of the good/positive and the evil/negative can the representational subject of Maoist discourse outline an indisputable totality of history. Historical modernity must rely upon the accordingly totalizing and rationalizing mode of discourse, which is literary modernity (radically different from literary modernism) in twentieth-century China. Since the political Mao-Deng phenomenon is precisely the cultural and historical modern applied in the practical domain, it must ground itself on the literary modernity essentialized by the representational subject.

Such a representational mode culminates in the Cultural Revolution novel *Hongnan zuozhan shi* [The warring history of Hongnan] (1972), which demonstrates the paradigm of omniscient narration to the extent of making a fifteen-page, direct remark on the ideas and thoughts of the hero, Hong Leisheng. Such excessive subjectivity is certainly on the verge of collapse, since the superfluous comments on the authorial intentions, on the ideas expressed in the work, and even on how the work is being written, expose—though unwittingly—self-referentiality, which signals the crisis of representational subjectivity as well as the crisis of modernity.

The Modern Subject and the Paranoid Narrator

The crisis of literary modernity is less obvious, but no less serious, in such paradigmatic modern works as Lu Xun's "A Madman's Diary." Since his birth, the madman has been deemed the harbinger of modernity, destined to lead the Chinese to "step into the *modern* from the middle age."[13] *Kuangren*, Lu Xun's original term for the madman, is intended to convey an implication of eccentricity, rather than real insanity.[14] On the other hand, the "I" is a real paranoid, searching continually for a universal understanding of everything around him. It is this totalizing symptom of paranoia that comprises the basic intellectual mentality in the paradigm of modern Chinese literature, a mentality striving to represent reality in a holistic way.

However, Lu Xun's (or the madman's) representational paranoia is the origin of the (self-)disruption of the subjective totalization. This is evident if one reads closely a hitherto neglected essay by Lu Xun. The essay, "Ji 'Yang Shuda jun' de xilai" (An account of 'Mr. Yang Shuda's abrupt visit) (hereafter "Account"), is like "A Madman's Diary" primarily in that it is also concerned with a madman and, moreover, defines the madman as feigning his madness. (In "A Madman's Diary," naturally, the one who feigns madness is Lu Xun himself.) What is different in "Account" is that Lu Xun does not portray the one who feigns madness as a hero but, on the contrary, as someone dispatched by an antagonistic faction to menace him. The essay records an event that occurs on 13 November 1924. A young student visits Lu Xun and assaults him with apparently insane words and actions. After critical scrutiny, Lu Xun "reveals" that the visitor is trying to force him to stop writing by feigning madness. This essay, published in the second issue of the weekly *Yusi* (Thread of talk) on 24 November 1924, was not the end of the story. A week later, in the third issue, there was another short article by Lu Xun, entitled "Guanyu Yang jun xilai shijian de bianzheng" (A rectification apropos of the event of Mr. Yang's visit), in which Lu Xun admits that, according to other students' statements, the visitor "was truly insane," and that he, Lu Xun, "was susceptible to suspicion too much . . . [t]he fact is the fact. . . . I can only wish that he soon returns to health."[15]

One can perceive that, indeed, Lu Xun is inclined to interpret all madness as feigned, for all his points of view (including the points of view he surmises other people would have) conform to the narratorial stance of "A Madman's Diary," that is to say, they start from the *rationality* of feigning madness.

Nevertheless, Lu Xun later asserts that "the account could remain there: this is an unexpected exposure of the real appearances of mutual suspicions between men—at least between him and me." [16] Lu Xun's self-critique in this passage is illuminating: his *self-identification* with the madman uncovers the fact that a writing with self-claimed or self-affirmed rationality potentially contains immense irrationality. Indeed, the narrative mode of the essay "Account" that exposes Lu Xun's paranoid mind is not much different from the narrative mode of "A Madman's Diary." (The incident is also recorded in the same way in Lu Xun's own diary on 13 November 1924, which truly amounts to "a madman's diary.")

That is to say, the intrinsic affinity between "An Account" and "A Madman's Diary" lies not simply in the shared madness of the madman and Yang, the psychotic student, but, surprisingly, in the *identically* paranoid symptoms of the narrators in the two narratives: the madman as Lu Xun's persona and Lu Xun as a real person. This is how Lu Xun, the subjectivity-laden narrator, describes the visitor in "Account": "Sure enough, he began to act, that is, quivered the corners of his eyes and mouth so as to show monstrosity and madness; but each time it was so laborious that his face finally calmed down before the tenth quiver." [17] Let us look at how the madman in "A Madman's Diary" narrates: "Sure enough! My elder brother came slowly out, leading an old man. There was a murderous gleam in his eyes, and fearing that I would see it, he lowered his head, stealing side glances at me from behind his glasses." [18] The stylistic similarity between the narrative of the madman created by Lu Xun and that of Lu Xun himself is more than clear. In the same paranoid mode of narration, both narratives ultimately undermine their own confidence in totalizing insofar as narratorial omniscience has slipped into ignorance. It is not unreasonable, then, to attempt an alternative reading of "A Madman's Diary" as staging a real paranoid, a paranoiac subject loaded with the discourse of modernity, which endows the subject with supreme discursive power while at the same time failing to maintain its legitimacy.

Lu Xun, at least unconsciously, implants a self-suspicious potential by equating the discourse of madness and the discourse of modernity. The representational mechanism, as a matter of fact, does suggest the untruth of the madman's narrative, which the canonical reading tends to ignore. For example, the "seven or eight others who discussed me in a whisper" and "were afraid of my seeing them" [19] are indeed furtively talking about the madness of the madman, but he interprets their behavior as preparing murder; likewise, when the doctor says "To be eaten at once!" [20] he is most likely referring to taking medicine, but the narrator, again, interprets the words as a message about eating him; the narrator's suspicion of the Zhaos' dog as an "accomplice" is even more unreliable. The canonical reading of the text, therefore, is perfectly reversible: in "A Madman's Diary," it can be revealed that all the madman-narrator's interpretations of the external occurrences are paranoid *misinterpretations*, and the whole narrative is constructed by *misrepresentations*.

Such a fact, as apparent as the misinterpretation that Lu Xun the narrator gives in his article "An Account," has hitherto escaped critical and scholarly observations—as the nakedness of the emperor escapes not only every spectator's notice, but also his own. It is true that a scenario of modernity is most likely what Lu Xun intends to offer, since in his preface to *Call for Arms*, Lu Xun explicitly indicates that his writing serves those who do not want anything pessimistic, let alone cynical. Yet a divergent or even cynical reading of his madman is not impossible, as it may well be Lu Xun's equivocal unconscious that undermines his intentional message. Ironically, the higher the representational fidelity is to the state of madness (produced by Lu Xun's realistic technique), the more liable the whole story becomes to the danger of self-problematization. Lu Xun's characterization of a paranoid madman, however rational the term *kuang* suggests, provides the basis for a double, or self-contradicting, meaning. As the paradigmatic work of Chinese modernity, "A Madman's Diary" can be regarded as an epitome of the omniscient paradigm of (mis)representation, a symptom that, in fact, self-disruptively undermines its claim to totalization. Herein lies postmodernity, which surfaces more intensely in avant-garde literature, in which the paranoid discourse of modernity is unmasked as a symptom of schizophrenia.[21]

Modernity Displaced and Fragmented

Since the mid-1980s, the paradigm of representational narrative in the twentieth century has been challenged by avant-garde writing, whose "postmodernity" began a mutiny within the literary discourse of modernity. The self-deconstructive specter that had haunted the entire history of modern Chinese literature came into the open.

Among the earliest avant-garde works of fiction is Can Xue's novella *Huangni jie* (Yellow mud street), which can well be read as a parody of the whole paradigm of Chinese literary modernity. Here, the grand history runs aground when the Maoist concept of class struggle does not develop into a triumphant, or at least tragic, climax but degenerates into boundless disturbances of discourses, which Can Xue renders as the incomprehensible essence of historical experiences. This incomprehensibility, then, is what Can Xue smuggles into representation, which fails to bring subjective confidence in attaining truth. Lu Xun's totalizing paranoia is ruthlessly uncovered as disordered schizophrenia, in which no absolute or determinant statement can be maintained. Without a totalistic vision, Can Xue's narrative is self-reversible in every detail: every utterance of the narrator or character is to be read as unsound. But the unsoundness of history and discourse is exactly what the narrative is intended to imply.

In *Yellow Mud Street*, madness appears in people's ignorance of the detachment of actions from their supposed goal or of the irrelevance of intentions to their realization. Everyone is obsessively concerned about the queer events and their (dis)connections to the "Wang Si-ma case," even though Wang Si-ma's very existence is either called into question—people keep asking "Is Wang Si-ma a real person?"[22]—or bluntly denied, though the nonexistence of Wang Si-ma is equally unprovable. Thus, the paranoia that drives one to totalize is explicitly disseminated as schizophrenia, which becomes a failure, or a parody, of paranoia.

The disintegration of the subjective comprehension of ultimate truth results from the malfunctioning operation of Maoist political apparatus, or to be more precise, from the chasm between the integrative discourse and the disintegrative social formations. As the grand subjective voice in the master discourse that claims absolute truths is invalidated, what remains is the debris of untruths, never again redeemable or capable of teleological perfection.

For Can Xue, since the given discursive system is not produced solely by a single authority—Mao or the Party, for example—but is actuated and practiced by a collective rhetoric that she evokes as the source of traumatic experiences, communication as such becomes nightmarish or even monstrous, disrupting its own logic and prohibiting any possibility of mutual understanding. Her novel *Tuwei biaoyan* (Breakout performances) (1988) is, in this sense, a melange of various self-conflicting and self-refutable micronarratives, which break up any monolithic truth-conveying subject.

The narrator of the novel is a stenographer (and thus a "realistic" author of incomprehensible text), who participates in the story to explore, among other residents of Five-Flavor Street, the case of "adultery" between Lady X and Gentleman Q. The fact/event of adultery (which the residents of the whole street are so zealous in discussing) seems to be the focus of the whole story; however, throughout the whole novel, nothing real is exposed. In a sense, the narrative of the stenographer is sincere and truthful: it neither fabricates facts without quoting in detail nor conceals anything related to the "actual" state of affairs. In fact, one of the most apparent features in *Breakout Performances* is the profuse use of direct quotations, which the stenographer-narrator records. In so doing, however, Can Xue denies the original, unitary truth of narrative, insofar as to narrate becomes nothing but to quote, restate, or paraphrase. The authorial subject is decentered and disseminated into numerous contending and discordant subjects.

At the beginning of the novel, a two-page discussion of Lady X's age sums up over twenty-eight different opinions and finally concludes by "postulat-ing it as thirty-five years old" for "convenience."[23] This opening description settles the basic mode of the entire novel, in which each statement is incon-gruous with another and the only truth is that nothing can be affirmed as truth. The stereotyped "block characterization" is parodied—for instance, in the narrator's conclusion about Lady X's appearance: "After various discus-sions about her age, we have now gotten such a contradictory vague impres-sion: Lady X is a middle-aged woman with white teeth and thin body, her neck is slender or wrinkly, her skin smooth or rough, her voice crisp and dissolute, her appearance sexy or not sexy at all."[24]

The "climax" of the novel is the description of the "adultery" between Lady X and Gentleman Q by which everyone has been intrigued. Although the narrator suggests at this point that "we are about to enter the core of the story,"[25] the chapter consists only of interviews with a few residents of Five-Flavor Street, none of whom can tell of the actual event. In any case, "The adultery did happen; though nobody can tell clearly where and when it hap-pened, everyone has affirmed this fact inwardly."[26] The novel culminates in the three Ph.D.s' dispute over the question "Who [the lady or the gentleman] took the initiative?":[27]

> We have imagined what Lady X and Gentleman Q did after they entered that pitch-dark barn at the time no one knows. Only one problem, the greatest, remains unresolved: Who took the initiative, i.e., who started first? In the black-room meeting, our experts produced three different opinions on this tricky problem. In the heated argument, the experts didn't side with the first speaker until after numerous setbacks. They achieved the conclusion through a vertical, macroscopic analysis of his-tory, a systematic study using the comparative method. . . . Gentleman Q looked so simple and innocent, we might absolutely conceive that it was Lady X who rushed ahead to strip off his clothes and manipulate him as if she were manipulating a puppet, so that he felt wronged and unable to wash off the infamy. But this is only the idea of common, me-diocre people; our experts on Five-Flavor Street are never misled by such superficial appearances.[28]

In his conclusion that it is Gentleman Q who started the adultery, Dr. A alleges, in a typical mode of Maoist discourse that postulates an omniscient cognitive subject, "When looking at a problem we must not look at its surface; we need to penetrate into the essence of the thing with eyes like swords."[29] Like any such subject, his "approach" to the adultery is neither concrete nor descriptive (his speech—or reasoning—does not even consist of any refer-ence to the real process of the occurrence) but is rationally analytic; however, all he gives us subsequently is a quaint discursive application of his idea of sexual relationship. The single "essence"—the one persistently maintained by the discursive system—has lost its subjective center and is thus bereft of its truth content. The three speakers' harangues—and in this sense, the characters' words in the novel, especially the narrator's—have dispersed any anticipation of an ultimate, central discourse.

The subjective heterogeneity of narration in avant-garde fiction challenges a literary modernity that establishes a centered, representational subjectivity. Yu Hua, another foremost avant-garde writer, proposes "perception against judgment" or "*selfless* mode of narration" [30] against the modern paradigm that absolutizes the authorial status. In "Yijiubaliu nian" (Nineteen eighty-six), Yu Hua does not simply indict the evil of the Cultural Revolution but reveals the repetitiveness and, more significantly, the incomprehensibility of that evil or the inability of the subject to exhaust the meaning of history. Not only does the protagonist of the novella show his madness ten years after the end of the Cultural Revolution, but the representation of madness, on the level of narratorial voice, appears insane. The subjective mode is parodied when direct characterization is imposed upon the course of self-mutilation that the mad protagonist follows. The narrator repeatedly uses "satisfied" or "smiling complacently" to describe the protagonist's feeling as he mutilates himself. He even reinforces the struggling tension between the desire to represent and the insufficiency of representing by misappropriating tropological devices. In the scene of the madman's cutting off his own nose, "The nose was dangling on the face like a swing." [31] The sound of the madman sawing his own leg is described like "he had been polishing a pair of pretty leather shoes." [32] Here, if the madness of the protagonist signals the fall of grand history, the madness of the narrative/narratorial subject effects the subversion against absolute representation and denies the illusion that the real we are confronted with can be comprehended and redeemed in a rational and complete way.

In other words, the narrator (unlike the one in Lu Xun's "New year's sacrifice") cannot distance himself from the point of view of the character, as they both suffer from the traumatic past. The identification between the narration and the insanity indicates the decline of the rational representational subject, in that the irrational narration has replaced an otherwise transcendental representation of irrationality (e.g., in "Account") or a discourse with rational purpose camouflaged under irrational utterances (e.g., in "The madman's diary"). The narrator simply shows what the character perceives in an equally irrational way without translating it into the rational:

> He saw a person lying somewhere around his feet. The man's feet somehow seemed connected to his own. He raised his foot and tried to kick

away the prostrate foot. But that foot unexpectedly recoiled almost before he had even lifted his leg to strike. When he put his foot down, the other foot shifted back to its original position next to his own. He couldn't help getting excited and lifted his own foot once more. He found that the foot on the ground had once again evaded his own at the same time and he felt that his rival was alarmed. Holding his foot motionless in the air until he saw that his rival's foot was also poised motionless in the air, he suddenly pounced, landing full force on the waist of that person. He heard a solid thump and looked down. The prone figure seemed unhurt and his feet still linked to his own.[33]

The narrative voice itself is preoccupied with the same susceptibility to threat as the madman himself, by visualizing from the madman's point of view without rationalizing it from a higher position. Therefore, if Lu Xun's paranoid subject forms an intended indictment (though ostensibly insane and thus practically dubious) against real oppression, Yu Hua adopts a subjective voice that points to nowhere except the agitation within the self. In Yu Hua's writing, the omniscient subject transforms into the displaced subject, which, within the mode of (parodied) omniscient narration, questions the function of subjective totality.

To a certain extent, the displacement of subjectivity in avant-garde literature results from a reawakening of traditional Chinese philosophy and aesthetics, especially Taoism and Chan (Zen) Buddhism, in which the subject can be seen as displaced and decentered. Ge Fei's short story "Jinse" (The ornamented zither), for example, revives the theme of a questionable self in Zhuang Zi and Li Shangyin, a non-Cartesian self that defies the unity of an absolute subject. The endlessly self-derivative, self-entangled narrative cycle of samsara borrows the title of a famous poem by the Tang Dynasty poet Li Shangyin.[34]

The third line of Li's poem is brought up more than once in Ge Fei's story by Feng Zicun, the protagonist fascinated by the idea of the "butterfly dream" of Zhuang Zi throughout his transmigrating lives.[35] While Zhuang Zi's parable is a questioning of the authenticity of reality and Li Shangyin's poem concerns the "obscurity" of memory, Ge Fei's narrative is a self-engulfing labyrinth that perplexes any integral, complete understanding of memory and history. Li Shangyin's poem predetermines the lyrical voice of Ge Fei's narrative subject, since Feng Zicun, like Li Shangyin, dwells on his speculation on the feeling of being lost in his memory/anamnesis. The lyrical subject, like Zhuang Zi, becomes an unstable and self-questioned one.

The *mise-en-abîme* structure is in accord with Zhuang Zi's parable: Zhuang Zi dreams his transformation into the butterfly, which, as conjectured, dreams in turn its transformation into Zhuang Zi. If Zhuang Zi's dream is the butterfly's reality, his reality must be the butterfly's dream. The mutual entanglement of reality and dream in narrative is part of traditional Chinese mysticism, which Ge Fei evokes against the historical subject in the grand narratives.[36]

In Ge Fei's "Ornamented Zither," narrative subjectivity is trapped in an endlessly involute cycle. Again, the lyrical quality of the narration brings back the self-mystified voices of the ancient philosopher/poet that challenge the modern teleological subjectivity. The frame narrative consists of a narrative that consists of another, and so on until the last, which actually consists of the initial narrative. One narrative subject is replaced by another that is supposedly subordinate, until the least subordinate subordinates the supreme. There is no subject, therefore, that is self-sufficient because, if each subject can be considered a metanarrative subject, there is no metanarrative subject at all, no absolute and transcendental subject that manipulates the narrative whole (which keeps "leaking" into consecutive and cyclic narrative funnels). The lyrical subject can no longer envision a teleological temporality or absolutize a rational history of emancipation. Rather, it is the successive recollections that motivate the narrative to move backward into the immemorial.

As a fictional subject, then, Feng Zicun transmits (if not transmigrates) himself successively as a narrative function in different times and locations, operates different functions, and never finds his original home. Such an un-canniness (*Unheimlichkeit* in the Heideggerian sense) in narrative and of narra-tive indicates the exiled situation of both the fictional and the narrative sub-jects. In Ge Fei, then, lyrical subjectivity is not only animated but decentered within the temporal self-involution. Therefore the modern concept of linear history is displaced by the intricate personal history of Feng Zicun, which cannot be grasped as an integrated whole. The narrative subject, ironically, fails to persist in its omnipotence and frequently exposes its own deficiencies, chasms, or self-suspicions, which, in turn, call into question the absolute reason of representational subjectivity.

The subjectivity in Chinese avant-gardism is, in every detail, unified and dispersed at one and the same time. The idea of the alienation of a frail indi-vidual self in face of the other is simultaneously decentered as part of the other to avoid a one-dimensionally self-righteous subjectivity. Modern Chinese nar-rative from Lu Xun to Can Xue, Yu Hua, and Ge Fei, then, is a process from a unifying subject doomed to break down into a subject self-exposed as split or displaced. Modernity, whose homogeneous cultural power has upheld the sociopolitical totality (and totalitarianism) in modern China, is challenged by the literary practice that questions its absolute mode of discourse. Thus rises the postmodernity of the Chinese avant-garde: a cultural/literary mode that corresponds to experience that is historically wounded by the atrocious and disastrous modern, in both political and cultural senses.

Answering the Question: What is the Postmodern/Post-Mao-Deng?

In his article "Answering the Question: What Is Postmodernism," Jean-François Lyotard proposes that "*Post modern* would have to be understood according to the paradox of the future (*post*) anterior (*modo*)."[37] Lyotard has repeatedly emphasized the link between the prefix *post* in the term *postmodern* and the Greek prefix *ana*, as in analysis, anamnesis, anagogy, and anamorphosis, that is, as a working through of the immemorial. What is immemorial, in the case of postmodernism, seems to be its overpowering, violent modernity. The prefix *post*, therefore, can well be associated with the German prefix *Nach*, as in the Freudian concept *Nachträglichkeit*, a deferred action that reactivates the traumatic experience of historical violence.[38] The postmodern, in this sense, is to be understood as the modern (the splendid idea fraught with bloody disasters) reactivated as a traumatic memory-trace, as a massive psychic burden that has been carried over (the meaning of *tragen* in the term *Nachträglichkeit*) to the present. The ambivalent attitude of attachment and resistance of the concept of *Nachträglichkeit* also implies that Chinese postmodernism does not launch an antagonistic literary movement. Without confronting political oppression from a self-assumed superior position, Chinese postmodernism is an implosion within the modern cultural paradigm, which serves as the basis of political authoritarianism.

The dissolution of a rational, omniscient subject in contemporary Chinese fiction attests to the psychohistorical phenomenon of postmodernity that is comparable to the post-Auschwitz cultural scene in the West. Therefore, my concept of Chinese postmodernism is radically different from, though not irrelevant to, that which has been either welcomed or repudiated over the past few years among Chinese scholars and critics. Chinese postmodernism, as I have elaborated it thus far, has more to do with the historical reality of the modern politico-cultural paradigm than with the global "postmodern" civilization. The latter, ironically, has been increasingly utilized by the central authority and successfully integrated into the project of Chinese modernity.

In China today it seems as if the concept of the postmodern cannot be understood unless associated with the sociocultural condition of postindustrialism, postcolonialism, late capitalism, and so on. From such a standpoint, postmodernism is only measured by the degree of the development of material civilization, or production-distribution mode, against the global background of transcapitalism.

Starting from this point, Zhang Yiwu argues, "The postmodern is a global cultural phenomenon, a condition culturally correspondent to postindustrialization and commercialization that the development of modern society is facing. It does not only function in the First and Second Worlds, but enters the Third World culture via the globalized communication and information." [39] By taking the "distribution of global power" into consideration, Zhang's conception of a global postmodern network has recently shifted toward a native "Third World" stance to confront "First World" oppression. Chinese postmodernism is presumed to counteract the so-called hegemony of Western discourses, from which contemporary Chinese culture is said to be suffering. Zhang thus asserts that "discontinuities, fragmentations, and instabilities" in contemporary Chinese narratives are "practical modes" "resisting the repression of the First World culture." [40]

To what extent, then, can the so-called First World culture be seen as a hegemonic threat to the less powerful Third World culture, Chinese culture in particular? The history of modern China has shown that the major Western discourse that has helped to legitimize the political totality is none other than the discourse of historical modernity. Zhang Yiwu, by accepting such contemporary *Western* theorists as Fredric Jameson and Edward Said while overlooking their self-critical stance, focuses on the First World's "absolute power of cultural distribution and knowledge production" [41] and assumes, again, a "repressed" and wronged nation that seeks sympathy. In this sense, such a theory of the postmodern amounts once more to the aspiration to a grand national subject that, in the name of resisting alien hegemonic forces, resists nothing but that which challenges the sociopolitical totality of the nation-state.

The supreme discursive power that strives to maintain social and ideological homogeneity in China today is not imposed by the West but is, rather, controlled by the central political authority. While the national subject that has recently recurred supports a discourse of national "emancipation," the real *native* problem and *endemic* malady are dodged. *Yaomohua Zhongguo de beihou* (Behind the demonization of China, [1996]), compiled by a number of domestic and overseas Chinese academics to lead a sweeping attack on American representations of China, reveals the danger of allying antioccidentalism with official nationalism. The attempt to oppose Western cultural colonization turns out to lead to the concealment of native political totality. The recurring grand subject that speaks for the nation, in effect, stands for the native/national political power, the most hegemonic power that "demonizes," or at least dehumanizes, the autonomous individuals of the nation. Insofar as the fact that modernity or modernization belongs exactly to the central national discourse is disregarded, the notion of the postmodern, overshadowed by the grand national subject, serves only to reinforce the rigid hegemony of the native authoritative discourse.

As long as we recognize that in China, for a long historical period, political factors have influenced social culture more significantly than the development of material civilization, the origin of postmodernity in Chinese avant-garde literature—for example, the deconstruction of totality and unity, the emphasis on indeterminacy and randomness, the implosion of a grand, absolute history—cannot be sought against the background of the globalization of the consumption society, the commercial society, or the information society. Commercialism and cultural massification are burgeoning in China under, or even in complicity with, its overshadowing political authoritarianism. The concept of the modern in China has depended heavily upon the entity of the modern nation-state as defined by Lenin and was comprehended in terms of economic and technological advancement until recent years. Chinese postmodernism has to do with the cultural psychology provoked by the indigenous culturopolitical condition, rather than global, or Westernized, civilization. Precisely from this point, "the post-Mao-Deng," a politico-historical notion, is correlated with "the postmodern," a concurrent and correspondent cultural paradigm intrinsically linked to this political environment.

If the political paradigm is itself understood as a cultural paradigm rather than simply an entity of the state apparatus or concrete policies, the political order of an age, particularly that of the contemporary China, can be regarded as a system based on the production of discourses. From this hypothesis, we are prepared to answer the question "In what sense can we use the prefix 'post-' in the notion 'the post-Mao-Deng?' " In terms of cultural production rather than production of material civilization, Mao's and Deng's ages do not belong to different political paradigms, even though they adopt different political schemes. That is to say, Deng's polity follows Mao's insofar as it has only "reformed" the instrument of discourse production. The consequence of such a reform is that the utopian discourse in terms of material economy replaces the utopian discourse in terms of spiritual community. After the collapse of Mao's spiritual community, Deng's polity resorts to the more vulgar but pragmatically more tangible and hedonic picture of elysium, by which the depressed citizens can be awakened to reconstruct a brave new world on the ruins of the previous utopia—or rather, dystopia. The crucial point is that it is the same *totalistic and teleological discourse of modernity* that becomes the culturopolitical sentry that bars any discourse in conflict to it.

It is thus clear that the notion of "the post-Mao-Deng" refers not to a political chronicle but to a cultural paradigm, which does not necessarily appear chronologically after Mao's and Deng's polities, just as the postmodern cultural paradigm does not appear after the modern age but indicates a deconstruction of the modern paradigm from within. Therefore, it is not far-fetched to place "the postmodern" (as cultural paradigm) and "the post-Mao-Deng" (as political mode) on a par, since "the post-Mao-Deng" tendency in culture and literature to challenge the simultaneously utopian and totalitarian political discourse is correspondent to the postmodern subversion against the grand narratives of modernity. Here, "the postmodern" is to be understood as a cultural paradigm generating within and defiant of the cultural paradigm of "the modern" without being confined in the material or economic structure of contemporary civilization.

Therefore postmodernism in Chinese avant-garde literature can be defined as both a psychic reaction to the discourses of modernity that are imbedded in the various versions of the Mao-Deng political agendas and a rhetorical reaction to the "modern" paradigm of twentieth-century Chinese literature. The political discourses of modernity and the literary paradigm of modernity share the mode of conceptualization. Historical modernity, which presupposes an absolute coherence between practice and telos and a transparent correspondence between representation and meaning, is certainly the most powerful concept propelling both political and literary modernity. The complicity of discursive/literary absolutization and political totalization in the Mao-Deng regimes can be traced back to their common origin.

Since the cultural modern, or the master discourse of the political Mao-Deng, lies in literary rationalization and absolutization, the prefix "post-" does not refer to a chronological subsequence but shows a temporal force of deferral and a spatial force of deviation within the repression and desire of the modern. The postmodern does not exist as a distanced critique of the modern but rather suggests a self-involvement in historical destiny. It thus implies simultaneously a preoccupation with and a deviation from the original or the primal. In other words, the postmodern is not a diachronic transcendence of the modern but a synchronic evocation and expulsion of its repression.

As an implosion of literary modernity within the subjective narrative that conforms to a political totality, literary postmodernity is a confession of the traumatizing violence of modernity within its deep formation. In this sense, the Chinese avant-garde is not only an affront to the external, imposing master discourse, but a working-through of the internalized discourse of modernity with which the subject has been culturally possessed. The impetus of the subjective self-critique stems from the fact that historical catastrophes in China cannot be simply imputed to external, historical evil forces but have to be examined within the collective/individual cultural subject, which adheres to the same paradigm of the discourse of the political power. The fact that it was always the intellectuals themselves who not only collaborated with, but elaborated, the persecutions of the intellectuals in the numerous political movements in the history of contemporary China is certainly a practical consequence of the supreme cultural and discursive paradigm of modernity or grand historicity shared by the so-called intellectuals and the political apparatus.

Postmodernity in Chinese literature can be primarily detected as the implosive disruption of the transparent, absolute genre that constructs the master discourse. The unifying modernity is still lurking, while at the same time it is whirled into the involute labyrinth of multiplied signifiers, the signifiers that fail to capture the signifieds in a transparent way. Then, to deal literarily with reality becomes, in the first place, to deal with the signifiers that are already culturally and historically intertextualized, overdetermined, contaminated and, in particular, entangled with the master discourse as something etiologically modern but pathologically/symptomatically postmodern. Thus, postmodernity in Chinese literature is certainly a postcatastrophic mentality, related to the disorder of rationality and subjectivity of the modern. The problematic subject in avant-garde narrative persists in the paradox of subjectivity: it has to resist its destruction by, ironically, self-consciously displaying its own quandary or disintegration. A postmodern subjectivity is a heterogeneous and self-questioning one, which breaches the absolute, rational, and totalistic oppression of both the external politico-historical Mao-Deng and the internal culturo-literary modern.

Notes

1 Liang Qichao, "Lun xiaoshuo yu qunzhi zhi guanxi" (On the relationship between fiction and the government of the people), in *Modern Chinese Literary Thought: Writings on Literature, 1893–1945*, ed. Kirk A. Denton (Stanford, Calif.: Stanford University Press, 1996), 74.

2 When the Literary Association and the Creation Society begin to advocate "literature for human life" and "revolutionary literature," the Crescent Society, traditionally considered a conservative literary coterie, offered an alternative way of literature that is, ironically, by no means antagonistic to the May Fourth cultural paradigm. In the quasi-manifesto of the Crescent Society (the piece harshly castigated by the Creation Society), Xu Zhimo, trained in a Anglo-American tradition rather than influenced by the Soviet Russian ideology, is equally concerned for the destiny of the nation and no less captivated by the discourse of the "reform of human life," even though his tone has not reached so high a revolutionary pitch as the Creation Society. Nonetheless, despite his own famous line "Thoughts are suffering from the rape of isms!" (*Xu Zhimo shiji* [Collected poems of Xu Zhimo] [Chengdu: Sichuan Renmin Chubanshe, 1981], 182), written in the previous year, Xu Zhimo also envisions a "creative idealism," which would be embodied in the practice of the awakening of the people and the struggling against the "insult to and violation of human dignity and health" (" 'Xinyue' de taidu" [The attitude of the "Crescent"], *Xinyue*

1, no. 1 [1928]: 10). The example of the Crescent Society shows that even the admittedly most "aesthetic" literary proposal contains a practical intention and thus the voice for the true autonomy of aesthetic value in literature is repressed to the minimum.

3   Lu Xun, "Wo zenme zuoqi xiaoshuo lai" (How I got to write fiction). *Lu Xun quanji* (Complete works of Lu Xun) (Beijing: Renmin Wenxue Chubanshe, 1993), vol. 4, 512. All translations are mine unless otherwise noted.

4   Other statements from the leading intellectuals in the May Fourth period attest to this observation. In his "General Introduction to the *Grand Anthology of Chinese New Literature*," Cai Yuanpei asks, "Why does transforming ideas have to be associated with literature? They do because literature is the instrument of transmitting ideas" (in *Jianshe lilun ji*, ed. Hu Shi [Constructive theories] [Shanghai: Liangyou Tushu Gongsi, 1935], 9). Similarly, Hu Shi insists that literary language be "used as a vehicle of new ideas and new mentalities" (*Hu Shi wenxuan* [Selected essays of Hu Shi] [Taipei: Yuanliu Chuban Gongsi, 1986], 174).

5   Jacques Derrida, *Of Spirit*, trans. Geoffrey Bennington and Rachel Bowlby (Chicago: University of Chicago Press, 1989), 26.

6   I focus more on the implicit authorial power of manipulating narration, despite the fact that, more than usually, a unified authorial voice hovers in narration. Mao Dun, though an advocate of realism, categorizes, or defines, the heroine Mei in his novel *Hong* (The rainbow) in the following way: "She is an extraordinary girl, she is a rainbow-like character, but her original wish is far beyond this, and far more unsatisfied, she is marching forward like a soldier only because the time is different! Her characteristic is 'marching forward!' Her only ambition is to conquer the environment and the destiny!" (*Hong* [Chengdu: Sichuan Renmin Chubanshe, 1981], 3). In his novel *Family*, Ba Jin is more notorious for implanting subjective intention into the narrative by exploiting the characters' utterances to express the authorial discourses: his characters directly define either their own roles—e.g., "Juehui . . . is a humanitarian" (*Jia* [Family] [Beijing: Renmin Wenxue Chubanshe, 1978], 10), "Qin is certainly a brave girl" (21), "My condition is even worse than yours" (18)—or society and history—e.g., "Sichuan has entirely too many feudal moralists, and their influence is very strong" (11), "I know that a high price must be paid for any reform to be put through, that many sacrifices must be made" (20). Obviously, all the voices are subsumed into, or subdued under, a single voice of the author in a homogeneous way. In all these canonical works, mimesis is replaced by diegesis, a narration that stresses telling in the authorial voice instead of showing without subjective involvement, even though mimesis is theoretically desired by such as Mao Dun. Subjective intervention may not necessarily mean direct insertion of authorial/narratorial statements. An authorial/narratorial voice could be hidden in the superficially spontaneous realistic representation. One of the most illustrative facts is the excess of modifiers that are intended to define what is represented, particularly, the modifiers that habitually condition the characters' actions. The most symptomatic examples can again be drawn from Ba Jin's *Family*, in which almost every speaking act is emotionally defined: "The more he talked the more excited he became," "The more she talked the more excited Qin became," "He said in an agitated voice" (18), "Qin . . . said in a trembling voice" (20), and so on. The metarepresentational modern subject is endowed with the absolute power of utilizing language to transmit messages that reject imagination, expel ambiguity, and impose determinacy.

7   Lu Xun, *Selected Works*, trans. Yang Xianyi and Gladys Yang (Beijing: Foreign Languages Press, 1980), vol. 1, 170.

8   Marston Anderson, *The Limits of Realism: Chinese Fiction in the Revolutionary Period* (Berkeley: University of California Press, 1990), 89.

9   Lu Xun, *Selected Works*, vol. 1, 170–73.

10 Mao Zedong, *Selected Works of Mao Tse-tung* (Peking: Foreign Languages Press, 1965), vol. 2, 337–38.

11 Mao, *Selected Works*, vol. 3, 272.

12 *The Book of Lieh-tzu*, trans. A. C. Graham (London: John Murray, 1960), 100.

13 Zhang Dinghuang, "Lu Xun xiansheng" (Mr. Lu Xun), originally published in *Xiandai pinglun* (Modern criticism), January 1925. See Li Zongying and Zhang Mengyang, eds., *Liushi nian lai Lu Xun yanjiu lunwen xuan* (Selected Essays in Lu Xun studies over the past sixty years) (Beijing: Zhongguo Shehuikexue Chubanhse, 1982), vol. 1, 33 (my emphasis).

14 The word *kuang* alludes to a story in *Analects* about Jieyu, the so-called *kuang*, who laughs at Confucius's political expectations. Zhu Xi comments, "Jieyu, the man of Chu, feigned madness and secluded himself from society" (*Sishu zhangju jizhu* [A variorum of the four Books] [Beijing: Zhonghua Shuju, 1983], 184). Traditionally, the word *kuangren* refers to a type of unruly person who attempts to resist the order of society with *intentional* mad behavior. Such a madman also appears in Nietzsche, whose influence on Lu Xun was immense. The 125th aphorism in *Die fröhliche Wissenschaft* (The gay science) describes a madman, through whose voice Nietzsche announces the murder of God by human beings. Lu Xun's own earliest use of *kuangren* can be found in his 1907 essay "On the Power of Mára Poetry," in which Percy Bysshe Shelley is referred to admiringly as a "madman" (*Lu Xun quanji* [Complete works of Lu Xun] [Beijing: Renmin Wenxue Chubanshe, 1993], vol. 1, 83).

15 *Lu Xun quanji* (Complete works of Lu Xun) (Beijing: Renmin Wenxue Chubanshe, 1993), vol. 7, 49–50.

16 Lu Xun, *Lu Xun quanji*, vol. 7, 49–50.

17 Lu Xun, *Lu Xun quanji*, vol. 7, 44.

18 Lu Xun, *Selected Works*, vol. 1, 43.

19 Lu Xun, *Selected Works*, vol. 1, 40.

20 Lu Xun, *Selected Works*, vol. 1, 44.

21 The sociocultural distinction between paranoia and schizophrenia is stated in Deleuze and Guattari's *Anti-Oedipus*, in which the two psychotic forms of desire are opposed to each other: schizophrenia displays a collage of fragmentary ruins of anarchical, heterogeneous elements, whereas paranoia attempts to impose a centralized, unified system upon disparate elements.

22 *Old Floating Cloud: Two Novellas*, trans. Ronald R. Janssen and Jian Zhang (Evanston, Ill.: Northwestern University Press, 1991), 32, 102, 108.

23 *Tuwei biaoyan* (Breakout performances) (Shanghai: Shanghai Wenyi Chubanshe, 1990), 5.

24 Can Xue, *Tuwei biaoyan*, 5–6.

25 Can Xue, *Tuwei biaoyan*, 149.

26 Can Xue, *Tuwei biaoyan*, 168.

27 Can Xue, *Tuwei biaoyan*, 214.

28 Can Xue, *Tuwei biaoyan*, 214–15.

29 Can Xue, *Tuwei biaoyan*, 216.

30 *Yu Hua zuopin ji* (The collected works of Yu Hua) (Beijing: Zhongguo shehuikexue chubanshe, 1995), vol. 2, 283 (my emphasis).

31 Yu Hua, *The Past and the Punishments*, trans. Andrew F. Jones (Honolulu: University of Hawai'i Press, 1996), 158 (translation modified).

32 Yu Hua, *The Past and the Punishments*, 159 (translation modified).

33 Yu Hua, *The Past and the Punishments*, 144 (translation modified).

34 Li's "Jinse" (The ornamented zither) reads as follows:

> The ornamented zither, for no reason, has fifty strings.
>
> Each string, each bridge, recalls a youthful year.
>
> Master Zhuang was confused by his morning dream of the butterfly;
>
> Emperor Wang's amourous heart in spring is entrusted to the cuckoo.
>
> In the vast sea, under a bright moon, pearls have tears;
>
> On Indigo Mountain, in the warm sun, jade engenders smoke.
>
> This feeling might have become a thing to be remembered,
>
> Only, at the time you were already bewildered and lost.
>
> (James Liu, *The Poetry of Li Shangyin: Ninth-Century Baroque Chinese Poet*
>
> [Chicago: University of Chicago Press, 1969], 1 [transliteration modified]).

35 The original passage from *Zhuang Zi* reads as follows: "Formerly, Chuang Chou [i.e., Zhuang Zi], dreamed that I was a butterfly, a butterfly flying about feeling that it was enjoying itself. I did not know that it was Chou. Suddenly I awoke and was myself again, the veritable Chou. I did not know whether it had formerly been Chou dreaming that he was a butterfly, or it was now a butterfly dreaming that it was Chou" (*Chuang Tzu: Genius of the Absurd*, arranged from the work of James Legge by Clae Waltham [New York: Ace Books, 1971], 60).

36 In this sense, Ge Fei's "The Ornamented Zither" also disputes the modern rationalization of Zhuang Zi's parable in, for example, Wang Meng's short story "Hudie" (The butterfly), in which a historical dialectic reorganizes the entangled times. Allegedly alluding to Zhuang Zi's parable, "The Butterfly" arrays a teleological temporality in which the personal history is a synecdoche of the national history. The basic thread of the narrative is woven by the protagonist Zhang Siyuan, who recalls his past (political) "lives" "transmigrating" from party secretary (before the political turbulence) via Old Man Zhang (during his exile to the village) to vice minister (after his rehabilitation). The "transmigration" here clearly contains the essence of dialectical history: it is only through the purgatory of the political turbulence that Zhang (or China as such) purifies his spirit and enters a new age of brightness in the end. Despite the stream-of-consciousness technique in Wang Meng's narrative, the linear progression of the story is highly tangible. On the contrary, the narrative unfolding of the transmigration in "The Ornamented Zither" is not progressive but retrogressive or involute.

37 Jean-François Lyotard, "Answering the Question: What Is Postmodernism?" trans. Régis Durand, in *The Postmodern Condition: A Report on Knowledge*, trans. Geoffrey Bennington and Brian Massumi (Minneapolis: University of Minnesota Press, 1984), 81 (italics original).

38 See also Lyotard's exposition of *Nachträglichkeit* in Jean-François Lyotard, *Heidegger and "the Jews,"* trans. Andreas Michel and Mark S. Roberts (Minneapolis: University of Minnesota Press, 1990), 15–17.

39 Zhang Guoyi, ed., *Shengcun youxi de shuiquan* (The rings of ripples of the game of existence) (Beijing: Beijingdaxue Chubanshe, 1994), 119.

40 Zhang Yiwu, *Zai bianyuanchu zhuixun: Disanshijie wenhua yu Zhongguo dangdai wenxue* (Pursuing at the margin: Third World culture and contemporary Chinese literature) (Changchun: Shidai Wenyi Chubanshe, 1993), 90.

41 Zhang Yiwu, *Zai bianyuanchu zhuixun*, 197.

xudong zhang

Epilogue: Postmodernism and Postsocialist Society—
Historicizing the Present

Throughout this essay I use two terms whose meanings are markedly distinct, terms that should be made clear at the outset. I define *postmodernism in China* as a global discourse of postmodernism and postmodernity, whose entry into China is via intellectuals who seek theoretical inspiration from, and discursive synchronization with, the West; this term is largely limited to small circles of literary and art criticism. Postmodern discourse in this sense is a continuation of the modernist trend in the 1980s. Its currency in the 1990s reflects the rapid growth of a consumer-oriented economy and the relentless process of globalization. Its content, however, is strictly foreign and technical, corresponding to the gleaming enclaves of international economic and cultural capital amid an extremely uneven Chinese reality. Its aesthetic and political excitement comes mainly from its vision (and, to an increasing degree, from the daily experience) of China as an integral part of the global market.

Contrary to this first term, *Chinese postmodernism* is a more nebulous yet productive discourse that is the focus of this essay. *Chinese postmodernism* pertains to Chinese everyday life as a producer of a culture of the postmodern. However, *postmodernism* as a theoretical discourse in this context seems vacuous except as a deliberate signifier (or an ad hoc stand-in) for an un-settled, postponed, living, and reconfiguring collective experience of revolution, modernity, statehood, and the masses. To this extent the "post" in Chinese postmodernism refers not so much to a sense that something is over but that something is finally ready to begin, along with the concomitant breakup of all kinds of rigid epistemological paradigms, aesthetic canons, historical periodizations, geographical hierarchies, and institutional reifications. Chinese postmodernism as a social discourse can therefore be considered a revolt against the modernist and modernization ideology of the New Era (1979–89); during this time modernism posed as a "new enlightenment" in opposition to Maoism as a form of Chinese feudalism, and thus sealed the legitimacy of Deng's China within the discourse of modernity. Modernity in the context of post-Mao Chinese history has its centrality in economic, bureaucratic, and social rationalization, which is congruent with a state-sanctioned integration with the capitalist world market and its hegemonic ideology. The social material environment created by the modernist thrust in the last two decades of the twentieth century also makes it possible, dialectically, for Chinese intellectuals to seek a broader understanding of modernity—one that is both more historically complex and theoretically supple as a concept of contradiction informing their daily encounter with change. The initial economic success of post-Mao Chinese society, the multicenteredness of global capital and production, and the survival of the Chinese socialist state allow ordinary Chinese to feel that one does not have to become a Westerner to enjoy a good life. This, to be sure, has profound implications for a whole range of quotidian, social, cultural, and political choices and aspirations. Like nationalism, postmodernism functions in China today as an empty net of "universal high culture," which often ends up with heavy catches from the water. Instead of projecting the Chinese reality into a timeless now, the notion of Chinese postmodernism, through its longing for a location and its struggle to break free from the tunnel vision of high modernism, is haunting the Chinese consumer masses with a past that has never been put to rest. Moreover, Chinese postmodernism reveals the conditions for the possibilities of a new life and its participating masses that have evaded analytical description. As the cultural form of the new market and consumer masses nurtured by the state, Chinese postmodernism becomes not only an important component of the mainstream ideology of Chinese society in the 1990s but also a utopian space for reconfigurations of social and class relations, the imagination of community, nation, freedom, and democracy, and a new universal culture of particularities.

In this essay I explore Chinese postmodernism in four steps: a discussion of its stylistic features; location of the discourse within a particular modernism-postmodernism shift in the post-Mao context and beyond; an analysis of the political stakes for the positions in the current intellectual debate; and, finally, the acquisition of a historical understanding of Chinese postmodernism as the culture of a postsocialist society.

Sense-Certainty of the Postmodern

Enthusiasts for Chinese postmodernism are nowadays put on the defensive by those who dismiss the issue as a Chinese problematic or who resist post-modernism in general. Yet the fact is often overlooked that at a pedestrian, journalistic level, identifying and inventorying Chinese postmodernist works in arts and criticism today is not difficult if one mechanically applies the standards established in Western critical and theoretical discourses. Nor has it been hard to describe radical paradigmatic shifts and profound sociocultural ruptures in the past two decades, because sweeping changes in post-Mao China are virtually the norm. However, the attempt to qualify and justify Chinese postmodernism at the empirical level may nonetheless be the right point of departure for any meaningful discussion. This is not so much because the restriction imposed by opponents of Chinese postmodernist discourse can be any more productive but because objectively, defining a historical *sense-certainty*—here I refer to the Hegelian notion *Sinnlichgewissheit* at the beginning of his phenomenology—may serve as a natural entry into a dialectical circle of interpretation and contestation.

When one describes the cultural-aesthetic landscape of Chinese postmodernism in the 1990s, one can easily say that the poetry of Chen Dongdong and Xiao Kaiyu, for example, and all the new generation poets, surged onto center stage by subverting the specific high modernist epic and the monolithic monumentality of the Menglong (Misty) authors, such as Yang Lian and Jiang He. In art, we can point to Zhang Peili, Wang Guangyi, Yu Youhan, and other political pop artists who have bestowed the nonconformist works of post-Mao Chinese art (pioneered by the Xing-xing movement, better known in the West as the Star Exhibitions) with a quasi-Warhol touch, while Xu Bing, Wang Jianwei, and other installation and conceptual artists continue to explore a more formalistic language, one that is both constitutively Chinese and conceptually experimental and that is exemplified by Xu's print shop production of a limitless amount of nonexistent—but ideographically possible—Chinese characters. In music, the academic avant-garde in the 1980s, represented by Tan Dun, Qu Xiaosong, and the like, itself inspired more by John Cage than by Arnold Schoenberg, has been pushed aside by numerous rock and roll bands in the 1990s, whose heroic precursor in the previous decade, Cui Jian, remains a powerful cultural icon emblematic of the cultural and political complexities and paradoxes of a postmodernism in a socialist or postsocialist country. In film, as Zhang Yimou and Chen Kaige became ranked among the most bankable suppliers of international art house motion pictures, the so-called Sixth Generation of Chinese filmmakers, such as Zhang Yuan and Wang Xiaoshuai, are struggling to invent a more documentary, more prosaic, and radically fragmented cinematic grammar compatible with post-Tiananmen Chinese everyday life. Furthermore, the new visual culture in China today has been thoroughly penetrated by advertisement and video; so that film has long ceased to be the standard bearer or fashion leader in the field. In architecture, we have not only the postmodern buildings designed mostly by American firms that have mushroomed in Chinese big cities but also the buildings of the younger generation Chinese architects, such as the American-educated and Beijing-based Zhang Yonghe (Chang Yung-ho). These projects have shown an amazing degree of sophistication in combining innovative design with commercial savvy, bringing a Chinese brand of postmodern architecture to their international and local nouveau riche clients. In the "traditional" world of fiction, while veterans from the 1980s such as Mo Yan and Yu Hua continue to defy categorization, an avalanche of new writers are busy replacing the modernist intensity and seriousness of their predecessors with various relaxed, free-floating, decentered, depth-shunning, antiheroic, and anti-idealist writings about everyday life of the Chinese 1990s. Not least, theoretical discourses, which in the 1980s depended either on European high philosophy or traditional culture (e.g., Neo-Confucianism) for their relevance and legitimacy, have finally become a cultural genre and intellectual fashion, rivaling the momentous renaissance of the personal essay, the daily bombardment of which, with their imported and homemade jargons, spurred the pejorative term "postology" (houxue). Indeed, to the startled and disgruntled opponents of Chinese "postology," such theoretical discourses of "cultural criticism" as feminism, postcolonialism, Neo-Marxism, cultural studies, and so forth are first and foremost a "postmodern" phenomenon.

If one acknowledges the fact that, despite the great theoretical sophistication seen in the past two decades, postmodernism is still understood by many as a cultural-aesthetic fashion with a Euro-American genealogy, then it is a natural, though unconvincing, first step to try to prove that there are credible, sufficient similarities between the postmodern fashion in China and its Euro-American archetypes. It is natural because there is no other way to enter the discursive or the symbolic system without a borrowed name. It is unconvincing because the question of Chinese postmodernism was born in the paradox that the technically postmodern features of contemporary Chinese culture and society, instead of qualifying the latter as postmodernism, often highlight the sense of irony emerging from the gap between an economic reality and its image or self-image in the symbolic and imaginary spheres. Thus any self-respecting argument for a Chinese postmodernism necessarily becomes an effort to bridge the opposites dialectically, to mediate between existing but ultimately distorting frameworks of experience and thinking in order to articulate something qualitatively new out of them. And to this extent postmodernism, as an idea and as a discourse, whose intervention in Chinese cultural and intellectual life is as aggressive as it is precarious, can be used as a theoretical hinge between a nameless reality and the system of naming that connects uneven and often discontinuous historical time and space.

Playing on the home ground of postmodernism, which is diverse, expansive, eclectic, and readily reproducible and disseminating, it seems only trivial, indeed misleading, to run down a list of essential characteristics and qualities, formal or otherwise, in order to prove one's authenticity, a notion dissolved by the very concept one tries to adopt. In practice, most critics and theoreticians of postmodernism in China seem to settle with a sort of loose family semblance, which for them justifies the debate of Chinese postmodernism as a cultural-political question. And, ever since Fredric Jameson's signature linking between postmodernism and consumer society (hence the notion of postmodernism as the "cultural logic of late capitalism") was popularized among various Chinese intellectual circles in the late 1980s, postmodernism has been seen by its Chinese students as primarily a sociohistorical change articulated culturally, whose becoming a particular Chinese problematic is conditioned first by the presence of a national discourse of high modernism, which the new rises to challenge and undermine, and, ultimately, by China's rapid economic growth, its decidedly mixed modes of production, and its incomplete but intensifying integration into the global capitalist market, which together provide a material, symbolic, and demographic environment for the postmodern, generally and minimally defined. From this perspective, one would find that those postmodern images and logos in contemporary Chinese art and culture, rather than being a fantasy of a few desperate international fashion chasers, are an integrated part of the thoroughly commercialized Chinese urban landscape, completed with Portman-designed hotels, McDonald's restaurants, karaoke bars, video compact disks (VCDs) of Hollywood or Hong Kong movies, shopping malls and wholesale clubs, the omnipresent advertisement of local or global brands, and the even more omnipresent consumer crowds.

But does that mean Chinese postmodernism is something for real? The question about the Real—to be precise, that the Real has become a question—is, ironically, perhaps one of the surest signs that we are actually dealing with the "postmodern," in and for which reality and history seem to have all but disappeared. That, however, should not divert us from the particularities of the issues coming with the still feeble discursive invention of Chinese postmodernism. If postmodernism as such is widely understood in today's media and academia as something, in its anti-essentialist way, essentially of depthless surface, unlimited reproducibility, and radical decenteredness, as something sustained by its appeal to the consumer masses everywhere and, as Baudrillard would tell us, containing virtually no relationship to reality whatsoever, it is not going to say much if one keeps reporting on the new fashions succeeding each other on the Chinese streets. In fact, those who oppose even the appearance of the term *postmodernism* in China maintain that, by borrowing or (re)producing those (Western-originated) simulacra, Chinese postmodernism and its proponents are threatening to obscure the urgent Chinese social, economic, and political imperatives known as modernity. Based on their respective notions of the modern, which are intensely although often implicitly political, opponents of postmodernism go on to press often contradictory charges, accusing Chinese postmodernism of being subversive (undermining the value system of the socialist state), complacent (legitimizing the state by affirming and celebrating the commercialized everyday culture under the former's ideological control), too Westernized (whoring after the academic fashions of the Western theory), too Chinese (harboring haughty nativism and nationalism), too leftist (criticizing capitalism and undermining the universal truth of modernity), too rightist (celebrating desire and commodities), and so forth.

One is tempted to admit that, in China, it is sometimes more interesting to study the resistance to and dismissal of Chinese postmodernism than cataloguing its aesthetic achievements; that the more productive discussions of the formal innovations of Chinese postmodernism will sooner or later end up in the political. The strong, often bitter objections to the idea of Chinese postmodernism must be considered a constitutive part of this discourse, its ideological-political contestedness part of the familiar, sensuous richness without which *Chinese postmodernism* as a term will be either too nebulous or too matter-of-fact. To give the issue of Chinese postmodernism any historical and theoretical sense-certainty, one has to start with the widely held view or conviction, rather, that, in China at least, the modern is far from over — or, as some still sincerely believe, has not yet begun. It is also important to remember that postmodernism, like other "isms" and "ologies," is an import from the West. As the most recent and least time-honored theoretical discourse from a foreign land, it tends to be singled out to shoulder the usual suspicion, even hostility, of those who are increasingly frustrated by following the West in ever closer range, or those who resent the Western discursive and theoretical licensing and hegemony, even though what they hold as good, solid, and genuinely Chinese knowledge systems are often little more than just older imports from nineteenth-century Europe, such as positivism, empiricism, historicism. The intellectuals' frustration reflects the powerlessness of this social group in the face of intensified globalization, on the one hand, and the surging confidence and self-assertion of the consumer masses, on the other. Once again, in the manner of the previous generations of the Chinese Enlightenment, they pledged their loyalty to the modern and, by doing so, denounce the postmodern as a harmful deviation or, at best, a premature, thus useless, present from their Western contemporaries. But it is precisely in its resistance to the postmodern that the Chinese modern reveals itself not as a totality, but as a differentiated, fragmented, and contradictory experience. Its prolonged discursive and ideological uniformity is not a historical given, but a historical contingency made possible by the persistence of the truly "premodern" elements in Chinese society (poverty, ignorance, superstition, chaos, repression, and the cultural and political backlash of the ultraconservatives who oppose not only the radical revolutions of 1919–49 but the Republican Revolution of 1911 as well) and, more recently, by the continued and renewed rivalry between socialism and capitalism, that is, between the two competing ideological claims on modernity in China in the post–cold war years. This only reminds us that the truth-content of Chinese postmodernism may very well lie in the intellectual and political stakes it has raised for all parties within the historical conjuncture of postsocialist China, in the ways it disrupts and demystifies entrenched positions in an increasingly differentiated cultural and social sphere after the disintegration of the reformist consensus among the state, intellectuals, and the masses, and among elite intellectuals themselves.

To those who entertain the idea of Chinese postmodernism and its complex, far-reaching implications, a diligent description of postmodernism in China will almost immediately turn into an analysis of a dazzling overlap of forms, discourses, and histories, a project that is inevitably more historical, theoretical, and ultimately political in nature than what it is ready to admit. In order to make sense of Chinese postmodernism (rather than merely postmodernism in China), we must show those Chinese images, or—if they are as genuinely postmodern in every aspect as their Western "originals"—Chinese simulacra in a historical situation, as something produced by a changing life experience and mode of production, and something that in turn offers a picture, a narrative, an ideological proof of socioeconomic relations, instead of a mirage in the global mirror-house of symbolic inflation and commodity fetishism. This means that even to see merely how China receives postmodernism one has to show how China produces it. A meaningful notion of Chinese postmodernism must be in-itself and for-itself a historical coming to terms with Chinese modernity as an admittedly unfinished project but one whose legitimacy, validity, and universal claim have already, for better or worse, come under fire. The perception, experience, and anxiety that modernity as an organizing principle, an all-encompassing, meaning-bestowing vision, is loosing its grip on Chinese daily life constitutes the sense-certainty for the incoming new.

Out of Modernism

The list of arts and artists at the beginning of this essay should make it clear that various artistic, literary, and theoretical styles in the Chinese 1990s are not only informed by postmodernism as an international discourse but also emerged more specifically against the cultural-intellectual mainstream of the Chinese 1980s, the so-called modernist-humanist paradigm of the New Era (1979–89). While high modernism had become an intellectual and formal institution in the Chinese metropolis before the Tiananmen incident, it has been thoroughly dismantled in the 1990s by the joint force of the market and the ideological apparatus of the state, as well as by a rising cultural populism and nationalism closely associated with the nascent urban middle class, its economic interest, and its increasing cultural and political assertiveness. In literature, for example, the modernist canon, established by waves of formal innovations in post-Mao era from Misty poetry via the Search-for-Roots movement to experimental or avant-garde fiction, while maintaining its prestige supported largely by its international recognition, has been swamped by an explosive literary market catering to the new, wealthier, and thoroughly depoliticized (except for an increasing nationalist sentiment) reading public that has little patience for stylistic experimentation and transhistorical contemplation. The emblem of post-Mao Chinese intellectual discourse, namely, its jargons à la Heidegger or Walter Benjamin and its metaphysical vision, is now replaced either by a journalistic genre designed for quick media exposure and consumer gratification or by a professionalist turn to the normality and standardization of academic production and promotion. All this passive or aggressive undermining of the previous cultural hegemony is true also of Euro-American postmodernism, which came into being in the 1960s and 1970s when it broke free from the establishment of high modernism (of Joyce, Le Corbusier, Kandinsky, and the like). Even those who carry on their uncompromisingly modernist or avant-garde style unabated—writers such as Ge Fei come readily in mind—are bound to be read in a different light, that is, in the context of the cultural market, in terms of a particular flavor or brand, of a uniquely marketable quality, not to mention that the brief moment of Chinese high modernism as a whole has already been subject to academic canonization and lost its shock value and subversiveness vis-à-vis the dominant taste and ideology of the reading public and the officialdom.[1]

There are reasons to believe that the modernism-postmodernism shift is more useful as a theoretical narrative pertaining to a sociohistorical periodization than as a chronological, discipline-based description of the developments in literature and the fine arts, especially in a context, such as the present one, where both modernism and postmodernism are derivative frameworks. Where the sociohistorical periodization owes its explanatory clarity and persuasiveness to the paradigmatic shift from modernism to postmodernism in literary and art history, the convoluted time-space implied in this formal change cannot be overlooked. Any critically meaningful study of Chinese postmodernism (or modernism, or for that matter, realism and romanticism as well) would involve not one but two pairs of formal and social histories, with each of the four subcategories of the double binary— for instance, Chinese realism and the Chinese revolution, European high modernism and European imperialism—striving for its own diachronic continuity and institutional realization while constantly getting mired in synchronic agitations and cross-cultural resonance. Together, they create an intense force field in which one thing readily becomes an allegory of another and in which historicity is overdetermined, overrepresented, repressed, forgotten, and eventually comes back with a vengeance.

Postmodernism, unlike previous styles in cultural history, does not seem to be conducive to the traditional comparative approach, as are studies of influence or parallelism, probably because its dependence on—indeed, symbiosis with—technologies of instantaneous reproduction and dissemination render such effort ineffective and unnecessary. That, however, only collapses the form to make comparison a laborious analysis of cultural fluidity conditioned by a multiplicity of socioeconomic and ideological contexts. With respect to the dialectic between form and content, one may contend that Adorno's thesis, based on his study of European classical music, that each new artistic paradigm contains, in and only in its aesthetic solution of tensions created in the history of form, a solution—or what we call articulation—of the social-moral dilemma of its time, still holds true, although only on an expanded historical horizon, with an added appreciation of the radical Other.[2]

Looking closely, many discussions of Chinese postmodernism actually talk about how postmodernism as such lands on the Chinese shores and establishes beachhead positions, although the effort is often confused, by readers and authors alike, with the attempt to show that a particular Chinese cultural form has emerged to address and articulate the globally determined, but locally conditioned, socioeconomic reality with a distinct Chinese accent. Even the crudest opponents of Chinese postmodernism can recognize the implied causal relationship between this cultural style and a socioeconomic reality that must be somehow more than the merely classical modern, hence their dismissal of Chinese postmodernism as unwarranted for an economically and technologically backward society unworthy of (or unable to afford) the pleasure, freedom, and prestige of the postindustrial (or information, or consumer) societies with which these critics do not seem to have an argument. But if we focus on the deconstruction of the moral, philosophical, and political systems of the Enlightenment and modernity, long seen as the core values and secret weapons of the modern imperial and colonial powers, and contemplate its effect on areas on the margins of an unevenly developed world system, then the modernism-postmodernism turn offers the possibility of a new discursive and ideological framework by which to continue the search for an alternative to the classical blueprint of modernity, namely the free market and liberal democracy. To this extent, postmodernism as an event may carry a revolutionary message in an era when the October-style revolution seems all but impossible. To push the Russian metaphor even further in the Chinese context, one may start to contemplate the breaking of the global chain of multinational capitalism at its weakest point, where postmodernism could come dangerously close to postsocialism, or vice versa.

If "postmodern" means—as the Japanese kanji translation of the term may suggest—departure, shedding off, coming out, breaking away, disengagement, exit, and freedom from the classical modern as the ruling ideology of the era of catch-up modernization and military dictatorship in East Asia in the late nineteenth and early twentieth centuries, then Chinese postmodernism, while challenging the ephemeral high modernism of the 1980s, uncunningly extends the epistemological and empirical boundary of modernism and modernity into the entire history of modern China, which has the socialist experience at its core. By doing so, it implicitly deconstructs, complicates, and even historicizes the ideological and simplistic opposition between socialist modernity and its bourgeois or counterrevolutionary alternative, despite the intention of the "liberal" position to highlight the revolutionary and socialist periods as an anomaly to the universal experience of modernity defined by the ideological hegemony of the post–cold war West.

To this extent, Chinese postmodernism, more than anything else, is an idea to be analyzed in the context of comparative history of ideas, an intellectual discourse to be reconstructed in its operations through concrete social and cultural domains. By its participation in the contemporary circulation of terms and discourses, the arrival of Chinese postmodernism simply reveals and destabilizes the ideological assumptions embedded in the premodern-modern order around which the foundational discourse of modern China evolves. In other words, the emergence of the term, like its Japanese counterpart, which took root in that ultraindustrial country in Asia, "testifies not so much to a transition from one period to another as to the shift or transformation of our discourse, as a result of which the supposed indisputability of the historico-geopolitical pairing (premodern and modern) has become increasingly problematic."[3] To this extent Chinese postmodernism, as reality or as fiction, adds a new twist, nuance, articulation to the tradition of antimodernist modernisms, including various forms of cultural traditionalism, nativism, rural communalism, nationalism, and populism, whose histories are as long as the history of modernity in China itself. Whereas the impulse to challenge western modernity and search for an alternative evolved in Japan, in the form of *kindai no chokoku*, or the "overcoming of the modern" during the Pacific War, in China the social energy and imagination found their political realization in socialism, which, in its Maoist form, brings a solution to the dilemma of non-Western modernities, which is how to address the geographical unevenness in terms of temporal evolution and simultaneously absorb the universal chronology hitherto invented and internalized in national-political terms.[4] The socialist experience of Chinese modernity is central to the historical determination of the discourse of Chinese postmodernism. While the addition of the third term or stage to the premodern-modern chronology suggests that the modern itself should be freed from the straitjacket of ideologies and social imaginaries into a larger historical constellation, different narratives are constructed by different social positions in the effort of breaking the Eurocentric grip on the notion of the modern that makes it possible for non-Europeans to imagine a native or modern in which one feels both contemporary and at home. All of them are predicated on the notion that modernity is an open-ended process that produces its own dispersal, alternative, subversion, and reversal, which has become popularized by the mass media. Thus a temporary discontinuity suggested by postmodernism allows one to pay attention to the spatial discontinuity or the uneven spread of the modern. This in turn gives rise to a world picture and a sense of one's individual and collective location, which creates the internal tension between postmodernism as a more ruthless force of global standardization and postmodernism as a pluralistic system that tolerates, even appreciates, spatial and temporal differences, as various local architectural or fashion styles and the distinctly postmodern genre of nostalgia may testify.

It is only in the context of postmodern nostalgia that we can explain the splashy return of Mao badges and Cultural Revolutionary songs to the streets of Chinese cities, the popularity and sometimes cult value of some Chinese socialist-realist film classics, the consumer appetite for yellowed black-and-white family photos from the simple everyday life under Mao, and numerous best-sellers made from the letters, diaries, memoirs of the rusticated students who spent their formative years in the remotest provinces of China during the Cultural Revolution, all of which are selflessly mingled with a flood of other cult images of nostalgia derived from the immediate past or the yester-years of prerevolutionary China.[5] One may even argue that it is only amidst the postmodern, postsocialist ruins or prosperity (depending on one's perspective) that Mao's China gets its afterlife as previously hidden, or carefully subdued, epic monumentality and the inhuman grandeur of an empire.[6] That such images and sentiments of nostalgia as a consumer-oriented cultural fashion should cause alarm and worry, not to mention political denunciations, should remind us that the ghosts from the past have not been dead for long, that Mao's China remains a huge presence in the collective unconscious of postsocialist China, capable of stirring up the uncontrollable imagination, and, last but not least, that the Chinese modern defined in classical liberal-democratic terms is far from a long, stable, and fully institutionalized tradition. At the same time, the postmodern liberation from the modern also exposes China—as a discourse, an invention, and an ideology—literally to an enlarged temporal genealogy and geographical territory. Even within the so-called cultural China, it readily inserts the PRC into the lingering, unsettled historical constellation of prerevolutionary China and postrevolutionary China and, geographically, in the context of other, usually much richer and intensely anticommunist, Chinese regimes, societies, and diasporic communities. Thus leaving the modern may also imply that the current Chinese government loses an important source of its legitimacy.

Where Chinese nationalists and critics of global capitalism want to emphasize that the economic transformation of China requires the strengthening of the nation-state and a pragmatic attitude toward the socialist legacy, for the enthusiasts of the global free market, a straight path to the future has been shown beyond any reasonable doubt. Not only the furious technological innovation and soaring stock market of the United States have set the tone of the perpetual growth (and the perpetual ideological present); the rise of Japan and later of the newly industrial countries of East and Southeast Asia—through their protected participation in what Eric Hobsbawm calls the "Golden Age" of twentieth century capitalism—has also proven that the capital can be multicentered, multinational, and multicultural. The postmodern (as the symbolic order of late capitalism) and the premodern (traditional or, more precisely, prerevolutionary China) tend to flirt with each other, as they do with the rhetoric of Neo-Confucianism, Confucian capitalism, or Asian values, in a way reminiscent of Freud's famous observation that the super-ego and the id tend to team up against consciousness. And in reality they unfailingly find their common enemy in Chinese socialism as an inheritor of the Chinese enlightenment and modernity.

Given the experience of Chinese socialism as a painful alternative and often desperate resistance to the hegemony of Western capitalism (and, one should add, social imperialism, as the state interest of the Soviet Union was called during and immediately after the Cultural Revolution), it should not be hard to understand that the unexpected arrival of the "postmodern" also keeps certain socialist or postsocialist imaginations and practices alive. In fact, Chinese postmodernism obtained its public fame or notoriety only when it had become an ideologico-discursive platform for the heated, public debate about Chinese economic, political, and social development in the 1990s, in which all the previous debates regarding Chinese modernization, socialist or otherwise, have been replayed against the nebulous yet unmistakable background of new global configurations, to which we will turn later.

The coexisting frames of reference result in the shifting characteristics of Chinese postmodernism, often frustrating its most sympathetic beholders. For instance, if Chinese postmodernism is to be viewed as a specific reaction against the established forms of high modernism, then one needs to bear in mind that modernism as a specific historical-aesthetic style has never been an "established form" in the history of modern China but always a cultural-intellectual striving and a transient, embattled, precarious movement, as in Beijing in the mid- and late 1980s, and, equally briefly, in Shanghai in the 1930s.[7] Moreover, the socioeconomic condition of the ephemeral Chinese high modernism, namely Chinese (bourgeois or socialist) modernity and modernization, is widely considered an ongoing project that has yet to run its full course in Chinese and world history. The fact that most of the criticism of the discourse of Chinese postmodernism (and its moral and political intensity) stems from an undivided loyalty to the unfinished projects of Chinese modernity and the Chinese nation-state indicates a temporal axis that fully collapses the discourse of Chinese uniqueness into the (liberal or Marxist) discourse of universal progress, an ideological conviction and discursive practice since the turn of the century. Compared to those universal values and institutions entailed in the Enlightenment, which are yet to be fully implemented in China (or in the West, one may want to add, as Jürgen Habermas's writings have reminded us), any celebratory and frivolous declaration that something is over will be cast in profound doubt and viewed as "ahistorical." In his essay "Theories of Postmodernism," Fredric Jameson reminds us of the "ungeneralizable" national situation in which Habermas offers his defense of high modernism against the ideological assault of the postmodern. Jameson seems to agree with Habermas that the classical European *Bürgerlichkeit* or the bourgeois public sphere remains to this day an only partially realized ideal even in the core Western democracies. That, however, does not prevent Jameson from analyzing the particular political and ideological repression in the formerly Federal Republic of Germany, where McCarthyism was a reality and where "intellectual intimidation of the Left and the silencing of a left culture (largely associated, by the West German Right, with 'terrorism') has been on the whole a far more successful operation than elsewhere in the West."[8] Self-styled liberals in China today quickly adopt the Habermasian model of the public sphere while preaching the Hayekian doctrine of the unlimited power of the free market based on the propertied individual. Through its political subversion of the discourse of socialist modernity, the liberal discourse has acquired not only a moral urgency but also a "forward-moving" posture (with a Fukuyama-style "End of History" as its goal) that allows it to see postmodernism as a main threat to the radical ideology of a conservative revolution, which seeks to reinsert China properly into the evolutionary chain of universal modernity.

If the postmodern, in China as anywhere else, signifies a sense of the radically new and, paradoxically, a certain loss of destiny or direction sociopolitically and historico-philosophically speaking, little wonder that the term would annoy most of those who see an ever clearer picture of world history rising on the horizon. The impassioned opponents of Chinese socialism are seeking to build an "alternative," that is, counterrevolutionary, discourse of modernization and modernity based on the law of the absolute free market. To such a conservative utopia and its demand for ideological clarity, teleological certainty, and moral intensity, Chinese postmodernism is certainly guilty of muddying the water, blurring the boundaries, and creating too much distraction, all of which seem to benefit both the survival of the current Chinese system and survival *under* it. What the champions of Chinese modernity are reluctant to acknowledge or fail to see is precisely the inconvenient fact that the "fiction" of Chinese postmodernism actually lays bare the very historical assumptions and teleology of modernity as such and therefore exposes the question of Chinese modernity—its rupture, omissions, discontinuity, and leap—in the new socioeconomic and cultural conditions at the end of the twentieth century. It might be very unsettling for some to see all the pillars of modern social-cultural institutions—from "nation-state" to "subjectivity," from the utopian design for an ideal society (or social space) to the absolute free market, and from a Eurocentric universal order to the unquestioned affirmation of cultural-ethnocentrism—have now been dragged into a seemingly endless process of deconstruction. But one can hardly make any convincing argument that it is more historical to ignore the new than to forget the old, and that the rise of the (postsocialist consumer) masses in China in the 1990s does not carry its own democratic and historic implications without requiring the prior establishment of the economic privilege and political institutions of the nineteenth-century bourgeoisie. In this respect, Hegel, the nineteenth-century philosopher who teaches us to think dialectically, that is, to see the old and the new in contradictions seeking to reach a solution before succumbing to new ones, may arguably be the first truly postmodern thinker.

Political Stakes

The inherent paradox of Chinese postmodernism lies in the fact that, by declaring the end of an era, it creates a sense of liberation from the past, hence of a limitless, indefinite future; yet by placing itself after something it intends to transcend, postmodernism—its novelty, innovativeness, and aesthetic appeal—can only be experienced and measured against established, dominant norms and institutions. To this extent, postmodernism inherits all the internal and historical ambiguities of modernism and thus becomes a new trope for the changing social-political space of post-Mao China. In a general sense, postmodernism, like modernism, is an endless and sometimes self-defeating struggle to become and remain the ever new. Like modernism, it lends its form to even its most determined opponents: there are postmodern anti-postmodernists, in the same way that there have been modernists of anti-modernism and revolutionaries of counterrevolution. Like modernism, postmodernism entails and is entailed by different socioeconomic and political orientations and positions. Like modernism, postmodernism encompasses radically different social ideals and political ideologies. Unlike modernism, however, postmodernism does not see everything as cosmologically, heroically new; rather its conept of newness or creation is hinged on a sophisticated, almost cynical sense that all the good and evil, in their most extreme forms, have been somewhere, somehow, and sometimes before, tried, and what is left for contemporary men and women is nothing more than shrewd and occasionally breathtaking eclecticism, synthesis, reproduction, and representation in the most literal sense. In this respect, there is nothing more indicative of the aesthetics of the postmodern than fashion or its concept of what is fashionable, which is fundamentally cyclical. This sense of relaxation if not freedom from the pressure of linear temporality (progress) and singular spatiality (Europe) can create new breaks, ruptures, and fluctuations as it shakes the very foundations of our notions of history, selfhood, meaning, and just about everything else. Taking place in real historical context, such shifts have profound political implications.

One of the curious things about Chinese postmodernism is its being labeled a *neoconservatism* (*xin baoshou zhuyi*) by its genuinely conservative critics. Initially coined by the London-based Chinese literary scholar Zhao Yiheng, *neoconservatism* as an attribute of Chinese postmodernism shows almost comically how stretched and misleading those Western-originated, Western-defined categories can be when enlisted in the Chinese political and cultural-political battles. While deploring postmodernism's fervor for replacing aesthetics and "ultimate truth" (*zhongji zhenli*) with politics, the new Right is unable to come up with any cultural vision, let alone theory, mainly because its own political positionality readily turns the cultural and the jargons of subjectivity into a tantalizing trope of private ownership (or the lack of it under communism).[9] What Zhao meant by *neoconservatism* here is nothing more than an alleged apology for the status quo or, more precisely, a reluctance and hesitation to scrap the existing system and its cultural legacies, by Chinese intellectuals who have equipped themselves with Western theoretical discourses of "postology" (poststructuralism, postcolonialism, postmodernism, etc.). Here, the backward-leaning tendency necessary to qualify the definition of *conservatism* is found by Zhao in two things. First, (postmodern) intellectuals have abandoned the elitist position independent and critical of the state power, thus allowing themselves to celebrate a mass culture and everyday life in China manipulated by both the (impure and underdeveloped) market and the (more supple but equally intrusive) government. Second, the implicitly or explicitly populist, nationalist, and even socialist tendency in the mass cultural affirmation of the everyday distracts, indeed, hinders the forward motion of Chinese enlightenment and progress, which in Zhao's context has become a code word for the political ideal of "market democracy," and from the vantage point of which the everyday reality of China cannot but be characterized as "conservative." The political sentiment and ideological conviction Zhao demonstrates achieved only their fantastic version, in the form of futurology, in China before 1989, but have since then evolved into a discourse of universal, realized (as in the post–cold war West) truth.

It will indeed be hard to understand how "abandoning the elitist position" can be used as evidence to prove someone's "conservatism," if the concrete ideological setting of Deng's China is missing, but by "elitism" Zhao clearly refers to the intellectual-bureaucratic consensus of the New Era, which was carried out by the "neoauthoritarian" (*xin quanwei zhuyi*) state. Such an express train to the universal destiny of the global market and modernism as an international language can be a smooth journey only when operated by the social engineers freed from the inconvenience of popular, local, and democratic debate on Chinese modernization and modernity. (Democracy, by the way, had never figured prominently in the pre-1989 intellectual lexicon, contrary to the popular impression derived from Western TV images of the Tiananmen "pro-democracy movement"). That, in retrospect, may explain the obsession of Chinese modernism with such aristocratic and/or politically reactionary modernists as T. S. Eliot, Ezra Pound, Martin Heidegger, and the twentieth-century Russian religious philosophers. The politicoeconomic message of such willed high modernism, to be sure, is a belated one, which finds its messengers in latecomers to contemporary Chinese intellectual life such as Fredrick von Hayek, even though in the economics and policy arena the penetration of neoliberal theology is earlier and more thorough, and is aided by another elitist intellectual camp, namely the "neoauthoritarianists" (*xinquan-weizhuyi zhe*). The emotional drama of Chinese high modernism in the New Era unwittingly travels along the historical path once described, with little emotional evalorization, by the sociologist Karl Mannheim as but another route of capitalization (which Mannheim quickly adds is not always necessarily in ideological agreement with the main push for modernization in the industrial, military, financial, and bureaucratic sectors).[10] For those Chinese "postmodernists," however, capitalization, marketization, privatization, and other forms of social rationalization are all part of the daily reality and thus need critical skepticism rather than sentimental reaffirmation. Even though the modernist-postmodernist conflict is implicitly or explicitly predicated on economics, the battle line is not clearly cut and is defined as much by taste and "common sense" as by ideological conviction. For instance, few modernists or former modernists in China are enthusiastic about the "Harvard boys do Russia" or "Chicago boys do Chile" models, even though Milan Kundera or Václav Havel remain their contemporary heros.

Still, it is clear that such accusation of Chinese postmodernism as "conservatism" (the prefix "neo" refers to its "postmodern," "postsocialist" appearance and postsocialist politics) can be established only in the ideological environment in which the radical, top-down revolutionary plan for sweeping, total socioeconomic change is desired. Such conservative revolution, intent on rooting out the evils of revolution and socialism once and for all, can find its model in the (postcommunist) Russia's 500-Day Plan, better known as the shock therapy prescribed by a group of Harvard economists to convert the Soviet command system into a free market system. By qualifying the cultural manifestations of the changing, radically heterogeneous realities of a China in transition as "conservative," Zhao reveals the fervor of the embrace of global post–cold war ideology by the Chinese liberals. Such ideology, nurtured in the Reagan-Thatcher years, continues to loom along with the climbing stock index on Wall Street. Yet its function as a utopia seeking its own realization in China today would be inconceivable without the "neoauthoritarianism" of a reformist regime and its elite intellectuals. Such a conservative utopia, to be sure, can only be elitist, "independent," and fundamentally antidemocratic in a big Third World and still residually socialist country like China, despite its advocates' pretense to democracy. While many Chinese postmodern works of art and theoretical discourse are recognizably—indeed, helplessly—symbiotic with a chaotic complex of economic and social relations in China today, their impatient and unimpressed critics seem to have a clean-cut, holistic plan that has figured out not only what to change but how to change it. Its implementation (i.e., the privatization of national wealth) will be inconceivable without the endorsement of powerful interest groups within the state bureaucracy, despite the "liberal intellectuals'" tired self-positioning as some kind of political dissidents.[11] Before the new system is created from scratch, anyone who wants to live and work risks being an apologist for the status quo. Here, "status quo," like its official name, "socialist market economy," can stand for the irreducible messiness and chaotic energy from which Chinese postmodernism evolved into a cultural form.

In today's environment of thorough commodification and manufactured consensus, the sentimental posture of a self-privileging heroism in Zhao's "insistence on elitist position" and "critique of vulgar mass culture" reveals in retrospect the deep yet hidden divide in the Chinese high modernism in the 1980s. While the stylistic intensity and formal autonomy of Chinese modernism (from Misty poetry to New Chinese Cinema) paradoxically make possible a posthumous articulation of the voluntarism and collective utopia of Mao's China, they also prepared a formal-discursive institution, as a temporary ideological void in pre-1989 China, awaiting its material and political realization through the final implantation of China in the evolution chain of world capitalism. Whereas Chinese modernism could have and did have a high cultural form of the collective, as indicated in the prevalent first-person plural figure *we* in early Misty poetry as well as in the social-political orientation of the early Fifth Generation film, it is also, historically speaking, the aesthetic den of the privileged individual and its inflated subjectivity in the imagined presence of global modernism and modernity, where the collective pronoun reveals the confidence of one's agency and leadership in a national self-transformation and cultural rebirth.[12] The grammatical figure of the discourse of Chinese postmodernism, however, is decidedly communal, if subjectless, as illustrated by both the poetry of new-generation wanderer tribes and the neorealist fiction of, say, Tan Ge and Liu Xinglong, a favorite subject of analysis by leading postmodernist literary critics such as Zhang Yiwu. The final split between the New Left (a pejorative label coined by its ideological and theoretical opponents, which includes Neo-Marxists, feminists, nationalists, as well as postmodernists) and the New Right vividly reveals the schizophrenic political unconscious of Chinese modernism and modernity, and to this extent marks the beginning of the political coming-into-being of post-Mao Chinese intellectuals, which is always, implicitly and explicitly, entangled with the question of Chinese socialism in the information age and the era of global capital.

The postmodern deconstruction of Eurocentric universality has been quickly picked up by the nativist current and various forms of intellectual, cultural "decolonization" in China in the 1990s. In theoretical discourse, such a sociocultural turn is marked by the disappearance of Heidegger, T. S. Eliot, Russian symbolists, Western Marxism, or the Vienna school as intellectual-cultural reference points, and, in their place, the rise to prominence in public discussions of Edward Said, postcolonialism, cultural studies, and postmodernism (whose first and by far the most authoritative theoretician known to Chinese, namely Fredric Jameson, is among the very few who enjoy both intellectual respect and ideological relevance in both worlds on either side of the modernist-postmodernist divide). The sociological or rather, politico-economical, message of the appearance of a Chinese postcolonial stance is unclear, however. Where it maintains its obvious progressive, critical edge vis-à-vis the conservative notion of universal modernity—now embodied by the self-styled Chinese liberals advocating the neoliberal ideal of "civil society" and the autonomous free market—such a posture may also reveal the emergence of a new power elite in new national and international class reconfigurations, who, as Arif Dirlik reminds us, may feel repressed and alienated in some ways but share, indeed, depend on, the very power they criticize in other ways.[13] Dirlik's observation is particularly to the point, given the structural disassociation of postcolonial discourse today from the earlier struggles of national and colonial liberation movements. In China, the half-century of socialist rule has rendered even the memory of imperialism and colonialism vague and lacking in concrete reference, whereas the ahistorical comparison between, say, Shanghai and Hong Kong, has given rise to a pervasive, philistine, historical regret that colonialism could have and would have provided a better route to individual well-being than socialism. However, except for very few scholars of Hong Kong or Taiwanese background, the celebration of in-betweenness, hybridity, and rootlessness associated with international mobility, now seen as a badge of privilege and success, has not caught up in Chinese postcolonialism, or for that matter, Chinese postmodernism in general. More importantly, since the postcolonial critics in China, as elsewhere, are deeply committed to the enlightenment and modernization, the convenient, if not only, intellectual room for them to engage in a critical rewriting of modernity tends to be defined in such ethnic, racial, sexual, and "cultural" terms that their overall theoretical and political challenge to the ideology of the modern is limited. This might be the reason why among Chinese intellectuals, the postcolonial discourse, having no difficulty associating itself with other theoretical subject-positions such as feminism, cultural studies, and so forth, tends to disdain Marxism and everything it deems as "grand narrative," whereas Chinese postmodernism, more populist and utopian, and tied closely to the Chinese everyday world, has demonstrated no such tendency.

As far as their knee-jerk reaction toward Chinese postmodernism is concerned, however, the Old Left and the New Right have much in common, both showing an instinctual distrust and fear of the new and the unknown in their dogmatic loyalty to reified institutions and doctrines as a sole path toward "universal truth." To this extent, despite its own ideological ambiguity, the theoretical discourse of Chinese postmodernism seems to touch upon an enormous yet nameless domain of historical happening, namely, the rising Chinese consumer mass and their incipient cultural and life forms. In this sense the debate against Chinese postmodernism has turned itself, unwittingly or not, into a contested claim on and bidding for this emergent style and its social agency. As the Old Left sees postmodernism as defying and undermining the discursive foundation of Marxism, revolution, socialism, and the party-state, the New Right senses in the emerging ideological centrism of the "socialist market economy" an ominous return of all the bad things, from realism in literature and art (as critics labeled the antimodernist genres as "neorealism," or *xin xieshi zhuyi*) to populism and consumer nationalism in the political domain. Whereas the Old Left perceives the changing fashions and unapologetic individualism in China today as indicative of the penetration of Chinese society by global capitalism, the New Right discovers an alarming complicity between ruthless state power and the affirmative, even celebratory nature of postmodern art works and theoretical discourses that legitimize the local hegemony and oppression, namely, the state, by celebrating the popular and the everyday under its yoke. In this respect conservative criticism in China in the 1990s takes its cue also from its Western counterparts, which now frequently use the strategies, tactics, and rhetoric of the Left, in this case the intellectual obligation to critique power at home, to formulate the right-wing agenda.[14]

That postmodernism, or merely the talking about it, has provided a new discursive, ideological, and cultural environment or atmosphere for living with the dilemma of Chinese modernity does not mean that what the latter entails can now be addressed or solved in a certifiably—that is, formally, superficially—postmodern fashion, if only because postmodernism as we know it has in its "cultural" core the assumption that politics, ideology, human experience, or history itself, no longer matter, indeed, no longer exist, an assumption which underscores the rise of a variety of postmodern cultural, identity (of ethnic or sexual varieties), or academic politics, often in the void of classically political categories such as class and nation. It is important to note that the strong form of intellectual opposition to postmodernism that can be found in China today is defined almost entirely in terms of national politics. It merely attacks postmodernism as a radical cultural theory, and by doing so *defends* the "enlightenment" agenda of the Chinese reform, which, in today's global ideological environment, has acquired its actualized form in the free market, the international power structure, and consumer society, all of which fall under the descriptive or analytical rubric of postmodernism, whose cultural-psychological sedimentation, or its *episteme,* is what the radical theory of postmodernism seeks to subvert and deconstruct. By "uncovering" the hidden relationship between such radical postmodern theorists as Michel Foucault, Jacques Derrida, Julia Kristeva, Roland Barthes, Louis Althusser, Pierre Bourdieu, and Fredric Jameson and the 1960s as a global period of radicalization, and between the 1960s and the Chinese Cultural Revolution (which is thoroughly stigmatized by the official ideology of the Reform regime), the opponents of Chinese postmodernism make more than a suggestion that postmodernism in China, in addition to being a frivolous academic mimicry of those Western masters, is a sinister reincarnation of the revolutionary and cultural revolutionary lunacy of Mao's China, a residue of the old political fantasy under the disguise of the fashionably new.[15]

In the context of intellectual politics of post-1989 China, the hostility toward Chinese postmodernism becomes a psychological and philosophical stand-in for something that is much older and has never made peace with Chinese revolution and socialism, two definitive elements of Chinese modernity.[16] Indeed the attack on Chinese postmodernism reveals the unsettled confrontation with the Chinese Revolution, a confrontation that acquires its urgency in the intellectual impulse to "return" to universal normalcy, namely a long delayed bourgeois modernity based on private ownership and parliamentary democracy, an otherwise "commonsensical" move now complicated by the ideological fuzziness of postmodernism and its incessant deconstructive operations. The Chinese critics of postmodernism are often expressly uninterested in the cultural fashions from the West, so long as the latter do not, in their original or borrowed forms, interfere, complicate, and disrupt the world picture of progress and its believed universal validity. On the other side of the coin, and along the reversed order of the same logic, there are arguments that Maoism, via the back door of sixties radicalism, remains current, in fact, prophetically postmodern which shows Chinese intellectuals a shortcut to the cultural critique of contemporary capitalism pursued by Western Marxists.[17] Such argument also conveniently forgets the very different economic, social, political, cultural, and national situations facing Mao as the leader of a communist state and the Western Marxists, poststructuralists, feminists, and other cultural critics of late capitalism.

But so long as postmodernism, as an everyday or popular cultural phenomenon, seems to nourish a social-ideological consensus of the consumer masses (a topic to which I will turn below), and, as an intellectual discourse, interrogates the assumptions, hierarchies, and power relations within the bodies of "universal truth," it will continue to be entangled with the issues of postsocialism, and, through this entanglement, lends a certain kind of legitimacy to the latter. To that extent, those who seek pleasure, freedom, and radical contemporaneity in Chinese postmodernism will continue to be bogged down and haunted by the specters of the Chinese Revolution and their own desire and obsession to overcome or forget about it.

Once the discourse of Chinese postmodernism is pitted against the holy trinity of modernization, modernity, and modernism, its aesthetic novelty and cultural gratification tend to disperse into a dense cloud of politics and underlining ideology. It is hardly surprising that postmodernism in China is facing harsh criticism from both the Left and the Right. In post-Mao, and now post-Deng, China, it is much easier to define the Right, which comprises mainly the followers of the neoliberal orthodoxy of sweeping marketization and privatization, than the Left, which occupies a diverse terrain and a more or less centrist ideology defined in terms of Chinese political reality. For those who still believe in the mandate of the enlightenment, modernization, and statehood, postmodernism is not only a heresy vis-à-vis the official or officially sanctioned intellectual discourse of the New Era, but more importantly an alternative mode of cultural production in the realm of mass culture that threatens the cohesiveness of the ideological-discursive hegemony of the state, including the technocratic and intellectual elite of the Reform establishment. The latter, through the voice of the self-styled "liberalists" (*ziyou zhuyi zhe*) such as Xu Youyu and Zhu Xueqin, has been particularly bitter in its denunciations against postmodernism, in which its own authoritarian tone can barely be concealed.

Postmodernism and Postsocialist Society

Such conservative critique of Chinese postmodernism, with its ideological self-righteousness and moral-psychological intensity, often manages to dislodge the postmodern debate by cornering it in a forced reductionist choice between socialism and capitalism, despotism and liberal democracy, state command and free market, "official" and "unofficial," popular culture and elitism, right and wrong. But to address the complexity and dynamism of the postmodern debate, it may be more productive to think not in terms of left and right, but in terms of the high and the low, that is, in terms of the structural transformation of Chinese society and culture in the 1990s, which allows us to consider the disoriented, divided intellectual discourse as a response to the everyday world of postsocialist China and its competing cultural and ideological forms.

If it is a valid observation that the debate on Chinese postmodernism has more to do with the historic situation of contemporary China than general formalistic features of the global cultural fashion, then it is only logical to try to understand the socioeconomic condition of Chinese society since the late 1980s in order to set this particular brand of postmodernism on its feet. It does not take a Marxist to see that, so long as the Chinese economy remains a shortage economy, so long as the average Chinese citizen perceives the wealth gap between his/her own country and that of the advanced industrial ones as cosmologically abstract, thus mythical and metaphysical, the nineteenth-century discourse of modernity, with all its trappings of teleology and hierarchy, and all the mythologies of presence, origin, and center, will remain intact and be held with equal passion by both the socialist and antisocialist, elitist and populist, nationalist and cosmopolitan elements of the Chinese state and society at large. It should be clear that not only Chinese postmodernism is conditioned by a fuller industrialization, a market economy, and, eventually, a commodity or consumer society, but the naming of Chinese postmodernism itself must be regarded as a cultural and political event made possible, even called for, by socioeconomic changes and ideological imperatives of postsocialist China. The tunnel vision of a single-minded modernism and its discursive self-autonomy would not and indeed did not disintegrate in front of newspaper reports and TV images about the postmodern *Lebenswelt*, let alone by the appearance of a few postmodern hotel or office buildings in one's childhood neighborhood, so long as the economic reality at home demands an undivided focus on and ideological valorization of modernization. Throughout the 1980s, such modernism, flanked by humanism in philosophy, realism in literature, and a reinvention of tradition in cultural discourse, was sustained by a social mentality compatible with the radical modernization or Reform programs. The first decade of China's post-Mao encounter with the (already postmodern, and, given the closer contact with Japan, Hong Kong, and overseas Chinese investors and visitors, already geographically multicentered) West was dominated by the urgency of modernization and modernity in virtually all areas of social, cultural, intellectual lives, which were still fully controlled by the newly established technocratic and intellectual elite of the Reform regime and their high cultural discourses. Simply put, a more relaxed and less simpleminded take on the ideal of the modern must be preconditioned by a certain degree of material wealth and security, which give rise to a certain degree of freedom and decadence, making it possible to look the other way, to wander, to explore, or simply to entertain different options, that is, to think in terms of "culture," not necessity. Before this moment arrives, the brutal, ruthless grip of the ideology of modernity on its believers is not something to be aware of, let alone talked away. Deng's economic reform and his creation of a "modestly affluent" (*xiao kang*) society have paved the way for the dissolution of not only Maoism as a utopianism but also an early-twentieth-century type of ideology of modernization shared by both Mao and Deng. Where postsocialism designates the ambiguous place of Chinese society in the grand narrative of the modern that has never left us, postmodernism signifies an emerging vision of a form of life corresponding and bringing cultural affirmation to such economic reality.

At any rate, Chinese postmodernism is simply inconceivable without readily available commodities and capital (including symbolic capital) flow, without new daily experiences based on a changed, and changing, material environment. While in societies formerly isolated from the capitalist world system—a category to which China in the early years of the Reform era still belonged—the mythological concept of wealth tends to be attached to concrete cult objects (from durable consumer goods such as television sets or portable stereo cassette players to the economic, political, and cultural institutions of contemporary capitalism), for a world in which daily life is intimately linked to the global market—where post-1992 China also belongs— that mythology becomes focused on that "sensuous abstraction" (to borrow Paul Valéry's phrase out of context), money. The social, collective recognition of money as the universally commensurate standard of wealth, success, freedom, and happiness in post-Mao China corresponds with the beginning of Chinese postmodernism, for under money the empirical world is once again unified, organized, and bestowed with meaning, not by cargo worship of specific and arbitrary objects and institutions but by a universally applicable concept, which, ironically, effectively allows the local, particular, and "cultural" elements to figure in the one and only game in town and which sets up the game situation where weighing one's options, advantages, and limits, and picking one's strategy under given historical conditions are not only legitimate but necessary. As a concrete abstraction of the extremely complex contemporary economic relations, money is a great equalizer, which unifies an uneven socioeconomic terrain. Once the logic and practice of financial capital become the terms by which to understand the world and according to which one organizes collective and individual experience, the cultural, psychological, and sociopolitical elements formerly considered incompatible with modernization and modernity can now be incorporated into the system according to their market value. That, more than anything else, lends a historic confidence to the cultural and social assertions of the Chinese world of life intertwined with socialism, and bestows on the latter (as well as on the presocialist and indeed, precapitalist historical moments, which have never been fully put to rest by the Chinese modernity) a membership in the perpetual presence of the global economic growth. Thus the Pacific (and increasingly "Greater China" as a shadowy empire of free-floating capital, commerce, and professionals) seems to have replaced the "West" as the anchor of a national imaginary, in which the long, bloody centuries of (European) industrialization are rendered unnecessary by the shining examples of economic miracles in East Asian "Little Dragons" and "Little Tigers," which have exported their way into the American Age.

Once China, with its extensive, if primitive, industrial power, educational capacity, bureaucratic network, and technological infrastructure, had committed itself to becoming a leading manufacturer of cheap commodities in the world, it rapidly took over its Southeast Asian neighbors as the biggest exporter to the West, mainly the United States, whose imports helped keep the post-Mao Chinese industry operating at full steam for more than a decade. The swelling Chinese foreign reserves (close to $150 billion by July 1999) and national saving (more than 6 trillion yuan, roughly $0.8 trillion) indicates not so much the rapidity of Chinese economic growth but rather the daunting discrepancy between the massive accumulation of products, services, and capital (all an increasingly integral part of the global market), on the one hand, and a populace that is still extremely poor and poorly protected by modern standards, and which constitutes the labor and domestic market, on the other. Where, as many believe, the high inflation caused by an overheated economy and lifting of price controls in 1988 may have contributed to the social disturbances resulting in the mass protest in 1989, a decade later the challenge facing the Chinese government is how to reverse a steady deflation, reduce huge factory inventories, and encourage Chinese consumers to buy just about anything from automobiles to stock shares to housing units. Somewhere in the process, the Chinese economy, whose core remains socialist or state-owned, became a surplus economy plagued by industrial overcapacity and insufficient domestic demand. Given its huge export-oriented industrial structure, its still very low wages and standard of living, and climbing savings due to a heightened sense of insecurity among working people, such overcapacity is as real as it is misleading. Once exports slow down due to fluctuations in the international market or intensified protections in the United States and the European Union, huge amounts of products flood the domestic market, which is unable to absorb this inward flow, an inability guaranteed by an artificial exchange rate that deflates the Chinese currency, slow wage growth, an artificially high real estate market due to land speculation often backed by government loans, and finally, by the determination of average consumers to hold on to their money and an almost certain further cutback of state welfare and labor security programs. This seems to be the way by which a phantom "postindustrial" prosperity has been created in China, which is characterized by low per capita income and consumption capacity and by an inflated hyperreality consisting of overinvestment, overproduction, conspicuous consumption by the new rich and corrupt bureaucrats (often the same individuals) and such enclaves of globalization as the special economic zones, luxury hotels and boutique stores, the tourist-oriented service industry, and so forth.

The surplus of commodities and capital is accompanied, to be sure, by a bubble economy of images, signs, and discourses. The saturation of media and mass cultural industry, the constant flow of truly international fashions and advertising, and the consumption of the latest MTV or Hollywood big hits virtually simultaneously with residents of American suburbia (made possible by digital technology and the Internet), all reinforce and amplify the impression that daily life in China today is an integral part of the timeless Now of global capitalism. It is no surprise that China has become the world's number one producer of the video compact disk player, a cheap, computer-based piece of hardware popular in China but virtually absent in the West, whose software supply relies almost completely on piracy. Thanks to the VCD, a great number of Chinese urban consumers now share the visual culture of the postmodern West at a much lower price than was possible before. It was rumored that a VCD version of Titanic appeared on the streets of Beijing and Shanghai a few days before the film had been released in the United States. Chinese postmodernism, like all varieties of this cultural trend, is made possible by and is almost exclusively dependent upon the technology of reproduction and representation, not that of production, where China has gained the reputation of being the world's biggest labor-intensive, heavily polluting workshop, instead of a significant player in the amazing contemporary advancement of science and technology. In this sense it might not be grossly inaccurate to call China a probational, virtual postmodern society.

The huge discrepancy between daily life under residual socialism and hyperreality in the fledging market is keeping Chinese society in a permanent state of economic mobilization and ideological agitation. At the same time, the drive for profit, and, with that, the leveling of the economic and psychological field by money has involved everything in market operations and gives everything its market value. Everything, that is, including the persistence of the socialist system, and, more relevant to our present subject, the unconscious of the rising consumer masses—their frustration, fear, resentment, their newly achieved freedom and sense of power, their obsession with the here and now, as well as their need for a new collective identity and social ideal. Market forces, with the presence and blessing of the communist party-state, have created a highly mixed mode of production. The coexistence of private, communal, state, and foreign joint-venture ownerships, the different forms of employment and job opportunities, and the residual egalitarian network of rural economy and the state welfare system make visible the choices, options, and optimal combinations in economic life. In economic and sociological terms, it is the overlap and coexistence of a dazzling variety of modes of production, social structures, political lexicons, ideological discourses, and value systems, not the growth rate itself, that constitutes the conditions of possibility of Chinese postmodernism.

It is important to remember that postsocialist China is conditioned not only by its place in the multinational capitalist environment, but also by its existing socioeconomic space, carved out during previous decades of revolution and socialism. The internal ambiguity of the logic of the Reform—indeed, of socialism understood as a historical experiment—lies in its double posture of transcending dogmatic socialism by embracing contemporary capitalist modes of production, while, in theory as well as in practice, transcending dogmatic capitalism by means of innovative, unprecedented ways of deconstructing and reconfiguring the old bundles of concepts, rights, and material forces. The implicit logic of the "advantage of the backward," which assumes that the institutional arrangements of advanced capitalist societies are sometimes only "second best" and are distorted by their internal flaws, is reminiscent of the historical appeal of socialism to Chinese intellectuals between the two world wars. Doubts about free-market capitalism, whose role in recent crises in Russia, Brazil, and East Asia has caused great alarm, find their cultural, theoretical formulations in postmodernism, in which all kinds of ideologies—from anticapitalist, anti-enlightenment conservatism to hypercapitalist futurism—can find their niches only in a deessentialized fashion, in which socialism, like Chinese postmodernism itself, cuts across the ideological lines rather than falls neatly along one and against the other.

It seems reasonable to assume that in trying to catch up with the West, the comparative frame of reference for China is often not the West itself, but China's neighboring countries: South Korea, Taiwan, Malaysia, and, in a different sense and to a different ideological and psychological effect, India and Russia. The nearly double-digit average growth rate of the Chinese economy of the past two decades has increasingly become a subject of study in recent years, a phenomenon crying for theoretical explanation. In the 1980s, the success of the economic reforms were considered to be due to a structural disengagement from socialist dogma and the embrace of the market mechanism. In the 1990s, however, the continued Chinese economic growth has more often than not been put in stark contrast to the collapse of the Russian economy, and, more recently, to the economic depression of all of East

Asia as a result of the speculative attack by international capital. Where the Russian situation declares the bankruptcy of any utopian dogma of absolute private ownership and the total autonomy of the free market, the East Asian economic crisis reveals the ruinous, predatory nature of unchecked freedom in the global financial market.[18] In both cases, it is the socialist character of the Chinese economy, its relative separation from the global system, that has sustained economic development in China. By the end of the 1990s, more and more scholars are ready to take the Chinese economy neither as an ad hoc, patchy, and half-measure free-market economy, nor as a chaotic, corrupt, and fading command system, but as an economic, social, and political alternative in the making, an experiment whose provisionality proves to be the norm. This way of thinking finds its most provocative voice in Cui Zhiyuan's call for "intellectual liberation" and his critique of "institutional fetishism."

Based on his collaborative research with Chinese scholars on the Nanjie village in the central Chinese province of Henan, Cui observes that the socialist infrastructure, economic or otherwise, can be creatively transformed in building a collective, cooperative model of economic development, in which "group rationality" and "individual rationality" may reach an optimal equilibrium through the mechanism of group incentives and mutual dependence.[19] This case study is just one example of Cui's effort to formulate a new theory of China's rural economy, which credits the phenomenal growth of the Chinese rural economy, above all of rural industry, to an innovative system of flexible production and specialization, cooperative ownership and democratic distribution of wealth, and the organic integration of rural China and industrialization. In doing so, Cui follows the footsteps of Fei Xiaotong, whose lifelong effort to theorize Chinese rural industrialization argues the compatibility of modern industrial technology and a decentered, flexible, and cooperative rural network of production. He also builds on Philip Huang's theory that the ruralization of industry provides a way out of the "involution" of rural Chinese economy in the past centuries, and that the socialist collectivization, accumulation, and protoindustrialization paved the way for rural China in the contemporary market environment.[20] Cui repudiates the prevalent view that economic vitality in rural China is a result of decollectivization and the reinstallation of private ownership or the "family responsibility system" by showing that the key to rural economic development is not increased agricultural production but the industrialization of rural China, which requires a heightened degree of social organization, specialization, and the concentration of capital. He also repudiates the equally conventional view that rural economic reforms amount to nothing more than local state corporatism, a view that, while admitting the huge vitality of rural industrialization, deplores the insufficient privatization or marketization that exists due to the presence of state and local government and the latter's command and control of re-sources, production, population mobility, and economic opportunities.[21]

For Cui, the innovativeness of rural Chinese industry lies in its being a de facto system of "flexible specialization" and "flexible production." The fact that the workers at rural industrial enterprises are also peasants who still hold on to their land under the contract-out system, that is, their double identity as worker/peasant, enhances the competitiveness of rural industry in the fluid market environment. Its rural and communal anchor allows rural enterprise to develop highly flexible technological, organizational, labor, and operation arrangements, thus giving it an advantage through efficient pro-duction when demand is uncertain. Borrowing Charles Sabel's notion of the Möbius strip, Cui thinks positively of the blurred, often messy, boundaries between enterprises and society, between private and collective ownerships, which are considered a sign of immature, insufficient privatization by neo-classical economics. Cui pays particular attention to the shareholding system developed by the Chinese peasants/workers, which, instead of dismember-ing and privatizing the collective property of the former people's communes, turns the collective assets into "collective shares," independent of the indi-vidual shares of the labor, while the representatives of the local community (i.e., village or township government) remain the legal owner of the collec-tive who coordinates the interests of its employees and those of other local residents.

Cui extends his theory of flexible production in (post)socialist China into many other areas of Chinese economy, but his choice of the rural industrial-ization as an entry point reflects the theoretical and political importance of this issue in China today. Not only do rural enterprises now represent close to 40 percent of the Chinese GNP, involve more than 100 million Chinese peasants, and remain the main driving force behind the improvement of the standard of living for the rural population, they are also poised to provide an alternative model of industrialization and urbanization, which, combined with the village election system, has far-reaching implications for Chinese socialism and Chinese (post)modernity. What concerns the theory of Chi-nese postmodernism most in Cui's writings are his two general concepts of intellectual liberation and institutional fetishism. By intellectual liberation, he means freedom from and more sophisticated ways to interrogate such tra-ditional binary opposites as private ownership versus state ownership, market versus plan, reformism versus conservatism, Sinocentrism versus wholesale Westernization. It is a way of thinking that, in Cui's own words, "expands the imaginary space for institutional innovation guided by the commitment to both economic and political democracy."[22] Calling for such intellectual lib-eration inspired by innovative theories such as analytical Marxism and critical legal studies, and above all by the changing Chinese reality, Cui criticizes various forms of institutional fetishism, which "immediately equalizes concrete institutional arrangements with abstract ideas, i.e., corporate America with 'market economy,' two party system with democracy." For Cui, such thinking endows concrete, historically conditioned institutional arrangements with superhistorical, mysterious "inevitability," thus fetishizes them.[23] The main thrust of such critical thinking, to be sure, is directed against such dominant mythologies, which identify private ownership with the market, and two- or multiple-party parliament politics or the appearance of a stable middle class with democracy. Here Cui's theoretical operations draw inspiration from Adam Przeworski, who regards socialism as political democracy combined with economic democracy; and Jon Elster, who considers current institutional arrangements of free-market capitalism as only "second best" for the development of productive forces. Moreover, Cui's wide-ranging account of a complex, diverse, and historically uneven reality bears an unmistakable sign of postmodernism, which deconstructs the previously held totalities into dividable bundles of qualities and relationships ready for reconfiguration under new historical circumstances, and which refutes the classical-modernist logic of identity to favor a more flexible, fuzzy, and dialectical thinking based on difference, resemblance, and free association.[24]

The postmodern logic of Cui's arguments, or, conversely, the prosocialist logic of Chinese postmodernism, as seen in Cui's theoretical operations, is something more readily grasped by his liberal-conservative opponents than by his New Left or postmodern allies, who have devoted their energy almost exclusively to charting the contours of the newly emergent Chinese everyday life and its cultural manifestations. But Cui's passionate commitment to economic and political democracy in China and his belief that socialism, via the route of intellectual liberation and institutional innovation, can create a better alternative to capitalism as we know it, proves to be an important intellectual anchor that supports the debate of Chinese postmodernism as a way of thinking beyond institutional fetishism in general and as a form of postsocialism in particular. Where multiple layers of private, communal, collective, and state ownership have been created and legitimized to free the productive force from the command economy of a formerly quasi-military state organization, individuals, communities, local regions, as well as enterprises themselves become shareholders as well as stakeholders in the new economic, social, and political environment. Scholars, notably Western scholars, are often more eager to gauge the extent to which economic liberalization dismantles socialism and nurtures capitalism than to analyze how socialism—a system created as an alternative to the lack of economic democracy in modern capitalism—is revitalized and, in its more decentered, deessentialized, flexible forms, becomes an integral, constitutive part of the daily reality of Chinese economic, social, political, and cultural life.

The politically contested nature of Chinese postmodernism, to be sure, is nothing but a reminder of the mixed modes of production, various articulations of a convoluted social and cultural history, of its many repressed and unrealized chapters and moments, their memory, and their participation in the new configuration of social and cultural forces in the present situation. Chinese postmodernism, on the other hand, rose with a distinctly Chinese mass culture nourished in the marketplace, and it entailed a conscious break from the previous modernist high cultural style. For those who want China to remain on the course of catching up with the phantom images of the nineteenth century, "classic" modernity, or those who, uncritically accepting postmodernism as a graduation certificate from the mandatory course of modernization and a one-way ticket to the timeless Now, the subject of Chinese postmodernism either threatens a premature ending of the national discourse of modernization or gives China undue prestige and the harmful illusion that it has passed the ordeals and tests of the modern. In China in the 1990s, postmodernism as a social-cultural question stems from the various ways through which the ideology of the modern becomes less and less capable of functioning as the organizing, rationalizing principle. In sociological terms, its arrival merely confirms the open secret that the Chinese economy and Chinese everyday life have already outgrown the administrative control and ideological tutelage of the Reform regime, whose popular support if not political legitimacy was badly damaged by the military crackdown in Tiananmen in 1989. For both its proponents and opponents, Chinese postmodernism, as both a cultural vision and a social ideology, is intertwined with the Chinese experience that neither socialism nor capitalism seems to provide satisfactory answers anymore, that innovative thinking is urgently needed, minimally to understand why, how, or how long the Chinese economic, social, and political structure can still manage to muddle through and, maximally, to articulate a new theory for a new social system and its cultural-intellectual discourse in the making. The modernism-postmodernism break, established in Western theoretical discourse, offers a symbolic framework by which to renegotiate the continuities and discontinuities of time and space, and therefore finds its currency in the intellectual effort to formulate a cultural, ideological reorientation, whose meaning in contemporary China is, however, always more political and socioeconomic than immediately "cultural."

If Chinese socialism is, as it is considered by Eric Hobsbawm, and, from the other end of the political spectrum, Lucian Pye, uniquely also a national and cultural (or "civilizational") project, then something radically historical can and must be found in this otherwise "ahistorical" space of a civilizational nation.[25] That is to say, if the political, historical meaning of Chinese social-ism is not merely considered rather cynically as a disposable tool for the resto-ration and sustenance of a "form of civilization," one must be ready to grapple with the changing Chinese politicoeconomic relations of today. In the con-text of Chinese postmodernism, these relations point to the theoretical pos-sibility, and its social-cultural implications, of "socialist market economy," of socialist postindustrialization, and the material and political cultures of the postsocialist consumer masses. The formation of the postsocialist national market, while involving the Chinese economy deeply in the world market, has also carved out a tangible national boundary, defined in terms of economic interest, in the mental map of the Chinese consumer masses, an imagina-tion that was to be sharpened by the latter's unhappy encounter with Western mass media's representation of China, a China at which the emerging urban middle-class now have a stake, and on which they want to lay claims.[26]

It is only fitting that such history or histories should find their new mode of expression in postmodernism, which is a style marked by internal schizo-phrenia, and which contains in its very texture a pastiche of previous and alien genres, styles, images, and languages. Where the historical legitimacy of Chi-nese postmodernism comes from both the realities of global capital and the realities of Chinese socialism, its imaginary self-affirmation often takes the form of a magical realist replaying of historical narratives, memories, and desires, which never want to miss any opportunity to seize upon the flying images and signs of the immediate now, only to turn them into allegorical expressions of something else. To this degree, it is impossible to understand Chinese postmodernism other than as a historical event. The playful phonetic similarity established between "postmodern" and "post-Mao-Deng" should be as telling to a diagnosis of contemporary China as a slip of tongue is to a psychoanalyst.[27]

The Historicity of the Postmodern

A look into the history of modern China will make it clear that the Chi-nese route to the modern has been a painful one; and in order to reorient a long, largely self-autonomous, and intensely self-centered civilization, mod-ern Chinese intellectuals probably practiced the most radical form of collec-tive rationalization in the history of modern culture by fighting a "cultural war" (against tradition) along deceptively value-free, logical lines, namely, by adopting and advocating evolution and pragmatism. This is the way by which Hu Shi defined and justified the Vernacular Revolution, that is, the attempt to create something plainly, unsentimentally useful.[28] The vernacular language is the medium for modern Chinese intellectuals and modern Chinese culture.

It is historically constructed as not only a signifying structure but a structure that signifies the metagrammar of a temporality understood in a world dominated by European powers and the iron law of instrumental reason. To this extent, the May Fourth movement shares the internal dialectic or dilemma of enlightenment in that it is both elitist in its task to mold a new nation by fostering a new culture, and anti-elitist in its commitment to the vernacular. The ensuing historical moments, from the Chinese Enlightenment in 1919 to the culmination of the Chinese Revolution in the statehood of the PRC, are nothing more than moments in the actualization of this logic of the modern in the material and cultural space called China. The challenge of postmodernism to this strong historical-intellectual genealogy of modern China cannot be effectively analyzed without a critical differentiation of this genealogy itself. Obviously, there is something in this genealogy, and in the challenge it is now facing, which is strictly parallel to the history of the modern-postmodern West, a parallel that vividly spells out the extent to which China has always been part of the world under the tightening grip of a modernity that has been steadily losing its European peculiarities to become something truly "universal," by coercion, power, and violence as well as through internalization and assimilation. On the other hand, there is something identifiably national if not "local," which stems from the particular, albeit by no means unique, Chinese response to the impact of the modern West, a response that always longs to "return" to its self-identity and permanence in a projected future point on the other end of the somewhat alienating process of change. Indeed, the perception of the modern as not only constantly new and changing but also ultimately ephemeral and merely transitional—a perception inconceivable without a long historical memory and measurement or the survival of a deeply rooted cultural and ethnocentrism—determines that the Chinese modern is always on the lookout for something that comes after the modern, or rather, for an even more plural world, in which one feels both modern and at home, for a contemporary identity that is thoroughly decolonized from the law of modernity as such. This deeply seated cultural unconsciousness can be found at work in the postmodern turn in contemporary Chinese culture, a paradigmatic shift from heroic creation (a classic modernist fixation) to enjoyment, pleasure, and suspicion toward any coercive or super-imposed uniformity, both domestic and international, the last of which may explain the strong and paranoiac Chinese opposition to NATO's "humanitarian" intervention in the former Yugoslavia, as that country shatters the expectations of the emerging Chinese urban middle class, for a more pluralistic world and reveals a new world order reminiscent of the one that, by means of its moral axiom that "might is right," drove China into the century of radical nationalist and socialist revolutions.

The cultural collective unconscious that perceives modernity as a moment of alienation—even though Chinese intellectuals in effect embrace the fundamentals of the modern, from industrialization to social rationalization, with an obsessive intensity—may help nurture a national consciousness more susceptible to the possibilities of eclecticism, synthesis, alternativity, pluralism, and negativity. Beliefs in evolution and pragmatism, although themselves products of an ideology of the modern, may also render the project of modernity more a matter of functional efficiency than one of deep emotional attachment when the rationale of the modern comes under doubt. Chinese communism, unquestionably the most radical and brutal form of Chinese modernity, is never a transparent unity but a bundle of sometimes contradictory ideals and convictions. Its mature and theorized form, namely Maoism, is itself a vernacular discourse of contradiction and praxis. Known as Marxism-made-Chinese or Sinified Marxism (makesi zhuyi zhongguohua), Maoism is a result of complex and highly dialectical negotiations not only between the West and the East but between high and low cultures as well. With its built-in passion for the masses and constant innovation, its profound disdain for discursive or institutional reifications, Maoism may be one of the ideological-philosophical foundations for the shift to the postmodern, whose utopian truth-content finds its legitimation/distortion in market ideology during the commercial Mao kitsch craze of the early 1990s. Furthermore, Chinese postmodernism, as a liberating force conditioned by new socioeconomic relations, may put an end to the ideological and political taboos leading to a rigid understanding of Maoism as a utopian totalitarianism. Insofar as utopian totalitarianism remains the centerpiece of a socialist modernity that the New Right seeks to subvert and replace with its own, and as long as "alternative" or "oppressed" modernity is used as a shorthand for unrealized bourgeois longings, liberal discourse will be unwilling and unable to cope with the emergence of a postmodern, postsocialist mass culture in urban China today. This inadequacy of discourse, however, may negatively endow Chinese postmodernism with a utopian, historic meaning it has so far been unable to embrace, namely, as the culture of the Fourth Estate ascending to the stage of world history.

Thus Chinese postmodernism may ultimately be used as an instrument of periodization for modern Chinese social, cultural, and intellectual history, as a way to mark a paradigmatic shift within the history of ideas of the modern, if only because it dissolves all the periods and their metaphysical properties in a keen sense of the perpetual now. Such a temporal structure, devoid of dogmas and taboos, in turn will provide us with a more effective framework to analyze the political ambiguities of Chinese postmodernism as an intellectual discourse and as a way to formulate a collective experience. In terms of the minute chronology of terminologies, the circulation of "postmodernism" is inseparable from the other, more historical marker, namely, the "post–New Era" (hou xinshiqi). Coined by the literary critic Zhang Yiwu, so far the most controversial, most productive, and in many ways the crudest theoretician of Chinese postmodernism, "post–New Era" is a defiant term to mark the ideological, intellectual, and (in terms of taste, habit, and behavior) cultural break from the New Era and its high-modernist–humanist discursive mainstream and hegemony. As a backlash to this nativist, plebeian celebration of the age of the masses and their everyday culture, there emerged an intellectual-cultural fashion of nostalgia for the New Era, that is, for the ideological, political, and intellectual consensus on "Reform," for the protected freedom and inwardness of the Chinese modernists, and for the exoticness of post-Mao Chinese society under the Western gaze.

To this gaze, and to this nostalgia, Chinese postmodernism offers a rude estrangement via the familiar—namely, commodities and the market—and a radical secularization or demystification through the irreducibly mundane, plebeian, and popular. Here, however, postmodernism no longer means the particular intellectual discourse of China in the 1990s, but its own conditions of possibility, above all the rise of the consumer masses and their own mode of cultural production and consumption.

It is important to keep a historical perspective in understanding the Chinese approach to the market, which, for the Chinese intellectual and state elite, is always a matter of rational choice and social engineering, and the very content of a continued enlightenment, as evidenced in the intellectual-social consensus of the New Era. Yet the expansion of the market and consumer-oriented everyday world and the impersonal, autonomous operations of market forces have quickly made it clear that those "spokesmen of the people" and pioneers of enlightenment, instead of controlling the system, are helplessly controlled, manipulated, and marginalized by the system which plays by its own rules. The day-to-day experience of many Chinese high intellectuals vis-à-vis the market is a textbook example of the destruction of the Subject in posthumanist, poststructuralist terms. Thus the resistance to the "postmodern" becomes part of internal intellectual politics and anxiety in the 1990s, which often sacrifices the analysis of the new for the sake of a self-privileging moral heroism with various ideological affiliations (anticommunism, religious fundamentalism, Chinese cultural traditionalism, liberal enlightenment, nostalgia for the Maoist utopian puritanism, and so forth).

But those who declared war on the rising consumer mass culture and its vulgarity often seem to forget the fact that the "postmodern" culture is merely a way to come to terms with a new economic, social, and political situation, and that the corrupt new culture is no more than the affirmation, celebration, self-indulgence, and self-projection of a nebulous new class occupying the social (and impoliticly, political) space that used to deny them entry. Contrary to the call for "opposing the secular world" (*zhan zai sushi de duilimian*) and "refusing to surrender" (*jujue touxiang*) by writers such as Zhang Chengzhi, Zhang Wei, and Han Shaogong, or the advocates for "restoring the humanist spirit" (*chongjian renwen jingshen*) by a group of scholars in Shanghai, the Chinese postmodernists offer their defense of the everyday sphere. For Zhang Yiwu, the moral indignation expressed by some Chinese intellectuals against the vulgar cultural carnival of Chinese postmodernism reveals a "fear of freedom" and the "anxiety of the modernity." In his view, such anxiety is rooted in an "internal contradiction of modernity":

> In fact, the objectives of the modern are quite concrete and tangible. The improvements of everyday life are indeed extremely secular, mundane goals. However, the processes by which those goals are to be achieved are of extreme grandeur and greatness. . . . If the worldliness of the human pursuit can be seen right away, many will be disappointed. In short, the modern is the pursuit of the ordinary by means of the great and the sublime. Today, Chinese society is moving toward further improvement of life in a worldly atmosphere, and that creates an acute sense of loss and formidable resistance.[29]

Zhang, in his dialogue with the writer Liu Xinwu, whom he credits for a literary chronology of the rise of commoners along with the transformation of Chinese economy, is enthusiastic about the emergence of the masses out of the political shadow (as a holy yet abstract concept) of the "people" in the 1990s, a process that can be traced to the economic and social reforms of the New Era, despite the era's obsession with the sublime and a total solution to all problems. Observing the ways by which the new mass culture penetrates and coexists with the state media, moving thus from the margins to the center, Zhang sees a "new relationship" between state and civil society, whose "shared social space," namely, the cooperations, consultations, and dialogue between the two, is the unique environment in which the culture of the "post–New Era" flourished. Such a shared social-cultural space, argues Zhang, conveys the cultural demand and imaginations of the consumer masses while carrying on the propaganda function of the state. This arrangement not only allows a clear hearing of the voices from the "civil society" but also helps nurture an "invaluable social consensus" in the expanded and developed "public sphere." Compared to the premature Chinese civil society of the late 1980s, which seemed on an almost inevitable collision course with the state, the present mature civil society is, Zhang argues, characterized by a "nonconfrontational" relationship to the state, despite the different and sometimes conflicting interests between the two. For Zhang, a new, mass-oriented, democratic, and consensual cultural paradigm is undoubtedly being nourished now, and the intellectual elite of the New Era will have little control over this booming field.[30]

Despite being vulnerable to the predictable accusation of endorsing the government and catering to the mainstream, Zhang's position is notably communitarian, populist, and nativist rather than explicitly political in terms of its positionality vis-à-vis capitalism. In fact, it is the political ambiguity of the central figure of Chinese postmodernism, namely, the postsocialist consumer masses, that determines the fundamental historical ambiguity of Chinese postmodernism as both a cultural paradigm and a social phenomenon. What Zhang shows us, often quite convincingly, is the way in which the imaginations, tastes, and demands of the newly emerging masses fuse with the bureaucratic and ideological operations of the state, and the way in which the state and Chinese civil society sometimes find their expression—cultural or political—in each other. But what is missing in this picture is a potent analysis of the dubious, makeshift category of Chinese civil society, which requires the breakdown of the nebulous postsocialist masses in terms of class interest and ideology, that is, we need to see the new class as a community, a form of life, a culture, and, ultimately, a political force. Liu Xinwu, Zhang's interlocutor in this context, occasionally tells a more detailed story of the rise of the "civil society" from outside the state system and on the margins of it, to the center of Chinese social life in the 1990s, a status backed by its swelling wealth and the new social ideology. But that only makes the very notion of a postsocialist Chinese civil society all the more nebulous, and its cultural and political influence exaggerated. If such a civil society, as Liu sees it, consisted initially of those who were "nowhere to be seen in the progress of history" and who exited as "fodder of society" (shehui tianchongwu), namely, unemployed, temporary workers, and other unclassifiable elements that the socialist economy and social organizations had failed to absorb, then the dramatic rise of this social group, that is, its newly found wealth in the marketplace, does not seem to be able to pose any major threat to the overall economic and social structure, despite its obvious, if traumatic, psychological effect on some state employees whose income fell or stagnated in the past decade.[31] In fact, the term shimin (urbanites) may unwittingly betray its true meaning of "marketplace people" (shi) (as opposed to those whose livelihood depends exclusively on the state system) whose activities constitute a "biosphere" of society that can no longer be described, not to mention analyzed, within the old binary of "official" and "unofficial" that some China scholars still hold to.[32] But if the market is considered the essential content of the so-called Chinese civil society, then "Chinese civil society" loses most of its classical social and political meaning as "bourgeois society," as it is embedded in the European origin of the term. Moreover, it loses its most desired (by the Chinese followers of Hayek), immediately political suggestion that there is an autonomous "society," based on and self-regulated by the market principle, which is subverting, replacing, and bringing an end to the Chinese state and the superstructures of socialist modernity. The most innovative part of Zhang and Liu's discussion of Chinese culture in the 1990s lies in its recognition that the overall market environment in China today is a product of the state, that the state shares the new economic, social, ideological, and cultural space being created in the market. That alone gives rise to very different implications of the rise of the (post)socialist consumer masses, and of Chinese postmodernism.

Thus the dramatic growth of the economic power of the former "social fodder" class, or the commoners at the bottom of the social hierarchy of Chinese socialism; their cultural affirmation, as manifested in Chinese mass cultural works, particularly TV soap operas, in the 1990s, can be regarded as a social metaphor for the economic and ideological reorientation of post-socialist Chinese society as a whole. It is theoretically problematic, therefore, to celebrate the rise of the masses and their culture without questioning their implicit ideological affiliations or at the very least offering a critical analysis of the possibility of them. Thus, for Chinese intellectuals more critical of the process of globalization and suspicious of the state's role in this process, Chinese postmodernism sometimes amounts to an uncritical celebration of the status quo, thus an implicit endorsement of the ideology of commodification by means of a populist affirmation of the social desire.[33] The critique of Chinese postmodernism from the Left is symmetrical with that from the Right and reveals a different kind of political anxiety that the (post)socialist state now functions as an agent of international capital and special interest groups at home.

Where it is evident that the rise of Chinese mass culture corresponds to a certain kind of upward social mobility of a certain social class, and in this process, a plebeian cultural imagination is steadily replaced by a middle-class aspiration, the newly emerged "social consensus" or the ideological mainstream is more complex, in political as well as historical terms. The post-modern vernacular culture, with its built-in rejection of the enlightenment ideology of Chinese intellectuals, proves to be more unruly and multidimensional than any other cultural paradigm in the history of modern China. At an existential level, Chinese postmodernism, speaking for Chinese mass culture and forms of everyday life in the 1990s, indicates the recognition of place and community as the only space or locale of collective survival and well-being, which is in stark contrast to the utopian embrace of and self-projection into the universal modern characteristic of the Chinese New Era. A regained sense of home, while vulnerable to all kinds of nativist, nationalist, and traditionalist impulses, does help nurture an appreciation of the particular, the local, the eclectic, the plural, and, in the opposite, a disdain and profound suspicion of anything dogmatic and radical, thus frustrating both Hayekian marketeers and spiritual fighters against the vulgar money society. Such thoroughly secular, deromanticized, and plebeian "social consensus," as it is manifested in the Chinese mass culture in the 1990s, also indicates a continuing national obsession with modernity, understood in postenlightenment (neo-enlightenment), postutopian, postintellectual, postsocialist, and probably equally postcapitalist terms. The very determination to explore a way different from that which has been pointed out by the ideologues of "market democracy" is considered a heresy in the post–cold war world; if Chinese modernization stands a chance to succeed, it will succeed only by blazing its own path in the wilderness, and in doing so creating its own form of life, its own culture, its own ideological, intellectual, and aesthetic discourse. To this extent, the Chinese revolution, the Maoist innovation of "making Marxism Chinese," remains a potent source of confidence, if not in the realm of repressed collective unconscious. The rise and fall of the Soviet Union, arguably the single most important event of the twentieth century, does not seem to have shaken that confidence, but only reinforced it (as "not to go down the Russian road" has become a national consensus). Such belated modernization, unfolding in the era of late capitalism (Mandel/Jameson), is bound to be "postmodern" if only for its active imagination which reevokes the old and the historical. For Gan Yang, Chinese postmodernism must be considered in the context of the historical arrival of Chinese modernity, namely the beginning of the "self-transformation" of peasant China as hundreds of millions of Chinese peasant workers entered History and started rewriting it.[34] In this respect, the ongoing Chinese revolution, now concentrated in the economic and cultural sphere, sees its historical precedents not in the Russian but in the French and American Revolutions. For Cui Zhiyuan, postmodernism would be the cultural expression of a new social system that combines economic democracy with political democracy, which the institutions of advanced capitalist societies fail to create. This, to be sure, is only a different way to say that the meaninglessness of Chinese postmodernism as one more instance of global cultural consumption can only be redeemed by the meaningfulness of postsocialist China already as a producer of a postmodern culture.

Chinese postmodernism, like China's "post–New Era," emerges with the anxiety-causing intensification and articulation of economic-social-class-political-ideological differentiations, contradictions, polarization, and fragmentation of Chinese society. Where the tidal wave of globalization rises, creating new nationalist and class consciousness, thus new social tensions at home, the persistence of socialism and national autonomy renders China an anomaly in the "history after ideology" and produces endless diplomatic and other frictions and confrontations with the United States, the self-appointed policeman of the post–cold war world. What proves to be most unsettling to those Chinese who have enjoyed two decades of rapid economic growth and relative social and international stability since the beginning of the New Era is the ominous looming of those old, loaded vocabularies of class, exploitation, oppression, imperialism, colonialism, hegemony, and power, for whose reappearance Chinese postmodernism is to blame.

What is implied here, however, is not so much the return of the old political society but the arrival of a new age, whose new configurations of wealth, power, and social relations demand a deconstruction and reconceptualization of previous moments of history and their ideological valorizations. At a level of historical generalization, and with a clarity that often escapes literary critics, Eric Hobsbawm observes: "All 'postmodernisms' had in common an essential scepticism about the existence of an objective reality, and/or the possibility of arriving at an agreed understanding of it by rational means. All tended to a radical relativism. All, therefore, challenged the essence of a world that rested on the opposite assumptions, namely the world transformed by science and the technology based upon it, and the ideology of progress which reflected it." [35] In the Chinese context, this "essential scepticism" is directed against the mythologized objectivity of both socialism and capitalism, although, obviously, its critical, if radically relativist, edge, is felt more acutely by those who think they have successfully replaced the official ideology of socialist modernity to claim the universal truth in its time-honored normality, namely in the image of liberal, free-market capitalism. And in this particular sense, postmodernism in China, in its seemingly ahistorical affirmation of the new, maintains, not eliminates, a unique sense of time and history or, rather, a unique temporal and historical tension, so long as all these different layers of collective experiences and memories still persist in the "status quo" of Chinese socialism. In other words, Chinese postmodernism, as a Chinese vision of the new at the end of the twentieth century, unwittingly becomes a buffer against the more radical and universal claim of the absolute market as a negation of the historical experience of Chinese modernity. The fundamental irony of Chinese postmodernism lies in that, by bestowing the status quo with a cultural space, it becomes a way of living history and its contradictions, rather than consuming it out of existence.

Notes

An abridged version of this chapter was published in *New Left Review*, no. 237, (September–October 1999): 77–105. The author wants to thank Richard Dienst and Moss Roberts for their comments on this version.

1 In an article recently published in the *Research Series of Modern Chinese Literature* (*Xiandai wenxue yanjiu congkan*), one of the backbone publications of the establishment of the field of modern Chinese literary studies in China, Yu Hua, the wonder boy of avant-garde fiction in the 1980s who spearheaded the violent "subversion" of the humanist-realist canon, is compared with Lu Xun, the ultimate canonical figure in modern Chinese literature, in their standing in and contribution to the paradigmatic development of modern Chinese literature. See Geng Chuanming, "Shilun Yu Hua xiaoshuo zhong de hou rendaozhuyi qingxiang ji qi dui Lu Xun qimeng huayu de jiegou" (On the posthumanist tendency in Yu Hua's fiction and its deconstruction of the enlightenment discourse of Lu Xun), *Xiandai wenxue yanjiu congkan* 72, no. 3 (1997), 79–93.

2 Cf. W. T. Adorno, *Philosophy of Modern Music*, trans. Anne G. Mitchell and Wesley V. Blomster (New York: Seabury, 1973).

3 Naoki Sakai, "Modernity and Its Critique: The Problem of Universalism and Particularism," ed. Masao Miyoshi and Harry Harootunian, *Postmodernism and Japan* (Durham, N.C.: Duke University Press, 1989), 94.

4 For an incisive analysis of the Japanese discourse of "the overcoming of the modern," see Harry Harootunian, "Visible Discourses/Invisible Ideologies," in *Postmodernism and Japan*, 63–92.

5 See Dai Jinhua, "Imagined Nostalgia," in this volume.

6 Svetlana Boym, *Common Places: Mythologies of Everyday Life in Russia* (Cambridge, Mass.: Harvard University Press, 1994), 247. The author, who initially thinks that the "sentiment of nostalgia is ancient and originates somewhere in the Homeric epic," admits that she was "surprised to find out that, in fact, the word 'nostalgia' was invented in the seventeenth century, roughly around the time of the famous quarrel between the Ancients and the Moderns, and that it is therefore only pseudo-Greek, or nostalgically Greek" (290). Nostalgia as a cultural fashion in postsocialist China, then, is a decidedly postmodern phenomenon, whose appearance is inconceivable without the disappearance of memory and the past in the process of rapid commodification.

7 For a critical examination of the Beijing-centered Chinese modernism of the 1980s, especially its formal-political negotiations with socialist modernity and global capitalism, see Xudong Zhang, *Chinese Modernism in the Era of Reforms* (Durham, N.C.: Duke University Press, 1997). For a historical study of the Shanghai-based modernism and middle class urban culture of the 1930s and early 1940s, see Leo Lee, "Shanghai Modern: Reflections on Urban Culture in China in the 1930s," in *Public Culture* 11, no. 1 (1999): 75–107. The article is a condensed version of two chapters from the author's book, *Shanghai Modern* (Cambridge, Mass.: Harvard University Press, 1999).

8 See Fredric Jameson, "Theories of Postmodernism," in *The Cultural Turn* (New York: Verso, 1998), 25–26.

9 In this particular sense, the "neoconservatism" label reminds us of the nationalists' (the Guomindang or KMT) calling the communists "reactionaries" in the late 1920s and early 1930s. I thank Arif Dirlik for this comment.

10 For a useful discussion of Mannheim's observations, see Fritz K. Ringer, *The Decline of German Mandarins* (Hanover, N.H.: University Press of New England, 1990), 2.

11 An in-depth analysis of Chinese liberalism as an antidemocratic conservatism can be found in Gan Yang, "A Critique of Chinese Conservatism in the 1990s," *Social Text* (summer 1998): 45–66.

12 For the paradox of Chinese modernism as an expressive vehicle for both a collective and an individual subjectivity, see relevant chapters on Misty poetry, Ge Fei and experimental fiction, and Fifth Generation film, especially chapter 10, "A Critical Account of Chen Kaige's *King of the Children*," in Xudong Zhang, *Chinese Modernism in the Era of Reforms*.

13 Arif Dirlik, *Postcolonial Aura: Third World Criticism in the Age of Global Capitalism* (Boulder, Colo.: Westview Press), 54–69.

14 For an observation on the Right's coopting Left tactics during the so-called Republican revolution in the United States in the early 1990s, see Stanley Aronowitz, "The Death and Rebirth of the American Left," *Social Text*, no. 44 (fall–winter 1995): 69–95.

15 For a particularly crude attack on Chinese postmodernism as a Western theory indebted to the Chinese Cultural Revolution and repudiated by Deng, see Guo Jian, "Wenge sichao yu 'houxue' " (The Cultural Revolution as an intellectual trend and "postologies"), in *Wenhua da geming: shishi yu yanjiu*, ed. Liu Qingfeng (The Cultural Revolution: Historical facts and researches) (Hong Kong: Chinese University of Hong Kong Press, 1996), 347–56. Guo did not bother to make the fine distinction between the influence of the Chinese Cultural Revolution on poststructuralists and their response to the events of 1968, which constituted a cultural revolution in its own right and occurred in a vastly different social and intellectual context. Similarly, he sees no need to tell the difference between theory rooted in such context and theory appropriated by a particular Chinese discourse in response to its own situations. For a discussion of postmodernism as a philosophy of defeat, see Terry Eagleton, *The Illusion of Postmodernism* (Oxford: Blackwell, 1996).

16 For a collection of essays analyzing the political differentiations of post-Mao Chinese intellectual discourse, see Xudong Zhang, ed., *Intellectual Politics in Post-Tiananmen China*, a special issue of *Social Text*, no. 55 (summer 1998).

17 This may be one of the central arguments of a forthcoming book, Liu Kang's *Aesthetics and Marxism: Chinese Aesthetic Marxists and Their Western Contemporaries* (Durham, N.C.: Duke University Press, 2000).

18 The Russian economy is believed to have shrunk about 50 percent between 1991 and 1999. In early 1998, when the artificially high real estate and stock market collapsed as a result of speculative attack by the free-floating international capital, almost all the newly industrialized countries of East Asia suddenly entered deep recession. In seven months, the "Asian Contagion" wiped out 30–50 percent of the currency and stock values of those "miracle economies" in Thailand, Malaysia, Indonesia, South Korea, and Hong Kong. Singapore and Japan were also hard hit. The Malaysian premier, Mahatir, bitterly accused international financial speculators, lead by George Soros, of robbing the savings of an entire generation in his country and thus setting the clock of its economic development back nearly thirty years. One dramatic estimate puts the loss of market value of the East Asian economies (excluding mainland China) on a par with the total economic loss of Europe during World War II.

19 Cf. Zhiyuang Cui et al., *Nanjiecun* (The Nanjie village) (Beijing: Gongshanglian Chubanshe, 1996).

20 Cf. Fei Xiaotong, *Peasant Life in China* (London: Routledge and Kegan Paul, 1939); *Xiang Tu Chung Jian* (Rural reconstruction) (Shanghai: Guancha, 1948); and *Rural Development in China* (Chicago: University of Chicago Press, 1989); Philip Huang, *The Peasant Family and*

Rural Development in the Yangzi Delta, 1350–1988 (Stanford, Calif.: Stanford University Press, 1990).

21 Cf. Jean Oi, Rural China Takes Off (Berkeley: University of California Press, 1999).

22 Zhiyuan Cui, Di er ci sixiang jiefang yu zhidu chuangxin (The Second intellectual liberation and institutional innovations) (Hong Kong: Oxford University Press, 1994), 13.

23 Zhiyuan Cui, Di er ci sixiang jiefang, 13.

24 Cui makes allusions and references to the philosophy of Mo Zi to highlight his position that "part of the effort of the second intellectual liberation is to rediscover the contemporary significance of ancient Chinese thought." Mo Zi is also the (admittedly fictional) sage featured, as Me-ti, in Brecht's writings about dialectical thinking and epic wisdom, a recent study of which is Fredric Jameson's Brecht and Method (London: Verso, 1998).

25 In his book on the "short twentieth century," Eric Hobsbawm observes that the sweeping success of Chinese communism after the Sino-Japanese war may be due to the Marxist-Leninist party organization's capacity of "bringing government policy from the centre to the remotest villages of the giant country—as, in the mind of most Chinese, a proper empire should do." The Age of Extremes: A History of the World, 1914–1991 (New York: Vintage Books, 1995), 465. Hobsbawm thinks that socialism in the Chinese context, even though more than empire survived, benefited historically and culturally "from the enormous continuities of Chinese history, which established both how ordinary Chinese expected to relate to any government enjoying the 'mandate of the heaven,' and how those who administered China expected to think about their tasks." He further quotes a "hard-nosed old China-watcher, a London Times correspondent" who predicted in the 1950s that "there would be no communism left in the twenty-first century, except in China, where it would survive as the national ideology." Hobsbawm, with the hindsight of a historian, adds: "For most Chinese this was revolution which was primarily a restoration: of order and peace; of welfare; of a system of government whose civil servants found themselves appealing to precedents from the T'ang dynasty; of the greatness of a great empire and civilization" (466). These views can be regarded as a development, in the context of the revolutions of the twentieth century, of Hobsbawm's own theory of nation and nationalism from his earlier work, Nations and Nationalisms since 1780 (Cambridge: Cambridge University Press, 1990), which contains only brief and scattered discussions on China.

Pye, from an opposite direction, and working from the assumption that the realization of universal modernity requires the actualization of the modern bourgeois nation-states, argues that China is "really a civilization pretending to be a nation-state," and that it still needs to turn itself from a political dinosaur into a qualified nation-state by following the classical European model. See Lucien Pye, "How Chinese Nationalism Was Shanghaied," in Chinese Nationalism, ed. Jonathan Unger (New York: M. E. Sharp, 1993), 86–112.

26 For a discussion of the market-born Chinese nationalism (with the global media as its midwife), see Xudong Zhang, "Mass Culture, Nationalism, and Chinese Intellectual Strategies in the 1990s," Social Text, no. 55 (summer 1998): 109–40.

27 The "postmodern" and "post-Mao-Deng" homophone can be found in the title of Yang Xiaobin's article included in this volume.

28 Cf. Hu Shi, "Bishang liangshan" (A forced rebellion), in Zhongguo xinwenxue daxi, jianshe lilun jii (The great anthology of modern Chinese literature), Collection on Theoretical Construction (Shanghai: Liangyou Tushu Yinshua Gongsi, 1935), 3–27.

29 Liu Xinwu and Zhang Yiwu, Liu Xinwu Zhang Yiwu duihualu (Dialogues between Liu Xinwu

and Zhang Yiwu: A post-century cultural outlook) (Guilin, Guangxi: Lijiang Chubanshe, 1996), 40.

30 Liu and Zhang, *Liu Xinwu Zhang Yiwu duihualu*, 56–57.

31 Liu and Zhang, *Liu Xinwu Zhang Yiwu duihualu*, chap. 3, "Shimin shehui de chengzhang" (The development of civil society), 43–61.

32 Two recent works, namely Michael Dutton's *Street Life China* (Cambridge: University of Cambridge Press, 1998), a theorically inspired sociological survey, and Gereme Barmé's *In the Red* (New York: Columbia University Press, 1999), an intimate cultural journalistic exposé, are among the first in English to grapple with those unclassifiable elements (such as *liumang*) in contemporary Chinese social and cultural life.

33 See Wang Hui, "PRC Cultural Studies and Cultural Criticism in the 1990s," trans. Nicholas A. Kaldis, *positions* 6, no. 1 (Spring 1998): 239–51. Wang shares many descriptive, analytical, and judgmental interests and positions with the "certifiable" postmodern critics. Even though he is certainly correct in pointing out that the arrival of postmodernism in Chinese in the 1990s is a "political event" (*zhengzhi shijian*), his generalization of Chinese postmodernism as the ideology of the complicity between the state and globalization needs to be checked in various concrete contexts. Wang's position is more helpful in highlighting the intellectual dilemma of contemporary China as it contemplates the continued validity of modernity, especially its critical tradition, in the face of the impatient move to go beyond the modern as an establishment and institution.

34 Gan Yang, "Shehui yu sixiang cong shu yuanqi" (preface to the Society and Thought Book Series), in Cui Zhiyuan, *Di er ci sixiang jiefang*, v–vi.

35 Eric Hobsbawm, *The Age of Extremes*, 517.

selected glossary
of terms and titles

bendi kongjian 本地空间
bensheng 本省
bianjibu de gushi 编辑部的故事
Bianyuan 边缘
bolaipin 泊来品
Canghe bairimeng 苍河白日梦
Changhenge 长恨歌
Chengshi jifeng 城市季风
Ci Qin 刺秦
dadao Beidao 打倒北岛
Dangdai dianying 当代电影
danwei 单位
Daoyu bianyuan 岛屿边缘
Didi nihao 弟弟你好
Dongbian richu xibian yu
    东边日出西边雨
Dongfang 东方
Dongwu xiongmeng 动物凶猛
dosan 多桑
duanlie 断裂

dushu 读书
Ershiyi shiji 二十一世纪
fan yuyan 反寓言
Feidu 废都
feifei zhuyi shipai 非非主义诗派
Fengyu liren 风雨丽人
Fengyue 风月
fenxiang jiannan 分享艰难
gaoya 高雅
geren zhuti 个人主体
gonggong kongjian 公共空间
guanfang 官方
gudian re 古典热
Guoba yin 过把瘾
guoxue 国学
Haishang jiumeng 海上旧梦
Hongfen 红粉
houxiandai zhuyi 后现代主义
hou xinshiqi 后新时期
houxue 后学

Huacheng 花城
huaijiu shuxi 怀旧书系
huaji mofang 滑稽模仿
Huangjin shidai 黄金时代
Huozhe
jindai 近代
Jishi yu xugou 记实与虚构
jujue touxiang 拒绝投降
Kewang 渴望
Lianai de jijie 恋爱的季节
liangwu 恋物
liumang 流氓
mazi de ren 码字的人
Meigui men 玫瑰门
Meili tao 美丽岛
minjian 民间
minzu guojia 民族国家
minzu yuyan 民族寓言
nan-chin 南进
Nanniwan 南泥湾
Nianlun 年轮
Pei-hai te jen 背海的人
pien-chiang 边疆
pien-tsui 边陲
pingmin yishi 平民意识
pintie 拼贴
Qianshou 牵手
Qianwan bie ba wo dang ren
    千万别把我当人
Qin song 秦颂
renwen jingshen de weiji
    人文精神的危机
Renwen jingshe xunsilu
    人文精神寻思录
Shanghai wangshi 上海往事
shangpinhua 商品化
shenhua shi de bianma 神话式的编码
shehui tianchongwu 社会填充物
Shenghuo wuzui 生活无罪
shengming gongtongti 生命共同体
shiluo 失落
shimin 市民
Siren shenghuo 私人生活
shou weituo de wenxue 受委托的文学
shuxie yiqianbian lantingxu
    书写一千遍兰亭序
Tangtai 当代
tongsu 通俗

Tongzhuo de ni 同桌的你
Tuanzhibu shuji 团支部书记
tung-fan 东番
waisheng 外省
wenhua re 文化热
wo ai wo jia 我爱我家
Wo de diwang shengya 我的帝王生涯
wuchang 无常
xiandai 现代
xianfeng xiaoshuo 先锋小说
xiangdui de kongjian 相对的空间
xiangzhen qiye 乡镇企业
xiaofei wenxue 消费文学
xiaokang 小康
Xiaoyao song 逍遥颂
xin baoshou zhuyi 新保守主义
xin jitizhuyi 新集体主义
xin quanwei zhuyi 新权威主义
xin ruxue 新儒学
xin tiyan xiaoshuo 新体验小说
xin wenrenhua 新文人画
xin xieshi zhuyi 新写实主义
xinxing minzu 新兴民族
xin zhuangtai 新状态
Yao a yao, yao dao waipo qiao
    摇啊摇，摇到外婆桥
yazhou jiazhi 亚洲价值
yangge 秧歌
Yangguang canlan de rizi
    阳光灿烂的日子
Ye shi 野事
Yigeren de zhanzheng 一个人的战争
yijia wenxue 议价文学
Yongshi woai 永失我爱
yu guoji jiegui 与国际接轨
Yu wangshi ganbei 与往事干杯
Yunmen 云门
Zaihuishou 再回首
Zaoyu zuotian 遭遇昨天
zhan zai sushi de duili mian
    站在俗世的对立面
zhengtixing 整体性
zhengzhi bopu 政治波普
zhongji zhenli 终极真理
Zhongshan 钟山
Zhongwai wenxue 中外文学
ziyou zhuyi zhe 自由主义者

contributors

MICHAEL BERRY is a Ph.D. student in the Department of East Asian Languages and Literatures at Columbia University.

EVANS CHAN is an independent filmmaker. He lives and works in Hong Kong and New York.

CHEN XIAOMING is Associate Professor of literature at the Chinese Academy of Social Sciences.

JUDY CHEN is a Ph.D. student in comparative literature at Rutgers University.

ARIF DIRLIK is Professor of History at Duke University. He is the author of several books, including *After the Revolution: Waking in the Global Capitalism* (1994); editor of *What Is the Rim? Critical Perspectives on the Pacific Region Idea* (1993); and coeditor, with Rob Wilson, of *Asia/Pacific as Space of Cultural Production* (1994).

DAI JINHUA is Associate Professor of Comparative Literature at Peking University.

ANTHONY KING is Professor of Art History at the State University of New York, Binghamton.

JEROEN DE KLOET is a Ph.D. research fellow at the Amsterdam School of Social Science Research in the Netherlands.

ABIDIN KUSNO teaches at the Metropolitan Studies Program, New York University.

WENDY LARSON is Professor of Chinese and Comparative Literature at the University of Oregon, Eugene.

CHAO-YANG LIAO is Professor of English at National Taiwan University.

PING-HUI LIAO is Professor of English at National Tsing-hua University.

SEBASTIAN HSIEN-HAO LIAO is Professor of English at National Taiwan University.

LIU KANG is Associate Professor of Comparative Literature at Pennsylvania State University.

SHELDON HSIAO-PENG LU is Associate Professor of Chinese, Film Studies, and Cultural Studies at the University of Pittsburgh.

ANBIN SHI is a Ph.D. student in comparative literature at Pennsylvania State University.

XIAOBING TANG is Associate Professor of Chinese literature at the University of Chicago.

WANG NING is Professor of English at the Beijing University of Languages and Cultures.

XIAOYING WANG teaches comparative literature at the University of Hong Kong.

XIAOBIN YANG is Assistant Professor of Chinese at the University of Mississippi.

XUDONG ZHANG teaches in the Department of Comparative Literature and East Asian Studies Program at New York University. He is the author of *Chinese Modernism in the Era of Reforms: Cultural Fever, Avant-garde Fiction, and the New Chinese Cinema* (1997).

ZHANG YIWU is Associate Professor of Chinese at Peking University.

index

Library of Congress Cataloging-in-Publication Data
Postmodernism and China : (journal into book) /
edited by Arif Dirlik and Xudong Zhang.
"Boundary 2 book".
"Postmodernism and China was created from a special
issue of Boundary 2 (23:3, 1997)".
Includes index.
ISBN 0-8223-2506-3 (cloth : alk. paper)
ISBN 0-8223-2544-6 (pbk. : alk. paper)
1. Popular culture—China.   2. Postmodernism—China.
3. China—Civilization—1976–
I. Dirlik, Arif.   II. Chang, Hsü-tung.
DS779.23 .P675 2000   951.05—dc21
99-042240